AN INTRODUCTION TO THEORIES OF LEARNING

Eighth Edition

MATTHEW H. OLSON
Hamline University

B. R. HERGENHAHN
Professor Emeritus
Hamline University

PEARSON
Prentice
Hall

Upper Saddle River, New Jersey 07458

Library of Congress Cataloging-in-Publication Data

Olson, Matthew H.
   An introduction to theories of learning / Matthew H. Olson and B. R.
Hergenhahn.—8th ed.
     p. cm.
   Previous ed. entered under B. R. Hergenhahn.
   ISBN-13: 978-0-13-605772-7
   ISBN-10:   0-13-605772-1
   1. Learning, Psychology of.   I. Hergenhahn, B. R.,   II. Title.
LB1051.H42 2009
370.15'23—dc22   2008006028

Editorial Director: Leah Jewell
Executive Editor: Jeff Marshall
Project Manager: LeeAnn Doherty
Associate Managing Editor: Maureen Richardson
Full Service Production Liaison: Joanne Hakim
Senior Marketing Manager: Jeanette Koskinas
Marketing Assistant: Laura Kennedy
Senior Operations Supervisor: Sherry Lewis
Cover Art Director: Jayne Conte
Cover Design: Bruce Kenselaar
Cover Photo/Illustration: Medioimages/Photodisc/
  Getty Images, Inc.

Director, Image Resource Center: Melinda Patelli
Manager, Rights and Permissions: Zina Arabia
Manager, Visual Research: Beth Brenzel
Manager, Cover Visual Research & Permissions:
  Karen Sanatar
Senior Image Permission Coordinator: Cynthia
  Vincenti
Full-Service Project Management: Kathy O'Connor/
  TexTech International
Composition: TexTech International
Printer/Binder: The Courier Companies
Cover Printer: Coral Graphics

Credits and acknowledgments borrowed from other sources and reproduced, with permission, in this textbook
appear on appropriate page within text.

Pearson Prentice Hall™ is a trademark of Pearson Education, Inc.
Pearson® is a registered trademark of Pearson plc
Prentice Hall® is a registered trademark of Pearson Education, Inc.

Pearson Education LTD., London
Pearson Education Singapore, Pte. Ltd
Pearson Education, Canada, Inc.
Pearson Education–Japan
Pearson Education Australia PTY, Limited

Pearson Education North Asia Ltd., Hong Kong
Pearson Educación de Mexico, S.A. de C.V.
Pearson Education Malaysia, Pte. Ltd.
Pearson Education, Upper Saddle River, New Jersey

10 9 8 7 6 5 4
ISBN-13: 978-0-13-605772-7
ISBN-10:   0-13-605772-1

In Memory of
B. R. Hergenhahn (1934–2007)
Esteemed Colleague,
Invaluable Mentor,
and
Cherished Friend

Ladies and Gentlemen,
one of the truly great characters of our time has left the building.

Brief Contents

Contents

Preface

As in previous editions, the four main goals of this textbook are to define learning and to show how the learning process is studied (Chapters 1 and 2), to place learning theory in historical perspective (Chapter 3), and to present essential features of the major theories of learning with implications for educational practices (Chapters 4 through 15). We have attempted to retain the best features of earlier editions while making revisions that reflect current research and scholarship. The most significant revisions include the following:

- The discovery of mirror neurons and their role in learning
- New findings concerning the role of dopamine in motivation and reward
- New research in the role of dopamine in reinforcement and learning
- Exciting developments in the discovery and exploration of silent synapses
- The role of neurogenesis in learning and in recovery from brain injury
- Extended research in evolutionary preparedness in learned fear
- Updated research and references throughout

I would like to express our gratitude to the individuals whose contributions helped shape this edition: William Timberlake, Indiana University; Linda Rueckert, Northeastern Illinois University; Darrell Smith, Tennessee State University; Randall Russac, University of North Florida; Krystine Batcho, Le Moyne College; R. H. Ettinger, Eastern Oregon University; Timothy Lionetti, Marywood University; Billy Smith, University of Central Arkansas; Todd Smith, Lake Superior State University; Mark Winkel, The University of Texas-Pan American.

I would also like to thank the outstanding faculty of the Psychology Department at Hamline University: Professors Dorothee Dietrich, R. Kim Guenther, Chuck LaBounty, and Robin Parritz; and Assistant Professor Serena King, who made it possible for Olson to devote time to this project. And I would like to thank Production Editor Kathy O'Connor, who provided outstanding assistance on behalf of Prentice Hall. Finally I would like to express gratitude to my patient wife, Marce Soderman-Olson, for reading too many drafts of new material and for her thoughtful and insightful editorial suggestions.

Finally, I express my heartfelt thanks to Bud Hergenhahn, who hired me more than thirty years ago, Ph.D. still in progress, to teach a handful of courses that, more or less, fit my training. My best and most critical editor did not get to contribute to the eighth edition. Bud did not live long after a massive heart attack, July 2007. My hope is that he would have approved of this edition of the text.

Any questions, suggestions, or comments about this text should be directed to Matt Olson in the Psychology Department at Hamline University, St. Paul, MN 55104, or by e-mail: mholson@gw.hamline.edu.

Matthew H. Olson

are capable of doing something that they could not do before learning took place. Second, this behavioral change is *relatively permanent;* that is, it is neither transitory nor fixed. Third, the change in behavior need not occur immediately following the learning experience. Although there may be a *potential* to act differently, this potential to act may not be translated into behavior until a later time. Fourth, the change in behavior (or behavior potentiality) results from *experience* or practice. Fifth, the experience, or practice, must be reinforced; that is, only those responses that lead to reinforcement will be learned. Although the terms *reward* and *reinforcement* are often used synonymously, there are at least two reasons why they should not be. In Pavlov's work, for example, a *reinforcer* is defined as any unconditioned stimulus, that is, any stimulus that elicits a natural and automatic reaction from an organism. In Pavlovian research, it is not uncommon for stimuli such as a mild acid solution or electric shock to be used as unconditioned stimuli. It is accurate to call such stimuli reinforcers, but they can hardly be considered rewards, if rewards are thought of as desirable. The Skinnerians also oppose equating the terms *reinforcer* and *reward.* For them, a reinforcer strengthens any behavior that immediately precedes the *reinforcer's* occurrence. In contrast, a reward is usually thought of as something that is given or received only for a worthy accomplishment that required a considerable investment of time and energy or for an act deemed desirable by society. Furthermore, because such desirable behavior typically occurs long before it is acknowledged by reward, reward cannot be said to strengthen it. For the Skinnerians, then, reinforcers strengthen behavior but rewards do not. Skinner (1986) elaborated on these points:

> The strengthening effect [of reinforcement] is missed . . . when reinforcers are called *rewards.* People are rewarded, but behavior is reinforced. If, as you walk along the street, you look down and find some money, and if money is reinforcing, you will tend to look down again for some time, but we should not say that you were rewarded for looking down. As the history of the word shows, reward implies compensation, something that offsets a sacrifice or loss, if only the expenditure of effort. We give heroes medals, students degrees, and famous people prizes, but those rewards are not directly contingent on what they have done, and it is generally felt that rewards would not be deserved if they had not been worked for. (p. 569)

In this text we acknowledge these concerns and do not equate the terms *reward* and *reinforcement.* Except where the term *reward* is appropriate as it is defined in Skinner's remarks in the preceding quotation, the terms *reinforcer* or *reinforcement* are used exclusively. Kimble's (1961) definition of learning provides a convenient frame of reference for discussing a number of important issues that must be confronted when attempting to define learning. We review these issues in the following sections of this chapter.

MUST LEARNING RESULT IN A BEHAVIORAL CHANGE?

As we see in Chapter 3, psychology has become a *behavioral* science for good reason. A science requires an observable, measurable subject matter, and in the science of

CHAPTER I

What Is Learning?

Learning is one of the most important topics in present-day psychology, yet it is an extremely difficult concept to define. The *American Heritage Dictionary* defines *learning* as follows: "To gain knowledge, comprehension, or mastery through experience or study." Most psychologists, however, would find this definition unacceptable because of the nebulous terms it contains, such as *knowledge, comprehension,* and *mastery.* Instead, we prefer a definition of learning that refers to changes in observable behavior. One of the most popular of these definitions is the one suggested by Gregory A. Kimble (1917–2006), which defines learning *as a relatively permanent change in* **behavioral potentiality** *that occurs as a result of* **reinforced practice** (Kimble, 1961, p.6). Although popular, this definition is far from universally accepted. Before reviewing sources of disagreement over Kimble's definition, let's look at it more carefully.

First, learning is indexed by a change in *behavior;* in other words, the results of learning must always be translated into observable behavior. After learning, learners psychology, that subject matter is behavior. Thus, whatever we study in psychology must be expressed through behavior, but this does not mean that the behavior we are studying *is* learning. We study behavior so that we can make *inferences* concerning the process believed to be the cause of the behavioral changes we are observing. In this case, that process is learning. Most learning theorists discussed in this book agree that the learning process cannot be studied directly; instead, its nature can only be inferred from changes in behavior. B. F. Skinner took exception to this contention. For Skinner, behavioral changes are learning, and no further process needs to be inferred. Other theorists say that behavioral changes result from learning. We have more to say about Skinner's antitheoretical point of view in Chapter 5.

Except for the Skinnerians, then, most learning theorists look on learning as a process that mediates behavior. For them, learning is something that occurs as the result of certain experiences and precedes changes in behavior. In such a definition, learning is given the status of an intervening variable. An intervening variable is a theoretical process that is assumed to take place between the observed stimuli and responses. Independent variables cause a change in the intervening variable (learning), which in turn causes a change in the dependent variable (behavior). The situation can be diagrammed as follows:

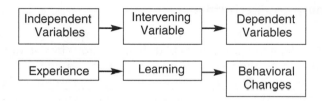

How Permanent Is Relatively Permanent?

Here we run into at least two problems. First, how long must a behavior change last before we say that learning has been demonstrated? This aspect was originally inserted into the definition to differentiate between learning and other events that may modify behavior, such as fatigue, illness, maturation, and drugs. Clearly, these events and their effects may come and go rapidly, whereas learning lingers until forgetting takes place over time or until new learning displaces old learning. Thus temporary states as well as learning modify behavior, but with learning the modification is relatively more permanent. However, the duration of the modification that results from either learning or temporary body states cannot be specified exactly.

A related problem is more serious. A number of psychologists have turned their attention to a phenomenon called **short-term memory** (see Chapter 14). They have found that if unfamiliar information, such as a nonsense syllable, is presented to human research participants who are prevented from rehearsing the information, they will retain the material almost perfectly for about three seconds. In the following fifteen seconds, however, their retention drops to almost zero (Murdock, 1961; Peterson & Peterson, 1959). Despite the fact that the information is lost over such a short period of time, we would hesitate to say that no learning occurred.

Accepting the qualification of "relatively permanent" in a definition of learning will also determine whether the processes of **sensitization** and **habituation** (see Chapter 14) are accepted as crude examples of learning. Sensitization is the process whereby an organism is made more responsive to certain aspects of its environment. For example, an organism that may not ordinarily respond to a certain light or sound may do so after receiving a shock. The shock, therefore, sensitized the organism, making it more responsive to its environment. Feeling "touchy" or hypersensitive following an upsetting experience is a form of sensitization with which we are all familiar.

Habituation is the process whereby an organism becomes less responsive to its environment. For example, there is a tendency for an organism to attend to novel stimuli as they occur in its environment. This tendency is referred to as the orienting reflex, and it is exemplified when a dog turns in the direction of a sound that suddenly occurs. After attending to the sound, however, the dog will eventually ignore it (assuming that it poses no threat) and go about its business. We say, in this case, that the dog's response to the sound has habituated. Similarly, Sharpless and Jasper (1956) found that a tone, when first presented, will arouse a sleeping cat. With repeated presentations, however, the tone loses its ability to arouse the cat. Again, we say that habituation has occurred.

Learning and Performance

As previously mentioned, what is learned may not be utilized immediately. Athletes, for example, may learn how to play their positions by watching films and listening to lectures during the week, but they may not translate that learning into behavior until game time. In fact, some players may be prevented from actually performing for a prolonged period of time because of an injury or an illness. We say, therefore, that the potential to act differently resulted from learning, even though behavior was not immediately affected.

This type of observation has led to the very important distinction between **learning** and **performance,** which is considered in detail in Chapters 6, 12, 13, and 14. *Learning* refers to a change in behavior potentiality, and *performance* refers to the translation of this potentiality into behavior.

Why Do We Refer to Practice or Experience?

Obviously not all behavior is learned. Much simple behavior is reflexive. A **reflex** can be defined as an unlearned or innate response in reaction to a specific class of stimuli. Sneezing in response to a tickling in your nose, producing a sudden knee jerk when your knee is tapped sharply, and instantly withdrawing your hand when it touches a hot stove are examples of reflexive behavior. Clearly, reflexive behavior is unlearned; it is a genetically determined characteristic of the organism rather than a result of experience.

Complex behavior can also be innate. When complex behavior patterns are genetically determined, they are generally referred to as examples of **instinct.** Instinctive behavior includes such activities as nest building, migration, hibernation, and mating behavior. For a while, psychologists explained complex behavior patterns by referring to them as instincts. We said birds and fish migrate because they possess a migration instinct, and birds build nests because of a nest-building instinct. Because the term *instinctive* was offered as an *explanation* of behavior, we now tend to use the term *species-specific behavior* (Hinde & Tinbergen, 1958) because it is more descriptive. Species-specific behavior refers to complex, unlearned, and relatively unmodifiable behavior patterns engaged in by a certain species of animal under certain circumstances.

Controversy continues, however, over whether species-specific behavior is completely determined by the makeup of the organism or whether some learning is involved. Do birds fly instinctively, or do they learn to fly? Some say that the young bird learns to fly through trial and error while falling to the ground from a tree. Others say that the birds respond reflexively to falling by flapping their wings and therefore fly without learning to do so.

A few examples, however, seem to demonstrate complex behavior that is clearly not influenced by learning. For example, many species of the cuckoo bird lay their eggs in other birds' nests, and the young cuckoo is raised by its foster parents. Because each adult cuckoo behaves in this way regardless of the foster parents' species, it is very difficult to imagine how such behavior could be learned.

Another example of what appears to be unlearned behavior is the nut-burying behavior of squirrels. Even when an infant squirrel is raised in isolation from other squirrels and sees a nut for the first time, it attempts to bury it. This nut-burying pattern of behavior occurs even if the nut is presented to the squirrel on a bare wooden floor. The squirrel makes scratching motions on the floor as if to dig a hole, tamps the nut with its nose in an apparent effort to push the nut into the floor, and then makes covering movements with its paws (Brown, 1965). Other research supports the contention that some species-specific behavior is both learned and innate (Hess, 1958; Lorenz, 1952, 1965, 1970; Thorpe, 1963). Lorenz found, for example, that a newly hatched duckling would form an attachment to any kind of moving object and follow it as its mother, provided the object was presented at just the right moment in the duckling's life. Lorenz demonstrated attachments between ducklings and a wooden box on wheels, a human being, and a bird of a different species. The formation of an attachment between an organism and an environmental object is called **imprinting.** Imprinting was found to occur only during a **critical period,** after which it was difficult, if not impossible, to imprint the duckling

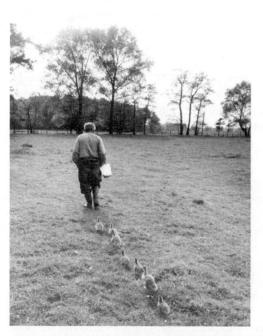

Konrad Lorenz and a group of ducklings that have imprinted on him. (Thomas McAvoy, Time-Life Picture Agency/Getty Images/Time Life Pictures.)

on anything. With imprinting, we have a combination of learned and instinctive behavior. It appears that the animal's genetic endowment causes it to be maximally sensitive to a moving object for a short period of time, during which it can learn the strong habit of following a specific object. If the learning does not occur during that interval, however, it may never occur. Furthermore, the strong habit of following an object does not seem to be built up over time with practice. Rather, the habit seems to be learned at full strength in a single trial. We have more to say about one-trial learning in Chapters 8 and 9.

Studies about imprinting raise a number of questions. The kind of learning, if any, involved in species-specific behavior and to what extent it is involved must be determined by future research. The main point to emphasize, however, is that to attribute a behavioral change to learning, the change must be relatively permanent and must result from experience. If an organism engages in a complex behavior pattern independent of experience, that behavior cannot be referred to as learned behavior.

Does Learning Result from a Specific Kind of Experience?

According to Kimble's (1961) definition, learning results from reinforced practice. In other words, only reinforced behavior will be learned. On this point, there is widespread disagreement among learning theorists. Theorists disagree not only over what constitutes reinforcement but also over whether it is a necessary prerequisite for learning to take place. In a sense, this book is an attempt to review various interpretations of the nature and importance of reinforcement. This is a subject, therefore, to which we return often.

A Modified Definition of Learning

We can now revise Kimble's (1961) definition of learning to make it neutral on the matter of reinforcement, thereby making it more widely accepted: *Learning is a relatively permanent change in behavior or in behavioral potentiality that results from experience and cannot be attributed to* **temporary body states** *such as those induced by illness, fatigue, or drugs.*

Such a definition still stresses the importance of experience but leaves it to the theorist to specify the kind of experience the theorist feels is necessary for learning to take place, for example, reinforced practice, contiguity between a stimulus and a response, or the acquisition of

Gregory A. Kimble. (Courtesy of Gregory A. Kimble.)

information. It also reminds us that experience can cause events other than learning that modify behavior. Fatigue is one such event.

ARE THERE DIFFERENT KINDS OF LEARNING?

Learning, as we have seen, is a general term that is used to describe changes in behavior potentiality resulting from experience. **Conditioning,** however, is a more specific term used to describe actual procedures that can modify behavior. Because there are two kinds of conditioning, **instrumental** and **classical,** many theorists conclude that there are at least two kinds of learning or that learning ultimately can be understood in terms of classical and instrumental conditioning. Although both conditioning procedures are discussed in detail later on in this book, we summarize both procedures here briefly.

Classical Conditioning

We look at classical conditioning in detail when we discuss Pavlov's views on learning in Chapter 7, but for now we can summarize classical conditioning as follows:

1. A stimulus, such as food, is presented to an organism and will cause a natural and automatic reaction, such as salivating. The stimulus causing this natural reaction is called the unconditioned stimulus (US). In this case, the food was the US. The natural, automatic reaction to the US is called the unconditioned response (UR). In this case, salivation was the UR.
2. A neutral stimulus (one that does not cause a UR), such as a tone or light, is presented to the organism just prior to the presentation of the US. This neutral stimulus is called the conditioned stimulus (CS).
3. After the CS and US are paired a number of times, with the CS always preceding the US, the CS alone can be presented, and the organism will salivate. This salivating response, similar to the organism's response to the US, now occurs in response to the CS, the tone or the light. We now say that a conditioned response (CR) has been demonstrated. In classical conditioning, the US is called reinforcement because the entire conditioning procedure depends on it. Note, however, that in classical conditioning, the organism has no control over reinforcement: It occurs when the experimenter wants it to occur. In other words, in classical conditioning, reinforcement is not contingent on any overt response made by the organism.

Instrumental Conditioning

The relationship between reinforcement and the organism's behavior is distinctively different in instrumental conditioning. With instrumental conditioning, the organism must act in a certain way *before* it is reinforced; that is, reinforcement is contingent on the organism's behavior. If the animal does not emit the desired behavior, it is not reinforced. Thus in instrumental conditioning, the animal's behavior is "instrumental" in getting it something it wants, that is, a reinforcer.

A small experimental test chamber called the **Skinner box** is often used to demonstrate instrumental conditioning (or a closely allied form of conditioning called operant conditioning). Such a box is a Plexiglas cage with a grid floor that can be electrified and a lever that, when pressed, activates a feeder mechanism that delivers food pellets to the animal inside. The experimenter introduces a hungry rat (for example) into the Skinner box. As the rat explores the enclosure, it will eventually activate the lever and receive a pellet of food. Soon the rat will associate lever pressing with the appearance of food, and its rate of lever pressing will increase. In this case, the rat must engage in lever pressing in order to get food. The lever pressing is the conditioned behavior; the food is the reinforcement. If the Skinner box is programmed so that when a hungry animal presses the lever it is given a pellet of food, the rate at which it presses the lever will increase.

Escape and avoidance conditioning are special kinds of instrumental conditioning. In **escape conditioning,** a rat is placed in the Skinner box and the electrified grid is activated. The animal must perform some response, such as jumping a small hurdle or climbing onto a small platform, to terminate the shock. The rat will associate the response with the termination of the shock. In this case, the response is the conditioned behavior, and the termination of shock is the reinforcement.

To demonstrate **avoidance conditioning,** let the Skinner box grid be activated at intervals, with a signal, such as a light, set up to precede the onset of shock by, say, five seconds. The rat will soon learn to associate the light with the onset of shock, and it will perform its response in order to avoid the shock whenever it sees the light go on. In avoidance conditioning, the lab animal learns to respond quickly so that it no longer experiences the actual shock.

Learning theorists have become increasingly aware that confining themselves to research involved with just classical and instrumental conditioning leaves out vast areas of human experience. For example, Gagné (1970) feels it is more realistic to assume that there are eight kinds of learning. Gagné believes that the eight kinds of learning are arranged in a hierarchy, with one sort being a prerequisite for the next. Thus, for Gagné, simple conditioning simply provides the basis for the more advanced kinds of learning. As we see in Chapter 12, Tolman took a similar position much earlier. Although many theorists believe that complex behavior ultimately can be understood in terms of classical or instrumental conditioning, other influential theorists oppose that contention.

LEARNING AND SURVIVAL

Throughout our long evolutionary past, our bodies have developed the capacity to respond automatically to certain needs. For example, we breathe automatically, and if our body temperature becomes too high or too low, mechanisms are triggered that cause sweating, which cools the body, or shivering, which raises body temperature. Likewise, if blood sugar is too low, the liver secretes sugar into the blood until the concentration of blood sugar is restored to a normal level. These automatic adjustment processes are called **homeostatic mechanisms** because their function is to maintain a physiological equilibrium, or *homeostasis*. In addition to the homeostatic mechanisms, we are also born with reflexes that facilitate survival. For example, most living organisms retreat reflexively from a painful stimulus.

Although both homeostatic mechanisms and reflexes are clearly conducive to survival, we would not survive long if we had to depend on them exclusively to meet our needs. For a species to *survive*, it must satisfy its needs for such things as food, water, and sex, and to do so it must interact with the environment. No organism would survive long if it did not *learn* which environmental objects could be used to satisfy its basic needs. Nor could an organism survive long if it could not learn which environmental objects were safe and which were dangerous. It is the learning process that allows organisms to do commerce with the environment in a way that allows for the satisfaction of the basic needs that cannot be satisfied by homeostatic mechanisms or reflexes.

It is also the learning process that allows an organism to adjust to a changing environment. Sources of satisfaction and of danger often change, and therefore, if an organism's adjustments to the environment were not dynamic, it could not survive. The learning process provides an organism with the flexibility it needs to survive under a wide variety of environmental conditions. To survive, an organism must learn which environmental objects are positive (conducive to survival), which are negative (detrimental to survival), and which are neutral (irrelevant to survival). In addition to learning whether stimuli are positive, negative, or neutral, the organism must learn to behave in such a way as to obtain or avoid these various stimuli. For example, strawberries may be valued positively because of their ability to reduce the hunger drive, but one may need to get a job and perform specific functions in order to be able to go into a store and buy them. Likewise, a bear may value honey positively but may need to learn to climb trees in order to obtain it.

In general, it is through classical conditioning that we learn which environmental objects are conducive to survival and which are not, and it is through instrumental or operant conditioning that we learn how to acquire or avoid desirable and undesirable objects. The adaptive value of classical conditioning is further demonstrated by the fact that it typically takes several pairings between a CS and a US before classical conditioning is established. Schwartz, Wasserman, and Robbins (2002) elaborate on this adaptive feature of classical conditioning:

> Indeed, if we conceive of Pavlovian conditioning as a kind of predictive analysis, we can even see virtue in the fact that it usually takes numerous CS–US pairings before an association is formed. Suppose we learned after a single pairing of CS and US. If we did, any stimulus that accidentally preceded, say, a shock, would produce conditioned fear. Because there is always some stimulus around when a shock (or some natural aversive event) occurs, we might end up walking around in fear of virtually everything. However, if conditioning requires *multiple* pairings, this most paralyzing and maladaptive possibility is largely eliminated. (p. 71)

Learning, then, should be looked on as a major tool in adapting to one's environment that supplements innate homeostatic mechanisms, reflexes, and at least in the case of nonhuman animals, unlearned adaptive behavior.

WHY STUDY LEARNING?

Because most human behavior is learned, investigating the principles of learning will help us understand why we behave as we do. An awareness of the learning process will allow greater understanding not only of normal and adaptive behavior but also of the circumstances that produce maladaptive and abnormal behavior. More effective psychotherapy might result from such an understanding.

Child-rearing practices can also utilize the principles of learning. Obviously, individuals differ from one another, and these individual differences may be explained in terms of differing learning experiences. One of the most important human attributes is language, and there is little doubt that specific language development results mainly from learning. No doubt many other human attributes are molded in a similar way by the interaction of the environment with the learning process. When parents know more about the learning experiences that create what they would call desirable traits, they may wish to organize the environment of their child so that it encourages these traits. Likewise, learning experiences that tend to produce socially maladaptive behavior can be avoided.

Moreover, there is a close relationship between the principles of learning and educational practices. In many cases, principles that have been uncovered while studying the learning process in the laboratory have eventually been utilized in the classroom. The widespread utilization of programmed learning, teaching machines, and computer-assisted instruction offers three examples of how research on learning influences teaching practices. The current trend in American education toward individualized instruction can also be considered a spin-off from research on the learning process. We may reasonably conclude that as our knowledge of the learning process increases, educational practices should become more efficient and effective.

DISCUSSION QUESTIONS

1. List the requirements that must be met before a change in behavior can be attributed to learning.
2. Describe the processes of sensitization and habituation as they have occurred in your life.
3. Differentiate between learning and performance.
4. Give a few examples of complex unlearned behavior. Do you feel that complex unlearned behavior exists on the human level? Explain.
5. Why was the term *instinct* replaced with the term *species-specific behavior*?
6. Differentiate between the terms *learning* and *conditioning*.
7. How many kinds of learning are there? Explain how you arrived at your answer.
8. What is meant by the statement "Imprinting seems to result from both learning and instinct"?
9. Describe the relationship between learning and survival.
10. Give a few reasons why it is important to study the learning process.

CHAPTER HIGHLIGHTS

avoidance conditioning

behavioral potentiality

classical conditioning

conditioning

critical period

escape conditioning

habituation

homeostatic mechanisms

imprinting

instinct

instrumental conditioning

learning

performance

reflex

reinforced practice

sensitization

short-term memory

Skinner box

temporary body states

CHAPTER 2

Approaches to the Study of Learning

We noted in Chapter 1 that most learning theorists contend that learning can be observed only indirectly through changes in behavior. Therefore, when we study learning, we observe behavior, and based on these observables, we infer that a particular type of learning has or has not occurred. The inaccessibility of learning is one reason why there are so many approaches to its study. Some feel, for example, that the best place to study learning is in the field rather than in the laboratory. This method of studying a phenomenon as it occurs naturally is called **naturalistic observation.** Using this technique, one would make detailed observations and recordings of what is being studied. Such research often results in a grouping or classification of the various elements of the phenomenon being investigated. For example, while using naturalistic observation to study learning in the classroom, one might classify learning to read or spell as verbal learning, the learning of athletic prowess as perceptual-motor skill learning, and the learning that requires complex mental processes as problem solving or concept formation.

Two major drawbacks of naturalistic observation become apparent. First, because the classroom situation is extremely complex, it is very difficult to observe and record accurately. Second, there is a tendency to classify events into chunks that may be too comprehensive; for example, what is classified as concept formation may in reality consist of many different phenomena whose distinctions get lost in the classifying process. Classifications that seem rather straightforward at first may become extraordinarily complex under closer scrutiny.

Naturalistic observation can be an important first step for a study of learning, but eventually the psychologist must break up the recorded chunks of behavior for closer and more detailed analysis; that is, the psychologist must become more elementistic in order to discover the various laws operating in the learning situation, and discovering laws usually involves experimentation. In other words, naturalistic observation may be important in isolating groups of events for further study, but these must then be reduced into smaller components for further analysis. Such an approach is called **elementism.**

THE SYSTEMATIC STUDY OF LEARNING

In modern times, that portion of psychology concerned with the learning process has become more scientific. We discuss in the next chapter that using the scientific method in the psychology of learning has been very productive. It is important, therefore, that we look at such a productive method in more detail.

What Is Science?

According to Hergenhahn and Olson (2007),

> **Science** combines two ancient philosophical positions on the origins of knowledge. One of these positions, called rationalism, contends that one gains knowledge by exercising the mind, in other words, by thinking, reasoning, and using logic. According to the rationalist, information must be sorted out by the mind before reasonable conclusions can be drawn. The other philosophical position, called empiricism, contends that sensory experience is the basis of all knowledge. In its extreme form, empiricism states that we know only what we experience. Thus the rationalist emphasizes mental operations whereas the empiricist equates knowledge with experience. Science combined the two positions thereby creating an extremely powerful epistemological tool. (p. 11)

Aspects of Theory

In the realm of science, empiricism and rationalism come together in **scientific theory** (Hergenhahn & Olson, 2007, p. 11). Scientific theories have two important aspects. First, a theory has a **formal aspect,** which includes the words and symbols the theory contains. Second, a theory has an **empirical aspect,** which consists of the physical events that the theory is attempting to explain. Although the relationship between the formal and empirical aspects of a theory is very complex, it should be noted that the formal part of a theory can make sense by itself even though it may make erroneous predictions about the physical world. The statement "All learning depends on drive reduction" makes sense formally but may not accurately explain learning. The point here is that a theory can sound valid, but it is devoid of scientific meaning unless it withstands the rigors of experimental tests. There is always the danger of being overly impressed by the wording of a theory and forgetting to check how accurately it predicts and describes empirical events. Most psychologists agree that astrology is a highly developed formal system that has little or no relationship to actual empirical events. In other words, astrology sounds good, but it adds virtually nothing to our understanding of human behavior. Stanovich (2001) says the following about scientific theories:

> A theory in science is an interrelated set of concepts that is used to explain a body of data and to make predictions about the results of future experiments. *Hypotheses* are specific predictions that are derived from theories (which are more general and comprehensive). Currently viable theories are those that have had many of their hypotheses confirmed. The theoretical structures of such theories are thus consistent with a large number of observations. However, when a data base begins to contradict the hypotheses derived from a theory, scientists begin trying to construct a new theory that will provide a better interpretation of the data. Thus, the theories that are under scientific discussion are those that have been verified to some extent and that do not make many predictions that are contradicted by the available data. They are not mere guesses or hunches. (pp. 24–25)

It is important to remember that no matter how abstract and complex a theory becomes, it must ultimately make contact with observable physical events. All scientific theories, no matter how abstract their formal aspects become, begin and end with statements about observable events. A **scientific law** can be defined as a consistently observed relationship between two or more classes of events. *All sciences seek to discover laws.*

From Research to Theory

As a general example of the use of theory in psychology, we can refer to research examining the relationship between food deprivation and rate of learning, with food as the reinforcer. In this case, learning rate will be indexed by the number of trials it takes for an animal to learn to turn left on every trial in a T-maze. After many separate experiments, a researcher finds that as hours of food deprivation go up, learning occurs more rapidly. That is, animals deprived of food the longest learn to turn left in a T-maze most rapidly.

These results can be looked on as the demonstration of a law. Here the observed relationship is between degree of food deprivation and performance on a learning task. The researcher turns next to study water deprivation and again finds that as hours of water deprivation go up, learning time goes down. Now we have a second law: As hours of water deprivation go up, an animal learns to turn left faster in a T-maze when the water is used as a reinforcer.

Next, the researcher turns to the study of sexual behavior. This time the opportunity to copulate is used as a reinforcer for the rat to turn left in the T-maze. Again, it is found that increased hours of sexual deprivation result in faster learning.

Although the goal of science is to discover laws (observed relationships between events), it is seldom enough simply to observe and record hundreds or perhaps thousands of empirical relationships. Scientists usually attempt to make sense of the laws they discover; that is, they attempt to group them in some coherent fashion. This grouping has at least two functions: (1) the **synthesizing function,** which attempts systematically to explain a large number of observations and (2) the **heuristic function,** which points the way to further research. At this point, therefore, the researcher may wish to go beyond the data. The researcher may make statements such as "Hungry animals tend to learn faster than food-satiated ones" or "Thirsty animals tend to learn faster than water-satiated ones." Both statements plunge the researcher into the realm of theory. Although the experiments involved specific situations (e.g., 2, 4, 6, and 8 hours of deprivation), the concept of hunger, which is an abstraction, covers all states of deprivation, even those not involved in the actual research (e.g., 26, 30, 37, and 50 hours of deprivation). Thus, by postulating the unobservable inner state of hunger, the researcher is at the same time attempting to tie together some of the observations and predicting the outcome of future research. The same is true when the concepts of thirst and sexual arousal are used.

The researcher can take an additional step and attempt to synthesize the three theoretical terms into still another theoretical term. The researcher can conclude, for example, that deprivation increases drive, and animals with high drive learn faster. Note that in taking this step the researcher is using the two functions of a theory: synthesis and prediction. By stating that "animals with high drive learn faster than animals with low drive," the researcher is suggesting research on oxygen deprivation, heat deprivation, and pain reduction. The relationship among the concepts of hunger, thirst, sexual arousal, and the empirical events from which they stem is shown in Figure 2–1.

The researcher could take still an additional step and postulate the even more general concept of motivation and include psychological factors (e.g., the need for achievement or for self-actualization) as well as the physiological ones we have been considering.

Theories as Tools

Because a theory is merely a research tool, it cannot be right or wrong; it is either useful or it is not useful. If a theory clarifies the various observations that have been made, and if it generates additional research, the theory is a good one. If it fails in either respect, the researcher is likely to search for a new theory.

If a hypothesis generated by a theory is confirmed, the theory gains strength. If a hypothesis generated by a theory is rejected, the theory is weakened and must either be revised or abandoned. Again we see how confirmation of a theory depends on empirical observation. Whether a theory is maintained, revised, or abandoned is

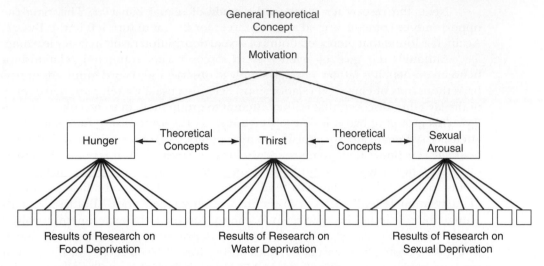

FIGURE 2–1   The relationship between theoretical concepts and the empirical events from which they stem.

determined by the outcome of the empirical research generated by the theory. Thus, we see that *theories must continually generate the very hypotheses that may prove they are ineffective.*

The Principle of Parsimony

We noted earlier that one characteristic of science is that it deals only with statements that are, in principle, empirically verifiable. Another characteristic of science is that it follows the **principle of parsimony** (sometimes called the principle of economy, Occam's razor, or Morgan's canon). This principle states that when two equally effective theories can explain the same phenomenon, but one explanation is simple and the other is complex, we must use the simpler explanation.

Summary of Characteristics of a Scientific Theory

1. A theory synthesizes a number of observations.
2. A good theory is heuristic; that is, it generates new research.
3. A theory must generate hypotheses that can be empirically verified. If such hypotheses are confirmed, the theory gains strength; if not, the theory is weakened and must be revised or abandoned.
4. A theory is a tool and as such cannot be right or wrong; it is either useful or it is not useful.
5. Theories are chosen in accordance with the law of parsimony: Of two equally effective theories, the simpler of the two must be chosen.
6. Theories contain abstractions, such as numbers or words, which constitute the formal aspect of a theory.

7. The formal aspect of a theory must be correlated with observable events, which constitute the empirical aspect of a theory.
8. All theories are attempts to explain empirical events, and they must, therefore, start and end with empirical observations.

THE LEARNING EXPERIMENT

In the previous section, we considered the course from research to theory; here we look briefly at the course from theory to research. First, we must delineate a subject matter. This usually takes the form of a general definition of learning or a general description of the phenomenon to be studied. Next, we attempt to specify the conditions necessary for the phenomenon to occur. Last, we must convert our theoretical statements about the learning process into terms of identifiable and repeatable activities or experimental performances. This way of measurably defining a theoretical term is called an **operational definition.** In other words, an operational definition relates what is being defined (in this case learning) to the operations used to measure it. For example, a common operational definition of learning rate is **trials to criterion,** which is the number of times an experimental subject needs to experience the material to be learned before being able to perform at some specified level, for instance, how many times the subject had to see a list of nonsense syllables before the entire list is recited accurately. Once researchers operationally define their theoretical terms, they are ready to experiment.

Every experiment involves something whose changes are measured, the **dependent variable,** and something the experimenter manipulates or controls to see its effect on the dependent variable, the **independent variable.** In the previously mentioned experiment concerning the relationship between the number of hours of food deprivation and rate of learning, rate of learning was measured and was, therefore, the dependent variable. Rate of learning was operationally defined as how many trials it took for the animal to learn to make a left turn in a T-maze a specified number of consecutive times. Thus, trials to criterion was used as the dependent variable. In learning experiments, the operational definition indicates the kind of behavior that will be used to index learning. Hours of food deprivation was systematically manipulated by the researcher, and it, therefore, was the independent variable.

Arbitrary Decisions in Setting Up a Learning Experiment

Science is often thought of as a cold, highly objective means for arriving at the "truth." Scientists, however, are often highly emotional and very subjective, and the truth they disclose is dynamic and probabilistic. This characterization can be seen in the number of arbitrary decisions that go into setting up any learning experiment. A number of these arbitrary decisions are summarized next.

1. What Aspects of Learning Should Be Investigated?   What aspects should be investigated, of course, are partially dictated by one's theory concerning learning. One can study learning in the laboratory, or one can observe learning as it occurs in a schoolroom via naturalistic observation. In addition, one can study instrumental conditioning, classical conditioning, concept formation, problem solving, or verbal or perceptual-motor learning. Although a theory of learning attempts to specify the conditions under which learning takes place, it is up to the experimenter to choose which of those conditions should be investigated.

2. Idiographic versus Nomothetic Techniques   Should researchers intensely study the learning process of a single experimental subject under a wide variety of circumstances (**idiographic technique**), or should they use groups of experimental subjects and study their average performance (**nomothetic technique**)? Although quite different, both techniques are respectable, and both yield useful information about the learning process. As we discuss later, Skinner used the idiographic technique, and Hull used the nomothetic technique. As we note in Chapter 9, the two techniques can result in entirely different conclusions about the nature of learning.

3. Humans versus Nonhuman Animals as Subjects   If researchers choose to use humans as their experimental participants, they are concerned about how their results generalize from the laboratory to the world outside. If, however, they use nonhuman subjects, such as rats, pigeons, or monkeys, they are also concerned about how the learning process generalizes from one species to another in addition to the first concern.

Why, then, use anything but humans? There are many reasons why researchers use nonhuman subjects instead of humans despite the difficulties involved.

1. Humans are often too sophisticated for certain learning experiments; that is, their previous experience interferes with a clear study of the learning process. The learning history of nonhuman subjects can be controlled with relative ease.
2. Often learning experiments are long and boring, and it would be difficult to find humans willing to participate in them. Nonhuman subjects do not complain.
3. Some experiments are designed to test the effects of genetics on learning ability. By using nonhuman subjects, the genetic background of subjects can be systematically manipulated.
4. The relationship between certain drugs and learning can be investigated with nonhuman subjects, whereas using humans for such research would be difficult or unethical, if not impossible.
5. Various surgical techniques can be used on nonhuman subjects, but not on humans. The surgical removal of certain brain areas and direct brain stimulation by electrodes implanted in the brain are only two examples. Likewise, humans cannot be sacrificed after the experiment to check on such things as neuronal effects of the treatment condition.

6. Last, but not least, humans sometimes miss appointments to run in experiments, whereas nonhuman subjects almost always show up.

4. Correlation Techniques Versus Experimental Techniques   Some researchers may use **correlational techniques.** They may, for example, correlate learning (operationally defined as a score on an achievement test) with intelligence (operationally defined as a score on an IQ test). Because this step involves correlating one response (performance on the achievement test) with another response (performance on the IQ test), the resulting relationship is called an R-R law (response–response law). R-R laws are *correlational* in that they describe how two classes of behavioral events vary together.

Other researchers may want to use **experimental techniques.** They vary systematically one or more environmental events and note their effect on the dependent variables. Because the relationship examined here is between environmental events (stimuli) and responses (changes on the dependent variable), it is said to be an S-R, or stimulus-response, law.

Although one may argue about the relative merits of correlational versus experimental techniques, the point here is that at least these two general approaches are available for doing research. Both approaches yield distinctly different information about learning. Which approach is taken depends on the preference of the individual researcher.

5. Which Independent Variables Should Be Studied?   Once learning is operationally defined, the dependent variable in an experiment is automatically set. If, for example, learning is operationally defined as "trials to criterion," this is what is measured in the experiment. Next, the researcher must ask, "What variable or variables are likely to have an effect on the behavior being measured?" The answer to that question may come from a long list of possible independent variables. A sample list follows:

Sex difference	Instructions
Age differences	Intelligence
Size of the stimulus materials used	Drugs
Rate of presentation	Intertrial interval
Meaningfulness of the material used	Interaction with other tasks

An additional function of a theory, by the way, is to give researchers some guidance in choosing their independent variable or variables.

6. What Levels of the Independent Variables Should Be Studied?   Once one or more independent variables are chosen, the researcher must consider how many levels of an independent variable should be represented in the experiment. For example, if age is chosen as an experimental variable, how many ages and which ones should be studied? There are some guidelines that could be used here to ensure that the levels of the independent variable chosen will have the greatest effect on the dependent variable (see Anderson, 1971), but this choice is basically arbitrary.

7. Choice of Dependent Variables   Common dependent variables in learning experiments include the following:

Scores on tests   Trials to criterion
Trials to extinction   Latency
Running speed   Probability of response
Rate of responding   Number of errors
Time to solution   Response amplitude

Because each potential dependent variable results from an operational definition of learning, it should be clear that many acceptable operational definitions of learning are available to the researcher. Although which is chosen is arbitrary, the choice may have a profound effect on the conclusions one draws about the outcome of an experiment. In experiments with two dependent variables, it is common for one variable to show an effect due to the independent variable and for the other to show no effect. For example, when investigating the transfer of training from one hand to the other in our laboratory, we consistently find that practice with one hand increases the speed with which a task can be performed with the other hand (speed of responding being one dependent variable). Using speed as our dependent variable, we find evidence for positive transfer of training from one hand to the other. If, however, we use number of errors as our dependent variable, we discover that practice with one hand does not facilitate performance with the other hand. Thus we conclude that no transfer of training took place—two altogether dissimilar conclusions resulting from our choice of the dependent variable.

8. Data Analysis and Interpretation   Once the data (scores on the dependent variable) have been gathered in an experiment, how does one analyze them? Although it is beyond the scope of this book to discuss them, the reader should be aware that many statistical techniques are available to the researcher for data analysis. Here again, the choice of a statistical test is somewhat arbitrary yet may have a significant effect on one's conclusions.

Once the experiment has been designed, run, and analyzed, it must be interpreted. There are usually many interpretations of the data provided by an experiment, and there is really no way of knowing if the one finally decided on is the best. It is possible that even after following the most rigorous scientific procedures in the gathering of experimental data, the interpretation of those data could be totally inadequate. For example, there is the story of the researcher who trained a flea to jump every time he said "jump." After this preliminary training, the researcher began pulling legs off the flea, and after the removal of each leg, he said "jump" and the flea jumped. The experiment continued in this manner until the flea's last leg had been pulled off. Now when the experimenter said "jump," the flea did not move. The researcher jotted his conclusion in his notebook: "Fleas without legs are deaf." We exaggerate only to stress the point that there are many possible conclusions to draw about the same experimental data.

It should be noted that although we refer to the decisions in this section as arbitrary, they are arbitrary only in the sense that there are a number of ways of arranging an experiment in a given area and any one of the ways might be scientifically correct. In a more practical sense, however, the choice of what to study, the kind of subject to use, independent and dependent variables, and the approach to data analysis and interpretation will be at least partially determined by such factors as cost, practicality, theoretical orientation, social and educational concerns, and availability of apparatus.

THE USE OF MODELS

The *Random House Dictionary of the English Language* defines **analogy** as "a partial similarity between like features of two things, on which a comparison may be based." In science, it is often useful to find that two things are analogous, especially when one thing is well known and the other is not. In such cases, we can use what is well known as a **model** in attempting to understand what is less known. At one time, noting the similarity between the functioning of mechanical pumps (about which a great deal was known) and the functioning of human hearts (about which less was known) provided a useful guide for heart research. Also, noting the similarities between lower animals and humans encouraged the intense study of lower animals in order to learn more about human processes.

In recent years, information-processing psychology has used the computer as a model in the study of human intellectual processes. Many information-processing psychologists state that computers and humans are analogous because both receive information (input) from the environment, process that information in one or more ways, and then act on that information (output). These information-processing psychologists say that the software programs determine how computers process the information fed into them. Likewise, humans are programmed by experience to process information in certain ways. Because of these similarities, some information-processing psychologists believe that much can be learned about how humans process information by assuming that computers and humans process information in similar ways; however, not all information-processing psychologists feel that the computer is a useful model for studying human cognitive processes.

Unlike a theory, a model is typically not used to explain a complicated process; rather, it is used to simplify the process and make it more understandable. The use of models involves showing how something is like something else. A theory, however, attempts to describe the processes underlying a complex phenomenon. Reinforcement theory, for example, is an attempt to explain why learning occurs. It is not an attempt to show what learning is *like*, as would be the case with a model. In the area of motivation, one might say that an organism acts like a mule with a carrot dangling before it, or one might say that the physiological state of hunger is interacting with previously learned habits, causing the organism to run. In the former case, a model is being used to *describe* behavior; in the latter case, a theory is being used in an attempt to *explain* behavior.

LEARNING IN THE LABORATORY VERSUS NATURALISTIC OBSERVATION

Remember that science deals in statements that are verified through experimentation. Contrasted with naturalistic observation, where the researcher has no control over what is being observed, an experiment can be defined as controlled observation. Information is both gained and lost in laboratory experimentation. On the plus side, the experimenter controls the situation and therefore is able to examine systematically a number of different conditions and their effect on learning. On the negative side, the laboratory creates an artificial situation that is much different from the circumstances under which learning would ordinarily occur. This always brings into question how information gained in the laboratory is related to learning situations outside the laboratory. Some researchers feel that combining naturalistic observation and laboratory experimentation is best. That is, one could make initial observations in the field, examine them in greater detail in the laboratory, and then observe the phenomenon again in the field with the greater understanding that resulted from the laboratory experimentation.

KUHN'S VIEWS OF HOW SCIENCES CHANGE

To portray science as an activity that gradually evolves toward an increasingly accurate understanding of nature, as we have done previously, may be somewhat misleading. In his 1973 book *The Structure of Scientific Revolutions,* Thomas Kuhn (1922–1996) presents a much different view of science. According to Kuhn, scientists working in a given area usually accept a certain point of view about what they are studying. For example, at one time most physicists accepted the Newtonian point of view in their study of physics. Kuhn calls a point of view shared by a substantial number of scientists a **paradigm.** A paradigm provides a general framework for empirical research and, as such, is usually more than just a limited theory. A paradigm corresponds more closely to what is called a school of thought or an "ism," such as *behaviorism, associationism,* or *functionalism* (these terms are explained in the next chapter).

The activities of scientists who accept a particular paradigm consist mainly of elaborating and verifying the implications of the framework it superimposes over the subject being studied. In other words, a paradigm is a way of looking at a subject that illuminates certain problems and suggests ways of solving those problems. Kuhn calls the problem-solving activities of scientists following a paradigm **normal science.** Normal science is what most of this chapter is about.

The positive result of a community of scientists following a certain paradigm is that a certain range of phenomena, those on which the paradigm focuses, are explored thoroughly. The negative result is that following a particular paradigm blinds the scientists to other, perhaps more fruitful, ways of dealing with their subject matter. Thus, whereas research generated by a certain paradigm results in depth, it may inhibit breadth.

According to Kuhn (1973), scientists following a particular paradigm, that is, those engaged in normal science, are providing little more than a "mop-up operation." Kuhn puts the matter as follows:

> Mopping-up operations are what engage most scientists throughout their careers. They constitute what I am here calling normal science. Closely examined, whether historically or in the contemporary laboratory, that enterprise seems an attempt to force nature into the preformed and relatively inflexible box that the paradigm supplies. No part of the aim of normal science is to call forth new sorts of phenomena; indeed those that will not fit the box are often not seen at all. Nor do scientists normally aim to invent new theories, and they are often intolerant of those invented by others. Instead, normal-scientific research is directed to the articulation of those phenomena and theories that the paradigm already supplies. (p. 24)

How then do new paradigms emerge? According to Kuhn, innovations in science come when scientists following a particular paradigm are consistently confronted with events that are inconsistent with the point of view they are holding. Eventually, as the anomalies persist, an alternative paradigm will emerge that will be able to explain the anomalies as well as the events supporting the previous paradigm. The new paradigm will usually be associated with one individual or a small group of individuals who attempt to convince their colleagues that their paradigm is more effective than its predecessor. Typically, the new paradigm meets with great resistance, and converts are won very slowly. Kuhn says that this resistance comes from the fact that a particular paradigm has implications for every aspect of one's scientific life, and therefore changing from one paradigm to another involves an enormous change in how one does science; for this reason, there is emotional involvement in the decision. Kuhn says, "Like the choice between competing political institutions, that between competing paradigms proves to be a choice between incompatible modes of community life" (p. 94). Because of this emotional involvement, scientists will usually do everything possible to make their accepted paradigm work before pondering a change. At some point, however, the older paradigm will be "overthrown," and the new one will replace it. The displacement of Newton's theory by Einstein's theory is one example, and the displacement of religious notions concerning the creation of human life by Darwin's theory of evolution is another.

According to Kuhn, then, a science changes (although it does not necessarily advance) through a series of **scientific revolutions,** which are similar to political revolutions, rather than through a continuous evolutionary process within a single theoretical framework. To Kuhn, the evolution of a science is at least as much a sociological phenomenon as it is a scientific phenomenon. We might add that because of the emotional involvement, it also appears to be a psychological phenomenon.

As valid as Kuhn's argument appears to be, it seems most forceful when applied to the physical sciences rather than the behavioral sciences. Within the more mature physical sciences, it is the rule that most scientists accept some prevailing paradigm, and therefore a change in paradigm tends to be revolutionary. In the younger behavioral sciences, however, many paradigms exist simultaneously. The book you are now reading provides a good example because it offers various ways of looking at the learning process. Every theory in this book is accepted to some extent

by a substantial number of researchers of the learning process. Although followers of one theory tend to form a camp, they still communicate and influence members of other camps. It would be difficult to find an area in physics for which this would be true. For example, one could not find a book on theories of gravity because there are not as many paradigms that exist simultaneously in that area.

Thus it seems that under the conditions that exist in the behavioral sciences, the revolutionary change of paradigms is less possible and less necessary. One possible exception to this contention would be the widespread acceptance of associationism, one of psychology's oldest and most widely accepted doctrines. In fact, most theories in this book assume some aspect of associationism. At the present time, there is growing dissatisfaction with the assumptions underlying associationism; thus we have the necessary condition for the kind of scientific revolution that Kuhn so eloquently describes in his book.

POPPER'S VIEW OF SCIENCE

As we have seen, science has traditionally been viewed as involving empirical observation, theory formation, theory testing, theory revision, and the search for lawful relationships. Like Kuhn, Karl Popper (1902–1994) was critical of this traditional view of science. According to Popper (1963), scientific activity does not start with empirical observation, as is so often claimed. Rather, it starts with the existence of a problem. For Popper, the idea that scientists wander around making empirical observations and then attempt to explain those observations was just plain silly:

> Twenty-five years ago I tried to bring home the same point to a group of physics students in Vienna by beginning a lecture with the following instruction: "Take pencil and paper: carefully observe, and write down what you have observed!" They asked, of course, *what* I wanted them to observe. Clearly the instruction, "Observe!" is absurd . . . observation is always selective. It needs a chosen object, a definite task, an interest, a point of view, a problem. (p. 46)

For Popper, then, problems determine which observations are made by scientists. The next step in scientific activity, according to Popper, is to propose a solution to the problem. A scientific theory is a proposed solution to a problem. What distinguishes a scientific theory from a nonscientific theory is the **principle of refutability** (sometimes called the **principle of falsification**). According to this principle, a scientific theory must make specific predictions about what will happen under certain circumstances. Furthermore, the predictions must be risky in the sense that there is a real possibility that the predictions will prove to be erroneous and thus refute the theory on which they were based. Einstein's theory of relativity made the risky prediction that as objects approached the speed of light, they would diminish in size and increase in mass. If these predictions were found to be false, Einstein's theory would have had to be revised or abandoned. It turns out, however, that his predictions were accurate.

Popper criticized a number of theories in psychology because they do not pass the test of refutability. Freud's theory, for example, makes no risky predictions. Everything that a person does can be "explained" by Freud's theory. If, for example, Freud's theory predicts that on the basis of early experience a man should hate women but is found to love them, the Freudian can say that he is displaying a "reaction formation." That is, he really does hate women on the unconscious level, and he is simply going overboard in the opposite direction to reduce the anxiety that his recognition of his true hatred of women would cause. Astrology suffers the same fate because there is no conceivable observation that could be made that would refute its claims. Contrary to common belief, if every conceivable observation agrees with a theory, the theory is weak, not strong.

Kuhn versus Popper

According to Popper, what Kuhn calls normal science is not science at all. For Popper, the subjective beliefs that Kuhn claims bind scientists to a paradigm inhibit effective problem solving. In his analysis of scientific activity, Kuhn stresses sociological and psychological factors, whereas Popper's analysis stressed the logical refutation of proposed solutions to problems. For Popper, either proposed solutions (theories) to problems pass the rigorous attempts to refute them or they do not; there is no room for subjectivity. Can the analyses of both Kuhn and Popper be correct? Robinson (1986) suggests that they can be, and we agree: "In a conciliatory spirit, we might suggest that the major disagreement between Kuhn and Popper vanishes when we picture Kuhn as describing what science has been historically, and Popper asserting what it ought to be" (p. 24).

DISCUSSION QUESTIONS

1. In what way(s) do you feel science differs from other fields of inquiry, such as philosophy and theology?
2. What is a *scientific law*? How does the scientific concept of law differ from how the term is used in a legal or a religious sense?
3. Discuss the strengths and weaknesses of naturalistic observation.
4. Briefly discuss the characteristics of a scientific theory.
5. Discuss the steps involved in going from experimentation to theory.
6. Discuss the steps involved in going from theory to experimentation.
7. What is a scientific model? Give an example of how a model has been used in psychology.
8. Differentiate between a theory and a model.
9. List and briefly describe the arbitrary decisions that are involved in setting up, running, and analyzing a learning experiment.
10. What does Kuhn mean when he says normal science is a "mop-up" operation?
11. Describe the process of scientific revolution as it is viewed by Kuhn.
12. Discuss Popper's criticisms of the traditional views of science.
13. How can the analyses of science offered by Kuhn and Popper be reconciled?

CHAPTER HIGHLIGHTS

analogy
correlational techniques
dependent variable
elementism
empirical aspect of a theory
experimental techniques
formal aspect of a theory
heuristic function of a theory
idiographic technique
independent variable
model
naturalistic observation
nomothetic technique

normal science
operational definition of learning
paradigm
principle of parsimony
principle of refutability (principle of
   falsification)
science
scientific law
scientific revolutions
scientific theory
synthesizing function of a theory
trials to criterion

CHAPTER 3

Early Notions about Learning

EPISTEMOLOGY AND LEARNING THEORY

Epistemology is a branch of philosophy that is concerned with the nature of knowledge. The epistemologist asks questions such as What is knowledge? What can we know? What are the limits of knowledge? What does it mean to know? and What are the origins of knowledge? Questions of this kind go back at least as far as the early Greeks. In fact, the views of Plato and Aristotle concerning the nature of knowledge set philosophical trends that persist until this day. Plato believed that knowledge was inherited and was, therefore, a natural component of the human mind. According to Plato, one gained knowledge by reflecting on the contents of one's mind. Aristotle, in contrast, believed that knowledge derived from sensory experience and was not inherited.

Although Plato believed that knowledge is inherited and Aristotle believed that it is derived from sensory experience, both exemplify **rationalism** because both believed that the mind is actively involved in the attainment of knowledge. For Plato, the mind must engage in active introspection to discover inherited knowledge. For Aristotle, the mind must actively ponder the information provided by the senses to discover the knowledge contained within that information. The term **nativism** can also be applied to Plato's position because he stressed that knowledge is innate. The position taken by Aristotle also exemplifies **empiricism** because he stressed the importance of sensory experience as the basis of all knowledge.

The philosophies of Plato and Aristotle show the difficulty in using such general philosophical terms as *rationalist, nativist,* and *empiricist.* A case can be made that all three labels accurately apply to any philosopher relevant to the history of learning theory. A rationalist maintains that the mind must be actively involved in the quest of knowledge (e.g., by thinking, reasoning, or deducing). Certainly both Plato and Aristotle were rationalists. The nativist maintains that some important trait or attitude is inherited. For Plato, one such attribute is knowledge. Aristotle, however, did not totally reject nativism. For him the reasoning powers used to abstract knowledge from sensory experience are innate. The empiricist maintains that sensory information is the basis of all knowledge, and because Aristotle believed this, he can be labeled an empiricist. This is not to say, however, that sensory information is unimportant in Plato's philosophy. For Plato the search for, or the awareness of, innate knowledge is often triggered by sensory experience.

Because the type of overlap just described is common among philosophers, it is important to remember that labels such as rationalist, empiricist, and nativist are applied to a philosopher because of the *emphasis* of that philosopher's work. There are no pure rationalists, empiricists, or nativists. In their explanations of knowledge, Plato can be called a nativist because he stressed inheritance, Aristotle can be called an empiricist because he stressed the importance of sensory information, and both Plato and Aristotle can be called rationalists because they stressed the importance of an active mind for the attainment of knowledge.

Because the views of Plato and Aristotle concerning the nature of knowledge have played such an important role in the history of learning theory, we look at them in greater detail.

PLATO

Plato (ca. 427–347 B.C.) was Socrates' most famous student. In fact, Socrates never wrote a word about his philosophy—it was written by Plato. This is a most significant fact because the early Platonic dialogues were designed primarily to show the Socratic approach to knowledge and were memories of the great teacher at work. The later dialogues, however, represent Plato's own philosophy and have little to do with Socrates. Plato was so upset by the execution of Socrates for impiety that he went on a self-imposed exile to southern Italy, where he came under the influence of the **Pythagoreans.** This fact has important implications for Western people and is directly related to all approaches to epistemology, including learning theory, that have occurred since.

The Pythagoreans believed that the universe was governed by numerical relationships that influenced the physical world. In fact, numbers and their various combinations *caused* events in the physical world. And both events, the number and the empirical event that it caused, were real. Thus, to the Pythagoreans, the abstract had an independent existence and was capable of influencing physical objects. Furthermore, physical events were thought to be only manifestations of the abstract. Although number and matter interact, it is matter that we experience with our senses, not number. This results in a dualistic view of the universe, in which one aspect can be experienced through the senses and the other cannot. Following this notion, the Pythagoreans made great strides in mathematics, medicine, and music. Through time, however, they developed into a mystical cult, allowing only a few individuals to become members and share their wisdom. Plato was one such individual.

Plato's later dialogues reflect complete acceptance of the dualistic universe in which the Pythagoreans believed. He developed a theory of knowledge based on the Pythagorean notion that the abstract has an independent and influential existence.

Reminiscence Theory of Knowledge

According to Plato, every object in the physical world has a corresponding abstract "idea" or "form" that causes it. For example, the abstract idea for *chair* interacts with matter to produce what we call a chair. The idea of *tree* interacts with matter to form what we see as a tree. All physical objects have such an origin. Thus what we experience through our senses is a chair, a tree, or a house, but not chairness, treeness, or houseness. The pure idea or essence of these things exists independent of matter, and something is lost when the idea is translated into matter. Therefore, if we attempt to gain knowledge by examining things that we experience through the senses, we will be misled. Sensory information provides only opinion; the abstract ideas themselves are the only bases of true knowledge.

But how do we obtain information about the ideas if we cannot experience them through the senses? Plato said we experience them through the "mind's eye." We turn our thoughts inward and ponder what is innately available to us. All human beings have in their mind complete knowledge of all the ideas that make up the world; thus true knowledge comes from introspection or self-analysis. We must learn to divorce ourselves from sensory information that can only deceive or, at best, remind us of what we already know.

How does one come to have knowledge of the ideas? Here Plato becomes mystical. All humans possess a soul. Before being placed in the body at birth, the soul dwells in pure and complete knowledge. Thus all human souls know everything before entering the body. Upon entering the body, the knowledge of the soul begins to be "contaminated" by sensory information. According to Plato, if humans accept what they experience through the senses as truth, they are doomed to live a life of opinion or ignorance. Only by turning away from the physical impure world to the world of ideas, pondered by the mind's eye, can we hope to gain true knowledge.

Thus all knowledge is **reminiscence,** or recollection of the experience our soul had in the "heaven which is beyond the heavens." Plato advises the astronomer to "let the heavens alone" and use "the natural gift of reason" (*Republic* VII, p. 296, from translation by Cornford, 1968).

As we have already seen, Plato was a nativist because he felt knowledge was inborn. He was also a rationalist because he felt this knowledge could be made available only through reasoning. As we discuss later, other rationalists were not as extreme as Plato in their negative attitude toward sensory information. However, it was Plato's philosophy that dominated Europe for the first twelve centuries of the Christian Era. It is largely through this early influence on Christianity that we still have remnants of Platonism in Western culture today.

ARISTOTLE

Aristotle (384–322 B.C.), one of Plato's students, first followed Plato's teachings quite closely and later broke away from them almost completely. A basic difference between the two thinkers was in their attitude toward sensory information. To Plato, it was a hindrance and something to be distrusted, but to Aristotle, sensory information was the basis of all knowledge. With his favorable attitude toward empirical observation, Aristotle compiled an extraordinarily large number of facts about physical and biological phenomena.

Aristotle, however, in no way abandoned reason. He felt that sense impressions were only the beginning of knowledge—the mind must then ponder these impressions to discover the lawfulness that runs through them. The laws that govern the empirical world are not knowable through sensory information alone but must be discovered by active reason. Thus Aristotle believed that knowledge was gained from sense experience *and* reasoning.

There are two major differences here between Aristotle's and Plato's theories of knowledge. First, the laws, forms, or universals that Aristotle was looking for did not have an existence independent of their empirical manifestation, as they did for Plato. They were simply observed relationships in nature. Second, for Aristotle all knowledge is based on sensory experience. This, of course, was not the case with Plato. It is because Aristotle contended that the source of all knowledge is sensory experience that he is labeled an empiricist.

In elaborating his empiricistic view of knowledge, Aristotle formulated his **laws of association.** He said that the experience or recall of one object will tend to elicit the recall of things similar to that object (law of similarity), recall of opposite things (law of contrast), or recall of things that were originally experienced along with that object (law of contiguity). Aristotle also noted that the more frequently two things are experienced together, the more likely it will be that the experience or recall of one will stimulate the recall of the second. Later in history this came to be known as the law of frequency. Thus, according to Aristotle, sensory experience gives rise to ideas. The ideas stimulated by sensory experience will stimulate other ideas in accordance with the laws of similarity, contrast, contiguity, and frequency.

Within philosophy the contention that the relationships among ideas can be explained by the laws of association is called **associationism.** An example of how ideas become associated through contiguity is shown in Figure 3–1.

Besides making empirical investigation respectable, Aristotle made several other contributions to psychology. He wrote the first history of psychology, which was entitled *De Anima.* He wrote extensively on the human sensory apparatus, which he listed as consisting of sight, hearing, smell, taste, and touch. He contributed greatly to later conceptions of memory, thinking, and learning. As we noted earlier, his associative principles of similarity, contrast, contiguity, and frequency later became the bases for the doctrine of associationism, which is still very much part of modern learning theory. In view of his immense contributions, we can forgive him for locating the mind in the heart and treating the brain as a system for cooling the blood. About Aristotle's great influence on learning theory, Weimer (1973) said,

> A moment's recollection . . . shows that Aristotle's doctrines are at the heart of contemporary thought in epistemology and the psychology of learning. The centrality of associationism as the mechanism of the mind is so well known as to require only the observation that not one single learning theory propounded in this century has failed to base its account on associative principles. (p. 18)

With Aristotle's death died the hope for the development of empirical science. In the centuries following Aristotle, there was no follow-up to the scientific study that Aristotelian thinking had promoted. The collapse of the Greek city-states, barbarian invasions throughout Europe, and the rapid spread of Christianity stunted the growth of scientific inquiry. Early medieval thinkers depended on the teachings of past authorities instead of seeking new information.

Plato's philosophy was an important influence on early Christianity. The conception of man that prevailed during these times is described by Marx and Cronan-Hillix (1987):

> Human beings were regarded as creatures with a soul possessed of a free will which set them apart from ordinary natural laws and subject only to their own willfulness and perhaps to the rule of God. Such a creature, being free-willed, could not be an object of scientific investigation.
>
> Even the human body was regarded as sacrosanct. Anatomists had to double as grave robbers, and that made anatomy a highly risky, or very expensive, occupation. The strictures against observation slowed the development of anatomy and medicine for centuries and allowed incredible misconceptions to persist for over a thousand years. A science of psychology could not flourish in such an atmosphere. (p. 28)

Religion has been defined as philosophy in the absence of dialogue; when Plato's views concerning the nature of knowledge were incorporated into Christian dogma, they could not be challenged. Some fifteen hundred years elapsed before the rediscovery of Aristotle's writings challenged the antiempiricism of the church. When inquiry into nature did begin again, it spread like wildfire. For psychology, the writings of René Descartes represent one of the most important examples of this renaissance.

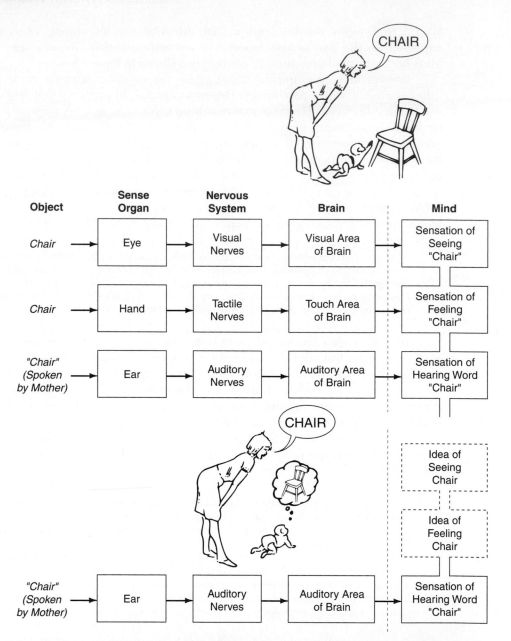

FIGURE 3–1   An example of how seeing and touching a chair and hearing the word chair become associated through contiguity. From *Introduction to Modern Behaviorism*, 3rd ed., by Howard Rachlin. Copyright ©1991 W. H. Freeman and Company. Reprinted with permission.

THE BEGINNING OF MODERN PSYCHOLOGY

René Descartes (1596–1650) tried to approach all philosophical inquiry with an attitude of complete doubt. "I can doubt everything," he argued, "except one thing, and that is the very fact that I doubt. But when I doubt I think; and when I think I must exist." He thus arrived at his celebrated conclusion, "I think; therefore I am." He went on from that point to prove the existence of God, and from there he inferred that our sensory experiences must be a reflection of an objective reality because God would not deceive us.

Descartes went on to postulate a separation between the mind and the body. He viewed the human body as a machine that moves in predictable ways; in this respect, we were the same as any other animal. The mind, however, is a uniquely human attribute. The mind was free and could decide the actions of the body. Descartes believed the pineal gland to be the point of contact between the mind and the body. The mind could move the gland from side to side and could thus open or close the pores of the brain. Through these pores, the "animal spirits" flowed down tiny tubes to the muscles, filling and swelling them and making them become short and thick, thus moving the parts of the body to which they were connected. Although physical action is what occurs when the mind causes behavior, sensory experience can also cause behavior. Motion outside the body exerts a pull on the "taut strings" that lead to the brain; the pull opens the pores of the brain, releasing the "animal spirits," which flow into the muscles and cause behavior. Therefore, the mind or the physical environment can initiate behavior. This description of *reflex action* was to have a long-lasting influence on psychology. Descartes can be considered a predecessor of the stimulus-response psychologists.

By comparing the human body to a machine, Descartes helped to make it accessible to scientific study. He urged physiologists to use the method of dissection to better understand the machinery of the body. Because Descartes believed that humans and animals were physiologically similar, the study of animals to learn about humans became respectable. Descartes, therefore, did much to pave the way for physiological and comparative psychology.

The mind, however, was free and possessed by humans alone. In explaining the working of the mind, Descartes relied heavily on **innate ideas,** thus showing Plato's influence on his philosophy. Innate ideas were not derivable from experience but were integral to the mind. Examples of innate ideas included the concepts of God and the self, the axioms of geometry, and the ideas of space, time, and motion. The question of innate ideas caused much philosophical discussion following Descartes.

Thomas Hobbes (1588–1679) opposed the notion that innate ideas are a source of knowledge. He maintained that sense impressions are the source of all knowledge. With this belief, Hobbes reopened the philosophical school of empiricism and its related associationism.

Hobbes believed that stimuli either help or hinder the vital functions of the body. A stimulus that aids in the vital functioning of the body causes a feeling of pleasure; therefore, the person seeks to experience this pleasure again. Stimuli that hinder the vital functioning of the body cause an aversive feeling, and the person seeks to retreat from it. According to Hobbes, human behavior is controlled by these "appetites" and "aversions." Those events approached by a person are called "good," and those avoided are called "evil." Thus the values of good and evil are individually determined; they are not abstract or absolute. Later Jeremy Bentham (1748–1832) said that human behavior was governed by the "pleasure principle," an idea that was picked up by Freud and later by the reinforcement theorists.

Hobbes was mainly interested in the political and societal conditions under which humans live. He felt that humans were basically selfish and aggressive, and if they were allowed to live in accordance with their nature, life would be characterized by self-satisfaction and war. Humans form political systems and societies because it is to our advantage to do so, not because we are by nature gregarious. Without agreed-on rules and regulations concerning conduct, human existence would be characterized by "continual fear, and danger of violent death; and the life of man, solitary, poor, nasty, brutish, and short" (Hobbes, 1962 [1651], p. 100). In other words, Hobbes believed that forming human societies was the lesser of two evils because it reduced the likelihood of constant struggle with other humans. This view of the function of society comes very close to the one held by Freud many years later.

John Locke (1632–1704) also opposed the notion of innate ideas. For him, the mind is made up of ideas, and ideas come from experience. He indicated that if ideas were innate, people everywhere would possess them, but they do not. Rather, different cultural groups differ markedly in what they think and believe. Thus, the infant mind at birth is a *tabula rasa,* a blank tablet, and experience writes on it. The mind becomes what it experiences; *there is nothing in the mind that is not first in the senses.* Simple ideas come directly from sense experience; complex ideas come from combining simple ideas.

Clearly, then, Locke was an empiricist. Note, however, that his philosophy had a major rationalistic component. Although simple ideas come from experience, they are combined by reflection, and reflection is a rational process. As Leibniz (1646–1716) said in summarizing Locke's philosophy, "There is nothing in the mind that is not first in the senses, *except the mind itself.*"

Like Galileo before him, Locke distinguished between primary and secondary qualities. Primary qualities are characteristics of the physical world powerful enough to cause accurate mental representations of themselves in the mind of a perceiver. Size, weight, quantity, solidity, shape, and mobility exemplify primary qualities. Secondary qualities are characteristics of the physical world too weak or minute to cause accurate mental representations of themselves in the mind of a perceiver. Electromagnetic energy, atoms and molecules, airwaves, and white corpuscles in the blood exemplify secondary qualities. Secondary qualities cause psychological experiences that have no counterparts in the physical world, for example, the experiences of colors, sounds, odors, tastes, and blood being entirely red.

Although it is not how Locke used the terms, it is often the case that *primary quality* is used to refer to physical objects and *secondary quality* to any psychological experience that has no exact counterpart in the physical world. In what follows we follow the latter convention. The distinction between primary and secondary qualities is often cited as the reason that psychology can never become a true science. It is claimed that because secondary qualities are purely cognitive, they cannot be objectively analyzed in the same way that primary qualities can be. For many, it is this inaccessibility of secondary qualities to direct objective study that causes them to be beyond the reach of scientific scrutiny. Many years later, this very concern caused many behaviorists to place the study of mental events off-limits in their analysis of human behavior.

George Berkeley (1685–1753) claimed that Locke did not go far enough. There was still a kind of dualism in Locke's view that physical objects cause ideas about them. Whereas Locke contended that there is an empirical world about which we have ideas, Berkeley claimed that we can experience only secondary qualities. Nothing exists unless it is perceived; *thus to be is to be perceived.* What we call primary qualities, such as shape and size, are really only secondary qualities or ideas. Ideas are the only things we experience directly and are therefore the only things we can be sure of. Despite such beliefs, Berkeley is still considered an empiricist because he believed the contents of the mind were derived from the experience of external reality. That external reality was not material or physical but rather God's perception: What we experience through our senses are God's ideas.

David Hume (1711–1776) carried the argument one step further. Although he agreed with Berkeley that we could know nothing for sure about the physical environment, he added that we could know nothing for sure about ideas. *We can be sure of nothing.* Mind, for Hume, was no more than a stream of ideas, memories, imaginings, associations, and feelings.

This is not to deny Hume's empiricist and associationist leanings. He believed strongly that human knowledge consists of ideas that somehow come from experience and come to be associated through the principles of association. Hume was saying, however, that we experience the empirical world only indirectly through our ideas. Even the laws of nature are constructs of the imagination; the "lawfulness" of nature is in our minds, not necessarily in nature. General concepts such as causation, for example, come from what Hume referred to as the "habitual order of ideas."

Needless to say, Hume upset everyone. To accept Hume was to question rational thought, science, psychology, and religion. All dogma, whether religious or scientific, now became suspect. Hergenhahn (2005) summarizes Hume's philosophy as follows:

> Hume had argued that all conclusions we reached about anything were based on subjective experience because that was the only thing we ever encountered directly. According to Hume, all statements about the nature of the physical world or about morality were derived from impressions and ideas and the feelings that they aroused, as well as from the way they were organized by the laws of association. Even causation, which was so important to many philosophers and scientists, was reduced to a habit of the mind in Hume's philosophy. For example, even if B always follows A and the interval between the two is always the same we cannot ever conclude that A causes B, because there is no way for us to verify an actual, causal relationship between the two events. For Hume, rational philosophy, physical science, and moral philosophy were all reduced to subjective psychology. Therefore, nothing could be known with

certainty because all knowledge was based on the interpretation of subjective experience. (pp. 175–176)

Immanuel Kant (1724–1804) claimed that Hume awoke him from his "dogmatic slumbers" and caused him to attempt to rescue philosophy from Hume's skepticism. Kant attempted to correct the impractical features of both rationalism and empiricism. Rationalism can involve only the manipulation of concepts, and empiricism confines knowledge to sensory experience and its derivatives. Kant attempted to reconcile both points of view.

Kant felt that careful analysis of our experience revealed certain categories of thought. For example, Kant indicated that we do have such ideas as causality, unity, and totality, but we never, as Hume had said, experience any of these things empirically. These categories of thought, or "faculties," are neither part of our sensory experience nor derived from it. If these thoughts are not the result of sensory experience, Kant reasoned, they must be **innate categories of thought.** These innate mental faculties are superimposed over our sensory experiences, thereby providing them with structure and meaning. Kant believed that there were twelve of these innate faculties that give meaning to our experiences of the physical world, including unity, totality, reality, existence, necessity, reciprocity, and causality.

What we consciously experience, according to Kant, is influenced by both sensory experience, caused by the empirical world, and the faculties of the mind, which are innate. The faculties of the mind transform sensory experience, thereby giving it greater organization and meaning. Any attempt to determine the nature of knowledge must, according to Kant, also take into consideration the active contribution of the mind. We see a current example of this point of view when we review Gestalt psychology in Chapter 10 and Jean Piaget's theory in Chapter 11. Kant's philosophy can be viewed as the antecedent of modern information-processing psychology and cognitive science. Flanagan (1991, p. 181) says, "When cognitive scientists discuss their philosophical forebears one hears the name of Immanuel Kant more than any other."

Thus Kant kept rationalism alive by showing that the mind is the source of knowledge. In other words, he kept alive an approach to explaining knowledge in terms other than its reduction to sensory experience. By taking a nativistic view—that much knowledge is inborn—Kant revived the Platonist view that had been losing ground since the time of Descartes.

John Stuart Mill (1806–1873) was disturbed by the contention of the early associationists, such as Hobbes and Locke, that complex ideas are nothing more than combinations of simple ideas. Although he remained an empiricist and an associationist, he made a very important revision in the position taken by other associationists. Accepting the notion that complex ideas are made up of simpler ideas, Mill added the notion that some simple ideas combine into a new totality that may bear little resemblance to its parts. For example, if we combine blue, red, and green lights, we get white. In other words, Mill believed that *the whole is different from the sum of its parts.* Thus Mill modified the empiricist contention that all ideas reflect sensory stimulation. For him, when some ideas combine they produce an idea that is unlike any of the elemental ideas that make up the emergent idea.

OTHER HISTORICAL INFLUENCES
ON LEARNING THEORY

Thomas Reid (1710–1796) also opposed the elementism of the empiricists, but his opposition took a different form than that of John Stuart Mill. Like Kant, Reid believed that the mind has powers of its own, which strongly influence how we perceive the world. He hypothesized twenty-seven faculties of the mind, most of which were thought to be innate. The belief in the existence of such faculties in the mind was later called **faculty psychology.** The faculty psychologist is a mixture of nativism, rationalism, and empiricism. Kant, for example, explored sensory experience (empiricism) in order to discover categories of thought (rationalism) that were innate (nativism).

Reid argued that Hume's contention that we cannot know anything directly about the physical world was ridiculous. Hergenhahn (2005) summarizes Reid's position:

> Reid argued that because all humans were convinced of the existence of physical reality, it must exist. . . . If Hume's logic caused him [Hume] to conclude that we could never know the physical world, then, said Reid, something was wrong with Hume's logic. We can trust our impressions of the physical world because it makes *common sense* to do so. We are naturally endowed with the abilities to deal with and make sense out of the world. (p. 173)

Reid gives examples of what life would be like if we denied the fact that our senses accurately represent physical reality: "I resolve not to believe my senses. I break my nose against a post. . . . I step into a dirty kennel; and after twenty such wise and rational actions, I am taken up and clapped into a madhouse" (Beanblossom & Lehrer, 1983, p. 86). Reid's contention that reality is as we perceive it is called **naive realism** (Henle, 1986).

Franz Joseph Gall (1758–1828) carried faculty psychology several steps further. First, he assumed that the faculties were housed in specific locations in the brain. Second, he believed that the faculties of the mind did not exist to the same extent in every individual. Third, he believed that if a faculty was well developed, there would be a bump or protrusion on the part of the skull corresponding to the place in the brain that houses that faculty. Likewise, if a faculty was poorly developed, a hollow or depression would be found on the skull. Armed with these assumptions, Gall set out to examine the shape of people's skulls. He developed an elaborate chart showing what faculties the various parts of the skull correspond to. Using this chart and analyzing the bumps and hollows of a person's skull, Gall and his followers believed they could tell which of the person's faculties were the most highly developed and which were underdeveloped. This analysis of mental attributes by examining the characteristics of the skull is called **phrenology.** A typical phrenology chart is shown in Figure 3–2.

Phrenology had two lasting effects on psychology, one good and one questionable. First, it led to research designed to discover the function of various parts of the brain. It was this very research, however, that disproved the assumptions on which

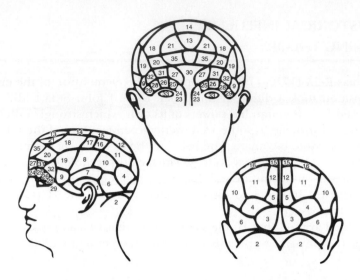

Affective Faculties   *Intellectual Faculties*

PROPENSITIES | SENTIMENTS | PERCEPTIVE | REFLECTIVE
? Desire to live | 10 Cautiousness | 22 Individuality | 34 Comparison
• Alimentiveness | 11 Approbativeness | 23 Configuration | 35 Causality
1 Destructiveness | 12 Self-Esteem | 24 Size
2 Amativeness | 13 Benevolence | 25 Weight and resistance
3 Philoprogenitiveness | 14 Reverence | 26 Coloring
4 Adhesiveness | 15 Firmness | 27 Locality
5 Inhibitiveness | 16 Conscientiousness | 28 Order
6 Combativeness | 17 Hope | 29 Calculation
7 Secretiveness | 18 Marvelousness | 30 Eventuality
8 Acquisitiveness | 19 Ideality | 31 Time
9 Constructiveness | 20 Mirthfulness | 32 Tune
 | 21 Imitation | 33 Language

FIGURE 3-2   A phrenology chart. (Suggested by G. Spurzheim, *Phrenology, or the Doctrine of Mental Phenomena*. Boston: Marsh, Capen & Lyon, 1834.)

phrenology was based. Second, many faculty psychologists believed that the faculties became stronger with practice, just like the biceps become stronger with practice. For this reason, the faculty psychologists were said to have taken a "mental muscle" approach to learning. Learning, to them, meant strengthening faculties by practicing those traits associated with them. One could improve one's reasoning abilities, for example, by formally studying such topics as mathematics or Latin. The belief that a particular course of training would strengthen certain faculties was called **formal discipline,** a concept that provides one answer to the question of how learning transfers from one situation to another. We have more to say about the transfer of training when we discuss E. L. Thorndike in Chapter 4. It should be noted here, however, that the idea of formal discipline, based on faculty psychology, dominated school curricula for many years and was used to justify requiring students to study

intensely the most difficult topics available, such as mathematics and Latin, regardless of their vocational aspirations. One suspects that many present-day educators still believe in the benefits of formal discipline. Indeed, there is some evidence that formal discipline is effective (see, e.g., Lehman, Lempert, & Nisbett, 1988).

Charles Darwin (1809–1882) supported the notion of biological evolution with so much evidence that it finally had to be taken seriously. The church bitterly opposed Darwin's notions. In fact, Darwin himself was so worried about the impact his findings would have on religious thought that he wished to have his research published only after his death.

The final acceptance of evolutionary theory by the scientific community marked a blow to the collective ego of humans equal only to the one dealt by Copernicus and the future one dealt by Freud. Evolution restored the continuity between humans and other animals that had been denied for centuries. No longer was there the clear-cut distinction between man and other animals that had been the cornerstone of so many philosophies, such as those of Plato, Aristotle, Descartes, and Kant. If we are biologically related to the "lower" animals, do they also have minds, souls, and innate categories of thought, and if so, to what extent? Obviously, animal research was now to take on much greater respectability. Descartes's thinking tolerated animal research as a way of finding out how the human body works, but from his point of view, it could not disclose anything concerning the human mind. Until Darwin, human behavior commonly was thought to be rational and animal behavior to be instinctive. With Darwin, that handy dichotomy was lost. Many questions arose, such as "Can an animal's behavior also be rational, at least in part?" and "Can humans' behavior be instinctive, at least in part?" A mind resulting from a long evolutionary process is looked at differently than a mind that is divinely implanted into the body by God.

Darwin changed all thoughts about human nature. Human beings were now looked on as a combination of their biological heritage and their life experiences. The pure associationism of the empiricists was now coupled with physiology in a search for the underlying mechanisms of thought, and the function of behavior as a way of adjusting to the environment was studied intensely. Individuality was appreciated as never before, and its study became popular. This new attitude was exemplified by Darwin's cousin, Francis Galton (1822–1911), who devised a number of methods, such as the questionnaire, free association, and correlation, specifically designed to measure individual differences. Probably the most famous person directly influenced by Darwin was Sigmund Freud (1856–1939), who explored the problems of the human animal attempting to live in a civilized world.

Such philosophic questions as "How do humans think?" and "What can humans know?" changed to "How do humans adjust to their environment?" and "Given certain circumstances, what do humans *do*?" Thus, the mood was set for a science of behavior. If human behavior was now to be studied like any other aspect of nature, the experimental approach that had been so successful in the physical sciences could be applied to the study of the human being.

Hermann Ebbinghaus (1850–1909) is said to have emancipated psychology from philosophy by demonstrating that the "higher mental processes" of learning

Hermann Ebbinghaus. (Courtesy of Corbis/Bettmann.)

and memory could be studied experimentally. Rather than assuming that associations had already been formed, and studying them through reflection, as had been the case for many centuries, Ebbinghaus studied the associative process as it was taking place. Thus he could systematically study the conditions that influenced the development of associations. He was an extremely careful researcher and repeated his experiments over a period of many years before he finally published his results in 1885. Many of his conclusions concerning the nature of learning and memory are still accepted.

An important principle of association was the law of frequency, which Ebbinghaus focused on in his research. The law of frequency stated that the more frequently an experience occurred, the more easily the experience was recalled. In other words, memory gains strength through repetition. To test this notion, Ebbinghaus needed material that was not contaminated by the subject's previous experience. To control for the effects of previous experience, he invented his now famous **nonsense material.** Nonsense material consists of syllables containing a vowel between two consonants (e.g., QAW, JIG, XUW, CEW, or TIB). Contrary to what is commonly believed, it was not the syllables in Ebbinghaus's research that were nonsense. The syllables he used often resembled words or actually were words. It was the relationships among the syllables that were meaningless. Thus we use the term *nonsense material* instead of *nonsense syllables*. The syllables were usually arranged in groups of twelve, although he varied group size to measure rate of learning as a function of the amount of material to be learned. He found that as the number of syllables to be learned became larger, it took a greater amount of time to learn them. Ebbinghaus was the first to demonstrate this fact that sounds so obvious to us today.

Using himself as a subject, Ebbinghaus looked at each syllable in the group for a fraction of a second and then paused fifteen seconds before starting through the group again. He continued in this manner until "complete mastery" had occurred, which meant he could recite each syllable in the group without making a mistake. At that point, he noted how many exposures to the group of syllables it took before mastery was reached. Also, he plotted the number of errors made as a function of successive exposures to the group of syllables, thus creating psychology's first learning curve.

At various intervals following original "mastery," Ebbinghaus went back and relearned a group of syllables. He noted the number of trials it took to relearn a group of syllables and subtracted that number from the number of exposures it took to learn the list originally. The difference was called **savings.** He plotted savings as a function of time elapsed since original learning, thus creating psychology's first

retention curve. His graph indicated that the rate of forgetting is very fast for the first few hours following a learning experience and very slow thereafter. He also found that *overlearning* reduces the rate of forgetting considerably. That is, if he continued to expose himself attentively to a group of syllables even after they had been mastered, they would be retained much longer than if his learning stopped with only one perfect recitation of the syllables.

Ebbinghaus also studied the effects of what is now called meaningfulness on learning and retention. He found, for example, that it took nine readings to memorize eighty syllables of material from Byron's *Don Juan* but about nine times as many exposures to learn eighty of his syllables. Not only was the learning rate much faster for the more meaningful material but also retention was far superior.

Ebbinghaus's research revolutionized the study of the associative process. Instead of hypothesizing about the law of frequency, he demonstrated how it functioned. Ebbinghaus brought the "higher mental processes" into the laboratory, where they have been ever since.

PSYCHOLOGY'S EARLY SCHOOLS

Voluntarism

Psychology's first school was **voluntarism,** and it was founded by **Wilhelm Maximilian Wundt** (1832–1920), who followed in the German rationalist tradition. Wundt's goals were to study consciousness as it was immediately experienced and to study the products of consciousness such as various cultural achievements. Wundt believed that immediate consciousness could be studied scientifically, that is, as a systematic function of environmental stimulation. One of his experimental goals was to discover the elements of thought, those basic elements of which all thoughts consist. Wundt founded what is generally considered to be psychology's first experimental laboratory in 1879, and its major goals were to discover the elements of thought and the basic processes that govern conscious experience.

For Wundt, however, experimental psychology was of limited usefulness in studying the human mind. The most important aspects of the mind could be studied only indirectly by studying its products, such as religion, morals, myths, art, social customs, language, and law. These products of the mind could not be studied experimentally but only through naturalistic observation. That is, they could be studied

Wilhelm Wundt. (Courtesy of Corbis/ Bettmann.)

only as they occurred historically or in the process of living. Wundt spent the last twenty years of his life writing his ten-volume *Völkerpsychologie* (group or cultural psychology), in which he described his observations concerning the cultural behaviors mentioned previously.

In accordance with the German rationalistic tradition, Wundt was primarily interested in the human will. He noted that humans could selectively attend to whatever elements of thought they wanted, causing those elements to be perceived clearly. Wundt referred to this selective attention as **apperception.** Also, the elements of thought could be willfully arranged in any number of combinations, a process Wundt referred to as **creative synthesis.** It was because of Wundt's emphasis on will that his school of psychology is called voluntarism.

Structuralism

When aspects of Wundt's voluntarism were transferred by his students to the United States, they were significantly modified and became the school of **structuralism. Edward Titchener** (1867–1927) created the school of structuralism at Cornell University. Structuralism, like the experimental aspect of Wundt's voluntarism, was concerned with the systematic study of human consciousness, and it, too, sought the elements of thought. In analyzing the elements of thought, the major tool the voluntarists and the structuralists used was **introspection.**

Experimental subjects had to be carefully trained not to misuse the introspective technique. They were trained to report their **immediate experience** as they perceived an object and not to report their interpretations of that object. In other words, Wundt and Titchener were interested in the subject's "raw" experiences but not in what they had learned about those experiences. In that sense, learning was looked on as more of a hindrance than a topic worthy of study for itself. When shown an apple, for example, the subject was supposed to report hues, brightnesses, and spatial characteristics rather than labeling the object as an apple. Naming the object of experience during an introspective report was called a **stimulus error,** for example, calling an apple an apple. In other words, the subject is reporting a compound idea rather than simple ones, and therefore the building blocks of the mind remain obscure. Clearly the voluntarists and the structuralists were more interested in the contents of the mind than with the origins of those contents.

A search for the elements of thought was essentially all that voluntarism and structuralism had in common. In explaining how the elements combine to form complex thoughts, voluntarism stressed the will, apperception, and creative synthesis— following in the rationalistic tradition. In other words, voluntarists postulated an active mind. In their explanation of the formation of complex thoughts, structuralists stressed the laws of association—following in the empiricistic tradition. In other words, they postulated a passive mind. Therefore, to equate voluntarism and structuralism, as is often done, is incorrect.

As a school of psychology, structuralism was short-lived and died within Titchener's own lifetime. There were many reasons for the death of structuralism, but the most important was probably the rising popularity of functionalism, which we consider in this chapter. The structuralists made a rather sterile attempt to use the methods of science to substantiate an ancient philosophical belief, that is, that simple ideas are combined into complex ones via the laws of association. It failed to take into consideration one of the most important developments in human history—the doctrine of evolution. As the importance of the evolutionary process became more apparent, increased attention was given to the organism's adaptation to its environment. Also, the doctrine of evolution made the study of "lower" animals a legitimate way of learning about people. Structuralism ignored both of these trends. It also ignored the growing evidence for the existence of unconscious processes that was being provided by researchers such as Freud. Finally, the structuralists opposed applied psychology, which was growing in popularity. They believed that knowledge concerning consciousness should be sought for its own sake without concern for its usefulness. For these and other reasons, structuralism came and went. It has been said that perhaps the most important thing about structuralism was that it appeared, it was tried, and it failed.

Functionalism

Functionalism also originated in the United States and initially coexisted with structuralism. Although functionalist beliefs diverged, their emphasis was always the same—*the utility of consciousness and behavior in adjusting to the environment.* Clearly the functionalists were strongly influenced by Darwin's doctrine of evolution.

The founder of the functionalist movement is usually thought to be **William James** (1842–1910). In his highly influential book, *The Principles of Psychology* (1890),

William James. (Courtesy of Library of Congress.)

James took the structuralists to task. Consciousness, he said, cannot be reduced into elements. Rather, consciousness functions as a unity whose purpose is to allow the organism to adjust to its environment. The "stream of consciousness" changes as total experience changes. Such a process cannot be reduced to elements because a person's conscious processes as a whole are involved with adaptation to that person's environment. The most important thing about consciousness, as far as James was concerned, was that it had a purpose. James also wrote about the importance of studying psychology scientifically. He emphasized that humans were both rational and irrational (emotional). He pointed out the importance of understanding the biological foundations of mental events and urged the study of lower animals to learn more about humans. Many of James's ideas are still current. It should be noted that James had a significant influence on psychology, both through his writings and through his ability as an inspirational teacher. Many consider James to be one of the greatest psychologists of all times.

In addition to James, two of the most influential members of the functionalist movement were John Dewey (1859–1952) and James R. Angell (1869–1949). In Dewey's (1896) famous article "The Reflex Arc Concept in Psychology," he attacked the growing tendency in psychology to isolate a stimulus-response relationship for study. He argued that isolating such a unit for study was a total waste of time because the purpose of behavior is overlooked. The goal for psychology should be to study the significance of behavior in adapting to the environment. Angell's main contribution was that he built up a department of psychology at the University of Chicago around the functionalistic point of view.

The main contribution the functionalists made to learning theory is that they studied the relationship of consciousness to the environment rather than studying it as an isolated phenomenon. They opposed the introspective technique of the structuralists because it was elementistic, not because it studied consciousness. The functionalists were not opposed to studying mental processes but insisted that they should always be studied in relationship to survival. Unlike the structuralists, the functionalists were very interested in applied psychology. Most functionalists believed that one of their major goals should be to furnish information that could be used to improve the human condition.

Behaviorism

The founder of **behaviorism** was **John B. Watson** (1878–1958), who noted that consciousness could be studied only through the process of introspection, a notoriously

unreliable research tool. Because consciousness could not be reliably studied, he said, it should not be studied at all. To be scientific, psychology needed a subject matter that was stable enough to be reliably measured, and that subject matter was behavior. Watson felt that the main concern for the psychologist should be behavior and how it varies with experience. Leave the study of consciousness to the philosophers, he said. Thus, what was the focal point of epistemological inquiry for thousands of years was looked on by the behaviorist as only a hindrance in the study of human behavior.

There should be no more introspection, no more talk of instinctive behavior, and no more attempts to study the human conscious or unconscious mind. Behavior is what we can see, and therefore behavior is what we study. According to Watson (1913),

John Broadus Watson. (Courtesy of Corbis/Bettmann.)

Psychology as the behaviorist views it is a purely objective experimental branch of natural science. Its theoretical goal is the prediction and control of behavior. Introspection forms no essential part of its methods, nor is the scientific value of its data dependent upon the readiness with which they lend themselves to interpretation in terms of consciousness. The behaviorist, in his efforts to get a unitary scheme of animal response, recognizes no dividing line between man and brute. The behavior of man, with all its refinement and complexity, forms only a part of the behaviorist's total scheme of investigation. (p. 158)

Elsewhere, Watson said (Watson & McDougall, 1929),

The behaviorist cannot find consciousness in the test tube of his science. He finds no evidence anywhere for a stream of consciousness, not even for one so convincing as that described by William James. He does, however, find convincing proof of an ever-widening stream of behavior. (p. 26)

Watson was enthusiastic about his work and its implications. He saw behaviorism as a means of stripping ignorance and superstition from human existence, thereby paving the way for more rational, meaningful living. Understanding the principles of behavior, he thought, was the first step toward that kind of life. Watson (1925) said,

I think behaviorism does lay a foundation for saner living. It ought to be a science that prepares men and women for understanding the first principles of their own behavior. It ought to make men and women eager to rearrange their own lives, and especially eager to prepare themselves to bring up their own children in a healthy way. I wish I had time more fully to describe this, to picture to you the kind of rich and wonderful individual we should make of every healthy child; if only we could let it shape itself properly and then provide for it a universe unshackled by legendary folk lore of happenings thousands of years ago; unhampered by disgraceful political history; free of foolish customs and conventions which have no significance in themselves; yet which hem the individual in like taut steel bands. (p. 248)

Clearly, Watson was a rebel. He took the various objective approaches to the study of psychology that were appearing here and there, and through his forceful writing and speaking, organized them into a new school of psychology. Unfortunately, Watson's career as a professional psychologist was cut short when he was asked to leave Johns Hopkins University because of marital troubles leading to divorce. The same year he left the university, he married Rosalie Rayner, with whom he did the famous study with the infant named Albert (we discuss this study in Chapter 7), and went into the advertising business. From that point on, instead of writing in professional journals, Watson published his ideas in *McCall's, Harper's,* and *Collier's* magazines.

Watson never wavered from his behaviorist outlook, and in 1936 he had the following to say about the position he took in 1912:

I still believe as firmly as ever in the general behavioristic position I took overtly in 1912. I think it has influenced psychology. Strangely enough, I think it has temporarily

slowed down psychology because the older instructors would not accept it wholeheartedly, and consequently they failed to present it convincingly to their classes. The young-
sters did not get a fair presentation, hence they are not embarking wholeheartedly
upon a behavioristic career, and yet they will no longer accept the teachings of James,
Titchener, and Angell. I honestly think that psychology has been sterile for several
years. We need younger instructors who will teach objective psychology with no reference to the mythology most of us present-day psychologists have been brought up
upon. When this day comes, psychology will have a renaissance greater than that which
occurred in science in the Middle Ages. I believe as firmly as ever in the future of
behaviorism—behaviorism as a companion of zoology, physiology, psychiatry, and physical chemistry. (p. 231)

Of course, the behaviorist's main point was that behavior should be studied
because it could be dealt with directly. Mental events should be ignored because
they could not be dealt with directly. Behaviorism had a profound effect on American learning theory. In fact, most of the theories of learning in this book can be
thought of as behavioristic. It is possible, however, to make subdivisions within the
behavioristic camp. Some theories concentrate on behavior related to an organism's survival. Such behavioristic theories can be called functional theories. Other
behavioristic theories are less concerned with adaptive behavior and explain all
learned behavior in terms of the laws of association. Such theories tend to treat
functional and nonfunctional behavior in the same way. Thus, under the general
heading of behaviorism we can list both functionalistic and associationistic theories.
Whether a behavioristic theory is labeled as functionalistic or associationistic
depends on the kind of behavior the theory concentrates on and how the theory
explains the origins of that behavior. Watson had two lasting effects on psychology.
First, he changed psychology's goal from attempting to understand consciousness
to the prediction and control of behavior. Second, he made behavior psychology's
subject matter. Ever since Watson, essentially all psychologists study behavior. Even
cognitive psychologists use behavior to index postulated cognitive events. For this
reason, it can be said that all contemporary psychologists are behaviorists.

SUMMARY AND OVERVIEW

From the brief history presented in this chapter, it can be seen that learning theory
has a rich and diverse heritage. As a result of this heritage, numerous viewpoints
concerning the learning process exist today. In Chapter 2, we referred to a point of
view shared by a substantial number of scientists as a paradigm. At least five such
points of view can be identified among modern theories of learning.

One paradigm we refer to as *functionalistic*. This paradigm reflects the influence of Darwinism in that it stresses the relationship between learning and adjustment to the environment. A second paradigm we refer to as *associationistic* because it
studies the learning process in terms of the laws of association. This paradigm originated with Aristotle and was perpetuated and elaborated on by Locke, Berkeley, and

Hume. The third paradigm we label *cognitive* because it stresses the cognitive nature of learning. This paradigm originated with Plato and came to us through Descartes, Kant, and the faculty psychologists. The fourth paradigm is referred to as *neurophysiological* because it attempts to isolate the neurophysiological correlates of such things as learning, perception, thinking, and intelligence. This paradigm represents a current manifestation of a line of investigation that started with Descartes's separation of the mind and the body. The current goal of most neurophysiological psychologists, however, is to reunite mental and physiological processes. The fifth paradigm is referred to as *evolutionary* because it emphasizes the evolutionary history of the learning organism. This paradigm focuses on the ways in which evolutionary processes prepare organisms for some kinds of learning but make other kinds difficult or impossible.

These paradigms should be viewed as only very crude categories because it is difficult to find any theory of learning that fits unambiguously into any one of them. We place a theory in a particular paradigm because of its major emphasis. However, within almost every theory, certain aspects of other paradigms can be identified. For example, even though Hull's theory is listed under the functionalistic paradigm in the following chart, it relies heavily on associationistic ideas. Similarly, Piaget's theory is listed under the cognitive paradigm only because of its major emphasis. Piaget's theory, as much influenced by Darwinism as any other, has a great deal in common with the theories listed under the functionalistic paradigm. Tolman's theory is also difficult to categorize because it has both functionalistic and cognitive elements. We list it as a cognitive theory only because the main emphasis of the theory is cognitive. Likewise, Hebb's theory, although its major emphasis is neurophysiological, also stresses cognitive events. In fact, Hebb's theory can be looked on as an effort to describe the neurophysiological correlates of cognitive experiences.

With these reservations in mind, the major theories of learning covered in this book are organized as follows:

Functionalistic Paradigm
Thorndike
Skinner
Hull
Associationistic Paradigm
Pavlov
Guthrie
Estes

Cognitive Paradigm
Gestalt theory
Piaget
Tolman
Bandura
Neurophysiological Paradigm
Hebb
Evolutionary Paradigm
Bolles

Which paradigm is correct? Probably all of them. No doubt they all emphasize certain truths about the learning process and ignore others. At this point in history, it appears that to obtain the most accurate picture of the learning process, one must be willing to view it from a number of different angles. We hope that this book will allow the student to do just that.

DISCUSSION QUESTIONS

1. Compare Plato's theory of knowledge with that of Aristotle's. Define the terms *rationalism, nativism,* and *empiricism* in your answer.
2. Summarize Descartes's influence on psychology.
3. Briefly describe what Kant meant by an "innate category of thought."
4. Summarize Reid's argument against Hume's skepticism.
5. Discuss phrenology and the theory of the mind on which it was based.
6. Discuss Darwin's influence on learning theory.
7. What was the significance of the work of Ebbinghaus as far as the history of learning theory is concerned?
8. Summarize the important features of the schools of voluntarism, structuralism, functionalism, and behaviorism.
9. What caused the downfall of structuralism?
10. What were the lasting effects of Watson's behaviorism on contemporary psychology?

CHAPTER HIGHLIGHTS

apperception
Aristotle
associationism
behaviorism
Berkeley, George
creative synthesis
Darwin, Charles
Descartes, René
Ebbinghaus, Hermann
empiricism
epistemology
faculty psychology
formal discipline
functionalism
Gall, Franz Joseph
Hobbes, Thomas
Hume, David
immediate experience
innate category of thought
innate ideas
introspection

James, William
Kant, Immanuel
laws of association
Locke, John
Mill, John Stuart
naive realism
nativism
nonsense material
phrenology
Plato
Pythagoreans
rationalism
Reid, Thomas
reminiscence theory of knowledge
savings
stimulus error
structuralism
Titchener, Edward
voluntarism
Watson, John B.
Wundt, Wilhelm Maximilian

CHAPTER 4

Edward Lee Thorndike

It is fitting that we begin our discussion of the major learning theorists with Edward L. Thorndike (1874–1949), perhaps the greatest learning theorist of all time. He did pioneer work not only in learning theory but also in educational practices, verbal behavior, comparative psychology, intelligence testing, the nature-nurture problem, transfer of training, and the application of quantitative measures to sociopsychological problems (e.g., he developed scales with which to compare the quality of life in different cities). Thorndike began this latter project, as well as many others, when he was more than sixty years old.

His research started with the study of mental telepathy in young children (which he explained as the unconscious detection on the part of the child of minute movements made by the experimenter). His later experiments involved chicks, cats, rats, dogs, fish, monkeys, and finally adult humans. He wanted to use apes also but could not afford to buy and maintain them.

Thorndike's scientific productivity was almost unbelievable. At his death in 1949, his bibliography comprised 507 books, monographs, and journal articles. Always attempting to measure everything, Thorndike reports in his autobiography that up to the age of sixty he had spent well over twenty thousand hours reading and studying scientific books and journals—this in spite of the fact that he was primarily a researcher rather than a scholar.

Thorndike was born in Williamsburg, Massachusetts, in 1874, and was the second son of a Methodist minister. He claims never to have seen or heard the word *psychology* until he was a junior at Wesleyan University. At that time he read William James's *Principles of Psychology* (1890) and was deeply impressed. Later, when he went to Harvard and took a course from James, they became good friends. When Thorndike's landlady forbade him to continue hatching chicks in his bedroom, James tried to get him laboratory space on the Harvard campus. When this failed, James allowed Thorndike to continue his studies in the basement of his home—much to the dismay of James's wife and to the delight of his children.

After two years at Harvard, where Thorndike earned a living by tutoring students, he accepted a fellowship at Columbia, working under James McKeen Cattell. Although he carried two of his "most educated" chicks with him to New York, he soon switched from chicks to cats. His years of animal research were summarized in his doctoral dissertation, "Animal Intelligence: An Experimental Study of the Associative Processes in Animals," which was published in 1898 and expanded and republished as *Animal Intelligence* (1911). The fundamental

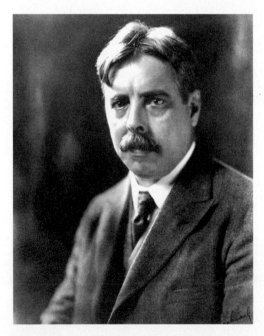

Edward L. Thorndike. (Courtesy of Teachers College, Columbia University.)

ideas in these documents permeate all of Thorndike's writings and, in fact, most of learning theory. The extent of Thorndike's influence is indicated by the following quotation from Tolman (1938):

> The psychology of animal learning—not to mention that of child learning—has been and still is primarily a matter of agreeing or disagreeing with Thorndike, or trying in minor ways to improve upon him. Gestalt psychologists, conditioned-reflex psychologists, sign-Gestalt psychologists—all of us here in America seem to have taken Thorndike, overtly or covertly, as our starting point. And we have felt very smart and pleased with ourselves if we could show that we have, even in some very minor way, developed new little wrinkles of our own. (p. 11)

ANIMAL RESEARCH BEFORE THORNDIKE

Descartes's contention that the bodies of both humans and nonhuman animals function according to the same mechanical principles did much to stimulate the anatomical investigations of nonhuman animals. It was Darwin, however, who suggested that humans and nonhumans are similar in all respects: anatomically, emotionally, and cognitively. Darwin's (1872) *The Expression of Emotions in Man and Animals* is generally considered the first text on comparative psychology. Not long after Darwin published this book, his friend **George John Romanes** (1848–1894) published *Animal Intelligence* (1882), *Mental Evolution in Animals* (1884), and *Mental Evolution in Man* (1885). The evidence that Romanes offered to support the continuity of intelligent and emotional behavior from lower animals to humans was largely anecdotal and often characterized by **anthropomorphizing,** or attributing human thought processes to nonhuman animals. For example, Romanes attributed the emotions of anger, fear, and jealousy to fish; affection, sympathy, and pride to birds; and slyness and reasoning to dogs. The following is one of Romanes's (1882, 1897) anecdotes:

> One day the cat and the parrot had a quarrel. I think the cat had upset Polly's food, or something of that kind; however, they seemed all right again. An hour or so later, Polly was standing on the edge of the table; she called out in a tone of extreme affection, "Puss, Puss, come then—come then, Pussy." Pussy went and looked up innocently enough. Polly with her beak seized a basin of milk standing by, and tipped the basin and all its contents over the cat; then chuckled diabolically, of course broke the basin, and half drowned the cat. (p. 277)

In an effort to describe animal behavior more objectively, **Conwy Lloyd Morgan** (1842–1936) gave the following advice to animal researchers in his book *An Introduction to Comparative Psychology* (1891). The advice became known as **Morgan's canon:** "In no case may we interpret an action as the outcome of the exercise of a higher psychical faculty, if it can be interpreted as the outcome of the exercise of one which stands lower in the psychological scale" (p. 53). As Hergenhahn (2005) points out, Morgan's canon is often misinterpreted as a warning against speculating about thoughts or feelings in nonhuman animals. In fact, Morgan did believe

Margaret Floy Washburn. (Courtesy of Archives of the History of American Psychology, The University of Akron.)

that nonhumans have cognitive processes. His canon tells us we cannot assume that human mental processes are the same as those experienced by nonhumans and that we should not attribute a behavior to a complex cognitive process when it can be explained with one that is less complex.

Although Morgan's explanation of nonhuman animal behavior was much more parsimonious than that of Romanes, it still depended on naturalistic observation. That is, Morgan was describing the behavior of animals as it occurred in the natural environment. For example, he described in great detail how his dog had learned to lift the latch of his garden gate, thereby escaping confinement. Morgan's research was an improvement over what had preceded it, but additional refinements were needed; animal behavior had to be studied systematically under controlled laboratory conditions. In other words, animal behavior had to be studied scientifically.

Margaret Floy Washburn (1871–1939), the first woman to earn the Ph.D. degree in psychology, took the study of nonhumans one step closer to the laboratory. Washburn's book, *The Animal Mind,* was first published in 1908, and new editions appeared regularly until 1936. In this text, Washburn reviewed and examined early sensory, perceptual, and learning experiments involving nonhumans and made inferences about consciousness based on the results of these studies, a strategy not unlike those used by many contemporary cognitive psychologists (Hergenhahn, 2005). Although Washburn drew her conclusions from experimental studies rather than from naturalistic observations, she did not identify, control, and manipulate the important variables related to learning. It was E. L. Thorndike who took this important next step. Galef (1998) summarizes Thorndike's research innovations:

> Thorndike's work contained a set of methodological innovations that were to revolutionize the study of comparative psychology: A representative sample of subjects was examined in a carefully described, standardized situation. Quantitative measures of performance were made. Comparisons were made of the performance, in the standard situation, of groups of subjects that had received different treatments before testing. Interpretations of implications of different outcomes of these comparisons were arrived at before experiments were begun. . . . In summary, Thorndike developed a methodology suitable not only for experimental study of animal learning but for much of animal and human behavior as well. (p. 1130)

MAJOR THEORETICAL CONCEPTS

Connectionism

Thorndike called the association between sense impressions and impulses to action a bond or a connection. This marked the first formal attempt to link sensory events to behavior. Earlier brands of associationism attempted to show how ideas became linked together; thus Thorndike's approach is quite different and can be regarded as the first modern theory of learning. His emphasis on the functional aspects of behavior is due mainly to the influence of Darwin. In fact, Thorndike's theory can be understood as a combination of associationism, Darwinism, and the methods of science.

Thorndike's concern was not only for stimulus conditions and tendencies to action but also for what held the stimulus and response together. He believed they were connected by a neural bond. His theory is called **connectionism,** the connection referred to being the neural connection between stimuli (S) and responses (R).

Selecting and Connecting

For Thorndike the most basic form of learning was **trial-and-error learning,** or what he originally called **selecting and connecting.** He reached this basic notion through his early experimentation, which involved putting an animal in an apparatus arranged so that when the animal made a certain kind of response, it escaped. The apparatus shown in Figure 4–1 was a small confining box with a pole sticking up in

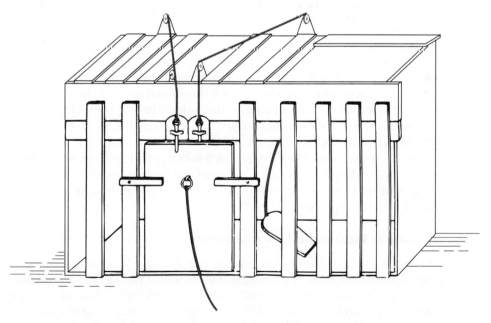

FIGURE 4–1   One kind of puzzle box that Thorndike used in his research on learning.

the middle or a chain hanging from its top. Pushing against the pole or pulling on the chain enabled the animal to escape. Some arrangements, however, required the animal to engage in a complex series of responses before it could escape. Different responses were called for at different times in Thorndike's experiments, but the idea was always the same—the animal had to perform in a certain way before it was allowed to leave the box. The following quotation from *Animal Intelligence* (1911) exemplifies his work with the puzzle box.

> The behavior of all but 11 and 13 was practically the same. When put into the box the cat would show evident signs of discomfort and of an impulse to escape from confinement. It tries to squeeze through any opening; it claws and bites at the bars or wire; it thrusts its paws out through any opening and claws at everything it reaches; it continues its efforts when it strikes anything loose and shaky; it may claw at things within the box. It does not pay very much attention to the food outside, but seems simply to strive instinctively to escape from confinement. The vigor with which it struggles is extraordinary. For eight or ten minutes it will claw and bite and squeeze incessantly. With 13, an old cat, and 11, an uncommonly sluggish cat, the behavior was different. They did not struggle vigorously or continually. On some occasions they did not even struggle at all. It was therefore necessary to let them out of the box a few times, feeding them each time. After they thus associate climbing out of the box with getting food, they will try to get out whenever put in. They do not, even then, struggle so vigorously or get so excited as the rest. In either case, whether the impulse to struggle be due to instinctive reaction to confinement or to an association, it is likely to succeed in letting the cat out of the box. The cat that is clawing all over the box in her impulsive struggle will probably claw the string or loop or button so as to open the door. And gradually all the other non-successful impulses will be stamped out and the particular impulse leading to the successful act will be stamped in by the resulting pleasure, until after many trials, the cat will, when put in the box, immediately claw the button or loop in a definite way. (pp. 35–40)

Thus, whether working for a piece of fish or for release from confinement, all his animals learned to do whatever was necessary to escape from the box.

Thorndike plotted the time it took the animal to solve the problem as a function of the number of opportunities the animal had to solve the problem. Every opportunity was a trial, and the trial terminated when the animal hit on the correct solution. A typical graph generated under these circumstances is shown in Figure 4–2. In this basic experimental arrangement, Thorndike consistently noted that the time it took to solve the problem (his dependent variable) systematically decreased as the number of trials increased; that is, the more opportunities the animal had, the faster it solved the problem.

Learning Is Incremental, Not Insightful

Noting the gradual decrease in time to solution as a function of successive trials, Thorndike concluded that learning was **incremental** rather than **insightful.** In other words, learning occurs in very small systematic steps rather than in huge jumps. He noted that if learning was insightful, the graph would show that the time to solution would remain relatively stable and high while the animal was in the unlearned state. At the point where the animal gained insight into the solution, the graph would

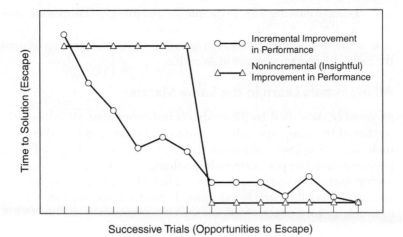

FIGURE 4-2   The figure exemplifies both the incremental improvement in performance observed by Thorndike and the nonincremental (insightful) improvement that Thorndike did not observe.

drop very rapidly and remain at that point for the duration of the experiment. Figure 4–2 also shows how the graph would look if the learning that took place was insightful.

Learning Is Not Mediated by Ideas

Based on his research, Thorndike (1898) also concluded that learning was direct and was not mediated by thinking or reasoning:

> The cat does not look over the situation, much less *think* it over, and then decide what to do. It bursts out at once into the activities which instinct and experience have settled on as suitable reactions to the situation *"confinement when hungry with food outside."* It does not ever in the course of its success realize that such an act brings food and therefore decide to do it and thenceforth do it immediately from decision instead of from impulse. (p. 45)

Elsewhere Thorndike (1911) made the same point with regard to monkeys:

> In discussing these facts we may first of all clear our way of one popular explanation, that this learning was due to "reasoning." If we used the word reasoning in its technical psychological meaning as the function of reaching conclusions by the perception of relations, comparison and inference, if we think of the mental content involved as feelings of relation, perceptions of similarity, general and abstract notions and judgments, we find no evidence of reasoning in the behavior of the monkeys toward the mechanisms used. And this fact nullifies the arguments for reasoning in their case as it did in the case of the dogs and cats. The argument that successful dealings with mechanical contrivances imply that the animal reasoned out the properties of the mechanisms, is destroyed when we find mere selection from their general instinctive activities sufficient to cause success with bars, hooks, loops, etc. There is also positive evidence of the absence of any general function of reasoning. (pp. 184–186)

Thus, following the principle of parsimony, Thorndike rejected reason in favor of direct selection and connection in learning. The demotion of reasoning and of the importance of ideas in learning was the beginning of what was to become the behavioristic movement in America.

All Mammals Learn in the Same Manner

Many were disturbed by Thorndike's insistence that all learning is direct and not mediated by ideas, especially because he also insisted that the learning of all mammals, including humans, follows the same laws. According to Thorndike, no special processes need be postulated when attempting to explain human learning. The following quotation serves both to point out Thorndike's (1913b) belief that the laws of learning are the same for all animals and to introduce other aspects of his theory, to which we turn next:

> These simple, semi-mechanical phenomena . . . which animal learning discloses, are the fundamentals of human learning also. They are, of course, much complicated in the more advanced states of human learning, such as the acquisition of skill with the violin, or of knowledge of the calculus, or of inventiveness in engineering. But it is impossible to understand the subtler and more planful learning of cultural men without clear ideas of the forces which make learning possible in its first form of directly connecting some gross bodily response with a situation immediately present to the senses. Moreover, no matter how subtle, complicated and advanced a form of learning one has to explain, these simple facts—the selection of connections by use and satisfaction and their elimination by disuse and annoyance, multiple reaction, the mind's set as a condition, piecemeal activity of a situation, with prepotency of certain elements in determining the response, response by analogy, and shifting of bonds—will as a matter of fact, still be the main, and perhaps the only, facts needed to explain it. (p. 16)

THORNDIKE BEFORE 1930

Thorndike's thinking about the learning process can be conveniently divided into two parts: one part consisting of his thoughts prior to 1930, and the second part consisting of his views after 1930, when some of his earlier views changed considerably.

The Law of Readiness

The **law of readiness,** proposed in his book *The Original Nature of Man* (Thorndike, 1913b), has three parts, abbreviated as follows:

1. When a conduction unit is ready to conduct, conduction by it is satisfying.
2. For a conduction unit ready to conduct, not to conduct is annoying.
3. When a conduction unit is not ready for conduction and is forced to conduct, conduction by it is annoying.

We notice some terms here whose subjectivity might worry the modern learning theorist. We must remember, however, that Thorndike was writing before the behavioristic movement and that many of the things he discussed had never been systematically analyzed before. It is also important to note that what appear to be subjective terms in Thorndike's writing may not be. For example, what he meant here by "a conduction unit ready to conduct" is merely a preparedness for action or goal directedness. Using current terminology, we can restate Thorndike's law of readiness as follows:

1. When someone is ready to perform some act, to do so is satisfying.
2. When someone is ready to perform some act, not to do so is annoying.
3. When someone is not ready to perform some act and is forced to do so, it is annoying.

Generally, we can say that interfering with goal-directed behavior causes frustration and causing someone to do something they do not want to do is also frustrating.

Even terms such as *satisfying* and *annoying* were defined to be acceptable to most behaviorists (Thorndike, 1911): "By a satisfying state of affairs is meant one which the animal does nothing to avoid, often doing such things as attain and preserve it. By a discomforting or annoying state of affairs is meant one which the animal commonly avoids and abandons" (p. 245). These definitions of satisfiers and annoyers should be kept in mind throughout our discussion of Thorndike.

The Law of Exercise

Before 1930, Thorndike's theory included the **law of exercise,** which had two parts:

1. Connections between a stimulus and a response are strengthened as they are used. In other words, merely exercising the connection between a stimulating situation and a response strengthens the connection between the two. This is the part of the law of exercise called the **law of use.**
2. Connections between situations and responses are weakened when practice is discontinued or if the neural bond is not used. This is the portion of the law of exercise called the **law of disuse.**

What did Thorndike mean by the strengthening or weakening of a connection? Here again he was ahead of his time, and on this issue he could be speaking today. He defined strengthening as an increase in the probability that a response will be made when the stimulus recurs. If the bond between a stimulus and a response is strengthened, the next time the stimulus occurs there is an increased probability that the response will occur. If the bond is weakened, there is a decreased probability that the next time the stimulus occurs the response will occur. In brief, the law of exercise says we learn by doing and forget by not doing.

The Law of Effect

The **law of effect,** before 1930, refers to the strengthening or weakening of a connection between a stimulus and a response as a result of the consequences of the response. If a response is followed by a **satisfying state of affairs,** the strength of the connection is increased. If a response is followed by an **annoying state of affairs,** the strength of the connection is decreased. In modern terminology, if a stimulus leads to a response, which in turn leads to reinforcement, the S-R connection is strengthened. If, on the other hand, a stimulus leads to a response that leads to punishment, the S-R connection is weakened.

The law of effect was a historical break from traditional associationistic theory that claimed frequency of occurrence or mere contiguity to be the determiners of the strength of an association. Although Thorndike accepted both the law of frequency and the law of contiguity, he went further by saying that the consequences of a response are important in determining the strength of association between the situation and the response to it. The importance of the consequences of an act in forming associations was only hinted at previously by philosophers such as Hobbes and Bentham. Here we see Thorndike's concern with the utility of behavior in helping the organism adjust to its environment, a concern that he shared with all the functionalists.

According to the law of effect, if a response results in a satisfying state of affairs, the S-R connection is strengthened. How can this happen, if the conduction unit has already fired before the satisfying state of affairs occurs? Thorndike attempted to answer this question by postulating the existence of a **confirming reaction,** which is triggered in the nervous system if a response results in a satisfying state of affairs. Thorndike felt that this confirming reaction is neurophysiological in nature and the organism is not conscious of it. Although Thorndike did not elaborate on the characteristics of this reaction, he did suspect that such a neurophysiological reaction was the true strengthener of neural bonds. We have more to say about the confirming reaction when we consider Thorndike's concept of belongingness.

Some learning theorists have attempted to answer the question of how reinforcement can strengthen the response that produced it by postulating the existence of a neural trace that is still active when the satisfaction occurs. In other words, for these theorists the conduction unit is still active at the time the organism experiences the satisfying state of affairs. Although the neural trace notion became a popular answer to the question, the problem of how reinforcement strengthens a response is still essentially unsolved.

SECONDARY CONCEPTS BEFORE 1930

Before 1930, Thorndike's theory included a number of ideas that were less important than the laws of readiness, effect, and exercise. These secondary concepts included multiple response, set or attitude, prepotency of elements, response by analogy, and associative shifting.

Multiple Response

Multiple response, or varied reaction, was for Thorndike the first step in all learning. It refers to the fact that if our first response does not solve the problem, we try other responses. Trial-and-error learning, of course, depends on the animal trying first one response and then another until it finds a response that works. When this happens, the probability of that response being made again increases. In other words, for Thorndike much learning depends on the fact that organisms tend to remain active until a response that solves an existing problem is made.

Set or Attitude

What Thorndike (1913a) called dispositions, preadjustments, or **sets (attitudes)** was his recognition of the importance of what the learner brings to the learning situation:

> It is a general law of behavior that the response to any external situation is dependent upon the condition of the man, as well as upon the nature of the situation; and that, if certain conditions in the man are rated as part of the situation, the response to it depends upon the remaining conditions in the man. Consequently, it is a general law of learning that the change made in a man by the action of any agent depends upon the condition of the man when the agent is acting. The condition of the man may be considered under the two heads of the more permanent or fixed and the more temporary or shifting, attitudes, or "sets." (p. 24)

Thus, individual differences in learning are explained by basic differences among people: by their cultural and genetic heritage or by temporary states such as deprivation, fatigue, or various emotional conditions. What acts as a satisfier or an annoyer depends on both the organism's background and its temporary body state at the time of learning. For example, animals with considerable experience in a puzzle box will probably solve new puzzle box problems faster than animals with no prior puzzle box training. Furthermore, animals that have been deprived of food for a considerable length of time will probably find food more satisfying than food-satiated animals. It is with his concept of set or attitude that Thorndike recognized that an animal's drive state will, to a large extent, determine what is satisfying and what is annoying to it.

Prepotency of Elements

Prepotency of elements is what Thorndike (1913b) called "the partial or piecemeal activity of a situation." It refers to the fact that only some elements of any situation will govern behavior:

> One of the commonest ways in which conditions within the man determine variations in his responses to one same external situation is by letting one or another element of the situation be prepotent in effect. Such partial or piecemeal activity on the part of a situation is, in human learning, the rule. Only rarely does man form connections, as the lower animals so often do, with a situation as a gross total—unanalyzed, undefined, and, as it were, without relief. He does so occasionally, as when a baby, to show off his little trick, requires the same room, the same persons present, the same tone of voice and the like. Save in early infancy and amongst the feeble-minded, however, any situation will most probably act unevenly. Some of its elements will produce only the response of neglect; others will be bound to only a mild awareness of them; others will connect with some energetic response of thought, feeling or action, and become positive determiners of the man's future. (pp. 26–27)

With the notion of prepotency of elements, Thorndike recognized the complexity of the environment and concluded that we respond selectively to aspects of it. In other words, we typically respond to some of the elements in a situation and not to others. Therefore, how we respond to a situation depends on both what we attend to and what responses are attached to what we attend to.

Response by Analogy

What determines how we respond to a situation we have never encountered before? Thorndike's answer, **response by analogy,** was that we respond to it as we would to a related situation that we previously encountered. The amount of **transfer of training** between the familiar situation and the unfamiliar one is determined by the number of elements that the two situations have in common. This is Thorndike's famous **identical elements theory of transfer** of training.

With his theory of transfer, Thorndike opposed the long-held view of transfer based on the doctrine of **formal discipline.** As we saw in Chapter 3, formal discipline was based on faculty psychology, which contended that the human mind was made up of several powers or faculties such as reasoning, attention, judgment, and memory. It was believed that these faculties could be strengthened with practice, for example, that practicing reasoning made one a better reasoner. Thus, the study of mathematics and Latin were justified because they strengthen the reasoning and memory faculties. It should be obvious why this position was referred to as the "mental muscle" approach to education because it claims that faculties of the mind are strengthened with practice just as people strengthen their biceps with exercise. This position also maintained that if students are forced to solve a number of difficult problems in school, they become capable problem solvers outside of school. Thorndike (1906) felt that there was little evidence that education generalized so readily. In fact, he believed that education resulted in highly specific skills rather than general ones:

> A man may be a tip-top musician but in other respects an imbecile: he may be a gifted poet, but an ignoramus in music; he may have a wonderful memory for figures and only a mediocre memory for localities, poetry or human faces; school children may reason admirably in science and be below the average in grammar: those very good in drawing may be very poor in dancing. (p. 238)

Thorndike and Woodworth (1901) critically examined the formal discipline theory of transfer and found little support for it. Instead, they found transfer from one situation to the next occurred only to the extent that both situations have elements in common. These elements, according to Thorndike, may be actual stimulus conditions, or they may be procedures. For example, looking up words in a dictionary in school may transfer to a variety of situations outside of school that have nothing to do with the exact words you were looking up in the classroom, but the ability to look things up may transfer. This is the transfer of procedure rather than of stimulus elements. Learning to pay attention for long periods and learning to be punctual are further examples of the transfer of procedures rather than stimulus elements.

Why is it, then, that the more difficult courses seem to produce brighter students? Because, said Thorndike, the brighter students went into these courses to begin with. Thorndike (1924) summarized his elaborate study with Woodworth on the transfer of training involving 8,564 high school students as follows:

> By any reasonable interpretation of the results, the intellectual values of studies should be determined largely by the special information, habits, interests, attitudes, and ideals which they demonstrably produce. The expectation of any large differences in general improvement of the mind from one study rather than another seems doomed to disappointment. The chief reason why good thinkers seem superficially to have been made such by having taken certain school studies, is that good thinkers have taken such studies, becoming better by the inherent tendency of the good to gain more than the poor from any study. When the good thinkers studied Greek and Latin, these studies *seemed* to make good thinking. Now that the good thinkers study Physics and Trigonometry, these seem to make good thinkers. If the abler pupils should all study Physical Education and Dramatic Art, these subjects would seem to make good thinkers. . . . After positive correlation of gain with initial ability is allowed for, the balance in favor of any study is certainly not large. Disciplinary values may be real and deserve weight in the curriculum, but the weights should be reasonable. (p. 98)

Concerning the question of how many elements two situations must have in common before the same behavior occurs in both, Thorndike (1905) said, "The case may be likened roughly to that of the direction taken by a four horse team at a fork in the roads, when the team has never traveled either road *as a team* but some one horse or a pair *has*. Their previous habit of taking, say, the left turn, will cause the whole team to go that way" (pp. 212–213).

Because all schools attempt to influence the way students behave outside of school, the problem of the transfer of training should be a central one for educators. Thorndike urged that the school curriculum be designed to include tasks similar to those students will perform when they leave school. Thus the study of mathematics should not be included because it strengthens the mind but because students will actually use mathematics when they leave school. *For Thorndike, schools should emphasize the direct training of those skills thought to be important beyond the school.*

The transfer of identical elements theory was Thorndike's solution to the problem of how we respond to a novel situation and to the problem of the transfer of training in general. Thorndike (1913a) offered what some thought was a weakness in his theory, namely, the fact that we respond smoothly to new situations, as supportive evidence for his theory: "There is no arbitrary *hocus pocus* whereby man's nature acts in an unpredictable spasm when he is confronted with a new situation. His habits do not then retire to some convenient distance while some new and mysterious entities direct his behavior. On the contrary, nowhere are the bonds acquired with old situations more surely revealed in action than when a new situation appears" (pp. 28–29). When attempting to explain how what is learned transfers from one situation to another, Thorndike's theory of identical elements and his more general position on transfer of procedure still remain highly influential (DeCorte, 1999, 2003; Haskell, 2001).

Associative Shifting

Associative shifting is closely related to Thorndike's identical elements theory of the transfer of training. The procedure for demonstrating associative shifting begins with a connection between a certain situation and a certain response. Then one gradually drops stimulus elements that are part of the original situation and adds stimulus elements that are not part of the original situation. According to Thorndike's identical elements theory, as long as there are enough elements from the original situation in the new situation, the same response will be given. In this way, the same response can be carried through a number of stimulus changes and finally be made to stimulating conditions totally dissimilar to those associated with the original response. Thorndike (1913a) said,

> Starting with response X made to *abcde,* we may successively drop certain elements and add others, until the response is bound to *fghij,* to which perhaps it could never otherwise have become connected. Theoretically the formula of progress, from *abcde* to *abfgh* to *afghi* to *fghij,* might result in attaching any response whatever to any situation whatever, provided only that we arrange affairs so that at every step the response X was more satisfying in its consequences than balking or doing anything else that the person could do. (pp. 30–31)

An example of associative shifting is found in the work of Terrace (1963) on discrimination learning. Terrace first taught pigeons to make a red-green discrimination by reinforcing them with grain when they pecked at a red key but not when they pecked at a green key. Next Terrace superimposed a vertical bar over the red key and a horizontal bar over the green key. Gradually the red and green colors were faded out, leaving only the vertical and horizontal bars on the keys. The discrimination previously associated with red and green was transferred without error to the vertical and horizontal bar discrimination. Now the pigeons pecked at the vertical bar and ignored the horizontal bar. The shifting process is shown in Figure 4–3.

The association shifts from one stimulus (red) to another (vertical bar) because the procedure allows enough elements from the preceding situation to guarantee that the same response is made to the new stimulus. This, of course, demonstrates transfer of training according to Thorndike's identical elements theory.

In a more general way, much advertising is based on the principle of associative shifting. The advertiser has only to find a stimulus object that elicits positive feelings, such as a picture of a beautiful woman or handsome man, a respected personality, a medical doctor, a mother, or a romantic outdoor scene. Then the advertiser pairs this stimulus object with the product—a brand of cigarettes, an automobile, or a deodorant—as often as possible so that the product will elicit the same positive feelings elicited by the original stimulus object.

In reading Thorndike, we should note that associative shifting is really quite different from trial-and-error learning, which is governed by the law of effect. Unlike learning that depends on the law of effect, associative shifting depends only on contiguity. Associative shifting represents, therefore, a second kind of learning that is similar to the theories of Pavlov and Guthrie, which we consider in Chapters 7 and 8.

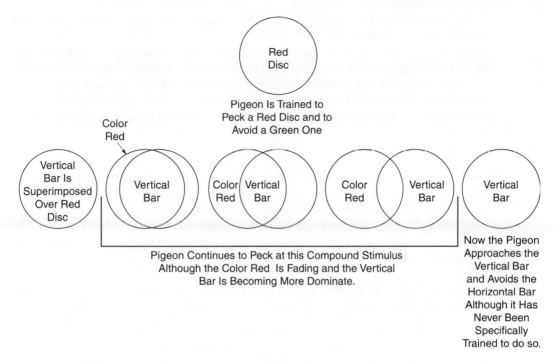

FIGURE 4–3 The process that Terrace used to shift a discriminatory response from one stimulus (the color red) to another stimulus (a vertical bar).

THORNDIKE AFTER 1930

In September 1929, Thorndike stood before the International Congress of Psychology in New Haven, Connecticut, and started his address by saying, "I was wrong." This admission points out an important aspect of good scientific practice: Scientists are obliged to change their conclusions if the data require it.

Revised Law of Exercise

Thorndike essentially renounced the entire law of exercise. The law of use, which states that mere repetition strengthened a connection, was found to be inaccurate. By the same token, simple disuse does not weaken a connection to any large extent. Although Thorndike still maintained that practice leads to minor improvement and that lack of practice leads to slight forgetting, for all practical purposes he discarded the entire law of exercise after 1930.

Revised Law of Effect

After 1930, the earlier law of effect was found to be only half true. The salvaged half states that a response followed by a satisfying state of affairs is strengthened. For the other half, Thorndike found that punishing a response has no effect on the strength of the connection. His revised law of effect states that *reinforcement increases the* **strength of a connection,** *whereas punishment does nothing to the strength of a connection.* This finding still has profound implications today. Thorndike's conclusion concerning the effectiveness of punishment is contrary to thousands of years of common sense and has numerous implications for education, child-rearing, and behavior modification in general. We often return to the question of the effectiveness of punishment as a means of modifying behavior in the following chapters.

Belongingness

Thorndike observed that in the learning of associations a factor in addition to contiguity and the law of effect is often involved. If the elements of an association somehow belong together, the association between them is learned and retained more readily than if the elements do not belong together. In one experiment designed to investigate this phenomenon, Thorndike (1932) read his experimental participants the following sentences ten times:

> Alfred Dukes and his sister worked sadly. Edward Davis and his brother argued rarely. Francis Bragg and his cousin played hard. Barney Croft and his father watched earnestly. Lincoln Blake and his uncle listened gladly. Jackson Craig and his son struggle often. Charlotte Dean and her friend studied easily. Mary Borah and her companion complained dully. Norman Foster and his mother bought much. Alice Hanson and her teacher came yesterday. (p. 66)

Afterward, participants were asked the following questions:

1. What word came next after *rarely?*
2. What word came next after *Lincoln?*
3. What word came next after *gladly?*
4. What word came next after *dully?*
5. What word came next after *Mary?*
6. What word came next after *earnestly?*
7. What word came next after *Norman Foster and his mother?*
8. What word came next after *and his son struggle often?*

If contiguity is the only influential factor, all sequences of words should be learned and remembered equally well. This, however, was not the case. The average number of correct associations from the end of one sentence to the beginning of the next was 2.75, whereas the average number of correct associations between the first and second word combinations was 21.50. Clearly, something is operating here beyond mere contiguity, and that something is what Thorndike called **belongingness;** that is, subjects and verbs belong together more than the last word in one sentence and the first in another.

Thorndike also related his notion of a confirming reaction, discussed earlier, to his concept of belongingness. He felt that if there is a natural relationship between the need state of the organism and the effect caused by a response, learning is more effective than if the relationship is unnatural. We say, for example, that a hungry animal finds food satisfying and a thirsty animal finds water satisfying. However, this is not to say that a hungry or thirsty animal would not find other things satisfying. Both still find escape from confinement and freedom from pain satisfying, but the existence of a powerful drive creates a class of events that are most satisfying at the moment. It was Thorndike's contention that an effect that belongs to the existing needs of the organism elicits a stronger confirming reaction than effects that do not belong to those needs, even though the latter effects may be powerful satisfiers under different circumstances.

We see, then, that Thorndike used the concept of belongingness in two ways. First, he used it to explain why, when learning verbal material, a person tends to organize what is learned into units that are perceived as belonging together. Second, he said that if the effects produced by a response are related to the needs of the organism, learning is more effective than if the effects produced by a response are not related to the organism's needs.

Many believed that with his concept of belongingness Thorndike was making concessions to the Gestalt psychologists who said organisms learn general principles and not specific S-R connections (see Chapter 10). Thorndike responded with his **principle of polarity,** which states that a learned response is most easily given in the direction in which it was formed. For example, almost everyone can recite the alphabet forward, but it is difficult to recite it backward. Likewise, almost any schoolchild can recite the pledge of allegiance forward, but it would be uncommon to find a child able to recite it backward. Thorndike's point was that if general principles and understandings are learned instead of specific S-R connections, a person should be able to perform what had been learned in either direction with almost equal ease. Thus, even with his concept of belongingness, Thorndike maintained his mechanistic, nonmental view concerning the learning process.

Spread of Effect

After 1930, Thorndike added another major theoretical concept, which he called the **spread of effect.** During one of his experiments, Thorndike accidentally found that a satisfying state of affairs not only increased the probability of recurrence of the response that led to the satisfying state of affairs but also increased the probability of recurrence of the responses surrounding the reinforced one.

One typical experiment demonstrating this effect involves presenting ten words, including *catnip, debate,* and *dazzle,* to participants who are instructed to respond with a number from 1 to 10. If the participant responds to a word with a number that the experimenter previously chose to go with that word, the experimenter says "right." If the subject responds with any other number, the experimenter says "wrong." The experiment proceeds in this fashion for several trials. Two important observations were made from this research. First, reinforcement (the experimenter saying "right") strongly increases the probability of the same number being repeated the next time the stimulus word is given, but punishment (the experimenter saying "wrong") does not reduce the probability of an incorrect number being repeated again. It was partially on the basis of this research that Thorndike revised his earlier law of effect. Second, it was found that the numbers preceding and following a reinforced number also increase in probability of recurring, even though they were not themselves reinforced and even if reporting these surrounding numbers had been punished previously. Thus, what Thorndike called a satisfying state of affairs apparently "spread" from the reinforced response to neighboring responses. He called this phenomenon the spread of effect. Thorndike also found that this effect diminishes with distance. In other words, the reinforced response has the greatest probability of recurring, then the responses next to the reinforced one, then the responses next to those, and so on.

In discovering the spread of effect, Thorndike felt that he had found additional confirmation for his revised law of effect because reinforcement not only increases the probability of a reinforced response but also increases the probability of neighboring responses, even though these may have been punished. He also felt that the spread of effect further demonstrates the automatic, direct nature of learning.

SCIENCE AND HUMAN VALUES

Thorndike was criticized for assuming determinism in the study of human behavior. Reducing human behavior to automatic reactions to the environment destroys human values, the critics said. Thorndike (1940) answered that on the contrary, the human sciences offered people their greatest hope for the future:

> The welfare of mankind now depends upon the sciences of man. The sciences of things will, unless civilization collapses, progress, extend man's control over nature, and guide technology, agriculture, medicine, and other arts effectively. They will protect man against dangers and disasters except such as he himself causes. He is now his own worst enemy. Knowledge of psychology and of its applications to welfare should prevent, or at least diminish, some of the errors and calamities for which the well-intentioned have been and are responsible. It should reduce greatly the harm done by the stupid and vicious. (p. v)

Elsewhere Thorndike (1949) said,

> Thus, at last, man may become ruler of himself as well as of the rest of nature. For strange as it may sound man is free only in a world whose every event he can understand and foresee. Only so can he guide it. We are captains of our own souls only in so far as they act in perfect law so that we can understand and foresee every response which we will make to every situation. Only so can we control our own selves. It is only because our intellects and morals—the mind and spirit of man—are a part of nature, that we can be in any significant sense responsible for them, proud of their progress, or trustful of their future. (p. 362)

Obviously, Thorndike was a very colorful person who expressed opinions on a wide variety of topics. In this chapter, we have concentrated on outlining his thoughts on the learning process and his views concerning the relationship between the learning process and educational practices. The student who is interested in knowing more about Thorndike is urged to read *The Sane Positivist: A Biography of Edward L. Thorndike* by Geraldine Joncich (1968).

THORNDIKE ON EDUCATION

Thorndike believed that educational practices should be studied scientifically. It was obvious to him that there should be a close relationship between the knowledge of the learning process and teaching practices. Thus, he expected that as more was discovered about the nature of learning, more could be applied to improve teaching practices. Thorndike (1906) said,

> Of course present knowledge of psychology is nearer to zero than to complete perfection, and its applications to teaching must therefore be often incomplete, indefinite and insecure. The application of psychology to teaching is more like that of botany and chemistry to farming than like that of physiology and pathology to medicine. Anyone of good sense can farm fairly well without science, and anyone of good sense can teach fairly well without knowing and applying psychology. Still, as the farmer with the knowledge of the applications of botany and chemistry to farming is, other things being equal, more successful than the farmer without it, so the teacher will, other things being equal, be the more successful who can apply psychology, the science of human nature, to the problems of the school. (pp. 9–10)

At many points Thorndike's thinking ran contrary to traditional notions about education; we saw one clear example in his identical elements theory of transfer. Thorndike (1912) also had a low opinion of the lecture technique of teaching that was so popular then (and now):

> The lecture and demonstration methods represent an approach to a limiting extreme in which the teacher lets the pupil find out nothing which he could possibly be told or shown. They frankly present the student with conclusions, trusting that he will use them to learn more. They ask of him only that he attend to, and do his best to understand, questions which he did not himself frame and answers which he did not himself work out. They try to give him an educational fortune as one bequeaths property by will. (p. 188)

He also said,

> The commonest error of the gifted scholar, inexperienced in teaching, is to expect pupils to know what they have been told. But telling is not teaching. The expression of the facts that are in one's mind is a natural impulse when one wishes others to know these facts, just as to cuddle and pat a sick child is a natural impulse. But telling a fact to a child may not cure his ignorance of it any more than patting him will cure his scarlet fever. (p. 61)

What then is good teaching? Good teaching involves first of all knowing what you want to teach. If you do not know exactly what it is you want to teach, you will not know what material to present, what responses to look for, and when to apply satisfiers. This principle is not as obvious as it sounds. Only recently have we realized the importance of behaviorally defining educational objectives. Although Thorndike's (1922) seven rules that follow were formulated for teaching arithmetic, they represent his advice for teaching in general:

1. Consider the situation the pupil faces.
2. Consider the response you wish to connect with it.
3. Form the bond; do not expect it to come by a miracle.
4. Other things being equal, form no bond that will have to be broken.
5. Other things being equal, do not form two or three bonds when one will serve.
6. Other things being equal, form bonds in the way that they are required later to act.
7. Favor, therefore, the situations which life itself will offer, and the responses which life itself will demand. (p. 101)

In more contemporary terms, Thorndike would have an orderly classroom with the objectives clearly defined. These educational objectives must be within the learner's response capabilities, and they must be divided into manageable units so that the teacher can apply "a satisfying state of affairs" when the learner makes an appropriate response. Learning proceeds from the simple to the complex.

Motivation is relatively unimportant, except in determining what will constitute a "satisfying state of affairs" for the learner. The learner's behavior is determined primarily by external reinforcers and not by intrinsic motivation. Emphasis is on bringing about correct responses to certain stimuli. Incorrect responses are to be corrected rapidly so that they are not practiced. Therefore, examinations are important: They provide the learner and the teacher with feedback concerning the learning process. If students learn their lesson well, they are to be reinforced quickly. If students have learned something incorrectly, their mistakes must be corrected quickly; thus examinations must be taken regularly.

The learning situation must be made to resemble the real world as much as possible. As we have seen, Thorndike believed that learning will transfer from the classroom to the environment outside only insofar as the two situations are similar. Teaching children to solve difficult problems does not enhance their reasoning capacity. Therefore, teaching Latin, mathematics, or logic is justified only when students will be solving problems involving Latin, mathematics, or logic when they leave school. Thorndike would approve of apprenticeship and internship programs and would be particularly enthusiastic about trade schools. He would not approve of curricula not involving experiential learning clearly linked to employment and the world outside of education.

The Thorndikian teacher would use positive control in the classroom, because satisfiers strengthen connections but annoyers do not weaken them. The Thorndikian teacher would also avoid lecturing and prefer dealing with students on a one-to-one basis.

One can see here the seeds of B. F. Skinner's attitude toward educational practices, which we consider in Chapter 5.

EVALUATION OF THORNDIKE'S THEORY

Contributions

Thorndike's pioneering work provides a distinct alternative for conceptualizing learning and behavior and differed radically from earlier approaches. Prior to Thorndike's studies, there simply was no systematic, experimental treatment of learning. He not only accounted for and synthesized the data available to him but also discovered and developed phenomena—trial-and-error learning and transfer of training, for example—that would define the domain of learning theory for years to come.

With his law of effect, Thorndike was the first to observe, under controlled conditions, that the consequences of behavior produce a backward-acting effect on the strength of that behavior. Questions about the reasons for the effect, its limits, its duration, and problems associated with its definition and measurement would direct research efforts in the behavioral tradition for the next fifty years, and they are still the topics of research and debate today. Thorndike was among the first to investigate the nature of forgetting in his early law of exercise and the suppression of behavior in his treatment of punishment, and he was clearly willing to discard early treatments of both phenomena when data contradicted his hypotheses. In his treatment of transfer of training, Thorndike was the first to rigorously question common assumptions in educational practices (formal discipline). And although he can be considered an early behaviorist, his notions of prepotency of elements and response by analogy foreshadowed contemporary cognitive theories of learning.

Criticisms

Although it has been demonstrated that some phenomena discovered by Thorndike—the spread of effect, for example—are due to processes other than those he identified (Estes, 1969b; Zirkle, 1946), the important criticisms of Thorndike's theory focus on two major issues. The first concerns the definition of satisfiers in the law of effect. The second, also related to the law of effect, concerns the starkly mechanistic definition of learning in the theory. Critics of the law of effect said that Thorndike's argument was circular: If the response probability increased, it was said to be due to the presence of a satisfying state of affairs; if it did not increase, it was claimed that no satisfier was present. Such an explanation was believed not to allow for a test of the theory because the same event (increased probability of a response) was used to detect both learning and a satisfying state of affairs. Later defenders of Thorndike argued that this criticism is invalid because once something has been shown to be a satisfier, it can be used to modify behavior in other situations (Meehl, 1950), but as we discuss in Chapter 5, this defense has failed.

A second criticism of Thorndike's law of effect concerned the way that S-R connections were thought to be strengthened or weakened. As we have seen, Thorndike believed learning to be an automatic function of a satisfying state of affairs and not the result of any conscious mechanism such as thinking or reasoning.

Clearly, Thorndike believed that an organism need not be aware of the relationship between a response and a satisfier in order for the satisfier to have an effect. Similarly, the intentions and strategies of the learner were considered nonessential for learning. Thorndike did not deny the existence of thoughts, plans, strategies, and intentions. Rather, Thorndike believed learning could be adequately explained without reference to such events. Contemporary students react negatively to this mechanical approach to the study of learning, as did many of Thorndike's contemporaries. William McDougall, for example, wrote in the 1920s that Thorndike's theory of selecting and connecting was a "theory of morons, by morons, and for morons" (Joncich, 1968). The debate concerning the nature of reinforcement and whether a learner must be aware of reinforcement contingencies before they can be effective continues today, and therefore we return to it often throughout this book.

DISCUSSION QUESTIONS

1. Summarize the nature of animal research prior to Thorndike's efforts. In what way was Thorndike's research different from that which preceded it? Include in your answer a discussion of Morgan's canon.
2. Do you agree with Thorndike's contention that the same laws of learning apply to both human and nonhuman animals? Explain.
3. Assuming Thorndike's revised law of effect to be valid, do you feel classroom practice in this country is in accordance with it? Child-rearing practices? Explain.
4. Summarize the revisions that Thorndike made in his theory after 1930.
5. Discuss Thorndike's concept of the confirming reaction.
6. Discuss the importance of sets or attitudes in Thorndike's theory.
7. According to Thorndike, what determines what will transfer from one learning situation to another?
8. Summarize Thorndike's criticisms of the formal discipline approach to education. How would you arrange schoolroom practices so that they take into consideration Thorndike's theory concerning the transfer of training?
9. Describe how you would reduce the probability of a child being fearful of a new situation, such as a new babysitter, using the procedure of associative shifting.
10. Discuss Thorndike's principles of belongingness and polarity.
11. Summarize what Thorndike learned from his research on the spread of effect.
12. What, according to Thorndike, provides humans with their greatest hope for the future?

CHAPTER HIGHLIGHTS

annoying state of affairs	belongingness
anthropomorphizing	confirming reaction
associative shifting	connectionism

formal discipline

identical elements theory of transfer

incremental learning

insightful learning

law of disuse

law of effect

law of exercise

law of readiness

law of use

Morgan, Conwy Lloyd

Morgan's canon

multiple response

prepotency of elements

principle of polarity

response by analogy

Romanes, George John

satisfying state of affairs

selecting and connecting

sets (attitudes)

spread of effect

strength of a connection

transfer of training

trial-and-error learning

Washburn, Margaret Floy

CHAPTER 5

Burrhus Frederic Skinner

Skinner (1904–1990) was born in Susquehanna, Pennsylvania. He received his master's degree in 1930 and his Ph.D. in 1931 from Harvard University. His B.A. degree was obtained from Hamilton College in New York, where he majored in English. While at Hamilton, Skinner had lunch with Robert Frost, the great American poet, who encouraged Skinner to send him a sample of his writing. Frost favorably reviewed the three short stories that Skinner sent, and Skinner decided definitely to become a writer. This decision was a great disappointment to his father, who was a lawyer and wanted his son to become a lawyer.

Skinner's early efforts to write were so frustrating that he thought of seeing a psychiatrist. He eventually went to work for the coal industry summarizing legal documents. In fact, his first book, coauthored by his father, concerned those legal documents and was entitled *A Digest of Decisions of the Anthracite Board of Conciliation.* After finishing this book, Skinner moved to Greenwich Village in New York City, where he lived like a Bohemian for six months before going to Harvard to study psychology. By that time, he had developed a distaste for most literary pursuits. In his autobiography (1967), he said, "I had failed as a writer because I had nothing important to say, but I could not accept that explanation. It was literature which must be at fault" (p. 395). When he failed in describing human behavior through literature, Skinner attempted to describe human behavior through science. Clearly, he was much more successful at the latter pursuit.

Skinner taught psychology at the University of Minnesota between 1936 and 1945, during which time he wrote his highly influential text, *The Behavior of Organisms* (1938). One of Skinner's students at the University of Minnesota was W. K. Estes, whose work has had a considerable impact

Burrhus Frederic Skinner. (Courtesy of Yousuf Karsh/Woodfin Camp & Associates, Inc.)

on psychology (see Chapter 9). In 1945, Skinner went to Indiana University as chair of the psychology department, and in 1948, he returned to Harvard, to which he remained affiliated until his death in 1990.

In a survey taken just prior to Skinner's death (Korn, Davis, & Davis, 1991), historians of psychology and chairpersons of graduate departments of psychology were asked to rank the ten most eminent (contemporary and all-time) psychologists. Skinner was ranked eighth on the all-time list but first among contemporary psychologists by historians of psychology; department chairs ranked Skinner first on both lists.

Through the years, Skinner was a highly prolific writer. One of his main concerns was to relate his laboratory findings to the solution of human problems. His work led to the development of programmed learning and teaching machines. Two representative articles in this area are "The Science of Learning and the Art of Teaching" (1954) and "Teaching Machines" (1958). Following his own ideas on this topic, he and his coauthor, Holland, produced a programmed text on his theoretical notions entitled *The Analysis of Behavior* (Holland & Skinner, 1961). In 1948 he wrote a Utopian novel called *Walden Two*. The title paid tribute to Thoreau's *Walden*. In *Walden Two* (1948), which Skinner wrote in only seven weeks, he attempted to utilize his principles of learning in the building of a model society. More recently Skinner wrote *Beyond Freedom and Dignity* (1971), in which he showed how a technology of behavior could be used in designing a culture. In *Beyond Freedom and Dignity*, he discussed why the idea of cultural engineering is met with so much opposition. Skinner's writings have been extended into the area of child development through the efforts of Bijou and Baer (1961, 1965). His thoughts have been related to the area of personality through the writings of Lundin (1974), who wrote *Personality: A Behavioral Analysis*, and to child rearing by Hergenhahn (1972), who wrote *Shaping Your Child's Personality*.

Most students of psychology are well aware of the widespread utilization of Skinnerian notions in the area of psychotherapy. For example, Lovaas's early work with autistic children relied heavily on Skinner's ideas. Behavioral engineering, however, is by no means limited to children. The technique has been successfully applied to the alleviation of a number of adult problems, such as stuttering, phobias, eating disorders, and psychotic behavior.

During World War II, while at the University of Minnesota, Skinner attempted to apply his theory to the problem of national defense. He trained pigeons to peck at disks on which moving pictures of enemy targets were being shown. The disks and the motion pictures were ultimately to be contained in a glider loaded with high explosives. The glider was called the *Pelican*, thus the name of the article describing these events, "Pigeons in a Pelican" (1960). The pecking of the pigeons closed various electronic circuits and thereby kept the vehicle on target. This American version of kamikaze fighter planes would involve no loss of human lives. Although Skinner demonstrated to a group of America's top scientists that he and his coworkers had perfected a homing device that was almost immune to electronic jamming, was capable of reacting to a wide variety of enemy targets, and was simple to build, their proposed project was turned down. Skinner speculated that the whole idea was simply too fantastic for the committee to cope with.

MAJOR THEORETICAL CONCEPTS

Radical Behaviorism

Skinner adopted and developed the scientific philosophy known as **radical behaviorism.** This scientific orientation rejects scientific language and interpretations that refer to **mentalistic events.** As we discuss, some behavioristic learning theorists use terms like *drive, motivation,* and *purpose* in order to explain certain aspects of human and nonhuman behavior. Skinner rejected these kinds of terms because they refer to private, mental experience and represent, in his view, a return to nonscientific psychology. For Skinner, observable and measurable aspects of the environment, of an organism's behavior, and of the consequences of that behavior are the critical material for scientific scrutiny. Ringen (1999) writes that

> Skinner holds that science is the search for causes, that the identification of causes enables prediction and control, and that experimental investigation, properly conducted, enables identification of causes. This much of Skinner's radical behaviorism is a rather traditional and unremarkable view of science. . . . What is unique, challenging and largely misunderstood about Skinner's radical behaviorism is Skinner's argument that this view of science provides a basis for skepticism about mentalism, in particular, and about various influential approaches to the development of theories of learning and intelligent action, in general. (p. 161)

Respondent and Operant Behavior

Skinner distinguished two kinds of behavior: **respondent behavior,** which is elicited by a known stimulus, and **operant behavior,** which is not elicited by a known stimulus but is simply emitted by the organism. Unconditioned responses are examples of respondent behavior because they are elicited by unconditioned stimuli. Examples of respondent behavior include all reflexes, such as jerking one's hand when jabbed with a pin, the constriction of the pupil of the eye when it is exposed to bright light, and salivation in the presence of food. Because operant behavior is *not* initially correlated with known stimuli, it seems to appear spontaneously. Examples include beginning to whistle, standing up and walking about, or a child abandoning one toy in favor of another. Most of our everyday activities are operant behaviors. Note that Skinner did not say that operant behavior occurs independently of stimulation; rather, he said that the stimulus causing such behavior is unknown and that it is not important to know its cause. Unlike respondent behavior, which is dependent on the stimulus that preceded it, operant behavior is controlled by its consequences.

Type S and Type R Conditioning

Along with the two kinds of behavior described previously, there are two kinds of conditioning. Type S conditioning is also called **respondent conditioning** and is identical to classical conditioning. It is called Type S conditioning to emphasize the importance of the stimulus in eliciting the desired response. The type of conditioning that involves operant behavior is called Type R because of the emphasis on the response. Type R conditioning is also called **operant conditioning.**

In Type R conditioning, the strength of conditioning is shown by *response rate,* whereas in Type S conditioning the strength of conditioning is usually determined by the *magnitude* of the conditioned response. We see, then, that Skinner's Type R conditioning very closely resembles Thorndike's instrumental conditioning, and Skinner's Type S conditioning is identical to Pavlov's classical conditioning. Skinner's research was concerned almost entirely with Type R, or operant, conditioning.

Operant Conditioning Principles

Two general principles are associated with Type R conditioning: (1) any response that is followed by a reinforcing stimulus tends to be repeated; and (2) a reinforcing stimulus is anything that increases the rate with which an operant response occurs. Or as we saw earlier, we say that a reinforcer is anything that increases the probability of a response's recurring.

Skinner (1953) did not provide a rule that one would follow in discovering what would be an effective reinforcer. Rather, he said that whether something is reinforcing can be ascertained only by its effect on behavior:

> In dealing with our fellow men in everyday life and in the clinic and laboratory, we may need to know just how reinforcing a specific event is. We often begin by noting the extent to which our own behavior is reinforced by the same event. This practice frequently miscarries; yet it is still commonly believed that reinforcers can be identified apart from their effects upon a particular organism. As the term is used here, however, the only defining characteristic of a reinforcing stimulus is that it reinforces. (p. 72)

In operant conditioning, the emphasis is on behavior and its consequences; with operant conditioning, the organism must respond in such a way as to produce the reinforcing stimulus. This process also exemplifies **contingent reinforcement,** because getting the reinforcer is contingent (dependent) on the organism emitting a certain response. We have more to say about contingent reinforcement in our discussion of superstitious behavior.

The principles of operant conditioning apply to a variety of situations. To modify behavior, one merely has to find something that is reinforcing for the organism whose behavior one wishes to modify, wait until the desired behavior occurs, and then immediately reinforce the organism. When this is done, the rate with which the desired response occurs goes up. When the behavior next occurs, it is again reinforced, and the rate of responding goes up further. Any behavior that the organism is capable of performing can be manipulated in this manner.

The same principles are thought to apply to the development of human personality. According to Skinner, we are what we have been reinforced for being. What we call personality is nothing more than consistent behavior patterns that summarize our reinforcement history. We learn to speak English, for example, because we have been reinforced for approximating the sounds of the English language in our early home environment. If we happened to be brought up in a Japanese or Russian home, we would learn to speak Japanese or Russian because when we approximated sounds in that language, we would have been attended to or reinforced in some way. Skinner (1971) said,

> The evidence for a crude environmentalism is clear enough. People are extraordinarily different in different places, and possibly just because of the places. The nomad on horse-back in Outer Mongolia and the astronaut in outer space are different people, but, as far as we know, if they had been exchanged at birth, they would have taken each other's place. (The expression "change places" shows how closely we identify a person's behavior with the environment in which it occurs.) But we need to know a great deal more before that fact becomes useful. What is it about the environment that produces a Hottentot? And what would need to be changed to produce an English conservative instead? (p. 185)

Skinner defined *culture* as a set of reinforcement contingencies. His answers to the questions he posed are that a particular set of reinforcement contingencies produces a Hottentot and another set produces the English conservative. Different cultures reinforce different behavior patterns. This fact must be clearly understood before an adequate technology of behavior can be developed. Skinner said (1971),

> The environment is obviously important, but its role has remained obscure. It does not push or pull, it *selects*, and this function is difficult to discover and analyze. The role of natural selection in evolution was formulated only a little more than a hundred years ago, and the selective role of the environment in shaping and maintaining the behavior of the individual is only beginning to be recognized and studied. As the interaction between organism and environment has come to be understood, however, effects once assigned to states of mind, feelings, and traits are beginning to be traced to accessible conditions, and a technology of behavior may therefore become available. It will not solve our problems, however, until it replaces traditional prescientific views, and these are strongly entrenched. (p. 25)

In Skinner's attempt to understand the causes of behavior, and thus to predict and control behavior, the analogy between operant conditioning and natural selection is an important one. Ringen (1999) writes,

> His main thesis is that the causal processes producing the behavior traditionally called purposive and intentional are instances of selection by consequences, a causal mode exhibited in the analogous processes of operant conditioning (the contingencies of reinforcement) and natural selection (the contingencies of survival). . . . He suggests that just as we learned that design could be produced without a designer we are learning that intelligence (and purpose) can be produced without mind. (p. 168)

If one controls reinforcement, one also controls behavior. However, this need not be looked on as a negative statement because behavior is constantly being influenced by reinforcement, regardless of whether we are aware of that fact. It is never a question of whether behavior is going to be controlled but a question of who or what is going to control it. Parents, for example, can decide to give direction to their child's emerging personality by reinforcing certain behavior, or they can let society rear their child by letting television, peers, school, books, and babysitters do the reinforcing. Giving direction to a child's life is difficult, however, and any parents wishing to do so must take at least the following steps (Hergenhahn, 1972):

1. Decide the major personality characteristics you want your child to possess as an adult. Let's say, for example, you want the child to grow up to be a creative adult.
2. Define these goals in behavioral terms. In this case you ask, "What is a child doing when he or she is being creative?"
3. Reward behavior that is in accordance with these goals. With this example, you would reward instances of creativity as they occurred.
4. Provide consistency by arranging the major aspects of the child's environment so that they, too, reward the behavior you have deemed important. (pp. 152–153)

Without knowledge of these principles, a parent could easily misapply them without knowing it. Skinner (1951) said,

> The mother may unwillingly promote the very behavior she does not want. For example, when she is busy she is likely not to respond to a call or request made in a quiet tone of voice. She may answer the child only when it raises its voice. The average intensity of the child's vocal behavior therefore moves up to another level. . . . Eventually the mother gets used to this level and again reinforces only louder instances. This vicious circle brings about louder and louder behavior. . . . The mother behaves, in fact, as if she has been given the assignment of teaching the child to be annoying. (p. 29)

According to Skinner, living organisms are constantly being conditioned by their environment. We can either allow the principles of learning to operate capriciously on our children, or, by systematically applying those principles, we can give some direction to their development.

FIGURE 5–1   A typical Skinner box. (Courtesy of Nina Leen/Getty Images/ Time Life Pictures.)

The Skinner Box

Most of Skinner's early animal work was done in a small test chamber that has come to be called the **Skinner box.** It is a direct descendant of the puzzle box used by Thorndike. The Skinner box usually has a grid floor, light, lever, and food cup. It is arranged so that when the animal depresses the lever, the feeder mechanism is activated, and a small pellet of food is released into the food cup. A typical Skinner box is shown in Figure 5–1.

The Cumulative Recording

Skinner used a **cumulative recording** to keep track of an animal's behavior in the Skinner box. A cumulative recording is quite different from other ways of graphing data in learning experiments. Time is recorded on the x-axis and total number of responses is recorded on the y-axis. The cumulative recording never goes down—the line either climbs or remains parallel to the x-axis. Let's say we are interested in how often the animal presses the lever. When the cumulative recording shows a line parallel to the x-axis, it indicates no responding; that is, the animal is not pressing the lever. When the animal makes a lever-pressing response, the pen goes up a notch and remains at that level until the animal makes another response. If, for example, the animal presses the lever when it is first placed in the Skinner box, the pen will go up a notch and remain there until the animal responds again, at which time the pen will go up another notch, and so on. If the animal responds very rapidly, the line will rise very rapidly. The rate with which the line ascends indicates the rate of responding; a very steep line indicates very rapid responding, and a line parallel to the x-axis indicates no responding. If at any time you want to know the total number of responses made by the animal, you just measure the distance between the line of the graph and the x-axis, which can easily be transformed into the total number of responses. Sample cumulative recordings are shown in Figure 5–2.

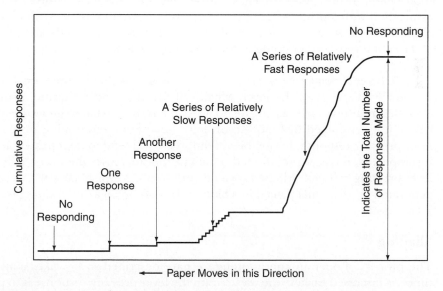

FIGURE 5–2 A cumulative recording. Note that the steeper the line, the faster the rate of responding. A line parallel to the baseline indicates no response.

Conditioning the Lever-Pressing Response

Typically, conditioning the lever-pressing response involves the following steps:

1. Deprivation   The experimental animal is put on a deprivation schedule. If food is to be used as the reinforcer, the animal is deprived of food for a twenty-three-hour period for a number of days prior to the experiment, or it is maintained at 80 percent of its free-feeding body weight. If water is to be used as the reinforcer, the animal is deprived of water for a twenty-three-hour period for a number of days prior to the experiment. (Some Skinner boxes are designed to deliver small pellets of food and others small drops of water.) Skinner does not say that these procedures "motivate" the animal; he even hesitates to say that they produce a drive state. Deprivation is simply a set of procedures that is related to how an organism performs on a certain task; nothing more needs to be said.

2. Magazine Training   After being on a deprivation schedule for a number of days, the animal is placed into the Skinner box. In **magazine training,** the experimenter uses an external hand switch and periodically triggers the feeder mechanism (also called the magazine), making sure the animal is not in the vicinity of the food cup when he or she does so (otherwise the animal would learn to remain near the food cup). When the feeder mechanism is activated by the hand switch, it produces a fairly loud clicking sound before delivering a pellet of food into the food cup. Gradually the animal associates the click of the magazine with the presence of a food pellet. At that point the click has become a secondary reinforcer through its association with a primary reinforcement (food). (We discuss secondary reinforcement in a later section.) The click also acts as a cue or signal indicating to the animal that if it responds by going to the food cup, it will be reinforced.

3. Lever Pressing   Now the animal can be left in the Skinner box on its own. Eventually, it will press the lever, which will fire the food magazine, producing a click that reinforces the bar press and also signals the animal to go to the food cup, where it is reinforced by food. According to operant conditioning principles, the lever-pressing response, having been reinforced, will tend to be repeated, and when it is repeated, it is again reinforced, which further increases the probability that the lever-pressing response will be repeated, and so on. A typical cumulative recording generated by an animal placed in a Skinner box after magazine training is shown in Figure 5–3.

Shaping

The process of operant conditioning we have described so far takes considerable time. As discussed earlier, one way to train the lever-pressing response is to place the deprived animal in the Skinner box and simply leave it there. The experimenter merely checks the cumulative recording periodically to see if the response has been learned. Under these conditions, the animal either learns or dies.

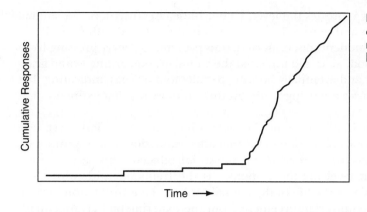

FIGURE 5–3 A typical
cumulative recording that
reflects the acquisition of a
lever-pressing response.

There is another approach to operant conditioning, referred to as **shaping,** that does not take as long as the procedure previously described. Again, the animal is placed on a deprivation schedule and is magazine trained, and again the experimenter uses the hand switch to trigger the feeder mechanism externally. This time, however, the experimenter decides to fire the feeder mechanism only when the animal is in the half of the Skinner box containing the lever. When the animal is reinforced for being near the lever, it will tend to remain in that part of the test chamber. Now that the animal remains in the vicinity of the lever, the experimenter begins to reinforce it only when it is still closer to the lever. Next it is reinforced only when it touches the lever, then only when it is putting pressure on it, and finally only when it is pressing the lever by itself.

The process is similar to a childhood game called You're Hot, You're Cold, in which a child hides something and the child's playmates try to find it. As they get closer to the hidden object, the child who hid the object says, "You're getting warm, you're warmer, you're boiling hot, you're on fire." As they get farther from the object, the child says, "You're getting cold, colder, very cold, you're freezing."

Shaping has two components: **differential reinforcement,** which simply means some responses are reinforced and others are not, and **successive approximation,** which refers to the fact that only those responses that become increasingly similar to the one the experimenter wants are reinforced. In our example, only those responses that successively approximated the lever-pressing response were differentially reinforced.

Recently it has been found that under certain circumstances, preexisting or even accidental contingencies between events in the environment and an animal's response automatically shape behavior. This phenomenon is called autoshaping, which we discuss later in this chapter.

Extinction

As with classical conditioning, when we remove the reinforcer from the operant conditioning situation, we produce **extinction.** During acquisition, the animal gets a pellet of food whenever it presses the lever. Under these circumstances, the animal learns to press the lever and persists in doing so until it is satiated with food. If the feeder mechanism was suddenly disconnected, thus preventing a lever pressing from producing a pellet of food, we would note that the cumulative recording would gradually become shallower and eventually become parallel to the *x*-axis, indicating that no lever-pressing responses are being made. At that point we say that extinction has occurred.

We are being somewhat inaccurate when we say that after extinction a response is no longer made; it is more accurate to say that after extinction, the response rate goes back to where it was before reinforcement was introduced. This baseline rate, also called the **operant level** for the response, is the frequency with which the response occurs naturally in the life of the animal without the introduction of reinforcement. When we remove reinforcement from the experimental arrangement, as in extinction, the response tends to go back to its operant level.

Spontaneous Recovery

After extinction, if the animal is returned to its home cage for a period of time and then brought back into the experimental situation, it will again begin to press the lever for a short period of time without any additional training. This is referred to as **spontaneous recovery.** A cumulative recording showing both extinction and spontaneous recovery is shown in Figure 5–4.

Superstitious Behavior

In our earlier discussion of operant conditioning, we briefly mentioned contingent reinforcement. Reinforcement following the lever-pressing response is an example of contingent reinforcement because the reinforcer is dependent on the response. What would happen, however, if the situation was arranged so that the feeder

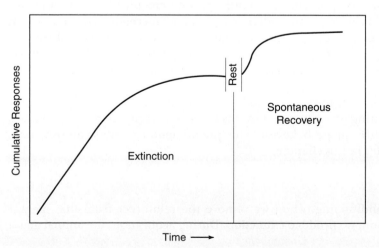

FIGURE 5–4   A cumulative recording that depicts the extinction and spontaneous recovery of a lever-pressing response.

mechanism would fire every now and then, independently of the animal's behavior? In other words, we are now going to arrange the situation so that the feeder mechanism randomly delivers a pellet of food *regardless of what the animal is doing.*

According to the principles of operant conditioning, we can predict that whatever the animal is doing when the feeder mechanism is activated will be reinforced, and the animal will tend to repeat the reinforced behavior. After a period of time, the reinforced behavior will recur when the feeder mechanism fires again, and the response will be strengthened. Thus the animal is apt to develop strange ritualistic responses; it may bob its head, turn in a circle, stand up on its back legs, or perform a series of actions, according to what it was doing when the feeder mechanism fired. This ritualistic behavior is referred to as superstitious because the animal looks as if it believes that what it is doing is causing a pellet of food to appear. Because the reinforcer in this situation is independent of the animal's behavior, it is referred to as **noncontingent reinforcement.**

One can think of numerous examples of **superstitious behavior** on the part of humans. Organized sports, for instance, are filled with many examples. Imagine what happens to the baseball player who, after stepping to the plate, adjusts his or her cap in a certain way and hits the very next pitch out of the ballpark. There will be a strong tendency on his part to adjust the cap in a similar way the next time he or she is at bat.

Discriminative Operant

Now we return to the Skinner box and discuss the light that we referred to earlier. After we have conditioned the animal to press the lever, we can make the situation more complex. We can arrange the situation so that the animal receives a pellet of food when the light in the Skinner box is on but not when the light is off. Under these conditions, we refer to the light as S^D, or a **discriminative stimulus.** The light being on defines the S^D condition, and the light being off defines the S^Δ condition (Δ = delta). With this arrangement, the animal learns to press the lever when the light is on and not to press when the light is off. The light, therefore, has become a signal (cue) for the lever-pressing response. We have developed a **discriminative operant,** which is an operant response given to one set of circumstances but not to another. The arrangement can be symbolized as follows: $S^D \rightarrow R \rightarrow S^R$, where R is the operant response and S^R is the reinforcing stimulus.

The concept of the discriminative stimulus allows a more detailed statement about which stimulus-response relationship is of interest in operant conditioning. For Thorndike, the association of interest was between a general environmental situation and a response effective in solving a problem. For Skinner, the relationship of interest can be diagrammed as follows:

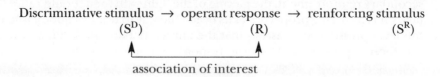

Discriminative stimulus $\rightarrow$ operant response $\rightarrow$ reinforcing stimulus
$\qquad (S^D) \qquad\qquad\qquad\qquad (R) \qquad\qquad\qquad\qquad (S^R)$

association of interest

There is some slight similarity between the discriminative operant and respondent conditioning. You will recall that respondent behavior is elicited by a known stimulus. The behavior occurs because of its association with the stimulus. Such behavior, as we have seen, is not under the control of its consequences. In the case of the discriminative operant, the light becomes a signal associated with a certain response that the organism has learned will be followed by reinforcement.

Operant behavior is emitted behavior, but Skinner (1953) said,

> Most operant behavior . . . acquires important connections with the surrounding world. We may show how it does so in our pigeon experiment by reinforcing neck-stretching when a signal light is on and allowing it to be extinguished when the light is off. Eventually stretching occurs only when the light is on. We can then demonstrate a stimulus-response connection which is roughly comparable to a conditioned or unconditioned reflex: the appearance of the light will be quickly followed by an upward movement of the head. But the relation is fundamentally quite different. It has a different history and different current properties. We describe the contingency by saying that a *stimulus* (the light) is the occasion upon which a *response* (stretching the neck) is followed by *reinforcement* (with food). We must specify all three terms. The effect upon the pigeon is that eventually the response is more likely to occur when the light is on. The process through which this comes about is called *discrimination*. Its importance in a theoretical analysis, as well as in the practical control of behavior, is obvious: when a discrimination has been established, we may alter the probability of a response instantly by presenting or removing the discriminative stimulus. (pp. 107–108)

Thus, the discriminative operant involves a signal that leads to a response, which in turn leads to reinforcement.

There are numerous examples of discriminative operants in everyday life. A certain time of the day (S^D) indicates that you must be in a certain place (R) to transact some business (S^R). As you're driving down the street, you encounter a red light (S^D), which causes you to stop (R), thereby avoiding a ticket or an accident (S^R). You see someone you don't care for (S^D), causing you to change the direction you are walking (R), thereby avoiding the person (S^R).

Secondary Reinforcement

Any neutral stimulus paired with a primary reinforcer (e.g., food or water) takes on reinforcing properties of its own; this is the principle of secondary reinforcement. It follows then that every S^D must be a secondary reinforcer because it consistently precedes primary reinforcement.

One way to demonstrate the reinforcing properties of a previously neutral stimulus is to wire the Skinner box so that a light comes on before the animal receives food for making a lever-pressing response. According to the principle of secondary reinforcement, the pairing of the light with food should cause the light to take on reinforcing properties of its own. One way to test this notion is to extinguish the lever-pressing response so that the animal presses the lever, and neither light nor food is produced. When the response rate decreases to its operant level, we arrange for the lever pressing to turn on the light but not deliver a pellet of food. We note that the response rate increases. Because the light alone has increased the response rate and thereby prolonged extinction, we say it has developed secondary reinforcing characteristics through its association with food during acquisition (training). A light not associated with a primary reinforcer will not produce a similar effect during extinction.

In addition to maintaining the lever-pressing response, we can now use the light to condition other responses. Once a previously neutral stimulus takes on reinforcing properties through its association with primary reinforcement, it can be used to reinforce any number of responses.

Keller and Schoenfeld (1950) provide an excellent summary of secondary reinforcement:

1. A stimulus that occasions or accompanies a reinforcement acquires thereby reinforcing value of its own, and may be called a conditioned, secondary, or derived reinforcement. A secondary reinforcement may be extinguished when repeatedly applied to a response for which there is no ultimate primary reinforcement.
2. A secondary reinforcement is positive when the reinforcement with which it is correlated is positive, and negative when the latter is negative.
3. Once established, a secondary reinforcement is independent and nonspecific; it will not only strengthen the same response which produced the original reinforcement, but it will also condition a new and unrelated response. Moreover, it will do so even in the presence of a different motive.
4. Through generalization, many stimuli besides the one correlated with reinforcement acquire reinforcing value—positive or negative. (p. 260)

Generalized Reinforcers

A **generalized reinforcer** is a secondary reinforcer that has been paired with more than one primary reinforcer. Money is a generalized reinforcer because it is ultimately associated with any number of primary reinforcers. The main advantage of the generalized reinforcer is that it does not depend on a certain condition of deprivation to be effective. Food, for example, is only reinforcing for an organism deprived of food, but money can be used as a reinforcer whether or not someone is deprived of food. Moreover, the very activities that once led to reinforcement may themselves become reinforcing. Skinner (1953) said,

Eventually generalized reinforcers are effective even though the primary reinforcers upon which they are based no longer accompany them. We play games of skill for their own sake. We get attention or approval for its own sake. Affection is not always followed by a more explicit sexual reinforcement. The submissiveness of others is reinforcing even though we make no use of it. A miser may be so reinforced by money that he will starve rather than give it up. (p. 81)

With these comments, Skinner came very close to Gordon Allport's concept of **functional autonomy.** Allport (1961) maintained that although an activity may once have been engaged in because it led to reinforcement, after a while the activity itself becomes reinforcing. In other words, the activity becomes independent of the reinforcer on which it was originally dependent. For example, a person might originally join the merchant marines in order to make a living but later in life go sailing because it is enjoyable to do so, even though sailing no longer provides an income. In this case we say that sailing is functionally autonomous; that is, it continues in the absence of the original motive. Skinner said that such an activity must ultimately result in primary reinforcement or it would extinguish. Allport, however, would say that the activity no longer depends on primary reinforcement.

Chaining

One response can bring the organism into contact with stimuli that act as an S^D for another response, which in turn causes it to experience stimuli that cause a third response, and so on. This process is referred to as **chaining.** In fact, most behavior can be shown to involve some form of chaining. For example, even the lever pressing in the Skinner box is not an isolated response. The stimuli in the Skinner box act as S^Ds, causing the animal to turn toward the lever. The sight of the lever causes the animal to approach it and press it. The firing of the feeder mechanism acts as an additional S^D, which elicits the response of going to the food cup. Consuming the food pellet acts as an S^D, causing the animal to return to the lever and again press it. This sequence of events (chain) is held together by the food pellet, which of course is a primary positive reinforcer. It can be said that various elements of a behavioral chain are held together by secondary reinforcers but that the entire chain depends on a primary reinforcer.

To explain how chaining comes about from Skinner's point of view, one must utilize the concepts of secondary reinforcement and associative shifting. Because of their association with the primary reinforcer, the events prior to the delivery of the food pellet take on secondary reinforcing properties. Thus the sight of the lever itself becomes a secondary reinforcer, and the response of looking at the lever is reinforced by the sight of the lever. Now, through a process similar to associative shifting (or higher-order conditioning, which we discuss in Chapter 7), other stimuli more remote from the lever develop reinforcing properties. Thus, after considerable training, when the animal is placed in the Skinner box, the initial stimuli it encounters will act as an S^D, causing the animal to orient toward the lever. The sight of the lever at this point acts both as a reinforcer and as an S^D, eliciting the next response in the chain. The situation is diagrammed in Figure 5–5.

Note that the development of a chained response always acts from the primary reinforcer backward. As more and more related stimuli take on reinforcing properties, the chain is extended. It is possible, for example, for the chain to extend gradually all the way back to the animal's home cage.

Occasionally rats have been trained to perform complex chained responses such as climbing a staircase, riding in a cart, crossing a bridge, playing a note on a

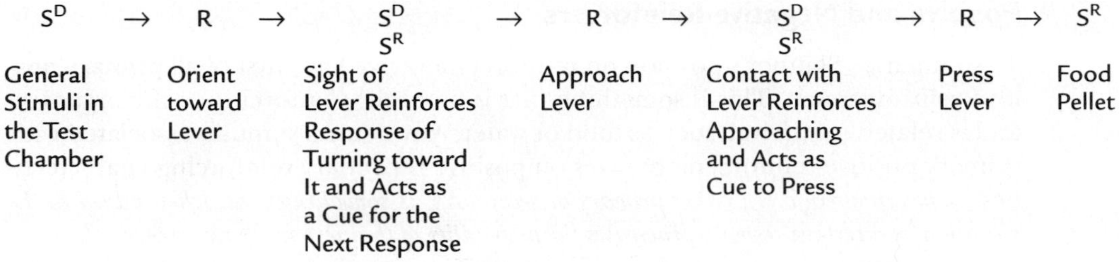

$$S^D \rightarrow R \rightarrow \begin{matrix} S^D \\ S^R \end{matrix} \rightarrow R \rightarrow \begin{matrix} S^D \\ S^R \end{matrix} \rightarrow R \rightarrow S^R$$

| General Stimuli in the Test Chamber | Orient toward Lever | Sight of Lever Reinforces Response of Turning toward It and Acts as a Cue for the Next Response | Approach Lever | Contact with Lever Reinforces Approaching and Acts as Cue to Press | Press Lever | Food Pellet |

FIGURE 5–5   An example of chained behavior.

toy piano, entering a small elevator, pulling a chain, riding the elevator down, and receiving a small pellet of food. This chain, too, is developed backward so that the events that precede the primary reinforcer gradually become secondary reinforcers. When they do, they reinforce the responses prior to them, and so on along the chain of behaviors.

Chained responses can also occur between two people. For example, seeing someone you know acts as an S^D to say "hello." Your hello acts as an S^D for your friend to say "hi." The response of "hi" acts not only as a reinforcer for your "hello" but also as an S^D for you to say "How are you?" This two-person chain can be diagrammed as follows:

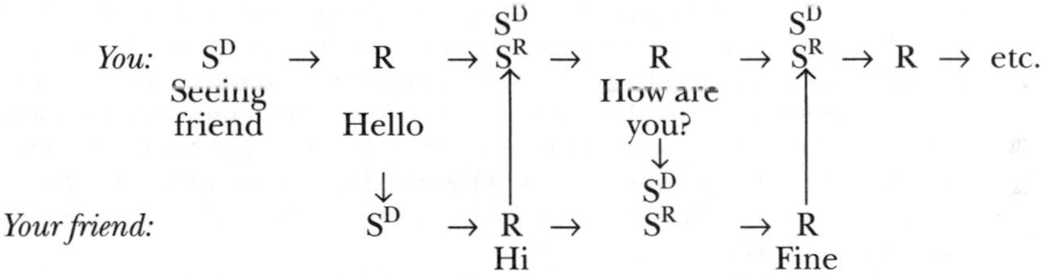

You: $\quad S^D \rightarrow R \rightarrow \begin{matrix} S^D \\ S^R \end{matrix} \rightarrow R \rightarrow \begin{matrix} S^D \\ S^R \end{matrix} \rightarrow R \rightarrow$ etc.

Seeing friend $\quad$ Hello $\qquad\qquad$ How are you?

Your friend: $\qquad\qquad S^D \rightarrow R \rightarrow \begin{matrix} S^D \\ S^R \end{matrix} \rightarrow R$

Hi $\qquad\qquad$ Fine

Not only do the consequences of certain responses act as cues for other responses but also certain thoughts can act as S^Ds for other thoughts. Skinner (1953) said,

> A response may produce or alter some of the variables which control another response. The result is a "chain." It may have little or no organization. When we go for a walk, roaming the countryside or wandering idly through a museum or store, one episode in our behavior generates conditions responsible for another. We look to one side and are stimulated by an object which causes us to move in its direction. In the course of this movement, we receive aversive stimulation from which we beat a hasty retreat. This generates a condition of satiation or fatigue in which, once free of aversive stimulation, we sit down to rest. And so on. Chaining need not be the result of movement in space. We wander or roam verbally, for example, in a casual conversation or when we "speak our thoughts" in free association. (p. 224)

Positive and Negative Reinforcers

To summarize Skinner's position on reinforcement, we have first of all **primary positive reinforcement.** This is something that is naturally reinforcing to the organism and is related to survival, such as food or water. Any neutral stimulus associated with primary positive reinforcement takes on positive secondary reinforcing characteristics. *A positive reinforcer, either primary or secondary, is something that, when added to the situation by a certain response, increases the probability of that response's recurrence.*

A **primary negative reinforcer** is something naturally harmful to the organism, such as an aversive high-pitched tone or an electric shock. Any neutral stimulus associated with a primary negative reinforcer takes on negative secondary reinforcing characteristics. A *negative reinforcer, either primary or secondary, is something that, when removed from the situation by a certain response, increases the probability of that response's recurrence.* For example, if a Skinner box is arranged so that an aversive tone is discontinued when the lever is pressed, the lever-pressing response will soon be learned. In this case, by pressing the lever the animal avoids experiencing an aversive stimulus. Notice that positive reinforcement is not positive because responses produce pleasant or desirable outcomes. Similarly, negative reinforcement does not earn its name because a response produces nasty or unpleasant outcomes. In addition, negative reinforcement should not be confused with punishment (Skinner, 1953):

> Events which are found to be reinforcing are of two sorts. Some reinforcements consist of *presenting* stimuli, of adding something—for example, food, water, or sexual contact—to the situation. These we call *positive* reinforcers. Others consist of *removing* something—for example, a loud noise, a very bright light, extreme cold or heat, or electric shock—from the situation. These we call *negative* reinforcers. In both cases the effect of reinforcement is the same—the probability of response is increased. We cannot avoid this distinction by arguing that what is reinforcing in the negative case is the *absence* of the bright light, loud noise, and so on; for it is absence after presence which is effective, and this is only another way of saying that the stimulus is removed. The difference between the two cases will be clearer when we consider the *presentation* of a *negative* reinforcer or the *removal* of a *positive*. These are the consequences which we call punishment. (p. 73)

Punishment

Punishment occurs when a response removes something positive from the situation or adds something negative. In everyday language we can say that punishment is either taking away something an organism wants, or giving it something it does not want. In either case, the outcome of the response temporarily decreases the probability of recurrence of that response. Skinner and Thorndike agreed on the effectiveness of punishment: It does not decrease the probability of a response. Although punishment suppresses a response as long as it is applied, it does not weaken the habit. Skinner (1971) said,

> Punishment is designed to remove awkward, dangerous, or otherwise unwanted behavior from a repertoire on the assumption that a person who has been punished is less

likely to behave in the same way again. Unfortunately, the matter is not that simple. Reward and punishment do not differ merely in the direction of the changes they induce. A child who has been severely punished for sex play is not necessarily less inclined to continue; and a man who has been imprisoned for violent assault is not necessarily less inclined toward violence. Punished behavior is likely to reappear after the punitive contingencies are withdrawn. (pp. 61–62)

A typical experiment that led Skinner to this conclusion was done by one of his students, Estes (1944). Two groups of eight rats each were trained to press the lever in a Skinner box. After training, both groups were placed on extinction. One group was extinguished in the regular way; that is, food was withheld following lever pressing. Rats in the second group, in addition to not receiving food, received a shock when they pressed the lever. Rats in this group were shocked an average of nine times. There were three extinction sessions, and the rats were shocked only during the first of the three sessions. The second and third sessions were the same for both groups. The punished group made fewer responses during the first extinction session than did the nonpunished group. The number of responses made during the second extinction session was about the same for both groups, with the nonpunished group making slightly more responses. From the data of the first two sessions, one can conclude that punishment was effective because the number of responses to extinction was much lower for the punished group. During the third extinction session, however, the previously punished group made many more responses than did the nonpunished group. Thus, in the long run the originally punished group caught up in the total number of responses to extinction to the nonpunished group. The conclusion was that simple nonreinforcement (extinction) is as effective in extinguishing a habit as nonreinforcement plus punishment. The results of the Estes study are summarized in Figure 5–6.

Skinner's main argument against the use of punishment is that it is ineffective in the long run. It appears that punishment simply suppresses behavior, and when the threat of punishment is removed, the rate with which the behavior occurs returns to its original level. Thus, punishment often appears to be very successful when, in fact, it has produced only a temporary effect. Other arguments against the use of punishment follow.

1. **It causes unfortunate emotional by-products.** The punished organism becomes fearful, and this fear generalizes to a number of stimuli related to those present as the punishment was occurring.
2. **It indicates what the organism should not do, not what it should do.** Compared with reinforcement, punishment conveys virtually no information to the organism. Reinforcement indicates that what was done is effective in the situation; therefore, no additional learning is required. Very often punishment informs the organism only that the punished response is one that will not work to bring reinforcement in a given situation, and additional learning is required to hit on a response that will work.

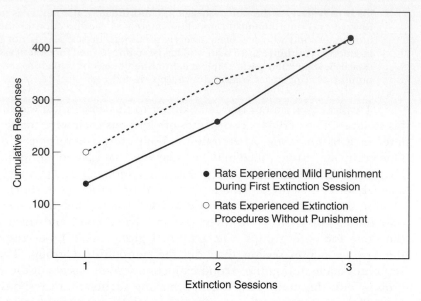

FIGURE 5–6   The results of Estes's research showing that the effect of punishment is to suppress the rate of responding only temporarily. (From W. K. Estes, An experimental study of punishment, *Psychological Monographs, 57,* Whole No. 263, 1944, 5.)

3. **It justifies inflicting pain on others.** This, of course, applies to the use of punishment in child rearing. When children are spanked, the only thing they may be learning is that under some circumstances it is justifiable to inflict pain on others.

4. **Being in a situation where previously punished behavior could be engaged in without being punished may excuse a child to do so.** Thus, in the absence of a punishing agent, children may swear, break windows, be disrespectful to elderly people, push smaller children around, and so on. These children have learned to suppress these behaviors when they could lead to punishment, but in the absence of a punishing agent, there is no reason to avoid engaging in these activities.

5. **Punishment elicits aggression toward the punishing agent and others.** Punishment causes the punished organism to become aggressive, and this aggression may cause additional problems. For example, our penal institutions, which use punishment as their major means of control, are filled with highly aggressive individuals who will continue to be aggressive as long as punishment or the threat of punishment is used to control their behavior.

6. **Punishment often replaces one undesirable response with another undesirable response.** For example, a child who is spanked for making a mess may now cry instead, just as a person punished for stealing may now become aggressive and commit even more crimes when the opportunity arises.

In their study of how 379 New England suburban mothers brought up their children from birth to kindergarten age, Sears, Maccoby, and Levin (1957) concluded the following concerning the relative effects of emphasizing reinforcement as opposed to punishment in child rearing:

> In our discussion of the training process, we have contrasted punishment with reward. Both are techniques used for changing the child's habitual ways of acting. Do they work equally well? The answer is unequivocally "no"; but to be truly unequivocal, the answer must be understood as referring to the kind of punishment we were able to measure by our interview method. We could not, as one can with laboratory experiments on white rats or pigeons, examine the effects of punishment on isolated bits of behavior. Our measures of punishment, whether of the object-oriented or love-oriented variety, referred to *Levels of Punitiveness* in the mothers. Punitiveness, in contrast to rewardingness, was a quite ineffectual quality for a mother to inject into her child training.
>
> The evidence for this conclusion is overwhelming. The unhappy effects of punishment have run like a dismal thread through our findings. Mothers who punished toilet accidents severely ended up with bedwetting children. Mothers who punished dependency to get rid of it had more dependent children than mothers who did not punish. Mothers who punished aggressive behavior severely had more aggressive children than mothers who punished lightly. They also had more dependent children. Harsh physical punishment was associated with high childhood aggressiveness and with the development of feeding problems.
>
> Our evaluation of punishment is that *it is ineffectual over the long term as a technique for eliminating the kind of behavior toward which it is directed.* (p. 484)

Why, then, is punishment so widely used? Because, said Skinner (1953), it is reinforcing to the punisher:

> Severe punishment unquestionably has an immediate effect in reducing a tendency to act in a given way. This result is no doubt responsible for its widespread use. We "instinctively" attack anyone whose behavior displeases us—perhaps not in physical assault, but with criticism, disapproval, blame, or ridicule. Whether or not there is an inherited tendency to do this, the immediate effect of the practice is reinforcing enough to explain its currency. In the long run, however, punishment does not actually eliminate behavior from a repertoire, and its temporary achievement is obtained at tremendous cost in reducing the over-all efficiency and happiness of the group. (p. 190)

It is interesting to note that Skinner himself was never physically punished by his father and only once by his mother, who washed his mouth out with soap for swearing (Skinner, 1967, p. 390).

Alternatives to Punishment

Skinner lists a number of alternatives to the use of punishment. The circumstances causing the undesirable behavior can be changed, thereby changing the behavior. For example, removing fine china from the living room will eliminate the problem of a child's breaking fine china. The undesirable response can be satiated by letting the organism perform the undesired response until it is sick of it, such as letting a child continue to light matches or eat candy (advice similar to that given by Guthrie, as we see in Chapter 8). If the undesirable behavior is a function of the child's developmental stage, it can be eliminated by simply waiting for the child to outgrow it. Skinner (1953) said about the latter approach, "It is not always easy to put up with the behavior until this happens, especially under the conditions of the average household, but there is some consolation if we know that by carrying the child through a socially unacceptable stage we spare him the later complications arising from punishment" (p. 192).

Another method is simply to let time pass, but this approach may take too long. Habits are not soon forgotten. For example, in his "Pigeons in a Pelican" project mentioned earlier, Skinner (1960) found that his trained animals "immediately and correctly" performed their task after six years of inactivity. Still another alternative to punishment is to reinforce behavior incompatible with the undesirable behavior (e.g., a child is reinforced for reading in the presence of matches rather than striking them). The best way to discourage an undesirable habit, however, is to ignore it (Skinner 1953):

> The most effective alternative process [to punishment] is probably *extinction*. This takes time but is much more rapid than allowing the response to be forgotten. The technique seems to be relatively free of objectionable by-products. We recommend it, for example, when we suggest that a parent "pay no attention" to objectionable behavior on the part of his child. If the child's behavior is strong only because it has been reinforced by "getting a rise out of" the parent, it will disappear when this consequence is no longer forthcoming. (p. 192)

Generally speaking, behavior persists because it is being reinforced; this is true of undesirable as well as desirable behavior. To eliminate objectionable behavior one needs to find the source of reinforcement and remove it. Behavior that does not lead to reinforcement extinguishes.

Comparison of Skinner and Thorndike

Although Skinner and Thorndike were in close agreement on a number of important issues such as control of behavior by stimuli in the environment and the ineffectiveness of punishment, there are important differences between them. For example, the dependent variable in Thorndike's learning experiments (his measure of the extent to which learning took place) was *time to solution*. Thorndike was interested in measuring how long it took an animal to perform whatever task was necessary to release it from confinement. Skinner, in contrast, used *rate of responding* as his dependent variable. Other differences between Skinner's operant conditioning and Thorndike's instrumental conditioning illustrate that the two approaches are quite distinct and that the terms *operant* and *instrumental* are not to be used interchangeably. In the history of learning theory, Skinner's operant conditioning differed so radically from Thorndike's instrumental conditioning that it was considered revolutionary. The differences between operant and instrumental conditioning are summarized in Table 5–1.

TABLE 5-1   Differences between Arrangements for Instrumental Conditioning
and for Operant Conditioning

CHARACTERISTIC	INSTRUMENTAL	OPERANT
Location of behavior	Maze, runway, puzzle box	Operant chamber
Methodology	Discrete trials	Free responding
Procedure	Subject is replaced in apparatus to begin each trial in a session	Subject is placed in the apparatus only to begin a session
Display	Learning curve	Cumulative record
Data display	On-trial performance against trials	Cumulative frequency against time
Data source	Average of performance of group of subjects	Individual-subject performance
Statistics?	Yes: significance test	No
Is a control used?	Yes: not administered the treatment variable or factor	Subject's pretreatment baseline serves as a comparison value

(Bringmann, W.G., Lück, H.E., Miller, R., & Early, C.E. [Eds.][1997]. *A pictoral history of psychology*. Carol Stream, Illinois. Quintessence Publishing Co.)

Schedules of Reinforcement

Although Pavlov (1927, pp. 384–386) did some work with partial reinforcement, using classical conditioning, it was Skinner who thoroughly investigated the topic. Skinner had already published data on the effects of partial reinforcement when Humphreys (1939a, 1939b) startled the psychological world by showing that the extinction process was more rapid following 100 percent reinforcement than after partial reinforcement. That is, if an organism receives a reinforcer every time it makes an appropriate response during learning and then is placed on extinction, it will extinguish faster than an organism who had only a certain percentage of its correct responses reinforced during acquisition. In other words, partial reinforcement leads to greater resistance to extinction than continuous, or 100 percent, reinforcement, and this fact is called the **partial reinforcement effect (PRE).**

Skinner studied the partial reinforcement effect extensively and eventually wrote a book with Ferster called *Schedules of Reinforcement* (Ferster & Skinner, 1957). This book summarized years of research on various types of partial reinforcement. Several schedules of reinforcement are commonly used:

1. Continuous Reinforcement Schedule   When a **continuous reinforcement schedule (CRF)** is used, every correct response during acquisition is reinforced. Usually in a partial reinforcement study, the animal is first trained on a 100 percent reinforcement schedule and then switched to a partial reinforcement schedule. It is difficult to bring about the acquisition of any response when partial reinforcement is used during the initial training period.

2. Fixed Interval Reinforcement Schedule   When a **fixed interval reinforcement schedule (FI)** is used, the animal is reinforced for a response made only after a set interval of *time.* For example, only a response following a three-minute interval is reinforced. At the beginning of the fixed time interval, the animal responds slowly or not at all. As the end of the time interval approaches, the animal gradually increases its speed of responding, apparently anticipating the moment of reinforcement. This kind of responding produces a pattern on the cumulative recording referred to as the *fixed-interval scallop.* Such a pattern is shown in Figure 5–7.

The behavior of an animal under this schedule is somewhat similar to the way a person behaves as a deadline approaches. After putting off a certain task as long as possible, the due date is rapidly approaching, and activity increases accordingly. Often a student preparing a term paper acts in this manner.

3. Fixed Ratio Reinforcement Schedule With a **fixed ratio reinforcement schedule (FR),** every *n*th response that the animal makes is reinforced. FR5, for example, means that the animal will be reinforced at every fifth response. Here the important factor in determining when a response is reinforced is the number of responses made. Theoretically, an animal on a fixed interval schedule could make just one response at the end of the interval and be reinforced each time it responds. With a fixed ratio schedule, this is not possible; the animal *must* respond a fixed number of times before it is reinforced.

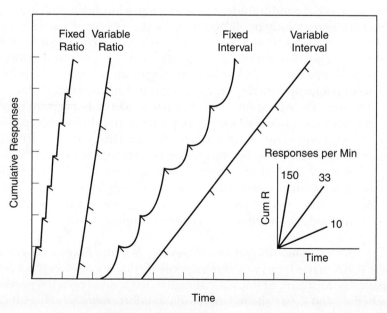

FIGURE 5–7 Typical cumulative recordings generated by fixed ratio, variable ratio, fixed interval, and variable interval reinforcement schedules. The slash marks in the recordings indicate a reinforced response.

For both the FI and FR reinforcement schedules, a reinforced response is followed by a depression in the rate of responding. This is called the *postreinforcement pause*. There is considerable speculation about why such a pause exists. Perhaps the animal learns that the responses immediately following a reinforced response are never reinforced. However, the scallop on the cumulative recording of an FI schedule is usually not found on that of an FR schedule. The FR schedule usually generates a steplike cumulative recording, indicating that the animal temporarily stops responding after a reinforced response and then, at some point, resumes responding at a rapid rate. Such behavior has been characterized as "break and run." A cumulative recording generated by an animal under an FR schedule is shown in Figure 5–7.

4. Variable Interval Reinforcement Schedule　With the **variable interval reinforcement schedule (VI),** the animal is reinforced for responses made at the end of time intervals of variable durations. That is, rather than having a fixed time interval, as with FI schedules, the animal is reinforced on the *average* of, say, every three minutes, but it may be reinforced immediately after a prior reinforcement, or it may be reinforced after thirty seconds or after seven minutes. This schedule eliminates the scalloping effect found in FI schedules and produces a steady, moderately high response rate. A typical cumulative recording generated by an animal on a VI schedule is shown in Figure 5–7.

5. Variable Ratio Reinforcement Schedule　The **variable ratio reinforcement schedule (VR)** eliminates the steplike cumulative recording found with the FR schedule and produces the highest response rate of the five schedules considered thus far. With the FR schedule, an animal is reinforced after making a specific number of responses, say, five. With the VR5 schedule, the animal is reinforced on the average of every five responses; thus, it might receive two reinforcers in a row or may make ten or fifteen responses without being reinforced. A cumulative recording produced by an animal under a VR schedule is shown in Figure 5–7.

The VR reinforcement schedule is the one governing the behavior of gamblers at a place like Las Vegas. The faster one pulls the handle of a slot machine, for example, the more frequently one is reinforced.

To summarize, continuous reinforcement yields the least resistance to extinction and the lowest response rate during training. All partial reinforcement schedules produce greater resistance to extinction and higher response rates during training than continuous reinforcement. Generally speaking, the VR schedule produces the highest response rate, FR produces the next highest rate, then VI, followed by FI, and finally CRF.

6. Concurrent Schedules and the Matching Law　Skinner (1950) trained pigeons to peck two operant keys that were available at the same time but that delivered reinforcements under different schedules. This procedure is referred to as a **concurrent**

Richard J. Herrnstein. (Courtesy of Susan G. Herrnstein.)

reinforcement schedule. He reported that the pigeons distributed their responses according to the schedules of reinforcement associated with each key and continued to do so during extinction. Ferster and Skinner (1957) also examined the effects of concurrent-schedule training, but in 1961, Richard Herrnstein (1930–1994) quantified the relationship between reinforcement and performance under concurrent schedules and provided direction for operant research for about the next thirty years. He refined Skinner's earlier observation by noting that under concurrent schedules, the relative frequency of behavior matches the relative frequency of reinforcement. This relationship is referred to as Herrnstein's **matching law.** The equation expressing matching is written as follows:

$$\frac{B_1}{B_1 + B_2} = \frac{R_1}{R_1 + R_2}$$

where B_1 is the frequency of pecking at key 1 and R_1 is the frequency of reinforcement for that behavior, and so on. Matching is illustrated in Figure 5–8.

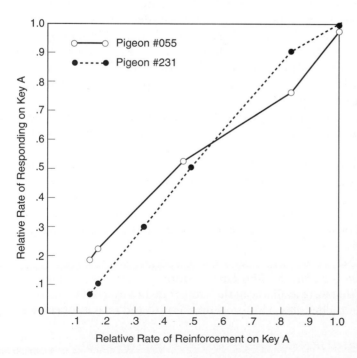

FIGURE 5–8   Results of two pigeons pecking on concurrent VI VI schedules. The pecking of key A is plotted relative to the pecking of key B. The total possible number of reinforcers from pecking both keys is 40 per hour; therefore, if pecking key A generated 10 percent of the reinforcers (4), pecking key B generated 90 percent (36). Notice that the relative rate of responding very nearly equaled the relative rate of reinforcement. (From R. J. Herrnstein, "Relative and Absolute Strength of Response as a Function of Frequency of Reinforcement," *Journal of the Experimental Analysis of Behavior*, 1961, 4, 267–272. Copyright 1961 by the Society for the Experimental Analysis of Behavior, Inc.)

In two subsequent papers, Herrnstein (1970, 1974) extended the implications of the matching law. First, he noted that even in a testing situation where there are two keys for pigeons to peck, the pigeons engage in behaviors other than pecking. He included these extraneous behaviors (B_e) and the reinforcements that maintained them (R_e) in the matching equation:

$$\frac{B_1}{B_1 + B_2 + B_e} = \frac{R_1}{R_1 + R_2 + R_e}$$

Furthermore, he made the assumption that in any given testing situation, the sum of the rates of all behaviors taken together is a constant (k). That is, $B_1 + B_2 + B_e = k$. It is possible, then, to write an equation that expresses the response rate for any single behavior:

$$B_1 = \frac{(k) R_1}{\Sigma R}$$

where ΣR is the summation of the frequencies of reinforcement for all behaviors occurring under the circumstances.

This expression is called **Herrnstein's equation** or Herrnstein's hyperbola, in reference to the function it generates for different values of (k) and R_e. As shown in Figure 5–9, Herrnstein's hyperbola is a form of the learning curve—a mathematical statement of Thorndike's law of effect. Figure 5–9 also reveals the logic of the mathematical expression as it applies to a simple situation with one operant behavior (B_1), two different values of extraneous behaviors (B_e), and associated extraneous reinforcements (R_es) but only one value of k. In the case illustrated on the left, there is

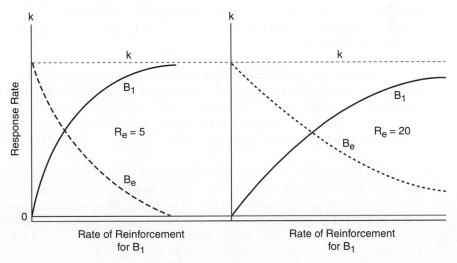

FIGURE 5–9 High levels of extraneous reinforcement (on the right) interfere with performance of a target operant behavior and prolong extraneous behaviors.

little extraneous behavior and reinforcement ($R_e = 5$). In the case on the right, there are increased effects of extraneous reinforcement ($R_e = 20$).

Recall that the sum of rates of all possible behaviors is a constant (k). Therefore, the asymptote, or maximum rate, of the operant behavior in either case is k. In each instance, as the rate of reinforcement for B_1 increases, more and more of the total behavioral output is in the form of B_1, and B_e necessarily decreases toward zero (0). Notice that the effect of extraneous reinforcement is distraction from B_1. When values of extraneous reinforcement and the accompanying extraneous behavior are high, the learning curve for B_1 rises more slowly and asymptotic performance is delayed. Similarly, when more extraneous reinforcements are available, extraneous behavior (B_e) decreases more slowly despite increased reinforcement for B_1.

As an example of the effects of extraneous behavior and reinforcement on human performance, imagine two piano students trying to master a difficult musical passage. One student is alone with the instructor. Contrary to the instructor's general policy, the other student has invited several friends to the lesson. The first student will be reinforced only by the instructor and will earn reinforcement only for correct musical performance. Therefore, extraneous behaviors and their reinforcements are minimized (as in Figure 5–9, where $R_e = 5$). The second student has available more sources and potential types of reinforcement (as in Figure 5–9, where $R_e = 20$) and can be reinforced for behaviors other than musical performance. That student may engage in a number of nonmusical activities to earn approval, attention, and respect from the observing friends. Herrnstein's equation accounts for the observation that the first student will improve faster and master the musical passage sooner than the second.

Development of the matching law continues, and the current body of literature evolving from Herrnstein's early matching observation is extensive. The matching equation has been used to explain effects of delay, magnitude, quality, and duration of reinforcements, as well as those of punishment (see Davison & McCarthy, 1988), and the mechanisms underlying matching phenomena continue to be debated (e.g., MacDonall, 1999, 2003).

7. Concurrent Chain Reinforcement Schedule   Whereas a concurrent schedule of reinforcement is used to investigate simple-choice behavior, a **concurrent chain reinforcement schedule** is used to investigate complex-choice behavior. With concurrent chain schedules, an animal's behavior during the initial phase of the experiment determines what schedule of reinforcement it experiences during the second, or terminal, phase.

One interesting finding using concurrent chain schedules is in the area of self-control. Under ordinary circumstances, organisms will clearly prefer small, immediate reinforcers over large, delayed reinforcers. With concurrent schedules, if response A is reinforced by small, immediate reinforcers and response B is reinforced by large reinforcers following a delay, response A will be overwhelmingly preferred. Likewise, using a concurrent chain schedule, if responding to alternative A switches in a schedule providing small, immediate reinforcers and responding to alternative B switches in a schedule producing large, delayed reinforcers, animals will show a strong preference for alternative A. Rachlin and Green (1972), however, showed that under certain circumstances, large, delayed reinforcers are preferred over small, immediate reinforcers. Rachlin and Green used a concurrent chain reinforcement schedule in which pigeons initially had a choice of pecking one of two white disks. Pecking the white disk on the left fifteen times (FR 15) was followed by a ten-second blackout and then a choice between a red and a green disk. Pecking the red disk produced two seconds of food (a relatively small reinforcer) immediately, and pecking the green disk produced four seconds of food (a relatively larger reinforcer) following a delay of four seconds. In the original choice phase of the experiment, if the white disk on the right was responded to fifteen times (FR 15), there was also a ten-second blackout and then the opportunity to peck a green disk. Pecking the green disk produced a four-second delay followed by four seconds of food. Under these experimental conditions, it was found that pigeons chose the white disk on the right 65 percent of the time, thus reversing the preference for small, immediate reinforcers. The experimental arrangement used by Rachlin and Green is shown in Figure 5–10.

What is it that changed the preference for small, immediate reinforcers to large, delayed reinforcers? The answer seems to be time. It has been shown that reinforcers lose their reinforcement value over time. Thus, an organism may opt for a small reinforcer if it is immediately available but will not plan to have one sometime in the future. If a delay is involved, organisms tend to choose larger reinforcers over smaller ones. Schwartz, Wasserman, and Robbins (2002) generalize these findings to humans:

> Consider, for example, the choice between going to the movies and studying on a particular evening. We could imagine that going to the movies involves a small but immediate reinforcement (an evening's entertainment), whereas studying involves a large delayed reinforcement (a good examination grade). Given the choice, at 7:45 P.M., between studying and an 8 P.M. movie, the student, like the pigeon, might choose the small immediate reinforcement. But if the choice were required at 9 A.M., so that now both reinforcers were going to be delayed, the student might choose to study. (p. 229)

Although it is beyond the scope of this book to explain how, it is interesting to note that the switchover in preference from small, immediate reinforcers to large, delayed reinforcers found by Rachlin and Green (1972) is predicted by Herrnstein's matching law (see Rachlin, 1991, pp. 585–586, for an explanation).

8. Progressive Ratio Schedules and Behavioral Economics   With a **progressive ratio reinforcement schedule (PR),** a lab animal begins with a low ratio schedule (usually FR), and the ratio of responses to reinforcements is systematically increased during subsequent training sessions. Although concurrent and concurrent chain schedules can be used to address relatively sophisticated problems of choice, the progressive ratio schedule provides a tool to study the complex problem of reinforcer efficacy.

How can we determine whether one reinforcer is more effective than another? It might seem, at first, to be a simple task. If we arrange one lever in a Skinner box so that it delivers water on an FR2 schedule and another lever so that it delivers a food pellet on the same schedule, doesn't the matching law, which indicates the frequency

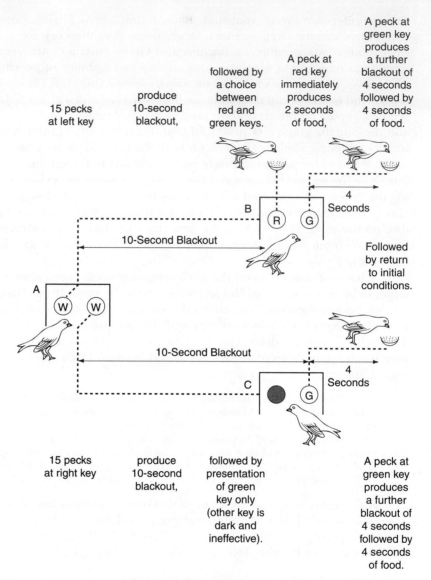

FIGURE 5–10   The concurrent-chain reinforcement schedule used by Rachlin and Green. (From H. Rachlin, *Behavior and Learning*, p. 584. Copyright © 1976 W. H. Freeman and Company. Reprinted with permission.)

of behavior for one reinforcer relative to the other, tell us which reinforcer is more effective? The answer is no. Of course, response rates will be affected by numerous factors such as the time required to consume one reinforcer relative to the other and the degree to which the lab animal has been either food or water deprived. To further complicate the problem, results observed under the FR2 schedule might not hold for a different reinforcement schedule. In recent years, a field called **Behavioral**

Economics (Hursh, 1991; Hursh & Bauman, 1987) has applied the progressive ratio reinforcement schedule to provide a solution—although not the only solution—to this problem (Bickel, Marsch, & Carroll, 2000).

In essence, the progressive ratio method requires a lab animal to indicate, in behavioral terms, the maximum it will "pay" for a particular reinforcer. Given that the only currency a lab animal has is its behavior, we increase the ratio of responses to reinforcers to determine how hard or how long an organism is willing to work to obtain reinforcement. We emphasize again that the problem of reinforcement efficacy is a complex one that may be addressed in a number of ways. The progressive ratio method approaches the problem by increasing behavioral requirements for reinforcement until the lab animal stops paying the price required to obtain a reinforcer. If an organism is willing to pay more for one type of reinforcer than for another, it tells us, in effect, that one type of reinforcer is more valuable and thus more effective than the other.

We begin by training a lab animal on a Fixed Ratio reinforcement schedule, an FR2, for example, such that every two responses earn a reinforcer. The FR2 is used for several days, and then the schedule is increased systematically. In our example, we begin by training a rat to press a lever to receive a food pellet on an FR2 schedule for three days. We then increase the response requirement by switching to an FR4 schedule on the fourth day, then to an FR8 schedule on the fifth day, then to a more demanding FR16 schedule on the next day, and so on. Conceptually, the responses per reinforcement reflect the *cost* the animal is willing to pay for a food pellet, and the graph that shows *reinforcement rate* (not response rate) as a function of the reinforcement schedule is referred to as a *demand function* (or demand curve). If an animal consumes five reinforcers per minute on an "inexpensive" FR2 schedule, it must double its response rate to maintain that level of consumption when we switch to a FR4 schedule. As the progressive ratio schedule is extended, the animal must increase its response rate dramatically in order to maintain the five reinforcer-per-minute consumption rate. Reinforcer efficacy can be assessed by looking at the *break point*, the schedule at which the animal indicates, by a significant decrease in response rate and thus a decrease in consumption, that the reinforcer has become too expensive. In Figure 5–11, we see two idealized demand functions (reinforcement rate plotted as a function of FR reinforcement schedule), one for a hypothetical reinforcer (Type A) and one for a different reinforcer (Type B), typically plotted on log-log coordinates. We can compare the demand functions for each kind of reinforcer as the FR schedules are increased. Both demand curves are horizontal when costs are low (low FR schedules), and in this example we see that when response requirements are low, reinforcer A is consumed at a greater rate than reinforcer B. We also see, however, that the demand curve for reinforcer A drops sharply when the reinforcement schedule increases to FR16, when 16 responses are required to earn a reinforcer. The curve for reinforcer B remains horizontal until the schedule increases to FR128, when 128 responses are required to obtain a reinforcer. Thus the break point for A occurs at the FR16 schedule, whereas the break point for B occurs at the FR128 schedule. Although reinforcer A seems more effective when costs are low, the lab animal is willing to pay eight times more for B than

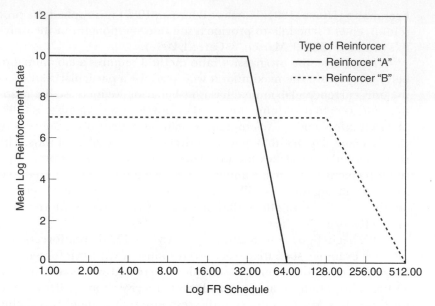

FIGURE 5–11 Hypothetical demand functions for two reinforcers: Demand for reinforcer "B" is inelastic relative to demand for reinforcer "A."

for A, and we can infer that, in behavioral terms, B is more valuable, thus more effective, than A.

Clearly, some reinforcers are necessary to maintain health and well-being, and although costs increase substantially, the animal will pay greater and greater numbers of responses in order to obtain those reinforcers. In human terms, we tend to maintain the level of consumption of gasoline or bread despite dramatic increases in the price of these commodities. The demand for these reinforcers is *inelastic,* because increased cost is tolerated in order to maintain a relatively constant quantity of the reinforcer. On the other hand, *elastic* demand is observed when reinforcers are consumed at a high rate when they are inexpensive but abandoned when cost increases. These reinforcers are luxuries that are not essential for the well-being of the organism. For humans this might include concerts or meals at fine restaurants. The pattern in Figure 5–11 is similar to that observed when we compare the reinforcing efficacy of heroin (reinforcer A) with food (reinforcer B) for baboons (Elsmore et al., 1980) or when we compare cigarette puffs (reinforcer A) with money (reinforcer B) for humans (Bickel & Madden, 1999).

The problem of understanding reinforcement efficacy is a complex one. Clearly, we cannot determine how well one reinforcer works relative to another unless we consider the deprivation conditions of the organism, the constraints imposed by the consumption of the reinforcer (licking a drinking tube versus chewing and swallowing a chow pellet), the cost of the reinforcer, and a number of other factors. When we take these factors into account, we discover a number of surprises about reinforcement efficacy. For example, a lab rat generates extraordinary response rates for electrical brain stimulation reinforcement (discussed in Chapter 14). On a continuous reinforcement schedule, the rat may press a lever hundreds of times per minute for two or three days to earn brain stimulation, neglecting both food and water. We are tempted to believe that brain stimulation reinforcement is much stronger than food or water reinforcement and that it may be the most powerful reinforcer yet discovered. The progressive ratio method shows, however, that the break point for brain stimulation comes much earlier than for natural, primary reinforcers like food (Hursh & Natelson, 1981) and that demand for this unusual reinforcer is extremely elastic.

Verbal Behavior

Skinner believed that verbal behavior (language) can be explained within the context of reinforcement theory. Talking and listening are responses that are influenced by reinforcement, just as is any other response. Any utterance, therefore, will tend to be repeated if it is reinforced. Skinner classified verbal responses in terms of how they were related to reinforcement, that is, in terms of what was being done in order to be reinforced. These classifications are discussed briefly next.

1. Mand   About the **mand,** Skinner (1957) said,

> A mand is characterized by the unique relationship between the form of the response and the reinforcement characteristically received in a given verbal community. It is sometimes convenient to refer to this relation by saying that a mand "specifies" its reinforcement. *Listen!, Look!, Run!, Stop!,* and *Say yes!* specify the behavior of a listener; but when a hungry diner calls *Bread!,* or *More soup!,* he is specifying the ultimate reinforcement. Frequently both the behavior of the listener and the ultimate reinforcement are specified. The mand *pass the salt!* specifies an action (pass) and an ultimate reinforcement (the salt). (p. 37)

The word *mand* comes from the fact that a demand is being made. When the demand is met, the utterance (mand) is reinforced, and next time the need arises, the person is likely to repeat the mand.

2. Tact   About the **tact,** Skinner (1957) said,

> This type of operant is exemplified when, in the presence of a doll, a child frequently achieves some sort of generalized reinforcement by saying *doll;* or when a teleost fish, or picture thereof, is the occasion upon which the student of zoology is reinforced when he says *teleost fish*. There is no suitable term for this type of operant. "Sign," "symbol," and more technical terms from logic and semantics commit us to special schemes of reference and stress the verbal response itself rather than the controlling relationship. The invented term "tact" will be used here. The term carries a mnemonic suggestion of behavior which "makes contact with" the physical world. A tact may be defined as a verbal operant in which a response of given form is evoked (or at least strengthened) by a particular object or event or property of an object or event. We account for the strength by showing that in the presence of the object or event, a response of that form is characteristically reinforced in a given verbal community. (pp. 81–82)

Generally speaking the tact involves naming objects or events in the environment appropriately, and its reinforcement comes from other people's reinforcement of the match between the environment and the verbal behavior.

3. Echoic Behavior   **Echoic behavior** is verbal behavior that is reinforced when someone else's verbal response is repeated verbatim. Echoic behavior is often a prerequisite to a more complicated verbal behavior; for example, first a child must imitate a word before the child can learn how that word is related to other words or other events. Thus, repeating something someone else has said is reinforced, and when this response is learned, it permits the speaker to learn more complex verbal relationships.

4. Autoclitic Behavior   According to Skinner (1957), "The term 'autoclitic' is intended to suggest behavior which is based upon or depends upon other verbal behavior" (p. 315). The main function of **autoclitic behavior** is to qualify responses, express relations, and provide a grammatical framework for verbal behavior.

The most severe critic of Skinner's explanation of verbal behavior has been Noam Chomsky (1959). Chomsky contends that language is too complex for a child to have learned. Some process other than learning must explain all the verbal utterances that, say, a three-year-old is capable of making. G. A. Miller (1965), in fact, points out that there are 10^{20} possible twenty-word sentences in the English language, and it would take one thousand times the estimated age of the Earth just to listen to them all. Obviously, says Chomsky, operant conditioning just does not explain the complexity of our language capabilities. Chomsky's explanation of language development is that our brain is structured to generate language. The underlying grammatical structure of all human languages reflects an underlying brain structure. That is, we are "wired" to produce grammatical utterances, just as a computer can be wired to produce moves in a chess game. Chomsky and Skinner seem to be continuing the nature-nurture debate launched by Plato and Aristotle: Chomsky's deep-brain structures theory of language acquisition represents the nature, or Platonic, side, and Skinner's view that verbal behavior is shaped by environment represents the nurture, or Aristotelian, side. We present more on the development of language in Chapter 15.

Contingency Contracting

Contingency contracting is an extension of Skinnerian thinking. Briefly, it involves making arrangements so that a person gets something wanted when that person acts in a certain way. Some arrangements can be simple and cover simple behavior, such as when a teacher says to a child, "If you sit quietly for five minutes, you can go out and play." Other arrangements can extend over a much longer period of time. For example, if a person has a weight problem and has difficulty losing weight, that person may wish to arrange the environment so that losing weight is reinforced. The person may, for example, sign over to another person something personally important such as money, a CD collection, a stamp collection, or favorite clothes. Taking money as an example, the person trying to lose weight may put up, say, 100 dollars and draw up an agreement whereby the other person gives back 10 dollars each week if three pounds are lost. Each week that at least three pounds are not lost, the person loses 10 dollars. The same kind of arrangement can be made by utilizing anything important to the person, and the behavior involved could as easily be smoking as losing weight.

The term *contingency contracting* comes from the fact that an agreement (contract) is made that certain activities will be reinforced that otherwise may not have been. In other words, the contract rearranges the reinforcement contingencies in the environment, causing them to be responsive to behavior patterns that one hopes to modify in some way.

Many behavior problems occur because our behavior is influenced more by immediate reinforcers than by distant ones. For example, for some the taste of food in the present is more reinforcing than the distant promise of a longer life if one eats in moderation. Likewise, the immediate effect of nicotine is more reinforcing than the promise of a longer life without smoking. Contingency contracting is a way of modifying behavior through current reinforcing contingencies rather than distant ones. It is hoped that as desirable behavior is shaped by using this procedure, the desirable behavior itself will be functional in obtaining reinforcers from the social environment. Not being overweight and not smoking both can be very reinforcing, but the problem is switching the overweight person and the smoker to another class of reinforcing experiences. Contingency contracting can be a very effective tool in accomplishing this switchover. Once the switch in reinforcement systems has been made, however, the desired behavior is usually sustained by the social environment, and therefore the artificial reinforcement contingencies are no longer needed.

Contingency contracting need not involve a second person; one can follow these procedures alone by giving oneself a "treat" of some kind each day one goes without smoking, drinking, or overeating. For a more detailed discussion of contingency contracting, see Homme, Csanyi, Gonzales, and Rechs (1970).

Skinner's Attitude Toward Learning Theory

Skinner believed that it is unnecessary to formulate complicated theories to study human behavior, and he believed it is unnecessary to know the physiological correlates of behavior. He believed that behavioral events must be described in terms of things that directly affect behavior and that it is logically inconsistent to attempt to explain behavior in terms of physiological events. For this reason, Skinner's method of research has been called "the empty organism approach."

Skinner also thought that complex theories of learning, such as Hull's (Chapter 6), are time-consuming and wasteful. Some day such theories may be useful in psychology, but not until we have collected much more basic data. Our main concern at this time should be, Skinner believed, to discover basic relationships between classes of stimuli and classes of responses. Therefore, the use of theory in studying the learning process cannot be justified (Skinner, 1950):

> Research designed with respect to theory is also likely to be wasteful. That a theory generates research does not prove its value unless the research is valuable. Much useless experimentation results from theories, and much energy and skill are absorbed by them. Most theories are eventually overthrown, and the greater part of the associated

research is discarded. This could be justified if it were true that productive research requires a theory—as is, of course, often claimed. It is argued that research would be aimless and disorganized without a theory to guide it. The view is supported by psychological texts which take their cue from the logicians rather than empirical science and describe thinking as necessarily involving stages of hypothesis, deduction, experimental test, and confirmation. But this is not the way most scientists actually work. It is possible to design significant experiments for other reasons, and the possibility to be examined is that such research will lead more directly to the kind of information which a science usually accumulates. (pp. 194–195)

Skinner's (1953) approach to research was to do a **functional analysis** between stimulating events and measurable behavior:

The external variables of which behavior is a function provide for what may be called a causal or functional analysis. We undertake to predict and control the behavior of the individual organism. This is our "dependent variable"—the effect for which we are to find the cause. Our "independent variables"—the causes of behavior—are the external conditions of which behavior is a function. Relations between the two—the "cause-and-effect relationships" in behavior—are the laws of a science. A synthesis of these laws expressed in quantitative terms yields a comprehensive picture of the organism as a behaving system. (p. 35)

Thus, Skinner manipulated hours of food or water deprivation and noted the effect on the rate with which the lever-pressing response was learned, or he observed the effect of schedules of reinforcement on response rate or resistance to extinction. In interpreting the results of his research, Skinner stayed very close to the data; that is, if partial reinforcement produces greater resistance to extinction than does 100 percent reinforcement, that is a fact, and that is all that can be said. In other words, Skinner did not attempt to explain why this is the case.

Even in deciding *what* to investigate, Skinner claimed he was not guided by theoretical notions but rather used a hit-and-miss process. He tried first one thing and then another. If he saw that one line of research was not producing anything worthwhile, he would shift to something that looked more fruitful, and he would continue in this trial-and-error fashion until he hit on something of value. This rather liberal attitude toward scientific investigation was summarized in Skinner's (1956) article "A Case History in Scientific Method."

The Need for a Technology of Behavior

Skinner felt very strongly that a carefully worked-out behavior technology could solve many human problems, yet many people would oppose such a technology because it seems to challenge a number of our cherished beliefs about ourselves, especially that human beings are rational, free, and dignified. Skinner (1971) believed that these beliefs were interfering with the solution of our major problems and also preventing the development of the very tool that could solve them:

What we need is a technology of behavior. We could solve our problems quickly enough if we could adjust the growth of the world's population as precisely as we adjust the course of a spaceship, or improve agriculture and industry with some of the confidence with which we accelerate high-energy particles, or move toward a peaceful world with something like the steady progress with which physics has approached absolute zero (even though both remain presumably out of reach). But a behavioral technology comparable in power and precision to physical and biological technology is lacking, and those who do not find the very possibility ridiculous are more likely to be frightened by it than reassured. That is how far we are from "understanding human issues" in the sense in which physics and biology understand their fields, and how far we are from preventing the catastrophe toward which the world seems to be inexorably moving. (p. 5)

Elsewhere, Skinner (1953) said,

The traditional view of human nature in Western culture is well known. The conception of a free, responsible individual is embedded in our language and pervades our practices, codes, and beliefs. Given an example of human behavior, most people can describe it immediately in terms of such a conception. The practice is so natural that it is seldom examined. A scientific formulation, on the other hand, is new and strange. Very few people have any notion of the extent to which a science of human behavior is indeed possible. In what way can the behavior of the individual or of groups of individuals be predicted and controlled? What are laws of behavior like? What over-all conception of the human organism as a behaving system emerges? It is only when we have answered these questions, at least in a preliminary fashion, that we may consider the implications of a science of human behavior with respect to either a theory of human nature or the management of human affairs. (pp. 9–10)

In an article entitled "What Is Wrong with Daily Life in the Western World?" Skinner (1986) renewed his plea for the utilization of behavior technology in solving human problems. In this article, Skinner argued that five cultural practices are eroding the strengthening effects of reinforcement contingencies: "(a) Alienating workers from the consequences of their work; (b) helping those who could help themselves; (c) guiding behavior with rules rather than supplying reinforcing consequences; (d) maintaining aversive sanctions of government and religions with long-deferred benefits for the individual; and (e) reinforcing looking, listening, reading, gambling, and so on, while strengthening few other behaviors" (p. 568).

According to Skinner, the many problems caused by these cultural practices could be solved by strengthening desirable behavior with the principles derived from an experimental analysis of behavior, that is, by using the principles described in this chapter.

Skinner's theory of learning has had, and is having, a profound influence on psychology. No matter what area of psychology one studies, one is apt to find reference to some aspect of Skinner's work. As we noted in Chapter 2, a characteristic of any good theory is that it generates research, and Skinner's theory has certainly done that. We now review the work of an important researcher who has been influenced by Skinner's work.

THE RELATIVITY OF REINFORCEMENT

David Premack

Traditionally, reinforcers have been thought of as stimuli. A primary reinforcer is usually thought of as being related to an organism's survival, and a secondary reinforcer is

David Premack. (Courtesy of David Premack.)

a stimulus that has been consistently paired with a primary reinforcer. Premack, however, has suggested that all *responses* should be thought of as potential reinforcers.

Specifically, he suggests that any response that occurs with a fairly high frequency can be used to reinforce a response that occurs with a relatively lower frequency. Using Premack's notion of reinforcement, one would allow an organism to engage freely in whatever activities it wanted to and carefully record what activities were engaged in and with what frequency. Afterward, the various activities that the organism engaged in would be arranged in a hierarchy. The activity that was engaged in most frequently would be listed first, the next most frequently engaged in activity would be listed next, and so on. By referring to this list, the experimenter would know exactly what could and could not be used to reinforce that particular organism. Say, for example, it was found that in a twenty-four-hour period, the activity engaged in most frequently by a rat was eating, then drinking, then running in an activity wheel, then grooming, and finally gazing out of the cage. According to Premack, allowing the animal to eat could be used to reinforce any of the other activities. For example, if the animal was allowed to eat each time it groomed itself, grooming would increase in frequency. Likewise, allowing the animal to groom itself could be used to reinforce the animal for looking outside the cage. The opportunity to look outside the cage, however, could not be used to reinforce any of the other activities because they all occurred with a greater frequency than the response of looking outside the cage.

According to Premack, the way to find out what can be used as a reinforcer is to observe the organism's behavior while it has the opportunity to engage in any number of activities, and the activities that it engages in most often can be used to reinforce the activities that it engages in less often.

In summary, we can say that if one activity occurs more often than another, it can be used to reinforce the activity that occurs less often. This is called the **Premack principle,** and it seems to hold for humans as well as for lower organisms.

To test his theory, Premack (1959) allowed thirty-one first-grade children either to play a pinball machine or to operate a candy dispenser as often as they wanted. Some of the children played mainly with the pinball machine, and they were called manipulators. The children who were primarily interested in the candy dispenser were called eaters. The first phase of the study merely determined the children's preferences for these two events.

In the second phase of the study, the groups of manipulators and eaters were each subdivided into two groups. One group was placed on manipulate-eat contingencies, in which the children had to play the pinball machine before they were allowed to operate the candy dispenser. The other group was placed on eat-manipulate contingencies, in which they had to operate the candy dispenser before they could play the pinball machine. It was found that for the manipulators the manipulate-eat arrangement made little difference in their behavior. They simply went right on playing the pinball machine as before. Under the eat-manipulate conditions, however, the frequency of eating went way up for the manipulators because they now had to eat in order to play the pinball machine. Likewise, for the eaters the eat-manipulate condition made little difference. They simply went on eating candy as before. But under the manipulate-eat conditions, their frequency of playing the pinball machine went way up. Thus, Premack found support for his contention that a less frequently engaged-in activity can be reinforced by the opportunity to engage in a more frequently engaged-in activity.

When preferences change, the reinforcers also change. For example, as long as an animal is hungry, it will eat frequently, and therefore the opportunity to eat can be used to reinforce any number of activities. When the animal is satiated, however, the frequency of its eating will decrease, and the opportunity to eat will become ineffective as a reinforcer. Premack (1962) demonstrated the reversibility of reinforcement in a study involving a running response and a drinking response. It was found that if animals were deprived of water for a considerable length of time, they would turn an activity wheel in order to gain access to water. But they would not increase their drinking to run in the activity wheel. That is, drinking reinforced running, but running did not reinforce drinking. This is what one would predict from traditional reinforcement theory. Premack also found that if an animal was allowed to drink all the water it wanted but was prevented from running in the activity wheel, the situation was reversed. Under these circumstances, drinking activity increased if it resulted in having the opportunity to run, but running did not increase if it allowed the animal to drink. That is, now running could reinforce drinking but not vice versa.

The implications of Premack's research are far-reaching. For one thing, what can act as a reinforcer becomes a very personal and continuously changing thing. The teacher can apply this knowledge by noticing individual children's preferences in a free-choice situation and determining their reinforcers accordingly. For one child, the opportunity to run and play may be a reinforcer; for another child, playing with clay may be a reinforcer. The idea of recess as a way to improve the performance of the class as a whole will need to be looked at more carefully. For examples of how the Premack principle can be used to control the behavior of schoolchildren, see Homme, DeBaca, Divine, Steinhorst, and Rickert (1963).

Revisions of the Premack Principle

You may remember from Chapter 4 that Thorndike's definition of a satisfier was criticized because it appeared to be circular. When Skinner defined a reinforcer as any event that increases the probability of a response, he neatly avoided the problems of describing physical, aesthetic, or chemical characteristics of reinforcers. Similarly, he

avoided the difficulties associated with describing the biological aspects of reinforcement. Unfortunately, his definition has also been criticized as circular. Walker
(1969) suggested that Skinner's operational definition has elusive and even "magi-
cal" qualities in that it suffices when a specific procedure produces reinforcing
effects, but it cannot explain cases in which that same procedure has no effect or
when it results in a decreased frequency of responding. Similarly, Gregory Kimble,
from whom we borrowed our initial definition of learning (see Chapter 1), indicates
that food is reinforcing at the beginning of a meal, is neutral midmeal, and is punishing at the end (Kimble, 1993). He even suggests facetiously that the concept of
reinforcement "suffers from terminal ambiguity and that it is a nominee for mercy
killing" (p. 254).

The traditional defense when Thorndike or Skinner is attacked as circular is
Meehl's (1950) "transituational" argument. According to this argument, a satisfier
or reinforcer in one situation can be shown to modify behavior in another situation.
It is argued that the transituational nature of reinforcers or satisfiers protects them
from claims that their definitions are circular. One of the important findings
derived from Premack's research is that the transituational argument is inadequate
if not entirely incorrect. For example, if an animal prefers to spend 30 percent of its
time eating, 20 percent drinking, and 10 percent in an activity wheel, the Premack
principle tells us that we can use drinking to reinforce activity in the wheel. In
a straightforward application of Premack's principle, we cannot use drinking to
reinforce eating in that specific animal, and we may not be able to use drinking to
reinforce wheel-running in an animal with different activity preferences. This
demonstrates a first flaw in the transituational argument. Research conducted by
William Timberlake and his associates (Timberlake, 1980; Timberlake & Allison,
1974; Timberlake & Farmer-Dougan, 1991) is instructive with respect to failure of
the transituational argument, the limits of the Premack principle, and the nature of
reinforcement.

William Timberlake

Timberlake (Timberlake, 1980; Timberlake & Farmer-Dougan, 1991) distinguishes
between the probability-differential hypothesis, the position taken by Premack, and
the **disequilibrium hypothesis,** a position that logically follows from Premack's
(1962) drinking–activity wheel study described earlier. In contrast with Premack's
suggestion that preferred activities can reinforce less preferred activities, the disequilibrium hypothesis states that any activity can be a reinforcer if a contingency
schedule constrains an animal's access to that activity. Imagine that we watch a freely
behaving rat for several days. Let us say that, as before, the rat spends 30 percent of
its waking time eating, 20 percent of its time drinking, and 10 percent of its time
running in an activity wheel. It distributes the remaining 40 percent of its time
among a number of other activities. According to Timberlake, this proportional distribution of activities constitutes an equilibrium, a state of activity-balance freely
maintained and preferred by the animal. If we establish a contingency schedule
such that time devoted to eating is reduced below the baseline of 30 percent, we

have created disequilibrium, a condition that will have motivational consequences. Under this condition of disequilibrium, eating can be used as a reinforcer for any other activity, and it will continue to have reinforcing properties until the animal has restored baseline equilibrium such that 30 percent of its time is allotted to eating.

On the other hand, the disequilibrium hypothesis predicts that wheel-running, the least probable of the activities listed, can also be a reinforcer. For this to happen, however, a schedule must somehow be imposed in which wheel-running is reduced below its 10 percent baseline, thus producing disequilibrium. As was the case with eating, wheel-running can be a reinforcer for any other behavior until wheel-running returns to 10 percent and equilibrium is restored.

The disequilibrium hypothesis also delineates conditions under which a specific activity can become punishing. To produce punishment, a schedule must be designed in which performance of one activity serves to increase another activity above its baseline. Imagine that the rat in our example is given food every time that it runs in the activity wheel. As long as eating takes less than 30 percent of the animal's time, food will reinforce wheel-running. However, if wheel-running produces conditions in which eating activity would exceed 30 percent of the animal's time, wheel-running will decrease under the wheel-food contingency. Eating has thus become a punisher.

Timberlake's position provides important new perspectives about reinforcement and reinforcement contingencies. Like Premack's, Timberlake's research shows clearly that the transituational argument concerning reinforcement is incorrect. Further, from this perspective the role of a contingency schedule is to produce disequilibrium rather than to provide information relating a response to a reinforcer or to provide contiguity between a response and a reinforcer. And finally, from Timberlake's research we see that deprivation of food or water per se is not essential to make these substances reinforcers. Rather, it is restriction of access to them that serves to make them reinforcers.

Although the positions taken by Premack and Timberlake are improvements on the older idea that "reinforcers are things that reinforce," we are still left with a number of unanswered questions. For example, neither position addresses the question of baseline preferences. Why should a rat spend more time eating than drinking? The answer can no longer be "Because it is more reinforcing to do so!"

There is no doubt that Skinnerian notions have had, and are having, far-reaching theoretical and practical implications. Recently, however, there has been a growing recognition of the limitations of operant principles in modifying behavior. In the next section, we examine why operant principles seem to have limited applicability.

THE MISBEHAVIOR OF ORGANISMS

We saw in the last chapter that Thorndike concluded that the same laws of learning apply to all mammals, including humans. Skinner, like many other learning theorists, agreed with Thorndike's conclusion. After observing how different species of animals performed under a certain schedule of reinforcement, Skinner (1956) commented,

"Pigeon, rat, monkey, which is which? It doesn't matter. Of course, these species have behavioral repertories which are as different as their anatomies. But once you have allowed for differences in the ways in which they make contact with the environment, and in the ways in which they act upon the environment, what remains of their behavior shows astonishingly similar properties" (pp. 230–231). Skinner went on to say that one can also add the performance of mice, cats, dogs, and human children, and the curves would still have more or less the same characteristics.

The alternative to believing that the same laws of learning apply to all mammals seems to necessitate going back to the concept of instinct, which the behaviorists attempted to bury forever. Those believing in the existence of instincts say that different species have different inborn tendencies that interact with or even negate the laws of learning. In other words, because of their innate behavior tendencies, certain species can be conditioned to do some things but not others. According to this point of view, some responses should be easier to condition for some species than for others because the responses of interest may occur more naturally for some species than for others.

Current interest in how innate behavior tendencies interact with learning principles has been stimulated by two of Skinner's ex-associates, Marian Breland (later Marian Bailey, 1920–2001) and Keller Breland. Armed with a knowledge of operant principles, the Brelands moved from Minnesota, where they had worked with Skinner, to Arkansas, where they started a business called Animal Behavior Enterprises. By using operant techniques, the Brelands were able to train a wide variety of animals to perform many different tricks, and their trained animals were put on display at fairs, at conventions, at amusement parks, and on television. As of 1961, the Brelands reported having conditioned thirty-eight species (totaling more than six thousand animals), including chickens, pigs, raccoons, reindeer, cockatoos, porpoises, and whales.

Everything seemed to be going fine for the Brelands until they began to experience breakdowns of conditioned behavior. Their problems became so pronounced that they were moved to report them in an article (Breland & Breland, 1961) whose title, "The Misbehavior of Organisms," was a parody of the title of Skinner's first major work, *The Behavior of Organisms* (1938).

The Brelands found that although their animals were initially highly conditionable, eventually instinctive behavior would appear and interfere with what had been learned. For example, an attempt was made to train raccoons to pick up coins and deposit them into a five-inch metal box. Conditioning a raccoon to pick up a single coin was no problem. Next, the metal box was introduced, and that is when the problem began. The raccoon seemed to have trouble letting the coin fall into the box. The animal would rub the coin inside of the container, take it back out, and hold it firmly for several seconds. Eventually, however, the raccoon released the coin into the box and received its food reinforcement. The next phase in training required the raccoon to place *two* coins into the metal box before receiving reinforcement. It was found that the raccoon could not let go of the two coins. Instead, it would rub them together, dip them into the container, and then remove them. The rubbing behavior became more and more pronounced, even though it delayed or even prevented reinforcement. The Brelands concluded that conditioning a raccoon to place two coins into a metal box was not feasible. It seemed that the innate behaviors associated with eating were too powerful to be overcome by operant conditioning principles. In other words, in this case a raccoon's innate tendency to wash and manipulate its food competed successfully with the learned response of placing one or more coins into a container.

Another example of the **misbehavior of organisms** involved training pigs to pick up large wooden coins and deposit them in a large "piggy bank." The coins were placed several feet from the bank, and the pig had to transport them to the bank before receiving reinforcement. Early conditioning was very effective, and the pigs seemed eager to perform the task. As time went on, however, the animals performed more slowly, and on their way to the piggy bank they would repeatedly drop the coin, root it (push it along the ground with their snouts), pick it up, drop it, root it, toss it in the air, and so on. The Brelands first believed that such behavior may have been the result of low drive, so they intensified the deprivation schedule that the animals were on, which only intensified the animal's misbehavior. Eventually it took the pigs about ten minutes to transport the coins a distance of about six feet, even when such delays postponed or eliminated reinforcement. Again, it appeared that the animal's instinctive behavior associated with eating became more powerful than the behavior it had learned.

From these and similar observations, the Brelands (1961) concluded, "It seems obvious that these animals are trapped by strong instinctive behaviors, and clearly we have here a demonstration of the prepotency of such behavior patterns over those which have been conditioned" (p. 684). The Brelands called the tendency for innate behavior patterns gradually to displace learned behavior **instinctual drift,** which they describe as follows:

> The general principle seems to be that wherever an animal has strong instinctive behaviors in the area of the conditioned response, after continued running the organism will drift toward the instinctive behavior to the detriment of the conditioned behavior and even to the delay or preclusion of the reinforcement. In a very boiled-down, simplified form it might be stated as "Learned behavior drifts toward instinctive behavior." (p. 684)

The Brelands feel that their work challenges three assumptions made by the behaviorists, namely, (1) that animals come to the learning situation as a *tabula rasa* (blank tablet), (2) that differences among various species are unimportant, and (3) that any response can be conditioned to any stimulus. Rather than making these assumptions, the Brelands (1961) conclude, "After 14 years of continuous conditioning and observation of thousands of animals, it is our reluctant conclusion that the behavior of any species cannot be adequately understood, predicted, or controlled without knowledge of its instinctive patterns, evolutionary history, and ecological niche" (p. 684).

Another phenomenon that seems to show the importance of instinctive behavior in a learning situation is **autoshaping.** We saw earlier in this chapter that the shaping process can be used to encourage an animal to make a response in a situation that it ordinarily would not make. To do so, the experimenter reinforces increasingly closer approximations to the desired behavior until the desired behavior is performed by the animal. In the case of autoshaping, however, the animal seems to shape its own behavior. For example, Brown and Jenkins (1968) found that if a pigeon was reinforced at certain intervals, regardless of what it was doing (noncontingent reinforcement), and if a disk was illuminated just prior to the presentation of the reinforcer (in this case, food), the pigeon learned to peck at the disk. The question is, Why did the pigeon learn to peck at the disk when it had never been reinforced for doing so?

One attempt to account for autoshaping has likened it to superstitious behavior, saying that the pigeon may have been pecking at the disk just before food was delivered, and therefore, pecking the disk would be maintained as a superstitious response. One problem with this explanation is that almost all pigeons peck the disk under these circumstances. It seems that if superstitious behavior were involved, some pigeons would peck the disk, others would turn in circles, others would peck other parts of the test chamber, and so on. A second explanation of autoshaping has been based on classical conditioning principles. According to this explanation, the illuminated disk becomes a secondary reinforcer because of its proximity to food, a primary reinforcer. Under the circumstances described thus far, this explanation is reasonable, except that it does not explain why the pigeon would peck at the disk. Earlier in this chapter we saw that, indeed, discriminative stimuli (S^Ds) become secondary reinforcers and thus can be used to maintain behavior, but why the animal should respond overtly to the secondary reinforcer as if it were the primary reinforcer is not clear.

An experiment by Williams and Williams (1969) casts further doubt on explanations of autoshaping as either a superstitious or a classical conditioning phenomenon. In their experiment, Williams and Williams arranged the situation so that pecking at the lighted disk actually *prevented* reinforcement from occurring. Food was presented to the pigeons every fifteen seconds, unless the pigeon pecked at the illuminated disk, in which case food was withheld on that trial. In this study, pecking at the illuminated disk was *never* followed by reinforcement. In fact, the more the pigeon pecked at the disk, the less food it received. According to the explanations of autoshaping in terms of both superstitious behavior and classical conditioning, the experimental arrangement in this study should have eliminated or, at least, drastically reduced disk pecking. It did not, however. The pigeons continued pecking at the disk at a high rate. In fact, for some pigeons disk pecking occurred so frequently that it virtually eliminated all reinforcement.

A study by Jenkins and Moore (1973) further complicates the situation. In their study, they found that if food was used as a reinforcer, pigeons responded to the disk with an eating posture, and if water was used as a reinforcer, pigeons responded to the disk with a drinking posture. In other words, when food was used as a reinforcer, the pigeons seemed to be eating the disk, and when water was used as a reinforcer, they seemed to be drinking the disk.

By the process of elimination, one is forced to view the autoshaping phenomenon as involving instinctive behavior patterns. It can be assumed, for example, that a hungry organism in a situation in which eating is possible will most likely exhibit responses related to eating. In the case of pigeons, pecking is such a response. Furthermore, it may be assumed that while in a high drive state, such behaviors can be easily elicited by any stimulus in the animal's environment that is vivid and on which an eating-related response could be easily released. A lighted disk in the environment of a hungry pigeon could be such a stimulus. According to this explanation, the lighted disk is simply eliciting instinctive behavior that has a high probability of occurring under the circumstances. Because disk pecking in autoshaping experiments is typically what the experimenter is looking for, it is not referred to as misbehavior, as were certain instinctive responses in the Brelands' work.

If one accepts the instinctive explanation of autoshaping, one needs to conclude that no learning takes place at all. The animal simply becomes hypersensitive in the situation and releases innate responses that are appropriate under the circumstances to the most vivid stimuli in its environment. This position, taken by Robert Bolles (see, e.g., Bolles, 1979, pp. 179–184), is discussed further in Chapter 15.

The work of the Brelands and the work on autoshaping are only two examples of a growing recognition in psychology that the innate response tendencies of an organism interact with the laws of learning. Thus, we are once again confronted with the age-old empiricism-nativism controversy: Is behavior learned, or is it genetically determined? The phenomenon of instinctual drift seems to indicate that at least for some species, behavior can be nudged only a limited amount from its instinctual basis before instinctual tendencies override learned tendencies as the most powerful determiners of behavior. What about humans? Do we have within us the remnants of our evolutionary past, toward which we periodically drift? The answer depends on who is being asked. Many learning theorists such as Skinner would say no. Others such as Bolles and the evolutionary psychologists would say yes.

SKINNER ON EDUCATION

Skinner, like Thorndike, was very interested in applying his theory of learning to the process of education. To Skinner, learning proceeds most effectively if (1) the information to be learned is presented in small steps, (2) the learners are given rapid feedback concerning the accuracy of their learning (i.e., they are shown immediately after a learning experience whether they have learned the information correctly or incorrectly), and (3) the learners are able to learn at their own pace.

Skinner learned firsthand that these principles were not being used in the classroom. He reflected on a visit he made in 1953 to one of his daughter's classes (Skinner, 1967): "On November 11, as a visiting father, I was sitting in the back of the room in an arithmetic class. Suddenly the situation seemed perfectly absurd. Here were twenty extremely valuable organisms. Through no fault of her own, the teacher was violating almost everything we knew about the learning process" (p. 406).

Skinner would insist that the course objectives be completely specified before teaching begins. Further, he would insist that the objectives be defined *behaviorally*. If a unit is designed to teach creativity, he would ask, "What are students *doing* when they are being creative?" If a unit is designed to teach the understanding of history, he would ask, "What are students *doing* when they are understanding history?" If educational objectives cannot be specified behaviorally, instructors have no way of knowing whether they have accomplished what they had set out to do. Likewise, if objectives are specified in terms not easily transformed into behavioral terms, it is next to impossible to determine to what extent the course objectives have been met.

Like most behaviorists, he would start with the simple and proceed to the complex. Complex behavior is thought to consist of simpler forms of behavior. Like Thorndike, motivation to Skinner was important only in determining what will act as a reinforcer for a given student. Secondary reinforcers are very important, too, because these are normally utilized in the classroom. Examples of secondary reinforcers include verbal praise, positive facial expressions, gold stars, feelings of success, points, grades, and the opportunity to work on what one wants to. Like Thorndike, Skinner stressed the use of extrinsic reinforcers in education. In fact, for the Skinnerian teacher, the main function of education is to arrange reinforcement contingencies so that the behavior that has been deemed important is encouraged. Intrinsic reinforcement is thought to be of minimal importance.

It is also important for the Skinnerian teacher to move from a 100 percent reinforcement schedule to a partial reinforcement schedule. During the early stages of training, a correct response is reinforced each time it occurs. Later, however, it is reinforced only periodically, which, of course, makes the response more resistant to extinction.

All the S-R behaviorists would prescribe a learning environment that allows for individual differences in learning rate. They would want to either deal with students individually or provide a group of students with material that allows individual self-pacing, such as teaching machines or specially constructed workbooks. The behaviorists would tend to avoid the lecture technique because there is no way of knowing when learning is taking place and therefore when to administer reinforcers. We have more to say about both individualized courses and the lecture technique later in this chapter.

Skinnerian teachers would avoid the use of punishment. They would reinforce appropriate behavior and ignore inappropriate behavior. Because the learning environment would be designed so that students experienced maximal success, they would usually attend to the material to be learned. According to the Skinnerians, behavior problems in school are the result of poor educational planning, such as failing to provide self-pacing, failing to use reinforcers appropriately, offering the material in chunks too large to be easily comprehended, using discipline to control behavior, having rigid plans that all students must follow, or making unreasonable demands on students (such as not moving or not making noise).

In his article "The Shame of American Education," Skinner (1984) insisted that the greater use of programmed instruction would not only facilitate student learning but also increase respect for teachers:

> Success and progress are the very stuff on which programmed instruction feeds. They should also be the stuff that makes teaching worthwhile as a profession. Just as students must not only learn but know that they are learning, so teachers must not only teach but know that they are teaching. Burnout is usually regarded as the result of abusive treatment by students, but it can be as much the result of looking back upon a day in the classroom and wondering what one has accomplished. Along with a sense of satisfaction goes a place in the community. One proposed remedy for American education is to give teachers greater respect, but that is putting it the wrong way around. Let them teach twice as much in the same time and with the same effort, and they will be held in greater respect. (p. 952)

SKINNER'S LEGACY: PSI, CBI, AND ONLINE LEARNING

The most common teaching technique is the lecture, and the lecture technique violates all three of the principles discussed previously. Skinner proposed an alternative teaching technique, **programmed learning,** which does incorporate all three principles. A device invented to present programmed material has been called a **teaching machine.** The advantages of using a teaching machine were outlined by Skinner (1958) as follows:

> The machine itself, of course, does not teach. It simply brings the student into contact with the person who composed the material it presents. It is a labor-saving device because it can bring one programmer into contact with an indefinite number of students. They may suggest mass production, but the effect upon each student is surprisingly like that of a private tutor. The comparison holds in several respects. (i) There is a constant interchange between program and student. Unlike lectures, textbooks, and the usual audio-visual aids, the machine induces sustained activity. The student is always alert and busy. (ii) Like a good tutor, the machine insists that a given point be thoroughly understood, either frame-by-frame or set-by-set, before the student moves on. Lectures, textbooks, and their mechanized equivalents, on the other hand, proceed without making sure that the student understands and easily leave him behind. (iii) Like a good tutor, the machine presents just that material for which the student is ready. It asks him to take only that step which he is at the moment best equipped and most likely to take. (iv) Like a skillful tutor, the machine helps the student to come up with the right answer. It does this in part through the orderly construction of the program and in part with techniques of hinting, prompting, suggesting, and so on, derived from an analysis of verbal behavior. . . . (v) Lastly, of course, the machine, like the private tutor, reinforces the student for every correct response, using this immediate feedback not only to shape his behavior most efficiently but to maintain it in strength in a manner which the laymen would describe as "holding the student's interest." (p. 971)

Programmed learning is a technique that is much more likely to be used by a behavioristically oriented teacher than a cognitively oriented one. Programmed learning incorporates many of the principles of reinforcement theory, although the technique was not invented by a reinforcement theorist. It was originally developed by Sidney L. Pressey (1926, 1927), whose "testing machine" was effective but did not become popular. Thus, we have an example of *Zeitgeist* (spirit of the times). Although Pressey's idea was good, it was not appropriate to the spirit of the time in which he proposed it. It was left to Skinner to rediscover programmed learning and make it popular.

Skinner's approach to programmed learning involves the following features derived from his theory of learning:

1. *Small steps.* Learners are exposed to small amounts of information and proceed from one **frame,** or one item of information, to the next in an orderly fashion. This is what is meant by a **linear program.**
2. *Overt responding.* **Overt responding** is required so that students' correct responses can be reinforced and their incorrect responses can be corrected.

3. *Immediate feedback.* Immediately after making responses, students are told whether they are correct. This **immediate feedback** acts as a reinforcer if the answers are correct and as a corrective measure if the answers are wrong.
4. *Self-pacing.* Students proceed through the program at their own pace.

There are a number of variations possible in this program. For example, some students may skip information if it is familiar. This procedure usually involves giving students a pretest on a certain section of the program, and if they perform adequately, they are instructed to advance to the next section.

Another kind of programming allows students to "branch" into different bodies of information depending on initial performance. After students have been presented with a certain amount of information, they are given a multiple-choice question. If they answer correctly, they advance to the next body of information. If they answer incorrectly, the branching program directs them to additional information, depending on the mistake that was made. For example, the program may say, "If you picked B as your answer, go back and review the material on page 24; if you picked D as your answer, repeat Section 3; if you chose A, you are correct; please proceed to the next section."

Is Programmed Learning Effective?   Schramm (1964) reviewed 165 studies of programmed learning. Of the 36 studies that compared programmed instruction with the more traditional kinds of instruction, 17 found programmed instruction to be more effective, 18 found both kinds of instruction to be equally effective, and only 1 found traditional techniques to be more effective. Therefore, the answer seems to be that programmed learning is effective, at least in the areas where it has been tried.

The question of why it is effective is not so easily answered. There was widespread disagreement concerning which aspect of programmed learning results in its effectiveness. Controversy also existed over the importance of all other aspects of programmed learning, for instance, the nature and importance of knowledge of results, what constitutes a small step, and the importance of self-pacing. At this time it can be concluded that programmed learning is an effective teaching device, but the essential ingredients that made it effective were never resolved.

Personalized Systems of Instruction

The approach called Personalized Systems of Instruction (PSI) was originally called the Keller Plan after Fred Keller (1899–1996), who developed it (Keller, 1968; Keller & Sherman, 1974). Like programmed learning, the PSI method is individualized and involves quick, frequent feedback on student performance. Offering an individualized course usually involves four steps, which can be summarized as follows:

1. Determine the material to be covered in the course.
2. Divide the material into self-contained segments.
3. Create methods of evaluating the degree to which the student has mastered the material in a given segment.
4. Allow students to move from segment to segment at their own pace.

The emphasis in PSI courses is on mastery of material within course segments, usually demonstrated by performance on short, focused examinations. Instructors can require that students master material completely before moving from one segment to another. Alternately, an instructor might require that a minimum criterion, 90 percent mastery, for example, be attained before a student progresses in the course. Even when complete mastery is not required, students in an individualized course will generally obtain As or Bs as a final grade because, in an individualized course, many personal factors that contribute variance to test scores are eliminated. If students are ill, emotionally disturbed, overloaded with other work, or for whatever reason are not ready to be tested, they simply postpone a segment test. Students are, within the time constraints imposed by a quarter or semester system, free to master course segments according to their personal timetables rather than meeting the deadlines of an instructor.

Are PSI Courses Effective?   Unlike many innovations in education, the results of the PSI format were exceptionally well documented. Sherman (1992) estimates the number of studies comparing PSI with traditional classrooms at more than two thousand. He notes that "the message was always the same" (p. 59). Study after study demonstrated that students in PSI format classes did as well as, if not better than, students in traditional courses and that they tended to retain material longer than students in traditional courses. (See also Kulik, Kulik, & Cohen, 1979.) In addition, students rated PSI classes as more enjoyable and more challenging than traditional classes. Why, then, didn't PSI courses become more popular? Sherman (1992) attributes the lack of significant adoption of the PSI format to the "inertia" of the educational system:

> The educational establishment is enormous, the constituencies are multiple and diverse, often with conflicting interests. The barriers to educational reform are formidable, even awesome. The power, the money, the investment in keeping things as they are may be impossible to overcome. Recommendations may be acceptable only if they don't change things very much. Improving instruction is the goal, but only in the context of not changing anything that is important to any vested interest. (p. 61)

Sherman cites the case of the psychology department at Georgetown University where, despite the evidence in support of PSI format classes, the department chair declared that half of class time must be devoted to lecturing, thereby "reducing the possibility of self-pacing to zero" and thus "effectively eliminated PSI courses" (p. 63).

What is left of self-pacing and immediate feedback is found in computer-based instruction (CBI), a topic to which we turn next.

Computer-Based Instruction

When a computer is used to present programmed or other kinds of instructional material, the process is called **computer-based instruction (CBI)** (also sometimes called computer-assisted instruction). Anyone who has recently purchased a new word-processing program, for example, has the option of doing a built-in set of tutorial exercises to introduce the features and capabilities of the software. Computer users who follow the tutorial are able to work at their own pace through small units intended to teach specific skills and applications. The tutorials require overt responding and active engagement with the materials. Help is available at the touch of a button, and feedback is immediate. The principles of learning found in Skinner's programmed learning and Keller's PSI classes are also found in CBI.

Not only can the computer be used to present instructional material but also it can evaluate how well that material has been learned. After a segment of a program has been completed, the computer can give an achievement test, grade it, and compare the score with the scores of others taking the program. Thus, the computer provides not only immediate feedback during the learning process but also the immediate results of achievement tests to both the students and the teacher. Depending on how students perform, the teacher can determine how well the instructional material is working and take whatever corrective measures that may be necessary. This step cannot be done as easily when a textbook and lectures are used to present the material and a midterm and final examination are used to evaluate student learning.

By providing immediate feedback, personal attention, exciting visual displays, and a gamelike atmosphere, CBI can motivate students to learn in ways that traditional instruction may not. There is considerable evidence that students learn more from CBI than from traditional instruction, and they do so in a shorter period of time. Linskie (1977), for example, reports that third-grade students learning math through CBI achieved much more than students taking traditional classes, and they did so with much greater enthusiasm:

> The students watched the clock to get down to the computer center on time. Once there, seated before the keyboard, the degree of concentration was almost unbelievable. No matter that the nine other students were typing away and that the nine other computers were typing back: nothing seemed to distract the students. The math period became almost like a daily relay race with students waiting impatiently for their own ten minutes with the machine. And there was no paper work to take home, no dirty smudges to displease the teacher, and no plague of broken pencils. . . . At the end of the year, the third-graders using the computer-assisted instruction showed a gain of just under two years in achievement while the third-graders taught by conventional methods progressed just over one year. When the experiment was tried in other schools, similar results were achieved through grade six. (p. 210)

Although CBI has been widely used to present various kinds of linear and branching programs, it can do much more. Programs have been written that allow the implications of different kinds of political and sociological systems to be studied, simulate a variety of psychological experiments, perform chemistry experiments without the need to handle equipment or chemicals (Bunderson, 1967), and teach problem-solving skills to engineers (Brown & Burton, 1975). A brief review of literature found more than four hundred published reports of CBI between 1993 and 1999.

Indeed, CBI is becoming so sophisticated that many believe that it can be used to teach anything that a good teacher is capable of teaching. It is claimed that even such topics as philosophy, religion, art appreciation, and creativity could be taught by CBI if instructional goals could be clearly specified. If we can get teachers to describe clearly what a student is doing when the student is being creative or appreciating art, say CBI enthusiasts, we can write a program that will teach those behaviors.

An educational format related to CBI is the "virtual classroom," sometimes referred to as **online education.** Given the sophisticated technology of computers and the Internet, it is now possible for a student to sit at a computer terminal miles from an instructor or the source of information and to interact, via the computer keyboard, with an actual instructor or with programmed materials. In this "distance learning" approach to education, a student has the opportunity to read text materials or lectures prepared by an instructor, to do exercises and lab assignments using the computer, to interact with the instructor and other students in computer "chat" sessions, or to engage in CBI that has been prepared by the instructor. Advances in computer technology make it possible to see and hear a class in progress, as well as to participate verbally. Reviews of the effectiveness of online classrooms indicate that they are as effective as traditional classrooms and that course ratings are comparable between the two approaches (see, for example, Hiltz, 1993; Spooner, Jordan, Algozzine, & Spooner, 1999).

Criticisms of CBI   CBI and online education meet with the same criticisms and difficulties that Sherman (1992) reports for PSI instruction. Many feel that these techniques do not exemplify "true" teaching because they minimize the role of the teacher. Sherman suggests, in fact, that the popularity of CBI lies in its being viewed as a supplemental educational activity that does not threaten the traditional role of the teacher. Critics say that the individualized approaches we have discussed create an instructional situation that is cold, mechanical, and dehumanizing. That is, the important, spontaneous interactions between teacher and students, and among students themselves, are absent from programmed learning, PSI, and CBI, and that criticism can be extended to some aspects of online learning. Some critics also say that the most important kind of educational material cannot be specified to the point where it can be programmed or arranged in segments. A related criticism concerns the usual demand on the part of those using programmed learning or CBI that course objectives be specified in behavioral terms. Many critics insist that the loftiest and most desirable educational objectives cannot be easily specified or measured and perhaps never fully reached. For example, Meek (1977) maintains that because individualized courses must have course objectives that are clearly specified and measurable, they generally do not have very important objectives. Meek offers the following suggestions about what the goals of any kind of course should be:

> The primary goals of such courses should involve an attempt to develop the ability of the student to think critically, to sort, to order, to choose among, to evaluate, and to interrelate competing ideals and ideas. The student must learn how to learn, how to evaluate ideas and data, and how to relate information acquired to her or his values and those that are present in the larger society. . . . It is basic nonsense to talk about the degree of "mastery" of such goals. (pp. 115–116)

In his now famous article, "Good-bye Teacher," Fred Keller described his individualized approach to education. Upon noting the superiority of this technique over the more traditional lecture technique, Keller (1968) concluded the following about the teacher of tomorrow:

> He becomes an educational engineer, a contingency manager, with the responsibility of serving the great majority, rather than the small minority, of young men and women who come to him for schooling in the area of his competence. The teacher of tomorrow will not, I think, continue to be satisfied with a 10 per cent efficiency (at best) which makes him an object of contempt by some, commiseration by others, indifference by many, and love by a few. No longer will he need to hold his position by the exercise of functions that neither transmit culture, dignify his status, nor encourage respect for learning in others. No longer will he need to live, like Ichabod Crane, in a world that increasingly begrudges providing him room and lodging for a doubtful service to its young. A new kind of teacher is in the making. To the old kind, I, for one, will be glad to say, "Good-Bye." (p. 89)

Keller's point, of course, is that instructors will need to become more concerned with how their students learn. The time is near when an instructor no longer will be able merely to dispense information and leave it up to the students to learn it. Tomorrow's instructor, whether cognitively or behavioristically oriented, will need to ponder various classroom formats to discover which one is optimally conducive to learning. The teacher will need to be converted from the traditional college professor to what Carl Rogers calls a "facilitator of learning" or what Keller calls either an "educational engineer" or a "contingency manager."

EVALUATION OF SKINNER'S THEORY

Contributions

B. F. Skinner's long and productive research program significantly influenced both applied and purely scientific psychology. Compared with many other learning researchers, Skinner's system was straightforward and could be easily applied to problems ranging from animal training to human behavior modification therapy. At another extreme, his work led to the matching law and had an indirect impact on current research in behavioral decision making.

Skinner's methodology was a departure from mainstream behaviorism. Verplanck (1954) noted that Skinner's approach "not only differs from the others in particulars of theoretical detail, but also represents a re-orientation toward the science" (p. 306). Whereas other researchers tended to conduct research on groups of subjects, making nomothetic comparisons between different experimental conditions, Skinner utilized an ideographic approach in which single experimental subjects were observed for prolonged periods. This approach, along with almost exclusive use of the cumulative record of responding, provided an alternative to the dominant research method(s) in the field, and it resulted in the creation of a specialized journal, *Journal of Experimental Analysis of Behavior.* The method allowed for detailed study and analysis of reinforcement schedules and yielded a number of new behavioral laws. Throughout his life, Skinner was steadfast in his insistence that psychologists should avoid theorizing, especially about cognitive events, and be content with descriptive accounts of behavior.

Criticisms

Some criticisms of Skinner's theory are more warranted than others. For example, Staddon (1995), who traces his lineage to Skinner as a former student of Richard Herrnstein, finds Skinner's influence in a number of societal problems. Most responsible are Skinner's contentions that punishment is ineffective and that, because humans have no free will, they cannot be held responsible for their behavior. Staddon believes that these Skinnerian beliefs have resulted in faulty parenting and flawed legal practices, which in turn have led to increased crime rates, illegitimacy, and illiteracy. Although we would not go so far as to blame Skinnerian behaviorism for complex social and economic problems, there are aspects of his position that can be legitimately criticized.

Although the ideographic method developed by Skinner allowed the examination of an individual's operant behavior in detail, it was very difficult to compare results from his procedure with results obtained in laboratories using the nomothetic method. A second criticism follows from Skinner's refusal to develop formal theory. As we noted in Chapter 1, a primary function of a theory is the explanation of existing data and phenomena. It is important to note, in the context of Skinner's position, that there is a great difference between describing a phenomenon and attempting to explain that phenomenon. In the first case, careful description is usually accurate, cannot be disputed, and tends to explain how and when behavior occurs. A theory, on the other hand, usually endeavors to explain why a behavior appears as well as the hows and whens. Theories, unlike descriptions, are often disputed, and such dispute may lead to scientific progress. Skinner's system did lead to progress, but it was a progress characterized by accumulation of behavioral phenomena rather than a deeper understanding of learning and motivation.

DISCUSSION QUESTIONS

1. Outline the procedure you would use while following Skinner's theory to increase the probability that a child would become a creative adult.
2. Would you use the same reinforcers to manipulate the behavior of both children and adults? If not, what would make the difference?
3. Are there some forms of adult human behavior for which you feel Skinner's theory is not applicable? Explain.
4. What would characterize the classroom procedures suggested by Skinner's theory of learning? List a few differences between these procedures and those now being followed in our schools.

5. Assuming the conclusions Skinner reached concerning the effectiveness of punishment are valid, what major change would they suggest in child rearing? Criminal behavior? Education?
6. What is the partial reinforcement effect? Briefly describe the basic reinforcement schedules that Skinner studied.
7. Propose an explanation for the partial reinforcement effect.
8. Describe concurrent and concurrent chain schedules of reinforcement, and give an example of each.
9. What is Herrnstein's matching law? For what aspects of reinforcement has the law been found to hold true? What are the implications of the law for dealing with human behavior problems?
10. What is contingency contracting? Give an example of how it could be used.
11. From Skinner's point of view, what are the advantages of programmed learning and teaching machines over the traditional lecture technique of teaching?
12. According to Skinner, why have we not developed a more adequate technology of behavior in this country? What would need to be done before we would be willing to utilize such a technology in solving our problems?
13. Give an example of how the Premack principle can be used to modify the behavior of a primary school child.
14. Discuss chaining from Skinner's point of view.
15. Explain language development from Skinner's point of view. Explain Chomsky's opposition to Skinner's explanation of language development.
16. Distinguish between positive reinforcement, negative reinforcement, and punishment.
17. Explain the difference between Premack's and Timberlake's views of reinforcers.
18. Describe the phenomenon of instinctual drift.
19. Describe autoshaping and attempt to account for it.

CHAPTER HIGHLIGHTS

autoclitic behavior
autoshaping
behavioral economics
chaining
computer-based instruction (CBI)
concurrent chain reinforcement schedule
concurrent reinforcement schedule
contingency contracting
contingent reinforcement
continuous reinforcement schedule (CRF)

cumulative recording
differential reinforcement
discriminative operant
discriminative stimulus (S^D)
disequilibrium hypothesis
echoic behavior
extinction of an operant response
fixed interval reinforcement schedule (FI)
fixed ratio reinforcement schedule (FR)
frame
functional analysis

functional autonomy

generalized reinforcers

Herrnstein's equation

immediate feedback

instinctual drift

linear program

magazine training

mand

matching law

mentalistic events

misbehavior of organisms

noncontingent reinforcement

online education

operant behavior

operant conditioning

operant level

overt responding

partial reinforcement
    effect (PRE)

Premack principle

primary negative reinforcer

primary positive reinforcer

programmed learning

progressive ratio reinforcement
    schedule (PR)

punishment

radical behaviorism

respondent behavior

respondent conditioning

shaping

Skinner box

spontaneous recovery of an operant
    response

successive approximation

superstitious behavior

tact

teaching machine

variable interval reinforcement
    schedule (VI)

variable ratio reinforcement
    schedule (VR)

CHAPTER 6

Clark Leonard Hull

Clark L. Hull (1884–1952) received his Ph.D. in 1918 from the University of Wisconsin, where he also taught from 1916 to 1929. In 1929, he moved to Yale, where he stayed until his death.

Hull's career can be divided into three separate parts. His first major concern was with the testing of aptitudes. He gathered material on aptitude testing while teaching a course on the topic at the University of Wisconsin, and he published

Clark Leonard Hull. (Courtesy of Library of Congress.)

Aptitude Testing in 1928. Hull's second major concern was hypnosis, and after a long study of the hypnotic process, he wrote *Hypnosis and Suggestibility* (1933b). His third concern, and the work for which he is most famous, was the study of the learning process. Hull's first major book on learning, *Principles of Behavior* (1943), radically changed the study of learning. It was the first attempt to apply comprehensive scientific theory to the study of a complex psychological phenomenon. We saw in Chapter 3 that Ebbinghaus was the first to use an experiment to investigate learning. But it was Hull who first utilized a rigorous theory to study and attempt to explain learning. Hull's theory, as presented in 1943, was extended in 1952 in *A Behavior System*. He intended to write a third book on learning but never did.

For his efforts, Hull received the Warren Medal in 1945 from the Society of Experimental Psychology. The award read,

To Clark L. Hull: For his careful development of a systematic theory of behavior. This theory has stimulated much research and it has been developed in a precise and quantitative form so as to permit predictions which can be tested empirically. The theory thus contains within itself the seeds of its own ultimate verification and of its own possible final disproof. A truly unique achievement in the history of psychology to date.

Hull was physically disabled most of his life by partial paralysis from childhood polio. In 1948, he had a coronary attack, and four years later he died. In the last book he wrote (*A Behavior System*), he expressed regret that the third book that he had intended to write on learning would never be written.

Even though Hull felt that his theory was incomplete, it has had a profound influence on learning theory throughout the world. Kenneth Spence (1952), one of Hull's many famous students, indicated that 40 percent of all experiments in the *Journal of Experimental Psychology* and in the *Journal of Comparative and Physiological Psychology* between 1941 and 1950 refer to some aspect of Hull's work, and when one looks only at the areas of learning and motivation, this figure rises to 70 percent. Ruja (1956) reports that in the *Journal of Abnormal and Social Psychology* between 1949 and 1952 there are 105 references to Hull's *Principles of Behavior,* and the next most popular reference was listed only twenty-five times. In fact, it is still quite common for the student of learning to come across numerous references to Hull's work while going through the psychological journals. By any measure, Clark Hull was a major contributor to our knowledge of the learning process.

Hull, like most functionalistic learning theorists, was significantly influenced by Darwin's writings. The purpose of Hull's theory was to explain adaptive behavior and to understand the variables affecting it. It can be said that Hull was interested in developing a theory that explained how body needs, the environment, and behavior interact to increase the probability of the organism's survival.

HULL'S APPROACH TO THEORIZING

As a first step in developing his theory, Hull completed an extensive review of previous research on learning. Next, he attempted to summarize those findings. Finally, he attempted to deduce testable consequences from those summary principles. We look at this approach to theory construction in somewhat more detail.

Hull's approach to theory construction has been called **hypothetical deductive** (or **logical deductive**). Rashotte and Amsel (1999) describe this approach:

> Following the natural sciences model, the behavioral scientist elaborates a set of postulates, or first principles, and uses them as premises in deducing, by rigorous logic, inferences or theorems about behavioral phenomena. . . . These postulates often involve hypothetical entities ("intervening variables"), invented by the theorist to organize his thinking about the relationships among experimental manipulations and measurements (independent and dependent variables) related to behavioral phenomena of interest. The theory can then be evaluated by translating the deductions from the theory into experimental operations and see how it fares in the laboratory. (p. 126)

This type of theorizing creates a dynamic, open-ended system. Hypotheses are constantly being generated; some of them are supported by experimental outcomes, and some are not. When experiments come out in a predicted direction, the whole theory, including postulates and theorems, is strengthened. When the experiments do not come out as predicted, the theory is weakened and must be revised. A theory such as Hull's must continually be updated in accordance with the outcome of empirical investigation. Hull (1943) wrote,

> Empirical observation, supplemented by shrewd conjecture, is the main source of the primary principles or postulates of a science. Such formulations, when taken in various combinations together with relevant antecedent conditions, yield inferences or theorems, of which some may agree with the empirical outcome of the conditions in question, and some may not. Primary propositions yielding logical deductions which consistently agree with the observed empirical outcome are retained, whereas those which disagree are rejected or modified. As the sifting of this trial-and-error process continues, there gradually emerges a limited series of primary principles whose joint implications are progressively more likely to agree with relevant observations. Deductions made from these surviving postulates, while never absolutely certain, do at length become highly trustworthy. This is in fact the present status of the primary principles of the major physical sciences. (p. 382)

As was mentioned in Chapter 2, any scientific theory is merely a tool that aids the researcher in synthesizing facts and in knowing where to look for new information. The ultimate value of a theory is determined by how well it agrees with observed facts or, in this case, with the outcome of experiments. The ultimate authority in science is the empirical world. Although a theory such as Hull's can become very abstract, still it must make statements concerning observable events.

No matter how elaborate and abstract a theory becomes, it must ultimately generate propositions that are empirically verifiable; Hull's theory does exactly that.

MAJOR THEORETICAL CONCEPTS

Hull's theory has a logical structure of postulates and theorems much like Euclid's geometry. The postulates are general statements about behavior that cannot be directly verified, although the theorems that follow logically from the postulates can be tested. We first discuss Hull's sixteen major postulates as they appeared in 1943, and then, later in the chapter, we turn to the major revisions Hull made in 1952.

Postulate 1: Sensing the External Environment and the Stimulus Trace External stimulation triggers an afferent (sensory) neural impulse, which outlasts the environmental stimulation. Thus, Hull postulates the existence of a **stimulus trace** (s) that continues for a few seconds after the stimulus event has terminated. Because this afferent neural impulse becomes associated with a response, Hull changes the traditional S-R formula to S-s-R, where s is the stimulus trace. For Hull, the association of interest is between s and R. The stimulus trace ultimately causes an efferent (motor) neural reaction (r) that results in an overt response. Thus we have S-s-r-R, where S is external stimulation, s is the stimulus trace, r is the firing of motor neurons, and R is an overt response.

Postulate 2: The Interaction of Sensory Impulses The **interaction of sensory impulses** ($\bar{s}$) indicates the complexity of stimulation and, therefore, the difficulties in predicting behavior. Behavior is seldom a function of only one stimulus. Rather, it is a function of many stimuli converging on the organism at any given time. These many stimuli and their related traces interact with one another, and their synthesis determines behavior. We can now refine the S-R formula further as follows:

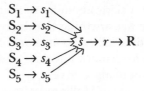

where $\bar{s}$ represents the combined effects of the five stimuli acting on the organism at the moment.

Postulate 3: Unlearned Behavior Hull believed that the organism is born with a hierarchy of responses, **unlearned behavior,** that is triggered when a need arises. For example, if a foreign object enters the eye, considerable blinking and tear secretion may follow automatically. If the temperature varies from that which is optimal for normal body functioning, the organism may sweat or shiver. Likewise, pain, hunger, or thirst will trigger certain innate response patterns that have a high probability of reducing the effects of those conditions.

The term *hierarchy* is used in reference to these responses because more than one reaction may occur. If the first innate response pattern does not alleviate a need, another pattern will occur. If the second response pattern does not reduce the need, still another will occur, and so on. If none of the innate behavior patterns is effective in reducing the need, the organism will have to *learn* new response patterns. Thus, according to Hull, learning is required only when innate neural mechanisms and their related responses fail to reduce an organism's need. Generally, as long as either innate responses or previously learned responses are effective in satisfying needs, there is no reason to learn new responses.

Postulate 4: Contiguity and Drive Reduction as Necessary Conditions for Learning   If a stimulus leads to a response and if the response results in the satisfaction of a biological need, the association between the stimulus and the response is strengthened. The more often the stimulus and the response that leads to need satisfaction are paired, the stronger the relationship between the stimulus and the response becomes. On this basic point, Hull is in complete agreement with Thorndike's revised law of effect. Hull, however, is more specific about what constitutes a "satisfying state of affairs." Primary **reinforcement,** according to Hull, must involve need satisfaction, or what Hull called **drive reduction.**

Postulate 4 also describes a secondary **reinforcer** as "a stimulus which has been closely and consistently associated with the diminution of a need" (Hull, 1943, p. 178). Secondary reinforcement following a response will also increase the strength of the association between that response and the stimulus with which it was contiguous. To summarize, we can say that if a stimulus is followed by a response, which in turn is followed by reinforcement (either primary or secondary), the association between that stimulus and that response is strengthened. It can also be said that the "habit" of giving that response to that stimulus gets stronger. Hull's term, **habit strength** $(_sH_R),$ is explained later.

Although Hull, like Thorndike and Skinner, was very much a reinforcement theorist, he was more specific about his definition of reinforcement. Skinner simply said that a reinforcer was anything that increased the rate with which a response occurred, and Thorndike talked about a nebulous "satisfying" or "annoying" state of affairs. For Hull, reinforcement was drive reduction, and reinforcers were stimuli that were capable of reducing a drive.

Habit strength is one of Hull's most important concepts, and as stated, it refers to the strength of the association between a stimulus and a response. As the number of reinforced pairings between a stimulus and a response goes up, the habit strength of that association goes up. The mathematical formula that describes the relationship between $_sH_R$ and number of reinforced pairings between S and R is as follows:

$$_sH_R = 1 - 10^{-0.0305N}$$

N is the number of reinforced pairings between S and R. This formula generates a negatively accelerated learning curve, which means that early reinforced pairings

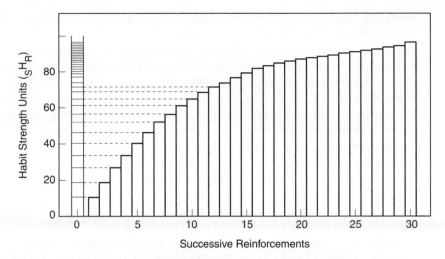

FIGURE 6–1 The relationship between gains in habit strength ($_sH_R$) and successive reinforcements. Hull, PRINCIPLES OF BEHAVIOR AND INTRODUCTION OF BEHAVIOR THEORY., 1st, © 1967. Electronically reproduced by permission of Pearson Education, Inc., Upper Saddle River, New Jersey.

have more of an effect on learning than do later ones. In fact, a point is reached where additional reinforced pairings have no effect on learning. Figure 6–1 shows that early reinforcements have more of an effect on learning than do later ones.

Postulate 5: Stimulus Generalization Hull says that the ability of a stimulus (other than the one used during conditioning) to elicit a conditioned response is determined by its similarity to the stimulus used during training. Thus, $_sH_R$ will generalize from one stimulus to another to the extent that the two stimuli are similar. This postulate of **stimulus generalization** also indicates that prior experience will affect current learning; that is, learning that took place under similar conditions will transfer to the new learning situation. Hull called this process **generalized habit strength ($_s\overline{H}_R$).** This postulate essentially describes Thorndike's identical elements theory of the transfer of training.

Postulate 6: Stimuli Associated with Drives Biological deficiency in the organism produces a **drive (*D*)** state, and each drive is associated with specific stimuli. Hunger pangs that accompany the hunger drive and the dry mouth, lips, and throat that accompany the thirst drive are examples. The existence of specific drive stimuli make it possible to teach an animal to behave in one way under one drive and another way under another drive. For example, an animal can be taught to turn right in a T-maze when it is hungry and to turn left when it is thirsty. As we see later in the chapter, the concept of drive stimuli became very important in Hull's 1952 revision of his theory.

Postulate 7: Reaction Potential as a Function of Drive and Habit Strength The likelihood of a learned response being made at any given moment is called **reaction**

potential ($_sE_R$). Reaction potential is a function of both habit strength ($_sH_R$) and drive (D). For a learned response to occur, $_sH_R$ has to be activated by D. Drive does not direct behavior; it simply arouses it and intensifies it. Without drive, the animal would not emit a learned response even though there had been a large number of reinforced pairings between a stimulus and a response. Thus, if an animal has learned to press a bar in a Skinner box in order to obtain food, it would press the bar only when it was hungry, no matter how well it was trained. The basic components of Hull's theory that we have covered thus far can be combined into the following formula:

$$\text{Reaction potential} = {_sE_R} = {_sH_R} \times D$$

Thus, reaction potential is a function of how often the response was reinforced in that situation and the extent to which a drive is present. By looking at the formula, it can be seen that if either $_sH_R$ or D were zero, $_sE_R$ would necessarily be zero. As we see in postulates 13 to 15, in addition to being related to response probability, $_sE_R$ is also related to resistance to extinction, latency, and amplitude of response.

Postulate 8: Responding Causes Fatigue, Which Operates against the Elicitation of a Conditioned Response Responding requires work, and work results in fatigue. Fatigue eventually acts to inhibit responding. **Reactive inhibition (I_R)** is caused by the fatigue associated with muscular activity and is related to the amount of work involved in performing a task. Because this form of inhibition is related to fatigue, it automatically dissipates when the organism stops performing. This concept has been used to explain the spontaneous recovery of a conditioned response after extinction. That is, the animal may stop responding because of the buildup of I_R. After a rest, the I_R dissipates, and the animal commences to respond once again. For Hull, extinction not only is a function of nonreinforcement but also is influenced by the buildup of reactive inhibition.

Reactive inhibition has also been used to explain the **reminiscence effect,** which is the improvement of performance following the cessation of practice. For example, if experimental subjects are trained to track a rotating disk with a stylus, their performances will gradually improve until some asymptotic (maximal) level is reached. If the subjects are allowed to rest for a few minutes after this asymptotic level is reached and then are asked to track the disk again, their performances will tend to exceed their previous asymptotic levels. This is called the reminiscence effect, and it is explained by assuming that I_R builds up during training and operates against tracking performance. After a rest, I_R dissipates and performance improves. Figure 6–2 presents an example of the reminiscence effect.

Additional support for Hull's notion of I_R comes from research on the difference between **massed** and **distributed practice.** It is consistently found that when practice trials are spaced far apart (distributed practice), performance is superior to what it is when practice trials are close together (massed practice). On a tracking task, for example, subjects resting between practice trials reach higher asymptotic levels of performance than subjects who go immediately from one practice trial to

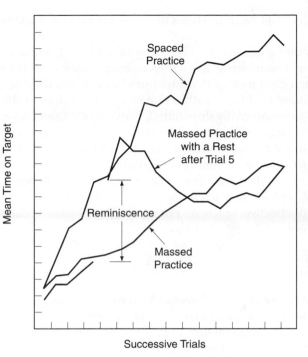

FIGURE 6–2 There were three groups of subjects in this experiment, which measured ability to track a rotating disk with a stylus. One group received distributed practice, another received massed practice, and a third group was first given massed practice, then a rest period, and then massed practice again. Clearly, the group receiving distributed practice performed much better than the other two groups. The vast improvement of the massed practice and rest group following the rest is an example of the reminiscence effect. (From *Principles of General Psychology*, 3rd ed., p. 290, by G. A. Kimble & N. Garmezy, 1968, New York: The Ronald Press Co. Copyright © 1968.)

the next. Figure 6–2 shows the difference in performance under massed and distributed practice conditions.

Although contemporary researchers may not agree with Hull's explanation, the effect remains robust. In a meta-analytical review of studies in verbal learning, Cepeda, Pashler, Vul, Wixted, and Rohrer (2006) examined 317 experiments and concluded that all demonstrated superiority of distributed practice over massed practice.

Postulate 9: The Learned Response of Not Responding   Fatigue being a negative drive state, it follows that not responding is reinforcing. Not responding allows I_R to dissipate, thereby reducing the negative drive of fatigue. The learned response of not responding is called **conditioned inhibition** ($_sI_R$). Both I_R and $_sI_R$ operate against the elicitation of a learned response and are therefore subtracted from reaction potential ($_sE_R$). When I_R and $_sI_R$ are subtracted from $_sE_R$, **effective reaction potential** ($_s\overline{E}_R$) is the result.

$$\text{Effective reaction potential} = {_s\overline{E}_R} = {_sH_R} \times D - (I_R + {_sI_R})$$

Postulate 10: Factors Tending to Inhibit a Learned Response Change from Moment to Moment   According to Hull, there is an "inhibitory potentiality," which varies from moment to moment and operates against the elicitation of a learned response. This "inhibitory potentiality" is called the **oscillation effect** ($_sO_R$).

The oscillation effect is the "wild card" in Hull's theory—it is his way of taking into consideration the probabilistic nature of predictions concerning behavior. There is, he said, a factor operating against the elicitation of a learned response, whose effect varies from moment to moment but always operates within a certain range of values; that is, although the range of the inhibitory factor is set, the value that may be manifested at any time could vary within that range. The values of this inhibitory factor are assumed to be normally distributed, with middle values most likely to occur. If, by chance, a large inhibitory value does occur, it considerably reduces the chance that a learned response will be made. This oscillation effect explains why a learned response may be elicited on one trial but not on the next. Predictions concerning behavior based on the value of $_s\bar{E}_R$ will always be influenced by the fluctuating values of $_sO_R$ and will thus always be probabilistic in nature. The $_sO_R$ must be subtracted from effective reaction potential ($_s\bar{E}_R$), which creates **momentary effective reaction potential ($_s\dot{\bar{E}}_R$).** Thus we have

$$\begin{array}{c}\text{Momentary effective}\\ \text{reaction potential}\end{array} = {}_s\dot{\bar{E}}_R = [{}_sH_R \times D - (I_R + {}_sI_R)] - {}_sO_R$$

Postulate 11: Momentary Effective Reaction Potential Must Exceed a Certain Value before a Learned Response Can Occur   The value that $_s\dot{\bar{E}}_R$ must exceed before a conditioned response can occur is called the **reaction threshold ($_sL_R$).** Therefore, a learned response will be emitted only if $_s\dot{\bar{E}}_R$ is greater than $_sL_R$.

Postulate 12: The Probability That a Learned Response Will Be Made Is a Combined Function of $_s\dot{\bar{E}}_R$, $_sO_R$, and $_sL_R$ In the early stages of training, that is, after only a few reinforced trials, $_sE_R$ will be very close to $_sL_R$, and therefore, because of the effects of $_sO_R$, a conditioned response will be elicited on some trials but not on others. The reason is that on some trials the value of $_sO_R$ subtracted from $_sE_R$ will be large enough to reduce $_s\bar{E}_R$ to a value below $_sL_R$. As training continues, subtracting $_sO_R$ from $_sE_R$ will have less and less of an effect because the value of $_s\bar{E}_R$ will become much larger than the value of $_sL_R$. Even after considerable training, however, it is still possible for $_sO_R$ to assume a large value, thereby preventing the occurrence of a conditioned response.

Postulate 13: The Greater the Value of $_s\dot{\bar{E}}_R$, the Shorter Will Be the Latency between S and R   Latency ($_st_R$) is the time between the presentation of a stimulus to the organism and its learned response. This postulate simply states that the reaction time between the onset of a stimulus and the elicitation of a learned response goes down as the value of $_s\dot{\bar{E}}_R$ goes up.

Postulate 14: The Value of $_s\dot{\bar{E}}_R$ Will Determine Resistance to Extinction   The value of $_s\dot{\bar{E}}_R$ at the end of training determines resistance to extinction, that is, how many nonreinforced responses will need to be made before extinction occurs. The greater the value of $_s\dot{\bar{E}}_R$, the greater the number of nonreinforced responses that have to be made before extinction takes place. Hull used n to symbolize the number of nonreinforced trials that occurred before extinction resulted.

Postulate 15: The Amplitude of a Conditioned Response Varies Directly with $_s\dot{\bar{E}}_R$
Some learned responses occur in degrees, for example, salivation or the galvanic skin response (GSR). When the conditioned response is one that can occur in degrees, its magnitude will be directly related to the size of $_s\dot{\bar{E}}_R$, the momentary effective reaction potential. Hull used A to symbolize response amplitude.

Postulate 16: When Two or More Incompatible Responses Tend to Be Elicited in the Same Situation, the One with the Greatest $_s\bar{E}_R$ Will Occur This postulate seems self-explanatory.

Summary of the Symbols Used in Hull's Theory

D = drive

$_sH_R$ = habit strength

$_sE_R$ = reaction potential = $_sH_R \times D$

I_R = reactive inhibition

$_sI_R$ = conditioned inhibition

$_s\bar{E}_R$ = effective reaction potential = $_sH_R \times D - (I_R + {_sI_R})$

$_sO_R$ = oscillation effect

$_s\dot{\bar{E}}_R$ = momentary effective reaction potential = $_s\bar{E}_R - {_sO_R}$

$\quad = [_sH_R \times D - (I_R + {_sI_R})] - {_sO_R}$

$_sL_R$ = the value that $_s\bar{E}_R$ must exceed before a learned response can occur

$_st_R$ = reaction time

p = response probability

n = trials to extinction

A = response amplitude

MAJOR DIFFERENCES BETWEEN HULL'S 1943 AND 1952 THEORIES

Incentive Motivation (K)

In the 1943 version of his theory, Hull treated the magnitude of reinforcement as a learning variable: The greater the amount of reinforcement, the greater the amount of drive reduction, and thus the greater the increase in $_sH_R$. Research showed this notion to be unsatisfactory. Experiments indicated that performance was dramatically altered as the size of reinforcement was varied *after* learning was complete. For example, when an animal trained to run a straight runway for a small reinforcer was switched to a larger reinforcer, its running speed suddenly went up. When an animal trained on a large reinforcer was shifted to a smaller reinforcer, its running speed went down. Crespi (1942, 1944) and Zeaman (1949) were two early experimenters who

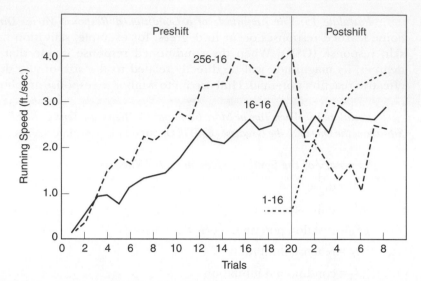

FIGURE 6–3   The results show that when animals are trained on a large reinforcer (256 pellets of food) and are then switched to a relatively small reinforcer (16 pellets of food), performance drops off rapidly. Likewise, when animals are trained on a small reinforcer (1 pellet of food) and then are switched to a relatively large reinforcer (16 pellets of food), performance improves rapidly. (From *Theory of Motivation*, p. 293, after Crespi, 1942, by R. C. Bolles, 1975, New York: Harper & Row: Copyright © 1967, 1975 by R. C. Bolles. Reprinted by permission of Harper & Row, Publishers, Inc.)

found that performance changed radically when the magnitude of reinforcement was changed. The results of Crespi's (1942) experiment are shown in Figure 6–3.

The changes in performance following a change in magnitude of reinforcement could not be explained in terms of changes in $_sH_R$ because they were too rapid. Moreover, $_sH_R$ was thought to be fairly permanent. Unless one or more factors operated against $_sH_R$, it would not decrease in value. Results like those found by Crespi and Zeaman led Hull to reach the conclusion that organisms learn as rapidly for a small incentive as they do for a large one, but they *perform* differently as the size of the incentive (K) varies. The rapid change in performance following a change in reinforcement size is referred to as the **Crespi effect,** after the man who first observed it.

Stimulus-Intensity Dynamism

According to Hull, **stimulus-intensity dynamism (V)** is an intervening variable that varies along with the intensity of the external stimulus (S). Stated simply, stimulus-intensity dynamism indicates that the greater the intensity of a stimulus, the greater the probability that a learned response will be elicited. Thus, we must revise Hull's earlier formula for momentary reaction potential as follows:

$$_s\dot{\bar{E}}_R = [_sH_R \times D \times V \times K - (I_R + {_sI_R})] - {_sO_R}$$

It is interesting to note that because $_sH_R$, D, V, and K are multiplied together, if any one had a value of zero, reaction potential would be zero. For example, there could have been many reinforced pairings between S and R ($_sH_R$), but if drive is zero, reinforcement is absent, or the organism cannot detect the stimulus, a learned response will not occur.

Change from Drive Reduction to Drive Stimulus Reduction

Originally, Hull had a drive reduction theory of learning, but later he revised it to a **drive stimulus reduction** theory of learning. One reason for the change was the realization that if a thirsty animal is given water as a reinforcer for performing some act, it takes a considerable amount of time for the thirst drive to be satisfied by the water. The water goes into the mouth, the throat, the stomach, and eventually the blood. The effects of ingesting water must ultimately reach the brain, and finally the thirst drive will be reduced. Hull concluded that the drive reduction was too far removed from the presentation of the reinforcer to explain how learning could take place. What was needed to explain learning was something that occurred soon after the presentation of a reinforcer, and that something was the reduction of **drive stimuli (S_D).** As mentioned earlier in this chapter, drive stimuli for the thirst drive include dryness in the mouth and parched lips. Water almost immediately reduces such stimulation, and thus Hull had the mechanism he needed for explaining learning.

A second reason for changing from a drive reduction theory to a drive stimulus reduction theory was provided by Sheffield and Roby (1950), who found that hungry rats were reinforced by nonnutritive saccharine, which could not possibly have reduced the hunger drive. About this research Hull (1952) said,

> Sheffield and Roby appear to have presented a critical case in point. . . . They showed that hungry albino rats are reinforced by water sweetened by saccharine which presumably is not at all nourishing (i.e., it does not reduce the need in the least). It may very well be that the ingestion of saccharine-sweetened water reduces hunger tension S_D for a brief period sufficient for a mild reinforcement, much as the tightening of the belt is said to do in hungry men, thus reinforcing that act. (p. 153)

Fractional Antedating Goal Response

You will recall that when a neutral stimulus is consistently paired with primary reinforcement, it takes on reinforcing properties of its own; that is, it becomes a secondary reinforcer. The concept of secondary reinforcement is vital in understanding the operations of the **fractional antedating goal response (r_G),** which is one of Hull's most important concepts.

Let us suppose we are training a rat to solve a multiple-component maze. We place the animal in the start box and eventually it reaches the goal box, where it is reinforced with food, a primary reinforcer. All the stimuli in the goal box that were experienced just prior to primary reinforcement (food) will, therefore, through the process of classical conditioning, become secondary reinforcers. Moreover, following classical conditioning principles, the rat will develop a conditioned response that closely resembles the unconditioned response. In our present example, the unconditioned response is that of salivation, chewing, and licking, caused by presenting food to a hungry animal. The conditioned response, also involving salivation, chewing, or

Before Pairing

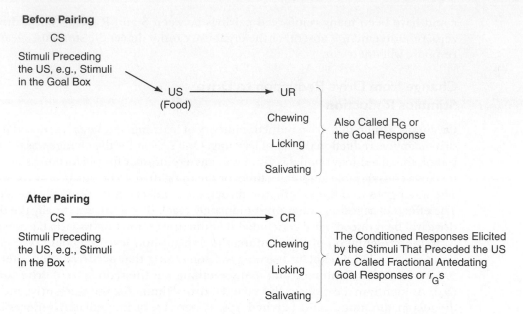

FIGURE 6–4　The development of the fractional antedating goal response (r_G).

licking, will be elicited by the various stimuli in the goal box as the rat approaches the food. The fractional antedating goal response is the conditioned response to stimuli, experienced prior to the ingestion of food. The development of r_G is shown in Figure 6–4.

In the chapter on Pavlov, we learn that neutral stimuli paired with secondary reinforcers come to have reinforcing properties of their own through the process of higher-order conditioning (a process similar to associative shifting). When applied to maze learning, this process causes stimuli prior to those occurring in the goal box to also become reinforcers, and then the stimuli before them, and so on. Gradually the process works backward until even the stimuli in the start box come to have reinforcing properties. When these previously neutral stimuli become secondary reinforcers, they perform two very important functions: (1) They reinforce the overt responses that bring the organism into contact with them, and (2) they elicit r_Gs.

Now as the animal leaves the start box, it comes into contact with a variety of stimuli, some with reinforcing properties, others without reinforcing properties. Those responses that bring the animal into close proximity to reinforcing stimuli will tend to be repeated, and other responses will extinguish. In this manner the animal learns to make the correct turns in the maze. *Thus, maze learning is thought to involve both classical and instrumental conditioning.* Classical conditioning produces the secondary reinforcers and r_Gs; instrumental conditioning produces the appropriate motor responses that bring the animal into proximity with both the primary and secondary reinforcers. Thus far, the explanation for maze learning is essentially the same as Skinner's explanation of chaining (see Chapter 5); but as we see next, Hull assigned the r_G a prominent role in the learning of chained responses.

Two characteristics of the r_G must be noted. First, the r_G must always be some fraction of the goal response (R_G). If the goal response involves eating, the r_G will be minute chewing movements and perhaps salivation. Second, and more important, *the r_G produces stimulation.* Overt responding causes the kinesthetic receptors in the muscles, tendons, and joints to fire, causing what Guthrie (see Chapter 8) called movement-produced stimuli. More technically, the firing of these kinesthetic receptors causes **proprioceptive stimuli.** Like any other response, the r_G is associated with stimulation. The proprioceptive stimulation caused by the r_G is symbolized s_G. The r_G and s_G are inseparable because whenever r_G occurs, so does s_G. Perhaps the most important aspect of the r_G is the fact that it produces s_G.

After a considerable amount of maze learning has taken place, the situation that emerges is as follows: The stimuli in the start box will become signals, or S^Ds, for leaving the start box because leaving it brings the animal into proximity with secondary reinforcers. A secondary reinforcer in this situation does three things: It reinforces the response the animal just made; it acts as an S^D for the next overt response, and it elicits an r_G. When the r_G is elicited, it automatically produces an s_G. The main function of the s_G is to elicit the next overt response. Thus, both the secondary reinforcers, which are external, and the s_Gs, which are internal, tend to elicit overt responses. The response that exposes the animal to the next secondary reinforcer most rapidly will be the one that finally becomes associated with the s_G. When the next secondary reinforcer is experienced, it reinforces the overt response made prior to it, and it elicits the next r_G. When the r_G is elicited, it triggers the next s_G, which triggers the next overt response, and so on. The process continues in this manner all the way to the goal box. The chaining process, as Hull saw it, is diagrammed in Figure 6–5. An example of chaining on the human level is shown in Figure 6–6.

It should be clear that Hull really had two explanations for chaining that he used simultaneously. One explanation, which emphasized external stimuli, was very much like Skinner's explanation of chaining. The other, which emphasized internal events, was very much like Guthrie's explanation of chaining, as we see in Chapter 8. Hull, then, combined the notions of Skinner and Guthrie and said that chained

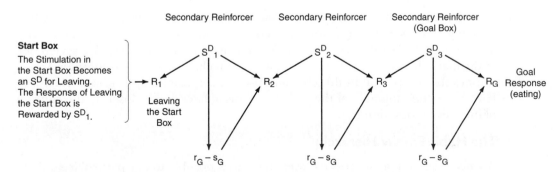

FIGURE 6–5 How S^Ds' overt responses (R), and the r_G-s_G mechanism combine to produce a chained response.

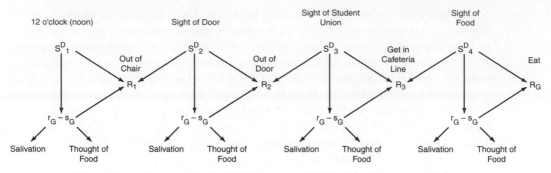

FIGURE 6–6   An example of chaining on the human level.

behavior is a function of either internal or external cues or, more probably, of both internal and external cues.

One might ask why it is important to postulate the r_G-s_G mechanism if Skinner's explanation of chaining is adequate. The answer is that the r_G-s_G mechanism is thought to be important because of the other things related to it. For example, the r_G-s_G mechanism can be thought of as the "mental" component of chaining. Generally speaking, the r_G-s_G concept provides an objective means of investigating thought processes. In the example in Figure 6–6, one can say that the time (noon) acted as an S^D, which triggered an r_G, which triggered the thought of food. Or one can say that the "expectation" of food was triggered, which keeps the person moving toward the food goal. Clearly, at this point, the behavioristic point of view and the cognitive point of view come very close together. In fact, it can be said that the main value of the proposed r_G-s_G is opening up research in the area of cognition. In this regard, Hull (1952) said,

> Further study of this major automatic device presumably will lead to the detailed behavioral understanding of thought and reasoning, which constitute the highest attainment of organic evolution. Indeed, the r_G-s_G mechanism leads in a strictly logical manner into what was formally regarded as the very heart of the psychic: interest, planning, foresight, foreknowledge, expectancy, purpose, and so on. (p. 350)

Thus Hull, in the tradition of Watson, Pavlov, and Guthrie, concluded that thinking consists of a minute internal representation of things that happen overtly. The "thought" of eating is nothing more than an s_G elicited by an r_G. We review one of the many theoretical extensions of the r_G-s_G mechanism when we consider Abram Amsel's theory later on in this chapter. Also, we see that Spence, who worked with Hull on the development of the r_G-s_G mechanism, later tied it closely to the concept of incentive motivation (K).

The Habit Family Hierarchy

Because there are many possible overt responses possible to any particular s_G, there are many alternative ways of reaching a goal. However, the route that is most likely is the one that brings the animal into proximity of reinforcement most rapidly. This fact was originally referred to as the "goal-gradient hypothesis" in Hull's early writings, but it appeared as a corollary to one of his postulates in 1952. The corollary concerned the delay of reinforcement (J) and read, "The greater the delay in reinforcement of a link within a given behavior chain, the weaker will be the resulting reaction potential of the link in question to the stimulus traces present at the time" (Hull, 1952, p. 126).

Here Hull is talking about a single link in a behavioral chain, but the same idea can be generalized to whole behavioral chains. Whether one is talking about a single response or a series of responses, delay of reinforcement has a deleterious effect on reaction potential. Likewise, either individual responses or chains of responses that are followed rapidly by reinforcement have relatively higher values of $_sE_R$ and are more likely to occur than those responses or behavioral chains with a longer delay between their occurrence and reinforcement.

The most direct route through a maze, whether a T-maze or a more complicated maze, has the greatest amount of $_sE_R$ because it results in less delay of reinforcement and also because there is less reactive and conditioned inhibition to be subtracted from $_sE_R$. But the shortest route through a maze is only one of many possible routes. The **habit family hierarchy** simply refers to the fact that in any learning situation, many responses are possible, and the one that is most likely is the one that brings about reinforcement most rapidly and with the least amount of effort. If that particular way is blocked, the animal will prefer the next shortest route, and if that is blocked, it will go to the third route, and so on.

There is a close relationship between the habit family hierarchy and how the fractional antedating goal response (r_G) and the stimulus to which it gives rise (s_G) operate in chaining. We noted earlier that any number of overt responses can follow the occurrence of an s_G. Some of these responses will result immediately in exposure to a secondary reinforcer, and others will not. Eventually the responses that bring the animal into contact with the secondary reinforcers most rapidly will be the ones made because they will have the highest values of $_sE_R$. Remember, the greater the delay of reinforcement (J), the lower the value of $_sE_R$. Thus, there is a hierarchy of possible responses associated with every s_G, and therefore there are a large number of routes through a maze. If the route consisting of the responses with the highest value of $_sE_R$ is blocked, the next one in the hierarchy will be chosen, and so on. The situation can be diagrammed as follows:

Hull's Final System Summarized

There are three kinds of variables in Hull's theory:

1. Independent variables, which are stimulus events systematically manipulated by the experimenter.
2. Intervening variables, which are processes thought to be taking place within the organism but are not directly observable. All the intervening variables in Hull's system are operationally defined (see Chapter 2).
3. Dependent variables, which are some aspect of behavior that is measured by the experimenter in order to determine whether the independent variables had any effect.

Figure 6–7 summarizes Hull's theory as it appeared in 1952. It should be noted that Hull's 1952 theory comprised seventeen postulates and 133 theorems. Therefore, the review of Hull in this chapter should be regarded as a brief introduction to a theory known for its thoroughness and complexity.

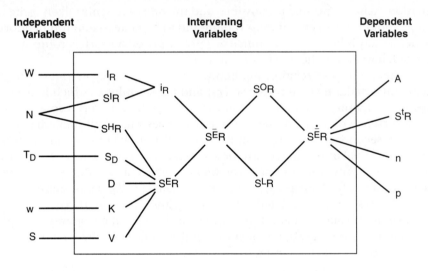

W = Work	V = Stimulus Strength	
N = Number of Prior Reinforcements	S^{E}R = Reaction Potential	
T$_D$ = Total Drive	S$\bar{^E}$R = Effective Reaction Potential	
w = Amount of Reinforcement	S^{O}R = Behavioral Oscillation	
S = Stimulus Intensity	S^{L}R = Response Threshold	
I$_R$ = Reactive Inhibition	S$\dot{\bar{^E}}$R = Momentary Effective Reaction Potential	
S^{I}R = Conditioned Inhibition	A = Response Amplitude	
i$_R$ = Combined Inhibitory Potential	S^{t}R = Response Latency	
S^{H}R = Habit Strength	n = Trials to Extinction	
S$_D$ = Drive Stimulus	p = Probability of a Response	
D = Drive		
K = Incentive Motivation		

FIGURE 6–7   Summary of Hull's theory of learning after 1952.

HULL ON EDUCATION

Although Hull was careful to restrict his theory and its implications to laboratory rats in carefully controlled experiments, we take the liberty of exploring the implications of Hull's theory for education. Hull's was a drive reduction, or a drive-stimulus reduction, theory of learning. As for the issues of specifiability of objectives, orderliness of the classrooms, and proceeding from the simple to the complex, Hull is in agreement with Thorndike. Learning for him, however, involves a reducible drive. It is hard to imagine how the reduction of a primary drive can play a part in classroom learning; however, some of Hull's followers (e.g., Janet Taylor Spence) have emphasized anxiety as a drive in human learning. From this line of reasoning, it follows that encouraging some anxiety in students that could subsequently be reduced by success is a necessary condition for classroom learning. Too little anxiety results in no learning (because there is no drive to be reduced), and too much anxiety is disruptive. Therefore, students who are mildly anxious are in the best position to learn and are therefore easiest to teach.

Practice would be carefully distributed so that inhibition would not be built up. The Hullian teacher would intersperse the topics to be taught so that the learner would not build up fatigue that interferes with learning. Likewise, topics would be arranged so that those that are maximally dissimilar follow one another. For example, one reasonable sequence of subjects might be math, physical education, English, art, and history.

Miller and Dollard (1941) summarized Hull's theory as it applies to education:

Drive:	The learner must want something.
Cue:	The learner must attend to something.
Response:	The learner must do something.
Reinforcement:	The learner's response must get him or her something he or she wants.

Spence's revision of Hull's theory suggested that students learn what they do. Thus, Spence was a contiguity theorist. His position is similar to that of Guthrie (Chapter 8). For Spence, incentives are important because they motivate students to translate what is learned into behavior. By relating incentives (reinforcers) to performance instead of to learning, Spence's position is close to the positions of Tolman (Chapter 12) and Bandura (Chapter 13).

EVALUATION OF HULL'S THEORY

Contributions

Hull's learning theory had an enormous impact on psychology. Marx and Cronan-Hillix (1987) put the matter aptly:

> Hull's most important contribution to psychology was his demonstration of the value of setting one's sights upon the ultimate goal of a thoroughly scientific and systematic behavior theory. He lived his own scientific life in pursuit of that goal, and thereby

influenced even those who disagreed most vehemently with the details of his work. Few psychologists have had so great an effect on the professional motivation of so many researchers. He popularized the strictly objective behavioristic approach as it had never been popularized previously. (p. 326)

Hull's theory addresses a vast number of behavioral as well as cognitive phenomena. The scope of the theory, coupled with precise definitions of variables, invited empirical scrutiny. Rashotte and Amsel (1999) say,

> Hull's plan for an S-R behaviorism was very ambitious. It aspired to predict the behavior of individuals in isolation, as well as in group settings. It aspired to conceptualize the bases for adaptive behavior in a broad sense, including certain cognitive processes and the performance differences between species and individuals. It aspired to be logically rigorous and mathematical as a way of ensuring that its assumptions and predictions were clear and available for comparison with competing theories. (pp. 124–125)

In Chapter 2 we saw that Popper's (1963) most important criterion for a scientific theory was that it made specific and testable predictions. Hull's is the first theory we encounter that meets Popper's criterion. Hull's insistence on precise definitions of concepts and exacting mathematical statements relating his concepts to behavior provided clear directions for testing the theory. For Hull, reinforcement hinged on the reduction of drive or drive stimuli produced by conditions of physiological need. The drive reduction hypothesis was the first attempt to break from the imprecise definitions of satisfiers/reinforcers that characterized both Thorndike's and Skinner's theories. Hull was also the first to make precise predictions about joint effects of learning and drive on behavior and about the effects of fatigue (via reactive and conditioned inhibition).

Criticisms

In spite of its overwhelming influence, Hull's theory did have its problems. It was criticized for being of little value in explaining behavior beyond the laboratory; for insisting too much that all concepts of interest be operationally defined; and, most important, for making inconsistent predictions. In his review of the final version of Hull's theory (1952), Hill (1990) says,

> Suppose we want to know how many successive nonreinforced trials it would take to produce complete extinction. One approach would be to use Postulate 16, which translates excitatory potential directly into trials to extinction. A second approach would be to use Postulate 9 to calculate the amounts of reactive inhibition and subtract it from excitatory potential. A third would be to note (Postulate 7) that when the amount of reward is zero, the value of K is also zero, which makes excitatory potential zero regardless of the values of the other intervening variables. It turns out that these three approaches, to the extent that they give precise answers at all, give conflicting ones. . . . When a theory makes incorrect predictions, it can be modified, as Hull intended that his theory should be. When a theory does not deal with a given issue at all, we can accept this limitation in its scope and hope that some day it may be expanded to include the neglected topic. However, when a theory is internally inconsistent, so that it

makes conflicting predictions about a given issue, its worth as a rigorous theory is seriously compromised. (pp. 63–64)

Despite his apparent willingness to subject his theory to critical tests, Koch (1954) suggested that Hull did not revise the theory enough in the face of problematic data and may have ignored many contradictory results. Later critics echoed that theme. Malone (1991), for example, portrays Hull as a researcher who used the power of his research facilities and talented students and his influence on journal editors to attack any opponents thus rendering "the self-correcting system more a self-perpetuating system!" (p. 165).

Even if such protective practices existed, subsequent research demonstrated that reinforcement occurred with or without reduction of drives or drive stimuli, and, as we discuss later in this chapter, the mathematical form of the theory was challenged by Kenneth Spence. One interesting suggestion is that Hull approached theory building backward. Shepard (1992) wrote,

> Rather than deducing empirically testable regularities from compelling first principles, Hull and Spence plotted empirically measured dependent variables . . . against experimentally manipulated independent variables . . . , searched for a mathematical function the shape of which seemed to approximate that of the plotted points, and then put forward the chosen function as a "postulate" of their theory. As George Miller once remarked . . . , Hull and his coworkers began by assuming what they should have ended up by deriving. (p. 419)

Yet with all its faults, Hull's theory was among the most heuristic in psychology's history. In addition to stimulating an unprecedented number of experiments, Hull's explanations of reinforcement, drive, extinction, and generalization have become standard frames of reference in discussions of these concepts today.

After Hull's death, the main spokesperson for the Hullian point of view was Kenneth W. Spence, who expanded and significantly modified Hull's theory (see Spence, 1956, 1960). Other important followers of Hull include Neal E. Miller, who extended Hull's theory into the areas of personality, conflict, social behavior, and psychotherapy (e.g., Dollard & Miller, 1950; Miller & Dollard, 1941); Robert R. Sears, who translated a number of Freudian concepts into Hullian terms and who also worked extensively in experimental child psychology (e.g., Sears, 1944; Sears, Whiting, Nowlis, & Sears, 1953); and O. Hobart Mowrer, who followed many of Hull's ideas while studying such areas as personality dynamics and the special characteristics of learning when fear or anxiety is involved. It is to Mowrer's work that we turn next.

O. HOBART MOWRER

O. Hobart Mowrer (1907–1982) was born in Unionville, Missouri, and received his Ph.D. from Johns Hopkins in 1932. During most of the 1930s, Mowrer was at Yale University, first as a postdoctoral fellow and then as an instructor of psychology. While at Yale, Mowrer was strongly influenced by Hull. In 1940, Mowrer joined the Harvard School of Education and remained there until 1948; he then moved to the University of Illinois (Urbana), where he stayed for the rest of his professional career.

The Problem of Avoidance Conditioning   Mowrer's career as a learning theorist began with his efforts to solve the problem that avoidance learning posed for Hullian theory. If an apparatus is arranged so that an organism receives an electric shock until it performs a specified response, it will quickly learn to make that response when it is shocked. Such a procedure is called **escape conditioning,** and it is diagrammed below:

$$\text{pain} \longrightarrow \text{R} \longrightarrow \text{escape from pain}$$
$$\text{(electric shock)} \qquad \text{(response)} \qquad \text{(reinforcement)}$$

Escape conditioning is easily handled by Hullian theory by assuming that the response is learned because it is followed by drive (pain) reduction. However, **avoidance conditioning** is not so easily explained by Hullian theory. With avoidance conditioning, a signal, such as a light, reliably precedes the onset of an aversive stimulus, such as an electric shock. Other than the presence of the signal that precedes the shock, the procedure is the same as for escape conditioning. The procedure used in avoidance conditioning is as follows:

$$\text{signal} \longrightarrow \text{pain} \longrightarrow \text{R} \longrightarrow \text{escape from pain}$$
$$\text{(light)} \qquad \text{(electric shock)} \qquad \text{(response)} \qquad \text{(reinforcement)}$$

With avoidance conditioning, the organism gradually learns to make the appropriate response when the signal light comes on, thus *avoiding* the shock. Furthermore, this avoidance response is maintained almost indefinitely, even though the shock itself is no longer experienced. Avoidance conditioning posed a problem for the Hullians because it was not clear what was reinforcing the avoidance response. In other words, what drive does such a response reduce? In his effort to solve this problem, Mowrer proposed a two-factor theory of learning.

O. Hobart Mowrer. (Courtesy of Archives of the History of American Psychology, The University of Akron.)

Mowrer's Two-Factor Theory of Learning Mowrer noted that the early stages of avoidance conditioning are arranged so that Pavlovian or classical conditioning occurs. The signal acts as a conditioned stimulus (CS) and the electric shock acts as an unconditioned stimulus (US), which elicits, among other things, fear. Eventually, the CS, through its pairings with the US, by itself elicits a response similar to the UR, that is, fear. Now when the light comes on, the organism experiences fear. Thus the first factor in Mowrer's **two-factor theory** is simply classical or Pavlovian conditioning. Mowrer called such conditioning **sign learning** because it explains how previously neutral stimuli, through their association with certain USs, become signs of danger and thus elicit fear.

Mowrer called the second factor in this two-factor theory **solution learning,** and it is what Thorndike and Hull called instrumental conditioning or what Skinner called operant conditioning. Solution learning involves learning to perform those activities that will either terminate aversive stimuli or those negative emotions, such as fear, elicited by stimuli that have become signs of danger through classical conditioning.

Others, such as Skinner, recognized two kinds of learning (respondent and operant conditioning), but Mowrer's contribution was in showing how the two are interrelated. Mowrer (1956) summarized his position as follows:

> Basically the two-factor, or two-process, hypothesis holds that *habits* are learned on the basis of the reinforcement provided by reward, or drive reduction, and that *fears* are learned (conditioned) on the basis of contiguous occurrence of a signal and punishment, in the sense of drive induction. Pavlov had held that *all* learning is a matter of conditioning or stimulus contiguity, while Thorndike and Hull had stressed habit formation on the basis of reward. Two-factor theorists, by contrast, have held that it is not here a matter of either-or but of *both:* both sign learning (conditioning) and solution learning (habit formation). (p. 114)

Thus Mowrer found the drive that the Hullians were looking for to explain avoidance conditioning, and that drive was conditioned fear. Mowrer believed that the onset of a CS associated with pain motivates an avoidance response, which is reinforced by the termination of the CS.

Decremental and Incremental Reinforcement   In 1960, Mowrer extended his theory to show how emotions other than fear become associated with various CSs. Which emotion becomes associated with a CS depends on the kind of US involved and at what time the CS is presented. In his analysis, Mowrer first distinguished between USs that produce an increment in drive, for example, shock, and those that produce a decrement in drive, for example, food. The latter are called **decremental reinforcers** because they reduce a drive, in this case hunger. The former are called **incremental reinforcers** because they produce or increase drive. For each of the two kinds of USs, it is possible to present a CS at its onset or at its termination. If a CS is presented prior to the onset of shock, it will come to elicit the emotion of fear. If a CS is presented prior to the termination of shock, it will come to elicit the emotion of relief. If a CS is presented prior to the presentation of food, it will come to elicit the emotion of hope. If a CS is presented prior to the removal of food, it will come to elicit the emotion of disappointment. The two kinds of USs and the emotions conditioned by various CS-US relationships are shown in Figure 6–8.

By suggesting that important learning can occur as the result of both drive induction (onset) as well as drive reduction (termination), Mowrer moved away from the Hullian tradition, which stressed drive reduction. As we discuss in Mowrer's final position, he moved even further away from Hullian theory.

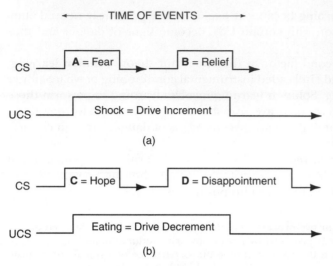

←——— TIME OF EVENTS ———→

CS ———— | **A** = Fear | ——→ | **B** = Relief | ——→

UCS ———— | Shock = Drive Increment | ——————→

(a)

CS ———— | **C** = Hope | ——→ | **D** = Disappointment | ——→

UCS ———— | Eating = Drive Decrement | ——————→

(b)

FIGURE 6–8 The emotion that becomes associated with a CS depends on which kind of US the CS is associated with and whether the CS is associated with the onset or termination of the US. Under the contingencies depicted, CS A will come to elicit fear, CS B will come to elicit relief, CS C will come to elicit hope, and CS D will come to elicit disappointment. BOWER, GORDON H.; HILGARD, ERNEST R., THEORIES OF LEARNING, 5th, © 1981. Electronically reproduced by permission of Pearson Education, In., Upper Saddle River, New Jersey.

All Learning Is Sign Learning   In the final version of Mowrer's (1960) theory, all learning was considered sign learning. Mowrer had already shown that external stimuli associated with positive USs, such as the termination of pain or the presentation of food, come to elicit the emotions of relief and hope, respectively. Likewise, external stimuli associated with negative USs, such as the onset of pain or the removal of food, come to elicit the emotions of fear and disappointment, respectively. Why, Mowrer asked, should not the same principles hold true for internal stimuli?

Internal body reactions, for example, proprioceptive stimuli caused by the firing of the kinesthetic receptors, always precede overt responses. When an organism is attempting to solve a problem, such as learning to escape from an aversive stimulus, learning to ride a bicycle, learning to speak a language, or learning to play tennis, certain overt responses lead to success, and others lead to failure. The body sensations that precede successful overt responses come to elicit hope for the same reasons that external stimuli elicit hope. The body sensations that precede unsuccessful or punished overt responses come to elicit fear, again, for the same reasons that external stimuli come to elicit fear. In this way, body sensations provide an internal guidance system in the sense that certain sensations signal impending failure, thus necessitating a behavioral correction, whereas other body sensations provide information that things are being done correctly and success is imminent. Thus, in Mowrer's final position, even solution learning, previously thought to be learned through drive reduction, was seen as governed by a sign learned because of its association with positive and negative outcomes. In other words, all learning was considered sign learning. Another way of phrasing Mowrer's final position is to say that organisms learn expectancies. That is, some signs, both external and internal, elicit the expectation of such things as pain or failure, whereas others elicit the expectation of such things as pleasure or success.

In the final version of Mowrer's theory, emotions were of central importance. Emotions elicited by both internal and external stimuli provide the primary guidance system for behavior. This emphasis on emotions was a major departure from traditional learning theory, but Mowrer (1960) felt no need to apologize for it:

> There has been a widespread tendency in Western civilization to look upon "the emotions" with a certain distrust and contempt and to elevate "the intellect" (reason, logic) high above them. If the present analysis is sound, the emotions are of quite extraordinary importance in the total economy of living organisms and do not at all deserve being put into opposition with "intelligence." The emotions are, it seems, themselves a high order of intelligence. (p. 308)

With his contention that all learning is sign learning, Mowrer created an essentially cognitive theory of learning. In particular, there is great similarity between Mowrer's final theory and Edward Tolman's cognitive theory, which is reviewed in Chapter 12.

KENNETH W. SPENCE

Although Hull had many ardent disciples, it was Kenneth W. Spence who became the major spokesperson for Hullian theory after Hull's death. For many years, Hull and Spence had a reciprocal influence on each other. It is clear that Hull had a profound influence on Spence, but it is also clear that Spence influenced Hull's evolving theory in several important ways. The two worked so closely together that it is not uncommon for their combined efforts to be referred to as the Hull-Spence theory of learning. In the end, however, Spence made several radical changes in the traditional Hullian theory, and in so doing he created a learning theory that was essentially his own.

Spence was born in Chicago on May 6, 1907, and died in Austin, Texas, in 1967. At the age of four, Spence moved to Montreal, Canada, where he remained until obtaining his B.A. degree in 1929 and his M.A. degree in 1930 from McGill University. Spence then moved to Yale, where he obtained his Ph.D. in 1933. After obtaining his doctorate, he remained at Yale as a research assistant and instructor until 1937. It was during his time at Yale that Spence came under the influence of Hull. Spence served on the faculty of the University of Virginia from 1937 to 1942, at which

Kenneth W. Spence. (Courtesy of Archives of the History of American Psychology—The University of Akron.)

point he moved to the University of Iowa. He remained there for twenty-six years, until 1964, when he moved to the University of Texas (Austin), where he remained until his premature death in 1967.

Spence made several contributions to learning theory, but we can summarize only what seem to be his more important ones here.

Discrimination Learning   In discrimination learning, an animal is typically presented with two stimuli and is reinforced for responding to one and not reinforced for responding to the other. It was within the area of discrimination learning that Spence defended Hull's theory against an attack by a group of cognitively oriented psychologists. This group contended that during discrimination learning animals learn principles (subjective strategies) rather than S-R associations, as Hull had maintained. We give more details of both the attack of the cognitive psychologists and Spence's reactions to it in Chapter 10, but in general here are the assumptions that Spence made about learning in a situation in which an organism must choose between two objects (Spence, 1936, 1937):

1. Habit strength ($_sH_R$) toward the stimulus that is reinforced increases with each reinforcement.
2. Inhibition (I_R and $_sI_R$) toward the stimulus that is not reinforced builds on each nonreinforced trial.
3. Both habit strength and inhibition generalize to stimuli that are similar to those that are reinforced and to those that are not reinforced.
4. The magnitude of generalized habit strength is greater than the magnitude of generalized inhibition.
5. Generalized habit strength and generalized inhibition combine algebraically.
6. Which stimulus is approached is determined by the algebraic summation of approach (habit strength) and avoidance (inhibition) tendencies.
7. When two stimuli are presented, the stimulus with the greatest net habit strength will be approached and responded to.

With these assumptions, Spence was able to use Hullian theory to explain phenomena that cognitive theorists offered as evidence against it. Not only did Spence's assumptions and the research they generated prevail against the arguments of the cognitive theorists but also they became the cornerstone of research on discrimination learning for many years.

Rejection of Reinforcement as a Necessary Condition for Instrumental Conditioning
The Hullians were having difficulties accounting for the results of **latent learning** experiments, which seemed to indicate that animals could learn without being reinforced. Thus, the term *latent learning* refers to learning that appears to take place in the absence of reinforcement. For example, Tolman and Honzik (1930) found that if rats were initially run through a maze without being reinforced in the goal box and were later reinforced for responding correctly, their performance rapidly

matched (or exceeded) that of rats that had been reinforced on every trial (see Chapter 12 for the details of this experiment). Tolman and his followers argued that such results indicated that learning occurred independent of reinforcement.

Spence replicated a number of these so-called latent learning experiments and confirmed Tolman's findings. For example, Spence and Lippitt (1940) ran rats that were neither hungry nor thirsty through a Y-maze, where water was consistently found in one arm of the Y and food in the other. After reaching one of the two goals, the rat was removed from the apparatus. The rats ran for several trials while satiated with both food and water. During the second phase of the experiment, half of the original group was deprived of food, and the other half was deprived of water. On the initial trial, the hungry rats went directly to the arm of the Y-maze where they had previously experienced food, and the thirsty rats went directly to the arm of the Y-maze where they had previously experienced water. The rats had obviously learned where the reinforcer appropriate to their drive state was located during the first phase of the experiment, but such learning could not have involved drive reduction because the animals were satiated at the time. Hull's explanation of these findings was that removing the animal from the apparatus following a goal response provides enough of a reinforcer for the animal to learn under the circumstances. The reader will recall that Hull believed that learning occurs at the same rate whether the size of the reinforcer (K) was large or small. Thus, according to Hull, even though the reinforcer in this situation was small, it was sufficient to cause the animals to learn where things were in the maze.

Spence agonized over Hull's interpretation of the latent learning experiments and eventually came up with his own explanation. Spence was not comfortable with Hull's assumption that in learning there is no difference between a very small reinforcer and a very large reinforcer, but there is a very important difference between a very small reinforcer and no reinforcer at all. Remember, for Hull, reinforcement was a necessary condition for learning, but *how much* reinforcement occurred was irrelevant.

In one sense, Spence's solution to the problem placed him in essential agreement with Guthrie's theory of learning (see Chapter 8) and in another sense, in agreement with Tolman's theory (see Chapter 12). Spence concluded that *instrumental conditioning occurs independent of reinforcement.* The animal learns a response simply by making it. Thus, as far as instrumental conditioning was concerned, Spence was not a reinforcement theorist (as Hull was); rather, he was a contiguity theorist (as Guthrie was). The law of contiguity is one of Aristotle's laws of association, which states that events become associated simply because they occur together. Spence (1960) summarized his position on instrumental conditioning as follows:

> The habit strength (H) of the instrumental response, it is important to note, is assumed to be a function of the number of occurrences of the response (N_R) in the situation and to be quite independent of the occurrence or non-occurrence of a reinforcer. Thus, if the response occurs there will be an increment in H regardless of whether a reinforcer does or does not result. This assumption, it is apparent, makes this formulation a contiguity and not a reinforcement theory. (p. 96)

It should be clear that Spence also accepted Aristotle's **law of frequency,** which states that the more often two events are experienced together, the stronger the association between them will become. We see in Chapter 8 that although Guthrie accepted Aristotle's **law of contiguity,** he did not accept his law of frequency.

Incentive Motivation   So, what function did reinforcement play in Spence's theory? According to Spence, reinforcement has an influence only through **incentive motivation (*K*).** Spence was largely responsible for Hull adding the concept of incentive motivation to his theory. In fact, it is widely believed that *K* was chosen as a symbol because it is the first letter in Spence's first name. It turns out, however, that Spence gave *K* a much more prominent role in his own theory than Hull gave it in his theory. In fact, Hull seemed to have problems with *K* because it was not clear to what physiological process it was related. Most of Hull's concepts were thought to have some physiological basis. For example, habit strength is tied directly to drive or drive stimulus reduction, and inhibition is tied directly to fatigue. However, it was not clear to Hull what physiological process *K* was related to, and that was troublesome.

Spence solved the problem by relating *K* directly to the r_G-s_G mechanism. As we saw earlier in the chapter, the r_G-s_G mechanism works back through a maze and eventually guides the animal's behavior from the start box to the goal box. Spence added the concept of incentive to this automatic guiding process. According to Spence, the strength of r_G-s_G is determined by *K,* and the stronger the r_G-s_G, the greater the incentive to traverse the maze. Simply restated, the r_G-s_G mechanism creates in the animal the expectation of reinforcement, which motivates it to run, and the greater the expectation, the faster the animal will run. By discussing the r_G-s_G mechanism as a means of providing the animal with expectations, Spence moved Hull's behavioristic theory closer to Tolman's cognitive theory. However, it should be noted that although Spence discussed expectations, he did so in mechanistic and not mentalistic terms. In fact, Spence believed that the same laws that apply to overt S-R associations apply to the r_G-s_G mechanism.

For Spence, then, *K* is the energizer of learned behavior. The habit strength of an instrumental response develops in accordance with the laws of contiguity and frequency but independent of reinforcement. However, according to Spence, the r_G-s_G mechanism requires reinforcement for its development, and it is this mechanism that determines whether an organism will perform a learned response and, if so, with what degree of enthusiasm. And so Spence, like Mowrer before him, ended up with a two-factor theory. As we have seen, a two-factor theory postulates two different kinds of learning, each governed by a different set of principles. As far as instrumental conditioning was concerned, Spence was a contiguity theorist and not a reinforcement theorist. As far as classical conditioning was concerned (the process by which the r_G-s_G mechanism develops), he was a reinforcement theorist. In other words, Spence believed that instrumental behavior is learned without reinforcement, but reinforcement provides the incentive to perform what has been learned.

A Change in Hull's Basic Equation   As the reader will remember, Hull combined the major components of his theory as follows:

$$_s\bar{E}_R = D \times K \times {}_sH_R - (I_R + {}_sI_R)$$

As we saw earlier in the chapter, this equation means that if either D or K equals zero, a learned response will not be emitted, no matter how high the value of $_sH_R$. In other words, for Hull, no matter how many times an animal has been reinforced for performing a response in a given situation, it will not perform the response if the animal is not in a drive state. Likewise, even if the animal is in a high drive state, it will not perform a learned response if there is no reinforcement for doing so. Again, Spence felt that Hull's assumptions were untenable and revised Hull's equation to read,

$$_s\bar{E}_R = (D + K) \times {}_sH_R - I_N$$

Note that Spence added D and K together rather than multiplying them as Hull did. The major implication of Spence's revision is that a learned response may be given in a situation even if no drive is present. For example, if one has eaten frequently at 6:00 P.M. in a certain location and one is in that location at 6:00 P.M., one may have the urge to eat even if one is not hungry. According to Spence's equation, as long as K and $_sH_R$ have a value greater than zero, a learned response will be emitted even if no drive is present. Thus, organisms sometimes eat when they are not hungry, drink when they are not thirsty, and perhaps even engage in sexual activities when they are not sexually aroused simply because they have developed strong tendencies to perform these acts under certain circumstances. Likewise, animals, including humans, may go on working for reinforcers that are no longer needed to satisfy basic drives, such as when a person continues to work to accumulate money, even though that person has more than enough to satisfy his or her basic needs.

Another implication of Spence's revised equation is that as long as D and $_sH_R$ have a value above zero, an organism should go on making a learned response, even if K equals zero. In other words, an organism should go on making a learned response even if there is no reinforcement for doing so. How, then, does Spence explain extinction?

The Frustration-Competition Theory of Extinction   The astute reader may have noticed in the previous equations that Hull's symbols for inhibition were I_R and $_sI_R$ and Spence's symbol was I_N. This apparently minor difference in symbols reflects a major theoretical difference between Hull and Spence concerning the nature of inhibition. For Hull, responding causes fatigue (I_R), which operates against the emission of a learned response. Likewise, when fatigue builds up, it is reinforcing the animal not to respond. Therefore, there is a learned tendency not to respond ($_sI_R$), which also operates against the emission of a learned response. Hull explains extinction by saying that when reinforcement is removed from the situation ($K = 0$), I_R and $_sI_R$ become the dominant influences of behavior, and the animal stops emitting the learned response.

Spence disagreed with Hull's explanation and proposed the **frustration-competition theory of extinction.** For Spence, nonreinforcement causes frustration, which elicits responses that are incompatible with the learned response and therefore compete with it. The frustration that occurs in the goal box when the animal finds the reinforcer missing is called **primary frustration (R_F).** With continued nonreinforced trials, the animal learns to anticipate frustration, the **fractional anticipatory frustration reaction (r_F),** just as it has learned to anticipate reinforcement during acquisition (r_G). As nonreinforced trials continue, r_F generalizes (just as r_G did) and occurs earlier and earlier in the behavioral chain that previously led to reinforcement. Just as r_Gs give rise to s_Gs, which stimulate behavior compatible with reaching the goal box, r_Fs give rise to s_Fs, which stimulate behavior that is incompatible with reaching the goal box. Eventually, the behavior stimulated by frustration and by the anticipation of frustration becomes dominant, and we say the learned response has extinguished.

Thus, Hull explained extinction in terms of the fatigue that results from responding in the absence of reinforcement, whereas Spence explained extinction as due to the active interference of learned behavior by the responses caused by frustration. Deductions from both of these positions have been tested experimentally, and Spence's explanation appears to fare best. For example, it has been found that using large reinforcers during acquisition produces more rapid extinction than using small reinforcers (Hulse, 1958; Wagner, 1961). According to Spence's theory, removing a large reinforcer produces more frustration than removing a smaller reinforcer; thus, more competing behavior is stimulated. Because the magnitude of the competing behavior is greater than it would be if a smaller reinforcer was removed, it generalizes more rapidly through the chain of behavior that has been previously learned; therefore, extinction occurs more rapidly. According to Hull, magnitude of reinforcement during acquisition should have little or no effect on the speed with which extinction occurs.

Most, if not all, of Spence's modifications made Hullian theory much more capable of dealing with the higher mental processes with which the cognitive theorists are concerned. Spence has made it possible to deal effectively with concepts such as expectation and frustration without sacrificing scientific rigor. Spence's theory can be considered behavioristic, but it is a behavioristic theory that is much more compatible with cognitive theory than was Hull's.

Next we turn to the work of Abram Amsel (1922–2006), a student of Spence's at the University of Iowa. Amsel's relationship to Spence was much like Spence's relationship to Hull; that is, Amsel and Spence had a reciprocal influence on each other. Although Spence was equating inhibition and frustration as early as 1936, it was Amsel who worked out many of the details of Spence's frustration theory of extinction and who used the theory to explain the partial reinforcement effect.

ABRAM AMSEL

Amsel's work combines Hull's ideas with those of Pavlov (see Chapter 7) to develop Spence's contention that extinction occurs because of competing responses caused

Abram Amsel. (Courtesy of Abram Amsel.)

by frustration. In this section we examine the frustration effect (FE) and the partial reinforcement effect (PRE), two of the phenomena addressed by Amsel's frustration theory (Amsel, 1958, 1962, 1992; Rashotte & Amsel, 1999).

Frustration theory identifies four properties that result from goal frustration. These properties are used to explain the various effects observed when a response that has been rewarded in the past is no longer rewarded. The first property of frustration, primary frustration (R_F), is a drivelike effect that follows nonreward. To begin, Amsel (1958, 1962, 1992) assumes that after an organism is reinforced a number of times in a given situation, it learns to expect reinforcement in that situation.

In informal terms, Amsel's theory assumed that when nonreward, reduced reward, or delayed reward occurs in place of an expected reward, the animal experiences a temporary, aversive motivational state [called] primary frustration . . . primary frustration (R_F), is a hypothetical unconditioned reaction to the frustrating event. The theory specifies that R_F will exert a transient motivational (energizing) effect on responses with which it coincides. (Rashotte & Amsel, 1999, pp. 150–151)

The energizing effect of R_F is expressed in behavior as a temporary increase in the speed, amplitude, or frequency of an instrumental response and is called the **frustration effect (FE).** The frustration effect was demonstrated in a classic experiment by Amsel and Roussel (1952) in which two straight alley runways were linked together. For the first eighty-four trials, the animals were reinforced at the end of each runway. After this preliminary training, however, the animals were run under conditions in which they were reinforced at the end of runway 1 on only 50 percent of the trials, whereas they continued to be reinforced at the end of runway 2 on each trial. It was found that running speed in runway 2 was significantly faster following nonreinforcement in runway 1 than it was following reinforcement in runway 1. This finding supports the contention that nonreinforcement causes frustration and that frustration is motivating, or drive inducing.

Further support for this contention was provided by a study by Bower (1962). Bower reasoned that the amount of frustration should be related to the amount of reinforcement reduction. To test his assumption, he used a two-runway apparatus similar to that used by Amsel and Roussel. In Bower's experiment, however, the rats were given four pellets of food at the end of each runway. The training phase of the experiment consisted of 6 trials a day for 24 days, or a total of 144 trials. After training, the conditions were changed so that the number of food pellets found at the end of the first runway was either 4, 3, 2, 1, or 0. The 4 food pellets found at the end of runway 2 remained constant throughout the experiment. Bower found that running speed in runway 2 was inversely related to the number of food pellets present in runway 1 (fewer food pellets, faster running). That is, the animals ran fastest in runway 2 when they received no reinforcement in runway 1; next fastest when they received only 1 pellet, then 2, then 3, and slowest after receiving 4 food pellets in runway 1. This experiment supports Bower's hypothesis that the amount of frustration is related to the amount of reinforcement reduction, and this is in accordance with Spence's and Amsel's view of frustration.

The second property of frustration is the internal stimulation resulting from R_F. Amsel assumed that the unlearned energizing reaction to nonreward has the effects of a naturally occurring drive, and in the Hullian tradition, it is assumed that R_F produces its own drive stimulus called the **frustration drive stimulus (S_F).** Like all drive stimuli, S_F is an aversive state that the organism will strive to reduce or eliminate. The fact that frustration initially energizes a nonrewarded response and helps to instigate repetition of the response may in itself be evidence that the animal seeks to eliminate S_F. The contention that the proposed state of frustration is aversive is further supported by studies demonstrating that animals will learn to perform a response that terminates a stimulus that was present when the animal experienced frustration (Daly, 1969; Wagner, 1963).

The third and fourth properties of frustration are the response that is conditioned to environmental stimuli that occur in the presence of R_F and the internal feedback stimuli produced by that conditioned response. These properties combine to produce **conditioned anticipatory frustration.** We learned earlier in this chapter that when the animal experiences primary reinforcement in a goal box, the stimuli in the goal box take on secondary reinforcing properties; that is, they develop the capacity to elicit r_Gs, which in turn elicit s_Gs. We also saw that through stimulus generalization or higher-order conditioning, these r_Gs slowly develop associations all the way back to the start box. Then, when the animal leaves the start box, its behavior is guided to the goal box by these r_Gs and the s_Gs that they elicit. According to Amsel, the same process is associated with primary frustration. That is, stimuli associated with primary frustration will develop the capacity to elicit a fractional anticipatory frustration reaction, or r_F, which is associated with an **anticipatory frustration stimulus** or s_F, just as an r_G necessarily is associated with an s_G. The r_G-s_G and the r_F-s_F mechanisms are associated with different behavior patterns, however. Whereas the r_G-s_G mechanism causes locomotion toward the goal box, r_F-s_F tends to cause avoidance of the goal box. In general, we can say that r_G is related to the expectancy of reinforcement, whereas r_F is related to the expectancy of frustration.

During extinction, the animal experiences nothing but frustration, which gradually generalizes backward to the start box through the r_F-s_F mechanism. When this happens, the animal experiences stimuli that elicit r_Fs either in the start box or shortly after leaving the start box, and they cause it to stop running. At that point we say that extinction has occurred.

Now we come to what is perhaps the most important aspect of Amsel's theory: its proposed explanation of the **partial reinforcement effect (PRE),** sometimes called the partial reinforcement extinction effect (PREE). The PRE refers to the fact that it takes longer to extinguish a response if it was intermittently reinforced during training than if it were continuously reinforced. In other words, PRE means that partial reinforcement yields greater resistance to extinction than does 100 percent reinforcement. A number of theories have been offered to explain the PRE, and Amsel's is one of the most widely accepted.

Amsel explains PRE as follows: First, the animal is trained to make a response, such as running down a straight alley. During this preliminary training, the animal usually experiences primary reinforcement (R_G) in the goal box on 100 percent of the trials. Under these circumstances, all the stimuli in the runway will eventually become associated with R_G through the r_G-s_G mechanism. Next the animal is placed on a partial reinforcement schedule in which it is reinforced on, say, only 50 percent of the trials. Because the animal developed a strong expectancy for reinforcement, it experiences primary frustration (R_F) on those trials when it does not receive reinforcement. As we saw before, the stimuli just prior to the experience of primary frustration will come to elicit r_Fs, which give rise to s_Fs. After several nonreinforced trials, a conflict develops because the same stimuli tend to elicit conflicting habits. When an r_G-s_G is elicited, the animal tends to run toward the goal box, but when an r_F-s_F is elicited, the animal tends to avoid the goal box. Because the animal had already developed a strong habit of running toward the goal prior to being switched to a partial reinforcement schedule, and perhaps because positive reinforcement is more influential than frustration, the animal continues to approach the goal box while under the partial reinforcement schedule. In other words, although there is an approach-avoidance conflict associated with the goal box, the approach tendency wins out.

Because the animal continues to approach the goal box even though it is not reinforced on some trials, eventually all the stimuli in the apparatus become associated with the running response, even those stimuli associated with frustration. In Amsel's (1992) terms, "instrumental counterconditioning" attaches the instrumental (approach) response to the aversive r_F-s_F mechanism (p. 51). Perhaps you have already anticipated Amsel's next step in his explanation of the PRE. When subjects trained on a continuous or 100 percent reinforcement schedule are switched to extinction, they experience frustration for the first time. For them, the effects of this frustration associate backward to the start box, and normal extinction occurs. Subjects trained on a partial reinforcement schedule, however, have already experienced frustration during training and have learned to run in the presence of the stimuli associated with frustration. The partial reinforcement subjects will therefore take much longer to extinguish—thus the PRE.

One could deduce from Amsel's proposed explanation of the PRE that great variation in behavior would accompany the conflict stage of partial reinforcement training. That is, when the same stimuli in the apparatus are eliciting both approach and avoidance tendencies, the running speed should vary from trial to trial. At the same time, when the stimuli become associated with the running response later in training, the running response should stabilize. Amsel (1958) found support for both deductions. One could also deduce from Amsel's theory that the PRE will occur only when there are a substantial number of preliminary training trials because his explanation depends on frustration, and the animal will not experience frustration unless it has learned to expect a reinforcer. Evidence supporting this contention was also found by Amsel (1958): The PRE resulted if animals had eighty-four preliminary training trials before being switched to a partial reinforcement schedule but did not if they had only twenty-four preliminary training trials.

Amsel's theory of frustrative nonreinforcement is only one of the many creative extensions of the Hull-Spence r_G-s_G mechanism. The student of psychology or education will discover a number of others in advanced courses. In fact, a review of the many uses of the r_G-s_G mechanism to explain various psychological phenomena would make an excellent independent study project.

Finally we turn to the contributions of Neal Miller, who studied with Hull and was strongly influenced by Hull's theory. Miller's work, which continues to make important contributions to contemporary psychology, was eclectic and not limited to explorations of learning theory.

NEAL E. MILLER, VISCERAL CONDITIONING AND BIOFEEDBACK

Among Hull's doctoral students at Yale was Neal E. Miller (1909–2002), a researcher who would extend Hullian influences into a variety of theoretical and applied areas.

Neal E. Miller. (Courtesy of AP Wide World Photos.)

Miller was born in Milwaukee, Wisconsin, in 1909. He completed his undergraduate work at the University of Washington, where he studied with Edwin Guthrie, whose theory we introduce in Chapter 8. He earned his M.A. at Stanford University in 1932 and his Ph.D. at Yale University in 1935. Upon completion of his doctorate, Miller spent several months at the Vienna Psychoanalytic Institute studying Freudian psychoanalysis. When he returned to the United States, Miller joined the faculty at Yale, where he remained until 1966. He then moved to Rockefeller University in New York, where he attained the status of professor emeritus. He maintained his relationships with Rockefeller and Yale until his death in 2002.

While at Yale, Miller conducted research in both Hullian and Freudian psychology and began a fruitful collaboration with John Dollard. In 1941, Miller and Dollard wrote *Social Learning and Imitation,* a behavioristic, reinforcement theory of observational learning and imitation that we discuss briefly in Chapter 13. In 1950, Dollard and Miller coauthored *Personality and*

Psychotherapy, an influential synthesis of Hullian behaviorism and Freudian psychodynamics. Among Miller's many contributions were demonstrations that autonomic, internal responses could be conditioned by using operant training procedures. These findings provided the groundwork for a therapeutic technique that is in use today and that remains the focus of research controversy.

Until the 1960s, it was believed that operant conditioning was possible only for responses that involve the skeletal or striped muscles. The smooth muscles and glands are controlled by the autonomic nervous system, and generally, it was believed that responses mediated by the autonomic nervous system could not be operantly conditioned.

There are now many experiments, a great number of them conducted by Neal E. Miller, demonstrating that both humans and nonhumans can control their own internal environment. For example, it has been found that individuals can control their own heart rate, blood pressure, and skin temperature.

To demonstrate that autonomic responses could be operantly conditioned, Miller and Carmona (1967) gave one group of thirsty dogs water whenever they salivated spontaneously. Another group of thirsty dogs was given water for going for long intervals of time without salivating. The rate of salivation went up for the former group and down for the latter group. Thus, it was demonstrated that salivation, which is governed by the autonomic nervous system, was modifiable through operant conditioning procedures. Other experiments demonstrated that conditioning of autonomic responses could be accomplished by using secondary reinforcers. For example, Shapiro, Turksy, Gerson, and Stern (1969) taught twenty male college students to raise or lower their blood pressure by showing them a picture of a nude female from *Playboy* whenever their blood pressure was altered in the direction desired by the experimenter. At the conclusion of the experiment, the students, with only two exceptions, were unaware of the fact that their blood pressure had been systematically altered.

In other studies of autonomic conditioning, the practical applications are readily apparent. Researchers have reported that heart patients can learn to control their cardiac abnormalities, that epileptics can learn to suppress abnormal brain activity, and that individuals suffering from migraine headaches can learn to avoid them by controlling the dilation of blood vessels surrounding the brain. For more detailed reviews of this research see DiCara, 1970; Jonas, 1973; Kimmel, 1974; and N. E. Miller, 1969, 1983, 1984.

In cases such as those mentioned in the preceding paragraph, a device is used to display to the patients the changes in the internal events that they are trying to control, for example, high blood pressure or irregular heart activity. Such a display is called **biofeedback** because it provides the patient with information about some internal biological event. Reinforcers like food or water are typically not used in this procedure. The information provided by the feedback device is all that is needed for learning to occur. In a sense, the information itself serves as the reinforcer. Usually after monitoring the biofeedback for a period of time, the patients become aware of their internal state and can respond accordingly—either raise or lower their blood pressure—without the aid of biofeedback. Obviously, this whole area of research, sometimes called **visceral conditioning,** has vast implications for the practice of medicine.

Early research clearly demonstrated that we can learn to control many autonomic functions in the laboratory, but there are serious questions about which autonomic functions are most readily controlled beyond the laboratory and, therefore, about which kinds of disorders should be treated with the technique.

For example, it is now suggested that biofeedback may be of limited use for certain disorders. A research team led by David M. Eisenberg examined data from 1,264 patients who suffer from essential hypertension, a disorder characterized by unusually high blood pressure. These researchers found that in twenty-six well-controlled studies, biofeedback techniques proved no more effective than two placebo techniques, including a phony biofeedback condition. The authors concluded that any type of relaxation technique, including biofeedback, was superior to leaving the condition untreated, but they did not recommend biofeedback as a replacement for medication (Eisenberg, DelBanco, et al., 1993).

Biofeedback has frequently been used to treat chronic headaches, although the therapeutic results, in some cases, have been attributed to nonspecific effects of positive expectations on the parts of both the patient and the practitioner (Roberts, 1994). Other studies seem to indicate that the efficacy of biofeedback for treatment of headache depends on the specific type of headache from which a patient suffers. Children who experience migraine headaches were taught to increase skin temperature with biofeedback and appeared to gain relief over a six-month period, compared with children who were on a headache clinic waiting list but were not treated (Labbe, 1995). Similarly, a meta-analysis (a mathematical analysis comparing experiments that test similar subjects and that use comparable procedures and controls) of studies using biofeedback for migraine headaches indicated that biofeedback treatment, coupled with progressive relaxation techniques, was more effective in treating migraine headaches than typically prescribed medications or drug placebos (Hermann, Kim, & Blanchard, 1995). In addition, patients who demonstrated greater skills in controlling either muscle tension or skin temperature by using biofeedback tend to reduce their migraine headaches more than patients who were less able to control those responses (Shellick & Fitzsimmons, 1989). On the other hand, individuals suffering from headaches typically attributed to general tension seem to be more susceptible to placebo or nonspecific effects, such as positive expectations (Blanchard, Kim, Hermann, & Steffek, 1994; Eisenberg, Kessler, Foster, & Norlock, 1993).

Biofeedback techniques are widely used today, but as the studies we have discussed indicate, we must be sure which disorders are most amenable to biofeedback treatment, particularly when biofeedback is offered as a cure for serious conditions ranging from alcoholism to neurological dysfunctions. In addition, further research will be required to determine which cures are best attributed to nonspecific placebo effects and which may actually result from patients learning to control autonomic functions.

DISCUSSION QUESTIONS

1. How would one overcome or minimize the negative contribution of work (I_R and $_sI_R$) in a learning situation?
2. According to Hull's theory, what effect would increasing the size of the reinforcer have on learning? Explain.
3. Describe a situation that would allow one to differentiate between learning and performance.
4. What would characterize classroom procedures designed in accordance with Hull's principles of learning? Give a few specific examples.
5. According to Hull's theory, who do you think would learn faster, high-anxious students or low-anxious students? Explain.
6. On what basic points would Skinner disagree with Hull? Where would the two most closely agree?
7. What do you think Hull means when he says "psychic phenomena" will someday be explained in terms of the r_G-s_G mechanism?
8. Explain chaining from Hull's point of view.
9. What is a habit family hierarchy?
10. Describe Hull's approach to theory construction. What is meant by the statement that Hull's theory is open-ended?
11. Diagram Hull's final version of his theory as it was presented in this chapter.
12. What kind of experiment could directly test Hull's contention that reinforcement depends on reduction of drives or drive stimuli?
13. You drive around a corner and see the house of the good friend you are about to visit, and you begin to smile. How would Hull explain this smiling behavior?
14. Describe the procedure used in avoidance conditioning.
15. Describe the two-factor theory that Mowrer developed to explain avoidance conditioning. In your answer, be sure to define sign learning and solution learning.
16. Discuss Mowrer's distinction between incremental and decremental reinforcement. Also discuss the ways that CSs can be made contingent on the two kinds of reinforcement and what emotions result from each contingency.
17. Summarize the final version of Mowrer's theory, and explain why it is considered basically cognitive in nature.
18. Summarize the evidence that caused Spence to change from a reinforcement theorist to a contiguity theorist with regard to instrumental conditioning.
19. In what sense did Spence remain a reinforcement theorist?
20. Describe the implications of $D \times K \times _sH_R$ versus $(D + K) \times _sH_R$.
21. Summarize the Spence-Amsel frustration-competition theory of extinction.
22. Summarize Amsel's explanation of the partial reinforcement effect.
23. What experimental findings might make us cautious when reading about successful uses of biofeedback techniques?

CHAPTER HIGHLIGHTS

anticipatory frustration stimulus (s_F)

avoidance conditioning

biofeedback

conditioned anticipatory frustration

conditioned inhibition $({}_sI_R)$

Crespi effect

decremental reinforcer

distributed practice

drive (D)

drive reduction

drive stimuli (S_D)

drive stimulus reduction

effective reaction potential $({}_s\bar{E}_R)$

escape conditioning

fractional antedating goal response (r_G)

fractional anticipatory frustration reaction (r_F)

frustration-competition theory of extinction

frustration drive stimulus (S_F)

frustration effect (FE)

generalized habit strength $({}_s\bar{H}_R)$

habit family hierarchy

habit strength $({}_sH_R)$

hypothetical deductive theory (logical deductive)

incentive motivation (K)

incremental reinforcer

interaction of sensory impulses $(\bar{s})$

latency $({}_st_R)$

latent learning

law of contiguity

law of frequency

massed practice

momentary effective reaction potential $({}_s\dot{\bar{E}}_R)$

oscillation effect $({}_sO_R)$

partial reinforcement effect (PRE)

primary frustration (R_F)

proprioceptive stimuli

reaction potential $({}_sE_R)$

reaction threshold $({}_sL_R)$

reactive inhibition (I_R)

reinforcement

reinforcer

reminiscence effect

sign learning

solution learning

stimulus generalization

stimulus-intensity dynamism (V)

stimulus trace (s)

two-factor theory

unlearned behavior

visceral conditioning

CHAPTER 7

Ivan Petrovich Pavlov

(continued)

Pavlov was born in Russia in 1849 and died there in 1936. His father was a priest, and originally Pavlov himself studied to become a priest. He changed his mind, however, and spent most of his life studying physiology. In 1904, he won a Nobel Prize for his work on the physiology of digestion. He did not begin his study of the conditioned reflex until he was fifty years old.

With Thorndike, we saw that scientists are obliged to change their views when the data require it, an important characteristic of the scientific enterprise. With Pavlov, we see the importance of serendipity, or accidental discovery, in science. Pavlov's method of studying digestion involved a surgical arrangement on a dog that allowed gastric juices to flow through a fistula to the outside of the body, where it was collected. This arrangement is shown in Figure 7–1.

Ivan Petrovich Pavlov. (Courtesy of Culver Pictures, Inc.)

Pavlov was measuring stomach secretions as the dog's response to such things as meat powder when he noticed that the mere sight of the food caused the dog to salivate. In addition, the mere sight of the experimenter or the sound of his or her footsteps would cause salivation. Originally Pavlov called such responses "psychic" reflexes. Being an extremely objective scientist and at heart a physiologist, Pavlov originally resisted investigating the "psychic" reflex. After a long personal struggle, however, and contrary to the advice of some of his colleagues, he finally decided to delve into the issue. He decided to study it, however, as a purely physiological problem to guard against any subjective element entering into his research. In fact, Pavlov's coworkers were fined if they used subjective, nonphysiological language in describing their research (Watson, 1978, p. 441). An apparatus like the one used by Pavlov to study the psychic reflex is shown in Figure 7–2.

Just as Pavlov started a second career at age fifty when he turned to the study of the

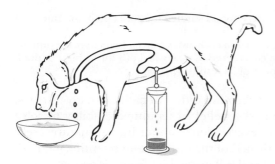

FIGURE 7–1 Dog with esophageal and gastric fistulae. Such an arrangement allowed the dog to be fed but prevented the food from reaching the stomach. Also, gastric juices flowing from the stomach could be measured. (From *Principles of General Psychology*, p. 208, by G. A. Kimble, N. Garmezy, & E. Zigler, 1974, New York: John Wiley & Sons, Inc.)

psychic reflex, he started a third career at age eighty when he turned to the application of his work on conditioning to mental illness. This work resulted in a book entitled *Conditioned Reflexes and Psychiatry* (1941), which many consider a significant contribution to psychiatry.

At the time Thorndike was developing his theory, American psychology was struggling to be objective. Structuralism, with its introspective method, was losing influence. In fact, consciousness per se was becoming a highly questionable subject matter. With his blending of associationism, Darwinism, and experimental science, Thorndike represented the best in American objective psychology. He was an important part of the functionalist movement, which as we have seen was one of the first major psychological movements in America. Under the influence of Darwin, the functionalist's main concern was survival, which of course involved adapting to the environment. The functionalists tried to discover how human actions, as well as thought processes, contribute to adaptation and survival.

At the time Thorndike was doing his major research, Pavlov was also investigating the learning process. He, too, was impatient with subjective psychology and, in fact, had almost decided not to study the conditioned reflex because of its "psychic" nature. Although Pavlov (1928) did not have a high opinion of psychologists, he had considerable respect for Thorndike and acknowledged him as the first to do systematic research on the learning process in animals:

> Some years after the beginning of the work with our new method I learned that somewhat similar experiments on animals had been performed in America, and indeed not

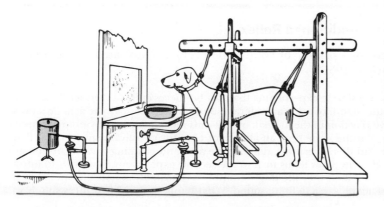

FIGURE 7–2 Dog with a tube entering its cheek. When the dog salivates, the saliva is gathered in the test tube and its quantity is recorded on the rotating drum to the left. From *Great Experiments in Psychology* by H. E. Garrett, which was published by Appleton-Century-Crofts in 1951.

by physiologists but by psychologists. Thereupon I studied in more detail the American publications, and now I must acknowledge that the honour of having made the first steps along this path belongs to E. L. Thorndike. By two or three years his experiments preceded ours, and his book must be considered as a classic, both for its bold outlook on an immense task and for the accuracy of its results. (pp. 38–40)

Thorndike and Pavlov, although traveling two different paths in many respects, shared an enthusiasm toward science and a belief in its ultimate ability to solve major human problems: "Only science, exact science about human nature itself, and the most sincere approach to it by the aid of the omnipotent scientific method, will deliver man from his present gloom, and will purge him from his contemporary shame in the sphere of interhuman relations" (Pavlov, 1928, p. 28). Pavlov never wavered from his scientific outlook, and in 1936 at the age of eighty-seven, he wrote the following letter to the young scientists of his country (Babkin, 1949):

> This is the message I would like to give to the youth of my country. First of all, be systematic. I repeat—be systematic. Train yourself to be strictly systematic in the acquisition of knowledge. First study the rudiments of science before attempting to reach its heights. Never pass on to the next stage until you have thoroughly mastered the one on hand. Never try to conceal the defects in your knowledge even by the most daring conjectures and hypotheses. Practice self-restraint and patience. Learn to do the drudgery of scientific work. Although a bird's wing is perfect, the bird could never soar if it did not lean upon the air. Facts are the air on which the scientist leans. Without them you will never fly upward. Without them your theories will be mere empty efforts. However, when studying, experimenting or observing, try not to remain on the surface of things. Do not become a mere collector of facts but try to penetrate into the mystery of their origin. Search persistently for the laws which govern them.
>
> The second important requisite is modesty. Never at any time imagine that you know everything. No matter how highly you are appreciated by others, have the courage to say to yourself, "I am ignorant." Do not let pride possess you.
>
> The third thing that is necessary is passion. Remember that science demands of a man his whole life. And even if you could have two lives, they would not be sufficient. Science calls for tremendous effort and great passion. Be passionate in your work and in your search for truth. (p. 110)

EMPIRICAL OBSERVATIONS

Development of a Conditioned Reflex

Exactly what is meant by a psychic or conditioned reflex is indicated by the following statement by Pavlov (1955):

> I shall mention two simple experiments that can be successfully performed by all. We introduce into the mouth of a dog a moderate solution of some acid; the acid produces a usual defensive reaction in the animal: by vigorous movements of the mouth it ejects the solution, and at the same time an abundant quantity of saliva begins to flow first into the mouth and then overflows, diluting the acid and cleaning the mucous membrane of the oral cavity. Now let us turn to the second experiment. Just prior to introducing the same solution into the dog's mouth we repeatedly act on the animal by a certain external agent, say, a definite sound. What happens then? It suffices simply to

repeat the sound, and the same reaction is fully reproduced—the same movements of the mouth and the same secretion of saliva. (p. 247)

The terms *Pavlovian conditioning* and *classical conditioning* are synonymous. The ingredients necessary to bring about Pavlovian or classical conditioning include (1) an **unconditioned stimulus (US),** which elicits a natural and automatic response from the organism; (2) an **unconditioned response (UR),** which is a natural and automatic response elicited by the US; and (3) a **conditioned stimulus (CS),** which is a neutral stimulus in that it does not elicit a natural and automatic response from the organism. When these ingredients are mixed in a certain way, a **conditioned response (CR)** occurs. To produce a CR, the CS and the US must be paired a number of times. First the CS is presented and then the US, and the order of presentation is very important. Each time the US occurs, a UR occurs. Eventually the CS can be presented alone, and it will elicit a response similar to the UR. When this happens, a CR has been demonstrated. The procedure can be diagrammed as follows:

Training procedure: CS → US → UR

Demonstration of conditioning: CS → CR

In Pavlov's example, the US was acid, the UR was salivation (caused by the acid), and the CS was a sound. The sound, of course, would not ordinarily cause the dog to salivate, but by being paired with the acid, the sound developed the capability to elicit salivation. Salivation as the result of hearing the sound was the CR.

Pavlov believed that the UR and the CR are always the same kind of response; if the UR is salivation, the CR must also be salivation. The magnitude of the CR, however, is always less than that of the UR. For example, Pavlov, who measured the magnitude of a response by counting drops of saliva, found that the US elicited more drops of saliva than did the CS. When we consider recent research on classical conditioning later in this chapter, we see that Pavlov's contention that CRs are smaller versions of URs has been found, at least in some cases, to be incorrect.

Experimental Extinction

A CR depends on a US for its existence, and that is precisely why the US is referred to as a *reinforcer*. Obviously, without the US a CS would never develop the capability of eliciting a CR. Likewise, if after a CR has been developed, the CS is continually presented without the US following the CS, the CR gradually disappears. When the CS no longer elicits a CR, experimental **extinction** is said to have occurred. Again, extinction results when the CS is presented to the organism and is not followed by reinforcement. In classical conditioning studies, reinforcement is the US.

Spontaneous Recovery

After a period of time following extinction, if the CS is again presented to the animal, the CR will temporarily reappear. The CR has "spontaneously recovered," even though there had been no further pairings between the CS and the US. Again, if there

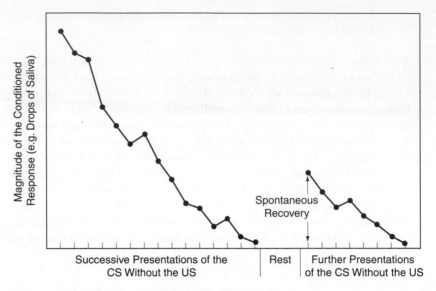

FIGURE 7–3   Typical curves showing the extinction and spontaneous recovery of a conditioned response.

is a delay following extinction and the CS is presented to the organism, it will tend to elicit a CR. The extinction and **spontaneous recovery** of a CR are shown in Figure 7–3.

Higher-Order Conditioning

After a CS has been paired with a US a number of times, it can be used much like a US. That is, through its pairing with the US, the CS develops reinforcing properties of its own, and it can be paired with a second CS to bring about a CR. Let us pair, for example, a blinking light (CS) with the presentation of food powder (US). Food powder will cause the animal to salivate, and after a number of pairings between the CS and the US, the blinking light presented alone causes the animal to salivate. That the animal salivates to the blinking light is, of course, a conditioned response.

Now that the blinking light elicits salivation, it can be paired with a second CS, say, a buzzer. The direction of the pairing is the same as in the original conditioning: First the new CS (buzzer) is presented, and then the old one (blinking light). Note that food is no longer involved. After a number of such pairings, the buzzer, when presented alone, causes the animal to salivate. In this example, the first CS was used much like a US is used to bring about a conditioned response. This is called *second-order conditioning.* We also say that the first CS developed *secondary reinforcing properties* because it was used to condition a response to a new stimulus. Therefore the CS is called a **secondary reinforcer.** Because secondary reinforcement cannot develop without the US, the US is called a **primary reinforcer.**

This procedure can be carried one more step. The second CS (buzzer) can be paired with one more CS, such as a 2,000-cps tone. The direction of the pairing is the same as before: first the tone, then the buzzer. Eventually, the tone presented alone will cause the animal to salivate. Thus, through its pairing with the blinking light, the buzzer also became a secondary reinforcer and therefore could be used to condition a response to another new stimulus, the 2,000-cps tone. This is *third-order conditioning*. Both second- and third-order conditioning come under the general heading of **higher-order conditioning.**

Because higher-order conditioning must be studied during the extinction process, it is very difficult, if not impossible, to go beyond third-order conditioning. In fact, such studies are quite rare. As one goes from first- to third-order conditioning, the magnitude of the CR becomes smaller, and the CR lasts for only a few trials. In this example, the tone elicits only a few drops of saliva and does so only the first few times it is presented to the animal.

Generalization

To illustrate **generalization,** we return to the basic conditioning procedure. We will use a 2,000-cps tone for our CS and meat powder for our US. After a number of pairings, the tone alone causes the animal to salivate; thus we have developed a CR. Once this has been accomplished, we enter the extinction phase of the experiment, only this time we will expose the animal to tones other than the original 2,000-cps tone. Some of the new tones will have a frequency higher than 2,000 cps, and some will have a lower frequency. Using the number of drops of saliva as our measure of the magnitude of the CR, we find that the CR has its greatest magnitude when the 2,000-cps tone is presented, but CRs are also produced for the other tones. The magnitude of the CR depends on the similarity of a given tone to the original training tone; in this case, the greater the similarity to the 2,000-cps tone, the greater the magnitude of the CR. An example of generalization is shown in Figure 7–4.

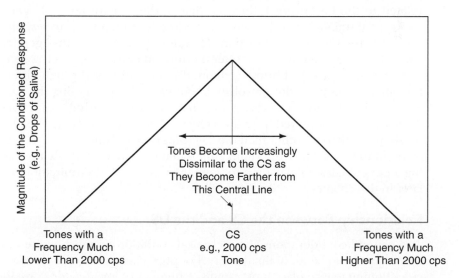

FIGURE 7–4 Idealized stimulus generalization curve showing that as stimuli become increasingly dissimilar to the one used as the CS during training, the magnitude of the CR goes down.

There is a relationship between Pavlov's concept of generalization and Thorndike's explanation of the transfer of training. With generalization, as the training and testing situations have more in common, there is a greater probability that the same response will be made to both. This statement could easily be subsumed under Thorndike's "identical elements" theory of transfer. Likewise, both generalization and transfer explain how we can have a learned reaction to a situation we have never encountered before; that is, we respond to a new situation as we respond to a similar situation with which we are familiar.

It is important to note the distinction between Thorndike's spread of effect and Pavlov's generalization. The spread of effect refers to the influence of reinforcement on responses neighboring the reinforced response, regardless of their similarity to the reinforced response. With the spread of effect, proximity is the important thing. Generalization describes the increased capability of producing a CR by stimuli related to the stimulus that actually preceded reinforcement. With generalization, similarity, not proximity, is the important thing.

Discrimination

The opposite of generalization is **discrimination.** As we saw previously, generalization refers to the tendency to respond to a number of stimuli that are related to the one actually used during training. Discrimination, by contrast, refers to the tendency to respond to a very restricted range of stimuli or to only the one used during training.

Discrimination can be brought about in two ways: prolonged training and differential reinforcement. First, if a CS is paired with a US many times, the tendency to respond to stimuli related to the CS, but not identical to it, decreases. In other words, if the minimum number of pairings between the CS and US necessary to develop a CR is used, there is a relatively strong tendency to respond to stimuli related to the CS during extinction; that is, there is considerable generalization. However, if training is prolonged, there is a reduced tendency to respond to stimuli related to the CS during extinction. Thus, it is possible to control generalization by controlling training level: the greater the amount of training, the less generalization.

The second way of bringing about discrimination is through differential reinforcement. This procedure involves, in our example, presenting the 2,000-cps tone along with a number of other tones that will occur during extinction. Only the 2,000-cps tone is followed by reinforcement. After such training, when the animal is presented with tones other than the 2,000-cps tone during extinction, it tends not to respond to them. Thus, discrimination is demonstrated. Pavlov's attempt at providing a physiological explanation for generalization and discrimination is considered later in this chapter.

Relationship Between the CS and the US

Two general considerations about classical conditioning must be mentioned. First, there appears to be an optimal interval of presentation between the CS and US for conditioning to take place most rapidly. A number of investigators have found that if the CS comes on a half second before the US, conditioning proceeds most efficiently.

The most common procedure is to have the CS come on and stay on until the US comes on. If the time between these two events is greater or less than 0.5 seconds, conditioning is relatively more difficult to establish. This explanation should be looked on as an oversimplification, however, because the optimal interval of time between the onset of the CS and the onset of the US for conditioning to occur depends on many factors, and it is the subject of a considerable amount of research. For example, when we consider research on taste aversion later in this chapter, we see that a phenomenon like classical conditioning occurs even when the delay between the CS and the US is several hours. Also, as we note in this chapter, there are circumstances in which a CS precedes a US at the optimal interval, yet no conditioning occurs.

The second matter is related to the first. Using traditional classical conditioning procedures, it was typically found that if the CS comes on *after* the US is presented, conditioning is extremely difficult, if not impossible, to establish. This is referred to as **backward conditioning.** One explanation for the apparent lack of backward conditioning is that a CS must be "informative" to the organism before conditioning will occur. Clearly, a CS that comes on after the US has already been presented cannot be used by the organism to predict the occurrence of the US. This would be true not only of the backward conditioning situation but also if CSs are redundant or unreliable. Evidence for this point of view is supplied by Egger and Miller (1962, 1963), who found that (1) if two CSs reliably predict a US, the first one presented will become conditioned, and the second one, which is redundant, will not; and (2) if two signals precede a US but one is always followed by the US and the other is only sometimes followed by the US, the more reliable signal becomes conditioned much more than the unreliable signal. It appears that stimuli that occur after the US or stimuli that are either redundant or unreliably correlated with the US cannot be used by the organism to predict the occurrence of primary reinforcements; that is, they have no **information value.** In general, Egger and Miller concluded that for classical conditioning to take place, the organism must be able to use the CS to predict whether reinforcement will occur. Egger and Miller's general conclusion is still widely accepted, but recent research on classical conditioning has necessitated a change in the beliefs about both backward conditioning and the circumstances under which a CS is informative. Later in this chapter, we discuss current research showing that CSs presented *after* the US are as informative as CSs that are presented *before* the US, and therefore backward conditioning is not only possible but also, under certain circumstances, as easy to establish as forward conditioning.

MAJOR THEORETICAL CONCEPTS

Excitation and Inhibition

According to Pavlov, the two basic processes governing all central nervous system activity are **excitation** and **inhibition.** Babkin (1949) said:

> The fundamental theoretical conception of Pavlov concerning the functional properties of the nervous system, and of the cerebral cortex in particular, was that they were

based on two equally important processes: the process of excitation and the process of inhibition. Very often he compared the nervous system with the ancient Greek god Janus, who had two faces looking in opposite directions. The excitation and the inhibition are only sides of one and the same process; they always exist simultaneously, but their proportion varies in each moment, at times the one prevailing, at times the other. Functionally the cerebral cortex is, according to Pavlov, a mosaic, consisting of continuously changing points of excitation and inhibition. (p. 313)

Pavlov speculated that each environmental event corresponds to some point on the cortex and that as these events are experienced, they tend either to excite or to inhibit cortical activity. Thus, the cortex is constantly being excited or inhibited, depending on what the organism is experiencing. This pattern of excitation and inhibition that characterizes the brain at any given moment is what Pavlov called the **cortical mosaic.** The momentary cortical mosaic determines how an organism will respond to its environment. As either the external environment or the internal environment changes, the cortical mosaic changes, and behavior changes accordingly.

A cortical mosaic can become a relatively stable configuration because, according to Pavlov, brain centers that are repeatedly active together form temporary connections, and the arousal of one will cause the arousal of the others. Thus, if a tone is consistently presented to a dog just before it is fed, the area of the brain aroused by the tone will form a temporary connection with the area of the brain that responds to food. When this connection is formed, the presentation of the tone will cause the animal to act as if food were present. At that point we say a conditioned reflex has been developed.

The Dynamic Stereotype

When events consistently occur in the environment, they come to have neurological representation, and responses to them become more probable and more efficient. Thus, responses to a familiar environment become rapid and automatic. When this happens, a **dynamic stereotype** is said to have been developed. Roughly, the dynamic stereotype is a cortical mosaic that has become stable because the organism has been in a highly predictable environment for a considerable length of time. As long as this cortical mapping accurately reflects the environment and produces appropriate responses, everything is fine. If, however, the environment is radically changed, the organism may find it difficult to change a dynamic stereotype. Pavlov (1955) said:

The entire establishment and distribution in the cortex of excitatory and inhibitory states, taking place in a certain period under the action of external and internal stimuli, become more and more fixed under uniform, recurring conditions and are effected with ever-increasing ease and automatism. Thus, there appears a dynamic stereotype (systematization) in the cortex, the maintenance of which becomes an increasingly less difficult nervous task; but the stereotype becomes inert, little susceptible to change and resistant to new conditions and new stimulations. Any initial elaboration of a stereotype is, depending on the complexity of the system of stimuli, a difficult and often an extraordinary task. (p. 259)

To summarize, certain environmental events tend to be followed by certain other environmental events, and as long as this relationship continues to be true, the association between the two on the neural level continues to grow stronger. (Note the similarity here to Thorndike's early thinking concerning the effect of exercise on a neural bond.) If the environment abruptly changes, new neural paths must be formed, and that is no easy matter.

Irradiation and Concentration

Pavlov used the term *analyser* to describe the path from a sense receptor to a certain area of the brain. An analyser consists of sense receptors, the sensory pathway from the receptors to the brain, and the area of the brain onto which the sensory activity is projected. Sensory information projected onto some area of the brain causes excitation in that area. Initially, there is an **irradiation of excitation;** in other words, this excitation spills over into neighboring brain areas. It is this process that Pavlov used to explain generalization. In our example of generalization described earlier, we noted that when an animal is conditioned to respond to a 2,000-cps tone, it responds not only to that tone but also to other related tones. The magnitude of the response is determined by the similarity between the tone presented and the actual CS used during training. As the similarity increases, the CR's magnitude increases.

Pavlov's explanation for generalization was that neural impulses travel from the sense receptors—in this case, from the ears—to a specific area of the cortex that reacts to a 2,000-cps tone. The activity caused by the 2,000-cps tone irradiates from this location out into the neighboring regions. Pavlov assumed that tones closest to the 2,000-cps tone are represented in brain regions close to the area corresponding to the one for the 2,000-cps tone. As tones become dissimilar, the brain regions representing them will be farther away from the area representing the 2,000-cps tone. In addition, Pavlov assumed that excitation diminishes with distance: It is strongest at the point corresponding to the CS and weaker farther away. Therefore, an association is made not only between the CS and the US but also with a number of stimuli related to the CS that are represented in neighboring brain regions. In addition to his hypothesis that excitation irradiates, or spreads, to neighboring regions of the cortex, Pavlov demonstrated, via generalization, that inhibition also irradiates.

Pavlov also found that **concentration,** a process opposite to irradiation, governs both excitation and inhibition. He asserted that under certain circumstances both excitation and inhibition are concentrated at specific areas of the brain. As the process of irradiation is used to explain generalization, the process of concentration is used to explain discrimination.

At first the organism has a generalized tendency to respond to a CS during conditioning. For example, if a signal is followed by a reinforcer, there is a learned tendency to respond to that and related signals. Likewise, if a signal is presented and is not followed by a reinforcer, there is a learned tendency not to respond to that and related signals. We say, therefore, that both excitation and inhibition have irradiated. With prolonged training, however, the tendencies to respond and not to respond become less general and increasingly specific to a narrow range of stimuli. In this case, we say the excitation and inhibition have been concentrated.

As we noted earlier in this chapter, discrimination, or the ability to respond differentially to related stimuli, can be brought about by prolonged training or differential reinforcement. If a large number of pairings are made between the CS and the US, the excitation begins to concentrate. After such training, one finds that the organism tends to respond only to the CS or to stimuli very similar to the CS. In other words, because excitation has been concentrated, very little generalization takes place.

Excitatory and Inhibitory Conditioning

Pavlov identified two general types of conditioning that follow directly from the preceding discussion. The first, **excitatory conditioning,** is observed when a CS-US pairing excites or produces a response: A bell (CS) is paired repeatedly with meat powder (US) so that presentation of the CS elicits salivation (CR); a tone (CS) is paired repeatedly with a puff of air (US) directed at the eye (which causes a reflexive eyeblink [UR]) so that presentation of the CS alone results in an eyeblink.

Conditioned inhibition is observed when training produces a CS that inhibits or suppresses a response. For example, Pavlov speculated that extinction might be due to inhibition that develops after a previously excitatory CS is repeatedly presented without a reinforcer. (Recent research, discussed shortly, indicates that this interpretation of extinction may not be correct.) The standard procedure for producing conditioned inhibition is to present a single CS (a tone, for example) paired reliably with a US and to present a *compound* CS (the tone together with a light) that is not paired with a US. We refer to the tone as "A$^+$," to indicate that it is always presented with the US, and to the compound tone plus light as "AX$^-$," to indicate that the tone-light combination is not paired with the US. The procedure for producing conditioned inhibition (CI training) is sometimes called A$^+$/AX$^-$ training (for example, see Rescorla, 2002). During the first stages of training, both A$^+$ and the compound AX$^-$ produce a CR. As training progresses, discrimination occurs; the response is observed after presentations of A alone (A$^+$) but not after AX$^-$. Thus the compound AX$^-$ and X itself become conditioned inhibitors. Later in this chapter, we will see how conditioned inhibition has been used to provide new directions in the study of classical conditioning. An additional type of inhibition documented by Pavlov reveals that conditioning is not a purely mechanical and unavoidable binding of stimuli to responses. If, after a dog acquires a stable salivation response to a tone, a new stimulus (e.g., a flashing light) is paired with the tone, the salivation response does not occur. **External inhibition** is the term that Pavlov used to describe the disruptive effect that occurs when a novel stimulus is presented along with an already established CS. The effect is not confined to conditioned excitation, however. If a CS is a conditioned inhibitor, introduction of an unexpected stimulus along with the CS produces **disinhibition,** which is the disruption of conditioned inhibition. In other words, if we pair a novel stimulus with a conditioned inhibitor, the inhibitor fails to inhibit.

Summary of Pavlov's Views on Brain Functioning

Pavlov saw the brain as a mosaic of points of excitation and inhibition. Each point on the brain corresponds to an environmental event. Depending on what is being experienced at the moment, a different pattern of excitation and inhibition occurs in the brain, and that pattern determines behavior. Some connections in the brain are between unconditioned stimuli and their associated responses, and some are between conditioned stimuli and their associated responses. The former are permanent, and the latter are temporary and change with varied environmental conditions.

When a temporary connection is first being formed in the brain, there is a tendency for a conditioned stimulus to have a very general effect in the brain. That is, the excitation caused by a conditioned stimulus irradiates over a relatively larger portion of the cortex. The same thing is true when an organism is learning not to respond to, or to avoid, a stimulus. The inhibitory effects of such a stimulus also irradiate over a fairly large portion of the brain in the early stages of learning. As learning proceeds, however, the excitation caused by a positive stimulus and the inhibition caused by a negative stimulus become concentrated in specific areas of the cortex. As the organism develops the connections between environmental events and brain processes that allow it to survive, a dynamic stereotype develops, which is a kind of neural mapping of the environment. The dynamic stereotype makes it easier to respond to a highly predictable environment but makes it difficult to adjust to a new environment.

Pavlov never explained how all of these processes interact to produce the smooth, coordinated behavior we see from organisms, but he did express amazement that systematic behavior did result from such a large number of influences. Pavlov (1955) put the matter as follows:

> Countless stimuli, different in nature and intensity, reach the cerebral hemispheres both from the external world and the internal medium of the organism itself. Whereas some of them are merely investigated (the orienting reflex), others evoke highly diverse conditioned and unconditioned effects. They all meet, come together, interact, and they must, finally, become systematized, equilibrated, and form, so to speak, a dynamic stereotype. What truly grandiose work! (p. 454)

The **orienting reflex** to which Pavlov referred here is the tendency for organisms to attend to and explore novel stimuli that occur in their environment. The orienting reflex has been the topic of considerable research in recent years.

First and Second Signal Systems

Until Pavlov, most physiologists and psychologists concerned themselves with the importance of the present or the past for the behavior of organisms. That is, they focused on reflexive responses elicited by current stimulating conditions or on how the memory of past events influences behavior. Pavlov's work on conditioning provided a framework for understanding how organisms anticipate *future* events. Because CSs precede biologically significant events (URs), they become signals for those events that allow an organism to prepare for and to engage in behavior that is appropriate to their occurrence. Anoklin (1968) makes this point concerning the anticipatory nature of conditioned reflexes:

> Pavlov . . . rated very highly the ability of the conditioned reaction to act as a "signal" reaction or, as he expressed it many times, a reaction of "warning character." It is this "warning" character which accounts for the profound historical significance of the conditioned reflex. It enables the animal to adapt itself to events which are not taking place at that particular moment but which will follow in the future. (p. 140)

Pavlov referred to the stimuli that come to signal biologically significant events (CSs) as the **first signal system** or "the first signals of reality." In addition, however, humans also utilize language, which consists of *symbols* of reality. Thus, one may respond to the word *danger* as one would respond to an actual dangerous situation. Pavlov referred to the words that symbolize reality as the "signals of signals" or the **second signal system.** Once established, these symbols can be organized into a complex system that guides much human behavior.

One example of how language complicates classical conditioning is found in the area of **semantic generalization** (sometimes called mediated generalization). Studies have shown that a response can be conditioned to the *meaning* of a stimulus rather than to the concrete stimulus itself. For example, if a response is conditioned to the number 4, human subjects will emit a conditioned response when they are confronted with such stimuli as $\sqrt{16}$, $8/2$, 2×2, $40/10$, and so forth. In other words, the number 4 elicits a conditioned response, but so will a variety of other stimuli that result in 4 after mental operations have been performed. The conclusion to be drawn is that for human subjects the true CS is the concept of "fourness." (See Razran, 1961, for additional examples of semantic conditioning.)

Semantic generalization also seems to vary as a function of age. In his work with children of different ages, Reiss (1946) found that after initial training, which involved visually presenting a word such as *right* as a CS, children generalized by exhibiting conditioned responses according to their level of language development. Eight-year-olds generalized to visually presented homophones (e.g., *rite*) eleven-year-olds generalized to antonyms (e.g., *wrong*), and fourteen-year-olds generalized to synonyms (e.g., *correct*).

Although the second signal system is clearly more complex than the first signal system, Pavlov felt that the same laws of conditioning govern both, and therefore they both could be studied objectively. In other words, the process by which we develop a reaction to an environmental event is the same process by which we develop a reaction to a word or a thought.

A COMPARISON BETWEEN CLASSICAL AND INSTRUMENTAL CONDITIONING

The kind of conditioning that Thorndike studied is now called instrumental conditioning because the response being observed was instrumental in getting the animal something it wanted (reinforcement). In the case of the cat in the puzzle box, the cat had to learn to perform a certain response that released it from the box and was reinforced with a piece of fish. If the appropriate response did not occur, the animal was not reinforced. To summarize, we can say that in instrumental conditioning, any response that leads to reinforcement tends to be repeated, and a reinforcer is something the animal wants.

Classical conditioning elicits a response from the animal, and instrumental conditioning depends on the animal's emission of the response. The former can be said to be involuntary and automatic, the latter to be voluntary and under the animal's control.

The function of reinforcement is also quite different for classical and instrumental conditioning. With instrumental conditioning, reinforcement is presented to the animal *after* the response of interest has been made. With classical conditioning, however, the reinforcer (US) is presented in order to *elicit* the response of interest. The two situations can be diagrammed as follows:

Instrumental Conditioning

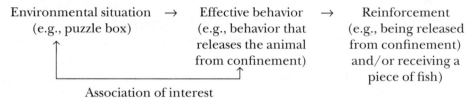

Classical Conditioning

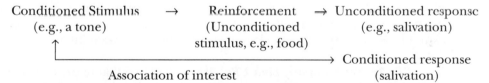

Pavlov felt that he had discovered the physiological basis for the associations that philosophers and psychologists had been talking about for so many years. To him, conditioned reflexes could explain how the mind works. Pavlov (1955) placed himself squarely among the associationists with the following statement:

> Are there any grounds . . . for distinguishing between that which the physiologist calls the temporary connection and that which the psychologist terms association? They are fully identical; they merge and absorb each other. Psychologists themselves seem to recognize this, since they (at least, some of them) have stated that the experiments with conditioned reflexes provide a solid foundation for associative psychology, i.e., psychology which regards association as the base of psychical activity. (p. 251)

Both kinds of conditioning enhance an organism's survival: classical conditioning by creating a system of signs and symbols that allow the anticipation of significant events; instrumental conditioning through the development of appropriate behavior patterns in response to those significant events. Both kinds of conditioning are also dependent on reinforcement. In classical conditioning, the US is the reinforcer, and if it is removed from the experimental arrangement, extinction occurs. In instrumental conditioning, the reinforcer is the "satisfying state of affairs" that *follows* an appropriate response. If reinforcement no longer follows a certain response, the probability of that response goes back to the point where it was before reinforcement was introduced. Classical and instrumental conditioning have in common not only the necessity of reinforcement (extinction follows when it is removed) but also the phenomena of spontaneous recovery, generalization, discrimination, and secondary reinforcement.

It should also be pointed out that it is impossible to separate instrumental and classical conditioning completely. For example, every instrumental conditioning study that utilizes a primary reinforcer (such as food or water) will necessarily produce classical conditioning. That is, all of the stimuli that consistently occur prior to the primary reinforcer will, through the process of classical conditioning, become secondary reinforcers.

RECENT RESEARCH ON CLASSICAL CONDITIONING

In his analysis of conditioning, Pavlov emphasized contiguity. That is, if a CS precedes a US, eventually a CS will elicit a CR. We saw earlier that the work of Egger and Miller (1962, 1963) cast doubt on this analysis by showing that CSs that are unreliable or redundant do not become conditioned to a US. More recently, several other researchers have also shown that factors other than simple contiguity are involved in classical conditioning. We review the work of these researchers, but first we discuss two possible inaccuracies in Pavlov's theory. The first is his view of CRs as smaller versions of URs; the second is his claim that extinction involves inhibition.

CRs Are Not Necessarily Little URs   Pavlov believed that in the course of conditioning the CS comes to substitute for the US, which is why classical conditioning has sometimes been referred to as stimulus substitute learning. It was assumed that because the CS acts as a substitute for the US, CRs were smaller versions of URs. Indeed, there are times when the CR and UR have much in common, as when the UR caused by food (US) is, among other things, salivation, and so is the CR. Also when the US is a puff of air to the eye, the UR is, among other things, an eye-blink, and a CS consistently paired with the US will eventually, when presented alone, cause an eye-blink. Often a CR does look like a smaller version of the UR. However, careful study of the nature of CRs has shown them to often be quite different from URs. For example, Zener (1937) carefully photographed a classical conditioning experiment and made the following observations:

> Except for the component of salivary secretion the conditioned and unconditioned behavior is not identical. (a) During most of the time in which the bell is reinforced by the presence of food, chewing generally occurs with the head raised out of the food-pan

but not directed either at the bell or into the food-pan, or at any definite environmental object. Yet this posture practically never, even chewing only occasionally, occurs to the conditioned stimulus alone. Despite Pavlov's assertions, the dog does not appear to be eating an imaginary food. (b) Nor is the behavior that does appear an arrested or partially unconditioned reaction consisting of those response elements not conflicting with other actions. It is a different reaction, anthropomorphically describable as a looking for, expecting, the fall of food with a readiness to perform the eating behavior which will occur when the food falls. The effector pattern is not identical with the unconditioned. (c) Movements frequently occur which do not appear as part of the unconditioned response to food: All the restless behavior of stamping, yawning, panting. (p. 393)

Not only has it been found that CRs and URs are often different in nature but also some researchers have found them to be antagonistic. Obrist, Sutterer, and Howard (1972) verified the fact that the typical UR, when shock is used as the US, is heart rate acceleration. And as Pavlov would have predicted, with minimal pairings of the CS and US, the CR is heart rate acceleration. With prolonged training, however, the CR became heart rate *deceleration*.

Another example of CR and UR being antagonistic is found when drugs are used as USs. Shepard Siegel (1979) describes a series of experiments in which morphine was used as a US. One reaction to morphine is analgesia—or a reduction in the sensitivity to pain. Under the influence of morphine, a rat will take significantly longer to remove its paw from a hot plate than a rat not under the influence of morphine. Because the injection itself precedes the experience of morphine (the US), it (the injection) can be viewed as a CS. Thus, after several injections of morphine, injecting the rat with plain water should reduce its sensitivity to pain. It turns out, however, that the opposite is true. Under the circumstances described above, rats become more sensitive to pain. That is, animals that were previously injected with morphine and are then injected with water remove their paws from a hot plate significantly *faster* than control animals that had never been injected with morphine. The CR (increased sensitivity to pain) appears to be opposite to the UR (decreased sensitivity to pain). Essentially the same results have been attained when lights or tones were used as CSs instead of the injection itself.

It has also been found (e.g., Holland, 1977) that even when the same US is used, CRs will take different forms when different CSs are paired with that US. Clearly the relationship between CRs and URs is much more complex than Pavlov had assumed. It turns out that sometimes CRs do mimic URs, sometimes CRs seem to prepare the organism for the US, and sometimes CRs are antagonistic to the UR. For a discussion of the different kinds of CR-UR relationships and the conditions that produce them, see Hilgard and Marquis (1940) and Hollis (1982).

Extinction Involves Interference   As we noted previously, Pavlov believed that during extinction, nonreinforced presentations of a CS result in conditioned inhibition that either suppresses or replaces previously learned excitatory associations between CS and US. Inhibition, rather than elimination of CS-US connections, was therefore the theoretical mechanism underlying experimental extinction of a conditioned response. A modified approach proposed by Bouton (1993, 1994) suggests

Mark E. Bouton. (Courtesy of Sally McCay/University of Vermont.)

that during extinction, presentation of a CS without a US results in new learning, usually including inhibition of the CR, that interferes with a previously learned CS-US association. Original CS-US associations thus remain intact and coexist with newly learned CS-extinction associations. However, the responses that occur under subsequent test conditions will depend on experimental-contextual cues other than the CS itself.

This argument rests heavily on three reliable learning phenomena. The first, spontaneous recovery, has already been described. The second, called the **renewal effect,** is observed when a response that has been conditioned in one experimental context is extinguished in another. When the experimental subject is returned to the original setting and the CS is presented, the CR is readily elicited (Bouton, 1984, 1991; Bouton & Bolles, 1979a; Bouton & King, 1983, 1986). The third effect, **reinstatement,** is observed when a US is presented after experimental extinction seems to be complete. After a few unpaired presentations of the US, the original CS again elicits a CR, although not at levels observed prior to extinction (Bouton, 1988, 1991; Bouton & Bolles, 1979b; Rescorla & Heth, 1975).

Bouton (1993, 1994) proposes that contextual factors, comprised of temporal (time) and physical/spatial stimuli present during conditioning, serve as memory retrieval cues for CS-US associations. During extinction, those same context cues come to retrieve CS-extinction associations. After extinction, the CS is "ambiguous"; it evokes both the responses learned during CS-US pairing and the responses learned during extinction. Contextual cues determine which response occurs, depending on which association they elicit. If context cues most resemble those stimuli that existed during conditioning, the CS elicits the CR; if they are most like the cues that existed during extinction, the CS elicits extinction responses other than the CR. Experimental manipulations that reduce ambiguity emphasize these conclusions.

For example, reinstatement is not observed if the postextinction US is presented in a context different than the one that existed during original conditioning (Bouton, 1984; Bouton & Bolles, 1979b; Bouton & Peck, 1989). In addition, spontaneous recovery is significantly reduced if a distinctive (non-CS) cue that was present during extinction trials is reintroduced during tests for recovery (Brooks & Bouton, 1993). Although research in the area continues, Bouton's contextual interpretation may be the most parsimonious way to explain spontaneous recovery, renewal, and reinstatement.

Overshadowing and Blocking   Pavlov (1927) observed that if he used a compound stimulus as a CS and one component of the stimulus was more salient than the other, only the more salient component is conditioned. This phenomenon is called **overshadowing.** If, for example, a compound CS consists of a light and a loud noise (presented together), all the conditioning occurs to the loud noise because it is the stronger or more salient element of the compound. When a compound stimulus is used as a CS, overshadowing is demonstrated when conditioning occurs to the dominant component of the stimulus but not to the weaker component. The phenomenon of overshadowing is of theoretical interest because both elements of the compound stimulus are presented contiguously with the US, and yet conditioning occurs only in the case of one element. Much of the current research on classical conditioning has been designed to explain the phenomenon of overshadowing and the related phenomenon of blocking, which we consider next.

In 1969, Leon Kamin reported an influential series of experiments on a phenomenon that he calls **blocking** (also called the **blocking effect**). Before discussing Kamin's work on blocking, we need to describe the **conditioned emotional response (CER),** which he used to demonstrate the blocking phenomenon. The CER was first described by Estes and Skinner (1941) as a method of measuring the strength of a CS-US association. The procedure involves first placing a rat in a Skinner box and shaping it to press a lever for food reinforcement. The rat is then switched to a variable interval schedule of reinforcement (e.g., a VI four-minute schedule) to produce a steady rate of responding. Next, the rat experiences one-hour experimental sessions during which a tone is sounded for three minutes at a time; on the termination of the tone, the rat receives a brief, unavoidable shock. Throughout the tone-shock sequences, the variable interval reinforcement schedule remains in effect. After several sessions, the rats greatly reduce their rate of lever pressing each time the tone is presented. The reduction in rate of responding during CS (tone) presentation is called **conditioned suppression.** It was found that the suppression lasts until the end of the shock that terminates each tone-shock sequence. After the shock is terminated, the response rate increases to its normal rate and continues at that rate until the tone comes on again. During the time that the tone is on, Estes and Skinner noted emotional responses such as defecation, squealing, and freezing. It is these conditioned emotional responses that are thought responsible for suppressing the response rate. With this procedure, the extent of classical conditioning (tone-shock relationship) can be indexed by changes in the rate at which an operant response is made.

Kamin (1969) used a variation in the CER procedure to demonstrate blocking. First, rats are trained to press a lever for food reinforcement. Next, the rats are exposed to sixteen trials in which a tone is followed by an electric shock. The result of this training is response suppression when the tone is presented. The next phase of the study involves pairing the tone from the previous phase with a light, thus creating a compound stimulus. The tone-light compound stimulus is presented to the rat on eight trials and is always followed by shock. The final phase of the study involves presenting only the light to the rat to see if it produces response suppression, and it does not. A control group indicates that if both the light and the tone

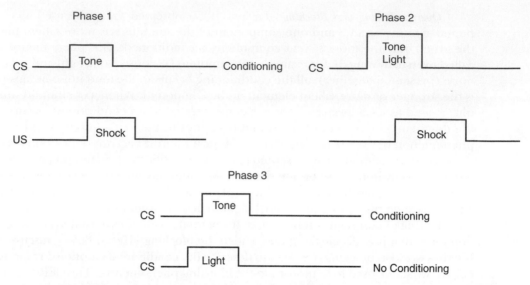

FIGURE 7–5   Kamin's blocking experiment. In Phase 1, a tone is paired with shock, and after several pairings, when presented alone, the tone causes response suppression. In Phase 2, the tone is paired with a light, and both precede a shock. Phase 3 shows that the tone continues to cause response suppression, but the light does not. In spite of the fact that the light was reliably paired with the shock in Phase 2, such pairing did not result in conditioning.

are paired with shock independently, both produce response suppression. If, however, the tone is first paired with shock and then is presented to the rat along with the light, little or no conditioning occurs to the light. Under these conditions, conditioning to the tone *blocks* conditioning to the light. (The blocking effect is also found if the light is used first and is then paired with the tone, in which case no conditioning occurs to the tone.) Kamin's procedure and results are summarized in Figure 7–5.

We examine possible explanations for blocking shortly, but it should be noted here that blocking, like overshadowing, exemplifies a situation in which stimuli are paired in accordance with classical conditioning principles and yet no conditioning occurs. Once again it is suggested that something more than mere stimulus contiguity is involved in classical conditioning.

The Rescorla-Wagner Theory of Classical Conditioning

Robert Rescorla and Allan Wagner have devised a theory that, in a sense, builds on the work of Egger and Miller (1962, 1963). The Rescorla-Wagner theory (see, e.g., Rescorla & Wagner, 1972; Wagner & Rescorla, 1972) provides an account of general classical conditioning phenomena, makes some unexpected predictions relevant to classical conditioning, and solves several critical problems associated with traditional classical conditioning theory. For example, it offers an explanation of blocking, which we consider shortly. The theory has guided research in associative learning since it was published, and Pearce and Bouton (2001) say that although "more than 25 years have passed since it was published, there is no sign of a decline in the influence of this theory" (p. 112).

The theory uses relatively simple mathematical and symbolic logic to summarize the dynamics of learning. First, as noted in Chapter 6, the learning curve increases gradually to a nearly level maximum, or asymptote. Rescorla and Wagner assume that the nature of the US determines the asymptotic, or maximum, level of conditioning that can be achieved. This maximum is symbolized by λ (lambda).

Next, associative learning acquired prior to a specific trial n is designated by V_{n-1}, and the *change* in learning due to conditioning on trial n is symbolized by ΔV_n. The symbol Δ (delta) indicates a change in V.

Finally, the Rescorla-Wagner theory includes two components that refer to the "conditionability" of a particular CS and US pair. The coefficient α (alpha) refers to the potential associative strength of a given CS. A loud tone, for example, will have a higher α value than a soft, inaudible tone. The coefficient β (beta) designates the potential associative strength of a specific US. A strong electric shock will elicit a more dramatic withdrawal reflex than a weak electric shock and therefore will have a greater value of β.

When we put all of these components together for a specified CS (CS_A) and US (US_A), we have

$$\Delta V_n = \alpha_A \, \beta_A (\lambda - V_{n-1})$$

This equation indicates that the change in strength of associative learning on any trial is a function of the *difference* between maximum possible learning and the amount already learned at the conclusion of the *preceding* trial.

Notice that because V_{n-1} grows with each trial and approaches λ, $(\lambda - V_{n-1})$ approaches zero, and ΔV_n is less on each successive trial. Thus, the function is asymptotic at the value of λ. It is not enough, however, for this expression to capture the shape of the learning curve; there are several mathematical expressions that can do the same (see, e.g., Chapter 6 or Chapter 9). The Rescorla-Wagner theory has the advantage of also accounting for anomalous findings in classical conditioning. Let us look, for example, at the way this theory explains blocking.

Recall that blocking occurs when a response is first conditioned to one CS_A (a light), then reinforced further with a compound CS_{AX}, made up of the initial CS_A (the light) and an additional CS_X (a tone). When the second element in the compound (the tone) is presented *alone,* it elicits little or no conditioned response. According to the theory, most of the conditioning possible for a particular US (e.g., a shock) is "used up" by the first CS.

In symbolic language, during initial conditioning, V_A approaches λ, and ΔV_A approaches zero. When we begin compound stimulus training, we have a condition in which

$$\Delta V_A = \alpha_A \beta \, (\lambda - V_{AX})$$

and

$$\Delta V_X = \alpha_X \beta (\lambda - V_{AX})$$

and according to the theory, $V_{AX} = V_A + V_X$. But remember that because of initial training with CS_A,

$$V_{AX} \cong V_A \cong \lambda$$

so V_X is functionally zero. If V_A has approached the value of λ, conditioning to CS_X is not possible because there is no conditioning left for the second CS. Essentially all the conditioning possible under the circumstances "belongs" to the first conditioned stimulus.

Contingency Not Contiguity

In his influential article "Pavlovian Conditioning: It's Not What You Think," Rescorla (1988) makes three observations about Pavlovian conditioning and delineates its importance in modern psychology.

First, like Egger and Miller (1962, 1963), he says it is essential that there be a correlation between US and CS that is more than mere coincidence or contiguity. Take, for example, a situation in which an animal experiences random USs and CSs over an extended period. There may be as many instances when the US and CS occur together (contiguity) as when they occur separately. Contrast this situation with one in which the US and CS are programmed so that they occur only together. These two conditions are represented in Figure 7–6, and it is important to notice that in both situations, CS and US occur together the *same* number of times.

Which CS-US relationship produces the best conditioning? It may seem intuitive, but it comes as a surprise to some psychologists that the latter situation produces the stronger classical conditioning, whereas the former produces weak conditioning, if any. Clearly, contiguity is not enough. Rescorla uses the term *contingency* to describe the relationship in which a CS provides a clear and informative marker for the US.

Robert A. Rescorla. (Courtesy of Robert A. Rescorla.)

Second, like Zener (1937), Rescorla (1988) says that the common claim that a CR is a "miniature" or "abbreviated" UR is either an oversimplification or entirely incorrect. A typical response to a US of electric shock in an open maze, for example, is increased activity or

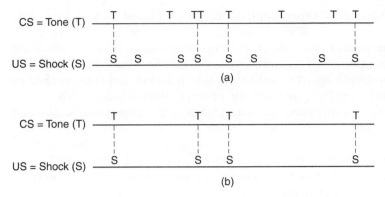

FIGURE 7–6 Although CS and US occur the same number of times in (a) and (b), the CS-US pairing in (a) produces little or no classical conditioning, but the CS-US pairing in (b) produces strong conditioning.

some version of a startle response. However, as seen in the conditioned suppression phenomenon described previously, if the CS used to signal shock is delivered during ongoing performance of a completely different response (lever pressing), the result is decreased activity. The CR can be several different responses, depending on the context in which the CS occurs.

These two points were clearly demonstrated when Rescorla (1966) trained dogs to jump over a hurdle in a shuttle box to avoid an electric shock that was delivered at regular intervals of thirty seconds. The situation was arranged so that the shock could be avoided if the dog jumped the hurdle before the end of the time interval. Each time the dog jumped over the hurdle, the clock was reset to zero and started running again. There was no external signal indicating when a shock would be delivered; the only signal was the animal's internal sense of the passage of time. All of the dogs in the experiment learned to jump often enough to avoid most of the shocks. The rate of jumping was then used as a frame of reference to judge the effects of other variables introduced into the experiment.

After this preliminary training, the dogs were removed from the hurdle-jumping apparatus and subjected to tones followed by electric shock. The dogs were divided into three groups. Group 1 received standard **forward conditioning,** in which a CS (a five-second tone) was always followed by a US (an electric shock). This procedure was called a positive contingency in Rescorla's study. Group 2 first experienced the US *and then* the CS. The situation for this group was arranged so that the CS was never paired with shock, nor was the CS ever followed within thirty seconds by the shock. The arrangement by which a CS *follows* a US, generally referred to as backward conditioning, was referred to as a negative contingency in Rescorla's study. This was an especially interesting experimental condition because it has been widely believed that when the CS follows the US, no conditioning occurs. Group 3 experienced the CS preceding the US and following it an equal number of times. By randomizing the occurrence of the CS relative to the US, a situation is created whereby there is no correlation between the two. That is, the US is as likely to occur following the presentation of the CS as it is when the CS does not occur. Therefore, for subjects in group 3, the CS had no predictive value.

In the final phase of the experiment, the dogs were placed back in the shuttle box and were again given avoidance training until the rate of their avoidance responses stabilized. At this point, the CS (tone) from the classical conditioning phase of the study was presented for five seconds a number of times. It was observed that when the CS was introduced to animals in group 1 (forward conditioning or positive contingency), they *increased* their rate of responding relative to what it was in the initial stage of the experiment. In fact, subjects in this group almost doubled their response rate when the tone came on. When the CS was introduced to animals in group 2 (backward conditioning or negative contingency), they *decreased* their rate of responding by about a third. When the CS was introduced to animals in group 3 (no correlation), their rate of responding remained essentially the same as in the initial phase of the experiment.

One crucial point to remember while interpreting the results of this experiment is that all animals received the same number of shocks during the classical conditioning phase of the experiment. What was varied was the relationship between the CS and the US. As we have seen, Rescorla (1966, 1967) says that it is contingencies that determine whether conditioning takes place and, if so, what kind of conditioning. In group 1, there was a positive contingency between the CS and the US, and therefore, the CS accurately predicted the occurrence of the US. This, according to Rescorla, is why the animals in this group jumped the hurdle more rapidly when the CS was presented. In group 2, there was a negative contingency between the CS and the US. That is, the CS was never paired with or followed by the US within thirty seconds. Thus, for subjects in this group, the CS became a signal for safety. Contrary to the common belief that no classical conditioning occurs under these conditions (backward conditioning), Rescorla found that the animals in this group indeed learned a contingency. They learned that the CS predicted the absence of the shock, and therefore, when the CS was introduced to these animals, they inhibited their rate of jumping. Rescorla says that it is important to realize that the procedure followed in group 2 is the most common "control" condition in classical conditioning studies. It has been commonly believed that because no facilitative conditioning occurs under these circumstances, no conditioning of any kind occurs, but this is clearly not the case. Because inhibitory conditioning does take place, this procedure cannot be used as a control group in classical conditioning studies. It is only the procedures followed in group 3 that provide a **truly random control group** for classical conditioning studies. In this group the appearance of the CS and of the US were independent of each other, and therefore, animals in this group could not use the CS to predict either the subsequent presence or absence of the US. Only under these conditions is there no contingency between the CS and US, and this is why, according to Rescorla, no classical conditioning occurs.

Again, Rescorla's explanation of his results is similar to the one offered earlier by Egger and Miller (1962, 1963). Both claim that for conditioning to take place, a CS must be informative; that is, it must provide the organism with useful information about the US. Rescorla expanded on Egger and Miller's work, however, by showing that negative contingencies are as informative as positive ones. According to Rescorla, it is only the truly random control procedure that creates an uninformative relationship between the CS and US and, thus, produces no conditioning.

Finally, Rescorla (1988) claims that Pavlovian conditioning is more than mere reflex learning and that it has a vital place in contemporary psychology. He insists that the emphasis he and his colleagues place on contingencies, rather than contiguity alone, reveals new and important information about the nature of associative learning. Therefore, he says, classical conditioning provides both a useful database and a theoretical orientation for two topics of current interest and activity in modern psychology. These topics, neuroscientific study of learning and computer simulation of neural networks, are discussed in Chapter 14.

LEARNED HELPLESSNESS

As we have just seen, Rescorla claimed that his truly random control group creates a situation in which there is no predictive relationship between the CS and the US, and therefore, no conditioning occurs. Indeed, Rescorla and others have demonstrated that no conditioning does occur in the truly random control condition, but perhaps they are looking at the wrong kind of behavior.

Martin Seligman (1969, 1975) provided convincing evidence that animals do indeed learn something very important under what Rescorla calls the truly random control condition. In his analysis, Seligman first points out that in a classical conditioning experiment, the organism is helpless, and it learns that it is helpless. To demonstrate that animals learn to be helpless as the result of classical conditioning, Seligman and his colleagues reversed the experimental procedures followed by Kamin and Rescorla and Wagner. Instead of first teaching animals an instrumental

Martin Seligman. (Courtesy of Martin E.P. Seligman.)

response and then exposing them to classical conditioning, Seligman gave his animals classical conditioning first and then attempted to teach them an instrumental response. It turns out that reversing the experimental procedures has a profound effect on the animals' behavior. Maier, Seligman, and Solomon (1969) reported the results of a number of studies in which classical conditioning (using a shock as a US) preceded an attempt to teach animals an instrumental response. The consistent finding is that exposing animals to a series of brief, intense, and unavoidable electric shocks renders animals unable to learn subsequently a simple instrumental response, like jumping a hurdle to escape from or avoid an electric shock. Furthermore, it does not matter how the CS is paired with the US. Animals were unable to learn a simple instrumental response in the second phase of the experiment, regardless of whether they had experienced what Rescorla referred to as a positive contingency, a negative contingency, or a truly random condition. Maier, Seligman, and Solomon contrast the abilities of dogs receiving classical conditioning with those of naive animals not experiencing classical conditioning:

> In a dramatic contrast to a naive dog, a dog which has experienced inescapable shocks prior to avoidance training soon stops running and howling and remains silent until shock terminates. The dog does not cross the barrier and escape the shock. Rather it seems to give up and passively accept the shock. On succeeding trials, the dog continues to fail to make escape movements and will take as much shock as the experimenter chooses to give.
>   . . . Such dogs occasionally jump the barrier and escape or avoid, but then revert to taking the shock; they fail to profit from exposure to the barrier-jumping-shock-termination contingency. In naive dogs a successful escape response is a reliable predictor of future, short-latency escape responses. (pp. 311–312)

According to Seligman, an animal learns that it is helpless in a classical conditioning situation precisely because it is helpless. Furthermore, the helplessness that is learned has nothing to do with the shock that is experienced per se; rather, it has to do with the animal's inability to control the shock. To demonstrate the importance of control, or lack of it, Seligman and Maier (1967) performed a two-phase experiment using dogs as subjects. During phase 1 of the experiment, subjects in group 1 were shocked while constrained in a hammock. Subjects in this group could terminate the shock by pressing a panel with their snouts. Subjects in group 2 were shocked whenever subjects in group 1 were shocked, but subjects in group 2 could do nothing to terminate the shocks. A third control group was placed in the hammock but was given no shock. Seligman and Maier hypothesized that during phase 1 of the experiment, subjects in group 1 learned that shock was potentially controllable through their behavior, whereas subjects in group 2 learned that their behavior could have no influence on the shock. For them, shock was inescapable.

To test their hypothesis, Seligman and Maier (1967) employed escape-avoidance training using a shuttle box in phase 2 of their study. Prompt response to a tone by jumping the hurdle between compartments was followed by the termination of the tone and the shock. Subjects in group 1 (escapable shock) and group 3 (no shock) quickly learned to avoid shock by jumping the hurdle. In vivid contrast, subjects in group 2 (inescapable shock) learned neither to avoid nor to escape the shock. When the shock came on in the shuttle box, they just took the shock and whined. Even when a member of this group occasionally blundered over the hurdle, thus escaping the shock, the response was not repeated when the shock next occurred. According to Seligman and Maier, these animals learned in phase 1 of the study that there was nothing that they could do to avoid shock, so in phase 2 of the study they tried nothing. When the belief that one can do nothing to terminate or avoid an aversive situation generalizes to other situations, it is called **learned helplessness.** Thus, learned helplessness is not caused by traumatic experience per se but by the inability, or perceived inability, to do anything about it. Animals that learned that they could not control an aversive situation became generally passive.

The phenomenon of learned helplessness has been found in many species of animals, including humans, using both appetitive and aversive USs. The symptoms

of learned helplessness include a reluctance to initiate any action to attain reinforcement or to escape punishment, general passivity, withdrawal, fearfulness,
depression, and general willingness to accept whatever happens. Seligman (1975)
has suggested that learned helplessness in humans may be experienced as depression and may characterize individuals who have been so thwarted in their attempts
in life that they become hopeless and withdrawn and finally just give up.

We see, then, that even in what Rescorla called a truly random control condition, organisms learn that they are helpless to avoid or escape an aversive situation
so they no longer try to do so. This feeling of helplessness generalizes beyond the
experimental situation and results in general passivity.

OTHER THEORETICAL ACCOUNTS
OF CLASSICAL CONDITIONING

The Importance of Attention   Nicholas Mackintosh (1975) theorizes that organisms seek information that predicts biologically significant events (e.g., USs). When
a predictive cue is found, attention is increasingly committed to that cue while
attention to irrelevant stimuli decreases. When there are multiple cues, the more
predictive cue becomes increasingly salient with each learning trial; less predictive
cues are increasingly ignored. Thus, Mackintosh's position relies on the active processing of information. A major difference between the position of Rescorla-Wagner
and that of Mackintosh is that the former views the organism as passively receiving
and recording information from the environment and Mackintosh does not. The
Rescorla-Wagner position represents a modern example of the older view of learning that sees the learning process as mechanical, automatic, and associative in nature.
Schwartz, Wasserman, and Robbins (2002) say of the Rescorla-Wagner theory:

> It provides a way of describing seemingly complex processes, involving the evaluation
> of probabilities and the selection of best predictors, in a mechanical, trial-by-trial fash-
> ion. The organism does not need to be able to consider its various experiences with CSs
> and USs over time and combine them in some complex fashion to be able to respond
> as though it were making these considerations. The Rescorla-Wagner theory gives the
> animal a simple solution to the complex problem of forming selective, informative
> associations. (p. 96)

Mackintosh's explanation of blocking follows from the assumption that more
predictive cues win a competition for attention. When one CS (a light) reliably predicts the occurrence of a biologically significant event (a shock), that CS becomes
more salient. When the light is paired with a second CS (a tone), the light remains a
superior predictor because of prior training, and the second CS loses whatever
salience it initially had. Thus, Mackintosh's theory accounts for the observation that
blocking becomes more effective the more frequently the first CS and second CS
are presented together. It may be remembered that the Rescorla-Wagner theory
explained the lack of conditioning to the newly inserted CS by saying that all the

conditioning that the US could support was "used up" by the first CS. So both the Rescorla-Wagner theory and Mackintosh's theory explain blocking, but they do so by making quite different assumptions about the nature of the learning process.

Surprisingness   In an effort to explain blocking, Kamin (1969) argued that when the US first comes on, the animal is surprised by it. If a CS reliably precedes the US, the animal gradually learns to expect the US shortly after the CS is presented. Eventually the animal is no longer surprised by the US, and no additional conditioning takes place. According to Kamin, when the CS elicits a memory of the US, the occurrence of the US is no longer surprising, and there is no reason to learn anything else under the circumstances. Thus, for Kamin, the mechanism that explains classical conditioning is surprisingness. When the onset of the US is a complete surprise, the animal searches its memory for an event that anticipated the US. When such an event is found, surprisingness diminishes, and so does conditioning. If the CS was such an event, it becomes associated with the US in the sense that when the CS comes on, it elicits a memory of the US. The elicited memory of the US will at first be weak but will become stronger with increased pairings of the CS and US. As the memory of the US elicited by the CS becomes more vivid, surprisingness diminishes, and so does conditioning.

Blocking is easily explained through the concept of surprisingness. Because stimulus A reliably predicts the US, the occurrence of the US is no longer surprising at the time stimulus B is introduced, and therefore no conditioning occurs to stimulus B. According to Kamin, no surprise means no conditioning. Wagner (1969, 1971, 1978) has elaborated on and substantiated Kamin's contention that surprisingness is reduced or eliminated to the extent that the CS elicits a memory of the US. Schwartz, Wasserman, and Robbins (2002) summarize the Kamin-Wagner theory as follows.

1. We learn about things only when we process them actively.
2. We process things actively only when they are surprising; that is, when we do not yet understand them.
3. As conditioning proceeds, the CS and the US become less surprising. As a result they get processed less, and we therefore learn less about them. (p. 104)

It is possible to relate the positions of Rescorla-Wagner with that of Kamin-Wagner by assuming that the difference between the maximum amount of conditioning possible and the amount of conditioning that has already taken place reflects the extent to which an organism is surprised by the onset of the US. When the amount of possible conditioning matches the amount of conditioning that has taken place, there is no longer any surprise. Also, because the amount of conditioning possible is directly proportional to the amount of surprise, it should be clear how the Kamin-Wagner theory accounts for the negatively accelerated curve that typically characterizes the learning process.

LEARNED IRRELEVANCE, LATENT INHIBITION, AND SUPERCONDITIONING

At least three phenomena pose problems for the Rescorla-Wagner theory, but they are readily explained by either Macintosh's or Kamin-Wagner's approaches. All of these effects entail preexposure of a CS before introducing a positive (excitatory) contingency between that CS and a US.

Recall that Rescorla (1966) used a truly random control condition in which both CS and US occurred but in which there was no contingency between them. If the CS that is first used in a random control condition is later paired in a contingent relationship with a US, conditioning is impaired. **Learned irrelevance** refers to the diminished efficacy of a CS that is used in a random control condition (Mackintosh, 1973).

This is a problem for the Rescorla-Wagner theory because according to it, preexposure to the CS should have no effect on conditioning. According to the Rescorla-Wagner theory, only characteristics such as the intensity of the CS will influence its subsequent association with the US, and those characteristics are not changed as the result of preexposure in a noncontingent relationship with a US. From Macintosh's perspective, organisms learn that a CS in the random control condition has no predictive value. In effect, it is ignored and is therefore an ineffective CS in a new learning context. The Kamin-Wagner position is similar. After the CS has been paired only randomly with a US, it is not processed actively; the organism ignores it.

The **latent inhibition effect** occurs when preexposing a CS (with no US whatsoever) retards conditioning when the CS and a US are subsequently paired (e.g., Baker & Mackintosh, 1977; Best & Gemberling, 1977; Fenwick, Mikulka, & Klein, 1975; Lubow & Moore, 1959). Once again, this is a problem for the Rescorla-Wagner theory because preexposure to the CS should have no effect on conditioning. Mackintosh and Kamin would explain the adverse effects of preexposure by saying that during the time that the CS is presented alone, the organism learns that it is irrelevant and therefore not correlated with any significant event. Once the CS is found to be irrelevant, it is ignored, thus retarding the formation of a predictive relationship if it is subsequently paired with a US. In an extension of Macintosh's notion of competition for attention, Moore and Stickney (1980) suggest that, although no reinforcement occurs during CS preexposure, there is still competition for attention among stimuli. Under most conditions, a preexposed CS competes for attention with stable, and therefore more predictive, environmental stimuli in the testing apparatus. Those stimuli gain salience, and the relatively meaningless CS loses salience, thereby reducing its subsequent effectiveness. Thus latent inhibition, like blocking, is explained by Macintosh as an organism's learning to attend to predictive stimuli and to ignore irrelevant or redundant information.

Finally, imagine that we use A^+/AX^- training to establish a CS as a conditioned inhibitor. One might expect that establishing a CS as a conditioned inhibitor impairs subsequent conditioning when the CS is paired with a US. The surprising result, however, is that conditioning is facilitated (Pearce & Redhead, 1995; Rescorla, 1971, 2002; Wagner, 1971; Williams & McDevitt, 2002). Researchers use the term **superconditioning** to describe the facilitation of conditioning that occurs when an established conditioned inhibitor (CS^-) is subsequently paired with a US. Rescorla (2002), for example, trained both rats and pigeons to respond to a CS paired with a strong US in what he called A^{++} training. The compound AX was trained as a conditioned inhibitor in AX^- training. Later, the compound AX was paired with a weak US (smaller amount of US or delayed presentation of US) in what Rescorla called AX^+ training. Both elements of the compound were then tested for their excitatory effects. Although both elements of the compound increased in their abilities to excite a response, the never-reinforced component of the compound, X, increased significantly more than the previously reinforced A component. Rescorla (2002) recognizes that the results "provide substantial challenges for all contemporary theories of compound conditioning" (p. 173). Williams and McDevitt (2002), who argue that superconditioning is the opposite of blocking, support an explanation similar to that in the Kamin-Wagner theory. That is, after a CS has become a conditioned inhibitor, its presentation with a US is surprising and therefore facilitates conditioning.

Conditioning as the Formation of Expectancies   Robert Bolles (1972, 1979) suggested that organisms do not learn any new responses during conditioning. Rather, they learn to execute species-specific reactions that are appropriate to the situation. According to Bolles, what organisms learn are expectancies that guide their unlearned behavior. A stimulus expectancy is formed when a CS is correlated with an important outcome such as the presence or absence of a US. In other words, the typical classical conditioning experiment creates a stimulus expectancy. A stimulus expectancy involves predicting the presence of one stimulus (US) from the presence of another stimulus (CS). Organisms also learn response expectancies, which are predictive relationships between responses and outcomes. According to Bolles, reinforcement does not strengthen behavior; rather, it strengthens the expectancy that a certain response will be followed by a reinforcer.

Bolles (1979) argued that recent findings call into question the traditional mechanistic-associationistic explanation of classical conditioning and proposes that his cognitive explanation be accepted instead:

> The unpredictability of the CR, the difficulty of not really knowing what kind of behavior to expect from a conditioned animal, suggests that what is learned in a Pavlovian situation is not a response at all. Perhaps what is learned is something else, perhaps something about the . . . CS-US relationship. Maybe what the animal learns then when the CS comes on is not to respond to it in some fixed manner but rather to expect the US. Whether or not we finally accept such a cognitive conclusion, it is clear that one of the oldest and most basic assumptions about the conditioning process is open to question. We can no longer take for granted that conditioning produces an automatic connection of some response to the CS. (p. 155)

In his explanation of conditioning, Bolles followed rather closely the theory of Edward Tolman (Chapter 12). Details and extensions of Bolles's theory are presented in Chapter 15.

In the last few sections, we have learned that the principles governing classical conditioning are still being disputed. Basic questions such as "What is learned during classical conditioning?" and "Under what circumstances is it learned?" are the focus of much current research, theory, and discussion, and it looks like this will be true for some time. In any case, it is now clear that classical conditioning is much more complex than was realized before. Rather than attempting to determine which account of classical conditioning is the correct one, it seems that it would be more accurate to conclude that all accounts accurately explain some aspect of classical conditioning. It seems reasonable to conclude that when the entire story is told, aspects of classical conditioning will be found to depend on predictability of cues, memory processes, the formation of expectancies, attentional processes, and the automatic formation of associations when there is a contingent relationship between CSs and USs.

CONDITIONED TASTE AVERSION: THE GARCIA EFFECT

For many years, anecdotal evidence suggested that pests, particularly rats and mice, escaped eradication because they quickly learned that some substances, poison baits, for example, made them sick and should be avoided. Similarly, people willingly share stories about a food or beverage they avoid because they associate it with nausea. Garcia and Koelling (1966) validated these anecdotal accounts of taste aversion by demonstrating an unusual phenomenon in classical conditioning. For now, we describe only one part of this important experiment, and in Chapter 15 we will explore the phenomenon in greater detail, with particular attention to its evolutionary and biological significance.

Garcia and Koelling exposed one group of rats to strong X-rays while the rats were drinking saccharine-sweetened water (CS). X-ray treatment causes nausea (US) in rats about thirty minutes after exposure. Another group of rats received painful electrical shocks as they drank the sweetened water. In subsequent tests, the rats in the first group refused to drink saccharine-sweetened water. The rats that received electrical shocks, however, showed no aversion to the flavored water. Garcia and Koelling concluded that the rats made ill by X-ray treatment learned an aversion to the flavor or taste associated with illness, a natural response that was conducive to their survival.

Although the Garcia and Koelling experiment seems to follow classical conditioning procedures, it presents a few problems when the results are interpreted as classical conditioning phenomena. First, the time delay between the CS (the taste of saccharin) and the US (nausea) greatly exceeds the time interval considered necessary for classical conditioning. The interval between the time an animal tastes a substance and then experiences illness can be several hours. Second, it is repeatedly found that a strong taste aversion can develop after only a few (sometimes only one) pairings of a substance and nausea. Ordinarily, it takes many pairings between a CS and a US to produce a conditioned response (CR). Sometimes when strong punishment is used, conditioning has been found to take place in one trial, but never when the interval between the CS and the US is as long as it typically is in taste aversion studies. Third, although taste aversions develop after long time delays and, in some cases, in just one trial, they are extremely resistant to extinction. Usually, resistance to extinction goes up as the number of pairings between the CS and the US goes up, but taste aversions seem to violate this principle. The effect observed by Garcia and Koelling was so unusual, relative to what was known about classical conditioning at the time, that their research report was initially rejected by a number of journals. Despite Garcia's twenty previous publications using X-ray technology in radiobiological research, one journal editor had the audacity to suggest that Garcia did not understand how X-rays worked (Garcia, 1981). However, Garcia and his colleagues persisted, and they replicated their earlier findings, first replacing the X-ray treatment with injection of lithium chloride, a chemical that produces nausea (Garcia, Ervin, & Koelling, 1966) and later demonstrating that rats learn aversions to taste cues but not to visual cues such as the size of food pellets (Garcia, McGowan, Ervin, & Koelling, 1968).

Thus, taste aversions are formed rapidly and last a long time, and these facts seem directly related to an organism's survival. The formation of taste aversions has so many unique features that the phenomenon has been given a name (Bolles, 1979): "The remarkable facility with which rats (and a number of other animals) learn about the relationship between the taste of a particular food substance and a subsequent illness we shall call the '**Garcia effect**'" (p. 167).

Cancer patients undergoing chemotherapy have been observed often to acquire long-lasting aversions to foods eaten prior to a treatment (Andresen, Birch, & Johnson, 1990; Bernstein, 1978). Drugs used in chemotherapy often produce nausea. From our knowledge of the Garcia effect, we would expect that flavor cues of foods eaten prior to treatment would become aversive, particularly if the subsequent chemotherapy treatment resulted in severe nausea. Longitudinal studies (Jacobsen et al., 1993) indicate that up to 50 percent of chemotherapy patients experience learned food aversions, but not all foods are likely to become aversive. Novel or unusual foods eaten prior to treatment tend to produce the effect more than familiar foods, and backward conditioning, aversion to foods eaten after treatments, is rare. Furthermore, taste aversions developed during the first few chemotherapy treatments are unstable and short-lived, whereas those developed later in the course of therapy tend to last longer. Interestingly, the severity of nausea induced by chemotherapy is not a good predictor of learned food aversions.

Does the Garcia effect have any practical implications? The answer seems to be yes. The Garcia effect has been used to control predators. Wild coyotes have long been a problem in the Western United States because they prey on lambs and other livestock. This problem has led to a debate between farmers and ranchers, who often want to kill the coyotes, and environmentalists, who want to save the coyotes for ecological reasons. Gustavson, Garcia, Hankins, and Rusiniak (1974) have shown that the Garcia effect can be used to control the eating habits of coyotes. In their study, three coyotes were fed lamb flesh treated with lithium chloride, which causes nausea, and three were fed rabbit flesh treated with the same substance. After only one or two experiences with the treated flesh, the coyotes avoided attacking the kind of animals whose flesh had made them ill but showed no avoid-ance of the other type of flesh. That is, those coyotes that ate treated lamb flesh avoided sheep but ate rabbits, and those coyotes that ate treated rabbit flesh avoided rabbits but ate sheep. Thus, it appears that we have a straightforward way of control-ling the eating habits of predators that satisfies the wishes of both ranchers and farmers and the environmentalists.

JOHN B. WATSON'S EXPERIMENT WITH LITTLE ALBERT

Before discussing the clinical applications of classical conditioning in the next sec-tion, we review **John B. Watson**'s famous experiment with an infant named Albert. We saw in Chapter 3 that Watson, the founder of the school of **behaviorism,** felt that psychology should be purged of all mentalistic concepts and explanations of human behavior based on instinct.

Watson was a radical environmental determinist. He believed that all we come equipped with at birth are a few reflexes and a few basic emotions, and through clas-sical conditioning these reflexes become paired with a variety of stimuli. Human emotion was, for Watson, a product of both heredity and experience. According to Watson, we inherit three emotions—fear, rage, and love. Through the conditioning process, these three basic emotions become attached to different things for differ-ent people. Personality was, to Watson, a collection of conditioned reflexes. He emphatically denied that we are born with any mental abilities or predispositions. The extreme to which Watson (1926) was willing to carry this position is exempli-fied by his following famous (or infamous) statement: "Give me a dozen healthy infants, well-formed, and my own specified world to bring them up in and I'll guar-antee to take any one at random and train him to become any type of specialist I might select—doctor, lawyer, artist, merchant, chief, and yes, even beggarman and thief, regardless of his talents, penchants, tendencies, abilities, vocations, and race of his ancestors" (p. 10).

To demonstrate how inborn emotional reflexes become conditioned to neu-tral stimuli, Watson and Rosalie Rayner (1920) performed an experiment on an eleven-month-old infant named Albert. In addition to Albert, the other ingredients in the experiment were a white rat, a steel bar, and a hammer. At the onset of the study, Albert showed no fear of the rat. In fact, he reached out and tried to touch it. During the initial part of the experiment, when Albert saw the rat and reached for it, the experimenter took the hammer and struck the steel bar behind the infant, making a loud noise. In response to the noise, Albert "jumped violently and fell for-ward." Again Albert saw the rat and reached for it, and again, just as his hand touched the rat, the bar was struck, making a loud noise. Again, Albert jumped vio-lently and began to whimper. Because of Albert's emotional state, the experiment was suspended for one week so Albert would not become too disturbed.

After a week, the rat was again presented to Albert. This time Albert was very cautious of the animal and watched it very carefully. At one point, when the rat came into contact with his hand, Albert withdrew his hand immediately. There were several more pairings between the rat and the sound, and eventually Albert developed a strong fear of the rat. Now when the rat was presented to Albert again, he began to cry and "almost instantly he turned sharply to the left, fell over, raised himself on all fours and began to crawl away . . . rapidly" (1920, p. 5).

It was also shown that Albert's fear generalized to a variety of objects that were not feared at the onset of the experiment: a rabbit, a dog, a fur coat, cotton, and a Santa Claus mask. Thus, Watson showed that our emotional reactions can be rearranged through classical conditioning. In this experiment, the loud noise was the US, fear produced by the noise was the UR, the rat was the CS, and the fear of the rat was the CR. Albert's fear of all white and furry objects showed that generalization also took place.

Bregman's Replication of Watson's Experiment   In 1934, E. O. Bregman replicated Watson's experiment and found that a child's fear could indeed be conditioned to a CS but that such conditioning took place only under certain circumstances. Bregman found that conditioning took place only if the CS was a live animal (as it was in Watson's experiment), but *no conditioning occurred if the CS was an inanimate object,* such as a block, a bottle, or even a wooden animal. Bregman's findings were inconsistent with Pavlov and Watson's claim that the nature of a CS should be irrelevant to the conditioning process. However, her findings were consistent with Seligman's contention that some associations are easier to form than others because of the biological preparedness of the organism. In this case, Seligman (1972) says that because animals have the potential to do harm, humans are biologically prepared to suspect them and therefore learn with relative ease to fear or avoid them.

Eliminating Conditioned Fears   Watson had demonstrated that an innate emotion, such as fear, could be "transferred" to stimuli that did not originally elicit that emotion, and that the mechanism for the transfer was classical conditioning. This was an extremely important finding, even if it would be demonstrated later that conditioning was easier with some stimuli than with others. If fears are learned, it should be possible to unlearn or extinguish them. Unfortunately, Watson and Rayner never removed Albert's fears because his mother removed him from the hospital where the experiment was being conducted shortly after fear was instilled (Harris, 1979, p. 152). Watson felt that his research had shown how learned fears develop, and no further research of that kind was necessary. Instead, his strategy was to find a child who had already developed a fear and then attempt to eliminate it. Watson, now working with Mary Cover Jones (1896–1987), found such a child—a three-year-old named Peter who was intensely frightened of, among other things, rats, rabbits, fur coats, frogs, and fish. Hergenhahn (2005) summarizes the efforts of Watson and Jones to eliminate Peter's fears:

> Watson and Jones first tried showing Peter other children playing fearlessly with objects of which he was frightened, and there was some improvement. (This is a technique called *modeling,* which Bandura and his colleagues employ today.) [See Chapter13 of this text.] At this point, Peter came down with scarlet fever and had to go to the hospital. Following recovery, he and his nurse were attacked by a dog on their way home

from the hospital, and all of Peter's fears returned in magnified form. Watson and Jones decided to try counterconditioning on Peter. Peter ate lunch in a room 40 feet long. One day as Peter was eating lunch, a rabbit in a wire cage was displayed far enough away from him so that Peter was not disturbed. The researchers made a mark on the floor at that point. Each day they moved the rabbit a bit closer to Peter until one day it was sitting beside Peter as he ate. Finally, Peter was able to eat with one hand and play with the rabbit with the other. The results generalized, and most of Peter's other fears were also eliminated or reduced. This is one of the first examples of what we now call **behavior therapy.** In 1924, Jones published the results of the research with Peter, and in 1974 she published more of the details surrounding the research. (p. 374)

The procedure Watson and Jones used to eliminate Peter's fear is quite similar to a procedure called systematic desensitization, which we will consider shortly.

Watson's Theory of Learning   Although Watson did as much as anyone to introduce Pavlovian psychology to the United States, he never fully accepted Pavlovian principles. For example, he did not believe that conditioning depended on reinforcement. For Watson, learning occurred simply because events followed each other closely in time. Classical conditioning occurs, not because the US reinforces the CS, but because the CS and US follow each other in close succession. Also, the more often events occur together, the stronger will be the association between them. Watson, then, accepted only the ancient laws of contiguity and frequency. For him, other learning principles were either mentalistic, like Thorndike's law of effect, or unnecessary, like the notion of reinforcement. In the next chapter, we review Guthrie's theory of learning and see that it is very similar to Watson's theory.

FURTHER APPLICATIONS OF CLASSICAL CONDITIONING TO CLINICAL PSYCHOLOGY

Extinction   Clinical practices based on classical conditioning assume that because behavior disorders or bad habits are learned, they can be unlearned or can be replaced by more positive behaviors. Let us assume that smoking and the excessive drinking of alcohol are behavior disorders, or at least bad habits. In such cases, the taste of alcohol or cigarettes can be considered CSs and the physiological effects of alcohol or nicotine are the USs. After many CS-US pairings, experiencing the CSs alone produces immediate pleasure (CR). One possible way to eliminate these habits is to present the CSs without presenting the USs, thus causing extinction. Schwartz, Wasserman, and Robbins (2002) point out the problems with this procedure:

> First, it is impossible to recreate completely in a laboratory setting the complex and idiosyncratic set of events that serve as CSs in the real world. . . . Second, . . . there is no evidence that extinction removes the underlying CS-US association; instead, extinction temporarily blocks CRs until conditions such as the passage of time (spontaneous recovery) or the reintroduction of either the US (reinstatement) or the training context (renewal) act to reestablish responding. . . . Finally, extinguished responses can always be retrained if drug use recurs. (p. 127)

Counterconditioning   A procedure more powerful than simple extinction is **counterconditioning.** In counterconditioning, the CS is paired with a US other than the original one. For example, a person is allowed to smoke or drink and then is given a drug that produces nausea. With repeated pairings, the taste of cigarettes or alcohol will produce conditioned nausea, which in turn will create an aversion to smoking or drinking. For example, Mount, Payton, Ellis, and Barnes (1976) injected Anectine into the arms of alcoholic clients immediately after they drank a glass of their favorite alcoholic beverage. Anectine produces a paralyzing effect on the respiratory system, which most people report as a frightening experience. After such treatment, only one of the nine individuals involved in this study started drinking again. Although counterconditioning has been found to be successful in a number of cases, the benefits from the procedure are often only temporary. Schwartz, Wasserman, and Robbins (2002) say,

> Ultimately, counterconditioning suffers from the same difficulties that plague extinction training. For one, counterconditioning in the laboratory or clinic may not generalize well outside these settings. Addicts may only learn that their drug of choice is unpleasant *when taken in this artificial environment*. . . . Second, any tendency to reuse the drug outside the clinic setting will result in the rapid reestablishment of the original conditioned responses. . . . Counterconditioning faces a further, unique difficulty. Even if the treatment were effective, convincing patients to undergo repeated exposures to shock or vomiting is no easy task. (p. 128)

Flooding   A major problem in treating phobias is the fact that individuals avoid or escape from frightening experiences. Because extinction is an active process (the CS must be presented and not followed by the US), avoiding fear-producing stimuli prevents extinction from occurring. If, for example, a person has a dog phobia, that person is never with a dog long enough to learn whether it is safe. Any CS that elicits fear will cause the organism to escape or avoid it, and such behavior prevents the organism from learning that the CS may no longer be associated with an aversive US. So how can such a phobia be extinguished? In the natural environment, it probably never would be. The only way of extinguishing a phobia is to force the organism to remain in the presence of the CS long enough to learn that nothing negative will follow. When such forced extinction is used to eliminate phobias, it is called **flooding.** Rimm and Masters (1979) report that flooding is a relatively fast way of eliminating phobias, but it produces results that are variable. With the flooding procedure, some individuals improve, but some get worse. That some individuals become worse is not surprising in light of the fact that they are forced to experience something that they had spent a good deal of their lives fearing and thus avoiding. Also not surprising is the fact that client dropout rates are higher when flooding is used than for systematic desensitization, the therapeutic technique that we consider next.

Systematic Desensitization   One of the most thorough attempts to apply classical conditioning principles to psychotherapy was undertaken by Joseph Wolpe (1958), who developed a therapeutic technique referred to as **systematic desensitization.** Wolpe's technique, which is used primarily for treating clients with phobias, involves three phases. The first phase is developing an **anxiety hierarchy,** which is done by taking a sequence of related anxiety-provoking events and ordering them from those that produce the greatest amount of anxiety to those that produce the least. Let us say that a person has an extreme fear of flying in an airplane. Such a person's anxiety hierarchy may look something like this:

1. Flying in an airplane
2. Sitting in an airplane while it is on the ground with its engines running
3. Sitting in an airplane while it is on the ground with its engines turned off
4. Being in close proximity to an airplane
5. Seeing an airplane at a distance
6. Being in an airport
7. Hearing the sound of airplane engines
8. Talking about being on an airplane
9. Planning a trip without airplanes involved
10. Hearing others plan a trip without airplanes involved

In the second phase of his procedure, Wolpe teaches his clients to relax. He teaches them how to reduce muscle tension and, in general, how it feels when one is not experiencing anxiety. In the third phase, the client first experiences deep relaxation and then is asked to imagine the weakest item on the anxiety hierarchy. While experiencing this item, the client is again asked to induce relaxation. When this is accomplished, the client is asked to ponder the next item on the list, and so forth through the entire list. Wolpe (1958) assumed that each time an item on the list is experienced along with relaxation (the absence of anxiety), a little bit of the phobic response associated with the terminal item on the list extinguishes. This procedure allows the client to gradually approximate the situation that was too frightening to ponder previously. Such an anxiety-provoking experience must be approached gradually and with a great deal of care; otherwise, the client will be unable to think about the feared item, and therefore fear of it will never extinguish. As we have seen, one problem that a person with a phobia has is avoidance of the very experiences that will eliminate the phobia. In other words, a person with a flying phobia typically avoids flying and all related experiences, the person with sex phobia avoids sexual and related experiences, and so on. If a phobia is ever going to extinguish, the feared item must be experienced in the absence of anxiety.

After this cognitive extinction has occurred, it is hoped that the person will be able to repeat the steps in the real world. After systematic desensitization, the client should be able to deal with his or her fear (or previous fear) more rationally and, in this case, fly in an airplane without experiencing disabling anxiety.

Whereas Wolpe had his clients move slowly closer to feared objects psychologically, Watson and Jones slowly moved a feared object physically closer to a child. Except for this difference the two approaches to extinguishing fears have much in common.

We compare in Chapter 13 the effectiveness of Wolpe's technique of systematic desensitization with that of other techniques used to treat phobias.

APPLICATIONS OF CLASSICAL CONDITIONING TO MEDICINE

The many research programs stimulated by Pavlov included one by Metalnikov (Metalnikov, 1934; Metalnikov & Chorine, 1926), who performed a series of unique experiments in classical conditioning. Using guinea pigs as subjects, Metalnikov paired either heat or tactile (touch) stimuli (CSs) with injections of foreign proteins (US). Metalnikov reported that after repeated pairings of CS and US, presentation of the heat or touch stimuli alone resulted in a variety of nonspecific immune responses. These early studies were basically ignored by learning theorists in the United States, perhaps because they lacked rigorous experimental controls and accurate assessment of the immune responses that were observed. Research by Robert Ader and his colleagues in the 1970s renewed interest in the topic and demonstrated clearly that the immune system could be conditioned. In doing so, these researchers effectively launched a new and exciting interdisciplinary area now called psychoneuroimmunology, an area concerned with interactions among psychological factors (learning, perception, emotion), the nervous system, and the immune system.

Ader (1974) was initially studying taste aversion by pairing a saccharin drinking solution (CS) with injection of a drug (US). The drug in this instance, cyclophosphamide, suppresses the immune system. After the initial taste aversion experiment, Ader noted an unusually high number of deaths in rats that continued to receive the saccharin solution (without the US). He suggested that conditioned suppression of the immune system, resulting in greater susceptibility to viral or bacterial infections, led to increased deaths. In a subsequent experiment, Ader and Cohen (1975) first paired the CS of saccharin-flavored water with the US of cyclophosphamide injection. Three days later, the rats were injected with a foreign protein (red blood cells of sheep), a procedure that produces long-term elevation of a highly specific antibody in healthy rats (Markovic, Dimitrijevic, & Jankovic, 1993). When aversion-conditioned animals were reexposed to the saccharin CS, their blood levels of sheep cell antibodies were found to be lower than those of animals in control groups that were not reexposed to either the CS or to the US. Ader and Cohen concluded that the saccharin CS had acquired the ability to suppress the immune system in a highly specific manner.

Since the publication of Ader's studies, many experiments have demonstrated classical conditioning in the immune system. Although few of these studies have been done with humans, work with nonhuman animals has demonstrated conditioned suppression, as well as conditioned elevation, of immune functions, along with extinction of these effects (for review, see Ader & Cohen, 2001). Researchers continue to examine conditioned immune responses to better understand communication between the sensory and nervous systems and the immune system and to better understand how this unique kind of classical conditioning occurs (Hiramoto et al., 1997). In the near future, psychoneuroimmunologists hope to detail the ways in which conditioning can assist patients with autoimmune disorders such as lupus or certain types of arthritis, to help prevent tissue rejections in patients who have undergone transplant surgeries, or perhaps to rally the immune system in cancer patients and patients with HIV or AIDS (Ader, 2001, 2003; Bovbjerg, 2003).

PAVLOV ON EDUCATION

Pavlovian principles are difficult to apply to classroom education, although they are no doubt operating all the time. In general, we can say that every time a neutral event is paired with a meaningful event, classical conditioning occurs; obviously, pairings of that kind take place all the time. When a cologne that was consistently worn by a favorite teacher is smelled later in life, it will tend to elicit favorable memories of school; learning math in a rigid, authoritarian atmosphere may create a negative attitude toward math; being made to write something over and over again as a disciplinary action may create a negative attitude toward writing; having difficult subjects in the morning may create at least a mild dislike for mornings; and a likable, knowledgeable teacher may inspire certain students to consider a teaching career. The feelings of anxiety associated with failure in school may create an aversion to problem-solving situations outside of school. You will remember that the Garcia effect showed that strong aversions to a situation can develop if a negative experience is associated with that situation. Thus, animals that eat a certain food and become ill develop a strong aversion to that food. It is possible that if classroom experiences are negative enough, students may develop lifelong aversions to education. In addition, students with this negative attitude toward education may be the ones who attack teachers, school property, or other students in order to vent their frustrations.

Although the influence of classical conditioning in the classroom is strong, it is usually incidental. The principles of classical conditioning, however, can be purposively utilized in an educational program, as they were in the case of Albert. When Pavlovian techniques are used to modify behavior, the situation appears to resemble brainwashing more than education. To find examples of Pavlovian principles used to modify attitudes, one needs only to observe television commercials carefully. The advertiser's procedure involves pairing a neutral object (the product) with something someone likes (e.g., wealth, health, youth, sex, or prestige). Gradually, the product will cause viewers to have the same feeling that they used to get only from the object or event it was paired with. Next, it is assumed that the viewer will feel successful by smoking Brand X cigarettes, be sexier by driving a certain kind of car, or be more youthful by using a certain hair preparation.

Again, these "incidental" aspects of education are no doubt occurring all the time that a child is in school. The modification of attitudes and emotions involved in learning based on classical conditioning must be taken into consideration in designing any truly effective educational program.

EVALUATION OF PAVLOV'S THEORY

Contributions

The questions that Pavlov formulated—and partly answered—concerning the dynamics of the CS-US relationship, the course of response acquisition, generalization and discrimination, and extinction and spontaneous recovery have continued to stimulate productive studies in contemporary psychology and in related medical research. By 1965, well over five thousand experiments following Pavlov's experimental procedures had been conducted in both basic research areas and clinical applications (Razran, 1965). Thus, Pavlov rivals Skinner and Hull in terms of specific experimental-procedural contributions to the field. And in this chapter, we saw that contemporary researchers such as Robert Rescorla and Mark Bouton continue to make discoveries in classical conditioning.

In the history of learning theory, Pavlov created the first theory concerned with anticipatory learning. His treatment of the CS as a signal event was unique compared with other learning theorists who treated stimuli either as causal events in S-R connections or as reinforcing events that follow responses. If we view habituation and sensitization as the simplest units of nonassociative learning, it is appropriate to consider the classically conditioned response as the fundamental unit of associative learning. Clearly, theorists other than Pavlov came to rely heavily on that fundamental, anticipatory unit.

Criticisms

Insofar as we can criticize Thorndike's, Watson's, or other S-R theories for their simplistic, mechanistic views of learning, we can apply the same criticisms to Pavlov's theory. Pavlov avoided explanations of learning that involved complex mental processes and assumed that a learner's awareness of CS-US relationships was not needed for learning to occur.

We might wonder if Pavlov's influence might have been greater if he actually intended to study learning. Windholz (1992) points out that although the fundamental discovery of classical conditioning occurred in 1897, Pavlov considered his work pertinent to discovery of basic nervous system functions and was unaware that his work was relevant to the development of learning theory in the United States until the early 1930s. By that time, he was already in his eighties. During the last few years of his life, he speculated about both reflex learning and about trial-and-error learning and, as we noted earlier in this chapter, gave credit to E. L. Thorndike for developments in that area.

DISCUSSION QUESTIONS

1. Briefly describe the following: acquisition of a conditioned response, extinction, spontaneous recovery, generalization, discrimination, and higher-order conditioning.

2. Briefly describe Pavlov's physiological explanation of conditioning, generalization, and discrimination.
3. What observations did Egger and Miller make that were contrary to Pavlov's explanation of classical conditioning?
4. According to Pavlov, what determines how we respond to the environment at any given time?
5. Discuss the major differences and similarities between instrumental and classical conditioning.
6. Provide evidence that CRs are not necessarily small versions of URs.
7. First define overshadowing and blocking, and then discuss how the phenomena are contrary to what the law of contiguity would predict.
8. Describe how conditioned emotional responses (CERs) are used to index the strength of CS-US associations.
9. Summarize the Rescorla-Wagner theory of classical conditioning.
10. How does the Rescorla-Wagner theory explain blocking?
11. Explain the distinction that Rescorla makes between contingency and contiguity as a necessary condition for classical conditioning to occur.
12. What experimental arrangement produces what Rescorla calls a truly random control condition? Why, according to Rescorla, is a truly random control group necessary in classical conditioning studies?
13. Describe what kind of conditioned behavior is produced by positive and negative contingencies.
14. What, according to Seligman, is learned helplessness? Describe the circumstances under which learned helplessness develops.
15. How, according to Seligman, can learned helplessness be avoided?
16. Discuss Mackintosh's theory of classical conditioning based on attention. Include in your answer Mackintosh's explanation of blocking.
17. Discuss Kamin and Wagner's theory of classical conditioning based on surprisingness. Include in your answer Kamin and Wagner's explanation of blocking.
18. Discuss Bolles's theory of classical conditioning based on expectancy formation. Why did Bolles claim that his theory is opposed to those theories of classical conditioning in the associationistic tradition?
19. What is the Garcia effect?
20. Summarize the problems involved in trying to explain the development of taste aversions as a classical conditioning phenomenon.
21. How can the Garcia effect be used to change the eating habits of predators?
22. If the Garcia effect exists on the human level, why do you suppose so many individuals continue to smoke or consume alcohol even though their initial experience with smoking or drinking alcohol made them extremely ill?
23. Explain emotional development from J. B. Watson's point of view.
24. Describe the procedure used by Watson and Jones to extinguish Peter's fear of rabbits.
25. Explain how extinction and counterconditioning are used as therapeutic techniques, and explain why these techniques have limited usefulness.

26. Discuss flooding as a therapeutic technique. Include in your answer the problems associated with flooding.
27. Summarize Wolpe's therapeutic technique of systematic desensitization.

CHAPTER HIGHLIGHTS

anxiety hierarchy

backward conditioning

behaviorism

behavior therapy

blocking (also called the blocking effect)

concentration

conditioned emotional response (CER)

conditioned inhibition

conditioned response (CR) (also called conditioned reflex)

conditioned stimulus (CS)

conditioned suppression

cortical mosaic

counterconditioning

discrimination

disinhibition

dynamic stereotype

excitation

excitatory conditioning

external inhibition

extinction

first signal system

flooding

forward conditioning

Garcia effect

generalization

higher-order conditioning

information value of a stimulus

inhibition

irradiation of excitation

latent inhibition effect

learned helplessness

learned irrelevance

orienting reflex

overshadowing

primary reinforcer

reinstatement

renewal effect

secondary reinforcer

second signal system

semantic generalization

spontaneous recovery

superconditioning

systematic desensitization

truly random control group

unconditioned response (UR)

unconditioned stimulus (US)

Watson, John B.

CHAPTER 8

Edwin Ray Guthrie

Guthrie was born in 1886 and died in 1959. He was professor of psychology at the University of Washington from 1914 until his retirement in 1956. His most basic work was *The Psychology of Learning*, published in 1935 and revised in 1952. His style of writing is easy to follow and humorous; it involves many homespun

Edwin Ray Guthrie. (Courtesy of Archives of the History of American Psychology—The University of Akron.)

anecdotes to exemplify his ideas. There are no technical terms or mathematical equations, and he firmly believed that his theory—or any scientific theory, for that matter—should be stated so that it would be understandable to first-year college students. He placed a great emphasis on practical application of his ideas and in this regard was very much like Thorndike and Skinner. He was not really an experimentalist himself, although he certainly had an experimental outlook and orientation. Along with Horton, he performed only one experiment related to his theory of learning, and we discuss that experiment later on. He was, however, clearly a behaviorist. As a matter of fact, he felt theorists like Thorndike, Skinner, Hull, Pavlov, and Watson were too subjective and that by carefully applying the law of parsimony, it was possible to explain all learning phenomena by using only one principle. As we discuss in this chapter, this one principle was one of Aristotle's laws of association. It is for this reason that we place Guthrie's behavioristic theory within the associationistic paradigm.

MAJOR THEORETICAL CONCEPTS

The One Law of Learning

Most learning theories can be thought of as attempts to determine the rules by which stimuli and responses become associated. Guthrie (1952) felt that the rules that had been generated by theorists like Thorndike and Pavlov were unnecessarily complicated, and in their place he proposed one law of learning, the **law of contiguity,** which he stated as follows: "A combination of stimuli which has accompanied a movement will on its recurrence tend to be followed by that movement. Note that nothing is here said about 'confirmatory waves' or reinforcement or pleasant effects" (p. 23). Another way of stating the law of contiguity is to say that if you did something in a given situation, the next time that you are in that situation, you will tend to do the same thing.

Guthrie (1952) explained why, although the law of contiguity may be true, prediction of behavior will always be probabilistic:

> Although the principle as it has just been stated is short and simple, it will not be clear without a considerable amount of elaboration. The word "tend" is used because behavior

is at any time subject to a great variety of conditions. Conflicting "tendencies" or incompatible "tendencies" are always present. The outcome of any one stimulus or stimulus pattern cannot be predicted with certainty because there are other stimulus patterns present. We may express this by saying that the final behavior is caused by the total situation, but we may not, in making this statement, flatter ourselves that we have done more than offer an excuse for a failure to predict. No one has recorded and no one ever will record any stimulus situation in its totality, or observed any total situation, so that to speak of it as a "cause" or even as the occasion of a bit of behavior is misleading. (p. 23)

In his last publication before he died, Guthrie (1959) revised his law of contiguity to read, "What is being noticed becomes a signal for what is being done" (p. 186). This was Guthrie's way of recognizing the enormous number of stimuli that confront an organism at any given time and the fact that the organism cannot possibly form associations with all of them. Rather, the organism responds selectively to only a small proportion of the stimuli confronting it, and it is that proportion that becomes associated with whatever response is being made. One can note the similarity between Guthrie's thinking and Thorndike's concept of "prepotency of elements," which also states that organisms respond selectively to different aspects of the environment.

There is nothing new about the law of contiguity as a principle of learning. In fact, as we noted in Chapter 3, it goes all the way back to Aristotle's laws of association. Guthrie, however, made the law of contiguity the cornerstone of his unique theory of learning.

One-Trial Learning

Another of Aristotle's laws of association is the law of frequency, which states that the strength of an association depends on the frequency with which it occurs. If the law of frequency is modified to refer to the association between a response that leads to a "satisfying state of affairs" and the stimulating conditions preceding the response, Thorndike, Skinner, and Hull would accept it. The more often a response is reinforced in a given situation, the greater the probability of that response being made when that situation recurs. If the association is between a CS and a US, Pavlov would accept the law of frequency. The greater the number of pairings between the CS and the US, the greater the magnitude of the conditioned response elicited by the CS.

Guthrie's (1942) principle of **one-trial learning** completely rejects the law of frequency as a learning principle: *"A stimulus pattern gains its full associative strength on the occasion of its first pairing with a response"* (p. 30). Thus, to Guthrie, learning is the result of contiguity between a pattern of stimulation and a response, and learning is complete (the association is at full strength) after only one pairing between the stimuli and the response.

The Recency Principle

The principles of contiguity and one-trial learning necessitate the **recency principle,** which states that the response performed *last* in the presence of a set of stimuli will be that which will be done when that stimulus combination next recurs. In other words, whatever we did last under a given set of circumstances will be what we will tend to do again if those circumstances are reencountered.

Movement-Produced Stimuli

Although Guthrie reasserted his belief in the law of contiguity throughout his career, he felt it would be misleading to think of the learned association to be exclusively between environmental stimuli and overt behavior. For example, an environmental event and the response that it produces sometimes are separated by a fairly large interval of time, and it would be difficult, therefore, to think of the two as contiguous. Guthrie solved this problem by postulating the existence of **movement-produced stimuli,** which, as the name implies, are caused by the movements of the body. If we hear a sound and turn toward it, for example, the muscles, tendons, and joints produce stimuli that are distinctly different from the external stimulation that cause us to move. The important fact about movement-produced stimuli is that responses can be conditioned to them. That is, after a response is initiated by an external stimulus, the body itself produces the stimulus for the next response, and that response furnishes the stimulus for the next one, and so on. Thus, the interval between the occurrence of an external stimulus and the response finally made to it is filled with movement-produced stimuli. Conditioning is still between contiguous events, but in some cases the contiguity is between movement-produced stimuli and behavior rather than between external stimuli and behavior. Guthrie (1935) gave the following example of how he believed movement-produced stimuli function:

> Such a movement as listening or looking is not over like a flash or an explosion. It takes time. The movement, once started, maintains itself by the stimuli it furnishes. When the telephone bell rings we rise and make our way to the instrument. Long before we have reached the telephone the sound has ceased to act as a stimulus. We are kept in action by the stimuli from our own movements toward the telephone. One movement starts another, then a third, the third a fourth, and so on. Our movements form series, very often stereotyped in the form of habit. *These movements and their movement-produced stimuli make possible a far-reaching extension of association or conditioning.* (p. 54)

A simplified version of the situation described in Guthrie's example could be diagrammed as follows:

External stimulation → Overt response → Movement-produced stimuli → (telephone ringing) (e.g., turning toward telephone)

Overt response → Movement-produced stimuli → Overt response → (e.g., rising from chair) (e.g., walking toward telephone)

Movement-produced stimuli → Overt response (e.g., picking up telephone)

Guthrie's contention that a response can provide stimulation for the next response became very popular among learning theorists and is still usually involved in an explanation of chaining. As we have seen in Chapter 5, Skinner's explanation of chaining emphasized external stimuli and their secondary reinforcing properties. In this chapter, we have seen that Guthrie's explanation of chaining emphasizes internal stimuli. Hull and Spence's explanation of **chaining,** covered in Chapter 6, can be looked on as a combination of Skinner's and Guthrie's views because it maintains that both internal and external stimulation are involved in chaining.

Why Does Practice Improve Performance?

To answer this question, Guthrie differentiated between **acts** and **movements.** Movements are simple muscle contractions; acts are made up of a large number of movements. Acts are usually defined in terms of what they accomplish, that is, what change they make in the environment. As examples of acts, Guthrie listed such things as typing a letter, eating a meal, throwing a ball, reading a book, or selling a car. Guthrie and Horton (1946) explained improvement as the result of practice as follows:

> We have taken the position that acts are made up of movements that result from muscular contraction, and that *it is these muscular contractions that are directly predicted by the principle of association.* We are assuming that such movements are subject to conditioning or associative learning and that this conditioning is in itself an "all or none" affair, and its degree is not dependent on practice. One experience is sufficient to establish an association.
>
> But the learning of an act does take practice. We assume that the reason for this is that the act names an end result that is attained under varied circumstances and by movements varied to suit the circumstances. Learning an act as distinguished from a movement does require practice because it requires that the proper movement has been associated with its own cues. Even so simple an act as grasping a rattle requires different movements according to the distance and direction and position of the object. One successful experience is not sufficient to equip the infant with an act because the one movement acquired on that occasion might never again be successful. (pp. 7–8)

Just as an act is made up of many movements, a skill is made up of many acts. Thus, learning a skill such as playing golf or driving a car consists of learning thousands of associations between specific stimuli and specific movements. For example, learning to putt a golf ball into the cup from ten feet away from a certain angle under specific conditions (wind coming from a certain direction at a certain velocity, temperature 85 degrees, and so on) is only one of thousands of responses that constitute the game of golf. Practice allows more and more of these specific associations to be made. The same is true of driving, playing the banjo, and all other skills. Guthrie (1942) said, "Learning occurs normally in one associative episode. The reason that long practice and many repetitions are required to establish certain skills is that these really require many specific movements to be attached to many different stimulus situations. A skill is not simple habit, but a large collection of habits that achieve a certain result in many and varied circumstances" (p. 59).

To summarize, a skill is made up of many acts, and acts are made up of many movements. The relationship between one set of stimuli and one movement is learned at full strength in one trial, but this learning does not bring about proficiency at a skill. For example, driving a car, operating a computer, or playing baseball are all very complicated skills consisting of a large number of stimulus-response associations, and any one of these bonds or associations is learned at full strength in one trial. But it takes time and practice for all the necessary associations to be made. Learning to type the letter *A* while looking at an *A* on a written sheet of paper alongside your computer might be considered a specific stimulus-response (S-R) association. Looking at the letter *B* and typing the letter *B* is another specific association, as is looking at and typing the letter *C*. These specific associations must be built up for the entire alphabet and then for the numbers and then for the capital letters and finally for the various symbols that occur on the keyboard. Also, we must learn to make these responses under a wide variety of circumstances, such as varying lighting and temperature, different angles of seeing the material, and different kinds of paper. When all these responses have been learned, we say the person has become proficient. Thus, a skill such as word-processing (or typing) involves an enormously large number of specific S-R connections, each of which is learned in a single trial.

According to Guthrie, the reason Thorndike found systematic improvement through successive trials was that he was studying the learning of a skill, not the learning of individual movements. Guthrie and Horton (1946) said,

> We believe that when the puzzle-box situation varies indefinitely, as it did in the Thorndike box with the hanging loop, it is necessary for the cat to establish a large repertoire of specific escape movements adjusted to the specific differences in the situation. In other words, the cat establishes a skill, rather than a stereotyped habit. But the skill is made up of many specific habits. The gradual reduction of time reported by Thorndike is a consequence of the varied situation confronting the cat. (p. 41)

Whether learning occurs after one experience, as Guthrie believed, or in small increments, as Thorndike believed, is still a controversial issue and one that we discuss in more detail in the next chapter.

Nature of Reinforcement

What is the place of reinforcement in Guthrie's theory? On this point, Guthrie took issue with Thorndike, who, as you remember, made the revised law of effect the cornerstone of his theory. According to Thorndike, when a response leads to a satisfying state of affairs, its probability of recurring increases. Guthrie felt the law of effect was completely unnecessary. For Guthrie, **reinforcement** was merely a mechanical arrangement, which he felt could be explained by his one law of learning. According to Guthrie, *reinforcement changes the stimulating conditions and thereby prevents unlearning.* For example, in a puzzle box, the last thing the animal does before receiving a reinforcer is to move a pole or pull on a ring, which allows it to escape from the box. Therefore, the response that allowed the animal to escape—moving the pole, in this case—changes the entire pattern of stimuli that the animal experiences. According to the recency principle, when the animal is placed back into the puzzle box, it will tend to move the pole again. In other words, being released from the puzzle box after moving the pole preserves the association between being in the puzzle box and moving the pole. In fact, the last response that was made in the puzzle box will be the response the animal makes when it is again placed into the box, *regardless of what that response was.* Guthrie and Horton (1946) said,

> In our opinion the second occasion tends to repeat the behavior of the first, errors and all, except in so far as remaining in the puzzle box for a long time tends to establish new responses to the puzzle-box situation. *The reason for the remarkable preservation of the end action leading to escape is that this action removes the cat from the situation and hence allows no new responses to become attached to the puzzle-box situation.* Escape protects the end action from relearning. (p. 39)

Elsewhere Guthrie (1940) said,

> The position taken in this paper is that the animal learns to escape with its first escape. This learning is protected from forgetting because the escape removes the animal from the situation which has then no chance to acquire new associations.
>   . . . What encountering the food does is not to intensify a previous item of behavior but to protect that item from being unlearned. The whole situation and action of the animal is so changed by the food that the pre-food situation is shielded from new associations. These new associations cannot be established in the absence of the box interior, and in the absence of the behavior that preceded latch-opening. (pp. 144–145)

The Guthrie-Horton Experiment

Guthrie and Horton (1946) carefully observed approximately eight hundred escapes by cats from a puzzle box. Their observations were reported in a small book entitled *Cats in a Puzzle Box.* The puzzle box they used was very similar to the apparatus that Thorndike used in his selecting and connecting experiments. Guthrie and Horton used a large number of cats as subjects, but they noted that each cat learned to escape from the puzzle box in its own peculiar way. The particular response learned by a particular animal was the one the animal had hit on just prior to being released from the box. Because that exact response tended to be repeated the next time the animal was placed into the puzzle box, it was referred to as **stereotyped behavior.** For example, cat A would hit the pole by backing into it, cat B would push it with its head, or cat C would move it with its paw. Guthrie said that in each case the door flying open was an abrupt change in the stimulating conditions. By changing the stimulating conditions, the response of backing into the pole, for example, is protected from unlearning. The last thing that the animal did before the chamber was opened was to back into that pole, and because it backed into the pole, the stimulating conditions changed. Thus, applying the law of recency, the next time we put that animal into the puzzle box, it should respond by backing into the pole, and this is exactly what Guthrie and Horton observed. A pictorial record of a typical cat's performance is shown in Figure 8–1.

Guthrie and Horton (1946) observed that very often the animal, after escaping from the puzzle box, would ignore a piece of fish that was offered to it. Even though the animal ignored the so-called reinforcement, it was just as proficient at leaving the box the next time it was placed in it. This observation, according to

K-1   K-2   K-3   K-4   K-5   K-6   K-7   K-8   K-9

K-10   K-11   K-12   K-14   K-16   K-17   K-18   K-19   K-20

K-21   K-22   K-23   K-24   K-25   K-26   K-27   K-28   K-29

K-30   K-33   K-34   K-35   K-36   K-37   K-38   K-39   K-40   K-41

K-42   K-43   K-44   K-45   K-46   K-47   K-48   K-49   K-50   K-51

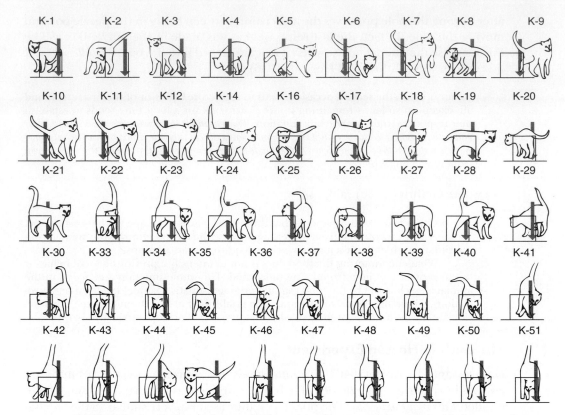

FIGURE 8–1 A pictorial record of a series of escape responses made by one of Guthrie's cats. The pictures were taken automatically when the cat moved the pole. Note that the cat tended to move the pole in the same way on each trial. (Reprinted from *Cats in a Puzzle Box,* by E. R. Guthrie & G. P. Horton, pp. 53–55, 1946.)

Guthrie, added further support to his contention that reinforcement is merely a mechanical arrangement that prevents unlearning. Guthrie concluded that any event following the desired response from an animal would change the stimulating conditions and thereby preserve that response under the preceding stimulating conditions. As we note in a later section, however, there are alternatives to Guthrie's interpretations of these observations.

Forgetting

Not only does learning occur in one trial but so does **forgetting**. All forgetting occurs, according to Guthrie, by causing an alternative response to occur in the presence of a stimulus pattern. After a stimulus pattern results in the alternative response, that stimulus pattern will thereafter tend to bring about the new response.

Thus for Guthrie, *all forgetting must involve new learning.* This is an extreme form of **retroactive inhibition**, which refers to the fact that old learning is interfered with by new learning. To demonstrate retroactive inhibition, let us suppose someone learns task A and then learns task B and then is tested for retention on task A. Another person learns task A, does not learn task B, and is tested on task A. It is generally found that the first person remembers less of task A than does the second person. Thus, it is demonstrated that learning something new (task B) has interfered with the retention of what was learned previously (task A).

Guthrie (1942) accepted an extreme form of retroactive inhibition. His position was that whenever something new is learned it must completely "knock out" something old. In other words, all forgetting is due to interference. *No interference, no forgetting:*

> The child who has left school at the end of the seventh grade will recall many of the details of his last year for the rest of his life. The child who has continued on in school has these associations of the schoolroom and school life overlaid by others, and by the time he is in college may be very vague about the names and events of his seventh-grade experience.
>
> When we are somehow protected from established cues we are well aware that these may retain their connection with a response indefinitely. A university faculty member's wife recently visited Norway, the original home of her parents. She had not spoken Norwegian since the death of her grandmother when she was five and believed that she had forgotten the language. But during her stay in Norway, she astonished herself by joining in the conversation. The language and atmosphere of her childhood revived words and phrases she could not remember in her American home. But her conversation caused much amusement among her relatives because she was speaking with a facile Norwegian "baby talk." If her family in America had continued to use Norwegian, this "baby talk" would have been forgotten, its association with the language destroyed by other phrases.
>
> Forgetting is not a passive fading of stimulus-response associations contingent upon the lapse of time, but requires active unlearning, which consists in learning to do something else under the circumstances. (pp. 29–30)

Summary of Guthrie's Theory as Presented Thus Far

Associations between stimulating conditions and movements are constantly made. An association between a stimulus and a response is made simply because the two occur together. The association can be either between external stimuli and overt responses or between movement-produced stimuli and overt responses. This association will continue until the same response occurs in the presence of other stimuli or until the same stimuli occur and the response is prevented from occurring. In a structured learning situation, such as a puzzle box, the environment is arranged so that there is an abrupt change in stimulation after a certain response is made. For example, if the cat hits the pole, the door opens, and it is allowed to escape. Guthrie said that after the cat hits the pole, the stimulus situation abruptly changes, and whatever association existed before that time is preserved. The most recent association before the abrupt change is between the stimulation in the puzzle box and the response that allows the animal to escape. According to the recency principle, when the animal is again placed in the puzzle box, it will tend to repeat that same response (it will tend to hit the pole again), and we say that the cat has learned how to escape from the box.

Unlike Thorndike, Skinner, Hull, and Pavlov, Guthrie was not a reinforcement theorist. Thorndike did, of course, discuss associative shifting, which he felt occurred independent of reinforcement. However, because Thorndike's main focus was on the kind of learning governed by the law of effect, he is generally considered a reinforcement theorist.

Of the theorists that we have covered thus far, Guthrie's theory is most similar to Watson's theory. Neither Watson nor Guthrie was a reinforcement theorist. Watson believed that all learning could be explained by employing the laws of contiguity and frequency. The main difference between Watson's theory and Guthrie's is that Watson accepted the law of frequency, whereas Guthrie did not.

HOW TO BREAK HABITS

A habit is a response that has become associated with a large number of stimuli. The more stimuli that elicit the response, the stronger the habit. Smoking, for example, can be a strong habit because the response of smoking has taken place in the presence of so many cues. Each cue present as a person smokes will tend to elicit smoking when next it is encountered. Guthrie (1952) indicated the complexities of a habit in the following quotation:

> The chief difficulty in the way of avoiding a bad habit is that the responsible cues are often hard to find, and that in many bad habit systems, they are extremely numerous. Each rehearsal is responsible for a possible addition of one or more new cues which tend to set off the undesired action. Drinking and smoking after years of practice are action systems which can be started by thousands of reminders, and which become imperative because the absence of the object of the habit, the drink or the smoke, results in a block to action and so in restlessness and tension. The desire, which includes tension in the muscles used in drinking or smoking, disrupts other action. The writer who "wants a smoke" is disturbed in his writing and the disturbed state will continue until the aroused action tendency is allowed to go through. The original wakening of the desire may be caused by any of the chance accompaniments of previous smoking—the smell of smoke, the sight of another person smoking, or of a cigar, the act of sitting back in the office chair, sitting down to a desk, finishing a meal, leaving the theater, and a thousand other stimulus patterns. Most smokers, while busily engaged in activities not associated with smoking, can go for long periods with no craving. Others find that the craving is strictly associated with such things as the end of a meal, if it has been their practice to smoke at that time. I once had a caller to whom I was explaining that the apple I had just finished was a splendid device for avoiding a smoke. The caller pointed out that I was smoking at that moment. The habit of lighting a cigarette was so attached to the finish of eating that smoking had been started automatically. (p. 116)

Threshold Method   To break a habit, the rule is always the same: Find the cues that initiate the bad habit, and practice another response in the presence of those cues. Guthrie listed three ways in which an organism can be made to make a response, other than an undesirable one, to a certain pattern of stimuli. The first technique is referred to as the **threshold method.** According to Guthrie (1938), this method involves

> introducing the stimulus at such weak strengths that it will not cause the response and then gradually increasing the intensity of the stimulus, always taking care that it is below the "threshold" of the response. A gradual introduction to the motion of a ship which, unfortunately, cannot be controlled by human means, but depends on the gradualness of change in the weather, can bring about tolerance of a considerable storm. Most children react to the taste of green olives by spitting them out. But if they begin with small nibbles, not enough to cause rejection, whole olives will eventually be taken with pleasure.
>
> . . . Members of families learn to make use of this type of associative inhibition in dealing with their housemates. The proposal to send the daughter to an expensive school is "broken gently" to the father. Casual mention of the school's advantages without directly submitting the issue, criticism of the present school, at first so mild that it will not stir defense, prepare the father so that when the question is at last put squarely before him he does not make a scene over the expense. He is by this time used to the idea and there will be no violent reaction. (pp. 60–61)

The threshold method can also be exemplified by what is ordinarily done when a horse is being broken. If you walk up to a horse that has never worn a saddle and attempt to throw a saddle on its back, it will no doubt start kicking and run away. The horse will do whatever it can to prevent you from putting that saddle on its back. If, instead of the saddle, you put a very light blanket on its back, chances are that it will not react violently. If the horse remains calm, you can gradually increase the weight on its back by using heavier and heavier blankets. You can then go from blankets to a light saddle and finally to the regular saddle. There is a process akin to this in psychotherapy. If the therapist is trying to help a patient overcome a phobia of some kind, he or she may use this method of approximation. If the patient has a terrible fear of a relative, for example, his or her mother, the therapist may first start out talking about people in general, then women, and then women who are related to the patient and, in this way, gradually build up to the point where they are talking about the mother without the patient being fearful. This method of treating a phobia is very much like Wolpe's technique of systematic desensitization, which was discussed in the last chapter.

Fatigue Method   The second method proposed by Guthrie is referred to as the **fatigue method.** Again, to take horse training as an example, the fatigue method would correspond to broncobusting, in which a saddle is thrown on the horse, the rider climbs on, and the horse is ridden until it gives up. That is, the horse is ridden until its fatigue causes it to do something other than buck while the saddle and the rider are on its back. Then, according to Guthrie, the response of riding calmly will replace the bucking response to the stimulus provided by the saddle and the rider. Once you get the animal to act calmly in the presence of the saddle and rider, then forevermore it will act calmly in their presence.

To break a dog of the habit of chasing chickens, all you have to do is to tie a chicken around the dog's neck and let it run around and try to get rid of it. When the dog eventually becomes fatigued, it will be doing something other than chasing in the presence of the chicken. The chicken has then become a cue for doing something other than chasing.

Another example that Guthrie used in describing the fatigue method involved a little girl who upset her parents by lighting matches. Guthrie's advice was to allow the girl (or perhaps force her) to continue to light matches to the point where it is no longer fun. Under these conditions, the sight of matches becomes a cue for avoidance rather than for lighting.

Incompatible Response Method   The third method of breaking a habit is the **incompatible response method.** With this method, the stimuli for the undesired response are presented along with other stimuli that produce a response that is incompatible with the undesired response. For example, a young child receives a panda bear as a gift, and her first reaction is fear and avoidance. In contrast, the child's mother elicits a warm, relaxed feeling in the child. Using the incompatible response method, you would pair the mother and the panda bear; it is hoped that the mother will be the dominant stimulus. If she is the dominant stimulus, the child's reaction to the mother–panda bear combination will be one of relaxation. Once this reaction has been elicited in the presence of the bear, the bear can be presented alone, and it will produce relaxation in the child. With the incompatible response method, both stimuli are presented to the learner: the one that causes the undesired response and a stronger stimulus that causes a response incompatible with the undesired response. The learner then tends to make a response other than the undesired one in the presence of the stimuli that previously elicited the undesired response. Because of this pairing, the stimuli that used to elicit the undesired response will now elicit the response associated with the stronger stimulus.

All three of these methods for breaking a habit are effective for the same reason. Guthrie (1938) said, "All three of these methods are, of course, only one method. All of them consist in presenting the cues of an undesirable action and seeing to it that the action is not performed. Since there is always other behavior going on when we are awake, the cues we present become stimuli for this other behavior and are alienated from the obnoxious response" (p. 62).

The three examples we gave of breaking a habit can be summarized as follows:

Threshold Method
1. Regular saddle → kicking
2. Light blanket → calm
3. Heavier blanket → calm
4. A still heavier blanket → calm
5. Light saddle → calm
6. Regular saddle → calm

Fatigue Method

1. Saddle → kicking
2. Passage of time
3. Saddle → calm

Incompatible Response Method

1. Panda bear → fear
2. Mother → relaxation
3. Panda bear and mother → relaxation
4. Panda bear → relaxation

We noted in our discussion of Thorndike's theory (Chapter 4) that he believed associative shifting to be a second kind of learning, one based on contiguity alone and not governed by the law of effect. Because Guthrie believed learning is dependent on contiguity alone, we would expect to find a great deal of similarity between Thorndike's concept of associative shifting and Guthrie's views about learning. In fact, Guthrie's entire theory can be looked on as an effort to describe how a response that is associated with one stimulus shifts over and becomes associated with another stimulus.

The incompatible response method of breaking a habit seems to represent one kind of associative shifting. Stimulus 1, the mother, elicits relaxation. Stimulus 2, the panda bear, elicits fear. When stimulus 1 is presented along with stimulus 2, the response previously associated with stimulus 1 now is elicited by stimulus 2, simply because the two stimuli are contiguous. Now the panda bear elicits the response that was previously associated with the mother.

The threshold method of breaking a habit also appears to represent a kind of associative shifting. Using the threshold method to eliminate the child's fear of the panda bear involves *gradually* associating the bear with the mother. To begin with, something only indirectly related to the bear, perhaps another of the child's toys, would be paired with the mother. Then the objects paired with the mother would become increasingly similar to the panda bear on successive pairings, and finally, the panda bear itself would be presented with the mother. Again, the end result is that the response once associated with mother "shifts over" to the panda bear.

Sidetracking a Habit

There is a difference between breaking a habit and sidetracking a habit. Sidetracking a habit can be accomplished by avoiding the cues that elicit the undesirable behavior. If you have accumulated a large number of behavior patterns that are not effective or for other reasons cause concern and anxiety, the best thing to do is leave the situation altogether. Guthrie advised going to an environment gives you a fresh start because you do not have many behavioral associations in a new environment. Going to a new environment releases you to develop new behavior patterns. This would be only a partial escape, however, because many of the stimuli causing your undesired behavior are internal, and you would, therefore, be taking them with you to the new environment. Also, stimuli in the new environment identical or similar to stimuli in the old environment will tend to elicit the responses previously attached to them.

Punishment

Guthrie said the effectiveness of **punishment** is determined by what it causes the punished organism to do. Punishment works, not because of the pain experienced by the individual, but because it changes the way the individual responds to certain stimuli. Punishment is effective only when it results in a new response to the same stimuli. Punishment succeeds in changing the undesired habit because it elicits behavior incompatible with the punished behavior. Punishment fails because the behavior caused by the punishment is not incompatible with the punished behavior.

Let us say that you have a dog that chases cars and you want it to stop. Guthrie (1952) said, get in your car and allow the dog to chase it. As it is running along the side of the car, reach down and slap its nose. This is likely to be effective. On the other hand, slapping its rear as it is chasing the car is not likely to be effective, although it can be assumed that a slap on the nose and a slap on the rear are equally painful to the dog. The difference is that the slap on the nose tends to make it stop and jump backward in the presence of the car, whereas the slap on the rear tends to make it continue forward, perhaps even a little more energetically. Thus one form of punishment causes incompatible behavior and is effective, and the other does not and is ineffective.

> What is learned will be what is done—and what is done in intense feeling is usually something different from what was being done. Sitting on tacks does not discourage learning. It encourages one in learning to do something else than sit. It is not the feeling caused by punishment, but the specific action caused by punishment that determines what will be learned. In training a dog to jump through a hoop, the effectiveness of punishment depends on where it is applied, front or rear. It is what the punishment makes the dog do that counts, or what it makes a man do, not what it makes him feel. The mistaken notion that it is the feeling that determines learning derives from the fact that often we do not care what is done as a result of punishment, just as long as what is done breaks up or inhibits the unwanted habit.
>
> . . . As the outcome of this discussion punishment and reward are not summarily to be ejected from the place they hold in public favor. No doubt whatever has been thrown on their general effectiveness. Children may still be spanked or caressed. But we shall have a much better insight into the uses of punishment and reward if we analyze their effects in terms of association and realize that punishment is effective only through its associations. Punishment achieves its effects not by taking away strength from the physiological basis of the connection . . . but by forcing the animal or the child to do something different and thus establishing inhibitory conditioning of unwanted habit. Punishment is effective *only in the presence of cues for the bad habit*.
>
> Furthermore, when the effect of punishment is only emotional excitement, punishment facilitates the stereotyping of the undesired habit. Punishment and reward are essentially moral terms, not psychological terms. They are defined not in terms of their effects on the recipient, but in terms of the purposes of the individual who administers them. Theory stated in their terms is bound to be ambiguous. (pp. 132–133)

Guthrie (1935, p. 21) talked about a ten-year-old girl who threw her hat and coat on the floor whenever she came home. Each time she did so, her mother scolded her and made her hang up her hat and coat. The situation continued until the mother guessed that her nagging had become the cue for the child to hang her clothes up. Realizing this, the next time the child threw her hat and coat on the floor, the mother made her pick them up and go back outside. Now as the girl came in the door, the mother insisted that she hang up her coat and hat immediately. This procedure was repeated a few times and soon the girl learned to hang up her hat and coat upon entering the house. Now the response of hanging up her clothes was attached to the stimuli present as she entered the house rather than to her mother's nagging. In this case, punishing the girl after her hat and coat were already on the floor could have no effect on the habit, except perhaps to strengthen it.

Guthrie and Powers (1950) also advise that a command should never be given if it could be disobeyed: "The skilled animal trainer never gives a command that he does not expect to be obeyed. In this he is like the army officer and the experienced teacher. If a teacher makes a request for silence in the room and it is disregarded, the request actually becomes a signal for disturbance" (p. 129).

Summary of Guthrie's Views on Punishment

Everything that Guthrie said about punishment is directly in accordance with his one law of learning—the law of contiguity. When stimuli and responses are paired, they become associated and remain associated unless the stimuli occur in the presence of another response, at which time they will become associated with the new response. While discussing ways of breaking a habit, we saw three mechanical arrangements that could be used to rearrange the associations between stimuli and responses. Punishment is another such arrangement. Punishment, when used effectively, causes stimuli that previously elicited an undesired response to elicit an acceptable response. Guthrie's views about punishment can be summarized as follows:

1. The important thing about punishment is not the pain it may cause but what it makes the organism do.
2. To be effective, punishment must cause behavior that is incompatible with the punished behavior.
3. To be effective, punishment must be applied in the presence of the stimuli that elicit the punished behavior.
4. If the conditions specified in 2 and 3 are not met, punishment will be ineffective or may even strengthen the undesired response.

Thus, when punishment is effective, it causes the organism to do something other than what it was punished for doing while the stimuli that elicited the punished behavior are still present. This response, of course, causes a new association to be formed, and the next time those stimuli appear, they will tend to elicit a favorable response instead of an unfavorable one.

Is there anything other than the anecdotal evidence that Guthrie offers to support his views on punishment? The answer is yes. Fowler and Miller (1963) trained rats to traverse a runway for food reinforcement. Subjects in the control group simply ran the runway and obtained food. Subjects in one experimental group were given a mild electric shock to the *front paws* just as they reached the food cup. Subjects in a second experimental group received a mild electric shock to the *hind paws* just as they reached the food cup. Relative to the running speed of the control subjects, subjects that had their front paws shocked as they reached the food cup ran slower on subsequent trials, whereas the subjects that had their hind paws shocked ran faster. Just as Guthrie predicted, shocking the rats on their hind paws actually facilitated running rather than inhibiting it. Because members of both experimental groups received the same intensity of shock, it was not the shock itself that facilitated or inhibited running speed. Rather, it was what the shock caused the animals to do. Shocking the front paws caused behavior incompatible with running whereas shocking the hind paws caused faster running.

Not all research on punishment has been supportive of Guthrie's theory, and it is now realized that Guthrie's account was at best incomplete. For a review of the complex topic of punishment see, for example, Walters and Grusec (1977).

Drives

Physiological **drives** provide what Guthrie called **maintaining stimuli** that keep the organism active until a goal is reached. For example, being hungry produces internal stimulation that continues until food is consumed. When food is obtained, the maintaining stimuli are terminated, and therefore, the stimulating conditions have changed, thus preserving the response that led to the food. However, physiological drives are only one source of maintaining stimuli. Any persistent source of stimulation, whether it is internal or external, provides maintaining stimuli. Guthrie (1938) said,

> To explain this requires that we first understand what a problem is. What makes the puzzle box or an unyielding parent a problem? The answer to this is that problems are persistent stimulus situations of such a nature that they keep the animal or the person disturbed and excited until some act is hit upon which removes the "maintaining stimuli" and allows the excitement to subside.
>
> Such persistent and disturbing stimuli are sometimes called "drives." In a hungry animal, the recurring spasms of the stomach serve to make the animal disturbed and to produce excitement. . . .
>
> The same behavior could be produced by some artificial and external stimulation. A paper bag fastened to the cat's foot with a rubber band will similarly activate the cat, and it will become disturbed and excited and this state will continue until some one of its movements eventually removes the bag. (p. 96)

He went on to say,

> And here is a point very apt to be overlooked. The next time that the disturbers are present, they will tend to call out, by virtue of their last association, the act that removed them. Other acts associated with them have been dissociated or unconditioned each by the next act. But after successful removal of the disturber, it is no longer there to be associated with a new act. The drive remains faithful to the act that removed it because that was its last association. After that no new associations could be established because the drive is gone. (p. 98)

Guthrie explained the habitual use of alcohol and other drugs in a similar way. Let us say, for example, that a person feels tense or anxious. In this case, tension or anxiety provides maintaining stimuli. If, under these circumstances, the person takes a drink or two, his or her tension may be reduced. According to Guthrie, this result ensures the relationship between tension and drinking. Therefore, the next time the person feels tense, he or she will tend to have a drink. Gradually tension will tend to elicit drinking (or drug taking) under a wider range of circumstances, with the result that the person becomes a habitual drinker or a drug addict.

Intentions

Responses that are conditioned to maintaining stimuli are called **intentions.** They are called intentions because maintaining stimulation from a drive usually lasts for a period of time (until the drive is reduced). Thus the *sequence of behavior* preceding the drive-reducing response is repeated next time the drive, with its related stimuli, occurs. The sequence of behavior associated with maintaining stimuli seems to be interrelated and logical and is, therefore, referred to as intentional. If an animal is hungry and is allowed to eat, it will do so. If, however, the direct satisfaction of the hunger drive is not possible, the animal will tend to perform whatever behaviors led to food the last time it was hungry: It may turn in a certain direction in a maze, press a lever, or move a pole. If a person is hungry and has a sandwich in her office, she will eat it; if, however, she forgot her lunch, she will get up, put on her coat, get into her car, find a restaurant, enter the restaurant, place an order, and so on. Different reaction patterns have been associated with the maintaining stimuli from hunger plus the stimuli from environmental circumstances, that is, having one's lunch or not. Behavior triggered by maintaining stimuli may look purposive or intentional, but Guthrie felt that it, too, could be explained by the law of contiguity.

Transfer of Training

It should be clear that Guthrie expected very little transfer of training. He said that if a child learns to add 2 and 2 at the blackboard, there is no guarantee that that child is going to know how to add 2 and 2 in his seat. The stimulating conditions under which that association was made are much different than those prevailing in a classroom seat.

Guthrie would say to the college student, if you want to get the most from your studies, you should practice in exactly the same situation—in exactly the same seat—in which you are going to be tested. The best place to study, according to Guthrie, is in the room where you are going to be tested because all the stimuli in that room will be associated with the information you are studying. If you learn something in your dorm room, there is no guarantee that this knowledge will transfer into the classroom. This is how Guthrie explained why a student may say after taking a test, "I don't know what happened to me; I went over that material a hundred times; I knew it quite well, and yet, it didn't come to me during the test." Guthrie said that there simply was not enough similarity between the conditions under which the student studied and the conditions under which she was tested.

Guthrie's advice is always to practice the exact behaviors that are going to be demanded of us; in addition, we should practice them in the exact conditions under which we are going to be tested or evaluated. If we want to utilize this information beyond the testing situation, we must go beyond the classroom and associate other stimuli with the behavior that the book or the class or the lecture caused us to do. Guthrie's advice to the student preparing for an essay examination is the same: In preparing for an essay test, write essay questions. Guess what the questions will be and answer them. Force yourself to respond to the questions under the time conditions that you are going to be exposed to during the test. Guthrie would give the same advice to the automobile mechanic or the electrician. If you want to learn how to fix engines, work on engines, and work on them under conditions similar to those that will prevail in real-life situations. This practice will maximize transfer.

Elsewhere, Guthrie (1942) said, "It is essential that the student be led to do what is to be learned . . . a student does not learn what was in a lecture or in a book. He learns only what the lecture or book caused him to do" (p. 55). According to Guthrie, *we learn what we do in the presence of specific stimuli.* This principle applies not only to the transfer of classroom learning to real-world behavior but also to all learning. An application of this principle appears in the investigation of birth order effects. Some researchers believe that birth order creates enduring traits that are observed both in the family and in a person's behavior beyond the family. Sulloway (1996), for example, argues that first-born children are more conservative and supportive of authority, and later-born children are more likely to be innovators and "rebels." Sulloway suggests that these birth order effects determine the character of the individual throughout life. Harris (2000), on the other hand, presents an argument with which Guthrie would vigorously agree. She suggests that learned behaviors such as conservatism, obedience to authority, and rebelliousness are restricted to the context of the family and are unlikely to transfer. Furthermore, she writes that "children learn separately how to behave in each of their social contexts" (p. 176) and adds that "there is little or no transfer of training because patterns of behavior acquired at home are likely to be inappropriate or irrelevant outside the home" (p. 177).

The notions of insight, understanding, and thinking had little or no meaning to Guthrie. The only law of learning is the law of contiguity, which states that when two events occur together, they are learned. All learning, whether it be nonhuman or human, simple or abstract, is subsumed under the law of contiguity and its related principles. There is no reference to conscious events in Guthrie's theory, nor is there any special interest in the survival value of learned behavior. According to Guthrie, incorrect responses are learned just as readily as correct ones, and the acquisition of both is explained by the same law of learning.

VOEKS'S FORMALIZATION OF GUTHRIE'S THEORY

As mentioned earlier, Guthrie did little research to test the validity of his own theory. Three explanations for Guthrie's lack of experimentation have been offered. First, Bolles (1979) suggested that Guthrie's theory minimized the roles of motivation and reinforcement, the two components of most other learning theories in the 1930s and 1940s that stimulated most of the research associated with them. Second, Carlson (1980) suggested that at the time Guthrie was at the University of Washington, psychology was offered only on the undergraduate level, and the theses and dissertations of graduate students, which were often used to test other theories experimentally, were not available to Guthrie. Third, as Guthrie himself realized, his principles of learning were stated in terms that were too general to be tested easily.

Virginia W. Voeks (1921–1989), who was a student at the University of Washington when Guthrie was influential there, attempted to restate Guthrie's theory in terms that were precise enough to be empirically verifiable. Voeks obtained her B.A. in 1943 from the University of Washington, where she was influenced by Guthrie, and her Ph.D. in 1947 from Yale, where she was apparently influenced by Hull. In fact, the outcome of Voeks's work was a theory whose structure was Hullian but whose content was Guthrian. After obtaining her doctorate, Voeks returned to the University of Washington, where she worked until 1949. In 1949, she moved to San Diego State College, where she remained until her retirement in 1971.

In Voeks's restatement of Guthrie's theory, there are four basic postulates, eight definitions, and eight theorems. The postulates attempt to summarize many of Guthrie's general principles of learning, the definitions attempt to clarify several Guthrian concepts (such as stimulus, cue, response, and learning), and the theorems are deductions from the postulates and definitions that are experimentally testable. Voeks tested a number of her deductions and found considerable support for Guthrie's theory.

Most of Voeks's formalization of Guthrie's theory, and the research that it stimulated, is too complex to be presented here. Voeks's four postulates, however, act both as a convenient summary and as a sample of her thoughtful formalization of Guthrie's theory.

Postulate I: Principle of Association (a) Any stimulus-pattern that once accompanies a response, and/or immediately precedes it by one-half second or less, becomes a full-strength direct cue for that response. (b) This is the only way in which stimulus-patterns not now cues for a particular response can become direct cues for that response (Voeks, 1950, p. 342).

Postulate II: Principle of Postremity (a) A stimulus that has accompanied or immediately preceded two or more incompatible responses is a conditioned stimulus for only the last response made while that stimulus was present. (b) This is the only way in which a stimulus now a cue for a particular response can cease being a cue for that response (Voeks, 1950, p. 344).

Postulate III: Principle of Response Probability The probability of any particular response's occurring . . . at some specified time is a . . . function . . . of the proportion . . . of the stimuli present which are at the time cues for that response (Voeks, 1950, p. 348)

Postulate IV: Principle of Dynamic Situations   The stimulus-pattern of a situation is not static but from time to time is modified, due to such changes as result from the subject's making a response, accumulation of fatigue products, visceral changes and other internal processes of the subject, introduction of controlled or uncontrolled variations in the stimuli present (Voeks, 1950, p. 350).

The reader should not conclude that Guthrie's theory of learning is of historical interest only. As we discuss in the next chapter when we consider the work of William K. Estes, one trend in modern learning theory is toward the greater use of mathematical models in explaining the learning process. It was Guthrie's theory of learning that formed the bases for the early mathematical models of learning and continues to be at the heart of most of them.

GUTHRIE ON EDUCATION

Like Thorndike, Guthrie would begin the educational process by stating objectives, that is, what responses are to be made to what stimuli. He would arrange the learning environment so that desired responses are elicited in the presence of the stimuli to which they are to be attached.

Motivation was even less important for Guthrie than it was for Thorndike. All that is necessary for Guthrie is that the student responds appropriately in the presence of certain stimuli.

Practice is important in that it causes more and more stimuli to elicit desired behavior. Because each experience is unique, one must "relearn" things over and over again. Guthrie would say that learning to add 2 and 2 at the blackboard is no guarantee that students will add 2 and 2 at their seats. Students must not only learn that 2 red blocks plus 2 more equals 4 red blocks, but they must make new 2-plus-2-equals-4 associations with apples, dogs, books, and so on. It is also possible that a student will learn to attach responses to the stimuli in the classroom and another set of responses to similar stimuli outside the classroom.

Essentially, Guthrie accepted Thorndike's identical elements theory concerning the transfer of training. The probability of making the same response to two different situations is determined by the similarity between the two situations. Like Thorndike, Guthrie rejected the formal discipline theory of transfer and felt that acceptance of such a position generated unfortunate classroom practices. Guthrie and Powers (1950) said,

> The teacher's acceptance or rejection of the formal discipline theory of transfer, the identical elements or generalization explanation, will be reflected in numerous day-to-day teaching practices. The subject-matter teacher no doubt would give evidence of an actual, if not verbal, acceptance of the formal discipline doctrine. Exposure to the content of certain courses becomes in itself, then, the objective of education; methods of teaching and the attempt to link content and the needs of the learner are of relatively secondary importance. The student must conform to subject matter requirements and must develop a docile, submissive role.
>
> A challenging or questioning attitude on the part of the teacher as regards the validity of the formal discipline doctrine paves the way for educational experimentation.

The teacher will ask what values, direct and indirect, are being served by pupil partici-pation in given curricular areas. He will be willing to revise content and method as facts regarding transfer are uncovered. The child will be viewed as a growing and developing organism constantly organizing and reorganizing experience into more or less effi-cient patterns of behavior. The discovery of the child's interests and wise use of effec-tive incentives in order to motivate participation become primary tasks of instruction. (p. 256)

Like Thorndike, Guthrie believed that formal education should resemble real-life situations as much as possible. In other words, the Guthrian teacher would have students do in school what they are expected to do when they leave school. Thus, like Thorndike, Guthrie would approve of internship or mentoring programs and would enthusiastically endorse professional trade school approaches to learning.

Guthrian teachers may sometimes use punishment in dealing with disruptive behavior, but they would realize that to be effective, punishment must be used as the disruptive behavior is occurring. Furthermore, the punishment must cause behav-ior that is incompatible with the disruptive behavior. In the best of cases, punishment should produce desirable behavior rather than simply terminating an undesirable behavior.

EVALUATION OF GUTHRIE'S THEORY

Contributions

Guthrie was unique in his insistence that learning resulted from contiguity between stimuli and responses and from contiguity alone. Even early reviewers of learning theory (Mueller & Schoenfeld, 1954) pointed out that Guthrie's simple contiguity approach could account for all of the basic phenomena addressed in Skinner's or Hull's analyses. The great appeal to scientists was the fact that Guthrie could explain learning, extinction, and generalization with a simple analysis, whereas other theo-ries approached these problems in more complex ways. In addition, extensions of this theory to practical application were straightforward generalizations of his single, simple learning principle and were revealed by Guthrie in pleasant anecdotal fash-ion rather than in stark therapeutic prescription.

Although Guthrie's theory did not generate research and controversy compa-rable with that instigated by Hull or Skinner, it provided an important alternative explanation of learning. In addition, it served as a constant reminder that a theory need not be extraordinarily complex to explain seemingly complex behaviors. As we see in the next chapter, William K. Estes was able to develop a diverse body of theory and research that extended into the 1990s by using the basic ingredients of Guthrie's position.

Criticisms

There is substantial appeal in a position that can explain escape learning, reward learning, extinction, and forgetting with the same principle. It is this ease of univer-sal explanation, however, that makes many psychologists uneasy about Guthrie's position. Recalling Popper's concern with theories that seem to be able to explain everything, we note that there are circumstances in which Guthrie's position becomes ambiguous and is too easily invoked to explain too many phenomena (Mueller & Schoenfeld, 1954).

Mueller and Schoenfeld (1954) also pointed out that although Guthrie was a strict critic of poor experimental methodology and of ambiguous language in other theories, he did not hold his own theory to the same standards. The Guthrie and Horton (1946) experiment, which was presented as an important demonstration of the theory, exemplifies Mueller and Schoenfeld's criticism. Moore and Stuttard (1979) suggest that, like most members of the cat family, including domestic cats, the cats in the Guthrie and Horton experiment were engaging in an instinctive nuzzling or rubbing behavior that is typically exhibited when a cat "greets" another (friendly) cat or a familiar human. These researchers observed that cats displayed the same consistent, stereotyped behavior reported by Horton and Guthrie (1946) even when rubbing against a vertical pole produced no reinforcement or change in stimulus conditions whatsoever.

DISCUSSION QUESTIONS

1. What law of association did Guthrie build his theory around? Describe this law and explain how the recency principle is deduced from it.
2. Given Guthrie's belief in one-trial learning, how did he explain the improvement in performance that results from practice? Include in your answer a distinction among movements, acts, and skills.
3. Is Guthrie's theory a reinforcement theory or not? Justify your answer.
4. How did Guthrie explain forgetting?
5. For Guthrie, what was the relationship between drives and "intentions"?
6. Explain how, according to Guthrie, the transfer of skills from where they are learned to where they are applied could be facilitated.
7. What suggestions did Guthrie offer for breaking a bad habit? Choose one of the suggestions, and show how it could be used to break the smoking habit.
8. How would Guthrie explain the phenomenon of regression, for example, the tendency to act as you did at a younger age under certain conditions, such as when you visit the house or room you grew up in?
9. How would Guthrie explain the tendency for someone to act like a "different person" under various conditions?
10. How would you revise your study habits so that they are in accordance with Guthrie's theory?
11. How would Guthrie explain the development of drug addiction?
12. Describe Guthrie's use of the term *reinforcement*.
13. According to Guthrie, under what circumstances would punishment be an effective technique in modifying behavior? Do you feel punishment is usually used as Guthrie said it should be? Explain.
14. What was Guthrie's purpose in introducing the notion of movement-produced stimuli?

15. Design an experiment to test Guthrie's contention that anything that disrupts a stimulus pattern will preserve the last response made to that stimulus pattern.
16. Discuss the key points of Voeks's restatement of Guthrie's theory.

CHAPTER HIGHLIGHTS

acts

chaining

drives

fatigue method of breaking a habit

forgetting

incompatible response method of breaking a habit

intentions

law of contiguity

maintaining stimuli

movement-produced stimuli

movements

one-trial learning

principle of association

principle of dynamic situations

principle of postremity

principle of response probability

punishment

recency principle

reinforcement

retroactive inhibition

stereotyped behavior

threshold method of breaking a habit

CHAPTER 9

William Kaye Estes

One current trend in learning theory is to move away from the broad, comprehensive theory and toward miniature systems. Researchers are marking off an area of interest and exploring it thoroughly. Breadth is sacrificed for depth. Exemplifying this trend are the so-called statistical learning theorists, who attempt to build a rigorous minisystem from which a restricted range of learning phenomena can be investigated. The most influential of these, and one of the earliest, was developed by Estes (1950). Estes, born in 1919, began his professional career at the University of Indiana. He moved first to Stanford University and then to Rockefeller University and completed his career at Harvard, where he was awarded honor as a professor emeritus. In 1997, Estes was awarded the Medal of Science, considered to be the highest honor bestowed by the National Science Foundation. The award recognizes him "for fundamental theories of cognition and

William Kaye Estes. (Courtesy of William Kaye Estes.)

learning that transformed the field of experimental psychology and led to the development of quantitative cognitive science. His pioneering methods of quantitative modeling and insistence on rigor and precision established the standard for modern psychological science."

In Chapter 5, we encountered some of the research on punishment that Estes performed while he was a student of Skinner at the University of Minnesota. It is for his development of statistical learning theory, however, that Estes is best known. His theory can be thought of as an attempt to quantify Guthrie's theory of learning. Guthrie's theory appears deceptively simple: Responses get attached to stimuli in a single trial. When one asks about the nature of learning in more detail, however, one soon realizes that the theory is much more complex than it appears to be at first. Estes investigates this complexity and offers a model that effectively deals with it.

MAJOR THEORETICAL CONCEPTS

Before giving an example of how Estes's **stimulus sampling theory (SST)** works, we look at the assumptions made by Estes:

Assumption I   The learning situation involves a large but finite number of stimulus elements, which are the many things that the learner could experience at the onset of a learning trial. These stimuli include experimental events, such as a light, a buzzer, verbal material presented in a memory drum, a bar in a Skinner box, or the runway in a T-maze. They also include changeable or transitory stimuli, such as the behavior of the experimenter, the temperature, extraneous noises inside and outside the room, and conditions within the experimental subject, such as fatigue or headache. All of these stimulus elements taken collectively are symbolized by S. Again, S is the total number of stimuli that accompany a trial in any learning situation.

Assumption II   All responses made in the experimental situation fall into one of two categories. If the response is one that the experimenter is looking for (such as salivation, an eye-blink, bar-pressing, turning right in a T-maze, or reciting a nonsense syllable correctly), it is called an A_1 response. If the response is anything other than the one the experimenter wants, it is incorrect and is labeled A_2. Thus, Estes divides all responses that may occur in a learning experiment into two classes: (A_1), the response in which the experimenter is interested—the "correct" response—or (A_2), all other responses. There are no gradations in between: An animal makes a conditioned response, or it does not; students recite a nonsense syllable correctly, or they do not.

Assumption III   All elements in S are attached to either A_1 or A_2. Again, this is an all-or-nothing situation: All stimulus elements in S are either conditioned to the desired or correct response (A_1) or to an irrelevant or incorrect response (A_2). Elements conditioned to A_1 elicit A_1 responses, and elements conditioned to A_2 elicit A_2 responses. At the beginning of an experiment, almost all of the stimuli will be conditioned to A_2 and will elicit A_2 responses. For example, in the early stages of an experiment, a rat engages in behaviors other than bar-pressing, an experimental participant does not respond when a CS is presented, and a student does not recall the correct nonsense syllable. The "correct" responses occur reliably only after they are attached to stimuli in the experimental context.

Assumption IV   The learner is limited in its ability to experience S. The learner experiences or samples only a small proportion of the stimuli available on any learning trial, and the size of the sample is assumed to remain constant throughout the experiment. *The constant proportion of S experienced at the beginning of each learning trial is designated by* θ (***theta***). After each trial, the elements in θ are returned to S. That is, Estes's theory assumes *sampling with replacement*. Those elements sampled on any given trial may be sampled again on subsequent trials.

Assumption V   A learning trial ends when a response occurs; if an A_1 response terminates a trial, the stimulus elements in θ are conditioned to the A_1 response. Following Guthrie, Estes accepts a contiguity explanation of learning. When an A_1 response occurs, an association is formed between that response and the stimuli that preceded it. In other words, because a proportion of the stimulus elements in S were sampled at the beginning of the trial, those elements are conditioned to A_1 through the principle of contiguity whenever an A_1 response terminates a trial. As the number of elements in S conditioned to A_1 increases, the likelihood that θ contains some of those elements increases. Thus, the tendency for an A_1 response to be elicited at the beginning of a learning trial increases over time, and stimulus elements initially attached to A_2 are gradually attached to A_1. This is what Estes calls learning. The **state of the system** at any given moment is the proportion of elements attached to A_1 and A_2 responses.

Assumption VI   Because elements in θ are returned to S at the conclusion of a trial, and because θ sampled at the beginning of a learning trial is essentially random, the proportion of elements conditioned to A_1 in S will be reflected in the elements in θ at the beginning of every new trial. If none of the elements in S are conditioned to A_1, θ will not contain any elements conditioned to the correct response. If 50 percent of the elements in S are conditioned to A_1, 50 percent of the elements in a random sample θ from S can be expected to be conditioned to A_1.

What determines whether an A_1 or an A_2 response occurs on a learning trial? How can Estes's theory reconcile his claim of all-or-none learning with the fact that performance is probabilistic—that the A_1 response will sometimes not occur even after several successful learning trials? The answer to these questions indicates why Estes's theory is called a *statistical learning theory*. The theory states that the probability of an A_1 response is equal to the proportion of stimulus elements in θ conditioned to A_1 at the beginning of a learning trial, and each θ is a random sample from S. If all elements in θ are conditioned to A_1, the response has a 100 percent chance of occurring. If, however, only 75 percent of the elements in θ are conditioned to A_1, we expect an A_1 response about 75 percent of the time and an A_2 response 25 percent of the time. In other words, the probability of observing an A_1 response depends on the *state of the system.*

Using these assumptions, we can derive a mathematical expression that summarizes the learning process as seen by Estes:

1. The probability of response A_1 on any trial n (P_n) is equal to the proportion of elements conditioned to A_1 on that trial (p_n).

$$P_n = p_n$$

2. From assumption II, all elements are either A_1 elements (with probability p) or A_2 elements (with probability q). And these constitute 100 percent of the elements in the situation.

$$p + q = 1.00$$

so

$$p = 1.00 - q$$

3. From assumption V, elements not conditioned to A_1 on any trial n (reflected in q) must be elements that were not preconditioned to A_1 prior to the first trial *and* that were not conditioned to A_1 on any previous trial. On any trial n, the probability that an element was not preconditioned on trial 1 is $(1 - P_1)$. Similarly, on any trial n, the probability that an element was not conditioned to A_1 on a *previous* trial is $(1 - \theta)^{n-1}$. The joint probability of two events occurring together (i.e., the probability that an element is not preconditioned *and* has not yet been conditioned) is the mathematical product of their individual probabilities. Therefore,

$$q = (1 - P_1)(1 - \theta)^{n-1}$$

4. Substituting from 3, we get

$$P_n = 1 - (1 - P_1)(1 - \theta)^{n-1}$$

How does Estes's theory relate performance and training? The following example might be helpful: Assume that we have two learners. One begins with $P_1 = 0$

and $\theta = .05$. The second also begins with $P_1 = 0$ but is able to sample a larger number of stimuli in the learning environment. For the second learner, $\theta = .20$.

For the first learner,

$$\text{on trial 1, } P_1 = 1 - (1)(1 - .05)^0 = 0$$
$$\text{on trial 2, } P_2 = 1 - (1)(1 - .05)^1 = .05$$
$$\text{on trial 3, } P_3 = 1 - (1)(1 - .05)^2 = .10$$

and performance approaches 100 percent ($P_n = 1.00$) at about 105 trials, assuming each of these trials terminates in an A_1 response.

For the second learner,

$$\text{on trial 1, } P_1 = 1 - (1)(1 - .20)^0 = 0$$
$$\text{on trial 2, } P_2 = 1 - (1)(1 - .20)^1 = .20$$
$$\text{on trial 3, } P_3 = 1 - (1)(1 - .20)^2 = .36$$

and performance approaches 100 percent ($P_n = 1.00$) at about 23–25 trials, again assuming each of the trials ends in an A_1 response.

The formula generates a negatively accelerated learning curve with an asymptote of 1 that can vary from case to case, as we have seen in the example, depending on the size of θ and the value of P_1. The learning curve produced by Estes's formula is essentially the same as the one generated by Hull's formula, described in Chapter 6 (see Figure 6–1). Both Estes and Hull assume that more learning takes place in the early stages of a learning experiment than in the later stages.

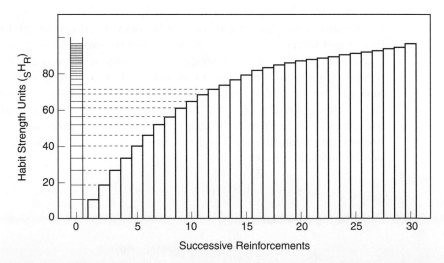

FIGURE 6–1   The relationship between gains in habit strength ($_sH_R$) and successive reinforcements. (From *Principles of Behavior,* p. 116, by C. L. Hull, 1943, Englewood Cliffs, N.J.: Prentice Hall.)

The **negatively accelerated learning curve** occurs, according to Estes, because trials in a learning experiment usually end with an A_1 response, and as a result, an increasing number of elements become conditioned to A_1. But there are diminishing returns. Taking as an example the situation in which, at the onset of an experiment, an A_1 response is highly unlikely (e.g., with eye-blinking conditioning), we see that almost all elements in S would be conditioned to A_2 (not blinking when a light is presented). Suppose, however, that blinking occurs at the end of trial 1. In this case, all the elements sampled on that trial (θ) switch from A_2 to A_1 because they were all conditioned to A_2 to begin with. On the next trial, a few elements will be conditioned to A_1, but most will still be conditioned to A_2. Therefore, it is now possible that some elements conditioned to A_1 will be sampled along with those conditioned to A_2. Thus the rate of changeover (from A_2 to A_1) will not be as great on trial 2 as it was on trial 1 because only those elements conditioned to A_2 can be transferred to A_1. As we saw earlier, this changeover from A_2 to A_1 is what constitutes learning. In the later trials, more and more elements are already conditioned to A_1; therefore, the number of elements conditioned to A_2 responses contained in θ on any given trial is small. It can be seen then that as learning trials progress, the rate of learning goes down. When all the elements in S are conditioned to A_1, no further learning can occur, and the probability that an A_1 response will occur is 1. Thus, we have a negatively accelerated learning curve, which again simply indicates that learning progresses more rapidly in the early stages than it does in the later stages. This negatively accelerated rate of changeover of the stimulus elements is diagrammed in Figure 9–1.

Generalization

Generalization from the original learning situation to other situations is easily taken care of by stimulus sampling theory. Estes takes the same position on transfer as did Thorndike and Guthrie. That is, transfer takes place to the extent that two situations have stimulus elements in common. If many of the elements previously conditioned to an A_1 response are present in a new learning situation, the probability is high that an A_1 response will be elicited in the new situation. If no elements are conditioned to A_1 at the onset of new learning situations, the probability of an A_1 response is zero. In a new situation, as with original learning, the probability of an A_1 response is equal to the proportion of stimulus elements in S conditioned to it.

Extinction

Estes handles the problem of extinction in essentially the same way as Guthrie did. Because in extinction a trial usually ends with the subject doing something other than A_1, the stimulus elements previously conditioned to A_1 gradually switch back to A_2. The laws for acquisition and for extinction are the same. In fact, in Estes's system, it does not make sense to speak of extinction. What is called extinction results whenever conditions are arranged so that stimulus elements are switched from an A_1 response to an A_2 response.

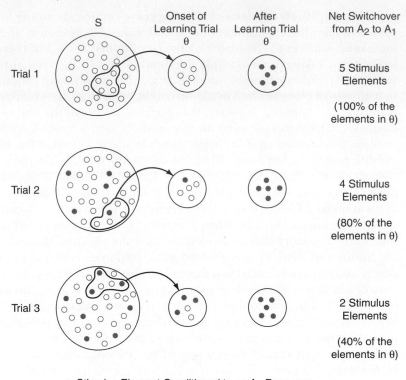

FIGURE 9–1   Estes's model of how stimulus elements change from the unconditioned state to the conditioned state.

Spontaneous Recovery

As you may remember from Chapter 7, spontaneous recovery refers to the reappearance of a conditioned response after that response has undergone extinction. To explain spontaneous recovery, Estes expands slightly on his notion of S. Earlier in this chapter, S was defined as the total number of stimulus elements present at the beginning of a trial in a learning experiment. We also noted that these stimulus elements include transitory events such as extraneous noises from the outside (e.g., a car backfiring, thunder, and loud voices) and temporary body states of the experimental subject (e.g., indigestion, headache, and anxiety). Because these and many other events are transitory, they may be part of S on one occasion but not on others. Likewise, when they are part of S, they are available to be sampled by the subject; when they are not part of S, they cannot be sampled. In other words, only those elements present in S can be sampled as part of θ.

Under these conditions, it is possible that during training A_1 responses become conditioned to many of these transitory elements. If it turns out that these elements are not available during extinction, the A_1 response conditioned to them cannot be switched to A_2 responses. Switching can occur only for stimulus elements actually sampled; thus if certain elements had been conditioned to A_1 responses during training and are subsequently not available during extinction, their status remains the same, that is, attached to A_1.

Now the importance of these transitory elements for spontaneous recovery becomes evident. It is entirely possible that many elements that were conditioned to A_1 during acquisition are not available during extinction but may reappear some time after extinction has taken place. Thus, if the subject is placed back into the experimental situation some time after extinction, a portion of these elements may now be present and would therefore tend to elicit an A_1 response. Spontaneous recovery is explained then by assuming that the extinction process (switching elements from A_1 to A_2) was never complete in the first place.

Probability Matching

For years, behaviorists puzzled over the phenomenon of **probability matching.** The traditional probability matching experiment involves a signal light that is followed by one of two other lights. When the signal light comes on, the subject is to guess which of the other two lights will come on. The experimenter arranges the situation so that the lights come on in any pattern he or she wishes, such as left light 75 percent of the time, right light 25 percent of the time or left light 100 percent of the time, right light zero percent of the time. The results of such an arrangement are usually that the subject ends up guessing the frequencies at which the lights come on almost exactly as the experimenter had arranged them; for example, if the right light comes on 80 percent of the time, the subject will predict that that light will come on about 80 percent of the trials. This is referred to as probability matching.

To handle these results, we need to add symbols for the two new stimulus events to Estes's theory:

$$E_1 = \text{left light going on}$$

$$E_2 = \text{right light going on}$$

In this case, an A_1 response is predicting E_1, and A_2 is predicting E_2. In Estes's analysis of probability matching, the subject's actual guess is irrelevant. It is assumed that when E_1 occurs, it evokes in the subject an implicit A_1 response, and when E_2 occurs, it evokes an implicit A_2 response. Thus, for Estes, the event itself acts as a "reinforcer" (see Estes & Straughan, 1954, for greater detail). The experimental situation can be diagrammed as follows:

Signal Light $\rightarrow$ | Guess A_1 A_2 | $\rightarrow$ | Event E_1 E_2 | $\rightarrow$ Implicit behavior terminates trail

Two additional symbols are necessary for Estes's analysis of probability matching:

$$\pi = \text{the probability of } E_1 \text{ occurring}$$
$$1 - \pi = \text{the probability of } E_2 \text{ occurring}$$

On a trial in which E_1 occurs, all elements sampled from S on that trial become conditioned to A_1, and on a trial on which E_2 occurs, the sample of elements will become conditioned to A_2.

As before, the probability of an A_1 response on any given trial (P_n) is equal to the proportion of elements in S that are conditioned to A_1, and the probability of an A_2 response is equal to the proportion of those elements not conditioned to A_1 or $(1 - P_n)$. As before, θ equals the proportion of elements sampled on each trial, and again, this value remains the same throughout the experiment.

The probability of an A_1 response after n trials is given by the following formula:

$$P_n = \pi - (\pi - P_1)(1 - \theta)^{n-1}$$

Because $(1 - \theta)$ is less than 1, with n getting larger, this equation yields a negatively accelerated curve with an asymptote of π. Thus, whatever the value of π, this formula predicts that the proportion of A_1 responses made by the subject will eventually match the proportion of E_1 occurrences set by the experimenter. In other words, Estes predicts probability matching by the subject, and this is what occurs. For more detail concerning the application of Estes's theory to probability matching, see Estes and Straughan (1954) or Estes (1964b).

ESTES'S MARKOV MODEL OF LEARNING

All statistical learning theories are probabilistic; that is, the dependent variable that they study is response probability. There is, however, a difference of opinion over what these changing response probabilities tell us about the nature of learning. The classic argument is over whether learning is gradual or complete in one trial. Thorndike concluded that learning was gradual and that it increased in small increments from trial to trial. Hull and Skinner went along with Thorndike on this matter. Guthrie differed by saying that learning occurred in an all-or-none fashion and only looked gradual because of the complexity of the task being learned. We discuss in Chapter 10 that Gestalt theorists, with their insight studies, also felt they demonstrated that the learner went from the unlearned state to the learned state very rapidly and not bit by bit.

Estes's early stimulus sampling theory accepted both an incremental (gradual) and an all-or-none point of view concerning the learning process. You will remember that only a small proportion of the total number of stimulus elements present during an experiment is sampled on any given trial. The sampled elements were conditioned in an all-or-none fashion to whatever response terminated the trial. However, because only a small portion of elements is conditioned on any given trial, learning proceeds bit by bit, and this is how the characteristic negatively accelerated learning curve is generated. To repeat, Estes's early position was that those stimulus elements that were sampled on a given trial were conditioned in an all-or-none manner, but because only a small number of them were sampled on a trial, learning proceeded in an incremental or gradual fashion. The probability of making an A_1 response changed gradually from one trial to the next, and if the total number of stimulus elements present in the experiment was large enough, the all-or-none nature of learning could not be detected. That is, with a large number of stimulus elements present in an experiment, there would be very small changes in response probabilities from one learning trial to the next, and when those probabilities were plotted, it would look *as if* learning was incremental rather than all-or-none in nature.

Later, Estes designed a number of studies that allowed the learning process to be observed in more detail (e.g., Estes, 1960, 1964a; Estes, Hopkins, & Crothers, 1960). These studies showed that when the number of elements to be sampled is very small, learning clearly occurs in an all-or-none fashion; in fact, it can be said that learning occurs completely on one trial or it does not occur at all—there appears to be no in between. This rapid change from the unlearned state to the learned state is said to correspond to a **Markov process,** which is characterized by an abrupt, stepwise change in response probabilities rather than a relatively slow, gradual change from trial to trial.

In one study, Estes (1964a) used *paired associates* to show the stepwise nature of learning. In **paired associate learning,** people learn pairs of items so that when they are shown the first member of the pair, they can respond with the other. Estes used a variation of paired associate learning in which people were shown the first member of the pair and had four responses to choose from, only one of which was correct. Thus, after they see the first member of the pair, the probability of their choosing the correct response by chance alone was .25 (1 in 4). Estes found that if a person guessed correctly on one trial, the probability of guessing correctly on the next trial went to 1 and stayed there. In other words, after guessing correctly, the person would be correct on 100 percent of the subsequent trials. People who did not guess correctly went on guessing at chance level until they guessed correctly, at which time their subsequent probability of being correct jumped to 1. The most important fact here is that different people learned the correct response at different points in the experiment; that is, when they learned, they learned completely, but this learning occurred on different trials for different people, as shown in Figure 9–2.

What happens when the individual instances of going from the unlearned to the learned state are overlooked and the data from all learners are pooled together? Under these circumstances, the probabilities of making a correct response for the people in the unlearned state would be combined with those in the learned state, and *average* probabilities would be plotted. For example, if there were five people in an experiment and three were in the unlearned state (probability of making a correct response = .25) and two were in the learned state (probability of making a correct response = 1), the average probability of making a correct response for the group would be .55. As more learning trials occur, more people will enter the learned state, and the average probability for the group would increase. This process is demonstrated in Figure 9–3. $P(C_{n+1}|N_n)$ is read as "the probability that learners will

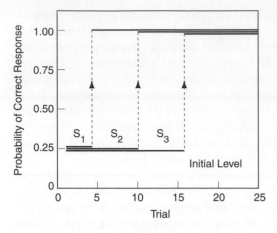

FIGURE 9–2 People go from chance-level performance to perfect performance in just one trial, but this process occurs at different times for different subjects. (From "All-or-None Processes in Learning and Retention," by W. K. Estes, 1964, *American Psychologist, 19,* pp. 16–25. Copyright by the American Psychological Association. Reprinted by permission of the publisher and author.)

be correct on trial $n + 1$, given that they were incorrect on trial n." $P(C_n)$ is the probability that learners will be correct on trial n.

Because the data are combined, one gets the impression that learning is gradual and improves slightly from trial to trial. When one looks at individual performance, however, the illusion of gradual learning disappears.

In an earlier study, Estes (1960) used another paired associate situation involving a nonsense syllable and a number. He ran forty-eight people on an eight-item paired associate list; that is, there were eight pairs of nonsense syllables and numbers. Each person was presented with each of the eight syllable-number pairs once and then tested by seeing the syllable alone and guessing the number that was associated with it. This time there was not a multiple choice, as there was in the other paired associate study previously mentioned.

To differentiate between the point of view that says learning is gradual and the one that says it is all or none, Estes hypothesizes four people who start the experiment with zero probability of being correct. These four hypothetical learners see a syllable

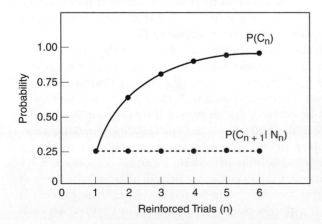

FIGURE 9–3 Even though individuals learned completely in one trial, when the data from a number of individuals are pooled, a negatively accelerated learning curve is generated. This curve gives the erroneous impression that learning is continuous and does not occur in an all-or-none fashion. (From "All-or-None Processes in Learning and Retention," by W. K. Estes, 1964, *American Psychologist, 19,* pp. 16–25. Copyright by the American Psychological Association. Reprinted by permission of the publisher and author.)

and a number paired once. When tested, one of the four anticipates the number correctly after seeing the nonsense syllable. Estes supposes that the probability of being correct on subsequent tests is raised from zero to .25 for the group. But this increase in the probability of being correct can occur in two ways: (1) Those who believe in the gradual nature of learning would say that the "associative strength" is increased in all four people, and therefore on subsequent tests all members of the group have a probability of being correct of .25 and a probability of being wrong of .75; (2) those who believe in all-or-none learning would say that one member of the group formed the correct association, whereas the other three did not. According to the principle of all-or-none learning, one person will always be correct on subsequent tests, and the other three will always be wrong. The difference between the associative strength point of view and the all-or-none point of view is diagrammed in Figure 9–4.

Now we return to the real experiment involving forty-eight people. Estes indicates that according to the associative strength point of view, how they perform on a second test should have little to do with whether they were correct on the first test. In other words, if the performance of people who were wrong on the first test is compared with the performance of those who were correct on the first test, it should show that they do about as well on the second test. The all-or-none point of view, however, says that all or most of the people who were correct on the first test should also be correct on the second test, and the people who were wrong on the

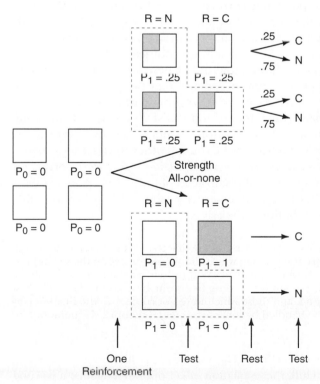

FIGURE 9–4 The diagram shows what the effects of a single reinforcement are thought to be according to the "associative strength" (upper part of diagram) and all-or-none (lower part of diagram) points of view. N = an incorrect response; C = a correct response; R = the response made on a test trial following one reinforcement. For example, $R = N$ means that the learner made an incorrect response on the test trial. (From "Learning Theory and the 'New Mental Chemistry,'" by W. K. Estes, 1960, *Psychological Review, 67*, pp. 207–223. Copyright 1960 by the American Psychological Association. Reprinted by permission of the publisher and author.)

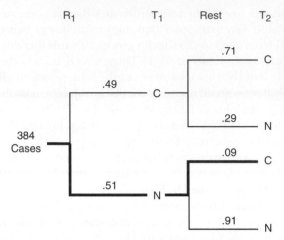

FIGURE 9–5   Results of paired associated learning experiment. See text for explanation. (From "Learning Theory and the 'New Mental Chemistry,'" by W. K. Estes, 1960, *Psychological Review, 67*, pp. 207–223. Copyright 1960 by the American Psychological Association. Reprinted by permission of the publisher and author.)

first test should also be wrong on the second test. Estes ran such a test, and the results are summarized in Figure 9–5.

It can be seen in Figure 9–5 that of the 384 possibilities of being correct (48 people × 8 paired associates), 49 percent of the responses on test 1 were correct and 51 percent were incorrect. Seventy-one percent of the items that were responded to correctly on test 1 were also responded to correctly on test 2, whereas only 9 percent of the items that were responded to incorrectly on test 1 were responded to correctly on test 2. This result lends support to the notion that when something is learned, it is learned completely; if it is not learned completely, it is not learned at all. Estes ran some trials with control groups that showed that the 51 percent of the items missed were just as difficult as the 49 percent not missed and that the people missing the 51 percent had the same average learning ability as the other participants.

As with most notions in learning theory today, Estes's work has not gone uncriticized. Underwood and Keppel (1962), for example, find fault with many aspects of the experiment we have just discussed. Among other things, they wonder, if the all-or-none point of view is correct, why were *all* the items that were correct on the first test not also correct on the second test instead of only 71 percent of them? Underwood and Keppel feel that Hull's incremental learning theory is better able to handle the data than Estes's all-or-none theory:

> It could be said that if an item were incorrect on the first test trial then it was below the performance threshold; there is no reason why it should be correct on the second test with no intervening study. Likewise, an item above threshold on the first test trial has a high probability of being correct on the second. Items which were correct on the first test trial but not on the second, and those which were not correct on the first but correct on the second, would be handled by some incremental theories via the notion of *oscillation.* (pp. 3–4)

As you will recall, the oscillation effect ($_sO_R$) was part of Hull's theory of learning (see Chapter 6). According to Hull, the oscillation effect operated against a learned response in varying amounts from trial to trial and in a random fashion. When the value of $_sO_R$ happened to be high, the probability of a learned response on that particular trial was low. When the value of $_sO_R$ was low, it had little effect on the elicitation of a learned response. Hull used the oscillation effect to explain why a learned response may occur on one trial but not on a subsequent trial.

ESTES AND COGNITIVE PSYCHOLOGY

Although Estes remains a contiguity theorist, in more recent years, he has been emphasizing cognitive mechanisms in his analysis of learning (see, e.g., Estes 1969a, 1969b, 1971, 1972, 1973, 1978). As we have seen, his earlier analysis followed Guthrie by assuming that whatever stimuli were present at the termination of a learning trial became associated with whatever response terminated the trial. Both Guthrie and Estes viewed learning as the mechanical, automatic association of contiguous events. Essentially, organisms, including humans, were viewed as machines that could sense, record, and respond. Although still mechanistic, Estes's current analysis of learning is much more complex because it considers the influence of cognitive events.

The Importance of Memory Earlier, Estes maintained that stimuli and responses become associated by contiguity, and once associated, when the stimuli recur, they will elicit the responses associated with them. Later, Estes added a third element to his analysis, namely, memory (see, e.g., Estes, 1969a, 1972, 1973, 1978). In Estes's more recent analysis, rather than stimuli leading directly to responses, stimuli elicit memories of previous experiences, and the interaction of current stimulation with memories of previous experiences produces behavior.

Estes (1976) describes what he believes occurs in a decision-making situation in which different responses are associated with different outcomes. For example, making an A_1 response will yield five points and making an A_2 response will yield three points. First, according to Estes, the person learns the value of each response, and this information is stored in memory. Subsequently, when given the opportunity to respond, the person will scan the situation to determine what responses are possible and recall what their outcomes are. Given this information, the person will choose to make the response that yields the most valuable outcome. Estes (1976) calls this the **scanning model of decision making.** In general, the model claims that in any decision-making situation, an organism will utilize whatever information it has stored in memory concerning response-outcome relationships and will respond in such a way as to produce the most beneficial outcome. It is this scanning model that Estes now uses to explain probability matching (see Estes, 1976).

Memory also plays a prominent role in Estes's analysis of higher-order cognitive operations such as those involving language. Following in the tradition of the British empiricists, Estes assumes that simple memories are combined to form complex memories. In learning a language, for example, first individual letters of the alphabet are learned and retained, then words, then sentences, and then other principles of organization. Language utilization, then, requires memories arranged in a hierarchy ranging from the memory of simple elements (e.g., letters) to the memory of complex grammatical rules and principles. Estes (1971) says that complex human behavior such as that involving language "is better understood in terms of the operation of rules, principles, strategies, and the like than in terms of successions of responses to particular stimuli" (p. 23). According to Estes, the interaction of such complex cognitive processes with sensory stimulation determines the response to a situation.

The Cognitive Array Model: Classifying and Categorizing

Estes sees stimulus sampling theory (SST) as a mathematical extension of Thorndike's identical elements theory of transfer. That is, it was developed to make precise predictions about transfer of learning from one situation to another, based on stimulus elements common to both. In recent work, Estes (1994) expands on a problem first explored by Medin and Shaffer (1978) and continues to develop Thorndike's identical elements approach. This time, however, the model is applied specifically to the behaviors of classification and categorization. Examining a creature, noting that it has feathers, that it flies, and that it lays eggs, and then calling it "bird" is one example of this kind of behavior. Physicians who gather data and diagnose a common cold, rather than pneumonia, and market analysts who declare a company to be a good investment, rather than a risky venture, are classifying or categorizing. Although Estes's approach to classification is strictly cognitive, we will see that there are similarities between the kinds of behaviors predicted by SST and by his model of classification. Furthermore, some of Estes's important assumptions about learning, made in his cognitive approach, are similar to those he made in the earlier development of SST.

Recall that in SST, learning occurs in an all-or-none, one-trial manner and that it requires only contiguity between stimuli and a particular response. On subsequent learning trials, people sample a limited number of stimulus elements from the stimulus set, and the resulting response depends on the proportion of stimuli in the sample that are attached to that response. If the sample contains no conditioned elements, either because of the random nature of sampling or because the environment has changed, the response is not elicited.

In Estes's cognitive model of classification, people are assumed to examine a complex stimulus and attend to (or sample) its important or salient features. As in SST, those stimulus features, along with information about their category or class membership, are learned all-or-none in one trial. At this point, Estes's cognitive approach, called the **array model,** differs from SST. In the case of the array model, the stimulus characteristics and category designation are stored in memory as a set—an array—that keeps the important features or attributes distinct and ready for comparison with attributes of other stimuli. When a new stimulus is encountered, salient features of the new stimulus are compared with previously learned and stored sets of features. Classification of a new stimulus is then based on the similarity of its attributes to stimulus attributes stored in memory arrays. There is an additional difference between SST and the array model that deserves mention. The focus of SST is on stimulus-response associations formed in the past and the way in which those associations were accumulated. The focus of the array model is on the classification of events that are encountered in the present or that will be encountered in the future. In noting that we do not acquire an exact, perfectly detailed memory record of situations previously encountered, Estes (1994) says,

> Situations never recur exactly, and therefore the record alone would be of no help to us in dealing with present problems or anticipating the future. Memory is essential to adaptive behavior because it is organized in ways that make information gained from past experience applicable to present situations. And the essence of memory is classification. . . . Suffice it to say that classification is basic to all of our intellectual activities. (p. 4)

SST Assumes Additive Stimulus Relationships Although both SST and the array model reflect Thorndike's identical elements theory of transfer, they do so in different ways. A simple example can help to illustrate these differences. Let us look first at a problem in which people learn to discriminate between two stimuli called "A" and "B" and the way that sampling theory deals with the problem of generalization of the "A" response. In our example, the stimuli will have three distinct features or sampling elements: size, color, and shape. The "A" stimulus is large, it is red, and it is a square. People learn to say "B" to a distinct second stimulus that is a small, blue circle. After discrimination training with these initial stimuli, people are tested on two new stimuli: a large, red circle and a small, blue square. The problem is displayed in Table 9–1.

As indicated on the lower right, we want to know how people will respond to the test stimuli, 2A and 2B, after discrimination has been learned with the training stimuli. Notice that the large, red circle shares two elements with the training stimulus that the person learned to call "A" but has only one element in common with the training stimulus called "B." Similarly, the small, blue square shares two elements with training stimulus "B" but only one element with "A." A basic prediction from SST, based on this straightforward *additive* combination of stimulus elements, is that people will call the large, red circle an "A" about 66 percent of the time because this stimulus shares two-thirds of the properties of the training stimulus that have been attached to response "A." They should also call the small, blue square an "A" about 33 percent of the time because one-third of its elements are attached to response

TABLE 9–1

TRAINING STIMULI		1A	1B	TEST STIMULI	2A	2B
Sampling Elements	1	large	small		large	small
	2	red	blue		red	blue
	3	square	circle		circle	square
RESPONSE		"A"	"B"		???	???
				Predicted:	(66% "A")	(33% "A")

"A" during initial discrimination training. This is a fairly straightforward demonstration of how Thorndike's idea of identical elements is used in SST to predict generalization, and the predictions for a very simple learning problem like this one are, in fact, quite accurate (cited in Atkinson & Estes, 1963, p. 193).

A significant problem with SST is that, in situations more complex than the one just described, the theory cannot account for large detrimental effects that are observed when either human or nonhuman learners are tested in contexts or with stimuli that are very different from those that existed during training. In *Classification and Cognition*, Estes (1994) indicates that the critical flaw is the assumption of additive stimulus effects—the conceptual and mathematical idea, demonstrated in our example, that stimulus elements combine in an additive manner in order to elicit learned responses. As an alternative, the array model assumes that elements combine *multiplicatively* to elicit responses.

The Array Model Assumes Multiplicative Stimulus Relationships   According to the array model, we judge the similarity of stimuli in a new context relative to the stimuli in the training situation by comparing stimulus attributes or elements. In each case of comparison, a factor called *s*, the similarity coefficient, describes the degree of similarity between pairs of stimulus attributes. Estes writes "We compare the two situations . . . feature by feature, applying a similarity coefficient of *unity* [italics added] if the features match and a coefficient with some smaller value *s*, if they differ. The measure of similarity is the *product* [italics added] of these coefficients" (p. 19). Therefore, the probability of response transfer from a training situation to a test situation is a function of the product of the similarity coefficients. If all stimulus element comparisons yield perfect matches, all similarity coefficients are equal to 1.00, and the measure of similarity will be $(1 \times 1 \times 1 \times 1 \ldots)$ or 1. The probability of response transfer is then 1.00, or certainty. Response probability decreases from certainty whenever there is a mismatch between the compared stimuli. In the earlier example, the similarity coefficients for comparisons of size and color are both 1.00 because both stimuli are large and red. The similarity coefficient for comparison of shape is *s*, some number less than 1.00, because the shapes do not match perfectly. Thus, the measure of similarity between stimuli 1A and 2A is $(1 \times 1 \times s)$ or *s*, and because the similarity measure for 1A and 2A is less than 1.00, we would not expect perfect response transfer between the two stimuli. Note that with an appropriate value of *s*, the array model can be applied to the generalization problem in Table 9–1 and make a prediction similar to that made by SST.

The array model is intended to describe and predict how people judge stimuli to be members of specific categories, not how a conditioned response is generalized or transferred to a new situation, and we can use the stimuli from our generalization problem to demonstrate the basics of the array model. In our example, the three stimulus attributes or elements are restricted so that they can each have only one of two values. With respect to size, a stimulus can be large (designated with a "+") or it can be small (designated with a "−"). It can be either red (+) or blue (−); and it can be either a square (+) or a circle (−). And in our basic, general description, *s* is assigned a single value for all attribute comparisons. The categorization rule that we

TABLE 9–2   Elements in Category A

	SIZE	COLOR	SHAPE
STIMULUS 1A	+	+	+
STIMULUS 2A	+	+	−
coefficient	1	1	s
PRODUCT: $(1 \times 1 \times s) = s$			

arbitrarily determine for this experiment is that all large, red things belong in category A; all small, blue things belong in category B. The stimuli will be presented one at a time, the participant will respond by categorizing the stimulus as "A" or "B," and the experimenter will indicate whether the categorical response is correct.

Items within a Category Are Similar to Each Other   The first step in developing the array model for this problem is to determine similarity of items within categories. We can see that two of our stimuli actually belong in category A. In Table 9–2, we show their coefficients of similarity and the product of those coefficients as a measure of the similarity of those items to each other. Keep in mind that the coefficient of similarity is 1 when the values of an element match (both + or both −) and is s, some value less than 1, when the values are different.

There are also two members of category B, and we show their similarity coefficients and the product for those stimuli in Table 9–3.

The measure of similarity of any stimulus with itself is, of course, 1.00 because all features match. In both categories A and B, the measure of similarity of the two stimuli within the category, indicated by the product of the similarity coefficients, is s and is less than 1.00 because, in each case, two features match perfectly but there is a mismatch with respect to shape. Note, however, that the measures of similarity between stimuli from different categories are even smaller than s. If two stimuli have one matching element and two mismatches, the product is $(1 \times s \times s)$ or s^2. If two stimuli mismatch on all three features, the product is $(s \times s \times s)$ or s^3. If we set $s = .7$ in this example (this setting is arbitrary and is used for illustration only), we see

two matches; one mismatch $= (1 \times 1 \times .7) = .7$
one match; two mismatches $= (1 \times .7 \times .7) = (.7)^2 = .49$
no matches; three mismatches $= (.7 \times .7 \times .7) = (.7)^3 = .34$

TABLE 9–3   Elements in Category B

	SIZE	COLOR	SHAPE
STIMULUS 1B	−	−	−
STIMULUS 2B	−	−	+
coefficient	1	1	s
PRODUCT: $(1 \times 1 \times s) = s$			

TABLE 9–4   Stimuli in Category A

	STIMULUS 1A	STIMULUS 2A	(SIMILARITY TO A)
STIMULUS 1A	1	s	$(1+s)$
STIMULUS 2A	s	1	$(1+s)$

Stimulus Items Represent a Whole Category   The next step in applying the array model is to determine the degree to which a particular stimulus is representative of its category as a whole. To do this, we construct a similarity coefficient matrix comparing elements within a category to other elements in that category, including comparison of a single stimulus with itself. The matrix for stimuli in category A appears in Table 9–4. In the far right column, we see that the similarity of stimulus 1A to all the items in category A is $(1 + s)$, the similarity of that item to itself plus the similarity of that item to the other member of the category. The similarity of 2A to all items in A is also $(1 + s)$.

Next, we can construct a matrix representing the similarity of items in A with items in B, thereby representing the similarity of each item in A to category B as a whole. The summed similarity of an item in A to each of the items in B is indicated in the far right column in Table 9–5.

Finally, we can make a probabilistic prediction about the correct categorization of a stimulus. This prediction is based on the similarity of a stimulus to its own (correct) category relative to the sum of its similarities to all possible categories. Thus, the probability of correctly categorizing stimulus 2A is calculated by dividing the similarity of stimulus 2A to category A by the similarity of stimulus 2A to categories A and B. That is, the probability of correctly recognizing stimulus 2A as a member of A is

$$\frac{(1 + s)}{(1 + s) + (s^2 + s^3)}$$

To see how the model might work with a concrete example, let's say that we train people on items 1A and 1B, and, as above, $s = .7$. The array model predicts that, when stimulus 2A appears, the probability that it will be categorized as an "A" is

$$\frac{(1 + .7)}{(1 + .7) + (.49 + .34)}$$
$$= \frac{1.7}{2.53}$$
$$= .67$$

TABLE 9–5   Stimuli in Category B

	STIMULUS 1B	STIMULUS 2B	(SIMILARITY TO B)
STIMULUS 1A	s^3	s^2	$(s^3 + s^2)$
STIMULUS 2A	s^2	s^3	$(s^2 + s^3)$

It might be a useful exercise for the reader to use the model to predict the probability of correct categorization of 2B under the same conditions. Note, however, that these mathematical manipulations are not just exercises so that experimenters can predict performance in categorical learning tasks. The theory assumes that people engage in cognitive processes that are captured in the mathematics of the theory. Estes (1994) writes:

> At the beginning of each trial after the first, the subject *computes* [italics added] the similarity of the exemplar presented to each member of the current memory array, *sums* [italics added] its similarity to all of the members associated with each category, *computes* [italics added] the probability of each category, and *generates* [italics added] a response based on these probabilities. It is not, of course, assumed that the individual carries out these calculations as a computer would do, only that the processing system accomplishes in some manner a set of computations leading to the same response probabilities as those produced by a computer programmed to simulate the model. (p. 46)

Clearly, with his more recent analyses, Estes has embraced cognitive psychology.

Estes's View of the Role of Reinforcement Estes's current view of reinforcement is also cognitive in nature. Estes has never been a reinforcement theorist, and he is not one now. His earlier position rejected the law of effect, which stated that reinforcement strengthened the bond or connection between a stimulus and a response. Following Guthrie, Estes believed that reinforcement prevented the unlearning of an association by preserving the association between certain stimuli and certain responses. Estes's more recent view of the role of reinforcement stresses the *information* that it provides to the organism (see, e.g., Estes, 1969b, 1971, 1978).

According to Estes, organisms learn not only S-R relationships but also R-O (response-outcome) relationships. That is, organisms learn, and remember, which responses lead to which consequences. In a given situation, some responses lead to reinforcement, some lead to punishment, and others lead to neither. Reinforcement and punishment do not strengthen or weaken behavior because R-O relationships leading to neither reinforcement nor punishment are learned as readily as those that do (Estes, 1969b). The organism simply learns what leads to what, and this information determines which response is preferred over others that are possible.

In his analysis of reinforcement, Estes makes the important distinction between learning and performance. For him, reinforcement and punishment are not learning variables because learning occurs in their absence. Rather, reinforcement and punishment are performance variables because they determine how material already learned will manifest itself in behavior.

Although Estes's position emphasizes cognitive mechanisms (e.g., memory) and views reinforcement and punishment as providing information to the organism, his position still views humans as machinelike. In this regard, the major difference between his earlier position and his recent one is that the machine has become much more complex. Hulse, Egeth, and Deese (1980) nicely summarize Estes's views on how reinforcement and punishment automatically guide behavior:

> The function of reinforcement, in Estes's theory, is not to strengthen directly the formation of new associations; simple contiguity suffices for that. In this regard he is in close

harmony with Guthrie. Instead, reinforcing events have their effects on *performance,* which, in Guthrie's terms, means the tendency for a given sequence of learned responses to run to some final conclusion. The function of reinforcement is to provide feedback based on the anticipation . . . of impending reward or punishment which summates with current stimuli (or stimuli recalled from memory) in the learning situation and so *guides* behavior preferentially along one path as opposed to another. In essence, in other words, Estes's theory emphasizes a cybernetic model for the influence of reinforcement upon performance: behavior is guided toward goals and away from aversive situations through positive or negative feedback from the reinforcing event. (pp. 73–74)

The term *cybernetic* in this quotation refers to a system that is automatically guided by feedback from the environment. Examples of cybernetic systems include the automatic pilot on an aircraft or a thermostat that regulates the temperature of a home.

With his informational interpretation of reinforcement and distinction between learning and performance, Estes aligns himself with the theories of Edward Tolman (see Chapter 12) and Albert Bandura (see Chapter 13). Estes, Tolman, and Bandura all believe that we learn what we observe and that how this information is translated into behavior depends on the goals of the organism. There is also a kinship between Estes's recent position and the information-processing approach to psychology. Information-processing psychology maintains that input from the environment (stimuli) interacts with one or more mental processes before it results in output (behavior). Like Estes, many information-processing psychologists accept a cybernetic model in explaining human behavior.

LEARNING TO LEARN

The controversy over the incremental versus the all-or-none position of learning (sometimes called the **continuity-noncontinuity controversy**) is still very much alive and promises to be for some time to come. As with most extreme positions, however, the truth will probably be found somewhere between the two. An example that seems to be satisfactory to both sides of the debate is Estes's earlier position that, with a complex learning environment, learning proceeds in an all-or-none fashion, only it does so a little bit at a time. In fact, logically, all incremental theories of learning can be reduced to all-or-none theories. What the theorists are really arguing over is the size of the chunk of material that is learned on any given trial.

Indeed, there is considerable evidence showing that the incremental and all-or-none positions are both correct. One example comes from the famous work of Harry Harlow. Harlow (1905–1981) received both his undergraduate and graduate education at Stanford University and then went to the University of Wisconsin, where he remained until his death. He was president of the American Psychological Association (APA) in 1957 and was given the Distinguished Scientific Contribution Award by the APA in 1960. Through the years, Harlow has used his creative research on monkeys to shed light on a variety of topics relevant to human behavior. It is his work on the learning process that concerns us here.

Harry F. Harlow. (Courtesy of Harlow
Primate Laboratory/University of Wisconsin.)

Using the Wisconsin General Test Apparatus shown in Figure 9–6, Harlow (1949) confronted monkeys with a total of 344 discrimination problems, including thirty-two practice problems. On each problem, they were to pick the one of two objects that had a reinforcer placed underneath it. Each of the 344 problems involved a different set of objects. Harlow's remarkable finding was that the more discrimination problems the monkeys solved, the better they became at solving them. It appeared that the animals were **learning to learn,** or forming what Harlow called a **learning set.** In the early discrimination problems, the monkeys tended to make a large number of errors, and improvement from problem to problem was fairly slow. The later problems, however, tended to be solved either with only one error or with none. On the last block of fifty-six problems, the monkeys chose the correct object 95 percent of the time by the second trial. It was as if they had developed the strategy of "win-stay, lose-shift." That is, if they picked the correct object on the first trial,

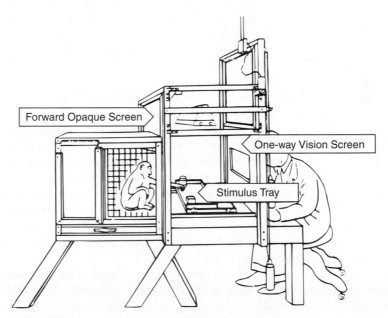

FIGURE 9–6 The Wisconsin General Test Apparatus. (From "The Formation of Learning Sets," by H. F. Harlow, 1949, *Psychological Review, 56,* p. 52. Copyright 1949 by the American Psychological Association. Reprinted by permission.)

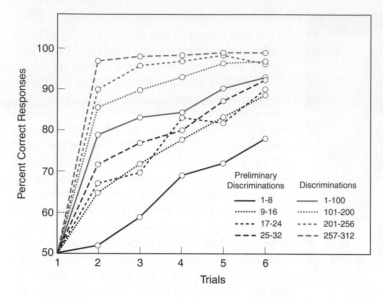

FIGURE 9–7   Harlow found a gradual improvement in the ability to solve discrimination problems. Although performance is relatively poor on early discrimination problems, later problems tend to be solved in just one trial. (From "The Formation of Learning Sets," by H. F. Harlow, 1949, *Psychological Review, 56*, pp. 51–65. Copyright 1949 by the American Psychological Association. Reprinted by permission.)

they stayed with it on the next; if their first choice was incorrect, however, they switched to the other object on the next trial. The percentage of correct responses for the first six trials of each of the discrimination problems is shown in Figure 9–7.

The gains from the early learning trials were slow and incremental in nature. Later learning, however, was very rapid and more like the all-or-none variety. Harlow (1949) said, "Before the formation of a discrimination learning set, a single training trial produces negligible gain; after the formation of a discrimination learning set, *a single training trial constitutes problem solution.* These data clearly show that *animals can gradually learn insight*" (p. 56).

To explain his results, Harlow (1950, 1959) used the concept of **error factors.** Error factors are erroneous strategies that have to be extinguished before a discrimination problem can be solved. In other words, error factors are response tendencies that lead to incorrect responses. One error factor could be the tendency to always choose the object on the left (position preference); another might be the tendency to continue to choose the same object although it is incorrect (stimulus preservation). For Harlow, learning was a matter more of eliminating incorrect strategies (error factors) than of strengthening a correct response. Thus, early learning is slow because it involves the elimination of error factors; later learning is rapid because it is based on a strategy that can be effectively applied to all two-choice discrimination problems.

Another theorist who accepts both the slow incremental and rapid all-or-none interpretations of learning is Donald Hebb. According to Hebb, learning that occurs very early in life is of the incremental variety, whereas later learning is cognitive, insightful, and more all-or-none in nature. We have more to say about Hebb's views of learning in Chapter 14.

THE CURRENT STATUS OF MATHEMATICAL MODELS OF LEARNING

Although we have minimized the mathematics in our coverage of Estes in this chapter, his approach is often referred to as a mathematical model of learning because he attempts to show how the learning process can be described in terms of various mathematical formulations. Mathematical models of learning are relatively new in psychology, and their newness is evident. Psychologists have always wanted to be scientific, and the language of science is mathematics. Therefore, when an opportunity comes along to use mathematics in a new way in psychology, it is met with considerable enthusiasm and optimism. One of the main contributions of the mathematical study of learning is that it allows a precise description of phenomena that have been studied for years in less precise terms. Outside this cleanup operation, however, mathematical models have provided little new information concerning the nature of the learning process. Currently, a large number of mathematical formulations, without any unifying theme running through them, describe different learning phenomena. To say that there is a lack of synthesis is not a criticism of mathematical models of learning; rather, it characterizes any new approach to the field. We explore another class of mathematical models, those dealing with learning in neural networks, in Chapter 14.

EVALUATION OF ESTES'S THEORY

Contributions

Shepard (1992) sees Estes as the primary influence in changing the directions of learning theory, moving it toward a new, more cognitively oriented field characterized by "formal elegance and conceptual precision . . . combined with a secure grounding in observation" (p. 210). Estes's citation for the Medal of Science, quoted at the beginning of this chapter, echoes this theme.

If we compare the mathematics of SST with Hull's extended formula, we see that Estes's approach is really quite simple, using only two factors that combine through the logical principles of probability theory. Like Guthrie, his learning theory requires only contiguity, and like Guthrie, he posits interference as the vehicle for extinction and forgetting.

In SST, however, it is the logic of probability and sampling that generates the predictions of the theory, including the familiarly shaped learning curve or the extinction curve. Similarly, it is the logic of probability theory that leads to explanation of categorical judgments in the more recent array model. Thus, we see Estes's approach as "top-down," beginning with a few fundamental principles and generating a variety of precise predictions about behavior.

Estes is credited by Shepard (1992) with a more important departure from the mainstream behaviorists of the 1950s. His theory was readily extended to learning in humans and was expanded into more and more complex kinds of learning, such as classification and concept learning (Estes, 1957, 1960), thus laying a groundwork for contemporary cognitive science. In addition, Bower (1994) writes,

> Therefore, in a broad historical perspective, although the specific assumptions and experimental paradigms of SST have been superseded and modified over the years, the current enthusiasm for parallel distributed, connectionist models of learning and cognition [Chapter 14] may be viewed as a partial outgrowth and legacy of the SST framework. It should come as no surprise that in the current scene one of the more creative and vigorous investigators of adaptive network models is that inimitable and indefatigable theorist, William K. Estes. (p. 298)

Criticisms

A number of criticisms have been raised against Estes's theory. The first, and the one most often noted by students of learning theory, concerns the restricted scope of the theory. Earlier theories were far more ambitious than Estes's theory, building grand structures that might account for all sorts of learning phenomena. Thorndike's theory began with the mechanisms underlying learning and extended into educational practices. Even Pavlov's theory stretches beyond the learning of simple reflexive responses and into such complex phenomena as language. Estes's theory represents a trade-off between scope and precision of predictions characteristic of many mathematical-psychological theories. Even in their restricted problem areas, there are occasions where such precisely formulated theories make extreme, and sometimes incorrect, predictions (Estes, 1994).

Shepard (1992) raises two additional criticisms of Estes's approach. First, Estes's theory, like Guthrie's, assumes no mechanism other than stimulus-response contiguity for strengthening learning connections, although both do assume that stimulus conditions must change when a correct response is emitted. Estes, however, does not make the important distinction between contiguity and contingency identified by Rescorla.

Second, Shepard (1992) observes that Estes and his colleagues allow the mathematical abstractions in the theory to severely constrain experimental conditions. If an experiment is so constrained as to become artificial, thus failing to reflect a real-world learning environment, then the results of that experiment may lack validity, and the theory itself is undermined.

DISCUSSION QUESTIONS

1. Categorize each of the following theorists as accepting either an incremental explanation of learning or an all-or-none explanation: Thorndike, Pavlov, Watson, Guthrie, Skinner, and Hull. Briefly explain your reason(s) for categorizing each theorist as you did.
2. Design an experiment that would allow one to determine clearly whether learning is incremental or all-or-none.

3. Discuss the importance of memory in the revised version of Estes's learning theory.
4. Describe Estes's scanning model of decision making.
5. Why is Estes's explanation of behavior referred to as a cybernetic model?
6. List some advantages and disadvantages of statistical learning theory.
7. From your everyday experience, do you feel that learning is incremental or all-or-none? What place do personal feelings of this kind have in science? Explain.
8. Do you feel that a process similar to "learning to learn" occurs in the life of the student? Explain becoming "testwise" in terms of learning to learn.
9. How does Harlow's error factor theory of learning compare with most of the other theories of learning you have read about in this book? For example, does his theory emphasize the "stamping in" of correct responses?
10. Regarding the learning process, briefly describe the incremental (continuity) position, the all-or-none (noncontinuity) position, and the compromise position that would accent both continuity and noncontinuity at different times or for different reasons.
11. How does the size of θ influence the learning process as Estes views it? List some factors you feel might influence the size of θ.
12. What stimulus features might be used in an array model to explain how we classify leaves as "oak" or "maple"?

CHAPTER HIGHLIGHTS

array model
continuity-noncontinuity controversy
error factors
learning set
learning to learn
Markov process
negatively accelerated learning curve

paired associate learning
probability matching
scanning model of decision making
state of the system
stimulus sampling theory (SST)
theta (θ)

CHAPTER 10

Gestalt Theory

- **Opposition to Voluntarism, Structuralism, and Behaviorism**
- **Major Theoretical Concepts**
  - Field Theory
  - Nature versus Nurture
  - Law of Prägnanz
- **The Brain and Conscious Experience**
- **Subjective and Objective Reality**
- **Gestalt Principles of Learning**
  - The Presolution Period
  - Insightful Learning Summarized
  - Transposition
  - The Behaviorists' Explanation of Transposition
- **Productive Thinking**
- **The Memory Trace**
  - Individual Trace versus Trace System
- **Gestalt Psychology on Education**
  - Was Popper a Gestalt Theorist?
- **Evaluation of Gestalt Theory**
  - Contributions
  - Criticisms

After J. B. Watson, behaviorism became the rage among American psychologists, and since his time, most eminent learning theorists, such as Guthrie, Skinner, and Hull, have been behaviorists. The behavioristic attack on the introspective method of Wundt and Titchener resulted in an almost complete abandonment of introspectionism. At about the same time the behaviorists were attacking introspection in America, a group of psychologists began attacking its use in Germany. This small group of German psychologists called themselves Gestalt psychologists. As the behavioristic movement is thought to have been launched by Watson's article "Psychology as the Behaviorist Views It," which appeared in 1913, the Gestalt movement is thought to have been launched by Max Wertheimer's article on apparent motion, which appeared in 1912.

Although Max Wertheimer (1880–1943) is considered the founder of Gestalt psychology, from its very inception he worked closely with two men who can be considered cofounders of the movement, Wolfgang Köhler (1887–1967) and Kurt Koffka (1886–1941). Köhler and Koffka participated in the first experiments performed by Wertheimer. Although all three men made significant and unique contributions to Gestalt psychology, their ideas were always in close agreement.

Apparently, the entire Gestalt movement started as the result of an insight Wertheimer had while riding a train heading for the Rhineland. It occurred to him that if two lights blink on and off at a certain rate, they give the observer the impression that one light is moving back and forth. He left the train and bought a toy stroboscope (a device that is used to present visual stimuli at various rates) with which he conducted numerous simple experiments in his hotel room. He substantiated the notion he had on the train that if the eye sees stimuli in a certain way, they give the illusion of motion, which Wertheimer called the **phi phenomenon.** His discovery was to have a profound influence on the history of psychology.

The importance of the phi phenomenon is that it is different from the elements that cause it. The sensation of motion cannot be explained by analyzing each of the two lights flashing on and off; somehow the experience of motion emerges from the combination of the elements. For this reason, the members of the Gestalt school believed that although psychological experiences result from sensory elements, they are different from the sensory elements themselves. In other words, phenomenological experience (e.g., apparent motion) results from sensory experience (e.g., flashing lights) but cannot be understood by analyzing the phenomenal experience into its components. That is, *the phenomenological experience is different from the parts that make it up.*

Thus, the Gestaltists, following in the Kantian tradition, believed that the organism adds something to experience that is not contained in sensory data, and that something is organization. **Gestalt** is the German word for

Max Wertheimer. (Courtesy of Archives of the History of American Psychology—The University of Akron.)

configuration or pattern. The members of this school believed that we experience the world in meaningful wholes. We do not see isolated stimuli but stimuli gathered together into meaningful configurations, or *Gestalten* (plural of *Gestalt*). We see people, chairs, cars, trees, and flowers. We do not see lines and contours and patches of color. Our perceptual field is a composition of organized wholes, or *Gestalten,* and these should be the basic subject matter of psychology.

The battle cry of the Gestaltists became "the whole is different than the sum of its parts" or "to dissect is to distort." You cannot really get the full impact of the *Mona Lisa* by looking at first one arm and then another, then the nose, then the mouth, and then trying to put all these experiences together. You cannot understand the experience of listening to a symphony orchestra by analyzing the separate contributions of each of the musicians. The music emanating from the orchestra is different from the sum of the notes played by the various musicians. The melody has an emergent quality, which is something different from the sum of the parts.

OPPOSITION TO VOLUNTARISM, STRUCTURALISM, AND BEHAVIORISM

The structuralists used the introspective method to discover the elements of thought. Influenced by the success of physical chemistry, they attempted to isolate the elements of thought that combined to produce our complex mental experiences. The structuralists, for example, were interested in studying the mental analogue to sensation; thus, they instructed their experimental subjects to avoid naming things and otherwise reading things into their experience. Instead, they were instructed to describe their raw experiences. The structuralists were associationists in that they believed that complex ideas were made up of simpler ideas that were combined in accordance with the laws of association. Their main concern was to discover the simpler ideas that supposedly were the building blocks of more complicated thoughts.

The functionalist movement, under the influence of Darwinian thought, was gaining momentum in America and began to challenge structuralism. The functionalists were primarily concerned with how human behavior or thought processes were related to survival, and they attacked the structuralists for ignoring that approach. Thus, the structuralists were criticized even before the behaviorists came along.

The behaviorists attempted to make psychology completely scientific, and being scientific necessarily involved measurement. They concluded that the only psychological subject matter that could be reliably and publicly measured was overt behavior. The description of conscious elements, as in voluntarism and structuralism, was unreliable because it was influenced by, among other factors, the verbal ability of the reporter. Because it can be studied only indirectly, the behaviorists found consciousness a dubious subject matter for a science.

The Gestalt psychologists maintained that the voluntarists, the structuralists, and the behaviorists were all making the same basic error in using an elementistic approach. They attempted to divide up their subject matter into elements in order to understand it; the voluntarists and the structuralists sought the elemental ideas that combine to form complex thoughts, and the behaviorists attempted to understand complex behavior in terms of habits, conditioned responses, or stimulus-response combinations.

The Gestaltists saw nothing wrong with the introspective method in general, but they felt the voluntarists and the structuralists misused it. Rather than using the introspective method to divide experiences, it should be used to investigate whole, meaningful experiences. It should be used to investigate how people perceive the world. When the technique is used in this way, it is found that a person's perceptual field consists of events that are organized and meaningful. The Gestaltists believed that these organized and meaningful events should be the subject matter of psychology. When these *Gestalten* are divided up in any way, they lose their meaning. Therefore, perceptual phenomena are to be studied directly and without further analysis. Because of this approach of studying perceptual phenomena directly (the term *phenomenon* means "that which is given"), Gestalt psychology has sometimes been called **phenomenology.** A phenomenologist studies meaningful, intact mental events without dividing them for further analysis. Following is a list of terms that have been used to describe both the Gestalt and the behavioristic approaches:

Gestalt	*Behavioristic*
holistic	atomistic, elementistic
molar	molecular
subjective	objective
nativistic	empiricistic
cognitive, phenomenological	behavioral

The only terms on the list whose meaning may not be obvious are *molar* and *molecular.* In general, *molar* means large, and *molecular* means small; when describing behavior, however, **molar behavior** refers to a large segment of behavior that is goal-directed and purposive, and **molecular behavior** refers to a small segment of behavior, such as a conditioned reflex, that is isolated for analysis. Obviously, the former is of more interest to the Gestalt psychologist than the latter. We have more to say about molar behavior in our discussion of Tolman in Chapter 12.

MAJOR THEORETICAL CONCEPTS

Field Theory

Gestalt psychology can be thought of as an attempt to apply **field theory** from physics to the problems of psychology. Roughly speaking, a *field* can be defined as a dynamic, interrelated system, any part of which influences every other part. The important thing about a field is that nothing in it exists in isolation. Gestalt psychologists utilized the concept of field on many levels. *Gestalten* themselves, for instance, can be thought of as small fields, the perceived environment can be looked on as a field, and a person can be thought of as a dynamic, interrelated system. Gestalt psychologists

Kurt Lewin. (Courtesy of M. I. T. Museum. Reprinted by permission.)

believed that whatever happens to a person influences everything else about that person. For example, the world simply does not look the same if one has a sore toe or an upset stomach. For the Gestalt psychologist, the emphasis is always on a totality or whole and not on individual parts.

Kurt Lewin (1890–1947), another early Gestalt psychologist, developed a theory of human motivation around field theory. He said that human behavior at any given time is determined by the total number of psychological facts being experienced at that time. A psychological fact, according to Lewin, is anything of which a person is conscious, including being hungry, a memory of a past event, being in a certain physical location, the presence of certain other people, or having a certain amount of money. A person's **life space** is the sum of all of these psychological facts. Some of these facts exert a positive influence on the person's behavior, and some a negative influence. It is the totality of these events that determines behavior at any given time. For Lewin, only those things consciously experienced can influence behavior; therefore, before anything experienced in the past can influence current behavior, the person must be conscious of it. A change in any psychological fact rearranges the entire life space. Thus, the causes of behavior are continually changing; they are dynamic. The person exists in a continually changing field of influences, and a change in any one of them affects all the others. This is what is meant by a psychological field theory.

Nature versus Nurture

The behaviorists tended to look on the brain as the passive receiver of sensations that, in turn, produce responses. In this view, the brain is a complex switchboard. Human nature, said the behaviorists, is determined by what we experience. The content of the "mind" is therefore the synthesis of our experiences, and little else. The Gestaltists assigned a more active role to the brain. For the Gestalt theorist, the brain is not a passive receiver and storehouse of information from the environment. The brain acts on incoming sensory information in such a way as to make it more meaningful and organized. This is not a learned function; it is the "nature" of the brain to impose organization and meaning on sensory information.

Because it is a physical system, the brain creates a field that influences information entering it, much like a magnetic field influences metal particles. This field of forces organizes conscious experience. What we experience consciously is sensory information *after* it has been acted on by the force fields in the brain. It is tempting to call the Gestaltists nativists because the brain's ability to organize experiences is not derived from experience. However, the Gestaltists pointed out that the brain's organizational abilities are not inherited; rather, such abilities characterize any physical system, the brain being but one example. In any case, the behaviorists postulated a passive brain that responded to and stored sensory information, and the Gestaltists postulated an active brain that transformed sensory information. With this distinction the behaviorists followed in the tradition of the British empiricists, and the Gestaltists followed in the Kantian tradition.

Law of Prägnanz

The Gestalt psychologists' main concern was always with perceptual phenomena. Through the years, well over one hundred perceptual principles have been studied by Gestalt theorists. One overriding principle, however, applies to all mental events, including the principles of perception, and that is the **law of Prägnanz** (*Prägnanz* is the German word for "essence"). Koffka (1963 [1935]) defined the law of Prägnanz as follows: "Psychological organization will always be as good as the controlling circumstances allow" (p. 110). By "good," Koffka meant such qualities as simple, complete, concise, symmetrical, and harmonious. In other words, there is a tendency for every psychological event to be meaningful, complete, and simple. A good figure, a good perception, or a good memory cannot be made simpler or more orderly through any kind of perceptual shift; there is nothing more we can do mentally that would make the conscious experience more organized. The law of Prägnanz was used by the Gestaltists as their guiding principle while studying perception, learning, and memory. Later it was also applied to personality and psychotherapy.

Of the many principles of perception studied by the Gestalt theorists, we discuss only the **principle of closure** because it relates directly to the topics of learning and memory. The principle of closure states that we have a tendency to complete incomplete experiences. For example, if a person looks at a curved line that is almost circular except for a small gap, the person will tend to fill in the gap perceptually and respond to the figure as a complete circle. This principle, like all the others, follows the general law of Prägnanz, which says that we respond to the world so as to make it maximally meaningful under existing conditions.

It is the field forces in the brain that provide these organized, meaningful experiences. Remember that it is sensory information after it has been transformed by field forces in the brain that we experience consciously. Thus, an incomplete circle may be what we experience sensorially, but consciously we experience a complete circle.

THE BRAIN AND CONSCIOUS EXPERIENCE

Every major psychological theory must in some way deal with the mind-body problem. The problem can be stated in many ways, for example, "How can something purely physical cause something purely mental?" or "What is the relationship between the body (brain) and consciousness?" No matter how elementistic one's answer becomes—even studying how individual brain cells respond to various forms of stimulation—the question concerning how the external world or patterns of neural activity are translated into conscious experience still remains.

The behaviorists solved the mind-body problem by ignoring it. In fact, they concentrated their investigations on behavior in order to avoid the mind-body problem. The voluntarists believed that the mind could willfully arrange the elements of thought into any number of configurations and that behavior was instigated by the resultant configurations. Thus, for the voluntarists an active mind profoundly influences behavior. Following in the tradition of British empiricism, the structuralists believed that body sensations passively give rise to, or cause, mental images. These mental images are thought to vary as a function of sensory experience and have no causal relationship to behavior. The belief that the contents of the mind vary passively as a function of sensory experience is referred to as **epiphenomenalism.** Thus, for the structuralists, there is a direct relationship between the body (sensation) and the mind (the ideas caused by sensations).

The Gestaltists took a different approach to the mind-body problem. They assumed an **isomorphism** between psychological experience and the processes in the brain. External stimulation causes reactions in the brain, and we experience those reactions *as they occur in the brain.* The main difference between this point of view and the one held by the structuralists is that the Gestaltists believe that *the brain actively transforms sensory stimulation.* The brain, therefore, organizes, simplifies, and adds meaning to incoming sensory information. We experience information only after it is transformed by the brain in accordance with the law of Prägnanz. Köhler (1947) said, "Experienced order in space is always structurally identical with a functional order in the distribution of underlying brain processes" (p. 61). Koffka (1963 [1935]) said, "Thus, isomorphism, a term implying equality of form, makes the bold assumption that the 'motion of the atoms and molecules of the brain' are not 'fundamentally different from thoughts and feelings' but in their molar aspects, considered as processes in extension, identical" (p. 62). Over and over, the Gestalt psychologists stated their belief that the phenomenal world (consciousness) is an accurate expression of the circumstances, that is, field forces, that exist in the brain.

With their concept of psychophysical isomorphism, the Gestaltists felt they had solved a major problem that the more mechanistic theories had not solved; that is, "How does the *mind* organize sensory information and make it meaningful?" The Gestalt psychologists answered this question by saying that the content of thought (consciousness) comes to us already organized; it is organized by the brain before we experience it or as we are experiencing it. Therefore, to the Gestaltists, *the activities of the brain correspond dynamically with the content of thought.* It should be made clear that from this point of view, the brain is much more than a complex switchboard. According to the Gestaltists, the brain actively transforms incoming sensory information according to the law of Prägnanz, and it is transformed information of which we are "conscious." The relationship among external stimulation, the brain, and conscious experience can be diagrammed as follows:

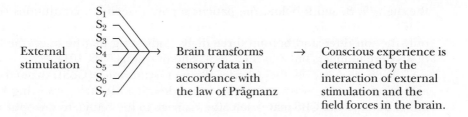

Because of their strong belief in an "active mind," the Gestaltists are clearly rationalists, and because they believe the "powers of the mind" are genetically determined, they are clearly nativists. These beliefs place them in the tradition of Plato, Descartes, and Kant.

As we shall see, one criticism of Gestalt psychology was that it did not develop the same kind of empirical tradition that occurred in the United States among the behaviorists. Many Gestalt principles—the principle of Prägnanz, for example— are demonstrable in an anecdotal manner but are difficult to approach by using laboratory-experimental techniques. There are, however, odd collections of data suggestive of the active, constructing brain posited by the Gestaltists.

First, we document the "blind spots" in the human visual fields. In each retina, there is an area with no photoreceptors (rods or cones). At this point, where the optic nerve exits the eye, we are technically unable to see. If you follow the instructions for the demonstration in Figure 10–1, you will see that, during normal visual processing, we are unaware of the blind spot; instead, the visual field seems complete, as if filled in by our active brains.

It may be the case that the active brain fills in the blind spots, or it may be the case that, because we have had the blind spots all our lives, we simply ignore them. In either case, the law of Prägnanz seems to be operating. The Gestalt position receives additional unexpected support when we examine patients who have had damage to their visual systems during adulthood and who develop large areas without visual sensation called *scotomas*. Ramachandran and Blakeslee (1998) describe a patient whose damage to his right occipital lobe resulted in a large scotoma in his left visual field. The patient reported that his vision seemed normal unless he paid careful attention, as if to search for missing visual details. When visually presented a discontinuous vertical line, such that the space in the line fell onto his scotoma, he first reported seeing two discontinuous line segments but then reported the two segments "growing toward each other" (p. 99). He reported the same phenomenon when he was shown a discontinuous column of a lowercase letter "x." When shown a discontinuous column of numbers, with the digits 1, 2, and 3 above the scotoma and

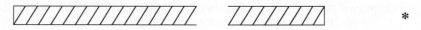

FIGURE 10–1   Blind spot demonstration: Close your right eye and look directly at the "*." Move the page so that the gap in the bar falls on the blind spot.

the digits 7, 8, and 9 below, the patient reported seeing a continuous column of numbers. Curiously, when he was asked to read the entire column, he could read only the top three and bottom three digits, indicating that he knew the "filled-in" digits were numbers but that they "look kind of strange" (p. 101).

Even stranger is the Charles Bonnet syndrome (CBS), named after an eighteenth-century Swiss philosopher who described it after observing his grandfather's symptoms. CBS may result after damage to the retina, to the optic nerve (or tract), or to deeper parts of the visual system. Patients with CBS experience hallucinations in their scotomas but suffer neither intellectual decline nor other psychiatric problems. Ramachandran and Blakeslee (1998) report patients whose scotomas are filled with laughing children, grazing cows, and in one case, a monkey neatly seated on Ramachandran's lap. Rovner (2002) describes a patient with CBS who reports "people coming and going, dressed in costumes like football or soldier uniforms . . . they put on galas, drive vehicles, and are very busy outside my house" (p. 45).

These perceptual phenomena are complex, and attempts to explain them are ongoing. For a Gestalt psychologist, however, the explanation is straightforward: The active brain fills in blank spaces, rather like a complex form of closure. If it is true that "nature abhors a vacuum," then it is true, from the Gestalt perspective, that the brain also abhors a vacuum and will actively fill it.

SUBJECTIVE AND OBJECTIVE REALITY

Because we can experience impulses from the physical world only after they have been transformed by the brain, what determines behavior? It cannot be the physical environment because, in a sense, we never experience the physical environment directly. For the Gestalt theorists, it is consciousness or subjective reality that determines behavior, and that fact has important implications. According to the Gestalt theorists, the law of Prägnanz is not the only thing that transforms and gives meaning to what we experience physically. Things such as beliefs, values, needs, and attitudes also embellish what we experience consciously. This means, of course, that people in exactly the same physical environment will vary in their interpretation of that environment and, therefore, in how they react to it. To make this point, Koffka distinguished between the **geographical environment** (objective or physical reality) and the **behavioral environment** (psychological or subjective reality). Koffka believed that to understand why people act as they do, it is more important to know their behavioral environments than it is to know their geographical environments. Koffka (1963 [1935]) used an old German legend to show the importance of subjective reality in determining behavior:

> On a winter evening amidst a driving snowstorm a man on horseback arrived at an inn, happy to have reached a shelter after hours of riding over the windswept plain on which the blanket of snow had covered all paths and landmarks. The landlord who came to the door viewed the stranger with surprise and asked him whence he came. The man pointed in the direction straight away from the inn, whereupon the landlord, in a tone of awe and wonder, said: "Do you know that you have ridden across the Lake of Constance?" At which the rider dropped stone dead at his feet.

In what environment, then, did the behavior of the stranger take place? The Lake of Constance? Certainly, because it is a true proposition that he rode across it. And yet, this is not the whole truth, for the fact that there was a frozen lake and not ordinary solid ground did not affect his behavior in the slightest. It is interesting for the geographer that this behavior took place in this particular locality, but not for the psychologist as the student of behavior; because the behavior would have been just the same had the man ridden across a barren plain. But the psychologist knows something more: since the man died from sheer fright after having learned what he had "really" done, the psychologist must conclude that had the stranger known before, his riding behavior would have been very different from what it actually was. Therefore the psychologist will have to say: There is a second sense to the word environment according to which our horseman did not ride across the lake at all, but across an ordinary snow-swept plain. His behavior was a riding-over-a-plain, but not a riding-over-a-lake.

What is true of the man who rode across the Lake of Constance is true of every behavior. Does the rat run in the maze *the experimenter* has set up? According to the meaning of the word "in," yes and no. Let us therefore distinguish between a *geographical* and a *behavioral* environment. Do we all live in the same town? Yes, when we mean the geographical, no, when we mean the behavioral "in." (pp. 27–28)

Thus, according to Koffka, beliefs are powerful determinants of behavior. In this regard, he was in close agreement with the theories of Tolman and Bandura, which will be covered in Chapters 12 and 13.

GESTALT PRINCIPLES OF LEARNING

The most significant work on learning by a member of the Gestalt school was done by Köhler between 1913 and 1917 at the University of Berlin Anthropoid Station on Tenerife, one of the Canary Islands. Köhler (1925) summarized his findings in *The Mentality of Apes*. While on Tenerife, he also studied the problem-solving ability of chickens, although this work is seldom mentioned.

Because Gestalt psychologists were primarily field theorists interested in perceptual phenomena, it is no surprise to find them looking at learning as a special problem in perception. They assumed that when an organism is confronted with a problem, a state of cognitive disequilibrium is set up and continues until the problem is solved. Therefore, to the Gestalt psychologist, cognitive disequilibrium has motivational properties that cause the organism to attempt to regain the balance in its mental system. According to the law of Prägnanz, cognitive balance is more satisfying than cognitive disbalance. On this point the Gestaltists are in close agreement with both Guthrie and Hull. It can be said that problems provide maintaining stimuli (or drive, to use Hull's term), which persist until the problems are solved, at which point the maintaining stimuli terminate (the drive is reduced). Support for this point of view was provided by the work of Bluma Zeigarnik, who found that uncompleted tasks were remembered longer and in greater detail than completed ones. She explained this phenomenon in terms of the motivational properties of a problem that persist until the problem is solved. The tendency to remember uncompleted tasks better than completed ones has come to be called the **Zeigarnik effect.**

Wolfgang Köhler. (Courtesy of Swarthmore College.)

Learning, to the Gestaltist, is a cognitive phenomenon. The organism "comes to see" the solution after pondering a problem. The learner thinks about all of the ingredients necessary to solve a problem and puts them together (cognitively) first one way and then another until the problem is solved. When the solution comes, it comes suddenly; that is, the organism gains an *insight* into the solution of a problem. The problem can exist in only two states: unsolved and solved. There is no state of partial solution in between. As we saw in Chapter 4, Thorndike believed that learning was continuous in that it increased systematically in small amounts as a function of reinforced trials. The Gestaltists believed that either a solution is reached or it is not; learning to them was discontinuous.

To test his notions about learning, Köhler used a number of creative experimental arrangements. One arrangement involved detour problems in which the animal can clearly see its goal but is unable to reach it directly. The animal must turn away from the sight of the object it wants and take an indirect route to reach it. A typical detour problem is diagrammed in Figure 10–2. With this type of problem, Köhler found that chickens had great difficulty in reaching a solution, but apes did so with relative ease.

A second kind of arrangement Köhler utilized necessitated using an implement of some kind in reaching a goal. For example, a banana was placed just out of the reach of an ape so that the ape must either use a stick to reach it or put two sticks together so that they are long enough to reach it. In either case, the animal had all the ingredients necessary to solve the problem; it was just a matter of putting them together in an appropriate manner.

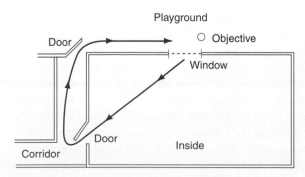

FIGURE 10–2   A typical detour problem. (From The *Mentality of Apes,* p. 21, by W. Köhler, 1925, London: Routledge and Kegan Paul Ltd. Reproduced by permission.)

The Presolution Period

Usually a rather lengthy period of time elapses before an insightful solution to a problem is reached. Describing what happens during this period, the Gestalt psychologists came close to the concept of trial-and-error learning, but the trial-and-error learning they referred to is cognitive rather than behavioral. The organism, they said, runs through a number of "hypotheses" concerning an effective way to solve the problem. The animal *thinks* about different possible solutions until it hits on one that works, and then it acts on that solution behaviorally. When the correct strategy is discovered, insight is said to have occurred. Of course, for insightful learning to occur, the organism must be exposed to all elements of the problem; if it is not, its behavior will seem to be blind and groping. This, said the Gestaltists, was the problem with Thorndike's research. Thorndike found what appeared to be incremental learning because important elements of the problem were hidden from the animal, thus preventing insightful learning. The reader can experience the "Aha" experience that usually accompanies insightful learning by trying to find the hidden cat in Figure 10–3.

Typically one searches through a good portion of the picture before finding the hidden shape. The problem creates a cognitive disequilibrium from which tension lasts until the problem is solved. In this case, discovering the cat restores cognitive equilibrium, relaxes the tension, and may make one feel like saying, "Aha."

Insightful Learning Summarized

Insightful learning is usually regarded as having four characteristics: (1) the transition from presolution to solution is sudden and complete; (2) performance based

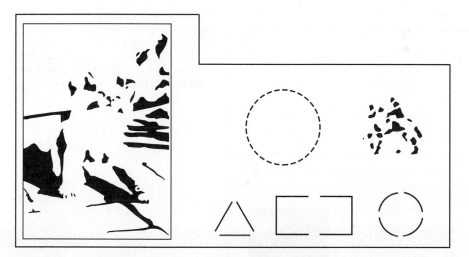

FIGURE 10–3   Examples of how incomplete figures are perceived as complete ones, thus exemplifying the principle of closure. From *Psychology: Understanding Human Behavior,* by Q. A. Sartain, J. A. North, R. J. Strange, & M. H. Chapman. Copyright © 1973. Reproduced by permission of McGraw-Hill.

on a solution gained by insight is usually smooth and free of errors; (3) a solution to a problem gained by insight is retained for a considerable length of time; (4) a principle gained by insight is easily applied to other problems. We see an example of this last characteristic in our discussion of transposition.

Transposition

When a principle learned in one problem-solving situation is applied to the solution of another problem, the process is referred to as **transposition.** Köhler's early work on transposition was done with chickens and apes. The typical experiment involved training an animal to approach one of two shades of gray paper; for example, chickens were fed on a dark shade of gray paper but not on a lighter shade. After such training, when the animal was given a choice between the two shades of gray, it approached the darker one. If the experiment was to end at this point, the behaviorists would be pleased because that is exactly how the animal should react, according to their point of view. It is the second part of the experiment, however, that the Gestaltists felt was most revealing.

After the preliminary training, the animal was given a choice between the dark paper on which it was trained and a still darker sheet of gray paper. The situation is diagrammed in Figure 10–4. How will the animal respond to the new situation?

The answer to that question depends on how one views the learning process. The Gestaltists felt that the behaviorists would predict that the animal would approach the lighter of the two shades of gray in the new situation because it is the exact one that had been reinforced in the first phase of the experiment. The Gestaltists, however, did not view learning as the development of specific habits or S-R

Stimuli: Used During Preliminary Training

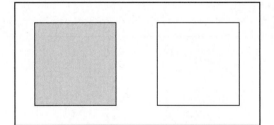

FIGURE 10–4   First the animal is taught to approach a dark gray stimulus and then is offered a choice between the dark gray stimulus and a still darker gray stimulus. If the animal chooses the darker of the two, transposition is said to have been demonstrated.

Stimuli: Used During the Transposition Test

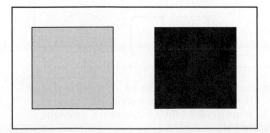

connections. To them what was learned in this kind of a situation was a relational principle; that is, they felt that the animal learned the principle of approaching *the darker of the two objects* in the first phase of the experiment and that the same principle would be applied in the second phase of the experiment. The Gestaltists predicted, therefore, that the animal would choose the darker of the two objects in phase 2, although they had been reinforced for choosing the other object in phase 1. Generally speaking, the prediction made by the Gestalt psychologists in this situation is accurate.

The Behaviorists' Explanation of Transposition

In the kind of learning situation described, the behaviorists tend to talk about the learning of specific S-R connections. As a result, their views on learning have been referred to as an **absolute theory.** In contrast, because the Gestalt view of learning emphasizes the comparison between the two stimuli, it has been referred to as a **relational theory.** Köhler's research created some problems for the absolute theory until Spence came up with his explanation of the transposition phenomenon based on S-R concepts (Spence, 1937).

Suppose, said Spence, that an animal is reinforced for approaching a box whose lid measures 160 square centimeters, and not reinforced for approaching a box whose lid measures 100 square centimeters. Soon the animal will learn to approach the larger box exclusively. In phase 2 of this experiment, the animal chooses between the 160-square-centimeter box and a box whose lid is 256 square centimeters. The animal will usually choose the larger box (256 square centimeters), even though the animal had been reinforced specifically for choosing the other one (160 square centimeters) during phase 1. This finding seems to support the relational learning point of view.

Spence's behavioristic explanation of transposition is based on generalization. As was mentioned in Chapter 6, Spence assumed that the tendency to approach the positive stimulus (160 square centimeters) generalizes to other related stimuli. Second, he assumed that the tendency to approach the positive stimulus (and the generalization of this tendency) is stronger than the tendency to avoid the negative stimulus (and the generalization of this tendency). What behavior occurs will be determined by the algebraic summation of the positive and negative tendencies. Spence's explanation is diagrammed in Figure 10–5.

Whenever there is a choice between two stimuli, the one eliciting the greatest net approach tendency will be chosen. In the first phase of Spence's experiment, the animal chose the 160-square-centimeter box over the 100-square-centimeter box because the net positive tendency was 51.7 for the former and 29.7 for the latter. In phase 2, the 256-square-centimeter box was chosen over the 160-square-centimeter box because the net positive tendency was 72.1 for the former and still 51.7 for the latter.

Spence's explanation has the advantage of making some unexpected predictions of transpositional phenomena. For example, his theory predicts that transposition breaks down at some point, and in the previous example the animal will choose the

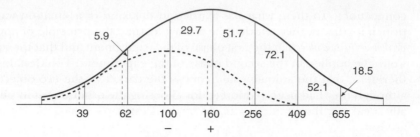

FIGURE 10–5   According to Spence's explanation of transposition, the tendency to avoid a stimulus (dashed curve) must be subtracted from the tendency to approach a stimulus (solid curve). It is the net value that results when these positive and negative influences are added algebraically that determines which of the two stimuli will be approached. (From "The Basis of Solution by Chimpanzees of the Intermediate Size Problem," by K. W. Spence, 1942, *Journal of Experimental Psychology, 31,* p. 259.)

smaller object in a pair of test stimuli. This choice occurs if the animal is presented with a 256-square-centimeter box and any box larger than 409 square centimeters. In all choices involving a 256-square-centimeter box and a box measuring 409 square centimeters or larger, the animal will choose the *smaller of the two,* thereby reversing the principle the animal was supposed to have learned. Likewise, if the animal is given a choice between a 160-square-centimeter box and one slightly larger than 409 square centimeters, the choices will be about equally divided because the net positive tendency for each box is about the same.

Because Spence's theory could predict both the successes and failures of the transposition phenomenon, his point of view was more widely accepted than the Gestalt point of view. Research on various aspects of transposition, however, has demonstrated that both S-R and Gestalt predictions fail under certain circumstances, and the matter is still unsettled.

PRODUCTIVE THINKING

During the later years of his life, Max Wertheimer was especially interested in applying Gestalt principles to education. His book *Productive Thinking,* which addressed educational issues, was published in 1945, two years after his death, and was expanded and republished in 1959 under the editorship of his son Michael. In his book, Wertheimer explored the nature of problem solving and the techniques that could be used to teach it, that is, **productive thinking.** The conclusions reached were based on personal experience, experimentation, and personal interviews with individuals such as Albert Einstein. For example, Chapter 10 in his book is entitled "Einstein: The Thinking That Led to the Theory of Relativity."

Wertheimer contrasted rote memorization with problem solving based on Gestalt principles. With the former, the learner learns facts or rules without truly understanding them. Such learning is rigid and easily forgotten, and it can be applied only to limited circumstances. Learning in accordance with Gestalt principles, however, is based on an understanding of the underlying nature of the problem. Such learning comes from within the individual and is not imposed by someone else; it is easily generalizable and remembered for a long time.

When one acts on memorized facts or rules without understanding them, one can often make stupid mistakes, such as when a nurse, while making her rounds on the night shift, wakes up patients to give them their sleeping pills (Michael Wertheimer, 1980). As a further example of what can result if basic principles are not understood, Wertheimer (1959 [1945], pp. 269–270) gave the example of a school inspector who was impressed by the children he had observed but wanted to ask one more question before departing. "How many hairs does a horse have?" he asked. Much to the amazement of both the inspector and the teacher, a nine-year-old boy raised his hand and answered, "3,571,962." "How do you know that your answer is correct?" asked the inspector. "If you do not believe me," answered the boy, "count them yourself." The inspector broke into laughter and vowed to tell the story to his colleagues when he returned to Vienna. When the inspector returned the following year for his annual visit, the teacher asked him how his colleagues had responded to the story. With disappointment the inspector said, "I wanted very much to tell the story but I couldn't. For the life of me, I couldn't remember how many hairs the boy had said the horse had." Although the story was admittedly hypothetical, Wertheimer used it to contrast memorized facts with the understanding of principles.

Wertheimer insisted that two traditional approaches to teaching actually inhibit the development of understanding. The first is teaching that emphasizes the importance of logic. Both inductive and deductive logic prescribe rules that must be followed in arriving at conclusions. Although such rules may have relevance for a narrow range of problems, they do not, according to Wertheimer (1959 [1945]), facilitate problem-solving ability. "Traditional logic is concerned with the criteria that guarantee exactness, validity, consistency of general concepts, propositions, inferences and syllogisms. The main chapters of classical logic refer to these topics. To be sure, sometimes the rules of traditional logic remind one of an efficient police manual for regulating traffic" (p. 6).

According to Wertheimer, reaching an understanding involves many aspects of learners, such as their emotions, attitudes, and perceptions, as well as their intellects. In gaining insight into the solution to a problem, a student need not—in fact, should not—be logical. Rather, the student should cognitively arrange and rearrange the components of the problem until a solution based on understanding is reached. Exactly how this process works will vary from student to student.

The second teaching strategy Wertheimer believed inhibits understanding is based on the doctrine of associationism. This approach to teaching typically emphasizes learning correct S-R connections through drill, memorization, and external reinforcement. Although Wertheimer believed that learning does occur under these circumstances, he believed it to be trivial compared with insightful learning. Wertheimer (1959 [1945]) made the following comment about teaching based on associationism: "Basically the items are connected in the way in which my friend's telephone number is connected with his name, in which nonsense syllables become reproducible when learned in a series of such syllables, or in which a dog is conditioned to respond with salivation to a certain musical sound" (p. 8).

Wertheimer believed that any teaching strategy based either on associationism or on logic could do little to enhance understanding but could do a great deal to inhibit it.

As an example of the difference between rote memorization of facts or rules and understanding based on insight, Wertheimer gave the example of students learning to determine the area of a parallelogram. The standard way of teaching children to find the area of a parallelogram is as follows:

1. First students are taught how to find the area of a rectangle by multiplying its altitude by its base.
2. Next a parallelogram is introduced, and the teacher demonstrates how it is converted into a rectangle by drawing three lines as follows:

3. Once converted into a rectangle, the area can be found by multiplying altitude times base.

Wertheimer discovered that after such training, students could find the areas of parallelograms presented in a standard way, but many were confused when figures were presented in a nonstandard way or when they were asked to find the areas of geometric forms other than parallelograms. An example of a figure that caused confusion in some students is shown in Figure 10–6.

Other students, however, seemed to grasp the principle behind the formula. They saw that a rectangle was a balanced figure that could be subdivided into

FIGURE 10–6   An example of a figure that caused confusion in students who attempted to find its area by dropping perpendicular lines from the two upper corners to the baseline. (From *Productive Thinking*, p. 15, by M. Wertheimer, 1959, New York: Harper & Row. Copyright © 1959 by Valentin Wertheimer; renewed © 1987 by Michael Wertheimer. Reprinted by permission of HarperCollins Publishers.)

columns and rows of small squares, which, when multiplied together, gave the number of squares in the entire rectangle, or its area. For example,

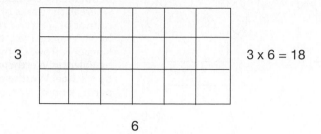

3   3 x 6 = 18

6

It was this conceptualization that was behind the formula altitude × base. Students with this insight knew that the manipulations done on the parallelogram merely rearranged the configuration so that the squares could be easily counted. Students understanding the "squares solution" were able to solve a wide variety of problems that the other students without such an understanding were unable to solve. The students who had gained insight into the nature of the problem knew that their task was to take whatever form was presented to them and rearrange it so that its area was represented as a rectangle.

Figure 10–7 shows three figures presented to students and how the students with an understanding of the principle involved found their areas as compared with

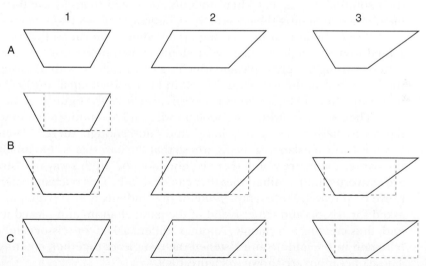

FIGURE 10–7 The portion of the figure labeled A indicates the forms presented to students. The portion of the figure labeled B shows how students with an understanding of the problem found the areas of the forms. The portion of the figure labeled C indicates how students without an understanding of the problem attempted to find the areas of the forms. (From *Productive Thinking,* p. 18, by M. Wertheimer, 1959, New York: Harper & Row. Copyright © 1959 by Valentin Wertheimer; renewed © 1987 by Michael Wertheimer. Reprinted by permission of HarperCollins Publishers.)

A   B

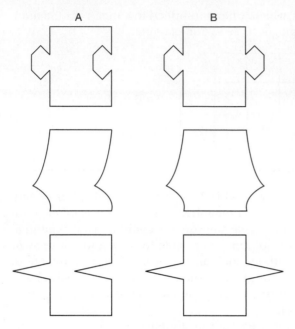

FIGURE 10–8   The areas of the forms in Column A can be found using the strategy of balancing excesses and discrepancies, whereas the areas of the forms in Column B cannot be. (From *Productive Thinking*, p. 19, by M. Wertheimer, 1959, New York: Harper & Row. Copyright © 1959 by Valentin Wertheimer; renewed © 1987 by Michael Wertheimer. Reprinted by permission of HarperCollins Publishers.)

the students who blindly attempted to apply the rule they had been taught to reach their solutions. Note that when students attempted to apply the formula they had memorized in finding the areas of these figures, their results were incorrect.

When the insight of rearranging a geometric form so that its area is represented as a rectangle is reached, students know which kinds of problems can be solved by using this principle and which cannot. Students with this insight know that the "excesses" in the forms on the left in Figure 10–8 equal the indentations, and therefore, they can be solved by using this principle; the figures on the right cannot.

The students solving the problems with understanding seem to see the various figures as having "too much here" and "not enough there." Their goal, then, becomes one of balancing the figures so that the part that is "too much" is placed in the part of the figure where there is "not enough." In this way the "strange" figures are converted into familiar ones they can deal with. This rearrangement can be cognitive or physical. For example, one of the students that Wertheimer worked with asked for scissors and cut one end of the parallelogram and placed it on the other end, thus creating a rectangle. Another student asked for scissors and cut the parallelogram in the middle and fastened the two pieces together, creating a rectangle. These operations are shown in Figure 10–9.

Wertheimer emphasized the same point over and over. That is, learning based on understanding is deeper and more generalizable than learning involving rote memorization. To truly learn, students must come to see the nature or the structure of the problem, and this they must do themselves. It is true that a teacher can guide students to such insights, but ultimately they must occur within the students themselves.

Cut

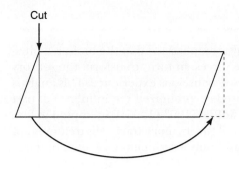

Cut

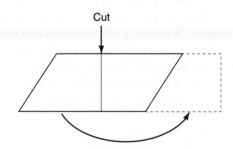

FIGURE 10–9 Two methods used by students to convert a parallelogram into a rectangle. (From *Productive Thinking*, p. 48, by M. Wertheimer, 1959, New York: Harper & Row. Copyright © 1959 by Valentin Wertheimer; renewed © 1987 by Michael Wertheimer. Reprinted by permission of HarperCollins Publishers.)

In closing this section, we offer one additional example of the difference between rote memorization and understanding. Michael Werthcimer (1980) describes an experiment performed by Katona in 1940. In this experiment, a slip with the following fifteen digits was handed to a group of subjects with the instruction that they study the digits for fifteen seconds:

$$149162536496481$$

After the subjects observed the list of digits, they were asked to reproduce the sequence of numbers in order. Most subjects were able to reproduce only a few of the numbers. After a week, most of the subjects remembered none of the digits. Another group of subjects was asked, prior to seeing the series of digits, to look for a pattern among the digits. Upon seeing the series, some of these subjects declared, "Those are the squares of the digits from 1 to 9." The subjects who saw the pattern were able to reproduce the series perfectly not only during the experiment but also weeks and months afterward. Thus we see again that learning based on an understanding of the principles involved in a problem-solving situation is very thorough and is retained almost perfectly for long periods of time. Also note that no external reinforcement was involved in this experiment. The only reinforcement was intrinsic and came when the learner gained an insight into the solution of the problem. The emphasis on intrinsic reinforcement as opposed to extrinsic reinforcement has characterized most of the cognitive theories since the early work of the Gestalt psychologists.

THE MEMORY TRACE

We mentioned earlier that Gestalt psychologists emphasized that the brain is a physical system that generates field forces. These forces, in turn, transform the sensory information entering them and thus determine conscious experience. This analysis gives the impression that the Gestaltists ignored or minimized the influence of past experience, but this impression is incorrect. Koffka (1963 [1935]) attempted to link the past with the present through his concept of the **memory trace.** His treatment of the memory trace is long and complicated, and only a rudimentary sketch of it can be presented here.

Koffka assumed that a current experience gives rise to what he called a **memory process.** The process is the activity in the brain caused by an environmental experience. This process could be simple or complex, depending on the experience it is based on. When a process is terminated, a trace of its effect remains in the brain. This trace, in turn, will influence all similar processes that occur in the future. According to this point of view, a process, which is caused by an experience, can occur only once in "pure" form; thereafter, similar experiences result from the interaction between the process and the memory trace. Thus, each time a process is aroused, it modifies the organism, and that modification influences future experiences. In fact, Koffka said, if one defines learning as a modification in behavior potential that results from experience, each elicitation of a process can be looked on as a learning experience.

What is the nature of the influence of the trace on the process? Koffka (1963 [1935]) answered that a trace "exerts an influence on the process in the direction of *making it similar to the process which originally produced the trace*" (p. 553). The stronger the memory trace, the stronger its influence on the process; therefore, one's conscious experience will tend to be more in accordance with the trace than with the process.

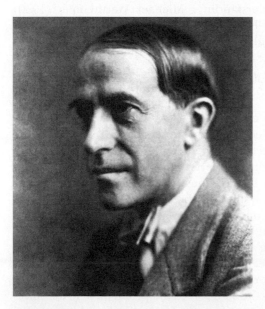

Kurt Koffka. (Courtesy of Archives of the History of American Psychology—The University of Akron.)

According to this point of view, if the last thing one did in a problem-solving situation was to solve the problem, the solution becomes "etched" in one's mind. The next time one is in a similar problem-solving situation, a process will occur that will "communicate" with the trace from the previous problem-solving situation. The trace then will influence the ongoing process in the direction just stated, making the problem easier to solve. With repetition, the trace becomes more and more influential over the process. In other words, as the animal solves more problems that are similar, it becomes a better problem solver. Koffka explained improvement in a skill as the result of the increasing influence of the trace on the process.

At this point in Gestalt theorizing, we see considerable agreement with Guthrie. It seems, for example, that Koffka accepted the recency principle, which states that what an organism did last in a situation is what it will do if the situation recurs. Likewise, as we discuss later, the Gestaltists are in essential agreement with Guthrie's explanation of how repetition results in improvement of a skill.

Individual Trace versus Trace System

Solving an individual problem is only a specific occurrence of problem-solving behavior, and learning to type the letters A, B, and C are only specific occurrences of the more general behavior we call typing. Every complex skill can be looked on as consisting of many processes and their corresponding traces, and yet each **individual memory trace** is related to the same skill. Numerous interrelated individual traces are referred to as a **trace system.** Koffka (1963 [1935]) assumed that through repetition, the trace system becomes more important than the individual traces that make it up. The "wholeness" quality of the skill comes to dominate the individual traces, thereby causing them to lose their individuality. This phenomenon may at first seem paradoxical; that is, repetition can help in learning, although it tends to destroy the traces of individual experiences:

> There is loss of consolidation of the *single individual* traces which we are apt to overlook because it is accompanied by a gain in the stability *trace system.* When we learn to type, the individual lessons will soon be forgotten, and the clumsy movements which we originally executed will at a later stage be impossible; i.e., the traces of the first lessons have become changed by the aggregate of traces which has been produced by the many repetitions and is responsible for the improvement of the skill. Similarly, when we stay in a room for any length of time, we get a great number of impressions of it by moving about or merely letting our eyes roam. But only a few of them can be recalled. (p. 545)

Just as the individual trace exerts a greater influence on future processes as it becomes more fixed, so does the trace system exert greater influence on related processes as it becomes more fixed. This contention has very interesting implications. For example, it is assumed that through the years we develop trace systems that correspond to similar experiences. Thus we develop trace systems that correspond to chairs, dogs, trees, males, females, or pencils. These trace systems will be a kind of neurological summation of all our experiences with objects in a certain class, such as cows or clowns. Because these trace systems become firmly established, they will have a profound effect on any individual experience we may have. For example, if we look at an individual elephant, the process aroused by that elephant will be influenced by the trace system that resulted from all of our other experiences with elephants. The resulting experience will be a combination of the two influences, with the trace system being the most important. Our memory of that event, then, will be one of "elephantness" that has little to do with any particular elephant but has more to do with what they have in common. This theory also serves to explain the phenomenon of closure. The individual experience of a partial circle is dominated by the trace system of "circleness," and the resulting experience is one of a complete circle.

Memory, like perception and learning, follows the law of Prägnanz. Memories tend to be complete and meaningful, even when the original experience was not.

Irregular experiences tend to be remembered as regular, unique events are remembered in terms of something familiar (e.g., a catlike object will be remembered as a cat), and minor flaws or discrepancies in a figure will tend to be forgotten. It is the enduring features of past experience, rather than uncommon occurrences, that guide our behavior. Again, the emphasis is on the pattern, the *Gestalt,* the wholeness of experience, and the recollection of experience. This theory is contrasted with the association theory of memory that is accepted by the behaviorists. The associationists accept the "bundle hypothesis," which states that complex thoughts are made up of simple ideas bound together by contiguity, similarity, or contrast. Memory occurs when one element in the bundle causes the recall of the other elements. The Gestaltists rejected association theory in favor of the law of Prägnanz in explaining all aspects of human experience, including perception, learning, and memory.

Behaviorism had nothing to say about perception, and early Gestalt theory had little or nothing to say about learning. But when the Gestaltists fled to America from Nazi Germany, they began to address the problem of learning because it was a major interest of American psychologists. Gestalt theory was clearly better able to handle problems in perception, mostly because behaviorism, in excluding mental events from its domain of study, ignored the topic of perception. So on the one hand, we had the Gestalt theorists attempting to expand their perceptual theory to cover learning, and on the other hand, we had the behaviorists ignoring perceptual learning. As usual, accepting a paradigm as an ideology blinded both the Gestaltists and the behaviorists to important aspects of the learning process. Fortunately, later thinkers have attempted to utilize the best of both paradigms. A good example of an effort to combine the two paradigms is Tolman's theory of learning, to which we turn in Chapter 12.

The healthy debate between the Gestalt psychologists and the behaviorists resulted in the modification of each point of view because of criticism from the other. Both positions were extreme, and both have left an indelible mark on psychology. Thanks, to a large extent, to the Gestalt psychologists, the study of cognitive processes is no longer taboo. However, cognitive processes currently are being studied under rigorous laboratory conditions under such headings as risk taking, problem solving, and concept formation. For the insistence on operationally defining these concepts and indexing them behaviorally, we can thank the behavioristic influence.

GESTALT PSYCHOLOGY ON EDUCATION

As we have seen, the Gestaltists view unsolved problems as creating ambiguity or an organizational disbalance in the student's mind, a condition that is undesirable. In fact, ambiguity is looked on as a negative state that persists until a problem is solved. Students confronted with a problem will either seek new information or rearrange old information until they gain insight into the solution. The solution is as satisfying to the problem solver as a hamburger is to a hungry person. In a sense, the reduction of ambiguity can be seen as the Gestalt equivalent to the behaviorist's notion of reinforcement. However, the reduction of ambiguity can be thought of as an intrinsic reinforcer, whereas the behaviorists usually stress external, or extrinsic, reinforcers.

Jerome Bruner (1966), while discussing curiosity as an innate human motive, comes close to what the Gestaltists refer to as a need to reduce ambiguity. Bruner says,

> Curiosity is almost a prototype of the intrinsic motive. Our attention is attracted to something that is unclear, unfinished, or uncertain. We sustain our attention until the matter on hand becomes clear, finished, or certain. The achievement of clarity or merely the search for it is what satisfies. We would think it preposterous if somebody thought to reward us with praise or profit for having satisfied our curiosity. (p. 114)

John Holt (1967) makes a similar point in his book *How Children Learn:*

> What we want to know, we want to know for a reason. The reason is that there is a hole, a gap, an empty space in our understanding of things, our mental model of the world. We feel that gap like a hole in a tooth and want to fill it up. It makes us ask How? When? Why? While the gap is there, we are in tension, in suspense. Listen to the anxiety in a person's voice when he says, "This doesn't make sense!" When the gap in our understanding is filled, we feel pleasure, satisfaction, relief. Things make sense again—or at any rate, they make more sense than they did. When we learn this way, for these reasons, we learn both rapidly and permanently. The person who really needs to know something, does not need to be told many times, drilled, tested. Once is enough. The new piece of knowledge fits into the gap ready for it, like a missing piece in a jigsaw puzzle. Once in place, it is held in, it can't fall out. (pp. 187–188)

Bruner and Holt share the Gestalt notion that learning is personally satisfying and that it need not be prodded by external reinforcement. The Gestalt-oriented classroom would be characterized by a give-and-take relationship between students and teacher. The teacher would help students see relationships and organize their experiences into meaningful patterns. Planning a Gestalt learning experience includes starting with something familiar and basing each step in the education process on those already taken. All aspects of the course are divided into meaningful units, and the units themselves must relate to an overall concept or experience. The Gestalt-oriented teacher might use the lecture technique but would insist that it allow for student-teacher interactions. Above all, rote memorization of facts or rules would be avoided. It is only when students grasp the principles involved in a learning experience that they truly understand them. When what is learned is understood instead of memorized, it can easily be applied to new situations, and it is retained for a very long time.

Was Popper a Gestalt Theorist?

In Chapter 2, we encountered Karl Popper's influential views of science. In *Learning from Error: Karl Popper's Psychology of Learning,* Berkson and Wettersten (1984) attempted to distill Popper's views of the learning process from his writings on the philosophy of science. We include Popper's views on learning here because they seem especially applicable to education from a perspective not unlike that of the Gestalt theorists.

Popper saw learning as problem solving. For Popper, a problem exists when an observation is contrary to what was expected. This discrepancy between observation and expectancy stimulates efforts to correct expectancies to make them compatible with the previously surprising observation. The newly formulated expectancies remain intact until observations are made that are incompatible with them, at which point they are revised again. This process of adjusting and readjusting one's expectations so that they agree with observation is an unending process. However, it is a process that, one hopes, makes expectancies and reality increasingly compatible. According to Popper, this process of adjusting one's expectations so that they agree with actual experience is motivated by an innate **cognitive hunger,** which refers to the fact that "we have been born with the task of developing a realistic set of expectations about the world" (Berkson & Wettersten, 1984, p. 16).

According to Popper, both scientific knowledge and personal knowledge grow in the same way and for the same reason. First, as we have seen, there is a problem (a discrepancy between what is observed and what is expected). Next, possible solutions to the problem are conjectured, and if possible, the proposed solutions are refuted. Solutions that survive serious attempts at *refutation* are retained until they, too, are contradicted by observation, at which point the process starts over. In the process of problem solving, Popper believed that conjectures should be bold and creative and attempts at refutation severe. Berkson and Wettersten (1984) summarize Popper's beliefs concerning how both scientific and personal knowledge grows and improves: "Because we do in fact learn by conjectures and refutations in an effort to solve problems, the best way to make progress in the growth of knowledge is to focus on and articulate problems, to conjecture solutions boldly and imaginatively, and to assess the proposed solutions critically" (p. 27).

The implications of Popper's theory of learning for education seem clear. A problem is presented to the class, and students propose solutions to the problem. Each proposed solution is critically analyzed, and those found ineffective are rejected. The process continues until the best possible solution is found. Problems could be scientific, sociological, ethical, philosophical, or even personal. The classroom atmosphere should be informal and relaxed enough to encourage bold conjecture, but at the same time, the participants should be encouraged to offer objective criticism when it is called for. "What is wrong with that proposed solution?" would be a recurring question. With appropriate adjustments for age levels, there is no reason why this classroom procedure could not be used from primary school to graduate school. Students involved in such exercises should be better able to articulate problems, more creative in seeking solutions to problems, and more capable of distinguishing between effective and ineffective solutions to problems.

EVALUATION OF GESTALT THEORY

Contributions

An important contribution of Gestalt psychology was its criticism of the molecular or atomistic approaches of S-R behaviorism. Crucial to this criticism were demonstrations that both perception and learning were characterized by cognitive processes that organized psychological experience. Like Kant, the Gestalt psychologists posited that the brain automatically transformed and organized experiences by adding qualities that were not inherent in the sensory experience. The organizational processes identified by Wertheimer and his colleagues have had an enormous impact on the fields of learning, perception, and psychotherapy, and they continue to influence contemporary cognitive sciences.

Gestalt psychology provided challenges that were productive even for behavioristic researchers. Spence's (1942) brilliant research on transposition, for example, was made necessary by Köhler's cognitive explanation of transposition. The Gestalt psychologists' focus on insightful learning also provided an alternative way of conceptualizing reinforcement. By drawing attention to the satisfaction that comes from discovery or from solving problems, Gestalt psychology turned our attention from extrinsic to intrinsic reinforcement. The debt owed to Gestalt psychology by contemporary cognitive psychology is often noted (for example, Murray, 1995).

Criticisms

Although Gestalt psychology did offer important challenges to behaviorism, it never attained mainstream status in learning theory. Behavioristic psychologists were interested in reducing the problem of learning to the simplest models possible, accumulating a vast store of data concerning the smallest problems in learning, and then building more global theories from tested elementary principles. When Gestalt psychologists joined the quest, they described learning in terms of "understanding," "meaning," and "organization," concepts that were themselves all but meaningless in the context of behavioristic research. Estes (1954) reflected the attitude of the dominant behavioristic school toward Gestalt learning theory:

> Typically the [Gestalt] theorists have developed their systems in other areas, then have attempted to collect the psychology of learning as an extra dividend without much additional investment. . . . From the writings of Köhler, Koffka, Hartmann, and Lewin one would gather that field interpretations of learning are demonstrably superior to all others. From the experimental literature on learning, on the other hand, one would conclude that if this view is correct, then the most superior theories of learning have had the least influence upon research. (p. 341)

DISCUSSION QUESTIONS

1. What was it about the structuralists and behaviorists' approaches to the study of psychology that the Gestalt theorists disagreed with?
2. What is meant by the statement "The law of Prägnanz was used by the Gestalt psychologists as an overriding principle in their explanation of perception, learning, memory, personality, and psychotherapy"?
3. Discuss the term *isomorphism* as it was used in Gestalt theory.
4. Distinguish between geographical and behavioral environments. Which of the two did the Gestalt theorists believe was the more important determinant of

behavior? Explain why you do or do not agree with the Gestalt theorists on this matter.

5. Discuss the topic of memory from the point of view of a Gestalt psychologist. Include in your answer the concepts of memory process, individual memory trace, and trace system.
6. Explain transposition from both a Gestalt and a behavioristic point of view.
7. Summarize the characteristics of insightful learning.
8. What is meant by the statement "For the Gestalt psychologist, learning is basically a perceptual phenomenon"?
9. List some differences between classroom procedures developed according to Gestalt principles and those developed according to S-R principles. In general, do you feel American public schools are based on a Gestalt model or a behavioristic model? Explain.
10. Summarize Wertheimer's thoughts on productive thinking. Include in your answer some of the differences between solutions to problems that are based on rote memorization and those based on an understanding of the principles involved in the problem.

CHAPTER HIGHLIGHTS

absolute theory	memory process
behavioral environment	memory trace
cognitive hunger	molar behavior
epiphenomenalism	molecular behavior
field theory	phenomenology
geographical environment	phi phenomenon
Gestalt	principle of closure
individual memory trace	productive thinking
insightful learning	relational theory
isomorphism	trace system
law of Prägnanz	transposition
life space	Zeigarnik effect

CHAPTER 11

Jean Piaget

Jean Piaget was born on August 9, 1896, in Neuchatel, Switzerland. His father was a historian whose specialty was medieval literature. Piaget showed early interest in biology, and when he was only eleven years old, he published a one-page article on a partially albino sparrow he had seen in a park. Between ages fifteen and eighteen, he published a number of articles on mollusks. Piaget noted that because of his many publications, he was accidentally offered the position of curator of the mollusk collection in the Geneva Museum while he was still a secondary school student.

As an adolescent, Piaget vacationed with his godfather, who was a Swiss scholar. Through these visits with his godfather, Piaget developed an interest in

Jean Piaget. (Courtesy of Getty Images Inc.—Hulton Archive Photos.)

philosophy in general and in **epistemology** in particular. (Epistemology is a branch of philosophy that is concerned with the nature of knowledge.) Piaget's interests in biology and epistemology continued throughout his life and were clearly evident almost everywhere in his theoretical writings.

Piaget received his Ph.D. in biology at the age of twenty-one, and by the time he was thirty, he had published more than twenty papers, mainly on mollusks but on other topics as well. For example, at the age of twenty-three, he published an article on the relationship between psychoanalysis and child psychology. After receiving his doctorate, Piaget held a variety of jobs, among them a position with the Binet Testing Laboratory in Paris, where he helped to standardize intelligence tests. The Binet Laboratory's approach to testing was to develop a number of test questions, which were then presented to children of different ages. It was found that older children could answer more questions correctly than younger children and that some children could answer more questions correctly than other children of the same age. The former children were considered to be more intelligent than the latter children. Thus, the child's intelligence quotient was derived from the number of questions a child of a certain age could answer correctly. During his employment at the Binet Laboratory, Piaget developed his interest in the intellectual abilities of children. This interest, as well as his interests in biology and epistemology, permeated all of Piaget's work.

While working on the standardization of intelligence tests, Piaget noted something that was to have a major influence on his later theory of intellectual development. He discovered that a child's *incorrect* answers to test questions were more informative than the correct answers. He observed that the same kind of mistakes were made by children of approximately the same age and that the kind of mistakes generally made by children of one age was *qualitatively* different from the kinds of mistakes made by children of different ages. Piaget observed further that the nature of these mistakes could not be explored adequately in a highly structured testing situation, in which children either answered questions correctly or they did not. Instead, Piaget employed the **clinical method,** which was an open-ended form of questioning. In the clinical method, Piaget's questions were determined by the child's answers. If the child said something of interest, Piaget formulated a number of questions designed to explore that item further.

During his employment at the Binet Laboratory, Piaget began to realize that "intelligence" could not be equated with the number of test items that a child answered correctly. To Piaget, the more basic question was why some children were able to answer some questions correctly and other children were not, or why a child could answer some items correctly but miss other items. Piaget began his search for the variables influencing the test performance of children. His search was to result in a view of intelligence that some consider to be as revolutionary as Freud's view of human motivation.

Piaget left Binet's laboratory to become director of research at the Jean-Jacques Rousseau Institute in Geneva, Switzerland, where he was able to pursue his own interests, using his own methods. Soon after his affiliation with the institute, his first major works on developmental psychology began to appear. Piaget, who never had a course in psychology, soon became an internationally known authority on child psychology. He continued his work, studying his own three children. He and his wife (a former student of his at the Rousseau Institute) made careful observations about their children over a long period and summarized their findings in several books. That Piaget's own children were used as sources of information in the development of his theory has often been criticized. The fact that more elaborate observations, involving large numbers of other children, have been in agreement with Piaget's earlier observations has tended, however, to still this criticism.

Piaget published about thirty books and more than two hundred articles and continued doing productive research at the University of Geneva until his death in 1980. His theory of intellectual development in the child was extensive and complicated, and in this chapter we merely summarize its essential features. It will become apparent that Piaget's explanation of the learning process is different from all the other explanations in this text.

The information in this chapter was compiled from several sources. The secondary sources were Beard, 1969; Flavfell, 1963; Furth, 1969; Ginsburg and Opper, 1979; and Phillips, 1975, 1981. The primary sources were Inhelder and Piaget, 1958; Piaget, 1966, 1970a, 1970b; and Piaget and Inhelder, 1969.

MAJOR THEORETICAL CONCEPTS

Intelligence

We noted earlier that Piaget was opposed to defining **intelligence** in terms of the number of items answered correctly on a so-called intelligence test. To Piaget, an intelligent act is one that causes an approximation to the conditions optimal for an organism's survival. In other words, intelligence allows an organism to deal effectively with its environment. Because both the environment and the organism are changing constantly, an "intelligent" interaction between the two must also change constantly. An intelligent act always tends to create optimal conditions for the organism's *survival under the existing circumstances*. Thus, for Piaget, intelligence is a dynamic trait because what is available as an intelligent act will change as the organism matures biologically and as it gains experience. Intelligence, according to Piaget, is an integral part of any living organism because all living organisms seek those conditions conducive to their survival, but how intelligence manifests itself at any given time will necessarily vary as conditions vary. Piaget's theory has often been referred to as **genetic epistemology** because it attempts to trace the development of intellectual capabilities. Here, the term *genetic* refers to developmental growth rather than biological inheritance. Piaget's views on how intellectual potential develops are summarized in the remainder of this chapter.

Schemata

A child is born with a few highly organized reflexes such as sucking, looking, reaching, and grasping. Rather than discussing individual occurrences of any one of these reflexes, Piaget chose to talk about the general potential to do such things as suck, look, reach, and grasp. The potential to act in a certain way was labeled **schema** (plural: *schemata*). For example, the grasping schema refers to the general ability to grasp things. The schema is more than a single manifestation of the grasping reflex. The grasping schema can be thought of as the cognitive structure that makes all acts of grasping possible.

When any particular instance of grasping is observed or described, one must talk in terms of a specific response to specific stimuli. These aspects of any particular manifestation of a schema are called **content.** Again, *schema* refers to a general potential to perform a class of behaviors, and *content* describes the conditions that prevail during any particular manifestation of that general potential.

Schema was an extremely important term in Piaget's theory. A schema can be thought of as an element in the organism's cognitive structure. The schemata available to an organism determine how it can respond to the physical environment. Schemata can manifest themselves in overt behavior, as in the case of the grasping reflex, or they can manifest themselves covertly. Covert manifestations of a schema can be equated roughly with thinking. We have more to say about covert manifestations of a schema later in this chapter. In both overt behavior and in thinking, the term *content* refers to the specifics of a particular manifestation of a schema.

Obviously, the way a child is able to deal with its environment changes as the child grows older. For new organism-environment interactions to occur, the schemata available to the child must change.

Assimilation and Accommodation

The number of schemata available to an organism at any given time constitutes that organism's **cognitive structure.** How an organism interacts with its environment depends on the kind of cognitive structure it has available. In fact, how much of the environment can be understood, or even responded to, is determined by the various schemata available to the organism. In other words, the cognitive structure determines what aspects of the physical environment can even "exist" for the organism.

The process of responding to the environment in accordance with one's cognitive structure is called **assimilation,** which refers to a kind of matching between the cognitive structures and the physical environment. The cognitive structure that exists at any given moment sets bounds on what the organism can assimilate. For example, if only the sucking, looking, reaching, and grasping schemata are available to a child, everything the child experiences will be assimilated into those schemata. As the cognitive structure changes, it becomes possible for the child to assimilate different aspects of the physical environment.

Clearly, if assimilation were the only cognitive process, there would be no intellectual growth because an organism would simply go on assimilating its experiences into its existing cognitive structure. However, a second, equally important process provides a mechanism for intellectual growth: **accommodation,** the process by which the cognitive structure is modified.

Every experience a person has involves both assimilation and accommodation. Events for which the organism has corresponding schemata are readily assimilated, but events for which the organism has no existing schemata necessitate accommodation. Thus, all experiences involve two equally important processes: recognition, or knowing, which corresponds to the process of assimilation, and accommodation, which results in the modification of the cognitive structure. Such modification can be roughly equated with learning. To put the matter still another way, we respond to the world according to our previous experience (assimilation), but each experience contains aspects unlike anything we had experienced before. These unique aspects of experience cause changes in our cognitive structures (accommodation). Accommodation, then, provides a major vehicle for intellectual development. Ginsburg and Opper (1979) give an example of how assimilation and accommodation are related:

> Suppose an infant of 1 months is presented with a rattle. He has never before had the opportunity to play with rattles or similar toys. The rattle, then, is a feature of the environment to which he needs to adapt. His subsequent behavior reveals the tendencies of assimilation and accommodation. The infant tries to grasp the rattle. In order to do this successfully he must accommodate in more ways than are immediately apparent. First, he must accommodate his visual activities to perceive the rattle correctly, for example by locating it in space. Then he must reach out, adjusting his arm movements to the distance between himself and the rattle. In grasping the rattle, he must mold his fingers to its shape; in lifting the rattle he must accommodate his muscular exertion to its weight. In sum, the grasping of the rattle involves a series of acts of accommodation, or modifications of the infant's behavioral structures to suit the demands of the environment. At the same time, grasping the rattle also involves assimilation. In the past the infant has already grasped things; for him, grasping is a well-formed structure of behavior. When he sees the rattle for the first time he tries to deal with the novel object by incorporating it into a habitual pattern of behavior. In a sense he tries to transform the novel object to something that he is familiar with—namely, a thing to be grasped. We can say, therefore, that he assimilates the objects into his framework and thereby assigns the object a "meaning." (p. 19)

Assimilation and accommodation are referred to as **functional invariants** because they occur at all levels of intellectual development. However, early experiences tend to involve more accommodation than later experiences because more and more of what is experienced will correspond to existing cognitive structures, making substantial accommodation less necessary as the individual matures.

Equilibration

One might ask what the driving force behind intellectual growth is. For Piaget, the answer is found in his concept of **equilibration.** Piaget assumed that all organisms have an innate tendency to create a harmonious relationship between themselves and their environment. In other words, all aspects of the organism are geared toward optimal adaptation. Equilibration is this innate tendency to organize one's experiences to ensure maximal adaptation. Roughly, *equilibration* is defined as the continuous drive toward equilibrium or balance.

The concept of equilibration is for Piaget what the concept of hedonism was for Freud or self-actualization was for Maslow and Jung. It is his major motivational concept, which along with assimilation and accommodation is used to explain the steady intellectual growth observed in children. We now describe how these three processes interact.

As we have seen, assimilation permits the organism to respond to a present situation in accordance with previous knowledge. Because the unique aspects of the situation cannot be responded to on the basis of previous knowledge, these novel or unique aspects of an experience cause a slight cognitive disbalance. Because there is an innate need for harmony (equilibrium), the organism's mental structures change to incorporate these unique aspects of the experience, thus causing the sought-after cognitive balance. As with the Gestalt psychologists, lack of cognitive balance has motivational properties that keep the organism active until a balance is attained. In addition to restoring the balance, however, this adjustment paves the way for new and different interactions with the environment. The accommodation described causes a change in mental structures, so that if those previously unique aspects of the environment were again encountered, they would not cause a disbalance; that is, they would be readily assimilated into the organism's existing cognitive structure. In addition, this new cognitive arrangement forms the basis for new accommodations because accommodation always results from a disbalance, and what causes a disbalance must always be related to the organism's current cognitive structure. Gradually, through this adaptive process, information that could not at one time be assimilated eventually can be. The dual mechanisms of assimilation and accommodation, along with the driving force of equilibration, provide for slow but steady intellectual growth. The process can be diagrammed as follows:

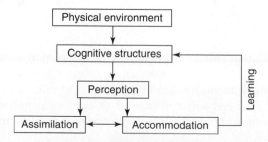

Interiorization

Children's early interactions with the environment are strictly sensorimotor; that is, they respond directly to environmental stimuli with reflex motor reactions. Children's early experiences, then, involve the use and elaboration of their innate schemata, such as grasping, sucking, looking, and reaching. The results of these early experiences are registered in the cognitive structures and gradually transform them. With increasing experience, children expand their cognitive structures, thereby enabling them to adapt more readily to an ever-increasing number of situations.

As a more elaborate cognitive structure develops, children are capable of responding to more complex situations. Also, they are less dependent on the here and now. For example, they are capable of "thinking" of objects that are not before them. Now, what children experience are functions of both the physical environment and their cognitive structures, which reflect their cumulative prior experiences. This gradual decreasing dependence on the physical environment and the increased utilization of cognitive structures is called **interiorization.**

As cognitive structures develop, they become increasingly important in the adaptive process. For example, elaborate cognitive structures make more complex problem solving possible. As more experiences are interiorized, thinking becomes a tool in adapting to the environment. Early in development, a child's adaptive responses are direct and simple and without thought. The child's early adaptive responses are mainly overt. As the process of interiorization continues, however, the child's adaptive responses become more covert; they involve internal actions rather than external ones. Piaget called these internal covert actions **operations,** and the term *operation* can be roughly equated with "thinking." Now, rather than manipulating the environment directly, the child can do so mentally through the use of operations.

The most important characteristic of any operation is that it is reversible. **Reversibility** means that once something is thought, it can be "unthought"; that is, an operation, once performed, can be mentally undone. For example, one can first mentally add 3 and 5, making a total of 8, and then mentally subtract 3 from 8, making a total of 5.

As we have seen, a child's first adjustments to the environment are direct and involve no thinking (operations). Next, as the child develops a more complex cognitive structure, thinking becomes more important. The early use of operations depends on those events the child can experience directly; that is, the child can think about those things that he or she can see. Piaget called these **concrete operations** because they are applied to concrete environmental events. Later operations, however, are completely independent of physical experience, and they therefore allow the child to solve purely hypothetical questions. Piaget called the latter **formal operations.** Unlike the concrete operation, the formal operation is not bound to the environment.

Interiorization, then, is the process by which adaptive actions become increasingly covert rather than overt. In fact, operations can be thought of as interiorized actions. Adaptive behavior, which first involves only sensorimotor schemata and overt behavior, evolves to the point where formal operations are utilized in the adaptive process. The use of formal operations characterizes the highest form of intellectual development.

Although intellectual growth is continuous, Piaget found that certain mental abilities tend to appear at certain stages of development. Note the word *tend*. Piaget and his colleagues found that although mental abilities appear around a certain age level, some children show the ability earlier and some later than other children. Although the actual age at which an ability appears may vary from child to child or from culture to culture, the order in which mental abilities appears does not vary because mental development is always an extension of what has already preceded. Thus, although children of the same age may have different mental abilities, the order with which the abilities emerge is constant. We summarize the various stages of intellectual development suggested by Piaget.

STAGES OF DEVELOPMENT

1. Sensorimotor Stage (Birth to about Two Years)　The **sensorimotor stage** is characterized by the absence of language. Because the children have no words for things, objects cease to exist when children are not dealing directly with them. Interactions with the environment are strictly sensorimotor and deal only with the here and now. Children at this stage are egocentric. They see everything with themselves as a frame of reference, and their psychological world is the only one that exists. Toward the end of this stage, children develop the concept of object permanence. In other words, they come to realize that objects go on existing even when they are not experiencing them.

2. Preoperational Thinking (about Two to Seven Years)　The preoperational thinking stage has two subdivisions:

A. Preconceptual thinking (about two to four years)　During this part of **preoperational thinking,** children begin rudimentary concept formation. They begin to classify things in certain classes because of their similarity, but they make a number of mistakes because of their concepts; thus, all men are "Daddy," all women are "Mommy," and all toys they see are "mine." Rather than being either inductive or deductive, their logic is transductive. An example of transductive reasoning is "Cows are big animals with four legs. That animal is big and has four legs; therefore, it is a cow."

B. Period of intuitive thought (about four to seven years)　During this part of preoperational thinking, the child solves problems intuitively instead of in accordance with some logical rule. The most striking characteristic of the child's thinking during this stage is his or her failure to develop **conservation.** Conservation is defined as the ability to realize that number, length, substance, or area remains constant, even though they may be presented to the child in a number of different ways. For example, a child is shown two containers filled to some level with some liquid.

Next, the contents of one container are poured into a taller, thinner container.

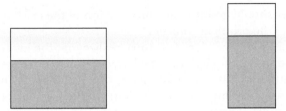

At this stage of development, the child, who observed that the first containers contained an equal amount of liquid, will now tend to say that the taller container has more liquid because the liquid is higher in the container. The child at this stage cannot mentally reverse cognitive operations, which means that he or she cannot mentally pour the liquid from the tall container back into the shorter one and see that the amount of liquid is the same in both.

For Piaget, conservation is an ability that occurs as a result of the child's cumulative experiences with the environment, and it is not an ability that can be taught until the child has had these preliminary experiences. As with all stage theories, teachability is a central issue. Do various capabilities come about because of certain experiences (e.g., learning), or do they unfold as a function of maturation along some genetically determined path? For Piaget it was both. Maturation provides the necessary sensory apparatus and brain structures, but it takes experience to develop the ability. The question of whether conservation can be taught before "its time has come" is still open; some say yes (e.g., LeFrancois, 1968), and some say no, thus agreeing with Piaget (e.g., Smedslund, 1961).

3. Concrete Operations (about Seven to Eleven or Twelve Years)   Children now develop the ability to conserve, along with the abilities to deal adequately with classes, with seriation (i.e., they can arrange things from smallest to largest and vice versa), and with number concepts. During this stage, however, the thought processes are directed to real events the child observes. The child can perform rather complex operations on problems, as long as the problems are concrete and not abstract.

The following diagram represents a typical problem given to children who are about eleven years old to study their thought processes. Their task is to determine

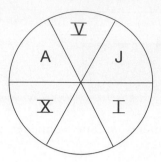

what letter should go into the empty section of the circle. Perhaps you would like to try to solve the problem yourself.

To solve the problem, one must realize that the letter of the alphabet opposite the Roman numeral *I* is *A*, the first letter of the alphabet. Also, the letter across from Roman numeral *X* is *J*, the tenth letter of the alphabet. Thus, the letter across from Roman numeral *V* must be the fifth letter of the alphabet, or *E*. At least two concepts must be utilized in solving such a problem: "one-to-one correspondence" and "opposite to." That is, it must be realized that Roman numerals and letters of the alphabet can be placed so that they correspond, and it must also be realized that the corresponding numerals and letters are placed opposite one another. If children do not have these concepts available, they cannot solve the problem. Likewise, if they can solve the problem, they must have the concepts available.

4. Formal Operations (about Eleven or Twelve to Fourteen or Fifteen Years)   Children can now deal with hypothetical situations, and their thought processes are not tied down exclusively to what is immediate and real. Thinking at this stage is as logical as it will ever become. Thus the mental apparatus one has is as sophisticated as it ever will be, but this apparatus can be directed toward the solution of a never-ending array of problems throughout one's life.

OPTIMAL CONDITIONS FOR LEARNING

Something that cannot be at least partially assimilated into an organism's cognitive structure cannot act as a biological stimulus. In this sense, the cognitive structures create the physical environment. As the cognitive structures become more elaborate, the physical environment becomes better articulated. Likewise, if something is so far from an organism's cognitive structure that it cannot be accommodated, no learning will take place. For optimal learning to take place, information must be presented that can be assimilated into the present cognitive structure but at the same time be different enough to necessitate a change in that structure. If the information cannot be assimilated, it simply cannot be understood. If it is completely understood, however, no learning is necessary. In fact, in Piaget's theory, assimilation and understanding mean about the same thing. This is what Dollard and Miller meant by their term **learning dilemma,** which points out that all learning depends on failure. According to Piaget, failure of previous knowledge to allow for assimilation of an experience causes accommodation, or new learning. Experiences should be moderately challenging to stimulate cognitive growth. Again, no such growth will occur if only assimilation occurs.

One must determine for each individual learner what kind of cognitive structures are available and slowly change these structures, one small step at a time. For this reason, Piaget would favor a one-to-one relationship between teacher and pupil. It should be obvious, however, that he would favor such a relationship for much different reasons than a theorist like Skinner, who also favors such a relationship.

Often Piaget is thought of as a nativist who believed intellectual development occurs as the result of biological maturation, but this is not entirely true. Piaget believed that maturation provides only the framework for intellectual development, but in addition to this framework, both physical and social experiences are indispensable for mental development. Inhelder and Piaget (1958) put the matter as follows: "The maturation of the nervous system can do no more than determine the totality of possibilities and impossibilities at a given stage. A particular social environment remains indispensable for the realization of these possibilities. It follows that their realization can be accelerated or retarded as a function of cultural and educational conditions" (p. 337). Elsewhere Piaget (1966) said,

> The human being is immersed right from birth in a social environment which affects him just as much as his physical environment. Society, even more, in a sense, than the physical environment, changes the very structure of the individual, because it not only compels him to recognize facts, but also provides him with a ready-made system of signs, which modify his thought; it presents him with new values and it imposes on him an infinite series of obligations. (p. 156)

Ginsburg and Opper (1979) summarize the ways in which Piaget felt that heredity influenced cognitive development: "(a) Inherited physical structures [e.g., the nervous system] set broad limits on intellectual functioning; (b) Inherited behavioral reactions [e.g., reflexes] have an influence during the first few days of human life but afterward are extensively modified as the infant interacts with his environment; and (c) The maturation of physical structures may have psychological correlates [e.g., when the brain matures to the point where language development is possible]" (p. 17). And as we have seen, equilibration, or the tendency to seek a harmony between one's self and the physical environment, is also inherited.

INTO WHAT CAMP DOES PIAGET'S THEORY FALL?

Clearly, Piaget is not an S-R theorist. As we have seen, S-R theorists attempt to determine the relationship between environmental events (S) and responses to those events (R). Most S-R theorists assume a passive organism that builds up response capabilities by accumulating habits. Complex habits, according to this point of view, are merely combinations of simpler habits. Certain S-R relationships are "stamped in," either by reinforcement or by contiguity. Knowledge, according to such a point of view, represents a "copy" of conditions that exist in the physical world. In other words, through learning, relationships that exist in the physical world come to be represented in the organism's brain. Piaget referred to this epistemological position as a *copy theory* of knowledge.

Piaget's theory is diametrically opposed to the S-R conception of knowledge. As we have seen, Piaget equated knowledge with cognitive structures that provide the potential to deal with the environment in certain ways. The cognitive structures provide a framework for experience; that is, they determine what can be responded to and how it can be responded to. In this sense, the cognitive structures are projected onto the physical environment and thus create it. In this way the environment is constructed by the cognitive structure. But it also is correct to say that the environment plays a large part in creating the cognitive structures. As we have seen, the interaction between the environment and the cognitive structures through the processes of assimilation and accommodation is of primary importance in Piaget's theory. Piaget (1970b) differentiated his views of intelligence and knowledge from those of empiricists as follows:

> In the common view, the external world is entirely separate from the subject, although it encloses the subject's own body. Any objective knowledge, then, appears to be simply the result of a set of perceptive recordings, motor associations, verbal descriptions, and the like, which all participate in producing a sort of figurative copy or "functional copy" (in Hull's terminology) of objects and the connections between them. The only function of intelligence is systematically to file, correct, etc., these various sets of information; in this process, the more faithful the critical copies, the more consistent the final system will be. In such an empiricist prospect, the content of intelligence comes from outside, and the coordinations that organize it are only the consequences of language and symbolic instruments.
>
> But this passive interpretation of the act of knowledge is in fact contradicted at all levels of development and, particularly, at the sensorimotor and prelinguistic levels of cognitive adaptation and intelligence. Actually, in order to know objects, the subject must act upon them, and therefore transform them: he must displace, connect, combine, take apart, and reassemble them.
>
> From the most elementary sensorimotor actions (such as pushing and pulling) to the most sophisticated intellectual operations, which are interiorized actions, carried out mentally (e.g., joining together, putting in order, putting into one-to-one correspondence), knowledge is constantly linked with actions or operations, that is, with transformations. (pp. 703–704)

There is both agreement and disagreement between Piaget's theory and Gestalt theory. Both agree that experiences are organized. Both believe that there is an innate need for a psychological balance and that a disbalance has motivational properties. Both believe that prior experience influences present experience. As we noted in the last chapter, the Gestalt theorists contended that as the memory trace becomes more fully established, it has an increased influence on conscious experience. Thus, when the memory trace of "circleness" is firmly established, an incomplete circle is experienced as a complete circle. The memory trace therefore "constructed" an experience that was not in accordance with physical reality. In a way, we can say that experiences are assimilated into existing memory traces, just as they are assimilated into existing cognitive structures. Just as cognitive structures are slowly changed by cumulative experiences, so are memory traces.

The major source of disagreement between the Gestalt theorists and Piaget is over the developmental nature of one's organizational ability. The Gestalt theorists believed that humans are born with a brain that organizes experiences according to the law of Prägnanz (see previous chapter). They believe that sensory data are experienced in an organized fashion at all stages of development. Piaget, in contrast, believed that the organizational abilities of the brain develop as the cognitive structures develop. To him, experience is always organized in terms of the cognitive structures, but the cognitive structures are always changing as a function of both biological maturation and sensory experience. Thus, Piaget used the term **progressive equilibrium** to describe the fact that the balance or organization that is sought is optimal under existing circumstances and that those circumstances are constantly changing.

The difference between Piaget and the Gestalt theorists on the matter of innate organizational abilities would result in a difference in educational practices. On the one hand, teachers attempting to utilize Gestalt principles in their teaching practices would tend to emphasize the "Gestalt" at all levels of education; seeing the total picture would be all-important. Such teachers would accept group discussions or even the lecture system. On the other hand, Piagetian teachers would be concerned about the individual student. These teachers would first attempt to determine the stage of development of a particular student before deciding what information to present. They would realize that knowing something about the student's cognitive structure would enable them to present the student with information that he or she would be ready to assimilate. There is a considerable difference, then, between assuming that the brain is constantly organizing experiences and assuming that organizational ability varies at different stages of development.

Piaget's theory is hard to classify in the traditional categories. It is empirical in the sense that knowledge depends on experience, but clearly it is not empirical in the same way that an S-R theory is. It is tempting to compare Piaget's theory of knowledge with that of Kant (see Chapter 3), but Kant's categories of the mind were innate whereas Piaget's were the result of maturation and cumulative experience. Piaget's theory is not entirely empirical, however. The concept of equilibration provides a nativistic component to his theory. It is this innate drive toward harmony between the internal and external environment that provides the basis of all intellectual growth. We see in Piaget's theory, then, a creative mixture of many points of view; for that reason, his theory is similar to that of Tolman, to which we turn in the next chapter.

PIAGET ON EDUCATION

According to Piaget, educational experiences must be built around the learner's cognitive structure. Children of the same age and from the same culture tend to have similar cognitive structures, but it is entirely possible for them to have different cognitive structures and therefore require different kinds of learning material. On the one hand, educational material that cannot be assimilated into a child's cognitive structure cannot have any meaning to the child. If, on the other hand, the material can be completely assimilated, no learning will take place. For learning to occur, the material needs to be partially known and partially unknown. The part that is known will be assimilated, and the part that is unknown will necessitate a slight modification in the child's cognitive structure. Such modification is referred to as accommodation, which can be roughly equated with learning.

Thus, for Piaget, optimal education involves mildly challenging experiences for the learner so that the dual processes of assimilation and accommodation can provide intellectual growth. To create that kind of experience, the teacher must know the level of functioning of each student's cognitive structure. We find, then, that both Piaget (a representative of the cognitive paradigm) and most of the behaviorists have reached the same conclusion about education, namely, that it must be *individualized*. Piaget reached this conclusion by realizing that the ability to assimilate varies from child to child and that educational material must be tailored to each child's cognitive structure. The behaviorists reached the conclusion through their recognition that reinforcement must be contingent on appropriate behavior, and the proper dispensing of reinforcers requires a one-to-one relationship between the student and the teacher or between the student and programmed educational material.

SUMMARY OF PIAGET'S THEORY

According to Piaget, children are born with a few sensorimotor schemata, which provide the framework for their initial interactions with the environment. The child's early experiences are determined by these sensorimotor schemata. In other words, children can respond to only those events that can be assimilated into these schemata, and they therefore set limits on their experience. Through experience, however, these initial schemata are modified. Each experience contains unique elements that the child's cognitive structure must accommodate. Through this interaction with the environment, the child's cognitive structure changes, allowing for an ever-growing number of experiences. This is a slow process, however, because new schemata always evolve from those that existed previously. In this way, intellectual growth that starts out with the child's reflexive response to the environment develops to the point where the child is able to ponder potential events and to explore mentally probable outcomes.

Interiorization results in the development of operations that free children from needing to deal directly with the environment by allowing them to deal with symbolic manipulations. The development of operations (interiorized actions) provides children with a highly complex means of dealing with the environment, and they are therefore capable of more complex intellectual actions. Because their cognitive structures are more articulated, so are their physical environments; in fact, their cognitive structures can be said to construct the physical environment.

It should be remembered that Piaget uses the term *intelligent* to describe all adaptive activity. Thus, the behavior of a child grasping a rattle is as intelligent as an older child solving a complex problem. The difference is in the cognitive structures available to each child. According to Piaget, an intelligent act always tends to create a balance between the organism and its environment under the existing circumstances. The ever-present drive toward this balanced state is called equilibration.

Although intellectual development is continuous during childhood, Piaget chose to refer to stages of intellectual development. He described four major stages: (1) sensorimotor, in which children deal directly with the environment by utilizing their innate reflexes; (2) preoperational, in which children begin rudimentary concept formation; (3) concrete operations, in which children use interiorized actions or thought to solve problems in their immediate experience; and (4) formal operations, in which children can ponder completely hypothetical situations.

Piaget's theory had a significant effect on educational practice. Many educators have attempted to formulate specific policies based on his theory (e.g., Athey & Rubadeau, 1970; Furth, 1970; Ginsburg & Opper, 1979). Others have attempted to develop an intelligence test in accordance with his theory (e.g., Goldschmid & Bentler, 1968). Clearly Piaget's theory opened new avenues of research that were either unnoticed or ignored by those accepting an associationistic point of view. As we noted in Chapter 2, one characteristic of a good scientific theory is that it is heuristic, and Piaget's theory is certainly that. In 1980, the year Piaget died, Jerome Kagan paid him the following tribute:

> Piaget uncovered a host of fascinating, handy phenomena which were under everyone's noses but which few were talented enough to see. The reliability of those discoveries (the eight-month-old who is suddenly able to retrieve a hidden toy and the shift at age 7 from a nonconserving to a conserving reply to the beakers of water) was so consistent across cultures that they resembled demonstrations in a chemistry lecture hall . . . few would question the conclusion that Piaget's writings have been a primary basis for the centrality of the cognitive sciences in contemporary psychology. . . . With Freud, Piaget has been a seminal figure in the sciences of human development. (pp. 245–246)

EVALUATION OF PIAGET'S THEORY

Contributions

Unlike many of the learning theorists we have studied, Piaget is not easily categorized as a reinforcement theorist, a contingency theorist, or a contiguity theorist. Like many researchers in what is loosely labeled the "cognitive" school, he assumes that learning happens more or less continuously and that it involves both acquisition of information and cognitive representation of that information. Piaget's unique contribution within this general perspective is his identification of the qualitative aspects of learning. Specifically, the concepts of assimilation and accommodation identify two different types of learning experience. Both are learning; both entail the acquisition and storage of information. Assimilation, however, is a static kind of learning, limited by the current cognitive structure; accommodation is a progressive growth of the cognitive structure that changes the character of all subsequent learning.

Criticisms

Many contemporary psychologists point out problems inherent in Piaget's research methodology. His clinical method can provide information that is not readily recorded in rigorously controlled laboratory experiments. It can be an ideal method to discover directions for further research under more carefully defined conditions, but one must be cautious when drawing inferences from observations made with the clinical method precisely because it lacks rigorous experimental controls. A related criticism concerns the extent to which Piaget's observations can be generalized, given that he did not observe children or adults from cultures that differed significantly from his own. For example, Egan (1983), writes

> If we find, for example, that most Australian Aborigine adults fail Piagetian tests of the conservation of continuous quantity, are we to believe that Aborigine adults will store water in tall thin cans in order to "have more water"; do they think they lose water when they pour it from a bucket into a barrel? That these confusions are not evident in their culture suggest that the classic Piagetian task, in such a context, is yielding obscure data that possibly have nothing much to do with general intellectual capacity. (pp. 65–66)

Although Piaget's notion of development through increasingly complex stages seems to be generally correct, there are indications that very young children are not as limited as was initially believed. Infants may well have a fundamental understanding of object permanence (Baillargeon, 1987, 1992; Bowers, 1989) and of certain physical laws such as the impossibility of passing a solid object through a physical barrier (Baillargeon et al., 1990; Keen, 2003). Children as young as four months are responsive to information in two-dimensional drawings of three-dimensional structures, and they discriminate between veridical and "impossible" figures (Shuwairi, Albert, & Johnson, 2007). In addition, there may be discontinuous development of understanding rather than the hierarchical accumulation suggested by Piaget (Berthier et al., 2000).

Perhaps more worrisome, adults may not attain formal operations even when faced with the kinds of experience that Piaget believed would lead to those structures. For example, Piaget and Inhelder (1956) devised a now well-studied water-level task. In this task, subjects are asked to indicate the orientation of liquid in a tilted container. Children tend not to realize that the liquid will remain horizontal with respect to the ground. Contrary to Piaget's expectations, nearly 40 percent of adults also fail to understand this (Kalichman, 1988). To make matters worse, twenty professional waitresses (working for breweries at the Oktoberfest in Munich) and twenty professional bartenders (employed at bars in Munich), all of whom would be expected to have substantial experience with liquids in tipped containers, perform more poorly at the water-level task than groups of students and other professionals (Hecht & Proffitt, 1995).

DISCUSSION QUESTIONS

1. How did Piaget's method of studying intelligence differ from the one used at the Binet Laboratory?
2. Explain why Piaget's view of intelligence is called genetic epistemology.
3. Give an example of an experience that involves both assimilation and accommodation.
4. What did Piaget mean by interiorization?
5. Explain how, according to Piaget, heredity and experience both contribute to intellectual growth.
6. Explain what Piaget meant when he said that the cognitive structures "construct" the physical environment.
7. Discuss the nature of knowledge from both the empiricist's point of view and Piaget's point of view.
8. Discuss Piaget's concept of progressive equilibrium.
9. Describe the educational implications of Piaget's theory.
10. Compare and contrast Piaget's theory of learning with any one of the associationistic theories covered in this book.
11. What do you suppose Piaget's views on the transfer of training would have been? In other words, according to Piaget, what would make it possible to utilize what was learned in one situation in other situations?
12. Outline the major stages of intellectual development according to Piaget.

CHAPTER HIGHLIGHTS

accommodation

assimilation

clinical method

cognitive structure

concrete operations

conservation

content

epistemology

equilibration

formal operations

functional invariants

genetic epistemology

intelligence

interiorization

learning dilemma

operation

preoperational thinking

progressive equilibrium

reversibility

schema

sensorimotor stage

CHAPTER 12

Edward Chace Tolman

Tolman (1886–1959) was born in Newton, Massachusetts, and received his B.S. degree from the Massachusetts Institute of Technology in electrochemistry in 1911. His M.A. (1912) and Ph.D. (1915) degrees were earned at Harvard University in psychology. He taught at Northwestern University from 1915 to 1918, at which time he was released for "lack of teaching success," but more likely it was because of his pacifism during wartime. From Northwestern, he went to the University of California, where he remained until his retirement. His stay at the University of California was interrupted, however, when he was dismissed for refusing to sign a loyalty oath. He led a fight against the loyalty oath as an infringement on academic freedom and was reinstated when the professors won their case.

Edward Chace Tolman. (Courtesy of University of California at Berkeley.)

Tolman was raised in a Quaker home, and his pacifism was a constant theme in his career. In 1942, he wrote *Drives toward War,* in which he suggested several changes in our political, educational, and economic systems that would increase the probability of world peace. In the preface, he stated his reasons for writing the book: "As an American, a college professor, and one brought up in the pacifist tradition, I am intensely biased against war. It is for me stupid, interrupting, unnecessary, and unimaginably horrible. I write this essay within that frame of reference. In short, I am driven to discuss the psychology of war and its possible abolition because I want intensely to get rid of it" (p. xi).

Tolman spent much of his life being a rebel. He opposed war when war was a popular cause, and as we discuss, he opposed Watsonian behaviorism when behaviorism was a popular school of psychology.

As we mentioned at the conclusion of Chapter 10, Tolman's theory of learning can be looked on as a blend of Gestalt theory and behaviorism. While still a graduate student at Harvard, Tolman traveled to Germany and worked for a short time with Koffka. Gestalt theory had a significant and lasting effect on his own theorizing. His favorable attitude toward Gestalt theory did not, however, preclude a favorable attitude toward behaviorism. Like the behaviorists, Tolman saw little value in the introspective approach, and he felt psychology had to become completely objective. His main disagreement with the behaviorists was over the unit of behavior to be studied. Behaviorists such as Pavlov, Guthrie, Hull, Watson, and Skinner represented, according to Tolman, the psychology of "twitchism," because they felt that large segments of behavior could be divided into smaller segments, such as reflexes, for further analysis. Tolman felt that by being elementistic, the behaviorists were throwing away the baby with the bathwater. He believed that it was possible to be objective while studying molar behavior (large, intact, meaningful behavior patterns). Unlike the other behaviorists, Tolman chose to study molar behavior systematically. It can be said that Tolman was methodologically a behaviorist but metaphysically a cognitive theorist. In other words, he studied behavior in order to discover cognitive processes.

MOLAR BEHAVIOR

The chief characteristic of **molar behavior** is that it is purposive; that is, it is always directed toward some goal. Tolman's major work was titled *Purposive Behavior in Animals and Men* (1932). Tolman never contended that behavior could not be divided into smaller units for the purposes of study; rather, he felt that whole behavior patterns had a meaning that would be lost if studied from an elementistic viewpoint. Thus, for Tolman, molar behavior constituted a Gestalt that was different from the individual "twitches" that made it up. In other words, purposive behavior patterns can be looked on as behavioral *Gestalten:*

> It will be contended by us (if not by Watson) that "behavior-acts," though no doubt in complete one-to-one correspondence with the underlying molecular facts of physics and physiology, have, as "molar" wholes, certain emergent properties of their own. And it is these, the molar properties of behavior-acts, which are of prime interest to us as psychologists. Further, these molar properties of behavior-acts cannot in the present state of our knowledge, i.e., prior to the working-out of many empirical correlations between behavior and its physiological correlates, be known even inferentially from a mere knowledge of the underlying molecular facts of physics and physiology. For, just as the properties of a beaker of water are not, prior to experience, in any way envisageable from the properties of individual water molecules, so neither are the properties of a "behavior-act" deducible directly from the properties of the underlying physical and physiological processes which make it up. Behavior as such cannot, at any rate at present, be deduced from a mere enumeration of the muscle twitches, the mere motions qua motions, which make it up. It must as yet be studied first hand and for its own sake. (pp. 7–8)

The type of behavior that Tolman (1932) labels as molar is exemplified in the following passage:

> A rat running a maze; a cat getting out of a puzzle box; a man driving home to dinner; a child hiding from a stranger; a woman doing her washing or gossiping over the telephone; a pupil marking a mental-test sheet; a psychologist reciting a list of nonsense

syllables; my friend and I telling one another our thoughts and feelings—*these are behaviors (qua molar)*. And it must be noted that in mentioning no one of them have we referred to, or, we blush to confess it, for the most part even known, what were the exact muscles and glands, sensory nerves, and motor nerves involved. For these responses somehow had other sufficiently identifying properties of their own. (p. 8)

PURPOSIVE BEHAVIORISM

Tolman's theory has been referred to as a **purposive behaviorism** because it attempts to explain goal-directed behavior, or **purposive behavior.** It must be emphasized that Tolman used the term *purpose* as purely descriptive. He noted, for example, that the searching behavior of a rat in a maze will persist until food is found; therefore, it looks "as if" its behavior is goal directed or purposive. For Tolman, the term *purposive* was used to describe behavior, just as the terms *slow, fast, correct, incorrect,* or *right turn* might be used to describe behavior. There is some similarity between Guthrie and Tolman on this point. For Guthrie, behavior persists as long as maintaining stimuli are being provided by some need state. For Tolman, behavior will look "as if" it is goal directed as long as the organism is seeking something in the environment. In both cases, the behavior will look purposive. Tolman (1932) said,

> It must . . . be emphasized that purposes and cognition which are thus immediately, imminently, in behavior are wholly objective as to definition. They are defined by characters and relationships which we observe out there in the behavior. We, the observers, watch the behavior of the rat, the cat, or the man, and note its character as a getting to such and such by means of such and such a selected pattern of commerces-with. It is we, the independent neutral observers, who note these perfectly objective characters as imminent in the behavior and have happened to choose the terms *purpose* and *cognition* as generic terms for such characters. (pp. 12–13)

Innis (1999) reinforces Tolman's claim that the

> "persistence until" character of the action, which can be directly observed, defines it as purposive. The selection of a particular route, or means, of reaching (or getting away from) the goal can also be directly observed, as can the disruption of this behavior if the situation is changed. In these observations, then, we have an objective measure of the animal's cognitions. (p. 101)

Although Tolman was freer with the terms he was willing to employ in his theory than most behaviorists, he remained a behaviorist, and an objective one. As we shall see, Tolman developed a cognitive theory of learning, but in the final analysis, he was dealing with what every other behaviorist deals with—observable stimuli and overt responses. Tolman (1932) said, "For a Purposive Behaviorism, behavior, as we have seen, is purposive, cognitive, and molar, i.e., 'Gestalted.' Purposive Behaviorism is a molar, not a molecular, behaviorism, but it is none the less a behaviorism. Stimuli and responses and the behavior-determinants of responses are all that it finds to study" (p. 418).

The Use of Rats

Some may think it strange for a cognitive theorist to use rats as experimental subjects, but Tolman had a special fondness for them. He stimulated the use of rats in psychological experiments at the University of California, and he dedicated his 1932 book to the white rat. Throughout Tolman's writings, one finds humor and wit, as exemplified by his following thoughts on the use of rats as experimental subjects:

> Let it be noted that rats live in cages; they do not go on binges the night before one has planned an experiment; they do not kill each other off in wars; they do not invent engines of destruction, and if they did, they would not be so inept about controlling such engines; they do not go in for either class conflicts or race conflicts; they avoid politics, economics, and papers on psychology. They are marvelous, pure, and delightful. (1945, p. 166)

Elsewhere Tolman (1938) said,

> I believe that everything important in psychology (except perhaps such matters as the building up of a super-ego, that is, everything save such matters as involve society and words) can be investigated in essence through the continued experimental and theoretical analysis of the determiners of rat behavior at a choice-point in a maze. Herein I believe I agree with Professor Hull and also with Professor Thorndike. (p. 34)

MAJOR THEORETICAL CONCEPTS

Tolman introduced the use of intervening variables into psychological research, and Hull borrowed the idea from Tolman. Both Hull and Tolman used intervening variables in a similar way in their work. Hull, however, developed a much more comprehensive and elaborate theory of learning than did Tolman. We consider the formal aspects of Tolman's theory later in this chapter, but first we turn to a few of his general assumptions about the learning process.

What Is Learned?

The behaviorists, such as Pavlov, Watson, Guthrie, and Hull, said that stimulus-response associations are learned and that complex learning involves complex S-R relationships. Tolman, however, taking his lead from the Gestalt theorists, said that learning is essentially a process of discovering what leads to what in the environment. The organism, through exploration, discovers that certain events lead to certain other events or that one sign leads to another sign. For example, we learn that when it's 5:00 P.M. (S_1), dinner (S_2) will soon follow. For that reason, Tolman was called an S-S rather than an S-R theorist. Learning, for Tolman, was an ongoing process that required no motivation. On this matter Tolman was in agreement with Guthrie and in opposition to Thorndike, Skinner, and Hull.

It should be pointed out, however, that motivation is important in Tolman's theory because it determines which aspects of the environment the organism attends to. For example, the hungry organism attends to food-related events in the environment, and the sexually deprived organism attends to sex-related events. In general, an organism's drive state determines which aspects of the environment will be emphasized in its perceptual field. Thus, for Tolman, motivation acts as a perceptual **emphasizer.**

According to Tolman, what is learned is "the lay of the land"; the organism learns what is there. It learns that if it turns to the left, it finds one thing, and if it turns to the right, it finds another thing. Gradually it develops a picture of the environment that can be used to get around in it. Tolman called this picture a **cognitive map.** On this point, Tolman was diametrically opposed to the other behaviorists. According to him, it is futile to look at individual responses or even individual routes to a goal. Once the organism has developed a cognitive map, it can reach a particular goal from any number of directions. If one commonly used route is blocked, the animal simply takes an alternate route, just as the human takes a detour on the way home from work if the route usually taken is not available. The organism will, however, choose the shortest route or the one requiring the least amount of work. This is referred to as the **principle of least effort.**

There is a great deal of similarity between Tolman's principle of least effort and Hull's notion of the habit family hierarchy. Both theorists concluded that after training, an organism can reach a goal through alternate routes. Tolman said that the organism's first choice is the route requiring the least amount of effort. Hull said that the organism prefers the shortest route because it has the shortest delay of reinforcement (J) and therefore the greatest amount of $_sE_R$. Furthermore, the response that has the greatest amount of $_sE_R$ will tend to occur in any given situation. Later in this chapter, we see some of Tolman's ingenious experimentation designed to show that animals respond according to cognitive maps rather than to simple S-R processes.

Confirmation versus Reinforcement

As with Guthrie, the concept of reinforcement was unimportant to Tolman as a learning variable, but there is some similarity between what Tolman called confirmation and what the other behaviorists called reinforcement. During the development of a cognitive map, the organism utilizes expectations. Expectations are hunches about what leads to what. Early tentative expectations are called **hypotheses,** and they are either confirmed by experience or not. Hypotheses that are confirmed are retained, and those that are not are abandoned. Through this process, the cognitive map develops.

An **expectancy** that is consistently confirmed develops into what Tolman referred to as a **means-end readiness,** or what is commonly referred to as a belief. When an expectation is consistently confirmed, the organism ends up "believing" that if it acts in a certain way, a certain result will follow, or if it sees a certain sign (stimulus), another sign will follow. Thus, the **confirmation of an expectancy** in the development of a cognitive map is similar to the notion of reinforcement, as other behaviorists may have used the term. Note, however, that the production, acceptance, or rejection of hypotheses is a cognitive process that need not involve overt behavior. Also, the hypothesis-testing process, so important to the development of a cognitive map, does not depend on any physiological need state of the organism. As mentioned earlier, learning is taking place constantly and does not depend on any motivational state of the organism.

Vicarious Trial and Error

Tolman noted a characteristic of rats in a maze that he took as support for his cognitive interpretation of learning. Often a rat pauses at a choice point and looks around as if thinking about the various alternatives available to it. Tolman called this pausing and looking around at the choice point **vicarious trial and error.** Instead of behavioral trial and error, in which first one response is tried and then another until a solution to the problem is reached, with vicarious trial and error, different approaches are tested cognitively rather than behaviorally.

Learning versus Performance

We saw in Chapter 6 that Hull distinguished between learning and performance. In Hull's final theory, the number of reinforced trials was the only learning variable; the other variables in his system were performance variables. Performance can be thought of as the translation of learning into behavior. Although the distinction between learning and performance was important for Hull, it was even more important for Tolman.

According to Tolman, we know many things about our environment but act on this information only when we need to do so. As mentioned earlier, this knowledge, which comes about through reality testing, lies dormant until a need arises. In a state of need, the organism utilizes what it has learned through reality testing to bring it into proximity to those things that will alleviate the need. For example, there may be two drinking fountains in your building that you may have passed many times without having paused for a drink, but if you become thirsty, you merely walk over to one of them and take a drink. You knew for some time how to find a drinking fountain, but you did not need to translate that knowledge into behavior until you became thirsty. We discuss the learning-performance distinction in more detail when we consider latent learning.

The points that we have made so far can be summarized as follows:

1. The organism brings to a problem-solving situation various hypotheses that it may utilize in attempting to solve the problem. These hypotheses are based largely on prior experience, but as we discuss later, Tolman believed that some problem-solving strategies may be innate.
2. The hypotheses that survive are those that correspond best with reality, that is, those that result in goal achievement.
3. After a while a clearly established cognitive map develops, and it can be used under altered conditions. For instance, when an organism's preferred path is blocked, it simply chooses, in accordance with the principle of least effort, an alternative path from its cognitive map.

4. When there is some sort of demand or motive to be satisfied, the organism makes use of the information in its cognitive map. The fact that information can exist but be utilized only under certain conditions is the basis for the very important distinction between learning and performance.

Latent Learning

Latent learning is learning that is not translated into performance. In other words, it is possible for learning to remain dormant for a considerable length of time before it is manifested in behavior. The concept of latent learning was very important to Tolman, and he felt he succeeded in demonstrating its existence. The now famous experiment that Tolman and Honzik (1930) ran involved three groups of rats learning to solve a maze. One group was never reinforced for correctly traversing the maze, one group was always reinforced, and one group was not reinforced until the eleventh day of the experiment. The last group was of the greatest interest to Tolman. His theory of latent learning predicted that this group would be learning the maze just as much as the group that was being regularly reinforced and that when reinforcement was introduced on the eleventh day, this group should soon perform as well as the group that had been continually reinforced. The results of the experiment are shown in Figure 12–1.

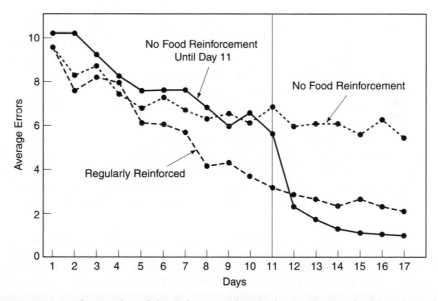

FIGURE 12–1 The results of the Tolman and Honzik experiment showing that when animals are reinforced after a period of nonreinforcement, their performance very rapidly equals or exceeds that of animals that had been reinforced from the onset of the experiment. (From "Introduction and Removal of Reward, and Maze Performance in Rats," by E. C. Tolman & C. H. Honzik, 1930, *University of California Publications in Psychology, 4,* pp. 257–275.)

By examining Figure 12–1, three things become apparent: (1) There is slight improvement in performance even in the group never receiving reinforcement; (2) the reinforced group shows steady improvement throughout the seventeen days of the experiment; and (3) when reinforcement was introduced on the eleventh day to the group not previously receiving reinforcement, their performance vastly improved. In fact, the last group performed even better than the group that was reinforced throughout the experiment. Tolman took the results to support his contention that reinforcement was a performance variable and not a learning variable.

The S-R theorists insisted that reinforcement was, in fact, not removed from the situation. Why, they asked, would the group never receiving food show slight improvement? They pointed out that simply being removed from the apparatus after reaching the goal box could act as a reinforcer for reaching the goal box. Another S-R interpretation of latent learning, one based on the concept of incentive motivation, is presented after our discussion of latent extinction.

Latent Extinction   It may be remembered that reinforcement theorists such as Pavlov, Hull, and Skinner viewed extinction as an active process. For them, for extinction to occur, a previously reinforced response must be made but not reinforced. Under these circumstances, the rate or magnitude of the previously reinforced response will go back to its previous level before reinforcement was introduced. But what does Tolman say? According to Tolman, learning occurs through observation and is independent of reinforcement. What an animal learns is to expect reinforcement if a certain response is made because it is this expectation that is confirmed during the acquisition phase of a learning experiment. Tolman's theory predicts that if an animal has learned an S-S expectancy (e.g., that a certain response will lead to the presence of food) and is given the opportunity to *observe* that that response will no longer lead to food, such observation will itself produce extinction. For example, if a rat that had previously learned to traverse a maze or a runway to obtain food is placed directly into a now-empty goal box, it will stop traversing the maze or runway on subsequent trials. Extinction that occurs under these circumstances is called **latent extinction** because it does not involve the nonreinforced performance of the previously reinforced response. Evidence for latent extinction has been found by many researchers, for example, Deese, 1951; Moltz, 1957; and Seward and Levy, 1949. Bower and Hilgard (1981) summarize these findings:

These . . . results . . . imply that the strength of an instrumental response sequence can be altered without *that response* occurring and receiving the altered conditions of reinforcement. . . . Such results create difficulties for an S-R reinforcement theory which supposes that responses can have their habit strengths altered only when they occur and are then explicitly punished or nonrewarded. The results seem to call for two assumptions; that at the start of a behavior sequence, organisms have available some representation of what goal they expect to achieve at the end of the response sequence; and that that goal expectation can be altered by direct experience with the goal situation without execution of the prior response sequence leading up to it. These, of course, are exactly the assumptions made in Tolman's theory. (pp. 340–341)

S-R theorists, such as Spence, explain latent extinction in terms of motivational factors. We saw in Chapter 6 that Spence believed that response learning occurred because of contiguity. That is, a goal response is learned simply because it is made. What reinforcement does, according to Spence, is provide an incentive for performing a response that had been learned independent of reinforcement. Furthermore, stimuli that occur prior to primary reinforcement take on secondary reinforcing properties, and these secondary reinforcers provide the incentive for the animal to traverse a maze or runway. According to Spence, what happens in the latent extinction situation is that the animal experiences these stimuli without primary reinforcement, and therefore their secondary reinforcing properties extinguish. Thereafter, when the animal is placed in the experimental apparatus, it has less incentive to perform the learned response. This is essentially the same explanation Spence would offer for latent learning; that is, animals learn a variety of responses in a maze or a runway simply by making those responses. When at some point reinforcement is introduced, it gives the animal the incentive to perform a response that it had previously learned through the law of contiguity. The question of whether latent learning and latent extinction are explained best in terms of expectancies or in terms of incentive motivation is yet unanswered.

Place Learning versus Response Learning

Tolman maintained that animals learn where things are, whereas the S-R theorists maintained that specific responses are learned to specific stimuli. Tolman and his collaborators performed a series of experiments designed to determine whether animals were place learners, as Tolman suggested, or response learners, as S-R theory suggested. A typical experiment in this area was done by Tolman, Ritchie, and Kalish (1946b). The apparatus they used is diagrammed in Figure 12–2.

Two groups of rats were utilized. Members of one group were sometimes started at S_1 and sometimes at S_2, but no matter where they started, they always had to turn in the same direction to be reinforced. For example, if the group was learning to turn right, the rat was fed at F_1 if it started at S_1 and was fed at F_2 if it started

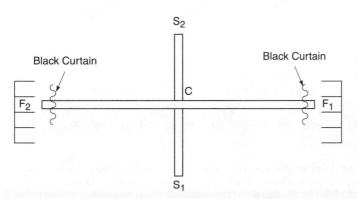

FIGURE 12–2 Apparatus used in the Tolman, Ritchie, and Kalish experiment on place versus response learning. S_1 and S_2 are starting points, F_1 and F_2 are food boxes, and C is the center point of the maze. (From "Studies in Spatial Learning II," by E. C. Tolman, B. F. Ritchie, & D. Kalish, 1946, *Journal of Experimental Psychology, 36,* p. 223.)

at S_2. This was the **response learning** group. Members of the other group were always fed at the same place (e.g., F_2). If a member of this group started at S_1, it had to turn left to be reinforced. If it started at S_2, it had to turn right. This was the **place learning** group.

The animals were given six trials a day for twelve days, or seventy-two trials. The criterion for learning was ten successive errorless trials. At the end of the experiment, only three of the eight rats in the response learning group had reached criterion, whereas all eight rats in the place learning group had reached criterion. In fact, the mean trials to criterion for the latter group was only 3.5, whereas it was 17.33 for the three response learners that reached criterion. The place learners solved their problem much faster than the response learners solved theirs. It appeared, therefore, that it was more "natural" for animals to learn places than to learn specific responses, and this result was taken as support for Tolman's theory. The results of the experiment are shown in Figure 12–3.

In another study by Tolman, Ritchie, and Kalish (1946a), animals were first trained in the apparatus shown in Figure 12–4. The animals had to learn to follow the route A, B, C, D, E, F, and G. H indicates the place where a five-watt bulb was located, the only illumination in the room during the experiment. After preliminary

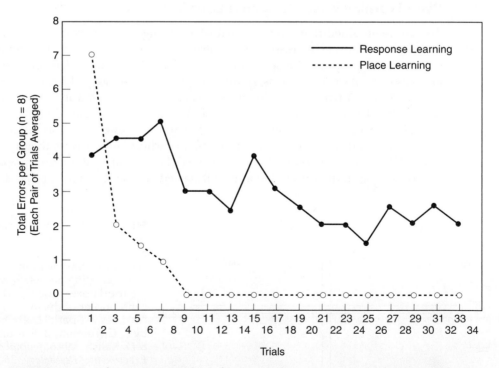

FIGURE 12–3   The average number of errors made on successive trials by place learning and response learning groups of rats. (From "Studies in Spatial Learning II," by E. C. Tolman, B. F. Ritchie, & D. Kalish, 1946, *Journal of Experimental Psychology, 36*, p. 226.)

training, the apparatus shown in Figure 12–4 was removed and replaced with the apparatus shown in Figure 12–5.

The path the animals were trained to take in the first phase of the experiment was now blocked, but the animals could choose among eighteen alternative paths.

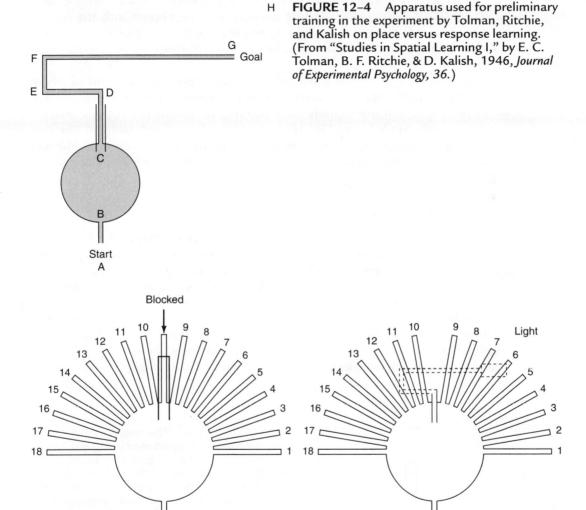

H **FIGURE 12–4** Apparatus used for preliminary training in the experiment by Tolman, Ritchie, and Kalish on place versus response learning. (From "Studies in Spatial Learning I," by E. C. Tolman, B. F. Ritchie, & D. Kalish, 1946, *Journal of Experimental Psychology, 36.*)

FIGURE 12–5 After preliminary training on the apparatus shown in Figure 12–4, the animals were allowed to choose one of the eighteen alleys shown in the figure to the left. The figure to the right shows the apparatus used for preliminary training superimposed over the test apparatus so that the relationship between the two can be seen. (From "Studies in Spatial Learning I" by E. C. Tolman, B. F. Ritchie, & D. Kalish, 1946, *Journal of Experimental Psychology, 36.*)

On the basis of S-R theory, one might expect that when the original path was blocked, the animals would choose the unblocked path closest to the original. This, however, was not the case. The most frequently picked was alley number 6, the one pointing directly to where the *goal* was during the first phase of the experiment. In fact, the alleys closest to the original alley were only infrequently chosen (alley 9 by 2 percent of the rats and alley 10 by 7.5 percent). Tolman, Ritchie, and Kalish (1946a) reported that the first pathway, the one chosen with the second greatest frequency, was the alley pointing to the place in the room where the animals had been fed in their home cages. The results of the experiment are shown in Figure 12–6.

Once again it looked as if the animals were responding in terms of where something was rather than in terms of specific responses. The S-R theorists felt that such experiments did not support place learning because it was entirely possible that the animals simply learned the response of running toward the light. The cognitive theorists refuted this interpretation by saying that if that were true, the animals would have chosen alleys 5 or 7 at least as often as alley 6, and this of course was not the case.

Reinforcement Expectancy

According to Tolman, when we learn, we come to know the "lay of the land." The term *understanding* was not foreign to him, as it was to other behaviorists. In a problem-solving situation, we learn where the goal is, and we get to it by following the shortest possible route. We learn to expect certain events to follow other events. The animal expects that if it goes to a certain place, it will find a certain reinforcer. The S-R theorist expects that changing reinforcers in a learning situation does not disrupt behavior as long as the quantity of reinforcement is not changed drastically. Tolman, however, predicted that if reinforcers were changed, behavior would be disrupted because in **reinforcement expectancy,** a particular reinforcer becomes a part of what is expected.

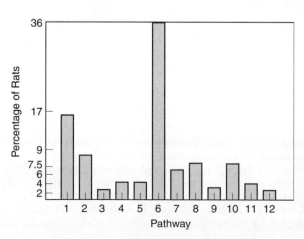

FIGURE 12–6 The results of the experiment diagrammed in Figures 12–4 and 12–5. It can be seen that the most frequently chosen path on the test trial was the one pointing directly to the goal. Tolman, Ritchie, and Kalish also pointed out that the second most frequently chosen path was the one that pointed to the animals' home cages, where they were fed. (From "Studies in Spatial Learning I" by E. C. Tolman, B. F. Ritchie, & D. Kalish, 1946, *Journal of Experimental Psychology, 36.*)

Tolman (1932, p. 44) reported an experiment by Elliott, who trained one group of rats to run a maze for bran mush and another to run a maze for sunflower seeds. On the tenth day of training, the group that had been trained on bran mush was switched to sunflower seeds. The results of Elliott's experiment are shown in Figure 12–7. We see that switching reinforcement considerably disrupted performance, thus supporting Tolman's prediction.

It should be noted, however, that the group trained on bran mush performed consistently better than the group trained on sunflower seeds before the switch. The Hullians said that because the bran mush had a larger incentive value (K) than did the sunflower seeds, reaction potential is greater. After the switch to sunflower seeds, K would go down accordingly. The Hullian explanation can only partially account for the results, however, because the group that switched to sunflower seeds performed much worse than the group consistently trained on sunflower seeds. Even correcting for the differences in incentive value, there still seems to be considerable disruption of performance that can be explained by the departure from what was expected.

The reader can certainly recall situations in which there has been a discrepancy between what was expected and what was experienced. Examples might include a good friend or relative acting "totally unlike himself," a familiar house torn down while you were on vacation, or receiving a pay raise either larger or smaller than you expected. In each case, the expected events were not the ones that actually occurred. If a person has important expectations, their failure in being realized could be traumatic. Leon Festinger (1957) constructed a theory of personality around this notion. According to Festinger, when a person's beliefs do not conform to what actually occurs, the person experiences a psychological state called **cognitive**

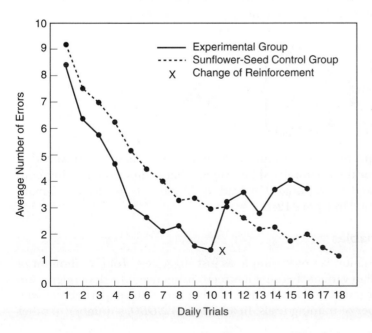

FIGURE 12–7 The results of an experiment by M. H. Elliott showing the effect of change of reward on the maze performance of rats (Brown, W., Tolman, E. C., Jones H. E., eds. University of California publications in psychology. Berkeley, CA: University of California press, 1932. Vol. IV, pp. 19–30).

dissonance. Cognitive dissonance is a negative drive state, and the person experiencing it seeks ways to reduce it, just as the person experiencing hunger seeks to reduce the hunger drive.

THE FORMAL ASPECTS OF TOLMAN'S THEORY

As an example of Tolman's (1938) more abstract theorizing, we summarize his article "The Determiners of Behavior at a Choice Point." In this example, the choice point is where the rat decides to turn either right or left in a T-maze. Some of the symbols we use are seen in the diagram of the T-maze shown in Figure 12–8.

In an experiment in which a rat was being trained to turn left in a T-maze, Tolman's dependent variable was a behavior ratio defined as follows:

$$\frac{B_L}{B_L + B_R}$$

This formula gives the percentage tendency to turn left at any stage of learning. If, for example, an animal turned left six times out of ten times, we would have

$$\frac{6}{6 + 4} = 60\%$$

Tolman felt that the behavior ratio was determined by the collective experiences that come from having turned both ways at the choice point on various trials. This experience allows the animal to learn what leads to what. The cumulative nature of these experiences was diagrammed by Tolman as follows:

$$\Sigma \; (O_c \; \overset{B_L}{\underset{B_R}{\Big\langle}} \; \begin{matrix} (O_L:O_{GL}) \\ \\ (O_R:O_{GR}) \end{matrix} \Bigg\} \; \rightarrow \; \frac{B_L}{B_L + B_R}$$

Rather than repeating this cumbersome diagram, Tolman abbreviated it ΣOBO, which stands for the accumulated knowledge that comes from making both B_L and B_R responses and seeing what they lead to. The events involved in T-maze learning are diagrammed in Figure 12–8.

Environmental Variables

Unfortunately, the situation is not so simple as just suggested. Tolman thought of ΣOBO as an independent variable because it directly influenced the dependent variable (i.e., the behavior ratio), and it was under the control of the experimenter who determined the number of training trials. In addition to ΣOBO, a number of other

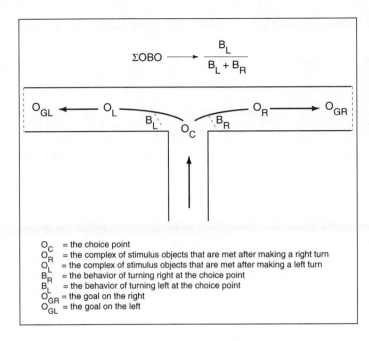

FIGURE 12–8   A diagram of a T-maze. (From "The Determiners of Behavior at a Choice Point," by E. C. Tolman, 1938. *Psychological Review, 45,* p. 1. Copyright © 1938 by the American Psychological Association.)

O_C = the choice point
O_R = the complex of stimulus objects that are met after making a right turn
O_L = the complex of stimulus objects that are met after making a left turn
B_R = the behavior of turning right at the choice point
B_L = the behavior of turning left at the choice point
O_{GR} = the goal on the right
O_{GL} = the goal on the left

independent variables could have an effect on performance. Tolman suggested the following list:

M = maintenance schedule. This symbol refers to the animal's deprivation schedule, for example, the number of hours since it has eaten.
G = appropriateness of goal object. The reinforcer must be related to the animal's current drive state. For example, one does not reinforce a thirsty animal with food.
S = types and modes of stimuli provided. This symbol refers to the vividness of the cues or signals available to the animal in the learning situation.
R = types of motor responses required in the learning situation, for example, running, sharp turns, and so on.
P = pattern of succeeding and preceding maze units; the pattern of turns that needs to be made to solve a maze as determined by the experimenter.
ΣOBO = the number of trials and their cumulative nature.

Here Tolman was no longer talking only about learning T-mazes but learning more complex mazes as well.

Individual Difference Variables

In addition to these independent variables, there are variables that the individual subjects bring into the experiment with them. The list of individual difference variables suggested by Tolman is as follows (note that their initials create the acronym HATE, a somewhat strange word for Tolman to use):

H = heredity
A = age
T = previous training
E = special endocrine, drug, or vitamin conditions

Each of the individual difference variables interacts with each of the independent variables, and a combination of all these variables working together is what produces behavior (seen in Figure 12–9).

Intervening Variables

Up to this point, we have been discussing the effects of observed stimulus variables (independent variables) on observed behavior (dependent variables). It would be possible, as Skinner suggested, to conduct thousands of experiments showing how those variables are related to each other in various combinations. The functional analysis suggested by Skinner, however, did not appeal to Tolman (1938), who wanted to move beyond the facts:

> But why, you may ask, can we not be satisfied with just experiments and the "facts" resulting from them? I find that there are two reasons. In the first place, an entirely factual empirical establishment of the complete functional relation, f_1, to cover the effects on $(B_L/B_L + B_R)$ of all the permutations and combinations of M, G, S, etc., would be a humanly endless task. We have time in this brief mortal span to test only a relatively limited number of such permutations and combinations. So, in the first place, we are forced to propose theories in order to use such theories to extrapolate for all these combinations for which we have not time to test.

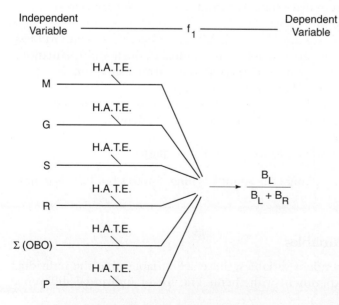

FIGURE 12–9 Illustration of the relationship among the independent variables, the individual difference variables, and behavior. (From "The Determiners of Behavior at a Choice Point," by E. C. Tolman, 1938, *Psychological Review, 45*, p. 8. Copyright © 1938 by the American Psychological Association.)

But I suspect that there is another reason for theories. Some of us, psychologically, just demand theories. Even if we had all the million and one concrete facts, we would still want theories to, as we would say, "explain" those facts. Theories just seem to be necessary to some of us to relieve our inner tensions. (pp. 8–9)

Tolman defined a theory as a set of intervening variables. An intervening variable is a construct created by the theorist to aid in explaining the relationship between an independent variable and a dependent variable. The example given in Chapter 2 was hunger. It has been found that performance on a learning task varies with hours of food deprivation, and that is an empirical relationship. If one says, however, that hunger varies with hours of deprivation and in turn influences learning, the concept of hunger is being used as an intervening variable. As Tolman said, such a concept is used to fill in the blanks in a research program.

For similar reasons, Tolman created an intervening variable to go along with each of his independent variables. In each case, the intervening variable was systematically tied to both an independent variable and a dependent variable. In other words, each of Tolman's intervening variables was operationally defined. **Maintenance schedule,** for example, creates a **demand,** which in turn is related to performance. Appropriateness of the goal object is related to *appetite,* which in turn is related to performance. Types of stimuli provided are related to the animal's capability for *differentiation,* and so on. A summary of Tolman's system, showing his use of intervening variables, is shown in Figure 12–10.

One can now see the similarity between Tolman and Hull in the use of intervening variables. Hull, as we have mentioned, borrowed the approach from Tolman, who introduced the use of intervening variables into psychology. The part of the system shown in Figure 12–10 that relates most closely to the main theme in Tolman's

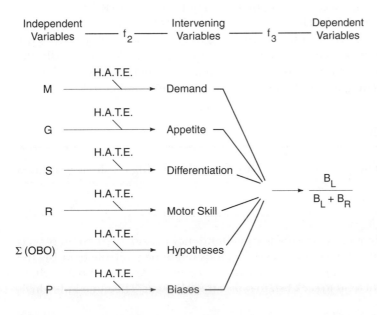

FIGURE 12–10 The relationship suggested by Tolman among independent variables, individual difference variables, intervening variables, and the dependent variable. (From "The Determiners of Behavior at a Choice Point," by E. C. Tolman, 1938, *Psychological Review, 45,* p. 16. Copyright © 1938 by the American Psychological Association.)

theory is the intervening variable of "hypotheses." As the result of previous experience (ΣOBO) hypotheses are developed that affect behavior ($B_L/B_L + B_R$). As these hypotheses are confirmed by experience, they become means-end readinesses, or beliefs. The function of an intervening variable is seen clearly at this point. It is an empirical fact that performance improves as a function of the number of learning trials, but the intervening variables are created in an effort to explain why this is the case. According to those who use intervening variables, the facts would be the same without their use, but our understanding of the facts would be severely limited.

MacCORQUODALE AND MEEHL'S FORMALIZATION OF TOLMAN'S THEORY

MacCorquodale and Meehl (1953) attempted to do for Tolman's theory what Voeks attempted to do for Guthrie's. That is, they attempted to make Tolman's terms more precise and his concepts more easily tested. Most of MacCorquodale and Meehl's restatement of Tolman's theory is beyond the scope of this book, but the following brief sample of their work nicely summarizes a few of Tolman's more important concepts.

MacCorquodale and Meehl (1953) describe Tolman's theory as an S_1-R_1-S_2 theory, where S_1 elicits an expectancy of some kind, R_1 indicates the manner in which the expectancy is acted on, and S_2 indicates what the organism thinks will happen as a result of its actions under the circumstances. In other words, the organism seems to think, "under these circumstances (S_1), if I do this (R_1), I will have a certain experience (S_2)." An example would be seeing a friend (S_1) and believing that saying "hello" (R_1) will result in a warm greeting from the friend (S_2). Or seeing a certain intersection (S_1) and believing that turning to the right (R_1) will result in finding a service station (S_2). The more often the S_1-R_1-S_2 sequence occurs, the stronger the expectation will become. Likewise, if S_1 and R_1 occur and S_2 does not follow, the expectation becomes weaker. MacCorquodale and Meehl handle the concept of stimulus generalization within Tolman's theory by saying that an expectancy that is elicited by S_1 will also be elicited by stimuli similar to S_1.

SIX KINDS OF LEARNING

In his 1949 article, "There Is More Than One Kind of Learning," Tolman proposed six kinds of learning.

Cathexes

Cathexis (plural, *cathexes*) refers to the learned tendency to associate certain objects with certain drive states. For example, certain foods might be available to satisfy the hunger drive of individuals who live in a particular country. Persons who live where fish is usually eaten will tend to seek fish to satisfy their hunger. The same individuals may avoid beef or spaghetti because, for them, those foods have not been associated with the satisfaction of the hunger drive. Because certain stimuli have been associated with the satisfaction of a certain drive, those stimuli will tend to be sought out when the drive recurs: "When a type of goal has been positively cathected it means that when the given drive is in force the organism will tend to apprehend, to approach, and to perform the consummatory reaction upon any instance of this type of goal which is presented by the immediate environment" (p. 146). When the organism has learned to avoid certain objects while in a certain drive state, a negative cathexis is said to have occurred. There is little difference between Tolman and the S-R theorists concerning this kind of learning.

Equivalence Beliefs

When a "subgoal" has the same effect as the goal itself, the subgoal is said to constitute an **equivalence belief.** Although this is close to what the S-R theorists call secondary reinforcement, Tolman (1949) felt that this kind of learning more typically involved the "social drives" rather than the physiological drives. He gave the following example: "Insofar as it can be demonstrated that with the reception of the high grades there is some temporary reduction in this student's need for love and approbation even without his going on to tell others about his grade, then we would have evidence for an equivalence belief. The A's would then be accepted by him as equivalent to the love or approbation to which they were originally a mere means" (p. 148).

Here again, there is little difference between Tolman and the S-R theorists, except that Tolman talked about "love reduction" as the reinforcement, and the S-R theorists would prefer to remain with the reduction of drives such as hunger or thirst.

Field Expectancies

Field expectancies are developed in the same way a cognitive map is developed: The organism learns what leads to what. Upon seeing a certain sign, for instance, it expects that a certain other sign will follow. This general knowledge of the environment is used to explain latent learning, latent extinction, place learning, and the use of shortcuts. This is not S-R learning but rather S-S, or sign-sign, learning; that is, when the animal sees one sign, it learns to expect another to follow. The only "reinforcement" necessary for this kind of learning to take place is the confirmation of a hypothesis.

Field-Cognition Modes

The kind of learning about which Tolman was least confident, a **field-cognition mode,** is a strategy, a way of approaching a problem-solving situation. It is a tendency to arrange the perceptual field in certain configurations. Tolman suspected that this tendency is innate but can be modified by experience. In fact, the most important thing about a strategy that works in solving a problem is that it will be tried in similar situations in the future. Thus, effective field-cognition modes, or problem-solving strategies, transfer to related problems. In that way they are similar to means-end readinesses (beliefs), which also transfer to similar situations. Tolman (1949) summarized his thinking about this kind of learning as follows: "In a word, I am trying to summarize under this fourth category all those principles as to the structure of environmental fields which are relevant to all environmental fields, and which (whether innate or learned) are carried around by the individual and applied to each new field with which he is presented" (p. 153).

Drive Discriminations

Drive discrimination simply refers to the fact that organisms can determine their own drive state and therefore can respond appropriately. For example, animals can be trained to turn one way in a T-maze when they are hungry and the other way when they are thirsty (Hull, 1933a; Leeper, 1935). Because Tolman believed in social as well as physiological drives, drive discrimination was an important concept to him. Unless an organism can clearly determine its own drive state, it will not know how to read its cognitive map. If an organism's needs are not clear, its goals are not clear, and therefore its behavior may be inappropriate. How people will act when they need love, for example, will be different from how they will act when they need water.

Motor Patterns

Tolman pointed out that his theory is mainly concerned with the association of ideas and is not overly concerned with the manner in which those ideas become associated with behavior. **Motor pattern** learning is an attempt to resolve this difficulty. Of all people, Tolman (1949) accepted Guthrie's interpretation of how responses become associated with stimuli. He did accept Guthrie reluctantly, however, which is exemplified by the following quotation: "In default of other experimental theories about the learning of motor patterns I am willing to take a chance and to agree with Guthrie that the conditions under which a motor pattern gets acquired may well be those in which the given movement gets the animal away from the stimuli which were present when the movement was initiated" (p. 153).

Tolman was truly an eclectic. Somewhere among the six kinds of learning he described, there is agreement with almost every other major theory of learning. Combining the ideas of Hull, Gestalt theory, and Guthrie in one system would have confused a lesser mind. As for his reason for postulating many kinds of learning rather than one or two kinds, Tolman (1949) said the following:

> Why did I want thus to complicate things; why do I not want one simple set of laws for all learning? I do not know. But I suppose it must be due to some funny erroneous equivalence belief on my part to the effect that being sweeping and comprehensive though vague, is equivalent to more love from others than being narrow and precise. No doubt, any good clinician would be able to trace this back to some sort of nasty traumatic experience in my early childhood. (p. 155)

Tolman's Attitude Toward His Own Theory

Tolman presented the final version of his theory in *Psychology: A Study of a Science,* edited by Sigmund Koch, which appeared in 1959, the year Tolman died. There is probably no better indication of how Tolman felt toward his own theory and toward science in general than the first and last paragraphs of his chapter in that volume. First, Tolman's (1959) opening statement:

> I would like to begin by letting off steam. If in what follows I have not done a very clear or useful job, I would plead some half-dozen reasons. First, I think the days of such grandiose, all-covering systems in psychology as mine attempted to be are, at least for the present, pretty much passé. I feel therefore, that it might have been more decent and more dignified to let such an instance of the relatively immediate dead past bury its dead. Secondly, I don't enjoy trying to use my mind in too analytical a way. Hence, I have found it frustrating and difficult to try to subject my system to the required sorts of analyses. Thirdly, I suppose I am personally antipathetic to the notion that science progresses through intense, self-conscious analysis of where one has got and where one is going. Such analyses are obviously a proper function for the philosopher of science and they may be valuable for many individual scientists. But I myself become frightened and restricted when I begin to worry too much as to what particular logical and methodological canons I should or should not obey. It seems to me that very often major new scientific insights have come when the scientist, like the ape, has been shaken out of his up-until-then approved scientific rules such as that food can be reached only by the hand and discovers "out of the blue," and perhaps purely by analogy . . . the new rule of using a stick (or a sign-Gestalt). Fourthly, I have an inveterate tendency to make my ideas too complicated and too high-flown so that they become less and less susceptible to empirical tests. Fifthly, because of increasing laziness, I have not of late kept up, as I should have, with the more recent theoretical and empirical discussions which bear upon my argument. If I had, the argument would have been different and better and also I would have given more credit to those to whom credit is due. Finally, to talk about one's own ideas and to resort frequently to the use of the first person singular, as one tends to do in such an analysis, brings about a conflict, at least in me, between enjoying my exhibitionism and being made to feel guilty by my superego. (pp. 93–94)

And Tolman's (1959) last statement about his theory was as follows:

> I started out, as I indicated in the introduction, with considerable uneasiness. I felt that my so-called system was outdated and that it was a waste of time to try to rehash it and that it would be pretentious now to seek to make it fit any accepted set of prescriptions laid down by the philosophy of science. I have to confess, however, that as I have gone along I have become again more and more involved in it, though I still realize its many weak points. The system may well not stand up to any final canons of scientific procedure. But I do not much care. I have liked to think about psychology in ways that have proved congenial to me. Since all the sciences, and especially psychology, are still immersed in such tremendous realms of the uncertain and the unknown, the best that any individual scientist, especially any psychologist, can do seems to be to follow his own gleam and his own bent, however inadequate they may be. In fact, I suppose that actually this is what we all do. In the end, the only sure criterion is to have fun. And I have had fun. (p. 152)

TOLMAN ON EDUCATION

In many respects, Tolman and the Gestaltists agree about educational practices: Both would emphasize the importance of thinking and understanding. For Tolman, it would be important to have the student test hypotheses in a problem situation. On this matter, Tolman is in close agreement with Harlow's error factor theory, which states that learning is not so much a matter of building up correct responses or strategies as it is a matter of eliminating incorrect responses or strategies. Both Tolman and the Gestalt theorist would encourage small groups for classroom discussions. The important thing is for students to have the opportunity, individually or as part of a group, to test the adequacy of their ideas. Hypotheses or strategies effective in solving a problem are those that are maintained by the student. The teacher, then, acts as a consultant to assist students in clarifying and then confirming or disconfirming hypotheses.

Like the Gestalt theorist, Tolman would also suggest that the student be exposed to a topic from different viewpoints. This process would allow the student to develop a cognitive map, which could be utilized to answer questions about that particular topic and related topics.

Finally, like the Gestalt theorists, Tolman would say that extrinsic reinforcement is unnecessary for learning to take place. Learning, according to Tolman, occurs constantly. Students, like everyone else, are attempting to develop expectancies or beliefs that reliably conform to reality. The Tolmanian teacher aids students in formulating the testing hypotheses and provides confirming experiences when hypotheses are accurate. In this way students develop complex cognitive maps that guide their activities.

EVALUATION OF TOLMAN'S THEORY

Contributions

When we look for the contributions that Tolman made to the study of learning, it is tempting to seize a single finding or important study and explore its importance. The demonstration of latent learning by Tolman and Honzik (1930) is one such example. Another, the radial-maze experiment by Tolman, Ritchie, and Kalish (1946b), in which it was demonstrated that rats learn spatial relations rather than simple responses, has been identified as the predecessor of current studies in comparative cognition (Olton, 1992). Tolman's investigations of spatial learning and cognitive maps continue to guide research about spatial learning in both humans and nonhumans (Hamilton, Driscoll, & Sutherland, 2002; Martin, Walker, & Skinner, 2003). Tolman's greatest contributions, however, lie less in specific research findings and more in his role as an antagonist against the dominance of Hullian neobehaviorism. Although Hull and others dismissed challenges by Gestalt psychologists and by Piaget, pointing to differences in both the experimental subjects and the methodologies, they were not able to ignore the well-designed and controlled experiments conducted in Tolman's laboratories. Tolman believed in the rigorous methods of behaviorism, and he extended that rigor to molar behavior and to mental events. With respect to Tolman's treatment of mentalistic terms, Innis (1999) writes,

> Rather than get rid of them, he wanted to give them objective, operational definitions. In place of the sterile mathematics and empty organisms of his competitors, Tolman proposed a rich theoretical structure in which purpose and cognition played well-defined parts as potentially measurable intervening variables. For him, actions were infused with meaning; behavior was goal-directed—that is, motivated and purposive. However, adopting this view did not mean that it was impossible to develop mechanistic rules to account for the behavior observed. (p. 115)

Tolman may have lost many skirmishes with the S-R behaviorists, but with the current emphasis in psychology on the study of cognitive processes, his theory may end up winning the war. The many current theories that emphasize the learning of expectancies and claim that the function of reinforcement is to provide information rather than to strengthen behavior owe a great debt to Tolman's theory. As we discuss, Bolles's is one such theory. In the next chapter, we see that Albert Bandura's theory is another.

Criticisms

Scientific criticisms of Tolman's theory are certainly valid. The theory is not easily subjected to empirical scrutiny. It involves such a large number of independent, individual, and intervening variables that it is extremely difficult to account for all of them. Unfortunately for scientific critics, Tolman anticipated such criticisms and, as reflected in his (1959) statement on the preceding pages, did not seem to care. And he did have fun.

Malone (1991) raises the serious criticism that, with his extensive introduction of intervening variables, Tolman actually caused regression of psychology back into the mentalistic orientations of the nineteenth century rather than progression of psychology through the twentieth century. As evidence of this claim, Malone pointed to the lack of practical applications generated by Tolman's theory. Although lack of applicability may be a valid issue, the claim that Tolman's theory is regressive may not be. As we see in upcoming chapters, contemporary cognitive theories and neural networks may not have immediate applicability to practical problems, and they are often encumbered by intervening constructs. Categorizing them as regressive, however, would be incorrect.

DISCUSSION QUESTIONS

1. Why can Tolman's theory be considered a combination of Gestalt psychology and behaviorism?
2. What is purposive behaviorism?
3. Why is Tolman's theory called an S-S theory rather than an S-R theory?

4. Describe a situation that would allow you to determine whether an animal is utilizing a cognitive map to solve a problem. Do not use any of the specific studies discussed in this chapter.
5. For Tolman, is reinforcement a learning or a performance variable? Explain.
6. Describe briefly the six kinds of learning proposed by Tolman.
7. Summarize the study performed by Tolman and Honzik on latent learning. What conclusions can be drawn from their results?
8. Describe a typical latent extinction experiment, and explain why the phenomenon of latent extinction was thought to support Tolman's theory.
9. Describe, according to Tolman, what events take place as an animal is learning to solve a maze. Incorporate as many of Tolman's theoretical terms into your answer as possible.
10. What would characterize classroom procedures designed in accordance with Tolman's theory?
11. Give instances from your own personal life that would either support or refute Tolman's theory of learning.

CHAPTER HIGHLIGHTS

cathexis

cognitive dissonance

cognitive map

confirmation of an expectancy

demand

drive discriminations

emphasizer

equivalence beliefs

expectancy

field-cognition modes

field expectancies

hypotheses

latent extinction

latent learning

maintenance schedule

means-end readiness

molar behavior

motor patterns

place learning

principle of least effort

purposive behavior

purposive behaviorism

reinforcement expectancy

response learning

vicarious trial and error

CHAPTER 13

Albert Bandura

Albert Bandura was born on December 4, 1925, in Mundare, a small town in Alberta, Canada. He obtained his B.A. from the University of British Columbia and his M.A. in 1951 and his Ph.D. in 1952, both from the University of Iowa. He did a postdoctoral internship at the Wichita Guidance Center in 1953 and then joined the faculty at Stanford University, where he has been ever since, except for the 1969–1970 year, when he was a fellow at the Center for the Advanced Study in the Behavioral Sciences. Bandura is currently the David Starr Jordan Professor of Social Science in Psychology at Stanford University.

Among Bandura's many honors are a Guggenheim Fellowship, 1972; a Distinguished Scientist Award from Division 12 of the American Psychological Association, 1972; a Distinguished Scientific Achievement Award from the California Psychological Association, 1973; presidency of the American Psychological Association, 1974; the James McKeen Cattell Award, 1977; the James McKeen Cattell Fellow Award from the American Psychological Society, 2003–2004; and the Gold Medal Award for Life Achievement in the Science of Psychology from the American Psychological Foundation, 2006. In addition, Bandura holds office in several scientific societies and is a member of the editorial boards of seventeen scholarly journals.

Albert Bandura. (Courtesy of Albert Bandura.)

While at the University of Iowa, Bandura was influenced by Kenneth Spence, a prominent Hullian learning theorist, but Bandura's major interest was in clinical psychology. At this time, Bandura was interested in clarifying the notions thought to be involved in effective psychotherapy and then empirically testing and refining them. It was also during this time that Bandura read Miller and Dollard's (1941) book *Social Learning and Imitation,* which greatly influenced him. Miller and Dollard used Hullian learning theory (see Chapter 6) as the basis of their explanation of social and imitative behavior. As we see later in this chapter, Miller and Dollard's explanation of imitative learning dominated the psychological literature for more than two decades. It was not until the early 1960s that Bandura began a series of articles and books that were to challenge the older explanations of imitative learning and expand the topic into what is now referred to as observational learning. Bandura is now looked on as the leading researcher and theorist in the area of observational learning, a topic that is currently very popular.

EARLIER EXPLANATIONS
OF OBSERVATIONAL LEARNING

Thorndike's and Watson's Explanations of Observational Learning

The belief that humans learn by observing other humans goes back at least to such early Greeks as Plato and Aristotle. For them, education was, to a large extent, selecting the best models for presentation to students so that the model's qualities may be observed and emulated. Through the centuries, **observational learning** was taken for granted and usually explained by postulating a natural tendency for humans to imitate what they see others do. As long as this nativistic explanation prevailed, little was done either to verify the fact that the tendency to learn by observation was innate or, indeed, to determine whether observational learning occurred at all.

Edward L. Thorndike was the first to attempt to study observational learning experimentally. In 1898, he placed one cat in a puzzle box and another cat in an adjoining cage. The cat in the puzzle box had already learned how to escape, so the second cat had only to observe the first cat to learn the escape response. However, when Thorndike placed the second cat in the puzzle box, it did not perform the escape response. The second cat had to go through the same trial-and-error process that the first cat went through before it also learned the escape response. Thorndike ran the same type of experiment with chicks and dogs, with the same results. No matter how long a naive animal watched a sophisticated one, the naive animal seemed to learn nothing. In 1901, Thorndike ran similar experiments with monkeys, but contrary to the popular belief that "monkey see, monkey do," no observational learning took place. Thorndike (1901) concluded, "Nothing in my experience with these animals . . . favors the hypothesis that they have any general ability to learn to do things from seeing others do them" (p. 42).

In 1908, J. B. Watson replicated Thorndike's research with monkeys; he, too, found no evidence for observational learning. Both Thorndike and Watson concluded that learning can result only from **direct experience** and not from indirect or **vicarious experience.** In other words, they said that learning occurred as a result of one's personal interactions with the environment and not as a result of observing another's interactions.

With only a few exceptions, the work of Thorndike and Watson discouraged further research on observational learning. It was not until the publication of Miller and Dollard's *Social Learning and Imitation* (1941) that interest in observational learning was again stimulated.

Miller and Dollard's Explanation of Observational Learning

Like Thorndike and Watson, Miller and Dollard sought to challenge the nativistic explanation of observational learning. However, unlike Thorndike and Watson,

Miller and Dollard did not deny that an organism could learn by observing the activities of another organism. They felt that such learning was rather widespread but that it could be explained objectively within the framework of Hullian learning theory. That is, if **imitative behavior** is reinforced, it will be strengthened like any other kind of behavior. Thus, according to Miller and Dollard, imitative learning is simply a special case of instrumental conditioning. Miller and Dollard (1941) divided imitative behavior into three categories:

1. **Same behavior** occurs when two or more individuals respond to the same situation in the same way. For example, most people stop at a red light, applaud when a play or concert is over, and laugh when others laugh. With same behavior, all the individuals involved have learned independently to respond in a particular way to a particular stimulus, and their behavior is triggered simultaneously when that stimulus, or one like it, occurs in the environment.
2. **Copying behavior** involves the guiding of one person's behavior by another person, such as when an art instructor gives guidance and corrective feedback to an art student who is attempting to draw a picture. With copying behavior, the final "copied" response is reinforced and thereby strengthened.
3. In **matched-dependent behavior,** an observer is reinforced for blindly repeating the actions of a model. As an example, Miller and Dollard describe a situation in which an older child learned to run to the front door upon hearing his father's footsteps as the father approached the house, and the father reinforced the child's efforts with candy. A younger child found that if he happened to be running behind his brother when he ran to the door, he (the younger child) would also receive candy from the father. Soon the younger child learned to run to the door whenever he saw his older brother doing so. At this point, the behavior of both children was being maintained by reinforcement, but each boy associated reinforcement with different cues. For the older child, the sound of the father's approaching footsteps triggered the running response, which was reinforced by candy. For the younger child, the sight of his brother running toward the door triggered running on his part, which was also reinforced by candy. Matched-dependent behavior also seems to characterize the behavior of adults who are in an unfamiliar situation. When one is in a foreign country, for example, one may avoid many problems by observing how the natives respond to various situations and then responding as they do, even if the rationale for the behavior is not clearly understood. Perhaps this is the rationale behind the old saying, "When in Rome, do as the Romans do."

Miller and Dollard (1941) also pointed out that imitation itself could become a habit. In the situation described previously, the younger child could have learned that imitating the behavior of his older brother had often led to reinforcement; therefore, the probability of his acting like his older brother in a wide variety of situations would have increased. Miller and Dollard referred to this learned tendency to imitate the behavior of one or more individuals as **generalized imitation.**

Miller and Dollard (1941) saw nothing unusual or special about imitative learning. For them, the role of the model was to guide the observer's responses until the appropriate one had been made or to demonstrate to an observer which response would be reinforced in a given situation. According to Miller and Dollard, if imitative responses are not made and reinforced, no learning takes place. For them, imitative learning was the result of observation, overt responding, and reinforcement. Nothing in these conclusions disagrees with those reached by Thorndike and Watson. Like their predecessors, Miller and Dollard found that organisms do not learn from observation alone. Perhaps, Miller and Dollard might say that the only mistake that Thorndike and Watson made was not placing the naive animal inside the puzzle box with the sophisticated animal. This placement would have allowed the naive animal to observe, to respond, and to be reinforced, and therefore imitative learning probably would have occurred.

Unlike the nativistic explanations of imitative learning that prevailed for many centuries, Miller and Dollard's explanation offered the first empirical explanation of the phenomenon. Their explanation was in accordance with a widely accepted theory of learning and was firmly supported by rigorous experimental research.

As we saw earlier, the work of Thorndike and Watson had laid interest in imitative learning to rest for more than three decades. Miller and Dollard's work had the same effect for more than two decades. Not until the early 1960s was the topic again scrutinized. It was at this time that Bandura challenged earlier explanations of imitative learning and began to formulate his own theory, which broke away from the behavioristic mold of the preceding theories. Bandura viewed observational learning as primarily a cognitive process, which involves a number of attributes thought of as distinctly human, such as language, morality, thinking, and the self-regulation of one's behavior.

The Skinnerian Analysis of Observational Learning

The Skinnerian explanation of observational learning is very similar to Miller and Dollard's. First, a model's behavior is observed, next the observer matches the response of the model, and finally the matching response is reinforced. Furthermore, once learning has occurred in this fashion, it is maintained by some kind of schedule of reinforcement in the natural environment. Thus, according to the operant analysis of observational learning, the model's behavior acts as a discriminative stimulus indicating which actions will result in reinforcement. Imitation, then, is nothing more than a discriminative operant (see Chapter 5).

Nonhumans Can Learn by Observing

Recent research indicates that the analyses of Thorndike, Watson, Miller and Dollard, and Skinner were incomplete. These newer studies are surprising because the data suggest that, despite claims to the contrary, some nonhumans can acquire fairly complex learning by observing other members of their species, and they can do so without direct reinforcement. In a study conducted by Nicol and Pope (1993), observer chickens were first paired with "demonstrator" chickens. Each observer watched as her demonstrator learned to peck one of two operant keys for food. When the observers were tested in the operant chamber, they showed a significant tendency to peck the key that had been reinforced for their demonstrators. In a similar study, Akins and Zentall (1998) reported that Japanese quail imitate a specific reinforced response made by "demonstrator" quail (pecking versus stepping on a lever) but do not imitate nonreinforced responses. In a series of studies with laboratory rats, a team of British researchers (Heyes & Dawson, 1990; Heyes, Dawson, & Nokes, 1992) trained a group of demonstrator rats to push a lever to either the right or the left to earn food. Observer rats tested with the joystick-lever tended to press the lever in the same direction that their demonstrators did, even though presses in either direction were reinforced. Similar results using Japanese quail instead of rats were reported more recently (Akins, Klein, & Zentall, 2002).

Nonhumans can also learn about extinction by observing. Heyes, Jaldow, and Dawson (1993) first trained rats to press the joystick either to the left or to the right. Observers then watched as demonstrator rats experienced extinction. One group of rats, trained to press to the right, watched as similarly trained demonstrators experienced extinction of the right-pressing response. Another group of right-pressing observers watched left-pressing demonstrators during extinction. (In experimental control conditions, left-trained rats also watched as their demonstrators extinguished either the same-directional or different-directional pressing responses.) The animals that watched same-directional extinction produced fewer responses during extinction than did those animals that watched different-directional extinction, and both observation groups extinguished faster than rats that did not observe extinction in demonstrators.

Zentall (2003) suggests that observational learning in nonhumans is a complex phenomenon that is neither reflexive (instinctive) behavior nor simple imitation. For example, quail can perform an observed response even when there is a thirty-minute delay between observation and performance (Dorrance & Zentall, 2001). Thus, they are able to maintain some sort of cognitive representation of behavior performed by a demonstrator. Although observational learning has not been observed in all nonhuman species, it is a phenomenon requiring more consideration than was given by learning theory pioneers.

BANDURA'S EXPLANATION OF OBSERVATIONAL LEARNING

Up to this point, we have been using the terms *imitation* and *observational learning* interchangeably; however, for Bandura a distinction must be made between the two concepts. According to Bandura, observational learning may or may not involve imitation. For example, while driving down the street you may see the car in front of you hit a pothole, and based on this observation, you may swerve to miss the hole and avoid damage to your car. In this case, you learned from your observation, but you did not imitate what you had observed. What you learned, according to Bandura, was *information,* which was processed cognitively and acted on in a way that was advantageous. Observational learning, therefore, is much more complex than simple imitation, which usually involves mimicking another person's actions.

If we had to choose a theory of learning that is closest to Bandura's, it would be Tolman's theory. Although Tolman was a behaviorist, he used mentalistic concepts to explain behavioral phenomena (see Chapter 12), and Bandura does the same thing. Also, Tolman saw learning as a constant process that does not require reinforcement, and Bandura believes the same thing. Both Tolman's theory and Bandura's theory are cognitive in nature, and neither are **reinforcement theories.** A final point of agreement between Tolman and Bandura concerns the concept of motivation. Although Tolman believed that learning was constant, he further believed that the information gained through learning was acted on only when there was reason for doing so, such as when a need arose. For example, one may know full well where a drinking fountain is but act on that information only when thirsty. For Tolman, this distinction between learning and performance was extremely important, and it is also important in Bandura's theory.

Empirical Observations

The learning-performance distinction is nicely demonstrated in a study performed by Bandura (1965). In this experiment, children observed a film in which a **model** was shown hitting and kicking a large doll. In Bandura's theory, a model can be anything that conveys information, such as a person, film, television program, demonstration, picture, or instructions. In this case, a film showed an adult modeling aggressiveness. One group of children saw the model reinforced for his aggressiveness; a second group of children saw the model punished for his aggressiveness. For a third group, the consequences of the model's aggressiveness were neutral; that is, the model was neither reinforced nor punished. Later, children in all three groups were exposed to the doll, and their aggressiveness toward it was measured. As might be expected, the children who saw the model reinforced for aggressiveness were most aggressive; the children who saw the model punished for aggressiveness were least aggressive; and the children who saw the model experience neutral consequences were between the two other groups in their aggressiveness. This much of the study is interesting because it demonstrates that the children's behavior was influenced by indirect or vicarious experience. In other words, what they observed another person experiencing had an impact on their own behavior. The children in the first group observed **vicarious reinforcement,** and it facilitated their aggressiveness; children in the second group observed **vicarious punishment,** and it inhibited their aggressiveness. Although the children did not experience reinforcement or punishment directly, it modified their behavior just the same. This result is contrary to Miller and Dollard's contention that observational learning will occur only if the organism's *overt* behavior is followed by reinforcement.

The second phase of this study was designed to shed light on the learning-performance distinction. In this phase, *all* the children were offered an attractive incentive for reproducing the behavior of the model, *and they all did so.* In other words, all the children had *learned* the model's aggressive responses, but they had *performed* differentially, depending on whether they had observed the model being reinforced, punished, or experiencing neutral consequences. The results of this study are summarized in Figure 13–1.

Note the similarity between the Bandura (1965) experiment and the one run by Tolman and Honzik (1930). In the latter study, it was found that if a rat that ran a maze without **reinforcement** was suddenly given reinforcement for making the correct goal response, its **performance** rapidly equaled that of a rat that had been reinforced on every trial. Tolman's explanation was that even the nonreinforced rats were learning the maze, and inserting reinforcement into the situation merely caused them to demonstrate the information that they had been accumulating all along. Thus, the purpose of Bandura's experiment was similar to Tolman and Honzik's, and the findings and conclusions about the distinction between learning and performance were also similar. The major finding from both experiments was

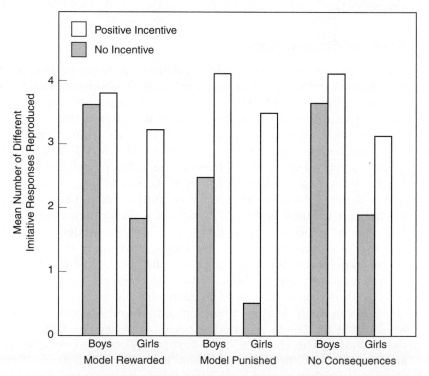

FIGURE 13–1 The influence of a positive incentive on the manifestation of responses learned by observation. (From "Influence of a Model's Reinforcement Contingencies on the Acquisition of Imitative Responses," by A. Bandura, 1965, *Journal of Personality and Social Psychology, 11,* p. 592. Copyright 1965 by the American Psychological Association. Reprinted by permission of the author.)

that reinforcement is a performance variable and not a learning variable. This, of course, is exactly opposite to the conclusion Hull reached about reinforcement. For him, reinforcement was a learning variable, not a performance variable.

Thus, Bandura disagrees sharply with Miller and Dollard's account of observational learning. For Bandura, observational learning occurs all the time. "After the capacity for observational learning has fully developed, one cannot keep people from learning what they have seen" (1977, p. 38). Also for Bandura, contrary to Miller and Dollard's contention, observational learning requires neither overt responding nor reinforcement.

Bandura finds several things incorrect about Skinner's and Miller and Dollard's explanation of observational learning. First, they do not explain how learning can occur when neither the models nor the observers are reinforced for their actions, which research has indicated is the case. Second, they do not explain **delayed modeling,** in which an observer exhibits learning that occurred from observations made at a much earlier time. Furthermore, the observer need not be reinforced for exhibiting this prior learning. Third, unlike Miller and Dollard and Skinner, who believe that reinforcement serves automatically and mechanically to strengthen behavior, Bandura (1977) believes that an observer must be aware of the reinforcement contingencies before they can have any effect: "Because learning by response consequences is largely a cognitive process, consequences generally produce little change in complex behavior when there is no awareness of what is being reinforced" (p. 18).

In short, Bandura maintains that all of the ingredients essential for an operant analysis of observational learning are missing; that is, there is often no discriminative stimulus, no overt responding, and no reinforcement.

MAJOR THEORETICAL CONCEPTS

To say that observational learning occurs independent of reinforcement is not to say that other variables do not affect it. Bandura (1986) lists four processes that influence observational learning.

Attentional Processes

Before something can be learned from a model, the model must be attended to. As was noted, Bandura thought learning to be an ongoing process, but he points out that only what is observed can be learned. Craighead, Kazdin, and Mahoney (1976) make this point in a rather humorous way:

> Suppose that you are holding a 4-year-old child on your lap while two other 4-year-olds play on separate areas of your living room floor and that, as child A gently pets your English sheepdog, child B inserts a butter knife into an electrical outlet. Everyone would learn something from this incident. Because it was directly associated with severe, unexpected pain and accompanying autonomic arousal, child B would learn to avoid using wall sockets as knife holders, and possibly, to stay away from electrical

outlets altogether. Child A might learn, or at least begin to learn, to avoid the sheepdog, or dogs in general. When child B suddenly screamed and cried, it startled child A, and since the occurrence of any strong, sudden, unexpected, and novel stimulus produces autonomic arousal, the harmless dog was associated with a strong, unconditioned response to a stressful stimulus. Depending upon the focus of his or her attention at the time, the child on your lap might later display avoidance of wall sockets (if he/she was watching child B), of dogs (if he/she was watching child A), or of you. Incidentally, since many of the principles of learning apply to both humans and animals, it is also possible that this sheepdog may subsequently try to avoid children. (p. 188)

So the question arises, what determines what is noticed? First, a person's sensory capacities will influence the **attentional processes.** Obviously, the modeling stimuli used to teach a blind or deaf person will need to be different from those used to teach a person with normal sight or hearing.

An observer's selective attention can be influenced by past reinforcements. For example, if prior activities learned through observation have proved functional in obtaining reinforcement, similar behaviors will be attended to in subsequent modeling situations. In other words, prior reinforcement can create a perceptual set in the observer that will influence future observations.

Various characteristics of models will also affect the extent to which they are attended to. Research has demonstrated that models will be attended to more often if they are similar to the observer (i.e., same sex, age, etc.), are respected, have high status, have demonstrated high competence, are thought of as powerful, and are attractive. In general, Bandura (1986) says, "[People] pay attention to models reputed to be effective and ignore those who, by appearance or reputation, are presumed to be ineffectual. . . . Given the choice, people are more likely to select models who are proficient at producing good outcomes than those who repeatedly get punished" (p. 54).

Retentional Processes

For information gained from observation to be useful, it must be retained. It is Bandura's contention that there are **retentional processes** in which information is stored symbolically in two ways, imaginally and verbally. The imaginally stored symbols are actual stored pictures of the modeled experience, which can be retrieved and acted on long after the observational learning has taken place. Here we have another point of agreement between Bandura's theory and Tolman's theory. Bandura says that behavior is at least partially determined by mental images of past experiences; Tolman said that much behavior is governed by a cognitive map, which is the mental representation of prior experiences in a given situation. The second, and for Bandura the more important, kind of symbolization is verbal:

> Most of the cognitive processes that regulate behavior are primarily conceptual rather than imaginal. Because of the extraordinary flexibility of verbal symbols, the intricacies and complexities of behavior can be conveniently captured in words. To take a simple example, the details of a route traveled by a model can be acquired, retained, and later performed more accurately by converting the visual information into a verbal code describing a series of right and left turns (e.g., RLRRL) than by reliance on visual imagery of the circuitous route, with its many irrelevant details. (1986, p. 58)

Although it is possible to discuss imaginal and verbal symbols separately, they are often inseparable when events are represented in memory. Bandura (1986) says,

> Although verbal symbols embody a major share of knowledge acquired by modeling, it is often difficult to separate representation modes. Representational activities usually involve both systems to some degree. . . . Words tend to evoke corresponding imagery, and images of events are often verbally cognized as well. When visual and verbal stimuli convey similar meanings, people integrate the information presented by these different modalities into a common conceptual representation. (p. 58)

Once information is stored cognitively, it can be retrieved covertly, rehearsed, and strengthened long after the observational learning has taken place. According to Bandura (1977), "It is the advanced capacity for symbolization that enables humans to learn much of their behavior by observation" (p. 25). These stored symbols make delayed modeling possible—that is, the ability to utilize information long after it has been observed.

Behavioral Production Processes

Behavioral production processes determine the extent to which that which has been learned is translated into performance. We may learn, by observing monkeys, how to swing from tree to tree by a tail, but we would be at a loss to replicate those behaviors without a tail. In other words, one may learn a great deal cognitively but be unable to translate that information into behavior for a variety of reasons; for example, the motor apparatus necessary to make certain responses may not be available because of one's maturational level, injury, or illness.

Bandura maintains that even if one is equipped with all the physical apparatus to make appropriate responses, a period of cognitive rehearsal is necessary before an observer's behavior can match that of a model. According to Bandura, the symbols retained from a modeling experience act as a template with which one's actions are compared. During this rehearsal process, individuals observe their own behavior and compare it with their cognitive representation of the modeled experience. Any observed discrepancies between one's own behavior and the memory of the model's behavior trigger corrective action. This process continues until there is an acceptable match between the observer's behavior and the model's behavior. Thus, the symbolic retention of a modeling experience creates a "feedback" loop that can be used to gradually match one's behavior with that of a model by utilizing self-observation and self-correction.

Motivational Processes

In Bandura's theory, reinforcement has two major functions. First, it creates an expectation in observers that if they act like a model who has been seen being reinforced for certain activities, they will be reinforced also. Second, it acts as an incentive for translating learning into performance. As we have seen, what has been learned observationally remains dormant until the observer has a reason to use the information. Both functions of reinforcement are *informational*. One function creates an expectancy in observers that if they act in a certain way in a certain situation, they are likely to be reinforced. The other function, the **motivational processes,** provides a motive for utilizing what has been learned.

This is a major departure from traditional reinforcement theories, which claim that only those responses that are overtly made and reinforced in a given situation are strengthened. According to Bandura, not only is reinforcement not necessary for learning to take place but also neither is direct experience. An observer can learn simply by observing the consequences of the behavior of others, storing that information symbolically, and utilizing it when it is advantageous to do so. Thus, for Bandura, *vicarious* reinforcement or punishment is as informative as direct reinforcement or punishment. In Bandura's theory, then, reinforcement and punishment are important but for much different reasons than they are for most reinforcement theorists. Most reinforcement theorists assume that reinforcement or punishment operates gradually, automatically, and usually without the awareness of the organism to strengthen or weaken an association between a stimulus and a response. For Bandura, however, learners gain information by observing either the consequences of their own behavior or of the behavior of others. The information gained by these observations can then be utilized in a variety of situations when a need to use it arises. Because actions, either one's own or someone else's, that bring about reinforcement or avoid punishment are especially functional, individuals will tend to observe and encode into memory those actions for future use. Armed with information gained by prior observations, individuals anticipate that if they act in certain ways in certain situations, certain consequences will follow. In this way, anticipated consequences at least partially determine behavior in any given situation. Nevertheless, anticipated *environmental* consequences are not the only determiners of behavior. Behavior is also partially influenced by anticipated *self-reactions,* which are determined by one's internalized standards of performance and conduct and by one's perceived self-efficacy. We have more to say about self-regulated behavior later in this chapter.

To summarize, we can say that observational learning involves attention, retention, behavioral abilities, and incentives. Therefore, if observational learning fails to occur, it could be that the observer did not observe the relevant activities of the model, did not retain them, was physically incapable of performing them, or did not have the proper incentive to perform them. Figure 13–2 summarizes the variables that Bandura feels influence observational learning.

Reciprocal Determinism

Perhaps the most basic question in all of psychology is "Why do people act as they do?" and depending on one's answer to this question, one can be classified as an environmentalist (empiricist), nativist, existentialist, or something else. Environmentalists (e.g., Skinner) said that behavior is a function of reinforcement contingencies in the environment, and therefore, if you change reinforcement contingencies, you change behavior. Nativists emphasize inherited dispositions, traits, or even ideas. Existentialists emphasize free choice; that is, people do more or less what they

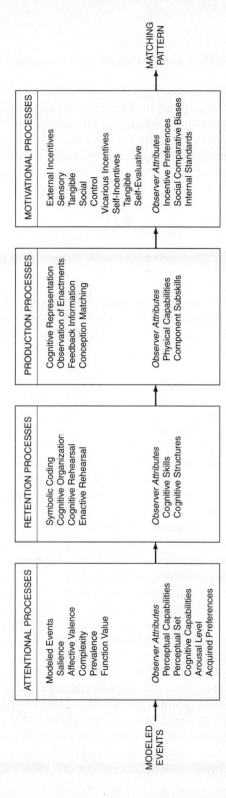

FIGURE 13–2 Summary of the various processes thought by Bandura to influence observational learning. BANDURA, ALBERT, *SOCIAL FOUNDATIONS OF THOUGHT & ACTION: A SOCIAL COGNITIVE THEORY*, 1st, © 1986. Electronically reproduced by permission of Pearson Education, In., Upper Saddle River, New Jersey.

choose to do. Thus most of the traditional answers to this question claim that behavior is a function of the environment, of certain traits or dispositions, or of the freedom that humans possess.

Bandura's answer to the question falls into the "something else" category. His answer is that the person, the environment, and the person's behavior itself all interact to produce the person's subsequent behavior. In other words, none of the three components can be understood in isolation from the others as a determiner of human behavior. Bandura (1986, p. 24) summarizes this three-way interaction as follows:

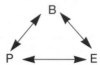

where P is the person, E is the environment, and B is the person's behavior. This position is referred to as **reciprocal determinism.** One deduction from this concept is that it is as valid to say that behavior influences the person and the environment as it is to say that the environment or the person influences behavior.

As an example of behavior influencing the environment, Bandura (1977, p. 196) describes an experiment in which a shock is scheduled to be delivered to a rat every minute unless it presses a bar, in which case the shock is delayed for thirty seconds. Those rats learning to press the bar with a certain frequency can avoid shock completely; those rats who fail to learn the response must go on experiencing periodic shocks. Bandura (1977) concludes, "Though the **potential environment** is identical for all animals, the **actual environment** depends upon their behavior. Is the animal controlling the environment or is the environment controlling the animal? What we have here is a two-way regulatory system in which the organism appears either as an object or an agent of control, depending upon which side of the reciprocal process one chooses to examine" (p. 196).

Bandura maintains that reinforcements, like punishments, exist only potentially in the environment and are actualized only by certain behavior patterns. Therefore, which aspects of an environment influence us are determined by how we act on that environment. Bandura (1977) goes further by saying that behavior can also *create* environments: "We are all acquainted with problem-prone individuals who, through their obnoxious conduct, predictably breed negative social climates wherever they go. Others are equally skilled at bringing out the best in those with whom they interact" (p. 197).

Thus, according to Bandura, people can influence the environment by acting in certain ways, and the changed environment will, in turn, influence their subsequent behavior. But Bandura points out that even though there is an interaction among people, the environment, and behavior, any of these components may be more influential than the others at any given time. For example, a loud noise in the environment may momentarily have more of an effect on a person's behavior than anything else. At other times, one's beliefs may be the most influential determiner of one's actions. In fact, many studies have shown that the behavior of humans is governed more by what they believe is going on than by what really is going on. For example, Kaufman, Baron, and Kopp (1966) ran a study in which all subjects were reinforced about once every minute (variable-interval schedule) for performing a manual response. Although all the subjects were *actually* on the same schedule of reinforcement, some were misled about their schedules. One group was told the truth about the schedule, another group was told that their behavior would be reinforced every minute (fixed-interval schedule), and a third group was told they would be reinforced after they had made on the average of 150 responses (variable-ratio schedule). Those subjects who believed they were on a fixed-interval schedule responded very slowly, those believing they were on a variable-ratio schedule responded very rapidly, and those who were told the truth about being on a variable-interval schedule responded with a rate between the other two groups. On the basis of this and similar studies, Bandura (1977) concludes, "Beliefs about the prevailing conditions of reinforcement outweighed the influence of experienced consequences" (p. 166).

Undoubtedly, it is best to have one's beliefs correspond to reality. In the experiment just summarized, the participants were misinformed, and they believed and acted on the misinformation. Many factors in everyday life can create non-adaptive beliefs in individuals, which can lead to ineffective or even bizarre actions. We consider these factors when we consider faulty cognitive processes later in the chapter.

To summarize, Bandura's concept of reciprocal determinism states that behavior, the environment, and people (and their beliefs) all interact and that this three-way interaction must be understood before we can understand human psychological functioning and behavior.

Self-Regulation of Behavior

According to Bandura (1977), "If actions were determined solely by external rewards and punishments, people would behave like weathervanes, constantly shifting in different directions to conform to the momentary influences impinging upon them. They would act corruptly with unprincipled individuals and honorably with righteous ones, and liberally with libertarians and dogmatically with authoritarians" (p. 128). The situation described in this quotation is obviously not the case, but if external reinforcers and punishers do not control behavior, what does? Bandura's answer is that human behavior is largely **self-regulated behavior.** Among the things that humans learn from direct or vicarious experience are **performance standards,** and once these standards are learned, they become the basis of self-evaluation. If a person's performance in a given situation meets or exceeds that person's standards, it is evaluated positively; if it falls short, it is evaluated negatively.

One's standards can arise from direct experience with reinforcement by placing a high value on behaviors that have been effective in bringing praise from the relevant individuals in one's life, such as one's parents. Personal standards can also develop vicariously by observing those behaviors for which others have been reinforced. For example, Bandura and Kupers (1964) found that children who were exposed to models who set high performance standards reinforced themselves only for superior performance, and children who were exposed to models who reinforced themselves for minimal performances also reinforced themselves for minimal performances.

Bandura (1977, p. 107) believes that the intrinsic reinforcement that comes from self-evaluation is much more influential than the extrinsic reinforcement dispensed by others. He gives several examples of cases in which extrinsic reinforcement for engaging in activities has *reduced* the motivation to engage in them. After reviewing a great deal of research on the relative effectiveness of extrinsic (externally administered) versus intrinsic (self-administered) reinforcement, Bandura concludes, "self-rewarded behavior tends to be maintained more effectively than if it has been externally reinforced" (p. 144).

Unfortunately, if one's standards of performance are too high, they can be a source of personal distress. Bandura (1977) says, "In its more extreme forms, harsh standards for self-evaluation give rise to depressive reactions, chronic discouragement, feelings of worthlessness, and lack of purposefulness" (p. 141). According to Bandura, working at goals that are too distant or too difficult can be disappointing: "Subgoals of moderate difficulty are therefore likely to be most motivating and satisfying" (p. 162).

Like internalized performance standards, **perceived self-efficacy** plays a major role in self-regulated behavior. Perceived self-efficacy refers to one's beliefs concerning what one is capable of doing, and it arises from a variety of sources, including personal accomplishments and failures, seeing others who are seen as similar to oneself succeed or fail at various tasks, and verbal persuasion. Verbal persuasion may temporarily convince people that they should try or avoid some task, but in the final analysis, one's direct or vicarious experience with success and failure will most strongly influence one's perceived self-efficacy. For example, a coach may fire up the team before a game by telling players how great they are, but the enthusiasm will be short-lived if the opposing team is clearly superior.

Persons with high perceived self-efficacy try more, accomplish more, and persist longer at a task than those with low perceived self-efficacy. The former also tend to experience less fear and less shame than the latter (Covert, Tangney, Maddux, & Heleno, 2003). Bandura (1980b) speculates that because people with high perceived self-efficacy tend to have more control over the events in their environment, they therefore experience less uncertainty. Because individuals tend to fear events over which they have no control and therefore are uncertain of, those individuals with high perceived self-efficacy tend to experience less fear.

One's *perceived* self-efficacy may or may not correspond to one's **real self-efficacy.** People may believe their self-efficacy is low when in reality it is high, and vice versa. The situation is best when one's aspirations are in line with one's capabilities. On the one hand, people who continually attempt to do things beyond their capabilities experience frustration and despair and may eventually give up on almost everything. On the other hand, if people with high self-efficacy do not adequately challenge themselves, their personal growth may be inhibited.

After reviewing nearly twenty years of research on perceived self-efficacy across many age groups and in both laboratory and real-world settings, Bandura and Locke (2003) say:

> Efficacy beliefs predict not only the behavioral functioning between individuals at different levels of perceived self-efficacy but also changes in functioning in individuals at different levels of efficacy over time and even variation within the same individual in the tasks performed and those shunned or attempted but failed. (pp. 87–88)

Moral Conduct

Like one's performance standards and one's perceived self-efficacy, one's **moral code** develops through interactions with models. In the case of morality, the parents usually model the moral rules and regulations that are ultimately internalized by the child. Once internalized, one's moral code determines which behaviors (or thoughts) are sanctioned and which are not. Departure from one's moral code brings **self-contempt,** which is not a pleasant experience, and thus one typically acts in accordance with one's moral code. Bandura (1977) says, "The anticipation of self-reproach for conduct that violates one's standards provides a source of motivation to keep behavior in line with standards in the face of opposing inducements. There is no more devastating punishment than self-contempt" (p. 154).

Bandura states his opposition to stage theories (e.g., Piaget and Kohlberg) and trait theories (e.g., Allport) rather forcefully. His primary reason for this opposition is that such theories predict a stability in human behavior that Bandura feels does not exist. Stage theories, for example, predict that a person's intellectual or moral capabilities are set by maturation, and therefore, those intellectual or moral judgments one can make are set by one's age. The same is true for type or trait theories, which say that people will act consistently in a wide range of situations because they are certain types of people or because they possess certain traits. Bandura maintains that human behavior is not all that consistent. Rather, he says, it is more circumstantial. In other words, Bandura believes that human behavior is determined more by the situation one is in and by one's interpretation of that situation than it is by one's stage of development, by one's traits, or by the type of person one is.

There is no better example of the situational nature of behavior than the topic of morality. Even though one has firm moral principles, there are several mechanisms that can be used to dissociate reprehensible acts from self-sanctions. These mechanisms make it possible for people to depart radically from their moral principles without experiencing self-contempt (Bandura, 1986, pp. 375–385):

1. Moral Justification In **moral justification,** one's otherwise reprehensible behavior becomes a means to a higher purpose and therefore is justifiable. "I committed the crime so that I could provide food for my family." Bandura gives another example:

> Radical shifts in destructive behavior through moral justification are most strikingly revealed in military training. People who have been taught to deplore killing as morally condemnable can be transformed rapidly into skilled combatants, who feel little

compunction and even a sense of pride in taking human life. . . . In justifying warfare, one sees oneself fighting ruthless oppressors who have an unquenchable appetite for conquest, protecting one's way of life, preserving world peace, saving humanity from being subjugated to an evil ideology, and honoring the country's international commitments. Such restructuring of circumstances is designed to get even considerate people to regard violent means as morally justifiable to achieve humane ends. (p. 376)

2. Euphemistic Labeling   By calling an otherwise reprehensible act something other than what it really is, one can engage in that act without self-contempt. For example, nonaggressive individuals are far more likely to be aggressive toward another person when doing so is called a game. Bandura gives other examples of how **euphemistic labeling** is used to make the reprehensible respectable: "Through the power of hygienic words, even killing a human being loses much of its repugnancy. Soldiers 'waste' people rather than kill them. . . . When mercenaries speak of 'fulfilling a contract,' murder is transformed by admirable words into the honorable discharge of duty" (p. 378).

3. Advantageous Comparison   By comparing one's self-deplored acts with even more heinous acts, one's own reprehensible acts look trifling by **advantageous comparison:** "Sure I did that, but look at what he did." Bandura offers examples:

Promoters of the Vietnamese War and their supporters . . . minimized the slaying of countless people as a way of checking massive communist enslavement. Given the trifling comparison, perpetrators of warfare remained unperturbed by the fact that the intended beneficiaries were being killed at an alarming rate. Domestic protesters, on the other hand, characterized their own violence against educational and political institutions as trifling, or even laudable, by comparing it with the carnage perpetrated by their country's military forces in foreign lands. (p. 379)

4. Displacement of Responsibility   Through **displacement of responsibility,** some people can readily depart from their moral principles if they feel a recognized authority sanctions their behavior and takes responsibility for it: "I did it, because I was ordered to do so." Bandura says, "Nazi prison commandants and their staffs felt little personal responsibility for their unprecedented inhumanities. They were simply carrying out orders. Impersonal obedience to horrific orders was similarly evident in military atrocities, such as the My Lai massacre" (p. 379).

5. Diffusion of Responsibility   A decision to act in a reprehensible manner that is made by a group is easier to live with than an individual decision. Where everyone is responsible—that is, when there is **diffusion of responsibility**—no single individual feels responsible.

6. Disregard or Distortion of Consequences   In **disregard or distortion of consequences,** people ignore or distort the harm caused by their conduct, and therefore, there is no need to experience self-contempt. The further people remove themselves from the ill effects of their immoral behavior, the less pressure there is to censure it. "I just let the bombs go and they disappeared in the clouds."

7. *Dehumanization* If some individuals are looked on as subhuman, they can be treated inhumanly without experiencing self-contempt. Once a person or a group has been **dehumanized,** the members no longer possess feelings, hopes, and concerns, and they can be mistreated without risking self-condemnation: "Why not take their land, they are nothing but savages without souls."

8. *Attribution of Blame* One can always choose something that a victim said or did and claim that it caused one to act in a reprehensible way. Bandura gives an example of the **attribution of blame:** "Rapists and males who acknowledge a proclivity to rape subscribe to myths about rape embodying the various mechanisms by which moral self-censure can be disengaged. . . . These beliefs hold rape victims responsible for their own victimization because they have supposedly invited rape by sexually provocative appearance and behavior and by resisting sexual assault weakly" (pp. 384–385).

Bandura (1977) attributes most misconduct to these dissociative mechanisms rather than to faulty moral codes: "Because internalized controls are subject to dissociative operations, marked changes in people's moral conduct can be achieved without altering their personality structures, moral principles, or self-evaluative systems. It is self-exonerative processes rather than character flaws that account for most inhumanities" (p. 158).

Determinism versus Freedom

Does the fact that much behavior is self-regulated mean that humans are free to do whatever they choose? Bandura (1986, p. 42) defines **freedom** in terms of the number of options available to people and their opportunities to exercise them. According to Bandura, constraints to personal freedom include incompetence, unwarranted fears, excessive self-censure, and social inhibitors such as discrimination and prejudice. Bandura (1989) elaborates:

> Given the same environmental conditions, persons who have developed skills for accomplishing many options and are adept at regulating their own motivation and behavior are more successful in their pursuits than those who have limited means of personal agency. It is because self-influence operates deterministically on action that some measure of self-directedness and freedom is possible. (p. 1182)

Thus, in the same physical environment, some individuals are freer than others. As we discuss, another constraint on personal freedom could be faulty cognitive processes, which may prevent people from interacting effectively with their environments.

FAULTY COGNITIVE PROCESSES

Bandura places great importance on cognitive processes in the determination of human behavior. We have seen how one's internalized performance standards, perceived self-efficacy, and moral codes play a major role in the self-regulation of behavior.

Further evidence for the influence of cognitive processes comes from the fact that we can *imagine* ourselves into almost any emotional state we wish. We can make ourselves nauseated, angry, peaceful, or sexually aroused simply by conjuring up appropriate thoughts. Thus, according to Bandura, behavior can be strongly influenced by one's own imagination.

Because one's behavior is at least partially determined by one's cognitive processes, it follows that if these processes do not accurately reflect reality, maladaptive behavior can result. Bandura gives several reasons for the development of **faulty cognitive processes.** First, children may develop false beliefs because they tend to evaluate things on the basis of appearance; they conclude that a tall, narrow beaker contains more water than a short, wider beaker because for them "taller" means "bigger." Piaget would say that a child reaching this conclusion has not learned the principle of conservation. Second, errors in thought can occur when information is derived from insufficient evidence. Bandura (1977) gives the following example: "Learning from the images conveyed by the mass media is a good case in point. People partly form impressions of the social realities with which they have little or no contact from televised representations of society. Because the world of television is heavily populated with villainous and unscrupulous characters it can distort knowledge about the real world" (p. 184). According to Bandura (1973), this distorted view of reality can sometimes result in criminal behavior: "Children have been apprehended for writing bad checks to obtain money for candy, for sniping at strangers with BB guns, for sending threatening letters to teachers and for injurious switchblade fights after witnessing similar performances on television" (pp. 101–102).

Bandura (1977) says that once false beliefs are established, they become self-perpetuating because those holding them seek out individuals or groups who share the same false beliefs. "The various cults and messianic groups that emerge from time to time typify this process" (p. 185). Furthermore, once false beliefs are established, they can be self-fulfilling prophecies. For example, if people believe that they are stupid, they will seek experiences and engage in activities that support their belief.

Third, fallacies in thinking can arise from faulty information processing. For example, someone who believes that all farmers lack intelligence would necessarily conclude that any particular farmer lacks intelligence. This deduction is false because the premise (belief) is false, but Bandura points out that one can also make erroneous deductions from correct information. In other words, even if people possess accurate information, their deductions may be faulty. An example would be correctly observing that unemployment is higher among black individuals than it is among white individuals but erroneously concluding from this fact that black individuals are less motivated than white individuals.

In some cases, faulty beliefs can cause bizarre behavior, such as when one's life is directed by the belief that one is "God." Also phobias can trigger extreme defensive behaviors, such as people who refuse to leave home because they are too frightened of dogs. In this case, the fact that most dogs do not bite can never be realized because these people never encounter dogs. What these phobics need, according to

Bandura, are "powerful disconfirming experiences," which will force them to change their expectations of how dogs behave. How observational learning is used to treat phobics is covered in the next section.

PRACTICAL APPLICATIONS OF OBSERVATIONAL LEARNING

What Modeling Can Accomplish

Modeling has several kinds of effects on observers. New responses may be acquired by watching a model being reinforced for certain actions. Thus, the **acquisition** of behavior results from vicarious reinforcement. A response that otherwise might be readily made in a situation is inhibited when a model is seen being punished for making that response. Thus response **inhibition** results from vicarious punishment. Seeing a model engage in a feared activity without experiencing any ill effects can reduce inhibitions in the observer. The reduction of fear that results from observing a model's unpunished participation in the feared activity is called **disinhibition.** A model may also elicit from an observer a response that has already been learned and for which there is no inhibition. In this case, by performing a response, the model simply increases the likelihood that the observer will make a similar response. This is called **facilitation.** Modeling can also stimulate **creativity,** which can be accomplished by exposing observers to a variety of models that cause the observer to adopt combinations of characteristics or styles. Bandura (1977) says,

> The progression of creative careers through distinct periods provides notable examples of this process. In his earlier works, Beethoven adopted the classical forms of Haydn and Mozart. . . . Wagner fused Beethoven's symphonic mode with Weber's naturalistic enchantment and Meyerbeer's dramatic virtuosity to evolve a new operatic form. Innovators in other endeavors in the same manner initially draw upon the contributions of others and build from their experiences something new. (p. 48)

Innovation can also be stimulated more directly by modeling unconventional responses to common situations. In this case, observers may already possess strategies that are effective in solving a problem, but the model teaches bolder, more unconventional problem-solving strategies.

With the possible exception of modeled creativity, the use of modeling to convey information has been criticized for stimulating only a response mimicry or imitation. That this is not the case is clearly demonstrated by **abstract modeling,** in which people observe models performing various responses that have a common rule or principle. For example, the models could solve problems by using a certain strategy or generate sentences that embody a certain grammatical style. Under these circumstances, observers typically learn whatever rule or principle is being exemplified in the diverse modeling experiences. After the observer learns the rule or principle, it can be applied to situations unlike any involved during the modeling. For example, once a problem-solving strategy is extracted from a number of modeling experiences, it can be used to solve problems that are different from anything experienced before. Thus abstract modeling has three components: (1) observing a wide variety of situations that have a rule or principle in common, (2) extracting the rule or principle from the diverse experiences, and (3) utilizing the rule or principle in new situations.

Because humans constantly encounter a wide variety of modeling experiences, it seems safe to conclude that most of the principles and rules that govern human behavior are derived from something like abstract modeling. Bandura (1977) says, "On the basis of observationally derived rules, people learn, among other things, judgmental orientations, linguistic styles, conceptual schemes, information-processing strategies, cognitive operations, and standards of conduct" (p. 42).

Inhibition, disinhibition, and facilitation all increase or decrease the probability of making a response that has already been learned. Acquisition, creativity, and rule or principle extraction involve the development of new learning through modeling.

In addition to acquisition, inhibition, disinhibition, facilitation, rule or principle extraction, and creativity, modeling has also been used to influence observers' moral judgments and their emotional responses. In fact, according to Bandura (1977, p. 12), *anything that can be learned from direct experience can also be learned by indirect or vicarious experience.* Furthermore, it can be learned more efficiently through modeling because much of the trial-and-error process involved in learning by direct experience is eliminated: "Observational learning is vital for both development and survival. Because mistakes can produce costly, or even fatal consequences, the prospects for survival would be slim indeed if one could learn only by suffering the consequences of trial and error. . . . The more costly and hazardous the possible mistakes, the heavier is the reliance on observational learning from competent examples" (p. 12).

Modeling in the Clinical Setting

According to Bandura, psychopathology results from dysfunctional learning, which causes incorrect anticipations about the world. The job of the psychotherapist is to provide experiences that will disconfirm erroneous expectations and replace them with more accurate and less disabling ones. Bandura has little patience with those psychotherapists who look for "insights" or "unconscious motivations" in their clients. Bandura (1977) feels that the clients of these therapists are used to confirm the therapists' own belief systems.

> Advocates of different theoretical orientations repeatedly discover their chosen motivators at work but rarely find evidence for the motivators emphasized by the proponents of competing views. In fact, if one wanted to predict the types of insights and unconscious motivators that persons are apt to discover in themselves in the course of such analyses, it would be more helpful to know the therapists' conceptual belief system than the clients' actual psychological status. (p. 5)

Bandura and his colleagues have run a number of studies to test the effectiveness of modeling in treating several psychological disorders. For example, Bandura,

Grusec, and Menlove (1967) showed children who had a strong fear of dogs a peer interacting fearlessly with a dog. The fear-provoking character of the model's behavior was gradually increased from session to session by relaxing the physical constraints on the dog and by varying the directness of the model's interactions with it. A control group of phobic children did not have the modeling experience. The approach behavior of all the children was measured for both the dog actually involved in the experiment and for an unfamiliar dog. Measures were taken immediately after treatment and one month later. Approach scores were determined by a graded sequence of interactions with the dogs; that is, children were asked to approach and pet the dogs, release them from their pen, take their leashes off, and finally spend time with the dogs in their pen. The children who had seen a peer model interact fearlessly with a dog were capable of significantly more approach responses than children in the control group. In fact, two-thirds of the children in the treatment group were able to remain alone with the dog in its pen, whereas none of the children in the control group could do so. The effects of treatment also generalized to the unfamiliar dog, and the effects were still present one month after the experiment.

It can be seen from this study that not only can new responses be learned by observing the consequences of models' behavior but also responses can be extinguished in the same way. Thus, **vicarious extinction** is as important as vicarious reinforcement in Bandura's theory. In this study, vicarious extinction was used to reduce or eliminate the avoidance response to dogs and thereby disinhibit the approach response to dogs.

In another study, Bandura and Menlove (1968) had three groups of children with dog phobias watch a series of films under three different conditions: **single modeling,** in which children saw a model interact with a single dog with increased intimacy; **multiple modeling,** in which children saw a variety of models interacting fearlessly with a number of dogs; and a *control condition,* in which children saw movies involving no dogs. Again, as in the 1967 study, the willingness of the children to approach the dog was measured. Both single and multiple modeling significantly reduced the children's fear of dogs, as compared with children in the control group, but only the children in the multiple-modeling group had their fear reduced to the point where they were able to be left alone with the dog in its pen. Again the effects of treatment generalized to other dogs and endured one month after the experiment. Comparing the results of this study with those of the 1967 study, Bandura concluded that although both **direct modeling** (seeing a live model) and **symbolic modeling** (seeing a model in a film) are both effective in reducing fears, direct modeling appeared to be more effective. However, the apparent reduced effectiveness of symbolic modeling was overcome by showing a variety of models instead of just one.

In the final study to be considered, Bandura, Blanchard, and Ritter (1969) compared the effectiveness of symbolic modeling, modeling with participation, and desensitization as techniques in treating a phobia. In this study, adults and adolescents with a snake phobia were divided into four groups. Group 1 (symbolic modeling) was exposed to a film showing children, adolescents, and adults interacting with a large snake. The scenes were graduated, showing increased interaction with the snake. Subjects in this group were trained in relaxation techniques and could stop the film whenever they became too anxious. When relaxed enough, they started the film again. Each subject continued in this manner until he or she could watch the film without anxiety. Group 2 (**modeling-participation**) watched a model handle a snake and then were helped by the model to actually come in contact with the snake. The model would first touch the snake and help the observer to do so also; then the model would stroke the snake and encourage the observer to do like-wise. This process continued until the observer could hold the snake in his or her lap without assistance. Group 3 received **desensitization therapy,** which consisted of asking subjects to imagine anxiety-provoking scenes with snakes, starting with imag-inary scenes that caused little anxiety and slowly progressing to imaginary scenes that caused great anxiety. Subjects were asked to continue imagining each scene until it no longer made them anxious. Group 4 received no treatment of any kind. The results of the study indicated that all three treatment conditions were effective in reducing the fear of snakes but that the modeling-participation method was by far the most effective (see Figure 13–3).

In fact, Bandura, Blanchard, and Ritter isolated all of the subjects who were unable to achieve the ability to hold the snake in their lap (including the control subjects) and used the modeling-participation method. In just a few sessions, each subject was able to hold the snake in his or her lap. Follow-up research indicated

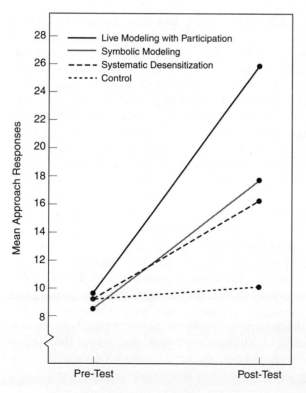

FIGURE 13–3   The tendency to approach a snake before and after various kinds of therapeutic treatments. (From "Relative Efficacy of Modeling Therapeutic Changes," by A. Bandura, E. B. Blanchard, & B. J. Ritter, 1969, *Journal of Personality and Social Psychology, 13,* p. 183. Copyright 1969 by the American Psychological Association. Reprinted by permission of the publisher and author.)

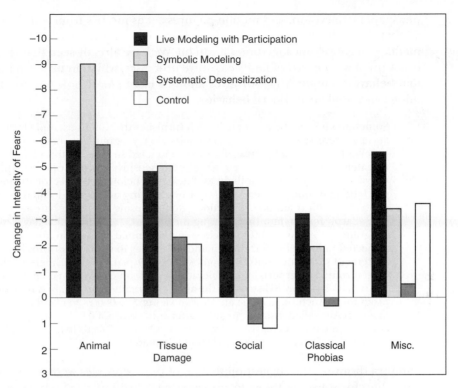

FIGURE 13–4 The generalized effects of various kinds of therapeutic treatments on the intensity of fears other than the one specifically treated. The higher the minus score, the greater the difference in the intensity of fear before and after treatment. (From "Relative Efficacy of Modeling Therapeutic Changes," by A. Bandura, E. B. Blanchard, & B. J. Ritter, 1969, *Journal of Personality and Social Psychology, 13,* p. 186. Copyright 1969 by the American Psychological Association. Reprinted by permission of the publisher and author.)

that not only did the effects of treatment endure but also they generalized to other phobias that had existed prior to the experiment. Bandura and his associates used a questionnaire to measure the magnitude of various fears before and after the experiment. The change in the magnitude of these fears as a function of the various treatment conditions is shown in Figure 13–4.

THE INFLUENCE OF THE NEWS
AND ENTERTAINMENT MEDIA

As we have seen, Bandura believes that we can learn as much from vicarious experiences as from observing the consequences of our behavior. We have also seen that Bandura defines a model as anything that conveys information. It follows, then, that newspapers, television, and motion pictures act as models from which we can learn a great deal. Of course, not everything learned from the news and entertainment media is negative, but sometimes it can be. We have already seen that television can cause the development of faulty cognitive processes, which in turn can lead to criminal behavior. Bandura (1986) gives another example of how television programming can stimulate antisocial behavior:

> Sometimes it is the fictional media that furnishes the salient example for the spread of an aggressive style of conduct. The television program *Doomsday Flight* provides an excellent illustration because of its novel modeled strategy. In this plot, an extortionist threatens airline officials that an altitude-sensitive bomb will be exploded on a transcontinental airliner in flight as it descends below 5,000 feet for its landing. In the end, the pilot outwits the extortionist by selecting an airport located at an elevation above the critical altitude. Extortion attempts using the same barometric-bomb plot rose sharply for two months following the telecast. . . . Moreover, a day or two after the program was rerun in different cities in the United States and abroad, airlines were subjected to further extortion demands of money to get the extortionists to reveal the placement of altitude-sensitive bombs allegedly planted in airliners in flight. Planes were rerouted to airports at high elevations, and some extortion demands were paid by airline officials, only to learn that the airliner contained no bomb. A rebroadcast of the program in Anchorage made an Alaskan viewer $25,000 richer, and a rerun in Sydney made an Australian instantly wealthy, after collecting $560,000 from Qantas. He added considerable force to his threat by directing Qantas officials to an airport locker where he had placed a sample barometric bomb he had built. (p. 173)

Bandura dismisses the suggestion that all of these episodes were mere coincidence and, therefore, had nothing to do with the television program *Doomsday Flight*. According to Bandura, the novelty of the strategy used for extortion and the timing of the episodes so soon after the program seem to preclude chance as an explanation.

In general, Bandura (1986) reaches the following conclusion concerning violence in fictional television: "Analyses of televised programs reveal that violent conduct is portrayed, for the most part, as permissible, successful, and relatively clean. . . . Witnesses to the violence in the dramatic presentations are more likely to approve of such behavior or to join in the assaults rather than to seek alternative solutions. Violence not only is shown to pay off but is readily used by superheroes, who dispose of their adversaries in a quick, perfunctory way as though slaying human beings was of no great concern" (p. 292).

As we have just seen, violence portrayed on fictional television can encourage violence in some viewers, but what about nonfictional television? According to Bandura (1986), nonfictional television, too, can encourage violence:

> There are several ways in which newscasts of violence can serve as an instrument of influence. . . . If televised reports convey detailed information about acts and strategies of aggression, they can contribute to the spread of the very methods they report through the instruction they provide. In addition, media reports of violent episodes can influence restraints over aggression by how the consequences are portrayed. Because each point in audience ratings means millions of dollars in advertising

revenue, the visual displays accompanying news reports are selected to attract and hold viewers, as well as to inform. The outcomes of aggression, especially collective actions, are easily misrepresented when dramatic pictorials are favored over less interesting but important consequences. Thus, showing people running off with appliances and liquor from looted stores during an urban riot is more likely to promote aggression in viewers living under similar circumstances than showing the terror and suffering caused by the massive destruction of one's neighborhood. (p. 292)

Pornographic Movies   Clearly not everyone exposed to violence on television or in the newspapers becomes violent. Similarly, not everyone exposed to sexually explicit literature or movies becomes a sexual deviant. In fact, erotic material has been used successfully to treat individuals with sexual problems. Bandura (1986) says, "Sexual modeling has been shown to have long-term effects when used for therapeutic purposes with persons suffering from sexual anxieties and dysfunctions . . . modeling of mutual pleasure alleviates sex anxieties, creates more favorable attitudes toward sex, and sparks inactive sex lives" (p. 294).

In the case of pornography, however, sexual aggression toward women is often modeled, and such modeling can stimulate similar behavior in some viewers. Bandura (1986) explains,

> Content analyses reveal an increase in abusive behavior toward women in pornographic depictions. . . . Research has added to our understanding of how violent erotica affects viewers. Males exposed to modeled sexual assault behave more punitively toward women than if exposed to modeled sexual intimacy devoid of aggressions. . . . Violent erotica often depicts women initially resisting but eventually relishing being raped. Such portrayals reinforce rape myths and weaken restraints over harshness toward women by indicating they enjoy being manhandled. Depictions of rape as pleasurable to women heighten punitiveness toward women regardless of whether males are angry or not. (pp. 294–295)

Although "humane living requires reducing social influences that promote cruelty and destructiveness" and "society has the right to regulate obscene materials that can cause harm" (Bandura, 1986, p. 296), the recognition and control of such influences and materials are complex matters. First, there is widespread disagreement over what is harmful and what is not. Second, there is concern that suppression of one form of expression (e.g., sexual expression) may threaten other forms of expression. Obviously, this is not a matter that will be resolved soon.

SOCIAL COGNITIVE THEORY

Although Tolman's and Bandura's theories are both cognitive in nature, Tolman concentrated almost exclusively on explaining the learning process; Bandura's cognitive theory is much more comprehensive. Dollard and Miller's theory focused on social behavior and incorporated Hullian learning theory. Bandura also concentrates on social behavior, but his theoretical orientation is not Hullian. Thus, to describe both Dollard and Miller's and Bandura's theories as *social learning theory,* as is often the case, is misleading. To differentiate his theory from those such as Tolman's and Dollard and Miller's, Bandura prefers the label **social cognitive theory.** In the preface to *Social Foundations of Thought and Action: A Social Cognitive Theory,* Bandura (1986) explains his choice of this label:

> The theoretical approach presented in this volume is usually designated as social learn-ing theory. However, the scope of this approach has always been much broader than its descriptive label, which is becoming increasingly ill-fitting as various aspects of the the-ory are further developed. From the outset it encompassed psychosocial phenomena, such as motivational and self-regulatory mechanisms, that extend beyond issues of learning. Moreover, many readers construe learning theory as a conditioning model of response acquisition, whereas within this theoretical framework learning is conceptual-ized mainly as knowledge acquisition through cognitive processing of information. The labeling problem is further compounded because several theories with dissimilar postulates [such as] Dollard and Miller's drive theory . . . bear the social learning label. In the interests of more fitting and separable labeling, the theoretical approach of this book is designated as *social cognitive theory.* The social portion of the terminology acknowledges the social origins of much human thought and action; the cognitive por-tion recognizes the influential causal contribution of thought processes to human motivation, affect, and action. (p. xii)

The current popularity of Bandura's theory can be partially explained by its recog-nition of the uniqueness of humans. It describes humans as dynamic, information-processing, problem-solving, and, above all, social organisms. Whether we learn from direct experience or from vicarious experience, most of our learning usually involves other people in a social setting. It is on the basis of our observations and interactions with other people that our cognitions, including our standards for per-formance and for moral judgment, are developed. In addition, Bandura's research typically reflects real-life situations and problems. His subjects are humans interact-ing with other humans, not humans learning lists of nonsense syllables or rats running mazes or pressing a lever in a Skinner box. According to Bandura (1977), it is the human capacity to symbolize that "enables them to represent events, to analyze their conscious experience, to communicate with others at any distance in time and space, to plan, to create, to imagine, and to engage in foresightful action" (p. vii).

Human Agency

In his more recent writings about social cognitive theory, Bandura (1999, 2000, 2001, 2002a, 2002b) emphasizes **human agency,** the conscious planning and inten-tional execution of actions that influence future events. In his words, "people are not just onlooking hosts of internal mechanisms orchestrated by environmental events. They are agents of experience rather than simply undergoers of experi-ences. The sensory, motor, and cerebral systems are tools people use to accomplish the tasks and goals that give meaning and satisfaction to their lives" (Bandura, 2001, p. 4). What Bandura calls an "agentic perspective" addresses questions in learning that other theorists in our book do not. For Bandura, the important problems in social cognitive theory concern future-oriented consciousness and cognition. He writes:

> The human mind is generative, creative, proactive, and reflective, not just reactive. . . . How do people operate as thinkers of the thoughts that exert determinative influence on their actions? What are the functional circuitries of forethought, planful proaction, aspiration, self-appraisal, and self-reflection? Even more important, how are they intentionally recruited? (Bandura, 2001, p. 4)

From the agentic perspective, many things we learn are planned in advance and guided by cognitive schemas. Such schemas include a focus on cognitively represented goals, anticipation of both positive and negative events that may occur, and self-corrective behaviors to maintain progress toward anticipated outcomes. In this sense, Bandura's theory of human agency places him fully within contemporary cognitive psychology and distances him most markedly from early behavioristic theorists. Next, we examine what Bandura refers to as the "core features" of human agency.

First, human agency is characterized by **intentionality,** which Bandura (2001) defines as a "representation of a future course of action to be performed" (p. 6). In other words, intentionality involves planning a course of action for some specific purpose. Thus, a person who wants to learn how to play golf or to play the piano makes a committed plan to take lessons, practice every Saturday morning, subscribe to an informative magazine, and so on. The plan itself, however, does not guarantee that the individual will actually learn the skill of interest; outcomes other than those anticipated may occur.

Second, human agency is characterized by **forethought,** which is defined as anticipation of the consequences of our intentions. This future-orientation guides behavior toward acquisition of positive outcomes and turns it away from negative ones, thus serving an important motivational function. Our future golfer anticipates joining a golf league, making new friends on the golf course, playing in amateur tournaments, and so on. Our would-be piano player may imagine playing at a recital or performing for friends at a social event. Bandura emphasizes that it is the *cognitive* representation of goals that provide motivation and guidance, given that the actual outcomes do not exist in the present. Furthermore, cognitive representations are subject to self-regulation by the learner's perceived self-efficacy, beliefs, and moral standards. In our examples, our imaginary future golfer does not imagine cheating or becoming a world-class professional; our imaginary would-be piano player does not aspire to plagiarize music and lyrics from a well-known composer or to play in a sold-out orchestra hall.

The third core feature of human agency is **self-reactiveness,** which provides a link between thought and action. Bandura (2001) writes that people "do things that give them self-satisfaction, and a sense of pride and self-worth, and refrain from behaving in ways that give rise to self-dissatisfaction, self-devaluation, and self-censure" (p. 8). Thus, once again, the important efficacy, belief, and value factors in social cognitive theory are invoked to provide guidance. In the case of foresight, they give structure and limitations to the planning of action. In the case of self-reactiveness, they guide the actual execution of behavior.

Finally, human agency is characterized by **self-reflectiveness,** the metacognitive capability to reflect on the directions, consequences, and meaning of our plans and actions. With respect to self-reflectiveness, Bandura is concise: "Efficacy beliefs are the foundation of human agency" (p. 10). As we have seen, Bandura believes that perceived self-efficacy is the most important determinant of the activities we choose, the intensity with which we pursue these activities, and our willingness to persist when frustrated or otherwise confronted with failure. Our intentional learning is therefore restricted by low perceived self-efficacy and extended by high perceived self-efficacy.

BANDURA ON EDUCATION

Bandura's theory has many implications for education. You may recall that Bandura believes that anything that can be learned by direct experience can also be learned from observation. Bandura also believes that models are most effective if they are seen as having respect, competence, high status, or power. In most cases, teachers can be highly influential models. Through careful planning of what is presented, teachers can do more than teach routine information. They can model skills, problem-solving strategies, moral codes, performance standards, general rules and principles, and creativity. Teachers can model conduct, which is then internalized by students and becomes the standard for self-evaluation. For example, internalized standards become the basis for self-criticism or self-praise. When students act in accordance with their own standards, the experience is reinforcing. When the actions of students fall short of their standards, the experience is punishing. Thus, for Bandura, as for the Gestalt theorists and Tolman, intrinsic reinforcement is far more important than extrinsic reinforcement. In fact, says Bandura, extrinsic reinforcement can actually reduce a student's motivation to learn. Reaching a personal goal is also reinforcing, and teachers should help students formulate goals that are neither too easy nor too difficult to achieve. This formulation, of course, needs to be done individually for each student.

To say that students learn what they observe is an oversimplification because observational learning is governed by four variables that the teacher must take into consideration. Attentional processes will determine what is observed by the student, and such processes will vary as a function of both maturation and the student's previous learning experiences. Even if something is attended to and learned, it must be retained if it is to be of any value; thus, retention processes are important. According to Bandura, retention is largely determined by one's verbal ability. A teacher must, therefore, take the verbal ability of the students into consideration when planning a modeling experience. Even if something is attended to and retained, the student may not have the motor skills necessary to reproduce a skill after it has been learned. Thus, a teacher must be aware of a student's behavioral production processes. Last, even if students attend to and retain what has been observed and are capable of behaviorally producing their observations, they must have an incentive for doing so. Thus the teacher must be aware of motivational processes. At this point, extrinsic reinforcement may be useful. For example, students may be willing to demonstrate what they have learned if they are offered points, stars, grades, or the admiration of the teacher. Note, however, that extrinsic reinforcement is being used to influence performance rather than learning.

We see then that observational learning has many educational implications, but to use it effectively in the classroom, the teacher must take into consideration the attentional, retentional, motor, and motivational processes of each student. With these things in mind, films, television, lectures, slides, tapes, demonstrations, and displays can all be used to effectively model a wide variety of educational experiences.

SUMMARY

The long avoidance of studies into observational learning was ended by Bandura's research, which first appeared in the literature in the early 1960s. Bandura disagreed with Miller and Dollard's earlier account of observational learning, which described it as a special case of instrumental conditioning. Bandura's explanation of learning is close to Tolman's, in that learning is assumed to be continuous and not dependent on reinforcement. For Bandura, as for Tolman, reinforcement is a performance variable, not a learning variable. Either direct or vicarious reinforcement provides information about what behaviors lead to reinforcement in various situations; when a need arises, this information is translated into behavior. Thus, reinforcement provides information that allows observers to anticipate reinforcement if they behave in certain ways. Reinforcement, according to Bandura, does not act directly to strengthen the responses that produce it. In fact, much, if not most, human learning occurs in the absence of direct reinforcement. Rather, human learning typically occurs by observing the consequences of the behavior of models. Such vicarious learning is made possible by the human capacity to symbolize and store information and then to act on that information at a later time.

Four major processes are thought to influence the course of observational learning: attentional processes, which determine which aspects of a modeling situation are attended to; retentional processes, which involve the imaginal and verbal coding of information so that it may be stored and utilized in the future; behavioral production processes, which involve the ability to make the responses necessary to translate what has been learned from observation into behavior; and motivational processes, which, because learning occurs continuously, determine which aspects of previously learned responses are translated into action. Reinforcement is the major motivational process because it not only causes an observer to focus on the functional aspects of a model's behavior but also provides an incentive for acting on the information gained by such observation. The information gained by observing reinforcement contingencies can come either from one's direct experience with reinforcement or by vicariously observing the consequences of a model's behavior.

One of Bandura's major concepts is reciprocal determinism, which states that there is a constant interaction among the environment, the behavior, and the person. According to Bandura, it makes as much sense to say that behavior influences the environment as it does to say that the environment influences behavior. In addition, the person influences both behavior and the environment.

Unlike traditional learning theorists, Bandura believes that much human behavior is self-regulated. Through direct and observational learning, performance standards develop that act as guides in evaluating one's own behavior. If one's behavior meets or exceeds one's performance standards, it is evaluated positively; if it falls short of one's standards, it is evaluated negatively. Likewise, one's perceived self-efficacy develops from one's direct and vicarious experiences with success and failure. Perceived self-efficacy influences self-regulated behavior in several ways: It determines what is attempted, how long one persists at a task, and what is hoped for. Intrinsic reinforcement (self-reinforcement) influences one's behavior more than extrinsic, or externally administered, reinforcement. One's moral behavior is governed by internalized moral codes. If one acts contrary to one's moral code, one experiences self-contempt, which acts as a severe punishment. However, Bandura describes a number of mechanisms that allow people to disengage themselves from their moral principles and thereby escape self-contempt for immoral behavior. These disengagement mechanisms include moral justification, euphemistic labeling, advantageous comparison, displacement of responsibility, diffusion of responsibility, disregard or distortion of consequences, dehumanization, and attribution of blame.

Faulty cognitive processes can develop from inaccurate perceptions, overgeneralization, or incomplete or erroneous information. Most phobias probably result from overgeneralization of one or more direct or vicarious painful experiences. One way to correct faulty cognitive processes, including phobias, is to provide powerful disconfirming experiences, which eventually reduce or eliminate one's inhibitions or fears. In addition to reducing or eliminating inhibitions, modeling can also be used to teach new skills, inhibit responses, facilitate responses, teach creativity, and teach general rules and principles.

Symbolic, live, and participant modeling in the clinical setting have been found effective in treating phobias. However, of all the methods tried, participant-modeling has been the most effective. The process of reducing one's fears by observing another person interacting fearlessly with a feared object is called vicarious extinction. Bandura provides evidence that news and entertainment media act as powerful models and can sometimes encourage aggressive, violent, and criminal behavior.

Bandura's theory is called a social cognitive theory because it emphasizes that most of the information we gain comes from our interactions with other people. Because of its emphasis on such cognitive processes as language and memory, its effectiveness as a guide in psychotherapeutic practices, its implications for child-rearing and educational practices, and its ability to stimulate new lines of research, Bandura's theory is very popular today and promises to become even more popular in the future.

EVALUATION OF BANDURA'S THEORY

Albert Bandura's work has had widespread influence among learning theorists, social psychologists, and cognitive psychologists. Like Estes, his work combines behaviorism and cognitive theory and continues to generate research. Even before Bandura's (1986) influential *Social Foundations of Thought and Action,* Bower and Hilgard (1981) recognized his approach as "the best integrative summary of what modern learning theory has to contribute to the solution of practical problems . . . a compatible framework within which to place information-processing theories of language comprehension, memory, imagery, and problem-solving" (p. 472).

Contributions

When Bandura's contributions are pointed out to contemporary readers, they often treat his theory as commonsense observations that we have all made at some time in the past. We must remember, however, that the foundations of Bandura's theory were developed at a time when most, if not all, learning theorists insisted that learning had its foundations in direct experience with the environment. As we noted at the beginning of this chapter, both Thorndike and Watson disregarded observational learning, and for Miller and Dollard, imitative learning was tied inevitably to reinforcement of actual imitated behavior. Even Piaget (1973) completely denied the role of observational learning in young children:

> It is absolutely necessary that learners have at their disposal concrete material experiences (and not merely pictures), and that they form their own hypotheses and verify them (or not verify them) themselves through their own active manipulations. *The observed activities of others, including those of the teacher, are not formative of new organizations in the child* [italics added]. (pp. ix)

Thus, Bandura's demonstrations that we learn by watching others and that such learning occurs with or without imitation and with or without reinforcement was a significant contribution to learning theory. A second major contribution is the three-way interaction represented in his notion of reciprocal determinism. Bandura (1983, 1986) points out that earlier, behavioristic theories tended to view behavior as an end product of person and environment or of person-environment interactions. Reciprocal determinism views behavior both as a product of person and environment and as an influence on person and environment, thereby shifting our perspective from a focus on behavior per se to the dynamic interplay of person, environment, and behavior.

Criticisms

Phillips and Orton (1983) have criticized the principle of reciprocal determinism on several grounds. They point out that systemic interaction is not new and may be traced back to philosophical, as well as scientific, writings in the nineteenth century. Second, they argue that, while Bandura claims to be a determinist, the principle of reciprocal determinism defies standard causal analysis. That is, if behavior causes changes in the person while the person causes changes in the behavior while the environment causes changes in behavior and the person and so on, the task of discovering what causes what becomes practically impossible.

A second criticism of Bandura's position falls in the category of "too much of a good thing." Whereas most theories of learning and cognition have become narrower in scope and more precise in their formulations over the last thirty years, Bandura's theory is similar to the broad, encompassing theories formulated by Skinner and Tolman. As we have seen, Bandura's cognitive social learning theory addresses problems in learning, memory, language, motivation, personality, moral conduct, psychological dysfunctions, and societal issues such as media influences on behavior. Whether such a theory can survive the many trends toward specialization remains to be seen.

DISCUSSION QUESTIONS

1. What conclusions did Thorndike and Watson reach about observational learning, and why did they reach them?
2. Describe Miller and Dollard's research on observational learning and their explanation for what they found.
3. Defend the statement "Bandura's theory of learning is not a reinforcement theory."
4. Describe the role of reinforcement in Bandura's theory. Include in your answer the ways in which Bandura's view of reinforcement differs from the views of traditional reinforcement theorists.
5. Define the terms *vicarious reinforcement* and *vicarious punishment,* and explain their importance to Bandura's theory.
6. Compare Bandura's theory to Tolman's theory.
7. Briefly describe attentional, retentional, behavioral production, and motivational processes, and describe their influence on observational learning.
8. Define and give examples of Bandura's concept of reciprocal determinism.
9. How, according to Bandura, is behavior self-regulated?
10. List several mechanisms that allow a person to act immorally without experiencing self-contempt.
11. Describe several ways in which faulty cognitive processes can develop. Give examples of the kinds of behavior that faulty cognitive processes can generate.
12. Describe how modeling can be used to produce each of the following: acquisition, inhibition, disinhibition, facilitation, creativity, and rule-governed behavior. Begin your answer by defining each of the terms.
13. Define each of the following terms: symbolic modeling, live modeling, multiple modeling, participant-modeling, desensitization therapy, and vicarious extinction.
14. Describe how modeling is used to reduce or eliminate a phobia. Which procedure did Bandura find most effective in treating phobias?

15. Explain why someone who accepts Bandura's theory would be very concerned about the content of children's TV programs.
16. Give a few examples of how Bandura's theory might be used in education and in child rearing.
17. Summarize Bandura's opposition to stage, type, and trait theories.
18. Based on Bandura's theory, do you feel a person would be more likely to respond to cries of help from an acquaintance or from a stranger? Explain.
19. Attempt to account for those occasions when a person does not learn from observation. For example, if you watched a brain surgeon performing an operation, would you be capable of performing such an operation? Why or why not?
20. Answer the following question from Bandura's point of view: "Why do children imitate some behaviors that they observe and not others?"
21. According to Bandura, what is probably learned by a child who is spanked by a parent for misbehaving?
22. In attempting to explain why people learn vicariously, it has been suggested that answering the question "What makes a horror movie horrifying to the observer?" would shed some light on the matter. Attempt to answer the question about horror movies, and then generalize your answer to the area of observational learning.

CHAPTER HIGHLIGHTS

abstract modeling

acquisition

actual environment

advantageous comparison

attentional processes

attribution of blame

behavioral production processes

copying behavior

creativity

dehumanize

delayed modeling

desensitization therapy

diffusion of responsibility

direct experience

direct modeling

disinhibition

displacement of responsibility

disregard or distortion of consequences

euphemistic labeling

facilitation

faulty cognitive processes

forethought

freedom

generalized imitation

human agency

imitative behavior

inhibition

intentionality

matched-dependent behavior

model

modeling-participation

moral codes

moral justification

motivational processes

multiple modeling

observational learning

perceived self-efficacy

performance

performance standards

potential environment

real self-efficacy

reciprocal determinism

reinforcement

reinforcement theory

retentional processes

same behavior

self-contempt

self-reactiveness

self-reflectiveness

self-regulated behavior

single modeling

social cognitive theory

symbolic modeling

vicarious experience

vicarious extinction

vicarious punishment

vicarious reinforcement

CHAPTER 14

Donald Olding Hebb

Donald O. Hebb (Courtesy of McGill
University, PR 000387.)

Specialized research, as well as general public interest, in the brain sciences has increased dramatically in recent years. Numerous psychologists studying abnormal behavior, psychotropic medications, personality, decision making, child development, memory, and of course, learning, have tethered theory to brain function. Many have contributed important foundations and findings in the brain sciences, and there are a number of potential candidates to represent the neurosciences in learning theory. We have chosen Donald O. Hebb as our representative for this tradition. His theoretical work, the contributions of his students and colleagues, and even his early speculations have been insightful and heuristic. This chapter attempts to present those contributions along with recent findings that, although not directly influenced by Hebb, are important links between brain science and learning.

Donald Olding Hebb was born on July 22, 1904, in Chester, Nova Scotia. Both his parents were medical doctors. His mother obtained her medical degree from Dalhousie University in Halifax, Nova Scotia, in 1896, making her only the third female to become a physician in the province of Nova Scotia at that time.

In 1925, Hebb received his B.A. from Dalhousie University with the lowest course average a person could have without actually failing. Because Hebb was one of psychology's most creative researchers and theorists, undergraduate grade point average, in his case, had no predictive value. After graduation, Hebb taught school in the village where he grew up. At the age of twenty-three, he read Freud and decided that psychology had a lot of room for improvement. Because the chair of the Psychology Department at McGill University in Montreal was a friend of his mother, he was admitted as a part-time graduate psychology student in spite of his poor undergraduate record. Hebb continued to teach elementary school while he was a graduate student, however, and had a compulsion to reform educational practices. In addition to wanting to become an educational reformer, another of Hebb's early passions was to write novels for a living, but like Skinner, his efforts failed.

During his years at McGill, Hebb was trained in the Pavlovian tradition, and he obtained his M.A. in 1932. In spite of his training, Hebb saw restrictions in Pavlovian theory and doubted its importance. While at McGill, Hebb read Köhler's *Gestalt Psychology* and Lashley's work on brain physiology (which we consider briefly) and found them both to his liking. In 1934, Hebb decided to continue his education at the University of Chicago, where he worked with Lashley and took a seminar from Köhler. Lashley's work cast doubt on the prevailing belief that the brain is a complex switchboard. This **switchboard** (or relay station) **conception of the brain** was held mainly by the behaviorists, for example, Thorndike, Hull, and Watson, and by

Karl Lashley. (Courtesy of Yerkes Regional Primate Research Center.)

the associationists, for example, Pavlov and Guthrie. Those holding this view assumed that sensory events stimulate specific areas of the brain and that learning causes a change in neural circuitry so that sensory events come to stimulate areas other than those they originally stimulated. Lashley's research, which used rats as subjects, raised serious questions about this conception of the brain. The most startling outcome of his research was his finding that the location of the destroyed portion of the brain was not as important as the amount of destruction. This consistent finding became Lashley's principle of **mass action,** which states that the disruption of learning and retention goes up as the amount of cortical destruction goes up, regardless of the location of the destruction. Lashley concluded that the cortex functions as a whole during learning, and if one part of the cortex is destroyed, other parts of the cortex take over the destroyed portion's function. This ability of one portion of the cortex to take over the function of another was referred to by Lashley as **equipotentiality.** Thus, mass action indicates that the amount of learning and memory disruption is a function of the amount of the cortical area destroyed, and equipotentiality indicates that the location of the cortical ablation is unimportant.

Clearly, these findings were not in accordance with Hebb's early training at McGill University, and his opposition to Pavlov, which was at first tenuous, now became outright disagreement. "I had all the fervor of the reformed drunk at a temperance meeting; having been a fully convinced Pavlovian, I was now a fully convinced Gestalter-cum-Lashleyan" (Hebb, 1959, p. 625). Once again, we are reminded that good scientists are willing to change their minds.

In 1935, Lashley accepted a professorship at Harvard, and he invited Hebb to go with him. In 1936, Hebb obtained his Ph.D. from Harvard and remained there an additional year as a teaching and research assistant.

In 1937, Hebb went to the Montreal Neurological Institute to work with the famous brain surgeon Wilder Penfield. Hebb's job was to study the psychological status of Penfield's patients after brain surgery. Much to Hebb's amazement, he found that even after substantial loss of tissue from the frontal lobes of the brain, there was no loss in intelligence, and in some cases, he even detected a gain in intelligence. Sometimes the tissue loss was as much as 20 percent. According to Hebb (1980), the questions raised by these observations acted as a stimulus for his subsequent work: "I could find no sign of loss after large amounts of brain tissue were removed from the frontal lobe. . . . It was this problem that set the main course for all my subsequent work" (p. 290).

After studying Penfield's patients for five years (1937–1942), Hebb (1980) reached a conclusion about intelligence that was later to become an important part of his theory: "Experience in childhood normally develops concepts, modes of thought, and ways of perceiving that constitute intelligence. Injury to the infant brain interferes with that process, but the same injury at maturity does not reverse it" (p. 292).

By now Hebb had made three observations that his later theory attempts to explain:

1. The brain does not act as a simple switchboard, as the behaviorists and associationists had assumed. If it did, destroying large amounts of brain tissue from the frontal lobes would have been more disruptive.
2. Intelligence comes from experience and, therefore, is not genetically determined.
3. Childhood experiences are more important in determining intelligence than adult experiences.

In 1942, Lashley accepted an appointment as director of the Yerkes Laboratories of Primate Biology in Orange Park, Florida, and again asked Hebb to join him. While at the Yerkes Laboratories (1942–1947), Hebb studied the emotions and personalities of chimpanzees and made several observations that further stimulated his own neurophysiological theory of learning and perception. In 1948, after five years at the Yerkes Laboratories, Hebb accepted an appointment as professor of psychology at McGill University, where he remained until his retirement. Among Hebb's many honors were eight honorary doctorates, the presidency of the Canadian Psychological Association (1952), the presidency of the American Psychological Association (1959), the Warren Medal (1958), and the distinguished scientific contribution award of the American Psychological Association (1961).

Once converted from the kind of behaviorism derived from Pavlov's theory, Hebb launched an attack on behaviorism that continued all his life. His first major book was *The Organization of Behavior* (1949). The initials of that book, OOB, bore a strange resemblance to the initials of Skinner's major book, *The Behavior of Organisms* (1938), which was affectionately known as BOO. A later publication, "Drives and the C.N.S. (Conceptual Nervous System)," showed Hebb's (1955) willingness to "physiologize" about psychological processes. His very readable *Textbook of Psychology* (1972) provides an excellent overview of his theory. A more technical account of Hebb's theory appears in *Psychology: A Study of a Science* (1959). Hebb's approach is diametrically opposed to Skinner's method of functional analysis, in which relationships between stimuli and responses are determined without any reference to internal events.

After his retirement from McGill University in 1974, Hebb moved back to a small farm near Chester, Nova Scotia, where he was born. He remained psychologically and physically active until he died on August 20, 1985, while in the hospital for what was thought to be routine hip surgery (Beach, 1987, p. 187).

MAJOR THEORETICAL CONCEPTS

Restricted Environments

Several experiments demonstrate the potentially disabling effects that a **restricted environment** has on early learning and development of the nervous system. The German ophthalmologist von Senden (1932) studied adults born with congenital cataracts who were suddenly able to see after the cataracts were surgically removed. These individuals could immediately detect the presence of an object, but they could not identify it by using visual cues alone. For example, although we might expect that a patient could easily discriminate between a circle and a triangle by comparing the rounded, continuous contour of the circle with the straight edges and corners of the triangle, von Senden's patients found the task exceedingly difficult, if not impossible. In addition, the patients had great difficulty learning cues to help them to make these difficult discriminations. These findings suggest that some kind of figure-ground perception is innate, but visual experience with various objects is necessary before objects can be differentiated. Gradually, with extensive practice, these previously blind individuals learned to identify objects in the environment, and their perceptions approached normality.

Austin Riesen (1947) reared infant chimpanzees in total darkness until they were about two years old. When they were finally taken from the darkness, they acted as if they were completely blind. Within a few weeks, however, they began to see, and eventually they behaved like chimpanzees reared normally. Hebb concluded that von Senden's patients and Riesen's chimpanzees *learned* to see.

Numerous other studies supported the conclusion that restricting early experience interferes with normal intellectual and perceptual development. Even the perception of pain, a phenomenon so essential for survival that we might expect it to be instinctive, may require critical early learning. A study run in Hebb's laboratory (Melzack & Thompson, 1956) showed that Scottish terriers reared in partial isolation were oblivious to pain, in addition to being less aggressive than their normally reared littermates.

Enriched Environments

If a severely restricted environment causes a disruption either in development or in normal functioning, is it possible that an **enriched environment,** one with wide varieties of motor and sensory experience, enhances development? The answer to this question seems to be yes. Hebb ran what was probably the first experiment designed to investigate the effects of different kinds of rearing conditions on intellectual development (1949, pp. 298–299). Two groups of rats were involved: One was reared in cages in Hebb's laboratory; the other was reared in Hebb's home by his two daughters. Rats in the latter group spent considerable time roaming around the house, presumably playing with Hebb's children. After several weeks, the "pet" rats were returned to the laboratory and compared with the cage-reared rats. The performance of the pet rats on a series of detour and maze problems was consistently superior to that of the rats reared in the laboratory.

Numerous studies support Hebb's early research. For example, a series of experiments by Bennett, Diamond, Krech, and Rosenzweig (1964) confirmed that rats reared in an enriched environment are faster learners than their littermates raised in relative isolation. In this research, the enriched environment was a large cage containing other rats and numerous toylike objects (see Figure 14–1). Control animals were reared alone in cages that contained no objects.

Are the effects of an impoverished early environment permanent? According to the research of Rosenzweig and his colleagues, apparently not. They found that the effects of an impoverished sensory environment are reversed by merely placing the animals in an enriched environment for only a few hours a day. Thus, damage done by a restricted early environment can be undone if conditions change for the better. As we will see later in this chapter, there does not appear to be a critical developmental stage beyond which the damage caused by a restricted sensory environment early in life cannot be remedied.

Hebb's explanation of these findings was straightforward. Greater sensory diversity provided by the enriched environment allowed the animals to build up more numerous and more complex neural circuits or networks. Once developed, these neural circuits were utilized in new learning. The austere sensory experiences in deprived environments restrict neural circuitry or delay its development altogether,

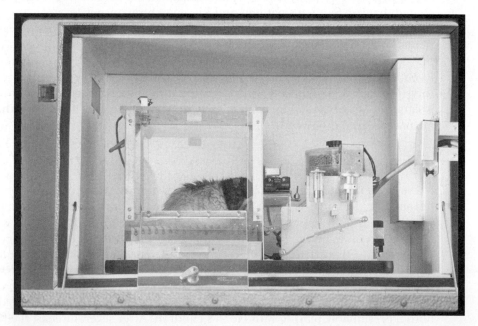

FIGURE 14–1   Animal being teared in an enriched environment. (Yoav Levy/ Phototake NYC)

and animals reared in those less stimulating environments were therefore inferior problem solvers. The implications of this research for education and child rearing are clear: Complex early sensory environments lead to superior problem-solving skills.

These observations strengthened Hebb's empiricist position: Intelligence, perception, and even emotions are learned from experience and therefore are not inherited, as the nativist claims. Hebb's theory proposes that infants are born with a neural network with random interconnections. Sensory experience causes this neural network to become organized and to provide a means of interacting effectively with the environment. The cell assembly and the phase sequence, two key concepts and basic elements in Hebb's proposed neural theory, are discussed next.

Cell Assemblies

According to Hebb, each environmental object we experience stimulates a complex pattern of neurons called a **cell assembly.** For example, as we look at a pencil, we shift our attention from the point to the eraser to the wooden shaft. As our attention shifts, different neurons are stimulated. When all neurons stimulated by different aspects of the pencil are stimulated, the result is our perception and identification of the pencil. On our first exposure to the pencil, however, the different aspects of this complex neural package will be independent. For example, as we look at the point of a pencil, a cell assembly corresponding to that event will fire. Initially, it will not influence the assemblies of neurons that correspond to the eraser or the wooden shaft. Eventually, because of the temporal contiguity between the firing of neurons in the assembly corresponding to the point and those corresponding to other parts of the pencil, the various parts of the neurological package become interrelated. Hebb's (1949) "neurophysiological postulate" suggests the mechanism by which initially independent neurons become linked into stable cell assemblies and by which assemblies become associated with other assemblies: "When an axon of cell A is near enough to excite a cell B and repeatedly or persistently takes part in firing it, some growth process or metabolic change takes place in one or both cells such that A's efficiency, as one of the cells firing B, is increased" (p. 62).

Hebb (1949) saw cell assemblies as dynamic, rather than fixed or static, systems of neurons. He posited mechanisms by which neurons could either leave or join cell assemblies, thus allowing assemblies to be refined through learning or development:

> In the integration which has been hypothesized . . . there would necessarily be a gradual change of the frequency characteristics of the system. The consequence would be a sort of fractionation and recruitment, and some change in the neurons making up the system. That is, some units, capable at first of synchronizing with others in the system would drop out: "fractionation." Others, at first incompatible, would be recruited. With perceptual development there would thus be a slow growth in the assembly, understanding by "growth" not necessarily an increase in the number of constituent cells, but a change. (pp. 76–77)

A cell assembly is an interrelated neurological package that can be fired either by external stimulation, internal stimulation, or a combination of the two. When a cell assembly fires, we experience the thought of the event the assembly represents.

To Hebb, the cell assembly is the neurological basis of an idea or thought. In this way, Hebb explains why houses, cows, or loved ones need not be present for us to think of them.

Phase Sequences

Just as different aspects of the same object become neurologically interrelated to form cell assemblies, so do cell assemblies become neurologically interrelated to form phase sequences. A **phase sequence** is "a temporally integrated series of assembly activities; it amounts to one current in the stream of thought" (Hebb, 1959, p. 629). Once developed, a phase sequence, like a cell assembly, can be fired internally, externally, or by a combination of internal and external stimulation. When any single cell assembly or combination of assemblies in a phase sequence is fired, the entire phase sequence tends to fire. When a phase sequence fires, we experience a stream of thought, that is, a series of ideas arranged in some logical order. This process explains how a few strains from a favorite song may trigger a pleasant memory, complete with characters and emotions. Hebb (1972) said the following about the development of phase sequences:

> Cell-assemblies that are active at the same time become interconnected. Common events in the child's environment establish assemblies, and then when these events occur together the assemblies become connected (because they are active together). When the baby hears footsteps, let us say, an assembly is excited; while this is still active he sees a face and feels hands picking him up, which excites other assemblies—so the "footsteps assembly" becomes connected with the "face assembly" and the "being-picked-up assembly." After this has happened, when the baby hears footsteps only, all three assemblies are excited; the baby then has something like a perception of the mother's face and the contact of her hands before she has come in sight—but since the sensory stimulations have not yet taken place, this is ideation or imagery, not perception. (p. 67)

For Hebb, there were two kinds of learning. One involves the slow buildup of cell assemblies early in life and can probably be explained by one of the S-R theories of learning, such as Guthrie's. This kind of learning is straight associationism. Likewise, the development of phase sequences can be explained with associationistic terminology. That is, objects and events that are related in the environment come to be related on the neurological level. After cell assemblies and phase sequences are developed, however, subsequent learning is more cognitive and can occur much more rapidly. Adult learning, for example, often characterized by insight and creativity, probably involves the rearrangement of phase sequences. Thus, Hebb maintained that the variables influencing childhood learning and those influencing adult learning are not the same. Childhood learning provides the framework for later learning. For example, learning a language is a slow, cumbersome process, which probably involves the building up of millions of cell assemblies and phase sequences. However, once a language has been learned, an individual can rearrange it in any number of creative ways, perhaps in the form of a poem or a novel. However, said Hebb, first come the building blocks and then come the insight and creativity that characterize adult learning.

Arousal Theory

We have all been in situations when, because of too much noise or commotion, we have not been able to think clearly. On the other hand, sometimes we must shake ourselves awake to maintain adequate performance. These reactions suggest that a level of stimulation that is neither too high nor too low is conducive to optimal cognitive functioning. Hebb explored this relationship between level of stimulation and cognitive functioning within the context of **arousal theory.**

Arousal theory involves the functioning of the **reticular activating system (RAS),** an area about the size of a finger that is located in the brain stem just above the spinal cord and just below the thalamus and hypothalamus. The RAS is involved in the processes of sleep, attention, and emotional behavior.

According to Hebb (1955), a neural impulse generated by the stimulation of a sense receptor has two functions. The **cue function of a stimulus** allows the organism to gain information about the environment. The **arousal function of a stimulus** is the potential for sensory impulses to change activity in the RAS. Hebb (1955) believed that for the cue function of a stimulus to have its full effect, there must be an **optimal level of arousal** provided by the RAS. When arousal level is too low, such as when the organism is drowsy, sensory information transmitted to the brain cannot be utilized. Likewise, when arousal is too high, too much information is relayed to the cortex, and the result can be confusion, response conflict, and irrelevant behavior. Thus a level of arousal that is neither too high nor too low is necessary for optimal cortical functioning and therefore optimal performance. The proposed relationship between arousal level and performance is shown in Figure 14–2.

Hebb speculated that different tasks require different levels of arousal for optimal performance. For example, a simple, well-practiced habit may be performed optimally across a wide range of arousal levels, whereas a highly skilled task may be performed optimally only at lower arousal levels. Gross behavioral skills, on the other hand, may be performed best under extremely high arousal. The proposed relationship between optimal performance on various tasks and arousal level is shown in Figure 14–3.

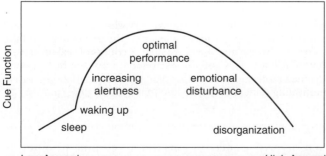

FIGURE 14–2   The relationship suggested by Hebb between arousal level and performance. (From *Textbook of Psychology,* 4th ed., p. 237, by D. O. Hebb & D. C. Donderi, 1987, Philadelphia: W. B. Saunders. Copyright © 1958, 1966, 1972 by W. B. Saunders Company. Reprinted by permission of Holt, Rinehart & Winston.)

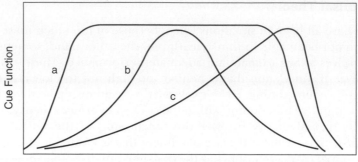

FIGURE 14–3   The relationship suggested by Hebb between arousal level and performance on three different kinds of tasks. Task a is a well-practiced habit such as giving one's name. Such a task is performed optimally over a wide range of arousal levels. Task b is a complex skill such as typing. Such a task is performed optimally only when arousal is neither too high nor too low. Task c is the kind of task that is relatively uncomplicated but requires the expenditure of a great deal of energy, such as weight-lifting or running a race. Such a task is performed optimally when arousal level is high. (From *Textbook of Psychology*, 4th ed., p. 237, by D. O. Hebb & D. C. Donderi, 1987, Philadelphia: W. B. Saunders. Copyright © 1958, 1966, 1972 by W. B. Saunders Company. Reprinted by permission of Holt, Rinehart & Winston.)

Arousal Theory and Reinforcement

According to Hebb, if arousal is too high, an organism will operate on the environment to reduce the arousal level. For example, if students are trying to study while an exciting television program plays in the background, they may modify the environment (i.e., turn off the television) or find a less arousing environment that is more compatible with studying. On the other hand, if it is too quiet and there is not enough sensory input to maintain an optimal level of arousal, students may increase arousal by turning on the radio, talking with friends, drinking coffee, and so on. Generally speaking, when the arousal level is too high, decreasing it is reinforcing, and when the arousal level is too low, increasing it is reinforcing. Unlike Hull's theory, which equates drive reduction with reinforcement, Hebb's theory equates reinforcement with either an increase or decrease in drive, depending on the circumstances. According to Hebb (1955), seeking excitement is a significant motive in human behavior:

> When you stop to think of it, it is nothing short of extraordinary what trouble people will go to in order to get into more trouble at the bridge table, or on the golf course; and the fascination of the murder story, or thriller, and the newspaper accounts of real-life adventure or tragedy, is no less extraordinary. This taste for excitement must not be forgotten when we are dealing with human motivation. It appears that, up to a certain point, threat and puzzle have positive motivating value, beyond that point negative value. (p. 250)

Sensory Deprivation

As we have seen, restricted sensory experience inhibits the development of neurophysiological assemblies that represent objects and events in the environment. But what happens if sensory experience is restricted *after* normal neurophysiological development has already taken place? A series of experiments were run at McGill University under Hebb's supervision to answer this question. In one of these experiments (Heron, 1957), a group of college students were paid twenty dollars a day to do nothing. They had only to lie on a comfortable bed with their eyes covered by translucent plastic, which permitted them to see diffuse light but not to recognize objects. A constant buzzing sound was transmitted to the subjects through earphones. To inhibit auditory perception further, air-conditioning equipment hummed monotonously in the background. The participants wore cotton gloves and cardboard cuffs, which extended over their fingertips, to minimize tactile stimulation. These conditions prevailed for almost twenty-four hours a day and were interrupted only when the students ate or needed to go to the washroom. This experimental arrangement is shown in Figure 14–4.

Most participants could stand the conditions for only two or three days (the longest was six). They typically became irritable and almost childlike in their limited interactions with the experimenter. Much to the surprise of Hebb and his coworkers, **sensory deprivation** produced an effect far beyond simple boredom. Hebb and Donderi (1987) summarize the results of the Heron experiment as follows:

> The experiment showed that humans can be bored, which we knew, but it showed too that boredom is too mild a word for some of the effects of sensory deprivation. The need for the normal stimulation of a varied environment is fundamental. Without it, mental functioning and personality deteriorate. The subjects in isolation complained of being unable to think coherently, they became less able to solve simple problems, and they began to have hallucinations. Some of them saw such things as rows of little men wearing black caps, squirrels marching with sacks over their shoulders, or prehistoric

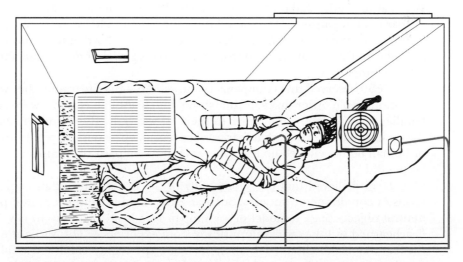

FIGURE 14–4   An experimental participant in Heron's sensory deprivation experiment. (From "The Pathology of Boredom," by W. Heron, 1957, January, *Scientific American,* p. 53. Courtesy of the Estate of Eric O. Mose. Reproduced by permission.)

animals in the jungle. These scenes were described as being like animated cartoons. More fundamentally disturbing were somesthetic hallucinations, when a subject perceived two bodies somesthetically or felt as if his head were detached from his body. . . . The subjects' very identity had begun to disintegrate. (p. 255)

Although other researchers have not replicated some of the more dramatic effects reported by Hebb (Suedfield & Coren, 1989; Zubek, 1969), later studies have shown that when the conditions of sensory deprivation are severe, people find them quite aversive and will tolerate them for only a short period of time. For example, when immersed in water (breathing through a snorkle tube) in complete darkness, experimental participants typically can last no more than a few hours before terminating their involvement in the experiment.

Hebb concluded from this research that not only is sensory experience necessary for proper neurophysiological development but also it is necessary for the maintenance of normal functioning. In other words, once the consistent events in a person's life are represented neurophysiologically in the form of cell assemblies and phase sequences, they require support from environmental events. If the sensory events that ordinarily occur in someone's life do not occur, the result is extreme and unpleasant arousal that is experienced as stress, fear, or disorientation. So, not only do consistent environmental events give rise to certain neurological circuits but also those same events must "confirm" those circuits. Thus, to the various needs that organisms have, such as the need for food, water, sex, and oxygen, Hebb added the need for stimulation. Even if all of one's other needs are satisfied, if one does not experience normal stimulation, severe cognitive disorientation results.

The Nature of Fear

While at the Yerkes Laboratories of Primate Biology, Hebb investigated the sources of **fear** in chimpanzees. He exposed the chimps to a wide variety of test objects, for example, a plaster cast of a chimpanzee head; a doll representing a human infant; a lifelike, full-sized human head from a window-display dummy; and an anesthetized infant chimpanzee.

Hebb observed that chimpanzees showed no sign of fear until they were about four months old. After that age, they showed no fear of objects that were completely familiar or completely unfamiliar to them. It was only when familiar objects were shown in unfamiliar ways that fear was expressed. For example, whole chimpanzee or human bodies elicited no fear, whereas models of parts of chimpanzee or human bodies did.

Hebb believed that the spontaneity of the fear ruled out an explanation in terms of conditioned responses. Such an explanation stresses repeated pairings of neutral objects (e.g., a model of a chimpanzee's head) with an aversive stimulus. Fear learned in this way develops slowly from experience. This was not the case in the fear that Hebb observed. Rather, the fear response was exhibited at full strength the first time an object was shown to a chimpanzee. Hebb's explanation involved cell assemblies and phase sequences. If a completely unfamiliar object is shown to an organism, no cell assembly is yet developed corresponding to that object. With repeated exposures, such an assembly gradually develops, and no fear is involved. Likewise, if a familiar object is shown to an organism, the neural circuits developed from prior experience with that object are activated, and there is no disruption of behavior. It is only when an object triggers an existing cell assembly or phase sequence and is subsequently not followed by the stimulus events that normally accompany the object that fear is elicited. The sight of an anesthetized chimpanzee, for example, will trigger the phase sequence associated with the sight of a normal, active chimpanzee, but the events that *should* follow are absent. Instead of the typical responses and sounds made by a chimpanzee, there is no movement and there is silence. Thus, a phase sequence is triggered but is not supported by the sensory events that originally caused its development. This lack of sensory support, according to Hebb, causes fear. Hebb explained the human reaction to dead or mutilated bodies in the same way. Thus Hebb (1946) reached the following conclusion about fear: "Fear occurs when an object is seen which is like familiar objects in enough respects to arouse habitual processes of perception, but in other respects arouses incompatible processes" (p. 268).

Long-Term and Short-Term Memory

Although G. E. Müller and A. Pilzecker suggested as early as 1900 that there are two distinct kinds of memory, Hebb more completely developed the distinction between different kinds of memory and speculated on underlying physiological mechanisms. Hebb (1949) made the distinction between permanent memory, which he attributed to physical-structural changes between neurons, and a transient, or short-term, memory that he attributed to ongoing activity in cell assemblies and phase sequences. Researchers now generally agree that there are two major kinds of memory: **short-term memory** and **long-term memory.** In this section, we discuss short-term memory and examine evidence suggesting the existence of different types of long-term memory.

It is generally assumed that sensory experience sets up neural activity that outlasts the stimulation that causes it. Hebb referred to this as **reverberating neural activity.** Although he recognized that some learning was both "instantaneously established and permanent" (1949, p. 62), he saw reverberating neural activity as the basis for what we call short-term memory *and* as the process that causes the structural changes underlying long-term memory. The contention that short-term memory is converted into long-term memory is referred to as **consolidation theory,** of which Hebb was a major proponent.

Contemporary cognitive psychologists conceive of short-term memory in ways that are similar to Hebb's. That is, short-term memory is seen as a relatively transient neural activity that is triggered by sensory stimulation but continues for some time after the sensory event is terminated. Hebb speculated that for phase sequences, reverberation might last from one to ten seconds (1949, p. 143), but how long short-term activity continues is not exactly known. In an empirical test of the duration of short-term memory, Peterson and Peterson (1959) read participants a consonant trigram (e.g., QHJ) and then instructed them to start counting backward immediately by 3s or 4s from a three-digit number they were given. Different participants had their counting interrupted at different times and were asked to repeat the consonant trigram that was read to them. The recall intervals were 3, 6, 9, 12, 15, and 18 seconds. The best retention was at a recall interval of 3 seconds, next 6 seconds, and so on. The worst recall occurred after 18 seconds. Thus, short-term memory seems to decay quickly as a function of time.

Because long-term memory is thought to depend on consolidation of short-term memory, it follows that anything that disrupts the former should also disrupt the latter. Based on this contention, Duncan (1949) trained rats to jump a barrier to avoid an electric shock. If they jumped from one side of an experimental chamber to the other side within ten seconds after they were placed in the apparatus, they could avoid being shocked. If they did not cross over to the "safe" side, they were shocked until they did. The animals were given one learning trial per day. Following each trial, each animal was given an **electroconvulsive shock (ECS)** through two electrodes clipped to its ears. The ECS causes convulsions much like those of an epileptic seizure. Depending on what group the animal was in, the shock occurred 20 seconds, 40 seconds, 60 seconds, 4 minutes, 15 minutes, 1 hour, 4 hours, or 14 hours after its learning trial. A control group received no ECS after learning. Training continued for eighteen days. Figure 14–5 shows for all groups the mean number of correct anticipations of the shock, that is, jumping to the safe side upon being placed in the apparatus.

The more closely the ECS follows a learning trial, the more it disrupts memory of the learning experience. For example, animals receiving ECS twenty seconds after a learning trial never learn the avoidance response. When the ECS is administered within an hour of the learning trial, it interferes with memory. After an hour, ECS apparently has no effect on memory. The animals receiving ECS an hour or

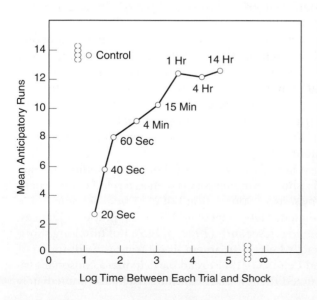

FIGURE 14–5　The results of Duncan's study show that as the delay between learning experience and an electro convulsive shock becomes longer, the disruptive effect of the shock on the retention of the learning experience goes down. (From "The Retroactive Effect of Electroshock on Learning," by C. P. Duncan, 1949, *Journal of Comparative and Physiological Psychology, 42,* p. 35. Copyright © 1949 by the American Psychological Association. Reprinted by permission.)

more after their learning trial perform as well as the control group that received no ECS. The results of Duncan's experiment lend support to consolidation theory and suggest that the consolidation period lasts about an hour. However, the moments immediately following a learning experience seem to be more important for consolidation than those after about the first minute.

Further evidence is provided for consolidation theory by the phenomenon called **retrograde amnesia,** which refers to the loss of memory for those events just prior to a traumatic experience, such as an automobile accident or a combat injury. This memory loss for events prior to a traumatic event may involve hours, days, or even months. Usually the memory of such events will slowly return except for those immediately prior to the traumatic event. Thus, the traumatic event has the same effect as Duncan's ECS.

Do ECS and other traumas to the brain disrupt consolidation of long-term memories because they interfere with neural reverberation (in cell assemblies and phase sequences) or because they interfere with neural processes that are necessary for consolidation but that are unrelated to reverberation? The question is not a trivial one, and it becomes particularly interesting when we consider the case of H.M., a surgical patient with a very special consolidation problem.

Consolidation and the Brain

A number of interrelated brain structures, collectively referred to as the **limbic system,** are important for the experience of various emotions. The **hippocampus** is one of the limbic structures that plays a critical role in learning. Brenda Milner, one of Hebb's students at McGill University, studied a patient known in psychology literature as H.M., who was recovering from surgery intended to correct his epilepsy (Milner, 1959, 1965; Scoville & Milner, 1957). During the surgical procedure, parts of both his right and left hippocampus (and related limbic structures) in his temporal lobes were damaged. After the operation, H.M. exhibited a severe case of **anterograde amnesia.** That is, he had little trouble recalling events that took place before the surgery, but he seemed to have great difficulty consolidating new long-term memories. Patients like H.M. perform well on intelligence tests and do very well on motor skills that were acquired before the damage to their hippocampus, and Milner reports no apparent personality change resulting from the brain damage. Such individuals may behave as if their short-term memory is functioning normally, but as soon as their attention is distracted from a task at-hand, the memory of it is lost. Patients like H.M. show us that reverbratory activity, including reverberation caused by mere repetition of information, is not sufficient to create long-term memory. The hippocampus and possibly other structures are therefore believed to be responsible for consolidation.

The problems experienced by H.M. and other patients with hippocampal damage are even more complex than researchers first imagined. Patients with brain damage like H.M.'s are able to learn certain complex procedural tasks, but they seem to be unaware that learning has occurred. For example, their performance on tasks such as puzzle building or inverted-mirror drawing improves with practice, thus demonstrating long-term learning, but the patients may claim that they have never seen or practiced the tasks in question. In addition, they have great difficulty with tasks that involve list learning and recall of new events and facts (Cohen & Eichenbaum, 1993; Cohen et al. 1999; Cohen & Squire, 1980; Squire, 1992). Researchers use the term **declarative memory** when referring to the type of long-term memory that is disrupted in patients like H.M. Declarative memory involves higher-order memory, including the memory that one has, in fact, learned something new. Damage to the hippocampus and other structures in the medial temporal lobe prevents consolidation of declarative memory, but, as we have noted, it does not impair a different type of long-term memory.

A set of neural structures called the **basal ganglia** were once thought to be involved primarily with control of muscle movement. Their roles in muscle control are evident in patients with either Huntington's disease or Parkinson's disease, both of which involve some degree of damage to the basal ganglia. Mishkin and his coworkers (Mishkin, Malamut, & Bachevalier, 1984; Petri & Mishkin, 1994) reported that patients with these disorders exhibit intact declarative memory but impaired consolidation of **procedural memory,** defined as memory for complex motor tasks such as puzzle building or inverted mirror drawing. More recent reports confirm the general finding, although they suggest that procedural memory is most impaired in patients with Parkinson's disease (Thomas-Ollivier et al., 1999; Vakil & Herishanu-Naaman, 1998). In contrast to patients with hippocampal damage (like H.M.), these patients show little or no improvement on puzzle tasks despite repeated practice, but they are aware of their failure to learn the tasks.

The conclusions drawn from observations of patients who have suffered damage to medial temporal lobe structures or to the basal ganglia are confirmed by studies utilizing brain-imaging technologies to study healthy experimental participants (Gabrieli, 1998; Gabrieli et al. 1997; Gabrieli, Brewer, & Poldrack, 1998): There are at least two kinds of long-term memory, declarative memory and procedural memory, each of which has its own neural mechanisms for consolidation. Furthermore, activities of the limbic system (for declarative memory) and the basal ganglia (for procedural memory), rather than reverberation itself, are needed to convert relatively unstable short-term memory into a permanent long-term memory.

Our overview of Hebb's theoretical contributions is now complete. Hebb opened lines of investigation in psychology that were previously ignored or did not exist, and he was one of the first to search for the neurophysiological correlates of psychological phenomena, such as learning. Due to a large extent to Hebb's efforts, neuroscience is very popular today and has expanded into many areas beyond those studied by Hebb and his students. We cannot here review the many fruitful lines of inquiry now pursued within the neurophysiological paradigm. What follows, however, represents a sample of such research. The first topic, reinforcement centers in the brain, is indirectly related to Hebb because it grew out of an accidental discovery made in Hebb's laboratory while the reticular activating system (RAS) was being studied. The next topic, learning at the cellular level, returns us to Hebb's fundamental notion of cell assemblies.

The final topic, cerebral asymmetry (the left-brain, right-brain issue) is not directly related to Hebb's theory, although one of his students made important research contributions in the area.

HEBB'S INFLUENCE ON NEUROSCIENTIFIC RESEARCH

Reinforcement and the Brain

As we have seen, Hebb's concept of optimal arousal provided an explanation of reinforcement that went beyond those offered by either Skinner or Hull. An accidental discovery in 1954 added a new and perplexing twist to the reinforcement puzzle. In our chapter on Pavlov, we noted that his discovery of the conditioned reflex was quite accidental. **Serendipity,** finding one thing while looking for another, has led to the discovery of important phenomena and sometimes to scientific breakthroughs. Another example of serendipity in science is the discovery of **reinforcement centers in the brain** by Olds and Milner (1954). Olds (1955), working in Hebb's laboratory at McGill University, described how the discovery was made:

> In the fall of 1953, we were looking for more information about the reticular activating system. We used electrodes permanently implanted in the brain of a healthy behaving rat. . . . Quite by accident, an electrode was implanted in the region of the anterior commissure.
>
> The result was quite amazing. When the animal was stimulated at a specific place in an open field, he sometimes moved away but he returned and sniffed around that area. More stimulations at that place caused him to spend more of his time there.
>
> Later we found that this same animal could be "pulled" to any spot in the maze by giving a small electrical stimulus after each response in the right direction. This was akin to playing the "hot" and "cold" game with a child. Each correct response brought electrical pulses which seemed to indicate to the animal that it was on the right track. (pp. 83–84)

The areas identified by Olds and Milner, scattered throughout the mammalian limbic system (part of the lower cortex, the hippocampus, the amygdala, the septum, and parts of the thalamus and hypothalamus), are called reinforcement centers because when they are electrically stimulated, animals tend to repeat the behavior that preceded the stimulation. Therefore, an animal with an electrode implanted in a reinforcement center can be trained to press a bar in a Skinner box simply by stimulating that area of the brain with a mild electrical current when the animal performs the appropriate response.

Olds and Milner (1954) are often credited with the discovery of the *pleasure center* in the brain. We intentionally use the term *reinforcement center* because substantial research suggests that the phenomenon discovered by Olds and Milner has less to do with pleasure than with the activational and motivational properties of reinforcers. First, we note that reinforcement by direct brain stimulation has some unusual characteristics and operates differently from primary reinforcers such as food or water. These characteristics are:

1. **No deprivation needed before training.** Unlike training involving food or water as a reinforcer, generally no deprivation schedule is needed when direct brain stimulation is used as a reinforcer. The animal does not need to be in a drive state. There are exceptions, however, and occasionally reinforcement centers are found that depend on the drive state of the organism.

2. **Satiation does not occur.** When food or water is used as a reinforcer, the animal will eventually satiate; that is, its need for food or water will be satisfied, and it will stop responding. With direct brain stimulation, however, the animal will go on responding at an extraordinarily high rate (for example, bar-pressing rates as high as 7,000 per hour have been reported) until it becomes physically exhausted.

3. **Takes priority over other drives.** Animals continue to press a bar for direct brain stimulation even when food is available and they have not eaten for a considerable length of time. Also, animals will often withstand a more intense electrical shock to obtain brain stimulation reinforcement than to obtain food, even if they have not eaten for twenty-four hours.

4. **There is rapid extinction.** Rather than the gradual extinction process observed when food or water is the reinforcer, extinction takes place almost immediately when direct brain stimulation reinforcement is terminated. Although extinction is rapid, the response rate recurs at full strength when the animal is again reinforced.

5. **Most schedules of reinforcement do not work.** Because extinction occurs very rapidly when brain stimulation is terminated, some partial reinforcement schedules cause the animal to stop responding. In general, only schedules of reinforcement that provide frequent reinforcement can be used with direct brain stimulation.

The role of dopamine   Current research concerning reinforcement centers is focused on a small part of the limbic system called the **nucleus accumbens.** In general, if a stimulating electrode causes cells in the nucleus accumbens to release the neurotransmitter dopamine, brain stimulation via that electrode will be reinforcing. If a stimulating electrode does not cause release of dopamine, reinforcing effects via that electrode are not observed (Garris et al., 1999). Salamone and Correa (2002) note that many researchers, textbooks, and even the popular media incorrectly equate release of dopamine in the nucleus accumbens with the pleasurable effects of biological reinforcers like food, water, or sex. Similarly, the euphoric effects of addictive drugs are also (mis)attributed to dopamine release by the nucleus accumbens. For example, nicotine, alcohol, cocaine, and heroin are very different from each other in terms of their *primary* chemical actions in the nervous system, yet what they and other addictive substances seem to have in common is their stimulation of nucleus accumbens dopamine (Leshner & Koob, 1999; Renaldi et al. 1999).

Several researchers (e.g., Berridge, 2005; Berridge & Robinson, 1995, 1998; Kalivas & Nakamura, 1999; Robinson & Berridge, 2000, 2001, 2003; Salamone & Correa,

2002; Salamone, Correa, Mingote, & Weber, 2003) suggest that dopamine activity in the nucleus accumbens mediates *anticipatory* or *motivational* aspects of reinforcers rather than the pleasure associated with them. The pleasurable effects associated with reinforcers, therefore, are not necessarily dopamine effects, but dopamine activity in the nucleus accumbens mediates what is common to all reinforcers: Animals want them and are motivated to attain them.

Importantly, dopamine-mediated motivational effects can be dissociated from pleasure/hedonic effects. Salamone and his colleagues (Aberman & Salamone, 1999; Salamone et al., 1995) first trained rats to lever-press for food reinforcement on a continuous reinforcement schedule. The rats were then injected with drugs that depleted nucleus accumbens dopamine. The animals continued to lever-press after dopamine depletion, indicating that the primary reinforcing characteristics of food were not affected by decreases in dopamine. Other researchers have demonstrated that injections of drugs that block dopamine in the nucleus accumbens do not interfere with the reward properties of sucrose (Ikemoto & Panksepp, 1996) or food (Nowend et al., 2001). Furthermore, injections of dopamine-blocking drugs in humans do not reduce the subjective euphoria caused by cocaine (Gawin, 1986; Haney et al. 2001; Nann-Vernotica et al., 2001) or by amphetamine (Brauer & DeWit, 1997). Even when dopamine is depleted, rather than blocked, human cocaine users report dose-dependent pleasure and euphoria but do not report craving or wanting the drug (Leyton et al., 2005).

Lab animals in which dopamine is either blocked or depleted become overly sensitized to work requirements of operant tasks. For example, if partial reinforcement schedules requiring sustained work are used, responding is significantly reduced (Aberman & Salamone, 1999; Correa et al., 2002). If given a T-maze choice between climbing a small hurdle for a large amount of food and obtaining a "free" but smaller amount of food, untreated animals climb the hurdle and eat a larger amount. After dopamine is blocked, animals choose the arm of the T-maze without the hurdle but continue to consume the food reinforcers (Cousins et al., 1996; Salamone, Cousins, & Bucher, 1994).

If the relationships between reinforcement, dopamine, and pleasure seem tenuous, consider the relationships between reinforcement, dopamine, and learning. Robinson, Sandstrom, Denenberg, and Palmiter (2005) conducted research with a strain of mice that are genetically engineered to be dopamine deficient. These mice are usually hypoactive, but their general inactivity can be reversed by injecting them with a drug that acts as a dopamine precursor. In a critical experiment, dopamine-deficient mice in three groups were reinforced to turn left or right in a T-maze. One group received no dopamine precursor, one received caffeine, and the third received the dopamine precursor. During the learning phase of the experiment, the untreated mice had to be assisted and placed in the correct arm of the T-maze (due to their hypoactivity); the caffeine-treated mice were active but showed no practice-related improvement in selecting the correct arm of the maze; and the mice treated with the dopamine precursor improved with each day of training. In a follow-up, test phase of the experiment, all mice were treated with the dopamine precursor. The mice that were untreated during the learning phase performed as well as the mice that were treated with the dopamine precursor during learning, but superior performance was observed in the mice that experienced the learning phase while treated with caffeine. The important observation here is that neither the untreated nor the caffeine-treated mice had dopamine during the learning phase. The data from the test phase indicate clearly, however, that learning did occur. These authors concluded that "dopamine is not necessary for liking rewards or for learning to make associations between rewards and salient cues. Rather, dopamine is necessary for reward-related cues to attain motivational significance such that they become wanted and therefore drive performance of goal-directed behavior" (p. 5).

Making Connections: Real Cells and Real Cell Assemblies

In the years since Hebb first wrote of recruitment, fractionation, cell assemblies, and phase sequences, psychologists have been surprised at the accuracy of his conjectures about the nervous system.

Appreciation of Hebb's speculations depends, in part, on an understanding of learning between two **neurons.** A neuron consists of a cell body; one or more extended processes called **axons,** which are specialized for carrying electrochemical information away from the cell; and many branching **dendrites,** specialized for receiving electrochemical information from other cells' axons. A simplified schematic pair of brain cells is represented in Figure 14–6.

The mammalian brain cell exists in a watery bath filled with ions of potassium, sodium, calcium, and chloride, as well as ionized protein molecules. We can think of a single brain cell as a fragile and sensitive mediator of a fluctuating electrochemical balance. In the case of a mammalian neuron, the cell is engaged in metabolic processes that function primarily to keep sodium ions outside the cell and to keep potassium ions inside. This particular state of "balanced tension" is called the **resting potential** of the cell, which refers to the electrical charge difference (an electrical potential) between the inside and the outside of the cell membrane. In the typical, resting mammalian neuron, the inside of the membrane is negatively charged relative to the outside, and the difference averages approximately seventy millivolts.

If this state of polarization is reduced, the electrical difference between the inside and outside of the cell membrane begins to move toward zero millivolts, and

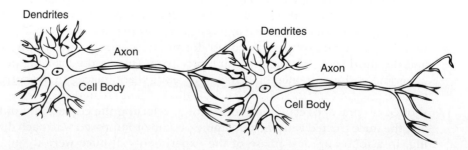

FIGURE 14–6   A simplified schematic drawing of two neurons. Cell bodies, dendrites, and axons are indicated.

the membrane may reach a millivoltage level called the **threshold,** at which level it can no longer maintain ion segregation. At that point, there is a slight reversal of the ionic distribution, primarily involving an exchange of the sodium and potassium ions. This causes the electrical condition of the cell membrane to reverse as well, with the inside becoming positively charged with respect to the outside. The cell then expends energy to reestablish the resting potential. The entire process of ionic reversal and "reloading" is referred to as the **action potential,** an event that actually travels from the cell body down the length of the axon.

The end or terminal of the axon responds to the arrival of an action potential by releasing a chemical **neurotransmitter** such as acetylcholine or dopamine into the extracellular space, or **synapse,** between it and other cells. **Receptors** on the dendrites and cell bodies of surrounding cells respond to released neurotransmitters with chemical reactions that move them toward or away from their own thresholds.

Brain cells exist in relationships with hundreds and perhaps thousands of other cells. Their individual excitatory and inhibitory activities are the result of continuous summation of chemical information from surrounding cells. We might imagine at the most fundamental level that learning entails a change in the relationship between two cells, and this is the level at which Hebb first focused. Specifically, learning consists of a change in a receiving cell's response to the neurotransmitter released by a sending cell. In a simplified example, we might imagine an unlearned receiving cell that does not generate its own action potentials in response to a neurotransmitter from a sending cell. We infer learning when the receiving cell begins to reliably and predictably generate an action potential in response to the sending cell's activity. Although Hebb suggested that the activity of one cell in contiguity with another might well change the relationship between them, he could only make conjectures about the processes involved. Recent research, however, has revealed mechanisms very much like those that Hebb anticipated.

Learning in *Aplysia*

A major obstacle to understanding the possible mechanisms of learning, recruitment, and fractionation lies in the sheer numbers of neurons involved in even the simplest behaviors in mammals. Eric Kandel, one of three winners of the 2000 Nobel Prize in Physiology or Medicine, and his associates (Castellucci & Kandel, 1974; Dale, Schacher, & Kandel, 1988; Kandel & Schwartz, 1982; Kupfermann et al., 1970) solved this problem by working with a shell-less sea mollusk called *Aplysia,* which has a relatively simple nervous system yet displays cell-assembly behaviors. The backside of this marine animal contains three external organs called the gill, the mantle shelf, and the siphon, and all three of these structures are reflexively withdrawn when either the mantel shelf or the siphon is touched.

When one of these reflex-triggering structures is stimulated weakly and repeatedly, the withdrawal response habituates. That is, it slowly disappears. Thus a circuit that was initially activated by an external input is "subtracted" from the larger pattern of neural activity. This process corresponds closely to Hebb's notion of fractionation, but how does this habituation occur?

Eric R. Kandel. (Courtesy of Eric R. Kandel.)

Kandel's research (Castellucci & Kandel, 1974) demonstrated that the critical event mediating habituation is a decrease in the release of neurotransmitter(s) from the sensory neuron, which serves to signal the motor neuron that triggers the reflexive withdrawal of the external organs. Exactly why and how the sensory neuron learns to ignore the weak, repetitive stimulation is not known, but the fact that the response is easily reactivated makes it clear that habituation is more than simple fatigue or depletion of neurotransmitter(s) (Kupfermann et al., 1970).

The reactivation process, called sensitization, occurs when, for example, an electric shock is delivered to the tail (near the organs) of the animal. After the shock, weak stimulation once again produces a withdrawal reflex. Sensitization is a more complex process than habituation. It involves an additional neuron, which is neither a sensory neuron nor a motor neuron. This **interneuron** stimulates the sensory neuron, causing it to release extra neurotransmitter onto the motor neuron controlling organ withdrawal (Cleary, Hammer, & Byrne, 1989; Dale, Schacher, & Kandel, 1988). Thus, sensitization seems to involve construction of a simple, three-element cell assembly composed of a sensory neuron, an interneuron, and a motor neuron, and provides a model for Hebb's notion of recruitment. As the reader might have anticipated, Kandel's studies have further demonstrated that an interneuron-mediated process similar to the one involved in sensitization underlies classical conditioning (Kandel & Schwartz, 1982).

Long-Term Potentiation

Kandel's work partly answers questions about how communication patterns between cells change. Additional mechanisms are revealed in the phenomenon called **long-term potentiation (LTP)** (Bliss & Lømo, 1973; Lømo, 1966). If part of the hippocampus, a structure already implicated in memory consolidation, is electrically stimulated with a single, weak electrical pulse, the strength of connections with other parts of the hippocampus can be inferred by recording the spread of neuro-electrical activity generated by the initial, weak pulse. More specifically, cells in an area of the hippocampus called the perforant path are stimulated, and the spread of that stimulation is recorded in and near another hippocampal area called the dentate gyrus. When the weak pulse is followed immediately by a burst of stronger, high-frequency electrical stimulation, the relationship between the perforant path cells and the dentate gyrus cells changes dramatically. Initially, the spread of the weak stimulation is slight, but after the high-frequency stimulation, a weak current applied to the perforant path produces much stronger activity in and near the dentate gyrus. The stronger, high-frequency stimulation is thus said to *potentiate* the effect of the initial, weak stimulation, and the effect can last for months (Figure 14–7).

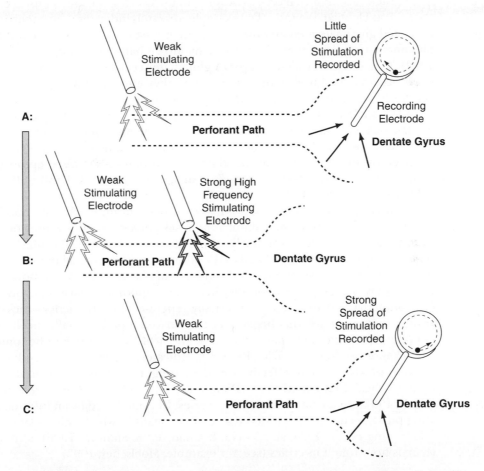

FIGURE 14–7 (A) Weak electrical stimulation of the perforant path has little effect on cells in the dentate gyrus. (B) Weak stimulation of the perforant path is followed by stronger, high-frequency, *potentiating* electrical stimulation. (C) Now weak stimulation of the perforant path spreads and readily excites cells in the dentate gyrus.

LTP occurs in some areas of the hippocampus as we have described. In other parts of the hippocampus, LTP will not occur unless the weak stimulation and the stronger, high-frequency stimulation occur simultaneously. Kandel (1991) has suggested that the two different LTP phenomena reflect the neural bases for nonassociative learning (habituation and sensitization) in the former case, and for associative learning in the latter. Note that associative LTP entails events described in Hebb's neurophysiological postulate. That is, a sending cell with weak influence on a receiving cell is active at the same time the receiving cell is stimulated by a different, more influential, sending cell. The simultaneous activity of the weaker sending cell and the receiving cell changes the electrochemical-sensitivity relationship between the two cells. Neuroscientists call the synapse between neurons in this arrangement a **Hebbian synapse.**

Much recent work has been devoted to uncovering the mechanisms of associative LTP at Hebbian synapses. For example, research indicates that a neurotransmitter called glutamate mediates the effect, but at least two different types of dendritic glutamate receptors are involved (Cotman, Monaghan, & Ganong, 1988; Nakanishi, 1992). One of them, called an NMDA glutamate receptor (named after the chemical procedure used to differentiate it from other glutamate receptors), cannot be activated unless nearby non-NMDA receptors on the same receiving cell are also stimulated by glutamate. If both receptor types are stimulated at the same time, NMDA receptors are activated and allow both calcium and sodium ions to enter dendrite sites. Researchers believe that the calcium ions initiate a series of enzymatic events that somehow increase the sensitivity of non-NMDA receptors (Bading, Ginty, & Greenberg, 1993; Baudry & Lynch, 1993; Lynch & Baudry, 1984, 1991; Schuman & Madison, 1991).

Initially, it was assumed that LTP would not occur unless the potentiating stimulus was of a high frequency, about 100 pulses per second. It was further assumed that, because the brain is unlikely to produce anything like the high-frequency, potentiating electrical pulses used in the laboratory, LTP was a laboratory phenomenon and nothing more. Interestingly, when a rat is in a complex and novel environment and is engaging in exploratory behavior (supposedly learning about the new environment), we can record an internally generated, low-frequency series of pulses (called theta rhythms) that begin near the perforant path and affect cells near the dentate gyrus—the same path studied in the artificially induced phenomenon of LTP (Vanderwolf et al., 1975). Research indicates that artificially produced theta rhythms produce LTP as effectively as the strong, high-frequency stimulation used in the typical LTP experiment (Diamond, Dunwiddie, & Rose, 1988; Staubli & Lynch, 1987). As a result of these discoveries, LTP, mediated by an internal potentiating pulse, is currently considered a possible means by which certain kinds of natural learning occur (Escobar, Alcocer, & Chao, 1998; Stanton, 1996), although this claim is not without its critics (see, for example, Hoelscher, 1997).

Long-Term Depression

Learning involves recruitment of new cell assemblies and phase sequences that are necessary for successful cognitive or motor behavior, but it also involves elimination of phase sequences that are unnecessary or that may actively interfere with smooth, efficient performance. LTP provides a mechanism by which neurons that are not part of an assembly or sequence might be stimulated and thereby recruited. A related phenomenon called **long-term depression (LTD)** provides a possible mechanism by which neurons that are initially part of an assembly can be eliminated. In LTD, when two sending cells stimulate a single receiving cell, the receiving cell becomes unresponsive to the activity of the sending cells (Kerr & Abraham, 1995). LTD has been demonstrated in the cerebellum, parts of the hippocampus (Akhondzadeh & Stone, 1996; Doyere et al., 1996), and parts of the cortex (Kirkwood et al., 1999). Currently, the role of NMDA receptors in LTD is uncertain, and neurotransmitters other than glutamate may be involved (Kirkwood et al., 1999).

Neuroplasticity

For many years, it was assumed that synaptic connections in the adult mammalian brain are relatively fixed and stable and that changes in the aging brain are due primarily to cell death and atrophy. Recent research shows that these assumptions are, at least partially, incorrect. **Neuroplasticity** (or brain plasticity) is the term used to describe the brain's capacity to reorganize or modify its connections as the result of experience. We have already examined several examples of neuroplasticity. They include learning, whether via a Hebbian synapse or another mechanism, LTP, and LTD. Findings from several laboratories indicate that many types of brain plasticity are maintained throughout adulthood (Azari & Seitz, 2000; Kolb, Gibb, & Robinson, 2003; Kolb & Whishaw, 1998). Today's leading plasticity researchers give credit to the heuristic function (see Chapter 2) of Hebb's theory for stimulating and guiding the research that reveals lifelong development of new synaptic connections (Gage, 2002; Kolb & Whishaw, 1998). Next, we explore the kinds of plasticity observed in the mammalian brain with special attention to learning.

Experience and Dendrite Development Previously, we saw that enriched environments facilitate learning. Several studies also show that enrichment-enhanced learning is associated with increased brain weight, increased levels of neurotransmitters, and other physical changes in the brain (Diamond, Lindner, & Raymond, 1967; Greenough & Chang, 1989; Kolb, Gibb, & Gorny, 2003; Rosenzweig & Bennett, 1978). Of specific interest are observations that experience changes both the length of a neuron's dendrites and the numbers of receptor sites on dendrites. Because up to 95 percent of a neuron's synapses occur on dendrites (Kolb, Gibb, & Robinson, 2003; Kolb & Whishaw, 1998; Schade & Baxter, 1960), increases in dendrite length or in numbers of receptors are likely to result in new synaptic connections and to be reflected in behavioral or cognitive changes. For example, *post mortem* examination of human brains by Jacobs, Schall, and Scheibel (1993) revealed that dendrites in the language areas of the brain are more complex in college-educated people than in people with high school educations. Similarly, the language areas of high school–educated individuals have more differentiated dendrites than comparable areas from people with less education. Women often score higher than men on tests of verbal ability, and these researchers also found more elaborate dendrite organization in the language areas of (deceased) women than in men. Other researchers have found that brain areas believed to control higher-order thinking have more differentiated dendrites than do areas representing the fingers, which have more differentiated dendrites than those brain areas representing the trunk of the body. Thus, those dendrites mediating very sophisticated cognitive processes are more elaborate than the dendrites controlling functions of intermediate complexity (finger dexterity) and so on. Furthermore, differences in dendrite organization between areas representing the fingers and areas representing the trunk of the body are more pronounced in people who have learned specialized skills requiring finger dexterity—piano playing, for example (Scheibel et al., 1990). Numerous studies with non-human animals have demonstrated predictable dendrite elaboration after exposure to experiences intended to stimulate specific parts of the brain (see Kolb & Whishaw, 1998, for a review).

It should not be inferred that increased dendrite development is always a good thing. Psychostimulants such as cocaine and amphetamines cause elaboration of the dendrites in the nucleus accumbens (Kolb et al., 2003; Li, Kolb, & Robinson, 2003; Robinson & Berridge, 2003), and these structural changes may underlie the cravings and compulsive behaviors of addicts and are, perhaps, implicated in cognitive difficulties experienced by addicts when they stop using psychostimulants (Hamilton & Kolb, 2005). Furthermore, prior exposure to psychostimulants, including nicotine, can block dendritic differentiation associated with more positive experiences, such as environmental enrichment (Hamilton & Kolb, 2005; Kolb et al., 2003).

The ultimate plasticity has been revealed by Gage and colleagues (Gage, 2002; Gage et al., 1995; Palmer, Ray, & Gage, 1995; Palmer et al., 1999), who have demonstrated that **neurogenesis,** the birth and development of new neurons, occurs well into adulthood in parts of the brains of many animals, including humans. Specifically, parts of the dentate gyrus of the hippocampus (already implicated in learning and memory) and parts of a forebrain structure connected to the olfactory bulb (the brain's sensory mechanism for olfaction or smell) have been shown to produce cells with stem cell properties. These cells can differentiate into neurons, glia, or even capillaries. This means that at least one part of the brain that is critical for learning, the hippocampus, can produce new neurons and support cells, possibly throughout the lifetime of the organism.

Some aspects of neurogenesis are quite predictable. For example, new learning—at least some types of new learning—require neurogenesis. Shors and colleagues (2001) demonstrated that a type of classical conditioning requiring intact hippocampus function is disrupted if neurogenesis is chemically blocked. Using a similar conditioning task, Leuner and associates (2004) reported that the best performing rats had more newly developed cells in the hippocampus than did the poor performers. A surprising "other side of the coin" is that some preexisting cells must die as part of the learning process. Thus, superior learning is indexed both by the birth of new cells and by elimination of old ones (Abrous, Koehl, & LeMoal, 2005).

Relearning after Brain Injury   Brain injuries like those caused by strokes result in the death of neurons, and these cells do not regenerate. After a stroke, loss of control of a hand or disruption of language skills is often due to the death of cells involved with hand-control or language, respectively. Despite the catastrophic nature of such injuries, some patients exhibit either partial or complete recovery of their stroke-induced losses. Researchers believe that this recovery is mediated by *recruitment* of neurons not typically involved with the skills in question. In Hebbian terms, recovery involves the development of new cell assemblies and phase sequences. Azari and Seitz (2000) used positron emission tomography (PET) scans to demonstrate that recovery after stroke is, in fact, due to the recruitment of synaptic patterns that are not typically observed in an uninjured brain. Cornelissen and colleagues (2003) used an alternative scanning technology called magnetoencephalography (MEG) with stroke patients exhibiting *anomia* (inability to name common objects). They saw development of new synaptic pathways for test stimuli presented in a special training procedure but not for control stimuli that were omitted from special training. Therefore, the new brain activity was attributed to specific learning rather than to recovery of a general object-naming process.

Work with laboratory rats has suggested that neurogenesis may also play a role in recovery from brain injury. Darsilai, Heldmann, Lindvall, and Kokaia (2005) induced strokes in rats by artificially blocking the middle cerebral artery. In general, the strokes induced neurogenesis in the rats, with older rats showing reduced neurogenesis in the hippocampus. Both old and young rats showed comparable neurogenesis in other areas, however. Thus not only learning but also a serious insult to the brain can induce neurogenesis, possibly as a repair mechanism.

Although damage caused by strokes is somewhat unpredictable, brain damage due to excess alcohol consumption is not. Chronic alcohol consumption produces cognitive impairment as well as changes in brain morphology, both of which are partially reversed when alcohol consumption ends. Working with laboratory rats, Nixon and Crews (2004) showed that neurogenesis is inhibited during a period of chronic alcohol consumption but that it increases dramatically during abstinence, thus suggesting a potential mechanism for recovery of cognitive function.

Complex Mechanisms   Numerous factors affect neuroplasticity, and many of these mechanisms may be operating simultaneously. There is widespread agreement that plasticity is modulated by growth-stimulating proteins called neurotrophins. Some of these, for example, nerve growth factor (NGF) and brain-derived neurotrophic factor (BDNF), enhance plasticity (Gottschalk et al., 1999; Kolb et al., 1996; Kolb et al., 1997; Lu, 2003). In addition, sex hormones play an important role in determining the morphology (shape) of neurons, and circulating levels of sex hormones are critical mediators of plasticity (Fernandez et al. 2003; Juraska, 1990; Juraska, Fitch, & Washburne, 1989; Kolb & Stewart, 1995; Stewart & Kolb, 1994). Stress reduces plasticity (Maroun & Richter-Levin, 2003; McEwen, 2001; Vyas et al., 2002), as does clinical depression (Laifenfeld, Klein, & Ben-Shachar, 2002; Sapolsky, 2000), but novel exercise and experience increase plasticity (Black et al., 1990).

An intriguing plasticity mechanism is the "silent synapse" (e.g., Atwood & Wojtowicz, 1999). A silent synapse is a synaptic connection that, for any number of reasons, might be otherwise nonfunctional but which becomes functional and active during learning. Such a synapse might be silent because no neurotransmitter is released from an axon terminal, even when a neuron generates normal action potentials. On the other hand, it may be silent because receptor sites are somehow deactivated. There is recent evidence for both mechanisms (Bekkers, 2005; Cabezas & Buño, 2006; Voigt, Opitz, & Dolabela de Lima, 2005; Voronin & Cherubini, 2004). Investigation into the mechanisms that transform a silent synapse into an active one is ongoing.

Mirror Neurons: Observational Learning

As we have seen, learning theories do not necessarily invoke brain mechanisms to explain learning, although some theories do so in varying degrees. Examples include Thorndike's neural bond, Pavlov's cortical mosaic, and Gestalt theory's principle of isomorphism. A neurophysiological theory of learning, however, must describe both a well-documented learning phenomenon *and* the neural events that underlie it. Because of their relative simplicity, we might expect that habituation, sensitization, and some types of classical conditioning are described with more precision by neurophysiological theories than are complex, cognitive learning phenomena. Surprisingly, recent findings in the neurosciences may reveal a relatively straightforward neural mechanism underlying social-cognitive learning, arguably one of the more complex types of learning we have presented.

Researchers at the University of Parma, Italy, were studying neurons that control motor functions in rhesus monkeys when the monkeys grasp or handle food. In yet another serendipitous moment, the researchers noticed that the neurons fired not only when the monkeys handled food but also when they *watched* researchers handling food. Subsequent controlled studies (di Pellegrino et al., 1992; Gallese et al., 1996; Rizzolatti et al., 1996) demonstrated clearly that these cells are active both when a monkey sees another monkey (or the experimenter) make a food-related grasping motion and when the monkey itself makes a comparable motion. These so-called **mirror neurons** reveal one way in which the brain encodes a behavior made by another animal, thereby facilitating execution of the same behavior. Using computer-imaging techniques, rather than single cell recording, researchers have demonstrated that humans also have mirror neuron systems, although they appear to be more complex than the food-grasping neurons observed in monkeys (Manthey, Shubotz, & von Cramon, 2003; Montgomery, Isenberg, & Haxby , 2007; Rizzolatti et al., 1996; Rizzolatti, Fogassi, & Gallese, 2001).

The discovery of mirror neurons has generated great enthusiasm among some researchers. Ramachandran (2000), for example, speculated that "mirror neurons will do for psychology what DNA did for biology: they will provide a unifying framework and help explain a host of mental abilities that have hitherto remained mysterious and inaccessible to experiments" (p. 1). He suggested, further, that the mirror neuron system may provide the neural mechanism that explains how we understand another's intentions or how we empathize with others. Although other researchers are more cautious in their speculations (Wilson & Knoblich, 2005), it is clear that the existence of the mirror system in humans has important implications for imitation and observational learning (see Chapter 13).

First, the mirror system appears to work more or less automatically. An observed action is directly mapped from the sensory cortex onto the motor cortex responsible for that action (Iacoboni et al., 1999). Consider, for example, the **chameleon effect,** the "nonconscious mimicry of the postures, mannerisms, facial expressions, and other behaviors of one's interaction partners" (Chartrand & Bargh, 1999, p. 893). In the chameleon effect, we adopt behavioral patterns, including vocal intonations, of those with whom we are interacting, and this unintended imitation tends to have facilitative social effects. This type of imitation appears to require no cognitive intervention or planning. We are not aware that we mimic, nor are we overtly attentive to those behaviors that have been "selected" for mimicry. Perhaps the mirror neuron system underlies this involuntary phenomenon (Wilson & Knoblich, 2005).

Second, although the mirror system allows immediate imitation of an observed behavior, as in the chameleon effect, it also allows storage of a behavior for execution at a later time. Clearly, there are occasions when immediate imitation is maladaptive. Imagine yourself at a job interview: Your future employer displays eccentric lip-licking and eyebrow-tugging behaviors, along with other idiosyncratic gestures that we cannot mention. As entertaining as these may be for you, mimicking them during the interview could be a costly mistake. Better to observe and store them now and then display them later, to the delight of your friends (after you have been hired, of course). Behaviors mapped onto mirror neurons can, therefore, be expressed or suppressed, depending on prevailing conditions.

Third, as in our job interview example, the behavior mapped by mirror neurons requires no reinforcement. It is simply the nature of these cells that they participate both in the observation of a significant behavior and in the subsequent execution of that behavior. No reinforcement or cognitive analysis intervenes between sensory representation and motor representation. As action is observed, its motor pattern is represented. Thus, as Bandura claimed, observational learning can occur constantly in social situations, but attention and performance are modulated, depending on the reinforcing or punishing outcomes of the observed behavior.

Research on the Split Brain

The **corpus callosum** is a large mass of fibers that connects the two halves of the cortex. For years, the function of the corpus callosum was unknown, but in the early 1960s, it was found to be instrumental in transferring information from one side of the cortex to the other. In a series of experiments that led to a share of the 1981 Nobel Prize in Medicine, Roger Sperry (1913–1994) noted that there were two possible routes for such a transfer—the corpus callosum and the optic chiasm (Sperry, 1961). The optic chiasm is the point in the optic nerve where information coming from one eye is projected to the side of the cortex opposite that eye. Sperry taught

Roger W. Sperry. (Courtesy of Keystone/ Hulton Archive/Getty Images.)

intact cats to make a visual discrimination with a patch over one eye. Following discrimination training, he tested for transfer by switching the patch from one eye to the other, and he found that the animal was able to perform just as well with either eye. In other words, complete interocular transfer was found.

Then Sperry (1961) began a search for the mechanism by which information was transferred from one side of the brain to the other. His first step was to ablate (cut) the optic chiasm, both before and after training, and again he found complete transfer of training from one eye to the other. Next, he ablated the corpus callosum *after* the discrimination training, and again he found no interference with the transfer of information from one eye to the other. His next step was to ablate both the optic chiasm and the corpus callosum before training, and he found that such a preparation prevented transfer from one eye to the other. Cutting both the optic chiasm and the corpus callosum created two separate brains, with one eye going to each and with no exchange of information between them. Sperry's split-brain preparation is seen in Figure 14–8.

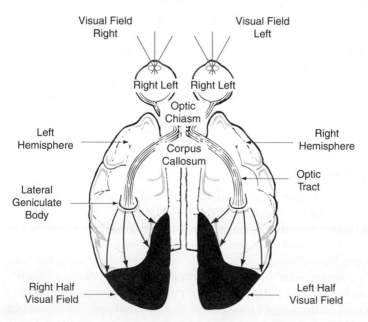

FIGURE 14–8   A diagram of Sperry's split-brain preparation. (From "The Great Cerebral Commissure," by R. W. Sperry, 1964, January, *Scientific American,* p. 46. Courtesy of the Estate of Eric O. Mose. Reproduced by permission.)

When the cat's brain was split and the cat was taught to make a visual discrimination with a patch over one eye, it had no recollection of that learning when tested with the other eye. The two halves of the split brain appeared to learn independently. In fact, with a patch over one eye, the animal could be taught to do one thing, such as approach a door with a cross on it, and with a patch over the other eye, it could be taught to approach the adjoining door with a circle on it; the two brains in the same skull learned contradictory habits. It is also possible to teach an animal to approach a stimulus (e.g., a circle) with a patch over one eye and to avoid the same stimulus with a patch over the other eye.

For various medical reasons, the **split-brain preparation** has been used on humans. The procedure has been instrumental in providing information about how the left and right hemispheres differ in the way they process information. It is to the differences between left- and right-brain functioning in humans that we turn next.

Left-Brain, Right-Brain Learning and Information Processing

In 1836, Marc Dax reported that loss of speech resulted from damage to the left cerebral hemisphere but not to the right. Dax's observation was essentially ignored, even after Paul Broca, a very prominent physician, made the same observation in 1861. In fact, we still refer to one of the language areas in the left hemisphere as Broca's area. The finding that, for the majority of people, a speech area exists on the left hemisphere but not on the right provided the first scientific evidence that the two cerebral hemispheres are asymmetrical in function.

Model   Patient's Copy

FIGURE 14–9 Attempts of a patient with right-brain damage to copy drawings of various objects. The incomplete copies exemplify the neglect syndrome. (From *Left Brain, Right Brain*, rev. ed., p. 160, by S. P. Springer & G. Deutsch, 1985, San Francisco, W. H. Freeman and Company. Copyright © 1981, 1985. Reprinted with the permission of W. H. Freeman and Company.)

Individuals with damage to their right hemispheres are likely to display difficulties related to attention or perception. They may be disoriented in familiar surroundings and have difficulty recognizing familiar faces and objects. Also, individuals with right-brain damage are more likely than patients with damage to the left hemisphere to display **neglect syndrome,** a disorder characterized by failure to see or attend to the left visual field or even to the left side of the body. Individuals exhibiting neglect syndrome have been known to shave only the right half of their faces or eat food only off the right side of a plate. When patients with right-hemisphere damage are asked to reproduce pictures placed in front of them, the results are often like those shown in Figure 14–9. The fact that these kinds of difficulties are more likely after damage to the right hemisphere was taken as further evidence that the two cerebral hemispheres function differently.

Hemispheric Functioning in Normal Brains

On the basis of the study of brain-damaged individuals and those whose brains were surgically split for medical reasons, it was clear that each hemisphere of the brain could perceive, learn, remember, and feel independently of the other hemisphere. One method used to determine how the two cerebral hemispheres function in individuals with normal, intact brains is **dichotic listening.** Although Broadbent used dichotic listening earlier to study selective attention, it was Doreen Kimura, a student of both Hebb and Brenda Milner, who used it as a safe and reliable method of studying cerebral asymmetry in normal subjects (Kimura, 1961, 1964, 1967).

The dichotic listening technique involves sending competing information, such as pairs of syllables or digits, to the left and right ears simultaneously through stereo headphones. For example, the syllable "ba" might be presented to the subject's left ear and the syllable "ga" to the right ear at the same time. In view of the fact that information presented to the left ear is projected mainly onto the right hemisphere and information presented to the right ear is projected mainly onto the left hemisphere, the question is which of the two simultaneously presented syllables or digits will be reported accurately. Under the circumstances just described, nearly all right-handers and most left-handers accurately report the digits or syllables presented to their right ears more often than those presented to their left ears. Therefore, the contention that in most humans, the left hemisphere is responsible for processing verbal information was again confirmed.

Doreen Kimura. (Courtesy of Doreen Kimura.)

Some have argued that instead of concluding from dichotic listening research that the left hemisphere is specialized for speech perception, it is more accurate to conclude that it is specialized for auditory perception in general or for general attention. However, the fact that most normal right-handers perceive melodies (Kimura, 1964) and environmental sounds such as dogs barking and automobile engines (Curry, 1967) better with their left ears (right hemispheres) does not support such an argument.

Speculations

Research into the differences between hemispheres generated a great deal of speculation concerning the role of cerebral asymmetry in everyday life. Bogen (1977) suggested that the dichotomous ways in which the world or thought processes are often described reflect the two kinds of hemispheric intelligence. According to Bogen, dichotomies such as those listed below are only manifestations of how the left and right brains process information (p. 135):

Left Hemisphere	Right Hemisphere
Intellect	Intuition
Convergent	Divergent
Realistic	Impulsive
Intellectual	Sensuous
Discrete	Continuous
Directed	Free
Rational	Intuitive
Historical	Timeless
Analytic	Holistic
Successive	Simultaneous
Objective	Subjective
Atomistic	Gross

The attempt to find dichotomies such as these and then explain their existence in terms of how the cerebral hemispheres process information has been called **dichotomania.** After reviewing the research on laterality, Beaton (1985) concluded that it is inappropriate to describe hemispheric functioning in terms of any dichotomies:

> There are certain problems in attempting to encapsulate some "fundamental" hemispheric difference in terms of . . . dichotomies. In the first place, virtually all investigators are agreed that cerebral asymmetry is not absolute but a matter of degree. It has not been shown, for example, that one hemisphere is totally incapable of carrying out the functions normally ascribed to its partner. Even with regard to language, the area in which left-right asymmetry is most unequivocal, it is evident that the right hemisphere possesses considerable powers of comprehension and can, under certain circumstances, demonstrate some expressive ability. . . .

Other dichotomies are even less securely founded. . . . There is, after all, no reason *why* the brain should have evolved so conveniently. . . . Perhaps then, a single dichotomy of brain function is inherently improbable. . . . It may, therefore, be profoundly misleading to assume that the relationship between the hemispheres as a whole can be described in terms of any single principle. (pp. 285–288)

Jerre Levy, a longtime researcher of left-brain, right-brain functioning, noted that although it is possible, under special circumstances, to demonstrate that the two hemispheres function differently, it is impossible to separate those functions in a normal, intact brain. In her article "Right Brain, Left Brain: Fact and Fiction," Levy (1985) said,

The two-brain myth was founded on an erroneous premise: that since each hemisphere was specialized, each must function as an independent brain. But, in fact, just the opposite is true. . . . Normal people have not half a brain nor two brains but one gloriously differentiated brain, with each hemisphere contributing its specialized abilities. . . . We have a single brain that generates a single mental self. (pp. 43–44)

Gazzaniga and LeDoux (1978) are less generous in their analysis. After extensive experimentation with split-brain patients, they concluded that the popular dichotomous misconception is a result of poorly designed experiments in which results are determined by "response bias" rather than by differences between the hemispheres. That is, experimental data are influenced by the type of response required of the experimental participant rather than by perceptual or cognitive processes preceding the response. Because of left-hemispheric language dominance in most patients, the left hemisphere performs best when tasks require speaking or writing. The right hemisphere is dominant when patients are required to respond by using their hands in three-dimensional space—drawing, building, touching/feeling, and so on. According to Gazzaniga and LeDoux, when experimenters assess hemispheric specialization by using tasks that minimize response bias, the differences between hemispheres are virtually eliminated. These investigators concluded that, although the two hemispheres have different response skills, they perceive, learn, and process in the same manner.

Investigation into the different functional properties of the two hemispheres continued (see Hellige, 1993; Ornstein, 1997), although it was no longer guided by earlier speculations about right-brain and left-brain functions. Interestingly, more recent work with split-brain patients has provided information about the hemispheres that would not have been predicted from the popular dichotomies of the 1970s and 1980s. For example, Cronin-Golumb (1995) presented "target" pictures of common objects to either the right or left hemispheres of patients. After seeing a target, the patients viewed a set of twenty additional pictures and selected those that were related to the target. When the patients used their right hemispheres for the task, they tended to select related pictures according to a linear ranking system. That is, the first picture selected was more related to the target than the second, the second more than the third, and so on. This type of ordering was not prevalent when patients used the left hemisphere. Findings also suggest that the right hemisphere has superior memory for details of visual patterns when compared with the left (Metcalfe, Funnell, & Gazzaniga, 1995) but that the left hemisphere has more sophisticated strategies for searching through a visual display (Kingstone et al., 1995).

Research on cerebral laterality has led to exciting discoveries, and it will continue to do so. However, because such discoveries tend to stimulate the imagination, it is important to concentrate on the actual research data so that the distinction between fact and fantasy is not blurred.

NEW CONNECTIONISM

Artificial Cells and Artificial Cell Assemblies

One place that Hebb would not have expected his ideas to appear is in the abstract world of computer simulation. The newest approach to understanding how neural systems learn, however, involves no actual neurons at all. Instead, computer models of brain cell activities serve to explore learning, memory, forgetting, and other brain activity. Two influential investigators in this research area, David Rumelhart and James McClelland, have named their approach parallel distributed processing (PDP) (McClelland & Rumelhart, 1988; Rumelhart, McClelland, & PDP Research Group, 1986) in reference to the assumption that the brain conducts simultaneous or parallel information-processing activities. This field has no agreed-upon name, but it has been called the new connectionism, and the models it uses are called **neural networks** (Bechtel & Abrahamsen, 1991).

The basic task in such computer simulations is first to define a set of computer neurons and their potential interconnections and relationships. Next, a number of simplified assumptions, drawn from our understanding of real neurons, are imposed on these artificial neurons. In addition, simple logical learning rules regulate the changes that occur in individual computer neurons and in their interconnections. Finally, the artificial neural system is "trained" and then observed to determine how it changes as a result of experience.

A simple example of a neural network, called a pattern associator (Bechtel & Abrahamsen, 1991; Hinton & Anderson, 1981; Rumelhart, McClelland, & PDP Research Group, 1986), may serve to demonstrate the idea, but keep in mind that much more complicated phenomena have been modeled in neural networks.

First, consider the simple set of elements in Figure 14–10. This particular network has only four elements: two input neurons and two output neurons. You may think of these as sensory neurons and motor neurons, respectively. There are also dashed lines representing possible neural connections between these elements.

Input from the environment (or a computer programmer) activates the input neurons. The output neurons will become active, depending on (1) the strength of the connections from the input units and (2) the number of input units that are connected with them. This output activation rule reflects the **summation** properties of actual neurons. Summation refers to the observation that a neuron adds the

Input 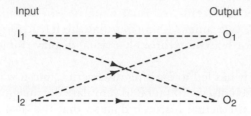 Output

FIGURE 14-10   Two input elements, two output elements, and their possible connections.

I_1

O_1

I_2

O_2

inputs from surrounding cells and that the summed total of inputs determines the cell's level of activity. The rule can be stated as follows:

$$A_o = \sum (w_{oi}) A_i$$

This equation means simply that the output activation (A_o) of a unit is the sum of its input activations (A_i) weighted by their connection strengths (w_{oi}). We can assume, at this point, that nothing has been learned in this hypothetical system—all w_{oi}s are zero—and that sensory input has no effect on motor output.

Let us say that we want to teach our network to discriminate between pine trees and spruce trees. In effect, we want this system to say "pine" whenever the input is the sight of a pine tree and to say "spruce" whenever it sees a spruce. Remember that in real nervous systems, written labels or tags are not attached to sensory input or motor output. In a simplified sense, sensory input representing the sight of a pine tree and the motor output representing the spoken word *pine* are nothing more than patterns of excitation and inhibition in the nervous system. It is in this sense that we will represent "pine" and "spruce" in our hypothetical neural network. We will arbitrarily give "pine" a sensory code of (+1, −1), indicating that the first sensory element has an excitatory activity of +1 and the second sensory element has an inhibitory activity of −1. In contrast, our "spruce tree" will have a sensory code of (−1, +1), indicating an inhibitory activity of −1 and an excitatory activity of +1 in the first and second sensory neurons, respectively.

You now know that (+1, −1) is "pine" and (−1, +1) is "spruce," and you can already reliably categorize these two types of trees. The problem, of course, is to teach the computer's neural network to categorize correctly and therefore exhibit discrimination between these two kinds of input. That is, when given (+1, −1) as sensory input, we want the first motor neuron to output +1 and the second to output −1 and to exhibit the opposite pattern for the "spruce" input. To accomplish these effects, we have to train the system. Specifically, we need to develop the connections between the sensory and motor elements so that the desired input-output relationship can occur. Note that the cells themselves do not learn to be excited (+1) or inhibited (−1). It is assumed that like real neurons, the abilities to be excited or inhibited are simple inherent properties of the cells. Learning occurs at the connections between cells, and it is both the kind and strength of the connections that are trained in neural networks.

At this point we must invoke a learning rule—a logical but arbitrary rule that our computer system will follow in order to change the connections between cells.

The most simple rule is called the **Hebb rule** (or the Hebbian rule). It is a mathematical statement that attempts to capture Hebb's contention that the connection between two cells that are active simultaneously will be strengthened or made more efficient. The Hebbian rule is written

$$\Delta w_{oi} = \text{lrate } (A_i)(A_o)$$

where

Δw is the *change* in the strength or *weight* of a connection between the input and output
lrate is a constant that reflects learning rate
A_i is the activation value level of the input unit
A_o is the activation value level of the output unit
and in our simple example, activation values will be either −1 or +1

The rule indicates that when two units are activated in the same direction (both +1 or both −1), the product of the mutual activity is positive, and therefore the connection weight becomes more positive. When they are simultaneously active in different directions (one element +1 and the other −1), the product is negative, and the connection weight becomes more negative. It will be easy to see how the connections change in our "pine" versus "spruce" example.

We will start with all weights or connections set at zero (0), and we will set learning rate (lrate) equal to $1/n$, where n is the number of input units. In other words, learning rate in our example is $1/2$. (This is an arbitrary setting that assures one-trial learning and is ideal for our simple example.)

We can begin by training or teaching the network "pine." The computer program sets the activation values of input to +1 and −1 for the first and second input units and sets the activation values of the output cells to the desired values of +1 in the first cell and −1 in the second. The matrix below shows the state of inputs, outputs, and weights (connection strengths) at the beginning of training.

Input

Units   Weights

(+1) I_1 0   0

Input values

(−1) I_2 0   0

O_1 O_2 Output units

(+1)   (−1)   Output values

We use the Hebbian rule to change the strengths of the connections from their initial zero values. For example, we can change the connection between input unit 1 and output unit 1 by simple substitution in the learning formula:

Δw is the amount of change (from zero) due to activation of the first input and first output neurons.

$$
\begin{array}{lll}
A_i & = & \text{activation of input } 1 = +1 \\
A_ô & = & \text{activation of output } 1 = +1 \\
\text{lrate} & = & {}^1\!/_2 \\
\text{therefore, } \Delta w & = & {}^1\!/_2\,(+1)\,(+1) = {}^1\!/_2\text{, or .50}
\end{array}
$$

The other weights will change accordingly, and after training the neural network, weights have the following values:

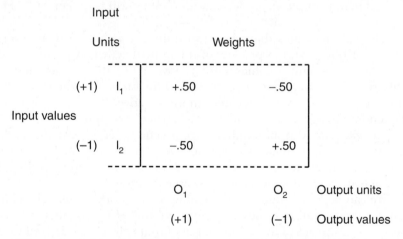

We can test this neural network to see if learning was effective by giving it an input and letting the network generate its own output according to the output activation (summation) rule. When given the input for "pine," $(+1, -1)$, output cell 1 adds $(.50)(+1) + (-.50)(-1)$ to yield $+1$; output 2 adds $(-.50)(+1) + (.50)(-1)$ to yield -1; and the network produces the appropriate $(+1, -1)$ response. This result occurs reliably because the weights or connection strengths were created from the "pine" input and output values. What might be surprising is the output that occurs when the trained system is given "spruce" $(-1, +1)$ as its input. Try it and see.

Back-propagation systems   Research in neural networks has reached levels of complexity that go well beyond the scope of this text, and the simple case of "pine" versus "spruce" provides only an introduction to an area that has already shown great promise. Imagine a network with, say, ten inputs and ten outputs plus a number of intermediate units. Our simple explanation and example can provide just a glimpse of the phenomena that might be mimicked by such a network, although the general summation principle remains much the same. The simple Hebbian learning rule, however, is usually replaced in more sophisticated networks by a form of the *delta rule* (McClelland & Rumelhart, 1988; Rumelhart, McClelland, & PDP Research Group, 1986), sometimes called a *back propagation rule*. The fundamental delta rule is

$$\Delta w_{oi} = \text{lrate } (d_o - A_o)(A_i)$$

Notice that it is similar to the Hebbian rule except that the output activation term is more complex. Here (d_o) refers to the desired output of a unit and (A_o) refers to the actual output. The system is programmed to change connection strengths so that the difference between desired and real output is minimized. It is, in a sense, a self-correcting learning rule that adjusts connection strengths until output matches a target state. If $(d_o - A_o)$ reaches zero, the weights no longer change, and learning is complete.

NETtalk (Sejnowski & Rosenberg, 1987) is a back propagation system that has received a great deal of attention among neural network researchers. The system consists of a computer scanning device with seven windows, each of which can scan a single printed letter from the English alphabet. Each scanning window is connected to 29 input units in the network. The output consists of 26 units, each of which represents a distinct phoneme in the English language. Each of the output units, in turn, is programmed through a voice synthesizer to produce its specific phoneme. There are 80 embedded or hidden units between the input units and the output units. Every input unit is connected to every hidden unit, and every hidden unit is connected to each of the outputs. There are therefore $7 \times 29 \times 80 \times 26$ or 18,320 weighted connections in NETtalk. Initially, weights are assigned randomly. And when a printed word is scanned as input, the output is a random garble of sound. A back-propagation rule is used to adjust weights so that the actual output of the system gets closer and closer to the desired output with each word presentation, and eventually NETtalk reads words aloud. Interestingly, after initial training with 1,000 words, NETtalk is able to accurately read words that are not in the training set, although it still makes mistakes common to novice readers. For example, if the word *rough* is in the training set, it will read the new word *tough* correctly, but will misread the new word *dough*.

Clark (1990) describes how NETtalk learns to read aloud.

> The network began with a random distribution of hidden unit weights and connections (within chosen parameters), i.e. it had no "idea" of any rules of text-to-phoneme conversion. Its task was to learn, by repeated exposure to training instances, to negotiate its way around this particularly tricky cognitive domain (tricky because of irregularities, subregularities, and context-sensitivity of text–phoneme conversion). And learning proceeded in the standard way, i.e. by a back-propagation learning rule. This works by giving the system an input, checking (this is done automatically by a computerized "supervisor") its output, and telling it what output (i.e. what phonemic code) it should have produced. The learning rule then causes the system to minutely adjust the weights on the hidden units in a way which would tend towards the correct output. This procedure is repeated many thousands of times. Uncannily, the system slowly and audibly learns to pronounce English text, moving from babble to half-recognizable words and on to a highly credible final performance. (p. 299)

It would be incorrect to conclude that research in neural networks is merely "computership," that is, skilled computer programmers making sophisticated computer programs that re-create phenomena we already know and understand. The new connectionism's networks begin with relatively simple assumptions: Hebb's learning rule and Lashley's contention that memory is distributed rather than localized in one or two neurons. From these starting points, neural networks have been constructed to simulate processes as simple as pattern recognition, demonstrated previously, and as complex as language learning or recovery from brain damage. Contemporary researchers are using neural networks to help us understand how the human brain detects the pitches or frequencies of different tones (May et al., 1999), how we learn to mentally represent concepts of number and counting (Anderson, 1998), and how disorders such as Parkinson's disease (Mahurin, 1998) and Alzheimer's disease (Tippett & Farah, 1998) affect the brain. We can expect to be reading more about neural networks for years to come.

HEBB ON EDUCATION

For Hebb, there were two kinds of learning. The first involves the gradual buildup of cell assemblies and phase sequences during infancy and early childhood. This early learning results in the objects and events in the environment having neurological representation. When this neural development has taken place, the child can think of an object or event, or a series of objects and events, when it is not physically present. In a sense, copies of those environmental objects now exist in the child's nervous system. During this early learning, an enriched environment would be important for the child, including a wide variety of sights, sounds, textures, shapes, objects, and so on. The more complex the environment, the more there is to be represented on the neurological level. The more that is represented on the neural level, the more the child can think about. Thus, the Hebbian teacher dealing with young children would create an educational environment with great variety. According to Hebb, during early learning certain associationistic principles may be operating. Those that seem most important for the development of cell assemblies and phase sequences are the principles of contiguity and frequency. For example, if a series of environmental events occurs often enough, it becomes represented neurologically as a phase sequence. Reinforcement appears to have nothing to do with it.

The second kind of learning, according to Hebb, is explained more by Gestalt principles than by associationistic ones. Once cell assemblies and phase sequences have been developed early in life, subsequent learning typically involves their rearrangement. In other words, once the building blocks have been established, they can be rearranged in almost an infinite number of configurations. Later learning then is perceptual, rapid, and insightful. The job of the teacher dealing with older children is to help them see what they have already learned in new, creative ways.

Hebb also said that the physical characteristics of the learning environment are very important. For any given task and for any given student, there is an optimal level of arousal that will allow most efficient learning. Because arousal level is controlled primarily by external stimulation, the level of stimulation in the learning environment will determine, to a large extent, how much learning takes place. If there is too much stimulation (e.g., commotion in the classroom), learning will be difficult. Likewise, if there is not enough stimulation (e.g., a deadly quiet classroom), learning will also be difficult. What is needed is an optimal level of stimulation for both the task and the student at hand.

Left-Brain, Right-Brain Learning Some educators, unaware of important progress in the research, were misled by speculations made in the 1970s and 1980s. We learned in this chapter that, except for individuals in whom the corpus callosum is severed, the left and right hemispheres do not learn or behave independently and that their differences are not well described by dichotomies. Although it is valid to criticize the content of a curriculum for its exclusive emphasis on the analytical or because it ignores special skills in different individuals, it is invalid to tie these criticisms to differences between the hemispheres. Because the normal brain functions as an interrelated whole, it is impossible to arrange an educational experience exclusively for one hemisphere. Levy (1985) makes this point: "Since the two hemispheres do not function independently, and since each hemisphere contributes its special capacities to all cognitive activities, it is quite impossible to educate one hemisphere at a time in a normal brain. The right hemisphere is educated as much as the left in a literature class, and the left hemisphere is educated as much as the right in music and painting classes" (p. 44).

SUMMARY

At the University of Chicago, while working with Lashley, Hebb was convinced that the brain did not work as a complex switchboard, as the behaviorists and associationists maintained; rather, it worked as an interrelated whole. This Gestalt conception of the brain was reinforced when Hebb, while working with Wilder Penfield, observed that large areas of the human brain could be removed without any apparent loss in intellectual functioning.

Hebb's major theoretical terms were *cell assembly* and *phase sequence*. A cell assembly is the neural package associated with an environmental object. If this neural package is stimulated in the absence of the object with which it is associated, an idea of the object is experienced. A phase sequence is a series of interrelated cell assemblies. If certain events typically occur together in a series in the environment, they become represented on the neural level as a phase sequence. The stimulation of a phase sequence causes a flow of related ideas. For Hebb, there were two kinds of learning. First, there is the slow buildup of cell assemblies and phase sequences early in life. Second, there is the more insightful kind of learning that characterizes adult life. Adult learning involves the rearrangement of cell assemblies and phase sequences rather than their development.

Arousal theory states that an environmental cue has two functions: (1) a cue function, which conveys information about the environment, and (2) an arousal function, which stimulates the reticular activating system (RAS). To allow optimal intellectual functioning, arousal must be neither too high nor too low. If arousal is too low for the optimal performance of a given task, anything that increases it is reinforcing; if arousal is too high for the optimal performance of a certain task, anything that decreases it is reinforcing.

Sensory deprivation disrupts normal cognitive functioning because it interferes with the relationship between neural circuits and environmental events. Results of sensory deprivation studies show that organisms need normal stimulation just as they need food, water, and oxygen. Research indicates that animals reared in enriched sensory environments are subsequently better learners than animals reared in relatively simple sensory environments. Hebb's explanation was that animals reared in enriched environments develop more complex neural circuitry, which later can be applied to new learning.

While studying fear, Hebb discovered that chimpanzees were not frightened of either completely familiar or completely unfamiliar objects. What did frighten the chimpanzees was a familiar object presented in an unfamiliar way. Hebb's explanation was that a familiar object triggered the neural circuits associated with it, but then subsequent events did not support or confirm those neural circuits; thus a conflict occurred, which stimulated fear. This theory could also explain why sensory deprivation is so disabling.

Hebb believed that there were two kinds of memory—short-term memory and long-term memory. Short-term memory lasts less than a minute and is associated with the reverberating neural activity caused by an environmental event. If an experience is repeated often enough, it is stored in long-term memory. The process whereby short-term memory is converted into long-term memory is called consolidation. If a traumatic experience occurs during the consolidation period, short-term memory is prevented from being transferred into long-term memory. Research indicates that the entire consolidation period lasts about an hour. Recent studies have shown different consolidation mechanisms for different types of long-term memory.

Hebb's theoretical work has stimulated many diverse studies of neurophysiological phenomena. While Olds and Milner were doing research in Hebb's laboratory on the arousal system, they accidentally discovered reinforcement centers in the brain. Sperry found that by ablating both the optic chiasm and the corpus callosum, he could create two independent brains in one skull. Such brains could be taught opposing habits, and one could be active while the other relaxed. Further work on the brain has indicated that although the left and right cerebral hemispheres are alike anatomically, they are dominant for different functions. Researchers like Eric Kandel, examining single neurons and small groups of neurons, have discovered the mechanisms by which actual cell assemblies and phase sequences might be built, and Hebb's theory has guided recent discoveries concerning adult plasticity in the nervous system. Computer scientists have used Hebb's ideas about the nervous system to build working computer models that mimic phenomena as diverse as human language learning, recovery from brain damage, and different disease processes in the human brain.

Although, with the exception of Hebb's work, research using the neurophysiological paradigm is often diffuse and unrelated, it is beginning to contribute to our further understanding of the learning process. In Chapter 3, it was said that our understanding of the learning process is enhanced when viewed from different angles. The neurophysiological paradigm provides us with one additional viewing angle.

EVALUATION OF HEBB'S THEORY

Contributions

Hebb's most important contribution was his conceptual demonstration that we could study higher cognitive processes by using single neurons and synapses as our fundamental tools. In this respect, Hebb differentiated his position from theories relying on abstract S-R bonds. Although contemporary students of psychology or neuroscience may take for granted the fundamental relationship between synaptic activity and all higher-order brain phenomena, Hebb was the first researcher to make that connection and to build simple models of how higher processes are constructed from synaptic events. More than fifty years after Hebb developed his theory, it continues to exert a heuristic influence in the neurosciences, as well as in computer research with neural networks.

Hebb's fundamental learning principle required only repetition and contiguity, and it was guided by a reasonable understanding of what neurons actually could do. Although he was willing to modify his basic neurophysiological postulate to include learning via reinforcement, Hebb's theory clearly does not need such a process. The postulate can account for everything from perceptual learning to conditioning via reinforcers to higher emotional and cognitive processes. In this respect, the theory has the same kind of elegance that we saw in Guthrie's theory and is scientifically appealing for its simplicity—not because it relies on biological or physiological mechanisms.

Like Tolman, Hebb saw the distinctions between motivation and learning and the difficulties inherent in separating the two by observing behavior. His development of arousal theory and the concept of optimal arousal did not resolve the problem, but it did provide a new way to conceptualize it. In doing so, Hebb provided resolution to questions about Hull's drive reduction hypothesis, explaining why we sometimes seek drive reduction and at other times seek drive induction. Thus, with his research concerning the nature of arousal, sensory deprivation, reinforcement, and fear, Hebb had an important influence on the study of motivation as well as the study of learning.

Criticisms

Hebb certainly was not the first to locate learning in the brain, and in some ways, his ideas concerning formation of associations between areas that are contiguously active are not that much different than Pavlov's. Similarly, he was not the first researcher to use his ideas about brain function to speculate about higher cognitive processes. It might be said that Hebb changed the level of analysis from larger areas of the brain to smaller numbers of neurons but maintained the general principle utilized by Pavlov.

A second criticism concerns Hebb's apparent unwillingness to change aspects of his theory in the light of important findings in the neurosciences. However, Hebb treated his system as a speculative model for a theory rather than as a finished, formal theory. Hebb may well have viewed the discoveries of numerous chemical neurotransmitters, physiological bases of reinforcement, and neural structures implicated in consolidation as interesting but irrelevant to his basic model or as transitional phases in the development of brain sciences. On the other hand, there is a single, rather simple issue that should have had major significance for Hebb.

As Quinlan (1991) indicates, Hebb's neurophysiological postulate relied exclusively on the phenomenon of excitation. As our understanding of the nervous system developed, however, it became increasingly clear that the majority of neural communications—and most neurotransmitters—are inhibitory. That is, the most frequent mode of action in the nervous system is that of one cell restricting the firing of a second cell. Certainly this fundamental fact is not a passing phase in the brain sciences, yet Hebb ignored it in the neurophysiological postulate. Neural networks must apply a Hebbian rule to change the strength of connections, but these models would not work if they relied strictly on the original learning postulate. It is interesting to note that the Pavlovian theory that Hebb rejected featured both excitation and inhibition in its analysis of brain functioning.

DISCUSSION QUESTIONS

1. Discuss several observations Hebb made during his early years as a psychologist that he later attempted to account for with his neurophysiological theory.
2. Discuss Lashley's concepts of mass action and equipotentiality.
3. Describe the switchboard conception of the brain. What was Hebb's opposition to such a conception, and what did he offer as an alternative?
4. Why, according to Hebb, were neurophysiological explanations of learning so unpopular at the time he accepted his professorship at McGill?
5. Discuss the concepts of cell assembly and phase sequence.
6. What, according to Hebb, is the difference between childhood learning and adult learning?
7. Describe the effects of sensory deprivation and Hebb's explanation of them.
8. How might Hebb explain dreams? For example, why might a backfiring car cause a person to have a crime-related dream?
9. How might Hebb explain the Gestalt principle of closure?
10. Summarize Hebb's research on fear. What did he find, and how did he explain what he found?
11. What does Hebb mean by an optimal level of stimulation?
12. Differentiate between the cue function and the arousal function of a stimulus.

13. Why, according to Hebb, do people sometimes go out of their way to seek stimulation?
14. Describe the relationship between arousal theory and reinforcement theory.
15. Differentiate between short-term and long-term memory. In your answer, include an explanation of consolidation and those things that interfere with consolidation.
16. Describe the unique characteristics of reinforcement by direct brain stimulation.
17. Cocaine stimulates release of dopamine in the nucleus accumbens. How might the reinforcing properties of cocaine be like the reinforcing properties of direct brain stimulation?
18. Summarize Sperry's research on the split brain.
19. Summarize the functions that appear to be associated with the left and right cerebral hemispheres.
20. Describe how Kimura used dichotic listening to study cerebral asymmetry.
21. Why may it be inappropriate to describe hemispheric functioning in terms of dichotomies?

CHAPTER HIGHLIGHTS

action potential

anterograde amnesia

arousal function of a stimulus

arousal theory

axons

basal ganglia

cell assembly

chameleon effect

consolidation theory

corpus callosum

cue function of a stimulus

declarative memory

dendrites

dichotic listening

dichotomania

electroconvulsive shock (ECS)

enriched environment

equipotentiality

fear

Hebb rule

Hebbian synapse

hippocampus

interneuron

limbic system

long-term depression (LTD)

long-term memory

long-term potentiation (LTP)

mass action

mirror neurons

neglect syndrome

neural networks

neurogenesis

neurons

neuroplasticity (or brain plasticity)

neurotransmitter

nucleus accumbens

optimal level of arousal

phase sequence

procedural memory

receptors

reinforcement centers in the brain

resting potential

restricted environment
reticular activating system (RAS)
retrograde amnesia
reverberating neural activity
sensory deprivation
serendipity

short-term memory
split-brain preparation
summation
switchboard conception of the brain
synapse
threshold

CHAPTER 15

Robert C. Bolles
and Evolutionary Psychology

In Chapter 1, we saw that learning and survival are closely related. In general, classical conditioning allows organisms to learn which stimuli signal events conducive to survival and which stimuli signal events detrimental to survival. Once these signals are learned, instrumental and operant conditioning allow organisms to learn appropriate reactions to those signals. Although associationistic theories such as Pavlov's clearly relate to survival, it was the functionalistic theories, such as those of Thorndike and Hull, that featured evolutionary theory in their explanations of learning. It is also possible to explore the relationship between *un*learned behavior and survival. During the heyday of behaviorism, **ethologists** were stressing the importance of species-specific (unlearned) behavior for survival. They included Karl von Frisch (1886–1982), Konrad Lorenz (1903–1989), and Nikolaas Tinbergen (1907–1988), all of whom shared the 1973 Nobel Prize in biology. Typically ethologists studied a specific category of behavior (such as aggression, migration, communication, or territoriality) in an animal's natural environment and attempted to explain that behavior in terms of evolutionary theory. As we will see, the methods advocated by the ethologists are reflected in the work of William Timberlake and his colleagues (Timberlake, 1997, 1999, 2001, 2002; Timberlake & Lucas, 1989; Timberlake & Silva, 1995), who advocate "animal-centered biological behaviorism," an approach that synthesizes biological, evolutionary, and physiological understandings of specific categories of behavior as they occur in a natural environment. The ethologists created an awareness that a complete understanding of behavior must take into consideration both learned and unlearned tendencies. This awareness paved the way for significant modifications in behaviorist theory that we discuss throughout this chapter.

Recently, the implications of evolutionary theory for understanding the learning process have been explored in great detail. For example, it has been observed that some species of animals learn with ease what other species learn only with great difficulty, if at all. Also, within a species, some relationships are learned with ease, whereas others are learned with great difficulty. Explaining these species-specific differences in learning is one of the concerns of **evolutionary psychology,** which explores in detail the implications of Darwinian and neo-Darwinian theory for explaining the behavior of organisms. In this chapter, we explore further the implications of evolutionary theory for an understanding of the learning process.

After a brief review of evolutionary theory, we feature the work of Robert C. Bolles (1928–1994), who, as much as anyone, attempted to explain the learning process in terms of evolutionary principles. This chapter concludes with a brief overview of the evolutionary psychological perspective on human learning.

DARWIN'S THEORY AND EVOLUTIONARY PSYCHOLOGY

Natural Selection and Adaptations

Although early biologists and naturalists pondered changes in species and in biological structures over time, it was Darwin's (1958 [1859]) *On the Origin of Species by*

Means of Natural Selection that provided the cause, **natural selection,** for such changes. The essential features of natural selection, and their relevance for evolutionary psychology, are summarized here.

First, there is natural variability within a species. This variability may be expressed in greater visual acuity in some members of a species, greater physical strength in others, or more rapid learning in others. These individual differences form the basic building blocks of the evolutionary process and are essential for its occurrence (Buss et al., 1998; Crawford, 1998).

Second, only some individual differences are heritable. That is, only some can be passed from parents to children, from those children to their children, and so on. As a general rule, variations caused by genetic mutations or by environmental events are not advantageous to members of a species and will not be passed to offspring. Similarly, learned variations in behavior, advantageous or not, may be transmitted to subsequent generations by learning but are not heritable. Evolutionary theory is concerned with heritable variability rather than behavioral variations that are the result of other phenomena.

Finally, the interaction between the attributes of an organism and the demands of the environment in which it lives allows natural selection to operate. Buss and colleagues (1998) say,

> Organisms with particular heritable attributes produce more offspring, on average, than those lacking these attributes because these attributes help to solve specific problems and thereby contribute to reproduction in a particular environment. . . . Differential reproductive success, by virtue of the possession of heritable variants, is the causal engine of evolution by natural selection. (p. 534)

An **adaptation** is defined as a physiological or anatomical structure, a biological process, or a behavior pattern that, historically, contributed to the ability to survive and reproduce (Wilson, 1975). By definition, an adaptation comes into existence through natural selection and must be heritable (Buss et al., 1998; Tooby & Cosmides, 1992). Thus, a particular genetic variant in a species—color vision, for example—may lead to greater survival rates and, more important, greater reproductive success among those individuals possessing that adaptation. As a result, the adaptation appears in increased numbers in subsequent generations, even if, at some time in the future, the adaptation no longer contributes directly to survival and reproductive success.

Misconceptions about Adaptations Crawford (1998) cautions against misunderstanding the concept of "survival of the fittest." It is commonly believed that natural selection favors the strongest, most aggressive members of a species and that evolutionary success entails violent struggles in which only dominant members of a species prosper. In some species, however, the successful members may be those whose adaptations include the ability to hide or avoid life-threatening confrontations. In other words, evolutionary **fitness,** defined in terms of reproductive success, often does not depend on an individual's physical fitness as we commonly think of the term.

Buss and associates (1998) also warn us to avoid the misconception that natural selection leads to optimal adaptations in a given situation. "Selection is not like an engineer who can start from scratch and build toward a goal. Selection works only with the available materials and has no foresight" (p. 538). Thus the slow process of evolution results in adaptations that solve a problem for a specific environment that may change in the future, using only the genetic materials provided by the organism within the constraints of other biological features of the organism. "Adaptations are not optimally designed mechanisms. They are better described as jerry-rigged, meliorative solutions . . . constrained in their quality and design by a variety of historical and current forces" (p. 539). It is also important to dispel the common notion that evolution has some ultimate goal toward which it is headed. For example, it is widely believed that evolutionary forces unfold according to some master plan. This is not true. Evolution does not necessarily mean progress. Natural selection means that organisms possessing adaptive traits in a given environment will tend to survive and reproduce *period*. As Buss and colleagues (1998) just reminded us, evolution has "no foresight."

Finally, Buss and colleagues (1998) and Gould (1991) caution against overuse of adaptationist explanations. The current use of a biological structure for a specific purpose does not necessarily mean that the structure evolved for that purpose. Gould, for example, points to the use of a bird's feathers for flight. According to Gould, feathers evolved as a mechanism to regulate a bird's body heat and were later co-opted for flying. He refers to the co-option of an adaptation (feathers) for a useful but unrelated purpose (flight rather than thermal regulation) as an **exaptation.**

Along with exaptations, there can be co-opted side effects called **spandrels** that may accompany a specific adaptation. For example, the increased capacity of the human brain provided many adaptive benefits. These benefits might have included improved problem-solving skills, superior tool making, and increased memory for locations of food or the territories of dangerous predators. The side effects of the larger brain might have included the abilities to make music, *written* language, and complex social rules—all of which might be incorrectly viewed as adaptations leading to survival and increased reproductive fitness.

Inclusive Fitness and Neo-Darwinian Theory

As we have seen, Darwin defined fitness in terms of the number of offspring produced by an organism. In 1964, William Hamilton (1936–2000) expanded Darwin's narrow definition by proposing the idea of **inclusive fitness.** In inclusive fitness, the focus broadens from the reproductive success of an individual member of a species to the perpetuation of that individual's genes and the genes it shares with other members of the species. Thus, we come to see parental behaviors or cooperative behaviors within a family group as adaptive because they promote the survival and possibly the reproductive success of shared, rather than individual, genes. Within the perspective provided by inclusive fitness, behaviors that may endanger specific individuals are now viewed as adaptive because the sacrifice of the individual may promote the survival of members of the species that share its genes.

Within neo-Darwinian theory, the concept of inclusive fitness has been extremely heuristic. In addition to explaining "altruistic" behavior, it has been employed to explain such diverse topics as suicide and homosexuality (for details, see Hergenhahn and Olson, 2007).

BOLLES'S THEORY OF LEARNING

Robert C. Bolles was born in Sacramento, California, in 1928, and he was schooled at home until he was twelve years old. He earned his B.A. at Stanford University in 1948 and completed his M.A. in mathematics at Stanford one year later. He was hired at the U.S. Naval Radiological Defense Laboratory near San Francisco, California, where he met future graduate school colleague and lifelong friend, John Garcia (discoverer of the Garcia effect), who was on leave from the doctoral program in psychology at the University of California at Berkeley (Garcia, 1997). Bolles soon joined Garcia in the psychology program at Berkeley, where they both studied under Tolman. During graduate school, Bolles and Lewis Petrinovich conducted the

early experiments that launched Bolles's interests in evolutionary learning theory (Bolles & Petrinovich, 1954; Petrinovich & Bolles, 1954). After earning his Ph.D. in 1956, Bolles assumed brief faculty appointments at the University of Pennsylvania and then at Princeton University. In 1959, he moved to Hollins College, and in 1964, he joined the faculty at the University of Washington, where he remained until his death from a heart attack on April 8, 1994.

During his career, Bolles wrote more than 160 research articles and three influential textbooks, including a text on learning theory. He served as editor of *Animal Learning and Behavior* from 1981 until 1984, and many of his students have gone on to make important contributions relating evolutionary processes to learning (for example, see Bouton & Fanselow, 1997).

Robert C. Bolles. (Courtesy of the Estate of Robert C. Bolles.)

Major Theoretical Concepts

Expectancies　For Bolles, learning involves the development of **expectancies.** That is, organisms learn that one kind of event reliably precedes another event. We have already seen in Chapter 7 that Bolles explained classical conditioning as the learned expectancy that, given one stimulus (CS), another stimulus (US) will follow. In everyday life, seeing lightning and expecting thunder exemplifies this kind of stimulus-stimulus, or S-S, expectancy. Whereas classical conditioning involves the development of S-S expectancies, operant conditioning and instrumental conditioning involve the development of response-stimulus or R-S expectancies (Bolles, 1972). For example, a rat learns to expect that if it presses the bar in a Skinner box, food will follow. In everyday life, expecting to hear the sound of a bell when a doorbell is pressed exemplifies an R-S expectancy. In discussing R-S expectancies, it helps to think of the S as an outcome produced by the response. Expectancy learning in Bolles's theory does not require reinforcement. In general, the temporal order and contiguity between two stimuli or between a response and its consequence determine the nature of the learned expectancy: A flash of lightning becomes a *predictor* for thunder, and pressing the button becomes a *predictor* for doorbell chimes—not the other way around (Staddon, 1988). Thus, we might call Bolles a "directional" contiguity theorist.

Innate Predispositions   Bolles's emphasis on expectancies shows the influence of Tolman (see Chapter 12). However, there were important differences between the two theorists. Whereas Tolman concentrated almost exclusively on learned S-S and R-S expectancies, Bolles emphasized *innate* S-S and R-S expectancies in his analysis of behavior, and it was his emphases on innate S-S and R-S expectancies that aligned him with other psychologists interested in evolutionary explanations of behavior. An example of an innate S-S relationship is when a young infant displays fear of a loud noise, suggesting that the infant expects a dangerous event to follow. Innate R-S expectancies are exemplified by the stereotyped behavior many species of animals show in the presence of food, water, danger, and other biologically significant objects or events.

According to Domjan (1997), the flaw in traditional, empirical learning theories, such as those developed by Thorndike, Watson, Skinner, and Hull, is an assumption known as the **empirical principle of equipotentiality** (not to be confused with Karl Lashley's Law of Equipotentiality). It states that the laws of learning "apply equally to any type of stimulus and any type of response" (p. 32). Thus, the empirical principle of equipotentiality led researchers to study learning in a given species without consideration of the evolutionary history of that species. Furthermore, it was incorrectly assumed that learning phenomena observed in one species, rats, for example, could be generalized to most, if not all, other species. In addition, when members of a species did not learn to perform a response under specified conditions, the disappointing outcome was attributed to equipment dysfunction or experimenter error, or it was disregarded as unexplainable "noise."

In contrast to the assumption of equipotentiality, Bolles (1988) stated

> I argue that there is much to be gained by assuming that there is some structure to the events an animal learns about, and that there is a corresponding structure in the organism that does the learning. . . . The way for an organism to succeed is to be able to

learn what needs to be learned. This involves not the random learning ability of the empiricist, but the genetically programmed learning ability of the nativist. (p. 5)

Later, we see how evolutionary psychology, which emphasizes innate, rather than learned, S-S and R-S expectancies, helps clarify many anomalies discovered during early research in learning. We have already seen one example of this in Chapter 5, where we discussed "the misbehavior of organisms."

Motivation Restricts Response Flexibility Some theorists that we have covered minimized or denied the role of motivation in the learning process (e.g., Guthrie and Tolman). Other theorists (e.g., Hull) placed great importance on the motivational state of the organism. Clearly, Bolles was in the latter camp. For him, motivation and learning were inseparable. However, in Bolles's approach, one must know both the motivational state of the organism *and* what the organism does *naturally* in that motivational state. According to Bolles (1979, 1988), although an organism may be somewhat flexible with respect to the S-S expectancies that it learns, R-S expectancies are more limited because motivation produces response bias. That is, an animal will have great difficulty learning a behavior that conflicts with a behavior that occurs naturally in the situation. For example, it will not learn escape-related behaviors in order to gain access to food, nor will it learn appetitive (approach) behaviors in order to escape from a painful or dangerous stimulus.

The Niche Argument Bolles (1988) argued that an understanding of learning must be accompanied by an understanding of the evolutionary history of the organism. He stated that

> animals have an obligation, an imperative, to learn this and to not learn that depending on their niche and how they fit into the overall scheme of things. We should expect some kinds of experience to be reflected in learning, and some not. . . . A learning task which violates an animal's a priori biological commitments to its niche, can be expected to produce anomalous behavior. A learning task which capitalizes on an animal's a priori predisposition to behave in certain ways is likely to be a glowing success. That is the niche argument. (pp. 12–13)

Other evolutionary psychologists expand on the niche argument with the idea of the **environment of evolutionary adaptedness (EEA),** a term that refers to the environment, both social and physical, in which a specific adaptation appeared (Bowlby, 1969; Tooby & Cosmides, 1990). These authors and others (e.g., Sherman & Reeve, 1997) emphasize that the EEA is not simply a prehistoric time or place that existed during the development of a species. Rather, it is a combination of environmental and social factors that existed during a given period, and it leaves open the possibility that different adaptations in a species may have had different EEAs. Furthermore, returning to the idea that evolution does not guarantee progress, they point out that today's organisms experience selection pressures that may be different than those that existed in a specific EEA. There are occasions when behaviors shaped by evolutionary influences are maladaptive in contemporary environments.

THE BIOLOGICAL BOUNDARIES OF LEARNING

In this section, we review evidence that casts further doubt on the contention that conditioning occurs automatically if a freely emitted response is followed by a reinforcer or if any CS is paired with a US. As we have seen, there is growing recognition that the genetic endowment of an organism must be taken into consideration in any learning experiment. In Chapter 5, the Brelands' concept of instinctual drift demonstrated the importance of instinctive response tendencies in the operant conditioning situation. We have seen that Bolles's theory is built on the idea that innate predispositions limit the associations that an organism can learn and the responses that the organism will make in specific situations. This idea is further supported by Seligman (1970), who maintains that some species learn associations more easily than other species do because they are biologically prepared to do so. Likewise, for some species an association may be difficult to learn because they are not biologically prepared to learn it. Thus, where an association falls on the **preparedness continuum** will determine how easily it will be learned.

Instrumental Conditioning

Problems with the empirical principle of equipotentiality appeared in some of the earliest studies of learning. Thorndike (1898), for example, reported that cats could learn a variety of responses using their paws to gain access to food but that they would not learn to groom themselves to earn a food reward. Clearly, this was a case in which a cat's natural response to hunger did not include grooming behavior. Or, as Seligman would have it, the cat was not biologically prepared to associate grooming with food. As Bolles (1988) commented concerning Thorndike's findings, "No one paid any attention" (p. 5). In the early 1950s, while they were graduate students at Berkeley, Robert Bolles and Lewis Petrinovich conducted research that initiated a new era of interest in the influence of evolution on learning.

In a preliminary experiment, Petrinovich and Bolles (1954) trained one group of rats to turn left and a second group to turn right in a T-maze. A T-maze is so named because it is shaped like a large T. The rat runs from a starting area at the base of the T to the choice point at the intersection of the vertical and horizontal sections, where it can turn left or right. Half of the rats in each group were deprived of water and were reinforced with water when they made the correct turning response; the remaining rats were deprived of food and earned a food reinforcement when they turned correctly. In this study, thirsty rats earning water reinforcers learned the task faster and made fewer errors than hungry rats working for food. This alone was interesting, for why would the kind of reinforcer (food versus water) influence learning efficiency?

In a second experiment, rats were again deprived of either water or food. They were reinforced with water or food, respectively, for whatever choice they initially made, turning right for example, on the first trial in the maze. On the second trial, they were reinforced only for making the opposite response—turning left in this example. On the third trial, they were reinforced only for making a response opposite to the choice on the second trial, and so on throughout the experiment. Thus, the rats were reinforced for left-right alternation. In this study, the hungry rats working for food learned the task faster than the thirsty rats working for water. The results of both experiments are shown in Figure 15–1.

Why did water reinforcement produce superior performance in the first experiment but not in the second? Theorists like Hull and Skinner would find it difficult to explain the results just described. An evolutionary explanation, however, solves the problem. Petrinovich and Bolles suggested that, because rats evolved as omnivorous, foraging animals, they would be biased against searching for food in the same location on successive trials. For foragers, food is a variable resource that is not likely to be found today where it was found yesterday. On the other hand, it would be adaptive for rats to search for water where it was found on previous occasions. Water is a more stable resource; a river or pond is not likely to disappear overnight. Thus, the rats in the experiment exhibited response biases as a result of their evolutionary history. Put another way, rats are prepared to go to the same place for water, but they are not prepared to go to the same place to find food.

Escape and Avoidance Organisms may exhibit a degree of response flexibility and exploration with respect to obtaining food or water. For example, hungry rats may press a lever, run a maze, poke their noses into a small cup, and so on to earn a food pellet. Bolles (1970) recognized, however, that there are occasions when an animal does not have the luxury of trial-and-error learning. Escape from a predator must be accomplished successfully in *one* trial if the organism is to survive. Thus, Bolles argued, innate R-S expectancies exist to provide solutions to environmental problems that pose an immediate threat to survival. Bolles (1988) wrote that

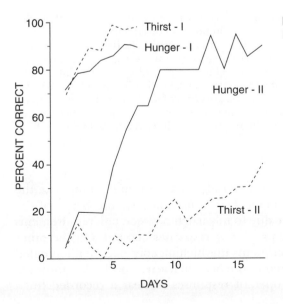

FIGURE 15–1 Performance curves for Problems I and II.

the rat's strategy is to use fixed patterns of behavior to protect itself, what I called species-specific defense reactions (Bolles, 1970). There just is very little flexibility in the response itself; the animal mainly only learns about stimuli; it learns which stimuli are dangerous and which are safe. (p. 11)

Bolles (1970, 1972) noted that for the rat, **species-specific defensive reactions (SSDRs)** include freezing, fleeing, screaming, leaping up, and aggressing toward some object. In the natural environment, one or more of these innate reactions may lead to safety, and if so, the problem is solved. Also, in a laboratory, if one of these innate reactions to pain allows the animal to escape pain, the escape response will be learned rapidly. In fact, under the circumstances just described, the animal really learns no new responses; the aversive stimulation simply elicits SSDRs.

Avoidance conditioning is a bit more complicated. According to Bolles, avoidance conditioning involves both S-S and R-S expectancies. Because in avoidance conditioning a signal precedes an aversive event (e.g., shock), the animal learns to expect pain when, say, a tone is sounded. Because the tone signals danger, it comes to elicit the same SSDRs that are elicited by the aversive stimulus itself. Thus, according to Bolles, either warnings of pain or pain itself elicits SSDRs.

An obvious prediction from Bolles's analysis is that the closer the response required of an animal in an experiment is to what that animal would do naturally in that situation, the more readily the response will be learned. If the required response is not part of the animal's innate response repertoire, it will be learned with great difficulty or perhaps not at all. An example is the fact that pigeons can easily be taught to fly from one perch to another to avoid shock, but it is almost impossible to teach pigeons to peck a key to avoid shock (Bolles, 1979, p. 185). Thus, the choice of the response required of an animal in a learning experiment is a major factor in determining the results of the experiment.

Even a casual look at rats in different avoidance learning situations reveals that what response we require of them is a tremendously important consideration; it can make the difference between some learning in one trial and no learning in 1000 trials. It is vastly more important than the reinforcement contingencies, various experimental parameters, the animal's prior experience, or different kinds of physiological interventions that might be made. The choice of what the response shall be is clearly not an arbitrary matter, or just a question of convenience, it is the governing factor in whether or how rapidly learning will occur. It is a serious indictment of our classical learning theories that they provide no hint that the choice of the response is so important. (p. 185)

Operant Conditioning

We saw in Chapter 5, in the work of the Brelands, that operant learning, like the types of learning just described, is limited by the natural response biases of the organism. Instances of operant failure due to mismatch between task requirements and naturally biased (or biologically prepared) responses abound. On the other hand, it is quite common to find experiments in which pigeons peck at illuminated keys for food reinforcement. Like pigeons, finches will learn to peck a key for food, and although they can learn some operant responses to hear a recorded finch birdsong, they will not learn to peck a response key to hear the recording (Stevenson-Hinde, 1973). Although pecking is a response that occurs naturally in the presence of food, finches are not biologically prepared to associate pecking with birdsong. Bolles, Riley, Cantor, and Duncan (1974) demonstrated that rats will learn to anticipate food if it is presented on a fixed-interval (FI) reinforcement schedule (once per day), but they are not prepared to learn to anticipate a painful electric shock if it occurs on the same FI schedule. Bolles (1988) wrote,

> Rats can readily learn to run back and forth to avoid shock. But they find it extraordinarily difficult to press a bar to avoid shock. Similarly, it was widely recognized that it was easy to teach the rat to press a bar to obtain food, but teaching a rat to press a bar to avert a negative consequence was quite a different matter. The literature was full of such anomalies. Pigeons, which are so adept at making subtle sensory discriminations in pecking a key to obtain food, had never been reported to solve its other biological problem [avoidance of negative consequences] in the same way. (p. 10)

Autoshaping

In Chapter 5, we presented the mystery of autoshaping. You may remember that, in an experiment conducted by Brown and Jenkins (1968), a pecking disk (or key) was briefly illuminated prior to behaviorally noncontingent presentation of food. Regardless of the behaviors that pigeons in this experiment exhibited in the interval prior to food presentation, virtually all pigeons in the study began to peck at the illuminated disk. No systematic shaping of the disk-pecking response was required. As noted in Chapter 5, Bolles's (1979) explanation suggested that autoshaping involved S-S learning but that no new response learning occurred. Rather, he interpreted the pecking behavior as an innate response to a stimulus that, because of its temporal contiguity with presentation of food, aquires food-related properties.

> We have been led to think of the key-peck response as an operant and as an arbitrary, convenient, easily measured response whose strength can be controlled by its consequences. But we can see in the autoshaping procedure . . . that the strength of the response is not controlled by its consequences. It is evidently controlled by the food-signaling property of the illuminated key. (p. 180)

J. E. R. Staddon (1988), who conducted his master's degree research under Bolles, emphasizes the predictive value of the illuminated pecking key and agrees with Bolles's analysis:

> [I]f each key illumination is followed by food (and food occurs at no other time), soon the light is classified as food-related. Small food-related objects induce pecking as a high-priority activity (autoshaping). If the apparatus arranges that pecking produces food, the correlation between light and food is further strengthened. . . . Food associated situations elicit food-related activities. (p. 68)

The maladaptive constraints of this type of S-S learning are illustrated in the work of Williams and Williams (1969), discussed in Chapter 5. Recall that, in this autoshaping experiment, pecking *reduced* the rate of reinforcement, but key-pecking continued nonetheless. Thus the illuminated disk acted as a signal for food and elicited food-related behavior regardless of the consequences of the behavior. As we indicated at the beginning of the chapter, evolution does not involve a master plan for progress. An adaptation that may have been successful in its niche (or EEA) may encounter problems in a modern environment—or in a laboratory—in which it fails.

Classical Conditioning

Conditioned Taste Aversion   In Chapter 7, we briefly introduced the Garcia effect. In this section, we present a more complete description of an experiment conducted by Garcia and Koelling (1966), and we examine the important contribution that the Garcia effect makes to the understanding of evolutionary influences on learning. Garcia and Koelling offered thirsty rats the opportunity to drink under four conditions. One group was offered bright, noisy water, and drinking it was immediately followed by an electric shock to the feet. The bright, noisy water was created by attaching an electrode to the drinking tube in a way that set off flashing lights and loud clicking sounds when the organism touched the drinking tube. A second group was offered the bright, noisy water, but instead of being shocked for drinking, they were exposed to strong X-ray treatment to induce nausea. A third group was given water without the flashing lights and clicking sounds but with the taste of saccharin; these animals, like those in the first group, were shocked through the feet immediately after drinking the saccharin solution. A fourth group was given the saccharin solution and then was made ill by X-ray treatment.

John Garcia. (Courtesy of John Garcia.)

Garcia and Koelling (1966) found that animals in group 1 developed an aversion to bright, noisy water, whereas animals in group 2 did not. In addition, animals in group 3 did not develop an aversion to saccharin-flavored water, whereas animals in group 4 did develop such an aversion. The experimental design and the results of the experiment are summarized as follows:

Group 1: Bright, noisy water → shock: Developed an aversion to the water

Group 2: Bright, noisy water → nausea: No aversion to the water

Group 3: Saccharin solution → shock: No aversion to saccharin

Group 4: Saccharin solution → nausea: Developed an aversion to saccharin

It can be seen that bright, noisy water became an effective CS when paired with shock but not when paired with nausea. Likewise, the taste of saccharin was an effective CS when paired with nausea but not when paired with shock. Garcia and Koelling (1966) explained their results by saying that there was a natural relationship between external events and the pain that the animals experienced. In other words, the pain was coming from "out there," and therefore the animals searched for an external predictor of that pain, which in this case was the lights and noise associated with drinking. Nausea, however, is experienced internally rather than externally. Therefore, the animals associated the taste of saccharin (which is internal) and not the bright, noisy water (which is external) with nausea. To use Seligman's terminology, we can say that the rats were biologically prepared to form an association between bright, noisy water and pain but not prepared to form an association between bright, noisy water and nausea. Likewise, the animals were biologically prepared to form an association between the taste of saccharin and nausea, but they were not biologically prepared to form an association between the taste of saccharin and pain.

A study by Wilcoxon, Dragoin, and Kral (1971) exemplifies Seligman's concept of preparedness as it applies to differences between species. In their study, rats and quail were given blue, salty water that was treated to make them sick. After drinking the water and becoming ill, both species were offered a choice between blue water or salty water. The rats avoided the salty water, whereas the quail avoided the blue water. This finding reflects the fact that rats rely on taste in an eating (or drinking) situation and quail rely on visual cues. Thus each species formed an association in accordance with its genetic makeup. In other words, although the US (treated, blue, salty water) and the UR (illness) were the same for both species, each species selected a CS in accordance with its genetic endowment. For the rats, the taste of salt became the CS, whereas for the quail, the color blue was the CS. In Seligman's terms, the rats were more biologically prepared to make the salt-illness association, but the quail were more biologically prepared to make the blue-illness association.

Garcia's research indicates that *within* a species, certain associations will be easier to form than others because of the evolutionary history of that species. The research of Wilcoxon, Dragoin, and Kral (1971) demonstrates differences *between* species: Different associations will be optimal for different species. However, as Logue (1988) and Rozin and Fallon (1981) point out, the last stimulus that an organism experiences prior to ingesting a toxic substance is the taste of that substance. Therefore, these authors argue, it would be highly adaptive if (most) organisms could acquire aversions to the flavor—rather than to the shape, color, or texture—of the food or beverage that made them ill. Indeed, despite the kinds of species differences described here, most vertebrates can learn aversions to flavor cues alone (Gustavson, 1977).

Like other conditioned responses, learned taste aversions can undergo extinction. In other words, if the flavor (CS) is repeatedly presented without ensuing illness (UR), organisms will again approach and consume a substance that was once avoided. Kathleen Chambers, one of Bolles's graduate students in the early 1970s, discovered that taste aversions extinguish faster in female rats than in male rats (Chambers, 1985; Chambers & Sengstake, 1976), and she has explored these sexual differences extensively in subsequent research (see, for example, Chambers et al., 1997). Her explanation for the difference in extinction rates, and the explanation with which Bolles agreed, is clearly an evolutionary one. She suggested that, because they are responsible for the survival of fetuses as well as newborn, nursing pups, it is extremely important that the females fulfill their nutritional needs. Therefore, it is adaptive for them to determine with some certainty if a previous illness was, in fact, associated with a specific food. That is, they are biologically prepared to "retest" a potentially nutritious food, given that the illness may have been caused by other factors.

For a taste aversion to extinguish, however, the organism must reexperience the flavor (CS) without experiencing the illness (UR). Given the nature of the Garcia effect, extinction may occur under laboratory conditions, but the organism in the wild may continue to avoid the CS, making extinction of the aversion impossible.

Biological Behaviorism

Recent work by William Timberlake (1999, 2001, 2002) extends and elaborates Bolles's niche argument. In his advocacy of what he calls "biological behaviorism," Timberlake attempts to reconcile the positions of the ethologists, whose research focuses primarily on naturally occurring behaviors of wild species, and experimental behaviorists, whose research focuses primarily on laboratory learning in domesti-

William Timberlake (Courtesy of William Timberlake.)

cated species. Timberlake credits the behavioral tradition for its important role in establishing standardized methods and measurement techniques for studying learning, and he recognizes the powerful logic of controlled experimentation that matured during the heyday of behaviorism. Like Bolles, however, Timberlake argues that attempts to discover abstract, general principles of learning neglect species-specific differences in prepared learning. Thus, if we do not understand an organism from a bioevolutionary perspective, phenomena such as those observed in autoshaping or "misbehavior" are often treated as errors and may lead us incorrectly to reject otherwise useful theories or methods.

Timberlake asserts that laboratory research in learning already makes accommodations for the natural propensities of species that are most frequently used in experiments. For example, Timberlake reminds us that the Skinner box has been "tuned" for the laboratory rat. The level at which the lever is located, delivery of food near the lever, and the operational requirements of the lever exploit the rat's natural food-seeking behaviors—scratching, nuzzling, probing, and so on. It is not arbitrary and artificial experimental design that requires pigeons to peck at eye-level lighted keys or that requires rats to run through mazes. Rats do not peck illuminated disks, and pigeons are not adept at negotiating mazes. The tasks that have become common in learning laboratories are widely used because they are compatible with both the natural behavioral abilities and the preparedness of the animals being tested. Most important, such procedures have become standard lab tasks because they produce reliable and consistent results.

The observations that successful laboratory manipulations capitalize on existing behavioral predispositions and that lab tasks have been finely tuned to produce reliable and robust responses in lab animals led Timberlake (2002) to the conclusion that much lab behavior is **overdetermined.** According to Timberlake, behavior is overdetermined if it occurs reliably in the absence of experimental manipulations such as food or water deprivation or response-reward contingencies and if a variety of sensory-motor patterns underly the behavior. For example, wild rats follow trails, whether in natural burrows and feeding areas or in the walls of a home that they have invaded. It is their bioevolutionary inclination to explore tunnels and small alley-like confinements. Trail following occurs as part of exploratory and social activities, and although it is used in foraging for food, it is also used for a variety of other purposes and is therefore independent of deprivation or the presence of primary reinforcers. In addition, trail following may utilize visual, olfactory, auditory, or other cues. Thus, Timberlake suggests that laboratory maze behavior is overdetermined.

As evidence for this argument, Timberlake and his colleagues reported decreased running times in rats that ran straight alley mazes without food reinforcement, regardless of deprivation conditions (Timberlake, 1983). Radial arm mazes (much like that used by Tolman and described in Chapter 12) are sometimes used to test for "efficient" search strategies in rats. An efficient strategy is one that avoids arms of the maze where food has already been consumed and that searches unexplored alleys. Timberlake and White (1990) demonstrated that food-deprived rats performed maze searches efficiently whether or not food reinforcers were used to bait the arms of the maze. Furthermore, Timberlake (2002) reports unpublished data indicating that undeprived, nonreinforced rats perform maze searches efficiently if tested at night when, as nocturnal animals, they are naturally most active.

Timberlake's overdetermination principle is not a condemnation of instrumental and operant procedures. It is an important caution about generalizing findings from one species to another, and it reminds us that we must be aware of the evolutionary preparedness of the learning organism. Keeping these ideas in mind, we next examine the role of evolutionary selection pressures and prepared learning in humans.

EVOLUTIONARY PSYCHOLOGY AND HUMAN BEHAVIOR

Although the previous section has focused on nonhuman research in our coverage of evolutionary psychology, evolutionary psychology has also been widely applied to the understanding of human behavior. In 1975, Edward O. Wilson published *Sociobiology: The New Synthesis,* which launched the field of **sociobiology,** a discipline that applied evolutionary principles primarily to the explanation of social behavior of animals, including humans. Subsequently, Wilson (1988, 1998) argued for unification of social sciences and natural sciences under the evolutionary paradigm. Stimulated by these early works, the field of evolutionary psychology emerged and, for the most part, separated from sociobiology. Its many articulate proponents include David Buss, Leda Cosmides, and John Tooby (Buss, 1995, 2004; Buss et al., 1998; Cosmides & Tooby, 1997; Crawford & Krebs, 1998; and Hergenhahn & Olson, 2007). In what follows, we limit our discussion to only a few of the topics that evolutionary psychology addresses, such as development of phobias, mate selection, parenting, family violence, "altruism" and moral behavior, and language development.

In many ways, the principles that guide evolutionary explanations of human behavior are parallel to the principles that Bolles (1972, 1988) invokes to apply evolutionary explanations to nonhuman behavior. Specifically, evolutionary psychology assumes that, despite the remarkable advances that the human species has made, particularly during the last two hundred years, we are still the product of thousands of years of evolution. Therefore, like other animals, we sometimes display innate *predispositions* to attend to some stimuli rather than to others and to learn some kinds of expectancies more readily than others. Like other animals, we are prone to innate response biases, particularly when guided by strong, biologically significant motivational states. In other words, Seligman's concept of preparedness applies to human learning just as it does to nonhuman learning. And finally, the niche argument applies to us just as it does to other animals. We can gain a more accurate understanding of human behavior if we consider a contemporary behavior relative to the EEA of that behavior. None of this says that humans are bound by inflexible instinctive behaviors. It does suggest, however, that the empirical principle of equipotentiality is inadequate to explain all of human learning, just as it is inadequate to explain the breadth of nonhuman learning.

The Development of Phobias

In recent years, investigations of fear responses in humans have revealed phenomena that seem best explained by evolutionary preparedness. Human phobias—unusually strong, fearful reactions to stimuli such as snakes and spiders—are difficult to explain in terms of classical conditioning, and attempts at such explanations are inevitably superficial. For example, few humans with snake or spider phobias have actually experienced the USs of snake or spider venom paired with visual CSs of snakes or spiders. Next, we will explore recent attempts to explain why some fears, like snake and spider phobias, are acquired so easily and why they are so resistant to change.

The following evolutionary explanation of the development of phobias offered by Lumsden and Wilson (1981) is very much in accordance with Seligman's concept of preparedness:

> The preparedness of human learning is most clearly manifested in the case of phobias, which are fears defined by a combination of traits. They are first of all extreme in response. . . . They typically emerge full-blown after only a single negative reinforcement [and] they are exceptionally difficult to extinguish. . . . It is a remarkable fact

that the phenomena that evoke these reactions consistently (closed spaces, heights, thunderstorms, running water, snakes, and spiders) include some of the greatest dangers present in mankind's ancient environment while guns, knives, automobiles, electric sockets, and other far more dangerous perils of technologically advanced societies are rarely effective. It is reasonable to conclude that phobias are extreme cases of irrational fear reactions that gave an extra margin needed to ensure survival. . . . Better to crawl away from a cliff, nauseated with fear, than to casually walk its edge. (pp. 84–85)

Öhman and Mineka (2001, 2003) argue that some phobias are acquired rapidly because they are mediated by nonconscious, automatic learning processes. They propose that a neural "fear module," a primitive, biological vestige of our mammalian evolutionary history, is responsible for the ease with which snake or spider phobias develop. Öhman and Mineka suggest that, as part of our evolutionary heritage, we share with other animals a neural mechanism that provides an automatic predisposition to learn fear responses to evolutionarily significant stimuli. These stimuli capture our attention, and we can learn about them without conscious information processing. This does not mean that all humans are naturally fearful of snakes, spiders, snarling dogs, and so on. It does suggest, however, that these kinds of stimuli are naturally salient for our species and that we are naturally prepared to learn snake or spider phobias even without personal experiences with traumatic USs.

First, these authors document the extreme fear of snakes observed among wild primates (e.g., King, 1997) to demonstrate the prevalence of such fears among other mammals. They also cite evidence that, although lab-raised monkeys do not seem to fear snakes innately, they quickly develop fear of snakes after watching the reactions of live or videotaped wild monkeys that are exposed to real (or toy) snakes (Cook & Mineka, 1990). More important, they present data from studies with human participants indicating that fear of snakes or spiders may not require conscious perception of these stimuli.

To explore how nonconscious learning might work, Öhman and his colleagues utilized a procedure called *backward masking*. In backward masking, a visual stimulus is displayed briefly, perhaps for only twenty or thirty milliseconds. This stimulus is followed almost immediately by a second visual display. The second visual display seems to act backward in time to interfere with, or "mask," conscious visual processing of the first stimulus. Thus, the second stimulus is the only one that is consciously perceived. This procedure is diagrammed below:

Brief Display → Brief interval → Masking Display → Perception

Picture A → Brief interval → Picture B → Only B is perceived

Öhman and Soares (1993) exposed one group of nonphobic participants to photos of snakes or spiders (CS) paired with electric shocks (US) to develop fear responses (indicated by changes in skin conductance). A control group saw photos of flowers or mushrooms (CS) paired with electric shocks (US). After acquisition of fear responses, the US was omitted and the CSs were presented as the first elements in a backward masking display. The first group of participants was shown snake/spider pictures masked by a picture of a snake or spider that had been cut into pieces and randomly reassembled. Thus the masking stimulus had spider/snake elements but not the complete configuration of the target stimulus. The control group saw pictures of flowers or mushrooms masked by randomly reassembled flower or mushroom pictures. Fear responses to the snake/spider photos, but not to the flower/mushroom photos, were observed. The results are important because the backward masking procedure prevents conscious perception of both snake/spider pictures and the neutral flower/mushroom pictures, yet only the evolutionarily significant stimuli evoked fear responses.

Group 1: Snake photo → Masking picture → Fear response occurs

Group 2: Flower photo → Masking picture → No fear response

To further explore these findings, Öhman and Soares (1994) tested already fearful participants by using the backward masking technique with photos of spiders or snakes. Even though the masking procedure made identification of the stimuli impossible, fear responses to masked spider photos occurred among those participants already fearful of spiders and to masked photos of snakes among those participants already fearful of snakes, but not vice versa. Additionally, fear responses can easily be conditioned to snake or spider photos when they are presented as the first elements in a backward masking display, although the same is not true of photos of flowers or mushrooms (Öhman & Soares, 1998).

Öhman, Flykt, and Esteves (2001) hypothesized that stimuli like snakes and spiders automatically capture our attention. For example, participants quickly find a picture of a snake embedded in an array of neutral stimuli but take significantly longer to find a picture of a flower embedded in an array of snake pictures. As might be expected, this effect is exaggerated among participants who are already fearful of snakes.

If fear-relevant stimuli like snakes and spiders capture or dominate our attention, it should be the case that attentional capture facilitates performance that benefits from directed attention. Lipp and Derakshan (2005) used a "dot-probe" task to demonstrate this phenomenon. These researchers showed participants two pictures, side by side, on a computer screen. One of the pictures was of a fear-relevant stimulus (snake or spider), and the other was of a neutral stimulus (flower or mushroom). The pictures were displayed on the screen for 500 milliseconds and then replaced immediately by a small dot, which appeared in the location of either the fear-relevant stimulus or the neutral stimulus. The participants were required to press a button as quickly as possible to indicate the side of the screen on which the dot appeared. They responded significantly faster when the dot appeared in place of the feared stimulus, supporting the contention that attention had been drawn to that location. On the other hand, if our attention is captured by a fear-relevant stimulus, our performance should suffer when we have to redirect our attention to search for a different stimulus. Lipp and Waters (2007) showed participants a nine-item picture matrix. Participants were instructed to search for a neutral target picture of a bird or fish. Participants were slower to find the target and made more errors when one of the nontarget pictures was a snake or a spider, and the effect was enhanced when the participants already had fears of snakes or spiders.

These data do not suggest that we learn fears only about evolutionarily significant stimuli or that we cannot learn fears of modern dangers. They do suggest, however, that we may learn fears about spiders and snakes *differently* than we learn fears about guns or identity theft. That is, if evolutionarily significant, fear-relevant stimuli are processed by a "fear module," such as the one proposed by Öhman and Mineka (2001, 2003), more modern dangers may be processed by different mechanisms. Mühlberger, Wiedemann, Herrmann, and Pauli (2006) recruited participants who were either spider-phobic or (airline) flight-phobic. The participants viewed pictures of spiders, airline crashes, or neutral stimuli while wearing headphones. The critical experimental manipulation was presentation of a loud, startling sound (US) paired with pictures of spiders or pictures of airline crashes (CS) for the spider-phobic and flight-phobic participants, respectively. Both sets of participants exhibited skin conductance responses, indicating arousal, when the startling noise was paired with their specific fear-relevant stimulus, but the arousal responses exhibited by the spider-phobic participants persisted throughout the experiment, and responses of flight-phobic participants did not. Furthermore, the covert skin conductance responses seen in the spider-phobic participants were accompanied by overt startle responses and widespread cortical evoked potentials (recorded via EEG electrodes). These phenomena were absent in the flight-phobic participants. Although the evidence is indirect, the data suggest that different brain mechanisms are activated by the types of feared stimuli particular to these two groups of phobic individuals. The authors concluded that fear of evolutionarily significant stimuli "is associated with a deeper and/or more biased processing" and that the mechanisms responsible for such fears "might be more widespread and might have stronger interconnections" (p. 587).

Mate Selection

Although there are societies in which marriages are arranged, men and women are usually active participants in courtship and mate selection. How do we choose, from many potential mates, the one (or ones) with whom we reproduce? The naive answer is simple: We seek long-term mating relationships with those individuals who are most attractive to us. How, then, do we develop ideas about what is attractive and what is not? It may seem, at one level of analysis, that there are as many standards for attractiveness as there are cultures, and even within a single culture, standards for physical attractiveness may vary. A social-cognitive learning theorist might suggest that definitions of attractiveness are learned by attending to salient models in our particular culture (our parents, peers, leaders, etc.) and, in technological societies, to those models that are deemed attractive by the media. However, from the perspective of evolutionary psychology, many socially transmitted standards are superficial. Social standards related to attractiveness are transient; for example, popular hairstyles, body-decorations, styles of dress, and even preferred body shapes can and do change. For the evolutionary psychologist, there must be mate-selection criteria that are more basic than social standards for physical attractiveness within any single culture and that are culturally universal.

David Buss, a preeminent researcher in mate selection, notes that

we never choose mates at random. We do not attract mates indiscriminately. . . . Our mating is strategic, and our strategies are specifically designed to solve particular problems required for successful mating. . . . Those in our evolutionary past who failed to mate successfully failed to become our ancestors. All of us descended from a long and unbroken line of ancestors who competed successfully for desirable mates, attracted mates who were reproductively valuable, retained mates long enough to reproduce, fended off interested rivals, and solved the problems that could have impeded reproductive success. (1998, p. 409)

The evolutionary perspective, therefore, suggests that an attractive mate will have characteristics that may be unrelated to physical attractiveness as portrayed by popular media. These more important characteristics might include value as a nurturer and provider, reproductive fitness, and worthiness as a partner and parent. In other words, an attractive mate will have characteristics that tell us that our mate will help to ensure our survival as well as produce, and enhance the survival of, our children.

Buss and his colleagues surveyed more than ten thousand people from thirty-seven diverse cultures to determine if there are *universal* features that are valued in potential mates (Buss, 1989, 1994, 1998; Buss & Schmitt, 1993). The results provide strong evidence that, despite the variability introduced by culture, evolution has selected features that we recognize (rather than learn) as being important characteristics of a good mate. As shown in Table 15–1, the most important characteristics identified by men or women are kindness and understanding, followed by intelligence, factors that should contribute to the survival of our mate, ourselves, and our offspring.

These similarities between males and females are noteworthy with only two important exceptions. Men tend to rank "physical attractiveness" higher than do women, and women tend to rank "good earning capacity" higher than do men. The evolutionary explanation for this difference is that females expend considerable biological resources carrying and delivering a child and, until recently, females continued to expend biological resources as the only parent capable of feeding a newborn. Thus, women place relatively greater value on a man's ability to protect and provide for the nuclear family while her resources (and strength) are otherwise occupied. Conversely, men should place greater importance on physical attributes that are predictors of a woman's

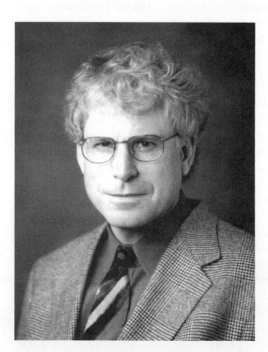

David Buss. (Courtesy of David M. Buss.)

TABLE 15–1   Characteristics Valued in a Mate

MALES AND FEMALES VALUE MOST HIGHLY
Kindness–Understanding
Intelligence

MALES VALUE MORE THAN DO FEMALES
Good looks
Youth

FEMALES VALUE MORE THAN DO MALES
Good Earning Capacity
Industriousness

Summarized from Buss (1989)

successful reproductive ability. In accordance with this prediction, Buss (1989) and Buss and Schmitt (1993) found that women place greater value than men on factors such as a mate's ambition, industriousness, social status, and athleticism. On the other hand, men attend more than women to factors such as a mate's age, general health, blemish-free skin, and clarity of eyes. Note that these "standards of beauty" are indicators of good health and are not restricted by transcient changes in style or preference for body-shape.

Parenting

Although the specific roles that parents play in educating, socializing, and disciplining children are shaped by cultural influences, they also reflect biological influences. For example, Tiger (1979) noted that being a parent entails sacrificing time and resources in "a set of radically unselfish and often incomprehensibly inconvenient activities" (p. 96). For evolutionary psychology, the task is to explain why two otherwise rational adults might deplete their biological and physical resources (thus putting their own survival at risk) for others who, as parents will attest, rarely say "thank you" and may not recognize the importance of their parents' unselfish and inconvenient acts for many years, if ever.

Kin Selection   An evolutionary explanation of parenting begins with the Neo-Darwinian principle of kin selection, the idea that evolutionary fitness involves perpetuation of not only our own genes but also those of individuals to whom we are related (inclusive fitness). **Hamilton's Rule** (Hamilton, 1964) suggests the guiding role of related genes as they pertain to **altruism,** an act of unselfish sacrifice for the benefit of another. Specifically, the rule says that altruistic behavior occurs when $rB > C$ and:

B = the *Benefit* gained by the recipient of an altruistic act
C = the *Cost* incurred by the altruistic actor
r = the *proportion* of genes shared by the actor and the recipient of the altruistic act

In the most simple and selfish case, consider an act that one does for one's own good. In this case, r = 1.00; that is, we share 100 percent of genes with ourselves. Hamilton's Rule suggests that we are likely to commit such an act on our own behalf even when the benefit of the act is barely greater than the cost. Thus, the probability of acting on our own behalf is always quite high. A child has half of the genes of a parent, so r = .50. This means that the benefit of an act must be more than twice its cost if an altruistic act is to occur. We are therefore less likely to commit an altruistic act for our children than for ourselves. In fact, unless the benefit-to-cost ratio is large, for example, when the child's health or life is in danger, Hamilton's Rule suggests that we will not extend an unselfish act. If we consider other relatives in the equation, we begin to see the sense of Hamilton's Rule. Our brothers, sisters, and parents also share 50 percent of our genes, but nieces, nephews, uncles, aunts, and grandparents share only 25 percent of our genes. For these latter individuals, the rule suggests that the benefit of an act must be more than four times the cost if an altruistic act is to occur. Thus, we are most likely to sacrifice for ourselves, next for our offspring and immediate family, and last for more distant relatives. The fewer genes we share with another individual, the less likely we are to extend an unselfish act, and the likelihood of an altruistic act being extended to an unrelated individual is, for all purposes, zero.

In this way, evolutionary psychologists see parenting not as a learned behavior but as an act that is predisposed by kin selection principles. Our offspring benefit because they are among those most likely to be recipients of our unselfish actions. As Krebs (1998) puts it, parents are "simply doing what they must to propagate their genes. Genetically speaking, they are helping themselves" (p. 353).

Sex Differences   Barash (1979) points out that parenting has been, and is, largely the job of the females:

> There is no human society, historically or in recent times, in which women have not borne the primary responsibility for child care. Parenting is a largely sex-linked occupation. In all societies, men do men things and women are left holding the babies. But why does this occur? Since one-half of the genes making up every individual have been contributed by each parent, then each parent should have the same interest in each child. Right? Wrong. (p. 108)

According to evolutionary psychologists, there are two primary reasons why women tend to be more involved in parenting than men. First, women have much more invested in their offspring than do men. Barash (1979) explains:

> Eggs are fertilized by sperm, not vice versa. And women become pregnant, not men. It is the woman who must produce a placenta and nourish her unborn child; who must carry around an embryo that grows in bulk and weight, making her more and more ungainly as her pregnancy advances; and, when the child is born, must nurse it. Because women become pregnant, they simply cannot produce as many children as can men. We may regret this fact, glory in it or simply accept it, but it remains, nevertheless, an indelible part of our biology. (p. 47)

Second, for self-sacrificing behavior to follow Hamilton's Rule, there must be mechanisms by which we can recognize relatives, including our own children, as carriers of our genes. Sex differences in parenting are believed to arise partly because men and women must rely on different kinds of cues to solve the problem of paternity (or maternity) uncertainty. For mothers, the problem is a simple one. As Buss (1998) notes, "No woman ever gave birth and wondered whether the baby that came out of her body was her own. In contrast, men can never be sure" (p. 415–416). It should be the case, therefore, that women are more predisposed than men to engage in parental behaviors. This does not mean that men cannot and do not sacrifice for their children. It does suggest, however, that they must rely on cues such as phenotypic (physical) appearance, cues that are less compelling than those a mother experiences (Krebs, 1998).

Family Violence An important implication of Hamilton's Rule and of kin selection in general is that violent behavior is unlikely to be directed toward those who share our genes. Violence within families, therefore, should be rare. Yet, it is a common observation that violence within families occurs daily. Gelles and Straus (1985), for example, warn that, except for military and law enforcement careers, an individual is "more likely to be hit or killed in his or her home by another family member than anywhere else or by anyone else" (p. 88).

Daly and Wilson (1982, 1998) argue that, despite nightly news reports and the claims of researchers like Gelles and Straus, kin selection exerts a strong guiding influence in family violence. Specifically, kin selection predisposes violent behavior against family members that are not genetically related. For example, in a compilation of homicide statistics from Detroit, shown in Figure 15–2, Daly and Wilson found that murder is more than twenty times more likely to be committed against a spouse (a nongenetic relative) or an unrelated individual than against one's child, parent, or other genetic relatives. Summarizing data from a variety of cultures, they write,

> Close genetic relationships are far more prevalent among collaborators in violence than among victim and killer. . . . Even in patrilineal social systems, in which brothers are one another's principal rivals for familial lands and titles, there is evidence that

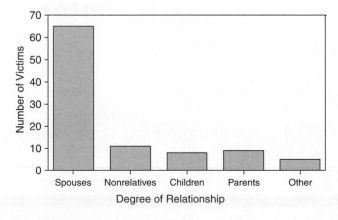

FIGURE 15–2 Homicide among cohabitants in Detroit, 1972. Summarized from Daly & Wilson (1982).

close genealogical relationship softens otherwise equivalent conflicts and reduces the incidence of violence. . . . Familial solidarity cannot be reduced to a mere consequence of proximity and familiarity. (1998, p. 440)

A troubling implication of Hamilton's Rule concerns the relationships between stepparents and their children. Pinker (1997) writes, "The stepparent has shopped for a spouse, not a child; the child is a cost that comes as part of the deal" (p. 433). Daly and Wilson (1998) pose the problem in the following way:

It is adaptive and normal for genetic parents to accept nontrivial risks to their own lives in caring for their young, but selection presumably favors much lower thresholds of tolerable cost in stepparenting. . . . Little wonder, then, that the exploitation and mistreatment of stepchildren is a thematic staple of folk tales all around the world. (p. 441)

But are these only folktales? Are stepchildren really more likely than genetic children to be selected as targets of violence? The answer is yes. In studies of homicides in Canada between 1974 and 1990, Daly and Wilson (1988, 1994) found that children, particularly those between birth and five years of age, were between fifty and one hundred times more likely to be killed by a stepparent than by a genetic parent. These dramatic findings are illustrated in Figure 15–3.

Altruism and Moral Behavior

The kind of altruism we have discussed so far is called **kin altruism,** and whether it occurs is determined by Hamilton's Rule. Evolutionary psychologists also discuss **reciprocal altruism,** which is helping behavior that occurs among individuals who are not genetically related. Reciprocal altruism is based on the fact that humans who cooperate are more likely to survive than those who do not (for example, in hunting or in warfare). Reciprocal altruism is based on the assumption that if one helps a member of the community, then at some future date, that member, or another member of the community, will respond in kind. Such altruism follows the maxim, "Do unto others as you would have them do unto you."

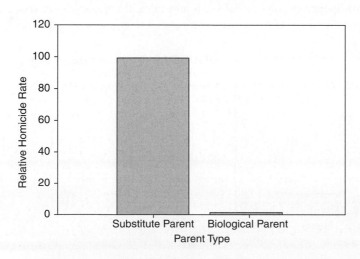

FIGURE 15–3 Parent-child homicide rates in the United States in 1976. From Daly & Wilson (1988).

Why, given that success is ultimately defined in terms of the survival of our genes or the genes of those who are related to us, should we extend cooperative behaviors for the welfare of those who are not related to us? Why should those behaviors that are the cornerstones of "moral behavior"—sharing, helping, cooperation, mercy—develop in the first place? Krebs (1998) provides one answer:

> The unconstrained pursuit of individual interests and the exploitation of others are ineffective interpersonal strategies for three main reasons. First, some resources are beyond the reach of individuals acting alone. Second, unconstrained selfishness may destroy the system of cooperation on which it feeds. Third, others are evolved to resist being exploited. In effect, individuals in cooperative groups agree to adopt moral strategies of interaction to maximize their mutual gain, although not necessarily consciously or explicitly. Moral rules uphold these strategies, defining the investments (e.g., duties) each individual is expected to make to obtain the returns (e.g., rights). (p. 339)

Among the moral strategies that people have adopted to maximize mutual gain and resist individual exploitation are deference to authority, adoption of systems of justice, and mechanisms to detect "cheating" (Cosmides & Tooby, 1992; Krebs, 1998).

Language

As we saw in Chapter 5, Skinner assumed that language learning could be explained by the principles of operant conditioning. In Chapter 7, Pavlov explained language by invoking higher-order classical conditioning principles. Although we did not address the problem in Chapter 13, Bandura's social-cognitive learning theory can be extended to language learning by attributing language acquisition to observational learning. For evolutionary psychologists, however, these learning theories are incomplete because they fail to address a diverse body of data that illustrates the role of preparedness in language acquisition. In fact, language learning may illustrate biological preparedness in human learning more dramatically than any of the phenomena that we have discussed thus far.

Although Noam Chomsky is skeptical of evolutionary explanations of language phenomena (1972, 1988), the argument against traditional learning-theory explanations of language begins with two important challenges he posed (1959, 1975). First, Chomsky points out that children generate unique word strings and sentences rather than merely repeating those words and sentences that have been reinforced. Similarly, children say things that have not, and in some cases could not, have been modeled in their environments. For example, it would be unlikely for a child to *learn* the confession "Yes, I eated the candy. I *dood* it!" Second, Chomsky argues that children develop *grammatical* comprehension without any formal instruction. That is, they understand and generalize the underlying rules of language and readily understand both typical and atypical sentences and phrases. Chomsky's position is that the brain is, in part, an organ naturally designed to generate and understand language. It therefore makes no more sense to talk about learning to have language than it does to talk about learning to have hands or a heart or any other biological organ.

Steven Pinker, in his influential book *The Language Instinct* (1994), takes the next logical step and marshals considerable evidence to place Chomsky's "organ of language" in the domain of evolutionary psychology. First, Pinker argues, there are language universals, rule characteristics common to every known language. Despite romantic notions we may have been led to believe about languages other than English, all languages recognize past, present, and future; all have pronoun references; and all have versions of subject/action (cause-effect) constructions. Similarly, all have simple rules for creating plural forms, even if there are exceptions to those rules. All languages have relatively simple rules for modifying statements to create questions, but no known language makes questions by reversing the word order of a statement. Early linguistic investigators found as many as forty-five grammar universals in thirty diverse languages (Greenberg, 1963), and subsequent investigations have found many more (e.g., Hawkins, 1988). These are exactly the kinds of findings that support Chomsky's claim that the brain is wired with an innate "Universal Grammar."

Second, Pinker shows that children are biologically prepared to create grammatical structure, even in the absence of models or instruction. Creole languages provide a demonstration of this innate invention (see, for example, Bickerton, 1981, 1984, 1998). When workers from several different cultures and language groups live together, for example, as farm laborers, they develop a functional, shorthand language called a **pidgin.** The pidgin language typically contains nouns and verbs from the various language groups represented but "no consistent word order, no prefixes or suffixes, no tense or other temporal or logical markers, no structure more complex than a simple clause, and no consistent way to indicate who did what to whom" (Pinker, 1994, p. 34). Children who grow up exposed to the pidgin language do not continue to use pidgin to speak with each other. Rather, they create complex grammatical rules, imposing structure that did not exist in their parents' pidgin, thereby creating a new language form called a **Creole.** Most important, the grammar that makes the Creole a real language is imposed by the children; it is not provided by parents or formal education. Thus, the children are biologically prepared to create grammatical systems by using the most fundamental linguistic tools at hand, even if the grammatical structure is not inherent in those tools. Recently, the transformation from pidgin to Creole has been observed in the sign language among deaf children in Nicaragua. In 1979, the first schools for the deaf were created in Nicaragua, and the children who attended those schools developed a form of pidgin sign language (despite a curricular emphasis on lip reading and speech). The second generation of deaf students made a grammatical leap from the pidgin to a more grammatically complex Creole sign language, much as Creoles did among people who rely on spoken language (Kegl & Iwata, 1989). Where do the grammatical rules come from if there is no formal grammatical instruction and no adults to model complex sentence structure, verb-tense changes, pronouns, and so on? Pinker's answer, like Chomsky's, is that grammatical learning is biologically prepared.

Finally, a strong argument for innately predisposed language would include evidence for a heritable, genetic mechanism. Of course, the complexity of language comprehension and production makes it unrealistic to assume that a single gene or even a small aggregate of genes underlies the language phenomenon. However, Pinker presents evidence of the next best thing, evidence for a genetic *inability* to learn grammatical structure. **Specific language impairment (SLI)** (Gopnik, 1990; Gopnik & Crago, 1991) is a heritable disorder that results in delayed language acquisition, poor articulation, and persistent grammatical errors without any evidence of general intellectual impairment. For example, normal four-year-old children succeed readily at the "Wug test." In this task, children are shown a line drawing of an imaginary creature and told that the thing is a "Wug." They are then told that there are now two (or more) of the creatures. Therefore there are two ____? Normal English-speaking four-year-olds typically fill the blank by saying "Wugs." Children and adults with SLI fail to solve this kind of problem correctly, but they exhibit no difficulties with mathematical or nonlinguistic tasks.

Although Pinker (1994) recognizes that much remains to be learned about the evolution of language, language development, and the role of the human brain in these phenomena, he is an enthusiastic advocate of an evolutionary psychological perspective:

> So we now know which biological traits to credit to natural selection and which ones to other evolutionary processes. What about language? In my mind, the conclusion is inescapable. Every discussion . . . has underscored the adaptive complexity of the language instinct. It is composed of many parts: syntax, with its discrete combinatorial system building phrase structures; morphology, a second combinatorial system building words; a capacious lexicon; a revamped vocal tract; phonological rules and structures; speech perception; parsing algorithms; learning algorithms. Those parts are physically realized as intricately structured neural circuits, laid down by a cascade of precisely timed events. What these circuits make possible is an extraordinary gift: the ability to dispatch an infinite number of precisely structured thoughts from head to head by modulating exhaled breath. (p. 362)

EVOLUTIONARY PSYCHOLOGY ON EDUCATION

Evolutionary psychology does not have implications for specific teaching techniques, but it does have implications for educational curricula in general. Evolutionary psychologists would agree with Thorndike and Piaget that children should be taught things when they are maturationally prepared or ready to learn them, but they might emphasize different kinds of learning than Thorndike or other theorists we have reviewed. For example, evolutionary psychology suggests that humans have natural predispositions toward selfishness, **xenophobia,** and aggression. Such dispositions will manifest themselves unless cultural resources are expended to inhibit them, and school curricula and activities, along with other cultural influences, such as child-rearing practices, must discourage these natural tendencies. Insofar as society values cooperative behavior, tolerance of ethnic and religious differences, and nonaggression, it needs to expend resources to discourage the natural tendencies to be selfish, prejudiced, and aggressive. In other words, children and young adults need to be taught to act in ways contrary to their natural predispositions.

On the other hand, the evolutionary psychologist also believes that humans are biologically prepared to learn things that a culture may value positively. Given the innate human predisposition to acquire language, for example, schools should stress bilingual learning even in the early stages of education.

Evolutionary psychologists remind educators to avoid "nothing-butism," the assumption that behavior is determined either by genes or by culture. Human behavior, they say, is always a function of both. This realization may be especially important when dealing with problem behaviors such as prejudice and aggression. Evolutionary psychology does not offer specific solutions for these problems, but it does suggest a reason why they are so persistent. Barash (1979) puts this reminder as follows: "Certainly there are many injustices and it is our right and duty to point them out when we see them, and to attempt some correction. Sociobiology helps us identify some of the possible roots of our injustice—male dominance, racism, and so forth. It surely has not created them. If any change is to occur, whether radical or merely cosmetic, we would do well to understand the biological nature of our species—what we really are (p. 235)."

EVALUATION OF EVOLUTIONARY PSYCHOLOGY

Contributions

Evolutionary psychologists make a distinction between **proximate explanations** and **ultimate explanations** of behavior. Proximate explanations include references to deprivation conditions, observable environmental stimuli, reinforcement contingencies, and the immediate learning history of the organism. Ultimate explanations emphasize traits and behaviors of organisms that have been shaped by natural selection. Most of the learning theories reviewed in this book emphasize the former and de-emphasize or completely ignore the latter. Perhaps the most important contribution Bolles and other evolutionary psychologists have made is the insistence that proximate explanations must be considered simultaneously with ultimate explanations. In a tribute to Bolles, Garcia (1997) notes that "Bolles went one step beyond Tolman. The contextual map and the subsequent sense impressions must be congruent with the evolution of the particular species under observation" (p. xiii). Bouton and Fanselow (1997) expanded on Bolles's contributions:

> His approach was molar rather than atomistic or reductionistic. Bolles expanded on Tolman's purposive approach by considering behavior in terms of both its immediate or proximal purpose and its ultimate or evolutionary one. He always put behavior in the context of its function. . . . The understanding is not complete until behavior can be placed in its functional context. (p. 5)

This is not to say that evolutionary psychology makes the task of psychologists easier. Plotkin (1998) writes:

> So, when natural selection enters into a causal explanation, that explanation is a great deal more complex than when it is not there because the proximate causes have not

disappeared. Instead they have been supplemented by a large number of other causes. . . . It is not only a more extensive causal story that must be told. It is also more complete. (pp. 16–17)

The benefit of this more complete story should be apparent. We have seen that research outcomes that appear to violate known learning principles are resolved when an evolutionary explanation is provided. Puzzling "exceptions to the rule" turn out not to be exceptions after all. In addition, evolutionary psychology has provided an important heuristic function. New research questions, including many that focus on human learning phenomena, have been stimulated, bringing us closer to a more complete understanding of learning that includes both nonhumans and humans.

Criticisms

Perhaps the most common criticism of evolutionary psychology, of the theory of evolution itself, is the claim that evolutionary arguments are circular. That is, critics claim that successful adaptations are defined as those physical or behavioral traits that survive natural selection (and are reproduced); therefore, if a behavior exists in a current generation, it must have been selected and is therefore a successful adaptation. Our earlier discussion of spandrels and exaptations demonstrates, however, that evolutionary psychologists have avoided the adaptationist trap and the problem of circularity.

A second criticism is that an evolutionary explanation of behavior embraces a doctrine of genetic determinism. That is, if we are the products of our genetic endowment, we are doomed to be the products of our selfish and greedy genes. However, as we have already seen, evolutionary psychology does not embrace "nothing-butism." Petrinovich (1997) points out that evolutionary psychology "does not involve genetic determinism because evolutionarily determined traits can be altered if the environment in which individuals develop is modified. A broad interactionist view is at the heart of modern sociobiology and evolutionary psychology" (p. 23).

Third, critics fear that evolutionary psychology represents a return to social Darwinism, a doctrine that justifies nepotism, racism, and perhaps even selective breeding. As we noted earlier, however, moral behaviors that include kindness to strangers and extension of helping behavior to others than our kin have evolved because it is to our benefit to engage in those behaviors. Again, Petrinovich (1997) defends evolutionary psychology:

> However, the importance of inclusive fitness does not mean that people are destined to benefit kin and friends to the detriment of all outsiders, thus condemning humans to an environment consisting of "us" and "them." It only means that there are propensities to communicate and cooperate with familiars more than with strangers. The fact that biases exist does not mean that people are hopelessly bound to follow their lead into the depths of xenophobia. (pp. 23–24)

Fourth, critics claim that genetic predispositions preclude learning. In effect, these critics say that if a behavior is the result of genetic processes, it is not learned. Situations merely elicit the behavior; thus all behavior is described as clusters of unconditioned responses. As we have seen, however, evolutionary psychology merely claims that evolutionary influences guide and bias learning. In rejecting the empirical principle of equipotentiality, evolutionary psychology merely says that learning is constrained by innate factors, not that it does not happen. As Pinker (1994) says, "Evolutionary psychology does not disrespect learning but seeks to explain it. . . . There is no learning without some innate mechanism that makes the learning happen" (p. 410).

DISCUSSION QUESTIONS

1. Discuss the primary features of evolutionary psychology.
2. Briefly summarize Darwin's theory of evolution.
3. Explain why exaptations and spandrels militate against the belief that all adaptations have been naturally selected.
4. Differentiate between inclusive fitness and Darwin's narrower definition of fitness.
5. How did Bolles expand Tolman's theory of expectancy learning to include evolutionary principles?
6. What is the empirical principle of equipotentiality? Why do evolutionary theorists disagree with it?
7. Briefly summarize Bolles's niche argument. Expand your summary to include the concept of the environment of evolutionary adaptedness (EEA).
8. Give examples of how biology constrains instrumental, operant, and classical conditioning. Include in your answer a discussion of Bolles's concept of species-specific defensive reactions (SSDRs).
9. Explain autoshaping in terms of evolutionary psychology.
10. Discuss the following categories of human behavior within the context of prepared learning: the development of phobias, mate selection, parenting, family violence, and altruism and moral behavior.
11. Differentiate beween kin altruism and reciprocal altruism, and give an example of each.
12. Discuss language development from the perspective of evolutionary psychology.
13. What have been the contributions of evolutionary psychology to an understanding of the learning process? For what has the approach been criticized?

CHAPTER HIGHLIGHTS

adaptation	ethologists
altruism	evolutionary psychology
Creole	exaptation
empirical principle of equipotentiality	expectancies
environment of evolutionary adaptedness (EEA)	fitness
	Hamilton's Rule

inclusive fitness

kin altruism

natural selection

overdetermined

pidgin

preparedness continuum

proximate explanations

reciprocal altruism

sociobiology

spandrels

species-specific defensive reactions (SSDRs)

specific language impairment (SLI)

ultimate explanations

xenophobia

CHAPTER 16

A Final Word

Chapter 1 presented an effort to define learning and differentiate it from other processes such as habituation, sensitization, and instinct. Chapter 2 discussed the characteristics of science as they apply to the study of learning. Chapter 3 outlined the historical antecedents of learning theory. Subsequent chapters provided detailed accounts of the major theories that grew out of this rich philosophical heritage. Each of the major theories was listed under one of five paradigms, depending on which historical theme it followed. The theories that were strongly influenced by Darwin were listed under the functionalistic and evolutionary paradigms. Those theories following in the tradition of Aristotle and Locke were listed under the associationistic paradigm. The theories following in the tradition of Plato, Descartes, Kant, and the faculty psychologists were listed under the cognitive paradigm. Hebb's theory was offered as an example of the neurophysiological paradigm, which also has its historical roots in the work of Descartes.

In this final chapter, we discuss what the trends seem to be within current learning theory. It in no way implies that the information in the preceding chapters is obsolete. Almost everything occurring in learning theory today is, in some way, an extension of one of the major theories of learning presented in this book. Understanding such an extension requires understanding the theory from which it is derived.

Thus, we have explored learning theory's past and present. In this chapter, we attempt to indicate where learning theory seems to be heading and ponder a few questions that it will need to address in the future.

CURRENT TRENDS IN LEARNING THEORY

At least four major trends can be seen in today's approach to the study of learning. First, today's learning theory is humbler in scope. Instead of attempting to explain all aspects of learning, today's theorist is content to investigate some aspect of the learning process. The theories of Estes in Chapter 9 offer examples of the reduced domain of contemporary learning theories.

Second is the increased emphasis on the neurophysiology of learning. As we saw in Chapter 14, neurophysiological explanations of learning have come from a position of obscurity during the peak of the behavioristic movement to one of the most popular approaches to the study of learning today, as seen by the enthusiasm for neural networks and the new connectionism.

Third, cognitive processes such as concept formation, risk taking, and problem solving are again a respectable and popular topic of study. Cognitive processes, because of their apparent close relationship to introspection, were largely ignored during the dominance of behaviorism. In turning again to cognitive processes, psychology is broadening its base, but it is not becoming unscientific. Behaviorism was an extreme reaction to the method of introspection and an attempt to make psychology a science by giving it a reliable, observable subject matter—behavior. There are those who maintain that behaviorism threw out the baby with the bathwater by defining behavior to exclude "higher mental processes," such as concept formation and problem solving or thinking in general. Currently, these areas are of vital interest to psychologists, and they are being explored scientifically. As with any other scientific research, the ultimate authority in research on cognitive processes is empirical observation. Theories are devised, hypotheses are generated, experiments are run, and as the result of the experiments' outcome, theories are strengthened or weakened. The method is the same as that of the traditional behaviorist; what has changed is the behavior that is being studied. Saltz (1971) says,

> After many years of very self-conscious empiricism, the psychology of human learning has begun to show signs of a vigorous interest in new (and often dramatic!) theoretical approaches. We find the postulations of multiple storage systems for memory; the distinction between learning systems and retrieval systems; the attempt to analyze "what is learned" into a complex system of interacting variables.
> Further, there is evidence to suggest that psychologists in the area of human learning may have lost some of their fear of studying complex processes. There has developed a

lively new interest in such issues as the nature of concept acquisition; the role of strategies in learning; and the more general question of the nature and function of variables like intention, meaning, and imagery. In short, there is a new interest in the role of the cognitive, information-processing variables in human learning. (p. vii)

The trend toward cognitive theory by no means indicates that behaviorism is dead. Behaviorism remains a powerful force in psychology (see, for example, Pearce & Bouton, 2001; Staddon & Cerlutti, 2003). Skinner (1974) said that true behaviorism has never really been tried. If it had, he maintained, many human problems could be solved. Skinner pleaded for the development of a technology of human behavior based on behavioristic notions. He claimed that older strategies for solving major human problems based on mentalistic or cognitive theories of behavior have been totally ineffective, and unless a more effective means of dealing with these problems is found, they will persist:

> I contend that behavioral science has not made a greater contribution just because it is not very behavioristic. It has recently been pointed out that an International Congress on Peace was composed of statesmen, political scientists, historians, economists, physicists, biologists—and not a single behaviorist in the strict sense. Evidently behaviorism was regarded as useless. But we must ask what the conference achieved. It was composed of specialists from many different fields, who probably spoke the commonsense lingua franca of the layman, with its heavy load of references to inner causation. What might the conference have achieved if it could have abandoned this false scent? The currency of mentalism in discussions of human affairs may explain why conferences on peace are held with such monotonous regularity year after year. (p. 250)

Skinner (1974) never waivered in his attack on cognitive psychology. At best, he said, cognitive psychology is simply old wine in new bottles: "Cognitive psychology is certainly in the ascendant. The word cognitive is sprinkled through the psychological literature like salt—and, like salt, not so much for any flavor of its own but to bring out the flavor of other things, things which a quarter of a century ago would have been called by other names" (p. 949).

At worst, cognitive psychology makes flagrant mistakes that retard our understanding of human behavior. Skinner (1987) listed the many mistakes he felt cognitive psychology was making in the form of accusations:

> I *accuse* cognitive scientists of misusing the metaphor of storage. The brain is not an encyclopedia, library, or museum. People are changed by their experiences; they do not store copies of them as representations or rules.
> I *accuse* cognitive scientists of speculating about internal processes which they have no appropriate means of observing. Cognitive science is premature neurology.
> I *accuse* cognitive scientists of emasculating laboratory research by substituting descriptions of settings for the settings themselves and reports of intentions and expectations for action.
> I *accuse* cognitive scientists of reviving a theory in which feelings and state of mind observed through introspection are taken as the causes of behavior rather than as collateral effects of the causes.
> I *accuse* cognitive scientists, as I would accuse psychoanalysts, of claiming to explore the depths of human behavior, of inventing explanatory systems that are admired for a profundity more properly called inaccessibility.

> I *accuse* cognitive scientists of speculation characteristic of metaphysics, literature, and daily intercourse, speculation perhaps suitable enough in such arenas but inimical to science.
>
> Let us bring behaviorism back from the Devil's Island to which it was transported for a crime it never committed, and let psychology become once again a behavioral science. (p. 111)

At present, Skinner's brand of behaviorism appears to be losing ground to cognitive psychology, but the battle is far from over.

Fourth, there is increased concern with the application of learning principles to the solution of practical problems. Recently, there have been many attempts to show how learning principles can be used to improve teaching and child rearing. Learning is currently being emphasized in the explanation of personality development. Some of the more effective psychotherapeutic techniques of today are based on learning principles. Learning principles are being used as a basis for redesigning mental and penal institutions. Learning principles are currently being investigated in their relationship to warfare, international relations, legal and judicial procedures, and public health. Learning is being explored as a means of modifying national attitudes toward pollution and population control. And related to the last point, learning is being studied as a means of instituting cultural change in general. No doubt the next decade will see an ever-growing concern with the application of learning principles to the solution of many human problems.

SOME UNANSWERED QUESTIONS ABOUT LEARNING

How Does Learning Vary as a Function of Maturation?

Many investigators (e.g., Piaget and Hebb) have found that the learning that occurs at one maturational stage is not the same as that which occurs at another maturational stage. Instead of thinking of learning as a unitary process that either occurs or not, we need to explore further how the learning process may change as a function of maturation. Indeed, such information will be vital in education and child rearing.

Does Learning Depend on Reinforcement?

Many learning theorists would say that learning does depend on reinforcement, but their opinions would vary about the nature of reinforcement. Thorndike's concept of reinforcement was "a satisfying state of affairs." Pavlov equated reinforcement with an unconditioned stimulus. For Guthrie, it was anything that causes an abrupt change in stimulating conditions. For Skinner, it was anything that increases the rate of responding. For Hull, it is anything that causes drive stimulus reduction. For Tolman, it was the confirmation of an expectancy. The Gestaltists likened reinforcement to the reduction of ambiguity. For Bandura, intrinsic reinforcement is the feeling one has when one's performance matches or exceeds one's internalized standards or when a personal goal is attained. Also for Bandura, as for Tolman and Spence, extrinsic reinforcers can be used to cause an organism to convert what had previously been learned into behavior. Thus for Bandura, Spence, and Tolman, extrinsic reinforcers influence performance, not learning. Although these definitions of reinforcement, in some cases, are substantially different, they all point out that some of our innumerable daily experiences "stick," and others do not. The process that causes some experiences to be retained can be loosely referred to as reinforcement. What, if anything, all these versions of reinforcement have in common has not yet been determined.

How Does Learning Vary as a Function of Species?

Bitterman (1960) observed that some species of animals cannot learn at all what others can learn with ease. As we saw in Chapter 7 and Chapter 15, some species are biologically prepared to learn certain associations; other species are contraprepared to learn them. Observations such as these raise questions concerning the extent to which we can generalize what we learn about learning from one animal species to another. What, for example, can studying the learning process in the rat tell us about the learning process in humans? The problem of the generalizability of research findings in learning is currently receiving wide attention.

Can Some Associations Be Learned More Easily Than Others?

Preparedness applies not only to differential learning among species but also to differential learning within a particular species. Thus the preparedness continuum is both an interspecies variable and an intraspecies variable. As evidence for the latter, Seligman (1970) offered the work of Garcia and his colleagues, who found within a species (e.g., coyote) that taste aversions are formed rapidly (sometimes in just one trial) and last for a very long period of time. Furthermore, Bolles, Garcia, and others found that some associations were "less natural" and were difficult to form, suggesting that those associations that are directly related to an organism's survival are easiest for the organism to form. Thus, we have another example of how an organism's genetic endowment interacts with the learning process. Which associations are easiest to learn for various species and why some are easier to learn than others are questions that are currently receiving considerable attention.

How Does Learned Behavior Interact with Instinctive Behavior?

We noted in Chapter 5 that the Brelands (1961) observed that animals that were conditioned to perform various tricks, such as placing coins in a bank, would eventually revert to behaviors that they would normally engage in under the circumstances.

For example, raccoons that were reinforced with food for dropping coins in a bank eventually refused to give up the coins. Instead, they would hold the coins and rub them together. In other words, they treated the coins as if they were food. This phenomenon was referred to as instinctual drift because it seemed that the organism's learned behavior gradually gave way to its instinctive behavior. Timberlake's (2002) overdetermination principle reveals additional interactions between the natural propensities of an organism and the constraints of a learning experiment. Such observations have led many psychologists to conclude that an organism's innate response tendencies may place limits on the extent to which its behavior can be modified through learning. The extent of these limits and whether such limits exist on the human level remain unanswered questions.

How Does Learning Vary as a Function of Personality Characteristics?

After operationally defining such traits as introversion and extroversion by using existing paper-and-pencil tests, is it possible that learning ability may be found to differ as a function of such traits? Research has shown, for example, that high-anxious subjects are conditioned more rapidly than low-anxious subjects (Taylor, 1951). In Taylor's research, high- and low-anxious subjects were distinguished by using the Taylor Manifest Anxiety Scale. How many other personality traits can be operationally defined and found to interact with learning rate? The answer to this question will be especially important in education. Because personality is currently thought of as the product of early learning, the question here is really how learning early in life affects later learning, or how the development of a cluster of strong habits influences the development of subsequent habits.

To What Extent Is Learning a Function of the Total Environment?

How does what children learn in school relate to what they learn from their parents, from television, from books, from toys and games, or from their peers? What happens when teachers encourage behavior that is not supported by anyone else in the children's lives? What happens if parents are encouraging certain behavior patterns in their children, but their peer groups encourage incompatible forms of behavior? Of concern here is how the many learning experiences a person has in a short period of time are related to one another.

How Do All of the Preceding Questions Interact with Type of Learning?

The term *interaction* is one of the most important terms in science. In general, two variables are said to interact when the effect of one variable is different at different levels of the second variable. Aspirin, for example, has different effects on people, depending on whether they consumed alcohol before taking it. Aspirin and alcohol, then, are said to interact. Lack of sleep may have no effect on weight lifting, but it may have a deleterious effect on typing. In this case, the effects of sleep loss on performance are said to interact with task complexity. That is, at one level of task complexity—weight lifting—loss of sleep has little or no effect, whereas at another—typing—it has a considerable effect.

Assuming that there is more than one kind of learning, it is possible that motivation (e.g., drive) may be important for one kind of learning but not for another. Drive may be important for instrumental conditioning but not for what Tolman called sign learning. It may be that the laws of classical and instrumental conditioning are the same for all species of animals, but other forms of learning occur only in animals high on the phylogenetic scale. It could be that some learning occurs in an all-or-none fashion, whereas other kinds of learning may be incremental. It may be that personality type also interacts with type of learning. For example, there may be a difference in learning rate between high- and low-anxious subjects in a classical conditioning situation but not in a problem-solving situation. A crisscross interaction is even possible in some cases. For example, high- and low-anxious subjects may perform in an opposite manner when the type of learning required of them is changed. This theoretical possibility is shown in Figure 16–1.

Obviously, it is possible that mediational processes are very important for concept formation and problem solving but may not be at all important for classical or operant conditioning. Thus, Thorndike's contention that learning is direct and independent of mediational processes would be true of only some kinds of learning. Likewise, the Gestalt contention that learning involves the conscious reduction of ambiguity would also be only partially true. Whether "thinking" is important may depend entirely on what kind of learning one is talking about.

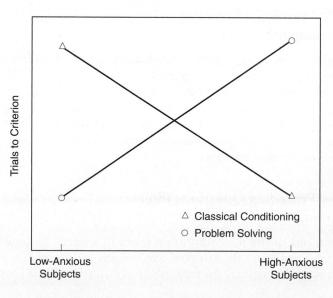

FIGURE 16–1 A theoretical interaction showing how anxiety level has a different effect on learning rate, depending on what kind of learning is involved. In this case, low-anxious subjects learn to solve a problem much faster than high-anxious subjects. When classical conditioning is examined, however, low-anxious subjects take much longer to condition than high-anxious subjects.

Also, it could turn out that everyone's notion of reinforcement is correct. Classical conditioning could, indeed, depend on the presentation of an unconditioned stimulus. Instrumental conditioning may depend on drive stimulus reduction, as described by Hull, or on a "satisfying state of affairs," as described by Thorndike. Other kinds of learning may be more conveniently explained by using the concept of reinforcement suggested by Guthrie, Skinner, Premack, Tolman, or the Gestaltists. The belief that there are a number of different kinds of learning, rather than one or two, makes all these positions plausible. This, of course, is the approach that Tolman (1949) was suggesting in his article "There Is More Than One Kind of Learning," and the possibility is raised again with empirical demonstrations of distinctions between procedural and declarative learning. As we have seen, learned behavior appears to interact with instinctive behavior. It is possible that when certain animals are in certain situations in which instinctive behavior is appropriate, learned behavior cannot compete. This may be true for only certain organisms and certain situations. Furthermore, it may not be at all true at the human level. Also, we have seen that for certain organisms, learning principles can be used to form some associations readily, but other associations are formed with great difficulty. Genetic endowment, the nature of the learning task, and learning principles all seem to interact in a complex way.

It seems that the more is known about any area, the easier it is to make finer distinctions within it. As more is known about the area of learning, it becomes more differentiated. The area of learning has become very heterogeneous, compared with the rather undifferentiated field it was not too many years ago. Like most subjects that we come to know more about, learning has become more complicated instead of less complicated. As it stands today, the field of learning can justify a number of different approaches to its study and a variety of explanations of its facts. As each of the new subdivisions of learning is studied more extensively, we will see more spin-offs from the general field of learning into separate autonomous fields, such as the neurophysiology of learning, cognitive learning, and mathematical models of learning. As these areas themselves become more differentiated, we will begin to see spin-offs from them, for example, Markov models of learning, learning and the single cell, and the effects of early experience on learning. And on it goes. This process of differentiation takes place in the evolution of any science.

NO FINAL ANSWERS ABOUT THE LEARNING PROCESS

There are no final answers concerning the nature of the learning process in this book. But that fact should not bother the student because in science there are never any final answers. In science, knowledge evolves, and evolution depends on variety. Clearly, most of what is now known about learning came out of the great debates among learning theorists in the 1930s and 1940s. Healthy criticism and defense of one's position seem to provide an atmosphere conducive to the growth of a young science. Fortunately, such an atmosphere still exists in psychology, but the debate among theorists is not as intense as it once was.

Where does this leave the student who is interested in learning about learning? Students have a smorgasbord of approaches to the study of learning before them. They can either choose the one that best satisfies their appetite and concentrate exclusively on it or sample from all of them. In building a house, sometimes a hammer is the most effective tool, sometimes a screwdriver, and at still other times a saw. The student who decides to sample from the smorgasbord is like the carpenter who selects different tools as different problems emerge. A third approach may result if a student cannot develop an appetite for any of the theories developed thus far. Such a student may someday develop his or her own theory. After all, this is what Thorndike, Pavlov, Skinner, Hull, Guthrie, Piaget, Tolman, Bandura, Bolles, Hebb, and the Gestalt psychologists did. At this stage of knowledge about the nature of learning, all three approaches are necessary.

In the determination of human behavior, there is no process more important than learning, and so one of the most worthwhile enterprises a person could engage in is to help unravel the mysteries of that process.

DISCUSSION QUESTIONS

1. Define the term *interaction*. Give a few examples of interactions not described in this chapter.
2. Discuss four major trends in learning theory today.
3. Summarize Skinner's opposition to cognitive psychology.
4. What is meant by the statement "The field of learning is becoming increasingly differentiated"?
5. List and briefly discuss the unanswered questions about learning.
6. Why, in your opinion, are there no final answers in science? Relate your answers to the study of the learning process.
7. What is the nature of the learning process? Respond in outline form.
8. Write what you feel is an acceptable definition of learning.

Glossary

absolute theory   The contention of the behaviorists that what an organism learns are specific responses to specific stimuli.

abstract modeling   The situation in which observers are presented with a variety of modeling experiences from which they extract a common rule or principle. Once extracted, the rule or principle can be applied to new situations.

accommodation   The modification of cognitive structures as the result of an experience that could not be assimilated into existing cognitive structures. Accommodation can be roughly equated with learning.

acquisition   The gaining of new information from one's observations.

action potential   A nerve "impulse" or "spike." During action potential, the conditions of resting potential are reversed and reset. (See also **resting potential** and **neurons.**)

acts   Complicated behavior patterns usually involving some goal accomplishment. Acts are made up of many individual movements.

actual environment   That proportion of a potential environment that is actualized by an organism's behavior.

adaptation   According to Darwin, any physiological or anatomical trait that allows an organism to survive and reproduce. According to Wilson, any physiological or anatomical trait or behavior pattern that contributes to an organism's ability to perpetuate copies of its genes into subsequent generations.

advantageous comparison   An attempt to escape from self-contempt by comparing one's immoral actions to another person's even more immoral actions.

altruism   Behavior that is apparently unselfish and self-sacrificing. (See also **kin altruism.**)

analogy   A partial correspondence or similarity between things otherwise dissimilar.

annoying state of affairs   A condition that an organism actively avoids. If such a condition occurs, the organism attempts to abandon it as soon as possible.

anterograde amnesia   Inability to consolidate new memories.

anthropomorphizing   Attributing human characteristics to nonhuman animals.

anticipatory frustration stimulus (s_F)   Proprioceptive (internal) stimuli that accompany the fractional anticipatory frustration reaction (r_F).

anxiety hierarchy   The initial stage of Wolpe's therapeutic technique of systematic desensitization, which involves taking a series of related anxiety experiences and ordering them from the experience that causes the greatest amount of anxiety to the experience that causes the least amount of anxiety.

apperception   According to Wundt, the clear perception that results from the willful force of one's attention.

Aristotle (384–322 B.C.)   Because he believed sensory experience to be the basis of all knowledge, he was the first major empiricist. He also proposed the laws of similarity, contrast, contiguity, and frequency to explain how ideas became associated with other ideas.

arousal function of a stimulus   That function of a stimulus that increases the activity of the reticular activating system, thereby increasing the electrical activity in certain higher centers of the brain.

arousal theory   The contentions that brain wave activity ranges from very fast to very slow with a rate in between that allows for the optimal performance of certain tasks.

array model   Estes's cognitive model of classification/categorization. Stimulus features are assumed to be stored and compared in a memory array.

assimilation   Responding to the physical environment in accordance with existing cognitive structures. Assimilation refers to a kind of matching between the cognitive structures and the physical environment. Assimilation can be roughly equated with recognition or knowing.

associationism   The philosophical belief that the relationships among ideas are explained by the laws of association.

associative shifting   The process whereby a response is "carried" from one set of stimulating conditions to another by gradually adding new stimulus elements and subtracting old ones. The result is that a response that was originally given to one set of circumstances is now given to an entirely new set of circumstances. Associative shifting is based on the principle of contiguity.

attentional processes   Those variables that determine what is attended to during observational learning.

attribution of blame   An attempt to escape self-contempt by saying the victim of one's immoral actions caused one to act as one did.

autoclitic behavior   Provides a grammatical framework for verbal behavior.

autoshaping   The observation that under certain circumstances the behavior of some organisms seems to be shaped automatically.

avoidance conditioning   The experimental arrangement whereby an organism can avoid experiencing an aversive stimulus by engaging in appropriate behavior.

axons   Extended processes of neurons that are specialized for carrying electrochemical signals away from the cell body. (See also **neurons.**)

backward conditioning   An experimental arrangement whereby the conditioned stimulus is presented to the organism after the unconditioned stimulus is presented.

basal ganglia   Neural structures responsible for control of motor movements and for consolidation of procedural memory. (See also **procedural memory.**)

behavior therapy   The utilization of learning principles in the treatment of behavior disorders.

behavioral economics   A discipline that uses behavioral techniques to study demand for reinforcers and reinforcer efficacy.

behavioral environment   According to Koffka, the environment as it is consciously experienced. Also referred to as subjective reality.

behavioral potentiality   The ability to perform some act, although the act is not being performed at the present time. Learning may result in a change in behavioral potentiality, although the learning may not be translated into behavior until some time after the learning has taken place.

behavioral production processes   Those variables that determine which aspects of what has been learned and retained cognitively can be produced behaviorally.

behaviorism   A school of psychology, founded by J. B. Watson, that completely rejected the study of consciousness. To be scientific, psychology needed a subject matter that could be reliably measured, and according to the behaviorist, that subject matter was behavior.

belongingness   Material is learned more readily when it is structured in certain ways. Contiguity alone does not determine how well something will be learned. How the material "fits together" must also be taken into consideration. Also, Thorndike maintained that learning is most effective when there is a natural relationship between the needs of an organism and the effects produced by a response.

Berkeley, George (1685–1753)   He said we can have no direct knowledge of the external world; we experience only the ideas that it causes us to have. His belief that nothing exists unless it is perceived led to his famous dictum "to be is to be perceived." What we call external reality is God's perception.

biofeedback   The information provided to individuals by some mechanical device concerning the status of one or more of their internal biological events. For example, a flashing light can be set to reflect heart rate, or an auditory signal can be triggered when blood pressure rises beyond a certain level.

blocking (also called the **blocking effect**)   When one CS (A) is paired with a US, it will become conditioned to that US. If, after initial conditioning, CS (A) is paired with a second CS (B) and presented to the organism as a compound stimulus CS (AB), little or no conditioning occurs to CS (B). It is as if the initial conditioning to CS (A) somehow blocked any conditioning to CS (B).

brain plasticity   See **neuroplasticity.**

cathexis   The formation of an association between a certain drive state, such as hunger, and certain stimuli, such as the foods one is accustomed to eating. When a drive occurs, one actively seeks out the stimuli that have been previously associated with its satisfaction. Cathexis is one of Tolman's six proposed kinds of learning.

cell assembly   The pattern of neural activity that is caused when an environmental object or event is experienced. When the cell assembly is well developed, the person is able to think of the entire event following the stimulation of the assembly, even if the object itself or the event is physically absent.

chaining   According to Skinner, chaining occurs when one response brings the organism into proximity with stimuli that both reinforce the last response and cause the next response. According to Guthrie, chaining is the process whereby the stimulation caused by one response acts as a stimulus for another response, that response in turn triggers another, and so on.

chameleon effect   Nonconscious mimicry of the postures, mannerisms, facial expressions, and other behaviors of one's interaction partners.

classical conditioning   An experimental arrangement whereby a stimulus is made to elicit a response that was not previously associated with that stimulus (i.e., the conditioned stimulus, CS, comes to elicit a response similar to the one elicited by the unconditioned stimulus, US).

clinical method   An open-ended form of questioning in which the researcher's questions are guided by the child's answers to previous questions.

cognitive dissonance   A psychological state experienced when there is a discrepancy between what is expected and what actually occurs.

cognitive hunger Popper's term for the innate desire to revise expectancies continuously so that they are increasingly accurate in reflecting reality.

cognitive map A mental picture of the environment.

cognitive structure The schemata that an organism has available at any given time to interact with the physical environment. Cognitive structure results from both biological maturation and cumulative experience. The cognitive structure not only is affected by experience but also determines what can be experienced. If a physical event cannot be at least partially assimilated into the organism's cognitive structure, that physical event cannot constitute a biological stimulus. The dual processes of assimilation and accommodation must always occur with the existing cognitive structure as a point of departure.

computer-based instruction (CBI) Utilization of computers to present and evaluate a wide variety of educational materials.

concentration Pavlov's contention that both excitation or inhibition can be focused or restricted to certain parts of the brain. He used this concept to explain discrimination.

concrete operations The stage of intellectual development in which children can deal logically with only those events that they can experience directly.

concurrent chain reinforcement schedule On such a schedule, the responses made during an initial phase determine what response alternatives and what reinforcement schedules are available during the terminal phase.

concurrent reinforcement schedule A schedule involving two alternative responses, each of which is maintained by an independent schedule of reinforcement.

conditioned anticipatory frustration Fractional anticipatory frustration reactions (r_F) and their stimuli (s_F) conditioned to environmental events that accompany primary frustration.

conditioned emotional response (CER) A procedure used to determine the strength of a relationship between a CS and a US that combines operant or instrumental conditioning and classical conditioning. In phase 1, animals learn an instrumental or operant response to the point that it is emitted at a steady rate. In phase 2, the classical conditioning phase, a CS is paired with a US a number of times. In phase 3, as animals are again performing the instrumental or operant response, the CS from phase 2 is presented, and its effect on the rate of responding is noted. Depending on how the CS and US were paired in phase 2, it is found that presenting the CS in phase 3 facilitates, inhibits, or has no effect on the rate with which the instrumental or operant behavior is emitted.

conditioned inhibition ($_sI_R$) In instrumental or operant conditioning, a learned response of not responding. Because responding produces fatigue (I_R) and fatigue is a negative drive state, not responding is reinforcing, hence conditioned inhibition. In classical conditioning, conditioned inhibition is conditioning observed when a CS-US pairing *suppresses* a response.

conditioned response (CR) (also called **conditioned reflex**) A response that is made to a stimulus not originally associated with the response. For example, salivation to the sound of a tone is a conditioned response because an organism would not ordinarily salivate to the sound of a tone.

conditioned stimulus (CS) A stimulus that before conditioning does not cause an organism to respond in any particular way. Before conditioning, the stimulus is a neutral stimulus. After conditioning, however, the conditioned stimulus elicits a conditioned response.

conditioned suppression The inhibition of a conditioned response caused by conditioned emotional responses (CERs).

conditioning An experimental procedure used to modify behavior. Most learning theorists believe that there are two kinds of conditioning—classical and instrumental—and that all learning involves conditioning. To those holding such a belief, *learning* is a term used to summarize a large number of conditioned responses.

confirmation of an expectancy When the prediction made about some future event is found to be accurate.

confirming reaction A neurophysiological reaction that is stimulated when a response produces a satisfying state of affairs. The confirming reaction was thought by Thorndike to be the true strengthener of a neural bond.

connectionism A term often used to describe Thorndike's explanation of learning because he assumed learning involved the strengthening of neural bonds (connections) between stimulating conditions and the responses to them.

conservation The realization that number, length, substance, or area has not changed, although it may be presented in a number of different ways. The ability to conserve requires the use of reversible operations.

consolidation theory The contention that a short-term memory is converted into a long-term memory following a period of consolidation.

content The ingredients that accompany a specific manifestation of a schema.

contingency contracting Making arrangements, sometimes with another person, so that certain behavior will be reinforced. For example, each time the person goes a week without smoking, the person receives ten dollars.

contingent reinforcement Reinforcement that occurs only if a specific response is made. If the response is not made, the organism is not reinforced.

continuity-noncontinuity controversy Another label for the debate over whether learning occurs gradually and in small increments or in large steps in an all-or-none fashion.

continuous reinforcement schedule (CRF) The condition in which the organism is reinforced each time it makes an appropriate response.

copying behavior A kind of imitative behavior studied by Miller and Dollard in which a sophisticated individual guides the behavior of a naive individual until an appropriate response is made.

corpus callosum A massive bundle of fibers that connects the two hemispheres of the cortex.

correlational techniques Research in which two response measures are related. Such research is usually interested in detecting how two kinds of behavior vary together. For example, how is performance on an IQ test related to performance on a creativity test? Correlational techniques generate R-R laws because two response measures are being related.

cortical mosaic The pattern of excitation and inhibition that constitutes the activity of the cortex at any given moment.

counterconditioning The technique used to eliminate undesirable behavior whereby a CS is paired with a US other than the one that originally reinforced the undesirable behavior. For example, if a CS was originally followed by shock, thus producing fear, the CS could be paired with food, thus producing a response incompatible with fear.

creative synthesis According to Wundt, the ability to willfully arrange the elements of thought into any number of configurations.

creativity The innovation that results from either synthesizing the influences of several models or from observing a single model demonstrate unconventional problem-solving strategies.

Creole A complex, grammatically complete language that is derived from a pidgin language. (See also **pidgin.**)

Crespi effect The rapid change in performance level as the size of reinforcement is varied.

critical period A period in an organism's life during which an important development occurs. If the development does not occur during that time, it may never occur. For example, if imprinting does not occur shortly after a duckling is hatched, it is difficult, if not impossible, to establish it. The period of time immediately following hatching, therefore, is the critical period for imprinting.

cue function of a stimulus That function of a stimulus that provides us with information about the environment.

cumulative recording A special kind of graphing technique used by Skinner. Each time a response is made, the cumulative recording rises one notch and remains at that level until another response is made. The steepness of the line, therefore, indicates rate of responding.

Darwin, Charles (1809–1882) He demonstrated the ability of behavior in adjusting to the environment and the fact that human development is biologically continuous with that of nonhuman animals. Both observations had a profound and lasting effect on psychology, especially on learning theory.

declarative memory Higher-order memory including the memory that one has learned something new.

decremental reinforcer According to Mowrer, an unconditioned stimulus that causes a reduction in drive, such as when food is given to a hungry animal.

dehumanize Make the victim of one's immoral actions appear to be less human in an attempt to escape self-contempt.

delayed modeling The case in which an observer does not display what has been learned from a modeling experience until sometime after the modeling experience has been terminated.

demand The intervening variable that corresponds to maintenance schedule. As the number of hours without eating goes up, for example, demand is thought to increase.

dendrites Extended processes of neurons that are specialized for receiving electrochemical signals from other neurons. (See also **neurons.**)

dependent variable The variable that is measured in an experiment, usually some kind of behavior (e.g., trials to criterion).

Descartes, René (1596–1650) He postulated that the mind and the body were governed by different laws. The mind was free and possessed only by humans, whereas the body was mechanical and its functions were the same for both humans and other animals. He was responsible for creating the duality of mind and body, stimulating interest in physiological and comparative psychology, and reviving Plato's belief in innate ideas.

desensitization therapy The procedure whereby clients are asked to imagine an anxiety-provoking thought until they are able to ponder the thought without experiencing anxiety.

dichotic listening The technique whereby conflicting information is simultaneously presented to the two ears of a subject.

dichotomania The tendency to explain the functioning of the left and right cerebral hemispheres in terms of two clearly delineated sets of functions.

differential reinforcement The condition in which some responses made by the organism are reinforced and others are not.

diffusion of responsibility An attempt to escape self-contempt by saying that the decision to engage in an immoral act has been made by a group.

direct experience The events that one experiences as a result of one's own personal interactions with the environment.

direct modeling The observation of a live model.

discrimination Learning to respond to one stimulus but not to other stimuli, although they may be related to the first. For example, through discrimination training a tone of 500 cps elicits a conditioned response, whereas a tone of 490 cps does not.

discriminative operant An operant response that is made selectively to one set of circumstances but not to another set of circumstances.

discriminative stimulus (S^D) A cue or signal indicating that if a certain operant response is made, it will be reinforced.

disequilibrium hypothesis Restricted access to a response makes access to that response reinforcing; excessive access to a response makes that response punishing.

disinhibition In classical conditioning, the disruptive effect caused by presenting a novel stimulus along with an established conditioned inhibitor. In observational learning, the removal or reduction of an inhibition to perform a certain response that results from either performing the response without experiencing negative consequences or from seeing a model perform the response without experiencing negative consequences.

displacement of responsibility An attempt to escape self-contempt by claiming that a person in a position of authority caused one to act immorally.

disregard or distortion of consequences An attempt to escape self-contempt by minimizing the harm caused by one's immoral actions.

distributed practice Learning a skill under the conditions in which practice trials are separated by a considerable length of time.

drive (D) The condition that exists when there is a biological deficiency in the body. For all practical purposes, the terms *drive* and *need* mean the same thing.

drive discriminations The fact that organisms can discriminate between various drive states and can therefore adjust their behavior so that appropriate goal objects can be experienced. Drive discriminations are one part of Tolman's six proposed kinds of learning.

drive reduction The satisfaction of a biological deficiency. Originally Hull thought it to be a necessary condition for learning. Hull later turned to a drive stimulus reduction theory of learning.

drive stimuli (S_D) The stimuli that characteristically accompany a certain drive, such as the dryness of the mouth, lips, and throat that accompany the thirst drive.

drive stimulus reduction The reduction or removal of the stimuli that accompany a drive. This usually occurs before the drive itself is actually reduced; for example, the dryness of the mouth, lips, and throat are eliminated before the effects of drinking water can reach the brain and thereby reduce the thirst drive.

drives Maintaining stimuli usually caused by some physiological need, such as hunger or thirst.

dynamic stereotype A cortical mapping of events consistently occurring in the environment. A stable environment comes to have neurological representation on the cortex.

Ebbinghaus, Hermann (1850–1909) He was the first to study learning and memory experimentally. Demonstrating how the law of frequency worked in forming new associations, he invented nonsense material to control for previous experience in a learning situation.

echoic behavior Repeating someone else's verbal utterances.

effective reaction potential ($_s\bar{E}_R$) Reaction potential ($_sE_R$) minus the effects of I_R and $_sI_R$.

electroconvulsive shock (ECS) A severe shock that causes convulsions, thereby preventing the electrical activity that appears to be necessary for consolidation to take place.

elementism The belief that the best way to study a complex phenomenon is to divide it into smaller components.

emphasizer A role that motivation plays in Tolman's theory. The motivational state of an organism determines which environmental events will be emphasized in that organism's perceptual field.

empirical aspect of a theory The empirical events that the theory purports to explain.

empirical principle of equipotentiality The idea, advocated by some early learning theorists, that the laws of learning apply to any stimulus and any response.

empiricism The philosophical belief that sensory experience is the basis of all knowledge.

enriched environment An environment that contains many objects and events, which, according to Hebb, stimulates the development of complex neural circuitry.

environment of evolutionary adaptedness (EEA) The physical and social environment that existed when a particular evolutionary adaptation appeared.

epiphenomenalism The belief that body sensations cause mental images. In other words, mental images are seen as the by-products of body experiences.

epistemology The study of the nature of knowledge.

equilibration Piaget's major motivational concept; the innate need for balance between the organism and its environment and within the organism itself. Disbalance has motivational properties that cause the organism to do whatever is necessary to regain balance.

equipotentiality The finding that the cortex functions as a whole and that if one part of the cortex is destroyed, any one of a number of cortical areas can take over its function.

equivalence beliefs Similar to the notion of secondary reinforcement, in that a previously neutral event develops the capability of satisfying a need. One of Tolman's six proposed kinds of learning.

error factors   False strategies that operate against the solution of a problem. According to Harlow, learning is a matter more of eliminating error factors than of strengthening correct responses.

escape conditioning   The experimental arrangement whereby an organism can terminate an aversive stimulus by engaging in appropriate behavior.

ethologists   Biological/behavioral scientists who study specific types of innate behavior in an organism's natural environment and attempt to explain that behavior in terms of evolutionary principles.

euphemistic labeling   An attempt to escape from self-contempt by calling an immoral act something other than what it really is.

evolutionary psychology   The discipline that considers psychological and behavioral phenomena (emotions, learning, cognition, etc.) as products of natural selection. (See also **natural selection.**)

exaptation   According to Gould, co-opting an adaptation for a purpose other than the one for which the adaptation originally occurred. (See also **adaptation.**)

excitation   An increase in brain activity. A stimulus that causes excitation is called a positive stimulus.

excitatory conditioning   Classical conditioning observed when a CS-US pairing *produces* a response.

expectancy   Learning that one event leads to another. A belief or hypothesis about the occurrence of a future event.

experimental techniques   Research in which one or more independent variables are systematically manipulated in order to detect their effects on one or more dependent variables. Because an experiment attempts to relate stimuli (independent variables) to responses (dependent variables), it is said to generate S-R laws. This process is contrasted with correlational techniques, which demonstrate R-R laws.

external inhibition   The term Pavlov used to describe the disruptive effect that occurs when a novel stimulus is presented along with an already established CS.

extinction   The procedure whereby a conditioned stimulus is presented but is not followed by reinforcement. Under these circumstances, the magnitude of the conditioned response gradually becomes smaller. When a conditioned response is no longer elicited by a conditioned stimulus, the conditioned response is said to have been extinguished.

extinction of an operant response   In operant conditioning, extinction involves the gradual decrease in the frequency with which a conditioned response occurs after it is no longer reinforced. When the frequency of an operant response returns to its operant level, it is said to be extinguished.

facilitation   The increased probability of making a previously learned response that results from observing another person making the response.

faculty psychology   The belief that the mind contains certain powers or faculties.

fatigue method of breaking a habit   Forcing an organism to continue to respond to a source of stimulation until it is fatigued. When it is fatigued, it will respond to the source of stimulation in a way different from the way it originally responded to it.

faulty cognitive processes   Those cognitive processes that prevent or inhibit effective and efficient interactions with the social or physical environment.

fear   According to Hebb, the emotion experienced when there is an incompatibility between ongoing neural activity and the environmental events that accompany it.

field expectancies   Similar to a cognitive map, in that the organism comes to know which events in a given environment lead to other events. Field expectancies are one part of Tolman's six proposed kinds of learning.

field theory   The belief that the environment consists of interdependent events. In psychology, field theory assumes that behavior or cognitive processes are a function of many variables that exist simultaneously, and a change in any one of them changes the effect of all the others.

field-cognition modes   Learned or inherited strategies that are utilized while attempting to solve problems. Field-cognition modes are one part of Tolman's six proposed kinds of learning.

first signal system   Physical events in the environment and the responses they produce.

fitness   According to Darwin, an individual's ability to survive and reproduce. (See also **inclusive fitness.**)

fixed interval reinforcement schedule (FI)   The condition in which only the response made after a certain interval of time has passed is reinforced.

fixed ratio reinforcement schedule (FR)   The condition in which only the *n*th response made is reinforced.

flooding   Because organisms typically avoid experiencing those things that frighten them, it is unlikely that unjustified fears would ever extinguish naturally. Using the technique of flooding, the organism is forced to experience feared CSs long enough to learn that an aversive experience will not follow, thus creating the conditions necessary for extinction.

forethought   Defined by Bandura as anticipation of the consequences of our intentions.

forgetting   All forgetting, according to Guthrie, involves blocking out old associations by forming new ones. This is an extreme form of retroactive inhibition.

formal aspect of a theory   The signs, symbols, or words that a theory contains.

formal discipline   The belief held by some faculty psychologists that specific training can strengthen a specific faculty. For example, practicing being friendly would strengthen the friendliness faculty, thereby making the person friendlier.

formal operations   The stage of intellectual development in which children can deal logically with hypothetical events in addition to those events that they can experience directly.

forward conditioning   An experimental arrangement whereby the conditioned stimulus is presented before the unconditioned stimulus.

fractional antedating goal response (r_G)   A response that is conditioned to the stimuli present prior to the ingestion of a primary reinforcer. The conditioned response (r_G) is always some fraction of the goal response (R_G). For example, if the goal response is eating, r_G would be minute chewing responses. Each r_G automatically produces a stimulus, which is symbolized by s_G. The r_G-s_G mechanism plays an important role in Hull's explanation of chained behavior.

fractional anticipatory frustration reaction (r_F)   Stimuli that precede primary frustration will develop the capacity to elicit some portion of the primary frustration response.

frame   Term used in programmed learning to describe the small amount of information presented to the learner. In a linear program, the learner proceeds through the program frame by frame until a body of information is mastered.

freedom   According to Bandura, the number of options available to a person and the opportunity to exercise them.

frustration drive stimulus (S_F)   Aversive proprioceptive (internal) stimuli that accompany primary frustration (R_F).

frustration effect (FE)   The increased vigor of responses following nonreinforcement. For example, rats run faster following nonreinforcement than following reinforcement.

frustration-competition theory of extinction   Spence's and Amsel's contention that extinction is caused by responses stimulated by frustration, which interfere with the performance of a previously learned response.

functional analysis   The investigation of how certain stimuli and certain responses vary together. Skinner's approach to research was to avoid theorizing and to deal only with the manipulation of observable stimuli and note how their manipulation affected behavior; sometimes called the "empty organism" approach to research.

functional autonomy   A term introduced by Gordon Allport to explain behavior that apparently occurs independently of external reinforcement. Such behavior, according to Allport, was originally dependent on reinforcement but eventually becomes autonomous or self-reinforcing.

functional invariants   Processes that are not stage-specific but are present at all stages of development, such as assimilation, accommodation, and equilibration.

functionalism   The primary goal of the functionalist was to discover how mental and behavioral processes are related to an organism's adaptation to its environment. Members of this school were strongly influenced by Darwin's writings.

Gall, Franz Joseph (1758–1828)   He believed that a person's strong and weak faculties could be detected by analyzing the bumps and depressions on the person's skull. This system of analysis was called phrenology.

Garcia effect   The name given to the observation that animals form strong taste aversions easily and in apparent contradiction to several principles of classical conditioning.

generalization   The tendency for an organism to respond not only to the specific stimulus it was trained on but also to related stimuli. For example, if an organism was trained with a 500 cps tone as a conditioned stimulus, such tones as 600, 550, and 490 cps will also tend to elicit conditioned responses.

generalized habit strength ($_sH_R$)   Habit strength from previous learning experiences that generalizes to a new learning experience because of the similarity between the new learning experience and older ones.

generalized imitation   The learned tendency to imitate the behavior of others in order to be reinforced.

generalized reinforcers   Stimuli that derive their reinforcement properties from being paired with more than one primary reinforcer. Generalized reinforcers have wide application because their effectiveness does not depend on any particular need of the organism.

genetic epistemology   A term often used to describe Piaget's theory. The term *genetic* means developmental rather than having anything to do with inheritance. Epistemology refers to the study of knowledge; thus the term *genetic epistemology* is used to describe the study of knowledge as a function of maturation and experience.

geographical environment   According to Koffka, the physical or objective environment. Also referred to as objective reality.

Gestalt   A German word meaning pattern or configuration.

habit family hierarchy   A hierarchy of responses arranged according to their values of $_sE_R$. When a particular response is thwarted, the animal makes the next response available in its response repertory. Responses that result in the most rapid reinforcement have the greatest value of $_sE_R$ and are, therefore, most likely to occur. If a response with the highest value of $_sE_R$ is blocked, the response with the next highest value of $_sE_R$ will occur, and so on.

habit strength ($_sH_R$)   A measure of the strength of association between a stimulus and a response. The magnitude of the $_sH_R$ depends on the number of reinforced pairings between the stimulus and the response. In the final version of Hull's theory, $_sH_R$

was the only learning variable; the other factors were performance variables. In other words, Hull believed that the only thing that affected learning directly was the number of reinforced trials.

habituation   The decreased tendency to respond to a stimulus that results from prolonged exposure to that stimulus.

Hamilton's Rule   Hamilton's mathematical expression stating that the tendency to extend altruistic behavior to another individual is proportional to the number of genes shared with that individual. (See also **kin altruism**.)

Hebb rule   A learning rule in computer simulation referring to Hebb's idea that when two cells are active together, the connection between them is strengthened.

Hebbian synapse   A synapse at which simultaneous activity of a weaker sending cell and a receiving cell induces a change in the electrochemical relationship between the two cells.

Herrnstein's equation   A mathematical expression derived from the matching law that describes the learning curve for a single operant behavior. It expresses response rate as a function of reinforcement rate.

heuristic function of a theory   A theory's ability to generate research.

higher-order conditioning   After classical conditioning has taken place, a second conditioned stimulus is paired with the first conditioned stimulus. After a number of such pairings, the second conditioned stimulus can also elicit a conditioned response. This is called second-order conditioning. Once the second conditioned stimulus has the power to elicit a conditioned response, it can be paired with a third conditioned stimulus to produce third-order conditioning.

hippocampus   A brain structure within the limbic system thought to be involved in the conversion of short-term memory into long-term memory.

Hobbes, Thomas (1588–1679)   He reasserted Aristotle's doctrine of associationism and also suggested that experiences of pleasure and pain influence how associations are formed.

homeostatic mechanisms   Automatic processes that function to keep the body operating within certain physiological limits, thus maintaining a physiological equilibrium, or homeostasis.

human agency   The conscious planning and intentional execution of actions that influence future events.

Hume, David (1711–1776)   He said we can know nothing with certainty. All ideas are products of the mind and do not necessarily relate to a reality outside the mind. Therefore, the so-called natural laws are more the result of "habits of thought" than of any lawfulness in nature.

hypotheses   Expectancies that occur in the early stages of learning.

hypothetical deductive theory (logical deductive)   A theory consisting of postulates and theorems. Postulates are assumptions that cannot be verified directly; theorems are deduced from the postulates, and they can be verified experimentally. If an experiment designed to test a theorem comes out in the predicted direction, its postulate is indirectly verified, and the theory gains strength. If the experiment does not come out in the predicted direction, the theory loses strength. A hypothetical deductive theory is constantly changing in light of experimental evidence.

identical elements theory of transfer   The theory that the likelihood of something learned in one situation being applied in a different situation is determined by the number of common elements in the two situations. As the number of common elements goes up, the amount of transfer between the two situations goes up. The elements can be either stimuli or procedures.

idiographic technique   The intense study of a single experimental subject.

imitative behavior   The learned tendency to mimic the behavior of a model whose behavior has been seen being reinforced. According to Bandura, imitative behavior is only one of many possible results of observational learning.

immediate experience   The raw psychological experience that was the object of introspective analysis; experience that was not contaminated by interpretation of any kind.

immediate feedback (also called immediate knowledge of results)   The arrangement whereby learners are informed about the accuracy of their answers immediately following a learning or testing experience.

imprinting   The rapid formation, during a critical period, of a close attachment between an organism and an environmental object.

incentive motivation (K)   Size of reinforcement. Originally (1943), Hull felt that K affected learning, but he later (1952) concluded that it affected only performance. For Spence, incentive motivation was extremely important. It worked through the r_G-s_G mechanism and was the energizer of learned behavior.

inclusive fitness   The neo-Darwinian contention that an organism's fitness is determined by its ability to perpetuate copies of its genes into subsequent generations. This can be accomplished either by producing offspring or by helping relatives survive and reproduce. (See also **fitness**.)

incompatible response method of breaking a habit   The stimulus for an undesired response is presented, along with another stimulus that will cause a response incompatible with the undesired one. Because of this pairing, the stimulus that originally elicited the undesired response will no longer do so.

incremental learning   Learning that occurs a little bit at a time rather than all at once.

incremental reinforcer According to Mowrer, an unconditional stimulus that causes an increase in drive, such as electric shock.

independent variable The variable that is systematically manipulated in an experiment. Typical independent variables include hours of deprivation, sex of subject, age, rate of presentation, and degree of meaningfulness.

individual memory trace The memory trace left by a specific experience.

information value of a stimulus The ability of a stimulus to act as a signal to an organism that a significant event is about to occur. For example, a stimulus that signals the occurrence of food for a hungry animal has information value.

inhibition A decrease in brain activity. A stimulus that causes inhibition is called a negative stimulus. For Bandura, the reduced probability of performing a previously learned response that results from either direct or vicarious punishment of that response.

innate category of thought According to Kant, a genetically determined faculty of the mind that molds our cognitive experiences by giving them greater structure and meaning than they otherwise would have.

innate ideas Ideas that are not derived from experience but rather are thought to be inherited as part of the mind.

insightful learning Learning that occurs very rapidly, is remembered for a considerable length of time, and transfers readily to situations related to the one in which the insightful learning took place.

instinct The inborn capacity to perform a complex behavioral task. In recent years, the term has been replaced by *species-specific behavior.*

instinctual drift The tendency for the behavior of some organisms, after prolonged conditioning, to revert to instinctual patterns of behavior.

instrumental conditioning An experimental procedure whereby the rate or probability of a response is changed from one value before conditioning to another value following conditioning. With instrumental conditioning, the organism must perform an appropriate response to be reinforced.

intelligence Intelligence is a complex term in Piaget's theory, but in general it can be said that an intelligent act always tends to create optimal conditions for an organism's survival under existing circumstances. Intelligence is always related to an organism's adaptation to its environment.

intentionality Defined by Bandura as a representation of a future course of action to be performed.

intentions Behavior patterns that are conditioned to maintaining stimuli.

interaction of sensory impulses ($\bar{s}$) Behavior is usually the result of many stimuli impinging on sensory receptors at any given time. The afferent (sensory) neural impulses caused by these stimuli interact, and their combined effect causes an efferent (motor) neural impulse and finally an overt response (R).

interiorization The increased tendency to rely more and more on mental operations in adjusting to the environment as the cognitive structure becomes more articulated. An operation is referred to as an "interiorized" action because it is an adaptive response that occurs mentally rather than overtly.

interneuron A neuron-mediating activity between a sensory neuron and a motor neuron.

introspection The reporting of one's own mental events while experiencing a certain object or situation; the technique employed by the structuralists to study the structure of the mind.

irradiation of excitation The tendency for excitation (or inhibition) in a specific area of the brain to spill over into neighboring brain regions.

isomorphism As used by the Gestalt psychologists, the relationship that exists between brain activity and consciousness.

James, William (1842–1910) The founder of the functionalist movement. He attacked the way that the structuralists used the introspective method to search for the elements of thought. Consciousness, he felt, could not be subdivided because it acted as a functional unit that was constantly changing. The most important thing about consciousness is that it aids human survival. He also encouraged psychology to embrace the scientific method, to search for the physiological correlates of mental processes, and to investigate human emotions as well as intellect.

Kant, Immanuel (1724–1804) He believed that the mind was active and not passive, as the empiricist-associationists had assumed. The mind has innate powers or faculties that act on sense impressions and give them meaning.

kin altruism Helpful or self-sacrificing acts that are extended to those who share our genes. (See also **Hamilton's Rule.**)

latency ($_s$t$_R$) The time between the presentation of a stimulus and the occurrence of a learned response.

latent extinction Extinction that occurs simply because an animal is allowed to observe that a reinforcer is no longer available. Such extinction does not depend on the performance of nonreinforced responses.

latent inhibition effect The decrement in acquisition of a CR due to preexposure of a CS.

latent learning Learning that appears to take place independent of reinforcement and that remains dormant until the organism is given an incentive for translating what has been learned into behavior.

law of contiguity When two or more events occur together, they become associated with one another. Guthrie's one law of learning, which states that when a pattern of stimuli is experienced along with a response, the two will become associated so that when that pattern of stimuli next recurs, it will tend to elicit that response. In 1959, Guthrie revised the law of contiguity to read "What is being noticed becomes a signal for what is being done."

law of disuse   That portion of the law of exercise that states that the strength of a connection diminishes when the connection is not used. Thorndike discarded the law of disuse after 1930.

law of effect   The law that states that the strength of a connection is influenced by the consequences of a response. Before 1930, Thorndike believed that pleasurable consequences strengthened a connection and annoying consequences weakened a connection. After 1930, however, he believed that only pleasurable consequences had an effect on the strength of a connection.

law of exercise   The law that states that the strength of a connection is determined by how often the connection is used. The law of exercise has two components: the law of use and the law of disuse.

law of frequency   The more often two events or more occur together, the stronger the association among them.

law of Prägnanz   The overriding principle in Gestalt psychology, which states that all mental events tend toward completeness, simplicity, and meaningfulness.

law of readiness   The law that states that when an organism is ready to act, it is reinforcing for it to do so and annoying for it not to do so. Also, when an organism is not ready to act, forcing it to act will be annoying to it.

law of use   That portion of the law of exercise that states that the strength of a connection increases with its use. Thorndike discarded the law of use after 1930.

laws of association   Principles such as similarity, contrast, contiguity, and frequency that are supposed to explain how one idea is related to another or how one experience elicits ideas related to it.

learned helplessness   When organisms learn that their behavior is independent of outcomes, they sometimes give up trying. Such animals become passive and withdrawn and seem to accept whatever happens to them. With humans, learned helplessness is often associated with the emotional state of depression.

learned irrelevance   Refers to the diminished efficacy of a CS that is used in a random control condition.

learning   A relatively permanent change in behavior or behavioral potentiality that comes from experience and cannot be attributed to temporary body states such as illness, fatigue, or drugs.

learning dilemma   Dollard and Miller's contention that for learning to occur, previously learned behavior and innate behavior patterns must be ineffective in solving a problem. In this sense, failure is a prerequisite for learning.

learning set   See **learning to learn.**

learning to learn   The tendency to become increasingly effective at solving problems as more problems are solved. Also called learning set.

life space   Kurt Lewin's concept to describe the simultaneous influences on a person at a given time. Anything that can affect behavior is called a "psychological fact," and the total number of psychological facts influencing a person at any given moment is that person's life space.

limbic system   A number of interrelated brain areas related to emotional experience.

linear program   A type of program that requires each student to go through the same sequence of information in the same order.

Locke, John (1632–1704)   He strongly opposed the notion of innate ideas and suggested that at birth the mind was a tabula rasa, or a blank tablet. He said that "there is nothing in the mind that is not first in the senses." He distinguished between primary qualities, the physical characteristics of an object, and secondary qualities, the psychological experience caused by a physical object, such as the experience of color or taste.

logical deductive (hypothetical deductive)   A theory consisting of postulates and theorems. Postulates are assumptions that cannot be verified directly; theorems are deduced from the postulates, and they can be verified experimentally. If an experiment designed to test a theorem comes out in the predicted direction, its postulate is indirectly verified, and the theory gains strength. If the experiment does not come out in the predicted direction, the theory loses strength. A hypothetical deductive theory is constantly changing in light of experimental evidence.

long-term depression (LTD)   A procedure whereby weak electrical stimulation of part of the hippocampus is made weaker or less effective. It occurs if the weak electrical stimulation is followed by a stronger, repetitive electrical pulse. (See also **long-term potentiation [LTP].**)

long-term memory   Also called secondary memory; the memory of an experience that lasts for a considerable length of time after the experience. Whereas short-term memory is usually measured by seconds, long-term memory can be measured by years.

long-term potentiation (LTP)   A procedure whereby weak electrical stimulation of part of the hippocampus is made stronger or more effective. It occurs if the weak electrical stimulation is followed by a stronger, repetitive electrical pulse. (See also **long-term depression [LTD].**)

magazine training   Training the animal to approach the food cup when it hears the feeder mechanism operate. Thus the click of the feeder mechanism is associated with food and thereby becomes a secondary reinforcer.

maintaining stimuli   Any source of stimulation that persists until some specific act is performed. For example, putting a rubber band around an animal's nose provides maintaining stimuli until it is removed, and the hunger drive provides maintaining stimuli until the animal eats.

maintenance schedule   The feeding schedule arranged by the experimenter for an organism during a learning experiment.

mand   A verbal command that is reinforced when the listener carries out the command. For example, the mand "pass the salt" is reinforced when the person receives the salt.

Markov process   The situation whereby the probability of a response increases and decreases in a stepwise fashion rather than in small, steady amounts.

mass action   The finding that disruption of learning and memory is a function of the amount of cortical tissue destroyed.

massed practice   Learning a skill under the conditions in which practice trials are separated by only a very short interval of time.

matched-dependent behavior   A kind of imitative behavior studied by Miller and Dollard in which the behavior of one person acts as a cue for another person to behave in a similar way. In operant terms, the first person's behavior acts as a discriminative stimulus for the second person that triggers a response that leads to reinforcement. According to the operant analysis, matched-dependent behavior is a kind of discriminative operant.

matching law   Herrnstein's observation that when two alternative responses are governed by two independent schedules of reinforcement, the relative rate of responding to the alternatives approximately matches the relative rate at which the alternatives are reinforced. The matching law holds not only for rate (frequency) of reinforcement but also for amount and delay of reinforcement. All other things being equal, organisms prefer schedules of reinforcement that produce frequent, large, and immediate reinforcers to schedules with infrequent, small, and delayed reinforcers.

means-end readiness   An expectancy that is consistently confirmed; sometimes referred to as a belief.

memory process   The brain activity that is caused by environmental stimulation.

memory trace   The remnants of an environmental experience after the experience is terminated.

mentalistic events   Private events that, traditionally, have been attributed to the mind, including purpose, intention, thinking, feeling, and motivation.

Mill, John Stuart (1806–1873)   An associationist who disagreed with his fellow associationists' contention that complex ideas are nothing more than a compound of simpler ones. He felt that ideas could fuse together, and the fusion could create an idea distinctly different from the simple ideas that made it up.

mirror neurons   Neurons in the motor cortex of primates and humans that are active both when a significant behavior is observed and when it is executed.

misbehavior of organisms   The term used by the Brelands to describe the tendency of some organisms to behave instinctually instead of as they had been conditioned to behave.

model   (1) When a fairly well-known situation is used to describe a relatively less known situation. Models are used to show that the two situations are alike in some respects. (2) Anything that conveys information to an observer. In Bandura's theory, a model can be a person, film, picture, instructions, description, animal, television, or newspaper.

modeling-participation   The situation in which a live model guides the behavior of an observer until an appropriate response is made. This is much like the copying behavior studied by Miller and Dollard.

molar behavior   A large segment of behavior that is goal directed and therefore purposive.

molecular behavior   A small segment of behavior, such as a conditioned reflex, that is isolated for detailed study.

momentary effective reaction potential ($_S\dot{\bar{E}}_R$)   Effective reaction potential ($_SE_R$) minus the effects of I_R, $_SI_R$, and $_SO_R$.

moral codes   The internalized criteria that come from direct or vicarious experience used to monitor and evaluate one's own ethical behavior. If one's behavior violates an internalized moral code, one experiences self-contempt.

moral justification   An attempt to escape from self-contempt by attributing one's immoral behavior to a higher cause.

Morgan, Conwy Lloyd (1842–1936)   An early comparative psychologist who attempted to be objective in his descriptions of animal behavior by carefully avoiding anthropomorphizing.

Morgan's canon   Morgan's rule that animal researchers should never explain animal behavior as resulting from a higher mental process, such as reasoning or thinking, if that behavior could be explained by a lower process, such as instinct, habit, or association.

motivational processes   Those variables that provide incentives for translating what has been learned and stored cognitively into behavior.

motor patterns   The learning of the overt behavior that the organism must utilize in reaching a desired goal. Motor patterns are one part of Tolman's six proposed kinds of learning.

movement-produced stimuli   Stimulation caused by the receptors found in the muscles, tendons, and joints of the body. As the body moves, these receptors fire, thereby providing a source of stimulation, or what Guthrie called movement-produced stimuli.

movements   Specific responses to specific stimuli. Acts are made up of many specific movements.

multiple modeling   The observation of two or more models.

multiple response   Refers to the fact that if one response does not solve the problem, the organism continues to try other responses until it hits on one that is effective in solving the problem; a prerequisite to trial-and-error learning.

naive realism   The belief that physical reality is as we perceive it.

nativism   The philosophical belief that a mental attribute is inherited and therefore is independent of experience.

natural selection   The process, proposed by Darwin, by which heritable variations (adaptations) within a species facilitate reproduction for individuals possessing those variations (adaptations) and thus appear with increasing frequency in subsequent generations of that species.

naturalistic observation   Studying a phenomenon as it occurs naturally in the environment.

negatively accelerated learning curve   A learning curve that shows the rate of learning to be more rapid during the early trials in a learning situation than in the later trials. In other words, as the number of successive learning trials increases, the rate of learning decreases.

neglect syndrome   The tendency for patients with damage to the right cerebral hemispheres to ignore or neglect the left side of their bodies or perceptual fields.

neural networks   Computer models used to study interrelationships among computer-simulated neurons.

neurogenesis   The birth and development of new neurons.

neurons   Brain cells (or nerve cells).

neuroplasticity (also called brain plasticity)   The brain's capacity to reorganize or modify its connections as the result of experience.

neurotransmitter   A chemical messenger released from the end of an axon. (See also **axons**.)

nomothetic technique   The study of a group of experimental subjects, the interest being in the average performance of the group.

noncontingent reinforcement   Reinforcement that occurs independently of the organism's behavior.

nonsense material   Material with little or no meaning, invented by Ebbinghaus to control for previous experience in a learning situation.

normal science   Those activities of scientists as they are guided by a particular paradigm.

nucleus accumbens   A part of the limbic system that is thought to mediate brain stimulation reinforcement and drug addiction.

observational learning   The process whereby information is acquired by attending to events in the environment.

one-trial learning   The contention that the association between a pattern of stimuli and a response develops at full strength as a result of just one pairing between the two.

online education   The so-called virtual classroom in which a student learns via computer terminal, either by participating in an ongoing class or by interacting with prepared materials.

operant behavior   Behavior that is simply emitted by the organism rather than elicited by a known stimulus. Operant behavior may come under the control of its consequences.

operant conditioning   Increasing the rate with which a response occurs or the probability of a response by arranging the situation so that the occurrence of that response is followed by reinforcement. Also called Type R conditioning.

operant level   The frequency with which an operant response occurs before it is systematically reinforced.

operation   Cognitive action. As a sensorimotor schema manifests itself in overt behavior, an operation manifests itself in covert behavior or thinking. An operation can be thought of as interiorized action.

operational definition of learning   A definition that states the procedures to be followed in determining whether, and to what extent, learning has taken place. Operational definitions of learning can range from grades on achievement tests to some behavioral measure in a learning experiment, such as trials to criterion or the number of errors in maze running.

optimal level of arousal   The level of brain activity that is most conducive to the performance of a certain task.

orienting reflex   The tendency for an organism to attend to and explore a novel stimulus as it occurs in its environment.

oscillation effect ($_sO_R$)   An "inhibitory potentiality" that opposes the emission of a conditioned response and whose value changes from moment to moment. The values of $_sO_R$ are normally distributed, and therefore the value that manifests itself at any given moment can be large or small but will most likely be a value that is neither very large nor very small.

overdetermined (behavior)   Behavior that occurs reliably in the absence of experimental manipulations such as food or water deprivation or response-reward contingencies and that has a variety of sensory-motor patterns underlying the behavior.

overshadowing   The observation that the most salient component of a compound stimulus will become conditioned to a US and the weaker component will not. It is as if a dominant component of a compound CS overshadows the weaker component.

overt responding   A response that can be observed by others, as opposed to a covert response, which is not publicly observable.

paired associate learning   Learning pairs of stimuli so that when people see the first member of the pair, they can respond by reporting the second member.

paradigm   A point of view shared by a substantial number of scientists that provides a general framework for empirical research. A paradigm is usually more than just one theory and corresponds more closely to what is called a school of thought or an "ism."

partial reinforcement effect (PRE)   The fact that a response that has been reinforced only sometimes takes longer to extinguish than a response that had been reinforced each time it occurred.

perceived self-efficacy   What a person believes he or she is capable of doing; often contrasts with real self-efficacy.

performance   The translation of what has been learned into behavior.

performance standards   The internalized criteria that come from either direct or vicarious experiences used to monitor, evaluate, and reinforce or punish one's own behavior.

phase sequence   A sequence of temporarily related cell assemblies. Cell assemblies that consistently follow one another in time form a unit or a phase sequence.

phenomenology   The study of intact, meaningful mental events. These intact, meaningful mental events are called phenomenological experiences, which structuralists wanted their subjects to actively avoid and Gestalt psychologists felt were the basic subject matter of psychology.

phi phenomenon   The experience of apparent motion that is caused by lights flashing on and off at a certain frequency. Wertheimer's discovery of apparent motion launched the Gestalt school of psychology.

phrenology   The study of the location of bumps and depressions on a person's skull in order to determine that person's strong and weak faculties.

pidgin   A makeshift language that contains nouns and verbs from various language groups but has no complex structure. (See also **Creole.**)

place learning   Learning where an object is located. According to Tolman, once the location of an object is known, it can be reached by any number of alternate routes.

Plato (427–347 B.C.)   He proposed a reminiscence theory of knowledge in which knowing was explained as remembering the pure knowledge that the soul had experienced before entering the body. Plato was the first major rationalist and the first nativist.

potential environment   The environmental events available to an organism if it acts in ways that actualize them.

Premack principle   The opportunity to engage in a frequently occurring activity can be used to reinforce a less frequently occurring activity.

preoperational thinking   The stage of intellectual development in which children begin to classify objects and events into rudimentary categories.

preparedness continuum   Seligman's observation that associations that are compatible with an organism's evolutionary history are learned more easily than those that are not.

prepotency of elements   Refers to the fact that different aspects of the environment evoke different responses; similar to what we now refer to as selective perception.

primary frustration (R_F)   The response that occurs when an organism experiences nonreinforcement after it had learned to expect reinforcement.

primary negative reinforcer   An aversive stimulus that, when removed from the situation following a response, increases the probability of the response's recurrence.

primary positive reinforcer   A stimulus related to an organism's survival that, when added to the situation following a response, increases the probability of the response's recurrence.

primary reinforcer   Something related to survival such as food, water, or sex. Pavlov believed that all conditioning ultimately depends on primary reinforcement. In classical conditioning, the primary reinforcer is the unconditioned stimulus.

principle of association   Voeks's first postulate, which states that when a stimulus and response occur together, they become associated and that only through such contiguity are S-R associations formed.

principle of closure   Tendency to complete incomplete experiences, thereby making them more meaningful.

principle of dynamic situations   Voeks's fourth postulate, which states that stimulus patterns are dynamic because they can be changed by such things as an organism's response, fatigue, or the systematic control of an experimenter.

principle of falsification (principle of refutability)   Popper's contention that for a theory to be scientific, it must make risky predictions that, if not confirmed, would refute the theory.

principle of least effort   The contention that a task will always be done in a manner that requires the least amount of effort or work.

principle of parsimony   When researchers have a choice between two equally effective theories, they are obliged to choose the simpler of the two.

principle of polarity   The observation that learned material is most easily performed in the same direction in which it was originally learned.

principle of postremity   Voeks's second postulate, which states that only the last response made in a situation is the response that will be made when the situation recurs and that other responses previously made in the situation will no longer be associated with it.

principle of refutability (principle of falsification) Popper's contention that for a theory to be scientific, it must make risky predictions that, if not confirmed, would refute the theory.

principle of response probability Voeks's third postulate, which states that the probability of a response being made in a given situation is a function of the number of cues in that situation associated with the response.

probability matching In a situation in which subjects are asked to guess whether an event will occur, the proportion of the trials in which they predict the event will occur comes approximately to match the proportion of the trials that it does actually occur. For example, if a light is illuminated on 60 percent of the trials, subjects will come to predict that it will be illuminated on about 60 percent of the trials.

procedural memory Memory for complex motor skills that may not include memory that the skill has been learned.

productive thinking Wertheimer's term for thinking that is based on the understanding of the principles involved in a problem rather than on logic or the rote memorization of facts or rules.

programmed learning A procedure that provides information to the learner in small steps, guarantees immediate feedback as to whether the material was learned properly, and allows the learner to determine the pace with which the learner goes through the material.

progressive equilibrium Living organisms constantly seek a balance between themselves and their environment. But according to Piaget, the cognitive structures of an organism are always changing as the result of maturation and experience. Therefore, a balance can never be absolute but must rather be a progressive equilibrium, which is a balance that is the best under the prevailing circumstances. As circumstances change, what an optimal balance is must change accordingly.

progressive ratio reinforcement schedule A lab animal begins with a low ratio schedule (usually FR), and the ratio of responses to reinforcements is systematically increased during subsequent training sessions.

proprioceptive stimuli The stimuli that result from the firing of the kinesthetic receptors in the muscles, joints, and tendons of the body. Also called movement-produced stimuli.

proximate explanations Explanations of behavior that emphasize events in an organism's immediate environment, such as its deprivation conditions and the reinforcement contingencies it is experiencing.

punishment The arrangement whereby a response either produces an aversive stimulus or removes a positive one. According to Guthrie, two conditions must be met before punishment will be effective: (1) The punishment must produce behavior that is incompatible with the undesired response, and (2) the punishment must be applied in the presence of the stimuli that elicit the undesired response.

purposive behavior Behavior directed toward some goal, such as going to the store, cooking a meal, or solving a maze.

purposive behaviorism A behavioristic approach that studies purposive behavior as such and does not attempt to reduce such behavior into smaller elements for further analysis.

Pythagoreans Followers of Pythagoras who believed abstractions, such as numbers, were just as real as physical objects and that these abstractions could influence the physical world. Such beliefs had a strong influence on the development of Plato's theory of knowledge.

radical behaviorism The scientific philosophy, adopted by Skinner, that rejects references to mentalistic events and other abstract, theoretical events that cannot be directly observed.

rationalism The philosophical belief that the mind must become actively involved before knowledge can be attained.

reaction potential $(_sE_R)$ Directly influences four response measures. As reaction potential goes up, the probability of a learned response being elicited by a stimulus goes up, resistance to extinction goes up, amplitude of a conditioned response goes up, and latency goes down.

reaction threshold $(_sL_R)$ The minimal value that the momentary effective reaction potential $(_sE_R)$ must exceed before a learned response can occur.

reactive inhibition (I_R) The fatigue caused by responding that operates against the emission of a conditioned response.

real self-efficacy What a person is actually capable of accomplishing; may or may not correspond to perceived self-efficacy.

recency principle The principle that the response that was last made in a situation is the response that will be made when that situation next recurs.

receptors Molecular structures on neurons that react with the neurotransmitters released by nearby neurons.

reciprocal altruism Helping behavior among individuals who are not genetically related. It is assumed that recipients of (reciprocal) altruisic behavior will respond in kind in the future.

reciprocal determinism Bandura's contention that the environment, the person, and the person's behavior all interact to produce behavior.

reflex An unlearned response to a specific class of stimuli.

Reid, Thomas (1710–1796) He believed that any philosophical position that denied that we can reliably experience the physical world was ridiculous. Reid argued that we can believe that our sense impressions, and the ideas they give rise to, accurately reflect the physical world because it makes common sense to do so.

reinforced practice Repeated performance under the conditions in which correct response is followed by reinforcement. Reinforced practice is thought by many learning theorists to be a necessary condition for learning to take place; other theorists do not agree.

reinforcement According to Bandura, reinforcement gives the observer information concerning what leads to what in the environment, so that the observer can anticipate certain outcomes from certain behaviors. According to Guthrie, one of many events that can change a stimulus pattern, thus allowing the association between the previous stimulus pattern and the last response made to it to remain intact. Reinforcement, to Guthrie, was nothing more than a mechanical arrangement that prevents unlearning. According to Hull, drive reduction or drive stimulus reduction.

reinforcement centers in the brain Areas of the brain that when stimulated cause the organism to repeat whatever behavior preceded their stimulation.

reinforcement expectancy The fact that an organism learns to expect a certain reinforcer if it engages in certain behaviors. Performance is disrupted when the original reinforcer used in a learning situation is replaced with a different reinforcer.

reinforcement theory Any theory that claims learning cannot occur without reinforcement. Bandura's is not a reinforcement theory.

reinforcer Anything that causes either drive reduction or drive stimulus reduction.

reinstatement A CR reappears after extinction if the US is again presented.

relational theory The contention of the Gestalt psychologists that organisms should learn principles or relationships and not specific responses to specific stimuli.

reminiscence effect The improvement of performance on a skill following a rest after cessation of practice.

reminiscence theory of knowledge The belief held by Plato that all knowledge is present in the human soul at birth; thus to know is to remember the contents of the soul.

renewal effect A CR, extinguished in an environment different from the environment in which it was learned, reappears if the organism is returned to the original learning environment.

respondent behavior Behavior elicited by a known stimulus.

respondent conditioning The same as classical conditioning; also called Type S conditioning.

response by analogy Refers to the fact that our response to an unfamiliar situation is determined by its degree of similarity to a familiar situation. Insofar as two situations are similar, they will tend to be similarly responded to. Thorndike describes similarity in terms of the number of elements that the two situations have in common. This observation is related to his identical elements theory of transfer of training.

response learning The learning of specific responses that are effective in solving a problem and thereby providing reinforcement.

resting potential The "ready" state of a neuron, during which sodium ions are outside the cell and potassium ions are inside the cell. The inside of the cell is −70 millivolts in relation to the outside.

restricted environment An environment lacking normal levels of stimulation or experience. According to Hebb, restricted environments fail to stimulate development and growth of cell assemblies.

retentional processes The variables involved in encoding certain observations for memory. Bandura believes that observations are stored in memory through imaginal and verbal symbols.

reticular activating system (RAS) A structure located in the brain stem that appears to be responsible for regulating the electrical activity in the higher centers of the brain.

retroactive inhibition The interference of old learning by new learning.

retrograde amnesia The inability to remember the events that took place just prior to a traumatic experience, such as an automobile accident.

reverberating neural activity A system of self-perpetuating neural activity that lasts for a few seconds after the source of stimulation has been removed. Reverberating neural activity is thought by some to be the basis of short-term memory.

reversibility An important characteristic of mental operations that refers to the process of reversing a thought. For example, one can mentally pour liquid from one container into another and then reverse the process by mentally pouring liquid back into the original container. Reversibility of mental operations is a necessary condition for conservation to occur.

Romanes, George John (1848–1894) An early comparative psychologist whose evidence for the continuity between nonhuman and human mental processes was anecdotal and replete with anthropomorphizing.

same behavior A kind of imitative behavior studied by Miller and Dollard in which two or more individuals respond in the same way to the same stimulus.

satisfying state of affairs A condition that an organism seeks out and attempts to preserve. Once such a condition exists, the organism does nothing to avoid it.

savings   The difference in the time it takes to relearn something as compared with the amount of time it took to learn it originally; a measure of retention used by Ebbinghaus.

scanning model of decision making   Estes's description of the decision-making process as involving first learning which responses lead to which outcomes. Given this knowledge of response-outcome relationships, the person in a choice situation will scan the response possibilities and then choose the response that will result in the most valuable outcome.

schema   The general potential to engage in a class of overt or covert actions. A schema can also be thought of as an element in an organism's cognitive structure.

science   A method of inquiry that involves the use of experimentation to test theories about various aspects of nature.

scientific law   A consistently observed relationship between two or more classes of empirical events.

scientific revolution   According to Kuhn, the displacement of one paradigm with another. Such a displacement usually occurs over a fairly long period and after great resistance. A paradigm is associated with the scientist's total view of science—what counts as a good problem, what counts as a good answer, what a good experiment is like, and so on. Thus, a change in paradigm is a widespread change for scientists that invalidates almost every aspect of their previous scientific life. There is, therefore, emotional involvement in such a change.

scientific theory   An interrelated set of concepts used both to explain data and to make predictions about results of future experiments.

second signal system   Symbols that represent environmental events. These symbols, which Pavlov referred to as "signals of signals," constitute human language and are responsible for complex interactions with the environment.

secondary reinforcer   A previously neutral stimulus that takes on reinforcing properties through its close association with primary reinforcement. After conditioning has taken place, a conditioned stimulus must necessarily be a secondary reinforcer.

selecting and connecting   See **trial-and-error learning.**

self-contempt   The self-imposed punishment that is administered when an individual's internalized moral code is violated.

self-reactiveness   Defined by Bandura as a link between thought and action that provides self-motivation and regulates behavior.

self-reflectiveness   Defined by Bandura as metacognitive capability to reflect on the directions, consequences, and meaning of our plans and actions.

self-regulated behavior   Behavior that is regulated by one's own performance standards, moral codes, or imagination.

semantic generalization   Generalization to symbols that have a meaning similar to the meaning of the conditioned stimulus used during training, although the physical characteristics of symbols may be totally dissimilar to those of the conditioned stimulus. For example, if human subjects are taught to salivate when they see the number 10, they will also salivate when they see $8\overline{|80}$ or $\sqrt{100}$. In semantic generalization, it is meaning that determines how much generalization occurs, rather than the physical similarity between stimuli.

sensitization   The tendency to be more responsive to the environment following an arousing experience.

sensorimotor stage   The initial stage of intellectual development in which children respond directly to events as they occur in the environment. During this stage of development, children adjust to the environment in terms of their schemata, such as grasping, looking, sucking, and reaching.

sensory deprivation   The condition whereby an organism's sensory stimulation is drastically reduced.

serendipity   Finding one thing while looking for something else.

sets (attitudes)   Temporary conditions, such as food deprivation, fatigue, or emotion, that determine what will be annoying or pleasurable to a given organism.

shaping   The process whereby a desired response is encouraged through the use of differential reinforcement and successive approximation rather than simply waiting for it to occur.

short-term memory   Also called immediate memory and primary memory; the memory of an experience that persists for only a short time after the experience.

sign learning   The kind of learning, in Mowrer's two-factor theory, whereby stimuli become signs of fear, hope, relief, or disappointment because of their proximity to various unconditioned stimuli.

single modeling   The observation of a single model.

Skinner box   An experimental test chamber usually consisting of a grid floor, lever, light, and food cup. Used to study instrumental or operant conditioning.

social cognitive theory   A term Bandura used to describe his theory.

sociobiology   A discipline founded by E. O. Wilson that applied evolutionary principles to social behavior.

solution learning   The kind of learning, in Mowrer's two-factor theory, whereby an organism learns the behavioral skills necessary to avoid aversive situations and to embrace positive ones.

spandrels   Side effects of adaptations that may be co-opted for the benefit of the organism. (See also **adaptation.**)

species-specific defensive reactions (SSDRs)   Innate reactions or escape responses that allow organisms to escape pain.

specific language impairment (SLI)   A heritable disorder that results in delayed language acquisition, poor articulation, and persistent grammatical errors without any evidence of general intellectual impairment.

split-brain preparation The arrangement whereby both the optic chiasm and the corpus callosum are severed, thereby causing the two halves of the cortex to function independently.

spontaneous recovery When a conditioned response is no longer elicited by a conditioned stimulus, extinction is said to have taken place. Following a delay after extinction, the conditioned stimulus again elicits conditioned responses, although there were no further pairings between the conditioned stimulus and the unconditioned stimulus.

spontaneous recovery of an operant response The increased frequency with which a conditioned operant response occurs following a delay after extinction and with no further training.

spread of effect The observation that reinforcement not only strengthens the response that produced it but also strengthens neighboring responses.

state of the system The proportion of stimulus elements in S that are conditioned to A_1 and A_2 responses at any given point in a learning experiment.

stereotyped behavior The tendency to repeat exactly the behavior patterns that were previously made in a situation.

stimulus error The error of naming an object while introspecting about it instead of reporting one's immediate experience.

stimulus generalization Stimuli similar to the one used during conditioning also elicit the conditioned response.

stimulus sampling theory (SST) A theory such as the one Estes developed that attempts to show how stimuli are sampled and attached to responses.

stimulus trace (s) The afferent (sensory) neural impulse that is caused by an external stimulus and continues for a short while after the external stimulus has ceased.

stimulus-intensity dynamism (V) The internal result of varying the magnitude of an external stimulus. A larger external stimulus will result in a larger stimulus trace, thereby increasing the probability that a learned response will be elicited.

strength of a connection Determined by how likely a certain response is in a given set of circumstances. In other words, the strength of a connection is equated with response probability.

structuralism Founded by Titchener, the goal of the school of structuralism was to discover the basic elements of thought by using the technique of introspection and to explain how those elements are held together by the laws of association.

successive approximation Reinforcing only those responses that become increasingly similar to the response that is finally desired; a component of the process of shaping.

summation The activity of single neurons is determined by the added or summed activity of the surrounding cells.

superconditioning Describes the facilitation of conditioning that occurs when an established conditioned inhibitor (CS⁻) is subsequently paired with a US.

superstitious behavior Behavior that looks as if it is governed by the belief that it must be engaged in before reinforcement can be obtained, whereas in reality the behavior has nothing to do with the presence or absence of reinforcement. Superstitious behavior results from noncontingent reinforcement.

switchboard conception of the brain The view that the brain acts only as a relay station between sensory events and responses.

symbolic modeling The observation of something other than a live model, such as a film or television.

synapse The space between the axon of one neuron and the dendrites or cell body of another neuron. (See also **axons** and **dendrites**.)

synthesizing function The explanatory, rather than predictive, function of a scientific theory.

systematic desensitization A therapeutic technique developed by Wolpe whereby a phobia is extinguished by having a client approach the feared experience one small step at a time while relaxing after each step.

tact The verbal behavior of naming things. Such behavior results in reinforcement when objects or events are named correctly.

teaching machine A device used to present programmed material.

temporary body state A temporary condition of the body, such as fatigue, illness, emotion, the presence of drugs, or sleep loss, that causes a modification in behavior. Such modifications in behavior are differentiated from those caused by learning.

theta (θ) The proportion of stimulus elements sampled from S at the onset of a trial in a learning experiment.

threshold The millivoltage difference between the inside and outside of a neuron at which the cell can no longer keep sodium ions outside the cell.

threshold method of breaking a habit A change in stimulating conditions is introduced so slowly that the organism does not notice it. Finally, the organism is reacting to the changed conditions in a manner other than it would have if the change had not occurred so slowly.

Titchener, Edward (1867–1927) Founder of the school of structuralism.

trace system A number of interrelated individual memory traces.

transfer of training When something learned in one situation is applied in another situation.

transposition The Gestalt version of transfer of training, which states that a principle that works in solving a problem will tend to be applied to the solution of similar problems.

trial-and-error learning The trying of different responses in a problem-solving situation until a response that solves the problem is found. Thorndike originally called this phenomenon selecting and connecting.

trials to criterion The number of trials an experimental subject requires to reach the criterion that the experimenter sets as a definition of learning. For example, if perfect recall of a list of nonsense syllables is defined as learning the list, then trials to criterion is the number of times the subject had to go through the list before recalling the items without error.

truly random control group Rescorla has shown that the only true control condition for classical conditioning studies is one in which there is no predictive relationship between a CS and a US. In other words, in a truly random control condition, a US precedes and follows a CS an equal number of times. Rescorla says that in such a condition there is no contingency between the CS and the US.

two-factor theory A theory that postulates one set of principles to explain one kind of learning and a different set of principles to explain another kind of learning.

ultimate explanations Explanations of behavior that emphasize traits and processes that have been shaped by natural selection. (See also **evolutionary psychology.**)

unconditioned response (UR) The natural and automatic response that is elicited when an unconditioned stimulus is presented to an organism. Withdrawing when stuck by a pin, salivating when food or acid is placed in the mouth, and the constriction of the pupil of the eye when light is shone into it are all examples of unconditioned responses.

unconditioned stimulus (US) A stimulus that causes a natural and automatic response from the organism. An object that causes pain to a certain part of the body will cause the organism to withdraw automatically from the source of pain. Pain, therefore, is an unconditioned stimulus. Shining a light into the pupil of the eye will cause the pupil to constrict automatically; the light, therefore, is an unconditioned stimulus.

unlearned behavior Associations between stimuli and responses that are genetically determined and therefore do not depend on experience for their development.

variable interval reinforcement schedule (VI) The condition in which only the response made after the passage of some average interval of time is reinforced.

variable ratio reinforcement schedule (VR) The condition in which a certain average number of responses needs to be made before the organism is reinforced.

vicarious experience The impact on one's own learning or behavior that comes from observing the consequences of another person's behavior.

vicarious extinction The extinction of a response that comes from observing that a model's performance of that response is not reinforced.

vicarious punishment The process by which observing another person's behavior being punished decreases the probability of the observer acting in a similar way.

vicarious reinforcement The process by which observing another person's behavior being reinforced increases the probability of the observer acting in a similar way.

vicarious trial and error The hesitation at a choice point in a learning situation, where it looks "as if" the animal is weighing the alternatives before it decides what to do.

visceral conditioning The conditioning of internal organs under the control of the autonomic nervous system, such as the stomach, intestines, heart, bladder, or arteries.

voluntarism The school of psychology founded by Wilhelm Wundt that emphasized willful attention (apperception) and the willful arrangement of conscious elements (creative synthesis). Wundt believed that experimental psychology had only limited usefulness and that the higher mental processes could be studied only indirectly by the naturalistic observation of human cultural behavior.

Washburn, Margaret Floy (1871–1939) The first woman to earn a Ph.D. in psychology, Washburn wrote about consciousness in nonhuman animals.

Watson, John B. (1878–1958) Founder of the school of behaviorism. According to Watson, the only reliable, observable, and measurable subject matter available to psychologists is behavior, and therefore behavior is all that psychologists should study. Watson relied heavily on Pavlov's theory of learning in his explanation of human behavior. Watson believed that except for a few basic emotions, human behavior was learned.

Wundt, Wilhelm Maximilian (1832–1920) Founder of the school of voluntarism; also founded psychology's first psychological laboratory in Leipzig, Germany, in 1879.

Zeigarnik effect The tendency to remember uncompleted tasks longer than completed ones.

References

ABERMAN, J. E., & SALAMONE, J. D. (1999). Nucleus accumbens dopamine depletions make animals more sensitive to high ratio requirements but do not impair primary food reinforcement. *Neuroscience, 92,* 545–552.

ABROUS, D. N., KOEHL, M., & LEMOAL, M. (2005). Adult neurogenesis: From precursors to network and physiology. *Physiological Reviews, 85,* 523–569.

ADER, R. (1974). Letter to the editor. *Psychosomatic Medicine, 36,* 183–184.

ADER, R. (2001). Psychoneuroimmunology. *Current Directions in Psychological Science, 10,* 94–98.

ADER, R. (2003). Conditioned immunomodulation: Research needs and directions. *Brain, Behavior, & Immunity. Special Issue; Biological mechanisms of psychosocial effects on disease: Implications for cancer control, 17,* S51–S57.

ADER, R., & COHEN, N. (1975). Behaviorally conditioned immunosuppression. *Psychosomatic Medicine, 35,* 333–340.

ADER, R., & COHEN, N. (2001). Conditioning and immunity. In R. Ader, D. L. Felten, & N. Cohen (eds.), *Psychoneuroimmunology* (3rd ed., Vol. 2, pp. 3–34). New York: Academic Press.

AKHONDZADEH, S., & STONE, T. W. (1996). Glutamate-independent long-term depression in rat hippocampus by activation of GABA–sub (A) receptors. *Life Sciences, 58,* 1023–1030.

AKINS, C. K., KLEIN, E. D., & ZENTALL, T. R. (2002). Imitative learning in Japanese quail (*Coturnix japonica*) using the bidirectional control procedure. *Animal Learning and Behavior, 30,* 275–281.

AKINS, C. K., & ZENTALL, T. R. (1998). Imitative learning in male Japanese quail (*Coturnix japonica*) using the two-action method. *Journal of Comparative Psychology, 110,* 316–320.

ALLPORT, G. W. (1961). *Pattern and growth in personality.* New York: Holt, Rinehart & Winston.

AMSEL, A. (1958). The role of frustrative nonreward in noncontinuous reward situations. *Psychological Bulletin, 55,* 102–119.

AMSEL, A. (1962). Frustrative nonreward in partial reinforcement and discrimination learning: Some recent history and a theoretical extension. *Psychological Review, 69,* 306–328.

AMSEL, A. (1992). *Frustration theory: An analysis of dispositional learning and memory.* Cambridge: Cambridge University Press.

AMSEL, A., & ROUSSEL, J. (1952). Motivational properties of frustration: 1. Effect on a running response of the addition of frustration to the motivational complex. *Journal of Experimental Psychology, 43,* 363–368.

ANDERSON, B. F. (1971). *The psychology experiment.* Belmont, CA: Brooks/Cole.

ANDERSON, J. A. (1998). Learning arithmetic with a neural network: Seven times seven is about fifty. In D. Scarborough & S. Sternberg (eds.), *An invitation to cognitive science, Vol. 4* (pp. 255–299). Cambridge, MA: MIT Press.

ANDRESEN, G. V., BIRCH, L. L., & JOHNSON, P. A. (1990). The scapegoat effect on food aversions after chemotherapy. *Cancer, 66,* 1649–1653.

ANOKLIN, P. K. (1968). Ivan P. Pavlov and psychology. In B. B. Wolman (ed.), *Historical roots of contemporary psychology* (pp. 131–159). New York: Harper & Row.

ATHEY, I. J., & RUBADEAU, D. O. (eds.). (1970). *Educational implications of Piaget's theory.* Waltham, MA: Ginn-Blaisdell.

ATKINSON, R. C., & ESTES, W. K. (1963). Stimulus sampling theory. In R. D. Luce, R. R. Bush, & E. Galanter (eds.), *Handbook of mathematical psychology, 2* (pp. 121–268). New York: Wiley.

ATWOOD, H. L., & WOJTOWICZ, J. M. (1999). Silent synapses in neural plasticity: Current evidence. *Learning and Memory, 6,* 542–571.

AZARI, N. P., & SEITZ, R. J. (2000). Brain plasticity and recovery from stroke. *American Scientist, 88,* 429.

BABKIN, B. P. (1949). *Pavlov: A biography.* Chicago: University of Chicago Press.

BADING, H., GINTY, D. D., & GREENBERG, M. E. (1993). Regulation of gene expression in hippocampal neurons by distinct calcium signaling pathways. *Science, 260,* 181–186.

BAILLARGEON, R. (1987). Object permanence in 3 1/2 and 4 1/2 month-old infants. *Developmental Psychology, 23,* 655–664.

BAILLARGEON, R. (1992). The object concept revisited. In *Visual perception and cognition in infancy: Carnegie-Mellon Symposium on Cognition, 23.* Hillsdale, NJ: Erlbaum.

BAILLARGEON, R., GRABER, M., DEVOS, J., & BLACK, J. (1990). Why do young infants fail to search for hidden objects? *Cognition, 36,* 225–284.

BAKER, A. G., & MACKINTOSH, N. J. (1977). Excitatory and inhibitory conditioning following uncorrelated presentations of CS and US. *Animal Learning and Behavior, 5,* 315–319.

BANDURA, A. (1965). Influence of a model's reinforcement contingencies on the acquisition of imitative responses. *Journal of Personality and Social Psychology, 11,* 589–595.

BANDURA, A. (1973). *Aggression: A social learning analysis.* Englewood Cliffs, NJ: Prentice Hall.

BANDURA, A. (1977). *Social learning theory.* Englewood Cliffs, NJ: Prentice Hall.

BANDURA, A. (1980b). Self-referent thought: The development of self-efficacy. In J. Flavell & L. D. Ross (eds.), *Cognitive social development. Frontiers and possible futures.* New York: Cambridge University Press.

BANDURA, A. (1983). Temporal dynamics and decomposition of reciprocal determinism: A reply to Phillips and Orton. *Psychological Review, 90,* 166–170.

BANDURA, A. (1986). *Social foundations of thought and action: A social cognitive theory.* Englewood Cliffs, NJ: Prentice Hall.

BANDURA, A. (1989). Human agency in social cognitive theory. *American Psychologist, 44,* 1175–1184.

BANDURA, A. (1999). A social cognitive theory of personality. In L. Pervin & O. John (eds.), *Handbook of Personality* (2nd ed.). New York: Academic Press.

BANDURA, A. (2000). Exercise of human agency through collective efficacy. *Current Directions in Psychological Science, 9,* 75–78.

BANDURA, A. (2001). Social cognitive theory: An agentic perspective. *Annual Review of Psychology, 52,* 1–26.

BANDURA, A. (2002a). Growing primacy of human agency in adaptation and change in the electronic era. *European Psychologist, 7,* 2–16.

BANDURA, A. (2002b). Social cognitive theory in cultural context. *Applied Psychology: An International Review. Special Issue on Psychology in the Far East, Singapore, 51,* 269–290.

BANDURA, A., BLANCHARD, E. B., & RITTER, B. J. (1969). Relative efficacy of modeling therapeutic changes for inducing behavioral, attitudinal and affective changes. *Journal of Personality and Social Psychology, 13,* 173–199.

BANDURA, A., GRUSEC, J. E., & MENLOVE, F. L. (1967). Vicarious extinction of avoidance behavior. *Journal of Personality and Social Behavior, 5,* 16–23.

BANDURA, A., & KUPERS, C. J. (1964). The transmission of patterns of self-reinforcement through modeling. *Journal of Abnormal and Social Psychology, 69,* 1–9.

BANDURA, A., & LOCKE, E. A. (2003). Negative self-efficacy and goal effects revisited. *Journal of Applied Psychology, 88,* 87–99.

BANDURA, A., & MENLOVE, F. L. (1968). Factors determining vicarious extinction of avoidance behavior through symbolic modeling. *Journal of Personality and Social Psychology, 8,* 99–108.

BARASH, D. (1979). *Sociobiology: The whisperings within.* London: Souvenir.

BARASH, D. P. (1986). *The hare and the tortoise: Culture, biology, and human nature.* New York: Penguin.

BAUDRY, M., & LYNCH, G. (1993). Long-term potentiation: Biochemical mechanisms. In M. Baudry, R. F. Thompson, &

J. L. Davis (eds.), *Synaptic Plasticity* (pp. 87–115). Cambridge, MA: MIT Press.

BEACH, F. A. (1987). Donald Olding Hebb (1904–1985). *American Psychologist, 42,* 186–187.

BEANBLOSSON, R. E., & LEHRER, K. (1983). *Thomas Reid's inquiry and essays.* Indianapolis, IN: Hackett.

BEARD, R. M. (1969). *An outline of Piaget's developmental psychology for students and teachers.* New York: Mentor.

BEATON, A. (1985). *Left side, right side: A review of laterality research.* New Haven, CT: Yale University Press.

BECHTEL, W., & ABRAHAMSEN, A. (1991). *Connectionism and the mind.* Cambridge, MA: Basil Blackwell.

BEKKERS, J. M. (2005). Presynaptically silent GABA synapses in hippocampus. *The Journal of Neuroscience, 25(16),* 4031–4039.

BENNETT, E. L., DIAMOND, M. C., KRECH, D., & ROSENZWEIG, M. R. (1964). Chemical and anatomical plasticity of brain. *Science, 146,* 610–619.

BERKSON, W., & WETTERSTEN, J. (1984). *Learning from error: Karl Popper's psychology of learning.* LaSalle, IL: Open Court.

BERNSTEIN, I. L. (1978). Learned taste aversions in children receiving chemotherapy. *Science, 200,* 1302–1303.

BERRIDGE, K. C. (2005). Espresso reward learning, hold the dopamine: Theoretical comment on Robinson et al. (2005). *Behavioral Neuroscience, 119,* 336–341.

BERRIDGE, K. C., & ROBINSON, T. E. (1995). The mind of an addicted brain: Neural sensitization of wanting versus liking. *Current Directions in Psychological Science, 4,* 71–76.

BERRIDGE, K. C., & ROBINSON, T. E. (1998). What is the role of dopamine in reward: Hedonic impact, reward learning, or incentive salience? *Brain Research: Brain Research Review, 28,* 309–369.

BERTHIER, N. E., DEBLOIS, S., POIRIER, C. R., NOVAK, J. A., & CLIFTON, R. K. (2000). Where's the ball? Two- and three-year-olds reason about unseen events. *Developmental Psychology, 36,* 394–401.

BEST, M. R., & GEMBERLING, G. A. (1977). Role of short-term processes in the conditioned stimulus preexposure effect and the delay of reinforcement gradient in long-delay taste-aversion learning. *Journal of Experimental Psychology: Animal Behavior Processes, 3,* 253–263.

BICKEL, W. K., & MADDEN, G. J. (1999). A comparison of measures of relative reinforcing efficacy and behavioral economics. *Behavioral Pharmacology, 10,* 627–737.

BICKEL, W. K., MARSCH, L. A., & CARROLL, M. E. (2000). Deconstructing relative reinforcing efficacy and situating the measures of pharmacological reinforcement with behavioral economics: A theoretical proposal. *Psychopharmacology, 153,* 44–56.

BICKERTON, D. (1981). *Roots of language.* Ann Arbor, MI: Karoma.

BICKERTON, D. (1984). The language bioprogram hypothesis. *Behavioral and Brain Sciences, 7,* 173–221.

BICKERTON, D. (1998). The creation and re-creation of language. In C. Crawford & D. L. Krebs (eds.), *Handbook of evolutionary psychology* (pp. 613–634). Mahwah, NJ: Lawrence Erlbaum Associates.

BIJOU, S. W., & BAER, D. M. (1961). *Child development, Vol. 1. A systematic and empirical theory.* Englewood Cliffs, NJ: Prentice Hall.

BIJOU, S. W., & BAER, D. M. (1965). *Child development, Vol. 2. The universal stage of infancy.* Englewood Cliffs, NJ: Prentice Hall.

BITTERMAN, M. E. (1960). Toward a comparative psychology of learning. *American Psychologist, 15,* 704–712.

BLACK, J. E., ISAACS, K. R., ANDERSON, B. J., ALCANTARA, A. A., & GREENOUGH, W. T. (1990). Learning causes synaptogenesis, whereas motor activity causes angiogenesis, in cerebral cortex of adult rats. *Proceedings of the National Academy of Sciences, 87,* 5568–5572.

BLANCHARD, E. B., KIM, M., HERMANN, C., & STEFFEK, B. D. (1994). The role of perception of success in the thermal biofeedback treatment of vascular headache. *Headache Quarterly, 5,* 231–236.

BLISS, T. V. P., & LØMO, T. (1973). Long lasting potentiation of synaptic transmission in the dentate area of the anaesthetized rabbit following stimulation of the perforant path. *Journal of Physiology, 232,* 331–356.

BOGEN, J. E. (1977). In M. C. Wittrock (ed.), *The human brain.* Englewood Cliffs, NJ: Prentice Hall.

BOLLES, R. C. (1970). Species-specific defense reactions and avoidance learning. *Psychological Review, 77,* 32–48.

BOLLES, R. C. (1972). Reinforcement, expectancy, and learning. *Psychological Review, 79,* 394–409.

BOLLES, R. C. (1975). *Theory of motivation* (2nd ed.). New York: Harper & Row.

BOLLES, R. C. (1979). *Learning theory* (2nd ed.). New York: Holt, Rinehart & Winston.

BOLLES, R. C. (1988). Nativism, naturalism and niches. In R. C. Bolles & M. D. Beecher (eds.), *Evolution and learning* (pp. 1–15). Hillsdale, NJ: Lawrence Erlbaum Associates.

BOLLES, R. C., & PETRINOVICH, L. (1954). A technique for obtaining rapid drive discrimination in the rat. *Journal of Comparative and Physiological Psychology, 47,* 378–380.

BOLLES, R. C., RILEY, A. L., CANTOR, M. B., & DUNCAN, P. M. (1974). The rat's failure to anticipate regularly scheduled daily shock. *Behavioral Biology, 11,* 365–372.

BOUTON, M. E. (1984). Differential control by contact in the inflation and reinstatement paradigms. *Journal of Experimental Psychology: Animal Behavior Processes, 10,* 56–74.

BOUTON, M. E. (1988). Context and ambiguity in the extinction of emotional learning: Implications for exposure therapy. *Behaviour Research and Therapy, 26,* 137–149.

BOUTON, M. E. (1991). Context and retrieval in extinction and in other examples of interference in simple associative learning. In L. Dachowski & C. F. Flaherty (eds.), *Current topics in animal learning: Brain emotion and cognition* (pp. 25–53). Hillsdale, NJ: Erlbaum.

BOUTON, M. E. (1993). Context, time, and memory retrieval in the interference paradigms of Pavlovian learning. *Psychological Bulletin, 114,* 80–99.

BOUTON, M. E. (1994). Context, ambiguity and classical conditioning. *Current Directions in Psychological Science, 3,* 49–52.

BOUTON, M. E., & BOLLES, R. C. (1979a). Contextual control of the extinction of conditioned fear. *Learning and Motivation, 10,* 445–466.

BOUTON, M. E., & BOLLES, R. C. (1979b). Role of conditioned contextual stimuli in reinstatement of extinguished fear. *Journal of Experimental Psychology: Animal Behavior Processes, 5,* 368–378.

BOUTON, M. E., & FANSELOW, M. S. (eds.). (1997). *Learning, motivation, and cognition: The functional behaviorism of Robert C. Bolles.* Washington, DC: American Psychological Association.

BOUTON, M. E., & KING, D. A. (1983). Contextual control of the extinction of conditioned fear: Tests for the associative value of the context. *Journal of Experimental Psychology: Animal Behavior Processes, 9,* 248–265.

BOUTON, M. E., & KING, D. A. (1986). Effect of context on performance to conditioned stimuli with mixed histories of reinforcement and nonreinforcement. *Journal of Experimental Psychology: Animal Behavior Processes, 12,* 4–15.

BOUTON, M. E., & PECK, C. A. (1989). Context effects on conditioning, extinction, and reinstatement in an appetitive conditioning preparation. *Animal Learning and Behavior, 17,* 188–198.

BOWER, G. H. (1962). The influence of graded reductions in reward and prior frustrating events upon the magnitude of the frustration effect. *Journal of Comparative and Physiological Psychology, 55,* 582–587.

BOWER, G. H. (1994). A turning point in mathematical learning theory. *Psychological Review, 101,* 290–300.

BOWER, G. H., & HILGARD, E. R. (1981). *Theories of learning* (5th ed.). Englewood Cliffs, NJ: Prentice Hall.

BOWERS, T. G. R. (1989). *The rational infant: Learning in infancy.* New York: Freeman.

BOWLBY, J. (1969). *Attachment and loss.* New York: Basic Books.

BRAUER, L. H., & DEWIT, H. (1997). High dose pimozide does not block amphetamine-induced euphoria in normal volunteers. *Pharmacology Biochemistry and Behavior, 56,* 265–272.

BREGMAN, E. O. (1934). An attempt to modify the emotional attitudes of infants by the conditioned response technique. *Journal of Genetic Psychology, 45,* 169–198.

BRELAND, K., & BRELAND, M. (1961). The misbehavior of organisms. *American Psychologist, 16,* 681–684.

BRINGMANN, W. G., LÜCK, H. E., MILLER, R., & EARLY, C. E. (eds.). (1997). *A pictorial history of psychology.* Carol Stream, IL: Quintessence Publishing Co.

BROOKS, D. C., & BOUTON, M. E. (1993). A retrieval cue for extinction attenuates spontaneous recovery. *Journal of Experimental Psychology: Animal Behavior Processes, 19,* 77–89.

BROWN, J. S., & BURTON, R. (1975). Multiple representations of knowledge for tutorial reasoning. In D. G. Bobrow & A. Collins (eds.), *Representation and understanding: Studies in cognitive science.* New York: Academic Press.

BROWN, P. L., & JENKINS, H. M. (1968). Auto-shaping of the pigeon's key-peck. *Journal of the Experimental Analysis of Behavior, 11,* 1–8.

BROWN, R. (1965). *Social psychology.* New York: Free Press.

BRUNER, J. S. (1966). *Toward a theory of instruction.* Cambridge, MA: Harvard University Press.

BUGELSKI, B. R. (1979). *Principles of learning and memory.* New York: Praeger.

BUNDERSON, V. (1967). The role of computer-assisted instruction in university education. *Progress Report to the Coordination Board of the Texas College and University System.* Austin: University of Texas Press.

BUSS, D. M. (1989). Sex differences in human mate preferences: Evolutionary hypotheses tested in 37 cultures. *Behavioral and Brain Sciences, 12,* 1–49.

BUSS, D. M. (1994). *The evolution of desire: Strategies of human mating.* New York: Basic Books.

BUSS, D. M. (1995). Evolutionary psychology: A new paradigm for psychological science. *Psychological Inquiry, 6,* 1–49.

BUSS, D. M. (1998). The psychology of human mate selection: Exploring the complexity of the strategic repertoire. In C. Crawford & D. L. Krebs (eds.), *Handbook of evolutionary psychology* (pp. 405–429). Mahwah, NJ: Lawrence Erlbaum Associates.

BUSS, D. M. (2004). *Evolutionary psychology: The new science of the mind.* Boston: Allyn & Bacon.

BUSS, D. M., HASELTON, M. G., SHACKELFORD, T. K., BLESKE, A. L., & WAKEFIELD, J. C. (1998). Adaptations, exaptation, and spandrels. *American Psychologist, 53(5),* 533–548.

BUSS, D. M., & SCHMITT, D. P. (1993). Sexual strategies theory: An evolutionary perspective on human mating. *Psychological Review, 100,* 204–232.

CABEZAS, C., & BUÑO, W. (2006). Distinct transmitter release properties determine differences in short-term plasticity at functional and silent synapses. *Journal of Neurophysiology, 95,* 3024–3034.

CARLSON, J. G. (1980). Guthrie's theory of learning. In G. M. Gazda & R. J. Corsini (eds.), *Theories of learning: A comparative approach.* Itasca, IL: Peacock.

CASTELLUCCI, V. F., & KANDEL, E. R. (1974). A quantal analysis of the synaptic depression surrounding habituation of the gill withdrawal reflex in *Aplysia. Proceedings of the National Academy of Sciences, U.S.A., 71,* 5004–5008.

CEPEDA, N. J., PASHLER, H., VUL, E., WIXTED, J. T., & ROHER, D. (2006). Distributed practice in verbal recall tasks: A review and quantitative synthesis. *Psychological Bulletin, 132(3),* 354–380.

CHAMBERS, K. C. (1985). Sexual dimorphisms as an index of hormonal influences on conditioned food aversions. *Annals of the New York Academy of Sciences, 443,* 110–125.

CHAMBERS, K. C., & SENGSTAKE, C. B. (1976). Sexually dimorphic extinction of a conditioned taste aversion in rats. *Animal Learning and Behavior, 4,* 181–185.

CHAMBERS, K. C., YUAN, D., BROWNSON, E. A., & WANG, Y. (1997). Sexual dimorphisms in conditioned taste aversions: Mechanism and function. In M. E. Bouton & M. S. Fanselow (eds.), *Learning, motivation, and cognition: The functional behaviorism of Robert C. Bolles* (pp. 195–224). Washington, DC: American Psychological Association.

CHARTRAND, T. L., & BARGH, J. A. (1999). The chameleon effect: The perception-behavior link and social interaction. *Journal of Personality and Social Psychology, 76(6),* 893–910.

CHOMSKY, N. (1959). [Review of *Verbal Behavior* by B. F. Skinner]. *Language, 35,* 26–58.

CHOMSKY, N. (1972). *Language and mind.* New York: Harcourt, Brace, Jovanovich.

CHOMSKY, N. (1975). *Reflections on language.* New York: Pantheon.

CHOMSKY, N. (1988). *Language and the problems of knowledge. The Managua lectures.* Cambridge, MA: MIT Press.

CLARK, A. (1990). Connectionism, competence, and explanation. In M. A. Boden (ed.), *The philosophy of artificial intelligence* (pp. 281–308). New York: Oxford University Press.

CLEARY, L. J., HAMMER, M., & BYRNE, J. H. (1989). Insights into the cellular mechanisms of short-term sensitization in *Aplysia.* In T. J. Carew & D. B. Kelley (eds.), *Perspectives in neural systems and behavior.* New York: Alan R. Liss.

COHEN, N. J., & EICHENBAUM, H. (1993). *Memory, amnesia, and the hippocampal system.* Cambridge, MA: MIT Press.

COHEN, N. J., RYAN, J., HUNT, C., ROMINE, L., WSZALEK, T., & NASH, C. (1999). Hippocampal system and declarative (relational) memory: Summarizing the data from functional neuroimaging studies. *Hippocampus, 9,* 83–98.

COHEN, N. J., & SQUIRE, L. R. (1980). Preserved learning and retention of pattern analysing skill in amnesia: Dissociation of knowing how and knowing that. *Science, 210,* 207–210.

COOK, M., & MINEKA, S. (1990). Selective associations in the observed conditioning of fear in rhesus monkeys. *Journal of Experimental Psychology: Animal Behavior Processes, 16,* 372–389.

CORNELISSEN, K., LAINE, M., TARKIAINEN, A., JÄRVENSIVU, T., MARTIN, N., & SALMELIN, R. (2003). Adult brain plasticity elicited by anomia treatment. *Journal of Cognitive Neuroscience, 15,* 444–461.

CORNFORD, F. M. (Trans.). (1968). *The republic of Plato.* New York: Oxford University Press.

CORREA M., CARLSON, B. B., WISNIECKI, A., & SALAMONE, J. D. (2002). Nucleus accumbens dopamine and work requirements on interval schedules. *Behavioural Brain Research, 137(1–2),* 179–187.

COSMIDES, L., & TOOBY, J. (1992). Cognitive adaptations for social exchange. In J. Barkow, L. Cosmides, & J. Tooby (eds.). *The adapted mind* (pp. 163–228). New York: Oxford University Press.

COSMIDES, L. & TOOBY, J. (1997). *Evolutionary psychology: A primer.* Santa Barbara: On-line Center for Evolutionary Psychology, University of California, Santa Barbara.

COTMAN, C. W., MONAGHAN, D. T., & GANONG, A. H. (1988). Excitatory amino acid neurotransmission: NMDA receptors and Hebb-type synaptic transmission. *Annual Reviews of Neuroscience, 11,* 61–80.

COUSINS, M. S., ATHERTON, A., TURNER, L., & SALAMONE, J. D. (1996). Nucleus accumbens dopamine depletions alter relative response allocation in a T-maze cost/benefit task. *Behavioural Brain Research, 74,* 189–197.

COVERT, M. V., TANGNEY, J. P., MADDUX, J. E., & HELENO, N. M. (2003). Shame-proneness, guilt-proneness, and interpersonal problem solving: A social cognitive analysis. *Journal of Social and Clinical Psychology, 22,* 1–12.

CRAIGHEAD, W. E., KAZDIN, A. E., & MAHONEY, M. J. (1976). *Behavior modification: Principles, issues, and applications.* Boston: Houghton Mifflin.

CRAWFORD, C. (1998). The theory of evolution in the study of human behavior: An introduction and overview. In C. Crawford & D. L. Krebs (eds.), *Handbook of evolutionary psychology.* Mahwah, NJ: Lawrence Erlbaum Associates.

CRAWFORD, C., & KREBS, D. L. (eds.). (1998). *Handbook of evolutionary psychology.* Mahwah, NJ: Lawrence Erlbaum Associates.

CRESPI, L. (1942). Quantitative variation of incentive and performance in the white rat. *American Journal of Psychology, 55,* 467–517.

CRESPI, L. (1944). Amount of reinforcement and level of performance. *Psychological Review, 51,* 341–357.

CRONIN-GOLOMB, A. (1995). Semantic networks in the divided cerebral hemispheres. *Psychological Science, 6,* 212–218.

CURRY, F. K. W. (1967). A comparison of left-handed and right-handed subjects on verbal and non-verbal dichotic listening tasks. *Cortex, 3,* 343–352.

DALE, N., SCHACHER, S., & KANDEL, E. R. (1988). Long term facilitation in *Aplysia* involves increase in transmitter release. *Science, 239,* 282–285.

DALY, H. B. (1969). Learning of a hurdle-jump response to escape cues paired with reduced reward or frustrative nonreward. *Journal of Experimental Psychology, 79,* 146–157.

DALY, M., & WILSON, M. I. (1982). Homicide and kinship. *American Anthropologist, 84,* 372–378.

DALY, M., & WILSON, M. I. (1988). Evolutionary social psychology and family homicide. *Science, 242,* 519–524.

DALY, M., & WILSON, M. I. (1994). Some differential attributes of lethal assaults on small children by stepfathers versus genetic fathers. *Ethology and Sociobiology, 15,* 207–217.

DALY, M., & WILSON, M. I. (1998). The evolutionary social psychology of family violence. In C. Crawford & D. L. Krebs (eds.), *Handbook of evolutionary psychology* (pp. 431–456). Mahwah, NJ: Lawrence Erlbaum Associates.

DARSILAI, V., HELDMANN, U., LINDVALL, O., & KOKAIA, Z. (2005). Stroke-induced neurogenesis in aged brain. *Stroke, 36,* 1790–1795.

DARWIN, C. (1859/1958). *On the origin of species by means of natural selection.* New York: New American Library.

DARWIN, C. (1872). *The expression of emotions in man and animals.* London: John Murray.

DAVISON, M., & McCARTHY, D. (1988). *The matching law: A research review.* Englewood Cliffs, NJ: Prentice Hall.

DeCORTE, E. (ed.). (1999). On the road to transfer: New perspectives on an enduring issue in educational research and practice (Special issue). *International Journal of Educational Research, 31(7).*

DeCORTE, E. (2003). Transfer as the productive use of acquired knowledge, skills, and motivations. *Current Directions in Psychological Science, 12,* 142–146.

DEESE, J. (1951). Extinction of a discrimination without performance of the choice response. *Journal of Comparative and Physiological Psychology, 44,* 362–366.

DEWEY, J. (1896). The reflex arc concept in psychology. *Psychological Review, 3,* 357–370.

DIAMOND, D. M., DUNWIDDIE, T. V., & ROSE, G. M. (1988). Characteristics of hippocampal primed burst potentiation *in vitro* and in the awake rat. *Journal of Neuroscience, 8,* 4079–4088.

DIAMOND, M. C., LINDNER, B., & RAYMOND, A. (1967). Extensive cortical depth measurements and neuron size increases in the cortex of environmentally enriched rats. *Journal of Comparative Neurology, 131,* 357–364.

DiCARA, L. V. (1970). Learning in the autonomic nervous system. *Scientific American, 222,* 30–39.

DI PELLEGRINO, G., FADIGA, L., FOGASSI, L., GALLESE, V., & RIZZOLATTI, G. (1992). Understanding motor events: A neurophysiological study. *Experimental Brain Research, 91(1),* 176–180.

DOLLARD, J. C., & MILLER, N. E. (1950). *Personality and psychotherapy.* New York: McGraw-Hill.

DOMJAN, M. (1997). Behavior systems and the demise of equipotentiality: Historical antecedents and evidence from sexual conditioning. In M. E. Bouton & M. S. Fanselow (eds.), *Learning, motivation, and cognition: The functional behaviorism of Robert C. Bolles.* Washington, DC: American Psychological Association.

DORRANCE, B. R., & ZENTALL, T. R. (2001). Imitative learning in Japanese quail depends on the motivational state of the animal at the time of observation. *Journal of Comparative Psychology, 115,* 62–67.

DOYERE, V., ERRINGTON, M. L., LaROCHE, S., & BLISS, T. V. P. (1996). Low-frequency trains of paired stimuli induce long-term depression in area CA1 but not in dentate gyrus of the intact rat. *Hippocampus, 6,* 52–57.

DUNCAN, C. P. (1949). The retroactive effect of electroshock on learning. *Journal of Comparative and Physiological Psychology, 42,* 34–44.

*EBBINGHAUS, H. (1913 [1885]). *On memory* (H. A. Ruger & C. Bossinger, trans.). New York: Teachers College Press.

EGAN, K. (1983). *Education and psychology: Plato, Piaget, and scientific psychology.* New York: Teachers College Press.

EGGER, M. D. & MILLER, N. E. (1962). Secondary reinforcement in rats as a function of information value and reliability of the stimulus. *Journal of Experimental Psychology, 64,* 97–104.

EGGER, M. D., & MILLER, N. E. (1963). When is a reward reinforcing? An experimental study of the information hypothesis. *Journal of Comparative and Physiological Psychology, 56*, 132–137.

EISENBERG, D. M., DELBANCO, T. L., BERKEY, C. S., KAPTCHUK, T. J., KUPELNICK, B., KUHL, J., & CHALMERS, T. C. (1993). Cognitive behavioral techniques for hypertension: Are they effective? *Annals of Internal Medicine, 118*, 964–972.

EISENBERG, D. M., KESSLER, R. C., FOSTER, C., & NORLOCK, F. E. (1993). Unconventional medicine in the United States: Prevalence, costs, and patterns of use. *New England Journal of Medicine, 328*, 246–252.

ELSMORE, T. F., FLETCHER, G. V., CONRAD, D. G., & SODETZ, F. J. (1980). Reduction of heroin intake in baboons by economic constraint. *Pharmacology Biochemistry and Behavior, 13*, 729–732.

ESCOBAR, M. L., ALCOCER, I., & CHAO, V. (1998). The NMDA receptor antagonist CCP impairs conditioned taste aversion and insular cortex long-term potentiation in vivo. *Brain Research, 812*, 246–251.

ESTES, W. K. (1944). An experimental study of punishment. *Psychological Monographs, 57* (Whole No. 263).

ESTES, W. K. (1950). Toward a statistical theory of learning. *Psychological Review, 57*, 94–107.

ESTES, W. K. (1954). Kurt Lewin. In Estes et al. (eds.), *Modern Learning Theory* (pp. 317–344). New York: Appleton-Century-Crofts.

ESTES, W. K. (1960). Learning theory and the new "mental chemistry." *Psychological Review, 67*, 207–223.

ESTES, W. K. (1964a). All-or-none processes in learning and retention. *American Psychologist, 19*, 16–25.

ESTES, W. K. (1964b). Probability learning. In A. W. Melton (ed.), *Categories of human learning*. New York: Academic Press.

ESTES, W. K. (1969a). New perspectives on some old issues in association theory. In N. J. MacKintosh & W. K. Honig (eds.), *Fundamental issues in association learning*. Halifax, Nova Scotia: Dalhousie University Press.

ESTES, W. K. (1969b). Reinforcement in human learning. In J. Tapp (ed.), *Reinforcement and behavior*. New York: Academic Press.

ESTES, W. K. (1971). Reward in human learning: Theoretical issues and strategic choice points. In R. Glaser (ed.), *The nature of reinforcement*. New York: Academic Press.

ESTES, W. K. (1972). An associative basis for coding and organization in memory. In A. W. Melton & E. Martin (eds.), *Coding processes in human memory*. New York: Halstead.

ESTES, W. K. (1973). Memory and conditioning. In E. J. McGuigan & D. B. Lumsden (eds.), *Contemporary approaches to conditioning and learning*. Washington, DC: Winston & Sons.

ESTES, W. K. (1976). The cognitive side of probability matching. *Psychological Review, 83*, 37–64.

ESTES, W. K. (1978). On the organization and core concepts of learning theory and cognitive psychology. In W. K. Estes (ed.), *Handbook of learning and cognitive processes* (Vol. 6). Hillsdale, NJ: Erlbaum.

ESTES, W. K. (1994). *Classification and cognition*. New York: Oxford University Press.

ESTES, W. K., HOPKINS, B. L., & CROTHERS, E. J. (1960). All-or-none and conservation effects in the learning and retention of paired associates. *Journal of Experimental Psychology, 60*, 329–339.

ESTES, W. K., & SKINNER, B. F. (1941). Some quantitative properties of anxiety. *Journal of Experimental Psychology, 29*, 390–400.

ESTES, W. K., & STRAUGHAN, J. H. (1954). Analysis of a verbal conditioning situation in terms of statistical learning theory. *Journal of Experimental Psychology, 47*, 225–234.

FENWICK, S., MIKULKA, P. J., & KLEIN, S. B. (1975). The effect of different levels of preexposure to sucrose on acquisition and extinction of conditioned aversion. *Behavioral Biology, 14*, 231–235.

FERNANDEZ, G., WEIS, S., STOFFEL-WAGNER, B., TENDOLKAR, I., REUBER, M., BEYENBURG, S., KLAVER, P., FELL, J., DE GREIFF, A., RUHLMANN, J., REUL, J., & ELGER, C. E. (2003). Menstrual cycle-dependent neural plasticity in the adult human hippocampus is hormone, task, and region specific. *Journal of Neuroscience, 23*, 3790–3795.

FERSTER, C. B., & SKINNER, B. F. (1957). *Schedules of reinforcement*. Englewood Cliffs, NJ: Prentice Hall.

FESTINGER, L. (1957). *A theory of cognitive dissonance*. Stanford, CA: Stanford University Press.

FLANAGAN, O. (1991). *The science of the mind* (2nd ed.). Cambridge, MA: MIT Press.

FLAVFELL, J. H. (1963). *The developmental psychology of Jean Piaget*. New York: Van Nostrand Reinhold.

FOWLER, H., & MILLER, N. E. (1963). Facilitation and inhibition of runway performance by hind- and forepaw shock of various intensities. *Journal of Comparative and Physiological Psychology, 56*, 801–805.

FURTH, H. G. (1969). *Piaget and knowledge: Theoretical foundations*. Englewood Cliffs, NJ: Prentice Hall.

FURTH, H. G. (1970). *Piaget for teachers*. Englewood Cliffs, NJ: Prentice Hall.

GABRIELI, J. D. E. (1998). Cognitive neuroscience of human memory. *Annual Reviews of Psychology, 47*, 87–115.

GABRIELI, J. D. E., BREWER, J. B., DESMOND, J. E., & GLOVER, G. H. (1997). Separate neural bases of two fundamental memory processes in human medial temporal lobe. *Science, 276*, 264–266.

GABRIELI, J. D. E., BREWER, J. B., & POLDRACK, R. A. (1998). Images of medial temporal lobe functions in human learning and memory. *Neurobiology of Learning and Memory, 70*, 275–283.

GAGE, F. H. (2002). Neurogenesis in the adult brain. *Journal of Neuroscience, 22*, 612–613.

GAGE, F. H., COATES, P. W., PALMER, T. D., KUHN, H. G., FISHER, L. J., SUHONEN, J. O., PETERSON, D. A., SUHR, S. T., & RAY, J. (1995). Survival and differentiation of adult neuronal progenitor cells transplanted to the adult brain. *Proceedings of the National Academy of Sciences, 92*, 11879–11883.

GAGNE, R. M. (1970). *The conditions of learning* (2nd ed.). New York: Holt, Rinehart & Winston.

GALEF, B. G., Jr. (1998). Edward Thorndike: Revolutionary psychologist, ambiguous biologist. *American Psychologist, 53(10),* 1128–1134.

GALLESE, V., FADIGA, L., FOGASSI, L., & RIZZOLATTI, G. (1996). Action recognition in the premotor cortex. *Brain, 119(2),* 593–609.

GARCIA, J. (1981). Tilting at the paper mills of academe. *American Psychologist, 36,* 149–158.

GARCIA, J. (1997). Robert C. Bolles: From mathematics to motivation. In M. E. Bouton & M. S. Fanselow (eds.), *Learning, motivation, and cognition: The functional behaviorism of Robert C. Bolles* (pp. xi–xiii). Washington, DC: American Psychological Association.

GARCIA, J., ERVIN, F. R., & KOELLING, R. A. (1966). Learning with prolonged delay of reinforcement. *Psychonomic Science, 5,* 121–122.

GARCIA, J., & KOELLING, R. A. (1966). Relation of cue to consequence in avoidance learning. *Psychonomic Science, 4,* 123–124.

GARCIA, J., McGOWAN, B., ERVIN, F. R., & KOELLING, R. A. (1968). Cues: Their relative effectiveness as a function of the reinforcer. *Science, 160,* 794–795.

GARRIS, P. A., KILPATRICK, M., BUNIN, M. A., MICHAEL, D., WALKER, Q. D., & WIGHTMAN, R. M. (1999). Dissociation of dopamine release in the nucleus accumbens from intercranial self-stimulation. *Nature, 398,* 67–69.

GAWIN, F. H. (1986). Neuroleptic reduction of cocaine-induced paranoia but not euphoria. *Psychopharmacology, 90,* 142–143.

GAZZANIGA, M. S., & LEDOUX, J. E. (1978). *The integrated mind.* New York: Plenum Press

GELLES, R. J., & STRAUS, M. A. (1985). Violence in the American family. In A. J. Lincoln & M. A. Straus (eds.), *Crime and the family* (pp. 88–110). Springfield, IL: Thomas.

GINSBURG, H., & OPPER, S. (1979). *Piaget's theory of intellectual development* (2nd ed.). Englewood Cliffs, NJ: Prentice Hall.

GOLDSCHMID, M. L., & BENTLER, P. M. (1968). *Conservation concept diagnostic kit: Manual and keys.* San Diego, CA: Educational and Industrial Testing Service.

GOPNIK, M. (1990). Dysphasia in an extended family. *Nature, 344,* 715.

GOPNIK, M., & CRAGO, M. (1991). Familial aggregation of a developmental language disorder. *Cognition, 39,* 1–50.

GOTTSCHALK, W. A., JIANG, H., TARTAGLIA, N., FENG, L., FIGUROV, A., & LU, B. (1999). Signaling mechanisms mediating BDNF modulation of synaptic plasticity in the hippocampus. *Learning and Memory, 6,* 243–256.

GOULD, S. J. (1991). Exaptation: A crucial tool for evolutionary psychology. *Journal of Social Issues, 47,* 43–65.

GREENBERG, J. H. (ed.). (1963). *Universals of language.* Cambridge, MA: MIT Press.

GREENOUGH, W. T., & CHANG, F. F. (1989). Plasticity of synapse structure and pattern in the cerebral cortex. In A. Peters & E. G. Jones (eds.), *Cerebral Cortex* (pp. 391–440). New York: Plenum.

GUSTAVSON, C. R. (1977). Comparative and field aspects of learned food aversions. In L. M. Barker, M. R. Best, & M. Domjan (eds.), *Learning mechanisms in food selection* (pp. 23–43). Waco, TX: Baylor University Press.

GUSTAVSON, C. R., GARCIA, J., HANKINS, W. G., & RUSINIAK, K. W. (1974). Coyote predation control by aversive conditioning. *Science, 1843,* 581–583.

GUTHRIE, E. R. (1935). *The psychology of learning.* New York: Harper & Row.

GUTHRIE, E. R. (1938). *The psychology of human conflict.* New York: Harper & Row.

GUTHRIE, E. R. (1940). Association and the law of effect. *Psychological Review, 47,* 127–148.

GUTHRIE, E. R. (1942). Conditioning: A theory of learning in terms of stimulus, response, and association. In N. B. Henry (ed.), *The forty-first yearbook of the national society for the study of education: Pt. II. The psychology of learning.* Chicago: University of Chicago Press.

GUTHRIE, E. R. (1952). *The psychology of learning* (rev. ed.). New York: Harper & Row.

GUTHRIE, E. R. (1959). Association by contiguity. In S. Koch (ed.), *Psychology: A study of a science* (Vol. 2). New York: McGraw-Hill.

GUTHRIE, E. R., & HORTON, G. P. (1946). *Cats in a puzzle box.* New York: Rinehart.

GUTHRIE, E. R., & POWERS, F. F. (1950). *Educational psychology.* New York: Ronald Press.

HAMILTON, D. A., DRISCOLL, I., & SUTHERLAND, R. J. (2002). Human place learning in a virtual Morris water task: Some important constraints on the flexibility of place navigation. *Behavioural Brain Research, 129,* 159–170.

HAMILTON, D. A., & KOLB, B. (2005). Differential effects of nicotine and complex housing on subsequent experience-dependent structural plasticity in the nucleus accumbens. *Behavioral Neuroscience, 119(2),* 355–365.

HAMILTON, W. D. (1964). The genetical evolution of social behavior. *Journal of Theoretical Biology, 7,* 1–52.

HANEY, M., WARD, A. S., FOLTIN, R. W., & FISCHMAN, M. W. (2001). Effects of ecopipam, a selective dopamine D1 antagonist, on smoked cocaine self-administration by humans. *Psychopharmacology, 155,* 330–337.

HARLOW, H. F. (1949). The formation of learning sets. *Psychological Review, 56,* 51–65.

HARLOW, H. F. (1950). Analysis of discrimination learning by monkeys. *Journal of Experimental Psychology, 40,* 26–39.

HARLOW, H. F. (1959). Learning set and error factor theory. In S. Koch (ed.), *Psychology: A study of a science* (Vol. 2). New York: McGraw-Hill.

HARRIS, B. (1979). Whatever happened to little Albert? *American Psychologist, 34,* 151–160.

HARRIS, J. R. (2000). Context-specific learning, personality, and birth order. *Current Directions in Psychological Science, 9,* 174–177.

HASKELL, R. E. (2001). *Transfer of learning: Cognition, instruction, and reasoning.* San Diego, CA: Academic Press.

HAWKINS, J. (ed.). (1988). *Explaining language universals.* New York: Blackwell.

HEBB, D. O. (1946). On the nature of fear. *Psychological Review, 53,* 259–276.

HEBB, D. O. (1949). *The organization of behavior.* New York: Wiley.

HEBB, D. O. (1955). Drives and the C.N.S. (Conceptual nervous system). *Psychological Review, 62,* 243–254.

HEBB, D. O. (1959). A neuropsychological theory. In S. Koch (ed.), *Psychology: A study of a science* (Vol. 1). New York: McGraw-Hill.

HEBB, D. O. (1972). *Textbook of psychology* (3rd ed.). Philadelphia: W. B. Saunders.

HEBB, D. O. (1980). [Autobiography]. In G. Lindzey (ed.), *A history of psychology in autobiography* (Vol. VII). San Francisco: Freeman.

HEBB, D. O., & DONDERI, D. C. (1987). *Textbook of psychology* (4th ed.) Hillsdale, NJ: Erlbaum.

HECHT, H., & PROFFITT, D. R. (1995). The price of expertise: Effects of experience on the water-level task. *Psychological Science, 6,* 90–95.

HELLIGE, J. B. (1993). *Hemispheric asymmetry: What's right and what's left.* Cambridge, MA: Harvard University Press.

HENLE, M. (1986). *1879 and all that: Essays in the history of psychology.* New York: Columbia University Press.

HERGENHAHN, B. R. (1972). *Shaping your child's personality.* Englewood Cliffs, NJ: Prentice Hall.

HERGENHAHN, B. R. (2005). *An introduction to the history of psychology* (5th ed.) Belmont, CA: Wadsworth.

HERGENHAHN, B. R., & OLSON, M. H. (2007). *An introduction to theories of personality* (7th ed.). Upper Saddle River, NJ: Prentice Hall.

HERMANN, C., KIM, M., & BLANCHARD, E. B. (1995). Behavioral and prophylactic pharmacological intervention studies of pediatric migraine: An exploratory meta-analysis. *Pain, 60,* 239–255.

HERON, W. (1957, January). The pathology of boredom. *Scientific American,* pp. 52–56.

HERRNSTEIN, R. J. (1961). Relative and absolute strength of response as a function of frequency of reinforcement. *Journal of the Experimental Analysis of Behavior, 4,* 267–272.

HERRNSTEIN, R. J. (1970). On the law of effect. *Journal of the Experimental Analysis of Behavior, 13,* 243–266.

HERRNSTEIN, R. J. (1974). Formal properties of the matching law. *Journal of the Experimental Analysis of Behavior, 21,* 159–164.

HESS, E. H. (1958). "Imprinting" in animals. *Scientific American, 198,* 81–90.

HEYES, C. M., & DAWSON, G. R. (1990). A demonstration of observational learning using a bidirectional control. *Quarterly Journal of Experimental Psychology, 42B,* 59–71.

HEYES, C. M., DAWSON, G. R., & NOKES, T. (1992). Imitation in rats: Initial responding and transfer evidence. *Quarterly Journal of Experimental Psychology, 45B,* 229–240.

HEYES, C. M., JALDOW, E., & DAWSON, G. R. (1993). Observational extinction: Observation of nonreinforced responding reduces resistance to extinction in rats. *Animal Learning and Behavior, 21,* 221–225.

HILGARD, E. R., & MARQUIS, D. G. (1940). *Conditioning and learning.* Englewood Cliffs, NJ: Prentice Hall.

HILL, W. F. (1990). *Learning: A survey of psychological interpretations* (5th ed.). New York: Harper & Row.

HILTZ, S. R. (1993). Correlates of learning in a virtual classroom. *International Journal of Man-Machine Studies, 39,* 71–98.

HINDE, R. A., & TINBERGEN, N. (1958). The comparative study of species-specific behavior. In A. Roe & G. G. Simpson (eds.), *Behavior and evolution.* New Haven, CT: Yale University Press.

HINTON, G. E., & ANDERSON, J. A. (eds.). (1981). *Parallel models of associative memory.* Hillsdale, NJ: Erlbaum.

HIRAMOTO, R. N., ROGERS, C. F., DEMISSIE, S., HSUEH, C., HIRAMOTO, N. S., LORDEN, J. F., & GHANTA, V. K. (1997). Psychoneuroendocrine immunology: Site of recognition, learning and memory in the immune system and the brain. *International Journal of Neuroscience, 92,* 259–286.

HOBBES, T. (1962 [1651]). *Leviathan.* New York: Macmillan.

HOELSCHER, C. (1997). Long-term potentiation: A good model for learning and memory? *Progress in Neuro-Psychopharmacology and Biological Psychiatry, 21,* 47–68.

HOLLAND, J. G., & SKINNER, B. F. (1961). *The analysis of behavior: A program for self-instruction.* New York: McGraw-Hill.

HOLLAND, P. C. (1977). Conditioned stimulus as a determinant of the form for the Pavlovian conditioned response. *Journal of Experimental Psychology: Animal Processes, 3,* 77–104.

HOLLIS, K. (1982). Pavlovian conditioning of signal-centered action patterns and autonomic behavior: A biological analysis of function. In S. Tosenblatt, R. A. Hinde, C. Beer, & M. Busnel (eds.), *Advances in the study of behavior* (Vol. 12). New York: Academic Press.

HOLT, J. (1967). *How children learn.* New York: Pitman.

HOMME, L., CSANYI, A. P., GONZALES, M. A., & RECHS, J. R. (1970). *How to use contingency contracting in the classroom.* Champaign, IL: Research Press.

HOMME, L. E., DE BACA, P., DIVINE, J. F., STEINHORST, R., & RICKERT, E. J. (1963). Use of the Premack principle in controlling the behavior of school children. *Journal of the Experimental Analysis of Behavior, 6,* 544.

HULL, C. L. (1928). *Aptitude testing.* Yonkers-on-Hudson, NY: World Book.

HULL, C. L. (1933a). Differential habituation to internal stimuli in the albino rat. *Journal of Comparative Psychology, 16,* 255–273.

HULL, C. L. (1933b). *Hypnosis and suggestibility: An experimental approach.* New York: Naiburg.

HULL, C. L. (1943). *Principles of behavior.* Englewood Cliffs, NJ: Prentice Hall.

HULL, C. L. (1952). *A behavior system: An introduction to behavior theory concerning the individual organism.* New Haven, CT: Yale University Press.

HULSE, S. H. (1958). Amount and percentage of reinforcement and duration of goal confinement in conditioning and extinction. *Journal of Experimental Psychology, 56,* 48–57.

HULSE, S. H., EGETH, H., & DEESE, J. (1980). *The psychology of learning* (5th ed.). New York: McGraw-Hill.

HUMPHREYS, L. G. (1939a). Acquisition and extinction of verbal expectations in a situation analogous to conditioning. *Journal of Experimental Psychology, 25,* 294–301.

HUMPHREYS, L. G. (1939b). The effect of random alternation of reinforcement on the acquisition and extinction of conditioned eyelid reactions. *Journal of Experimental Psychology, 25,* 141–158.

HURSH, S. R. (1991). Behavioral economics of drug self-administration and drug abuse policy. *Journal of the Experimental Analysis of Behavior, 56,* 377–393.

HURSH, S. R., & BAUMAN, R. A. (1987). The behavioral economics of demand. In L. Green & J. H. Kagel (eds.), *Advances in behavioral economics* (Vol. 1, pp. 117–165). Norwood, N.J. Ablex.

HURSH, S. R., & NATELSON, B. H. (1981). Electrical brain stimulation and food reinforcement dissociated by demand elasticity. *Physiology and Behavior, 26,* 509–515.

IACOBONI, M., WOODS, R. P., BRASS, M., BEKKERING, H., MAZZIOTTA, J. C., & RIZOLATTI, G. (1999). Cortical mechanisms of human imitation. *Science, 286,* 2526–2528.

IKEMOTO, S., & PANKSEPP, J. (1996). Dissociations between appetitive and consummatory responses by pharmacological manipulations of reward-relevant brain regions. *Behavioral Neuroscience, 110,* 331–345.

INHELDER, B., & PIAGET, J. (1958). *The growth of logical thinking from childhood to adolescence* (A. Parson & S. Milgram, trans.). New York: Basic Books.

INNIS, N. K. (1999). Edward C. Tolman's purposive behavior. In W. O'Donohue & R. Kitchener (eds.), *Handbook of behaviorism* (pp. 97–117). San Diego, CA: Academic Press.

JACOBS, B., SCHALL, M., & SCHEIBEL, A. B. (1993). A quantitative dendritic analysis of Wernecke's area, II: Gender, hemispheric, and environmental factors. *Journal of Comparative Neurology, 237,* 97–111.

JACOBSEN, P. B., BOVBJERG, D. H., SCHWARTZ, M. D., ANDRYKOWSKI, M. A., FUTTERMAN, A. D., GILEWSKI, T., NORTON, L., & REDD, W. H. (1993). Formation of food aversions in cancer patients receiving repeated infusions of chemotherapy. *Behavior Research and Therapy, 31,* 739–748.

JAMES, W. (1890). *The principles of psychology* (2 vols.). New York: Henry Holt.

JENKINS, H. M., & MOORE, B. R. (1973). The form of the autoshaped response with food or water reinforcers. *Journal of the Experimental Analysis of Behavior, 20,* 163–181.

JONAS, G. (1973). *Visceral learning: Toward a science of self-control.* New York: Viking Press.

JONCICH, G. (1968). *The sane positivist: A biography of Edward L. Thorndike.* Middletown, CT: Wesleyan University Press.

JONES, M. C. (1924). A laboratory study of fear: The case of Peter. *Pedagogical Seminary, 31,* 308–315.

JONES, M. C. (1974). Albert, Peter, and John B. Watson. *American Psychologist, 29,* 581–583.

JURASKA, J. M. (1990). The structure of the cerebral cortex: Effects of gender and the environment. In B. Kolb & R. Tees (eds.), *The cerebral cortex of the rat* (pp. 483–506). Cambridge, MA: MIT Press.

JURASKA, J. M., FITCH, J. M., & WASHBURNE, D. L. (1989). The dendritic morphology of pyramidal neurons in the rat hippocampal CA3 area: Effects of gender and experience. *Brain Research, 333,* 115–121.

KAGAN, J. (1980, September). Jean Piaget's contributions. *Phi Delta Kappan,* pp. 245–246.

KALICHMAN, S. C. (1988). Individual differences in water-level performance. *Developmental Review, 8,* 273–295.

KALIVAS, P. W., & NAKAMURA, M. (1999). Neural systems for behavioral activation and reward. *Current Opinion in Neurobiology, 9,* 223–227.

KAMIN, L. J. (1969). Predictability, surprise, attention, and conditioning. In B. A. Campbell & R. M. Church (eds.), *Punishment and aversive behavior.* Englewood Cliffs, NJ: Prentice Hall.

KANDEL, E. (1991). Cellular mechanisms of learning and the biological basis of individuality. In E. R. Kandel, J. H. Schwartz, & T. M. Jessell (eds.), *Principles of neural science* (3rd ed., pp. 839–852). New York: Elsevier.

KANDEL, E. R., & SCHWARTZ, J. H. (1982). Molecular biology of learning: Modulation of transmitter release. *Science, 218,* 433–443.

KAUFMAN, A., BARON, A., & KOPP, R. E. (1966). Some effects of instructions on human operant behavior. *Psychonomic Monograph Supplements, 1,* 243–250.

KEEN, R. (2003). Representation of objects and events: Why do infants look so smart and toddlers look so dumb? *Current Directions in Psychological Science, 12,* 79–83.

KEGL, J., & IWATA, G. A. (1989). *Lenguage de signos Nicaraguense (Nicaraguan sign language): A pidgin sheds light on the "creole" ASL.* Proceedings of the 4th annual meeting of the Pacific Linguistics Society, Eugene, OR.

KELLER, F. S. (1968). Good-bye teacher. *Journal of Applied Behavior Analysis, 1,* 69–89.

KELLER, F. S., & SCHOENFELD, W. N. (1950). *Principles of psychology.* New York: Appleton-Century-Crofts.

KELLER, F. S., & SHERMAN, J. G. (1974). *PSI: The Keller plan handbook.* Menlo Park, CA: W. A. Benjamin.

KERR, D. S., & ABRAHAM, W. C. (1995). Cooperative interactions among afferents govern the induction of homosynaptic long-term depression in the hippocampus. *Proceedings of the National Academy of Sciences, 92,* 11637–11641.

KIMBLE, G. A. (1961). *Hilgard and Marquis' conditioning and learning* (2nd ed.). Englewood Cliffs, NJ: Prentice Hall.

KIMBLE, G. A. (1993). A modest proposal for a minor revolution in the language of psychology. *Psychological Science, 4,* 253–255.

KIMBLE, G. A., & GARMEZY, N. (1968). *Principles of general psychology* (3rd ed.). New York: Ronald Press.

KIMMEL, H. D. (1974). Instrumental conditioning of autonomically mediated responses in human beings. *American Psychologist, 29,* 325–335.

KIMURA, D. (1961). Cerebral dominance and the perception of verbal stimuli. *Canadian Journal of Psychology, 15,* 166–171.

KIMURA, D. (1964). Left-right differences in the perception of melodies. *Quarterly Journal of Experimental Psychology, 16,* 355–358.

KIMURA, D. (1967). Functional asymmetry of the brain in dichotic listening. *Cortex, 3,* 163–178.

KING, G. E. (1997, June). The attentional basis for primate responses to snakes. Paper presented at the annual meeting of the American Society of Primatologists, San Diego, CA.

KINGSTONE, A., ENNS, J. T., MANGUN, G. R., & GAZZANIGA, M. S. (1995). Guided search is a left hemisphere process in split-brain patients. *Psychological Science, 6,* 118–121.

KIRKWOOD, A., ROZAS, C., KIRKWOOD, J., PEREZ, F., & BEAR, M. F. (1999). Modulation of long-term synaptic depression in visual cortex by acetylcholoine and norepinephrine. *Journal of Neuroscience, 19,* 1599–1609.

KOCH, S. (1954). Clark L. Hull. In Estes et al. (eds.), *Modern learning theory* (pp. 1–176). New York: Appleton-Century-Crofts.

KOFFKA, K. (1963 [1935]). *Principles of Gestalt psychology.* New York: Harcourt, Brace, and World.

KÖHLER, W. (1925). *The mentality of apes.* London: Routledge & Kegan Paul.

KÖHLER, W. (1947). *Gestalt psychology: An introduction to new concepts in modern psychology* (rev. ed.). New York: Liveright.

KOLB, B., COTE, S., RIBEIRO-DA-SILVA, A., & CUELLO, A. C. (1996). NGF stimulates recovery of function and dendritic growth after unilateral motor cortex lesions in rats. *Neuroscience, 76,* 1139–1151.

KOLB, B., GIBB, R., & GORNY, G. (2003). Experience-dependent changes in dendritic arbor and spine density in neocortex vary with age and sex. *Neurobiology of Learning and Memory, 79,* 1–10.

KOLB, B., GIBB, R., & ROBINSON, T. E. (2003). Brain plasticity and behavior. *Current Directions in Psychological Science, 12,* 1–5.

KOLB, B., GORNY, G., COTE, S., RIBEIRO-DA-SILVA, A., & CUELLO, A. C. (1997). Nerve growth factor stimulates growth of cortical pyramidal neurons in young adult rats. *Brain Research, 751,* 289–294.

KOLB, B., GORNY, G., LI, Y., SAMAHA, A. N., & ROBINSON, T. E. (2003). Amphetamine or cocaine limits the ability of later experience to promote structural plasticity in the neocortex and nucleus accumbens. *Proceedings of the National Academy of Sciences, 100(18),* 10523–10528.

KOLB, B., & STEWART, J. (1995). Changes in neonatal gonadal hormonal environment prevent behavioral sparing and alter cortical morphogenesis after early frontal cortical lesions in male and female rats. *Behavioral Neuroscience, 109,* 285–294.

KOLB, B., & WHISHAW, I. Q. (1998). Brain plasticity and behavior. *Annual Review of Psychology, 49,* 43–64.

KORN, J. H., DAVIS, R., & DAVIS, S. F. (1991). Historians' and chairpersons' judgments of eminence among psychologists. *American Psychologist, 46,* 789–792.

KREBS, D. L. (1998). The evolution of moral behaviors. In C. Crawford & D. L. Krebs (eds.), *Handbook of evolutionary psychology* (pp. 337–368). Mahwah, NJ: Lawrence Erlbaum Associates.

KUHN, T. S. (1973). *The structure of scientific revolutions* (3rd ed.). Chicago: University of Chicago Press.

KULIK, J. A., KULIK, C. L. C., & COHEN, P. A. (1979). A meta-analysis of outcome studies of Keller's personalized system of instruction. *American Psychologist, 34,* 307–318.

KUPFERMANN, I., CASTELLUCCI, V., PINSKER, H., & KANDEL, E. (1970). Neuronal correlates of habituation and dishabituation of the gill withdrawal reflex in *Aplysia. Science, 167,* 1743–1745.

LABBE, E. E. (1995). Treatment of childhood migraine with autogenic training and skin temperature biofeedback: A component analysis. *Headache, 35,* 10–13.

LAIFENFELD, D., KLEIN, E., & BEN-SHACHAR, D. (2002). Norepinephrine alters the expression of genes involved in neuronal sprouting and differentiation: Relevance for major depression and antidepressant mechanisms. *Journal of Neurochemistry, 83,* 1054–1064.

LEEPER, R. (1935). The role of motivation in learning: A study of the phenomenon of differential motivational control of the utilization of habits. *Journal of Genetic Psychology, 46,* 3–40.

LEFRANCOIS, G. R. (1968). A treatment for the acceleration of conservation of substance. *Canadian Journal of Psychology, 22,* 277–284.

LEHMAN, D. R., LEMPERT, R. O., & NISBETT, R. E. (1988). The effects of graduate training on reasoning: Formal discipline and thinking about everyday-life events. *American Psychologist, 43,* 431–442.

LESHNER, A. I., & KOOB, G. F. (1999). Drugs of abuse and the brain. *Proceedings of the Association of American Physicians, 111,* 99–108.

LEUNER, B., MENDOLIA-LOFFREDO, S., KOZOROVITSKIY, Y., SAMBURG, D. GOULD, E., & SHORS, T. J. (2004). Learning enhances the survival of new neurons beyond the time when the hippocampus is required for memory. *Journal of Neuroscience, 24,* 7477–7481.

LEVY, J. (1985, May). Right brain, left brain: Fact and fiction. *Psychology Today,* pp. 38–39, 42–44.

LEYTON, M., CASEY, K. F., DELANEY, J. S., KOLIVAKIS, T., & BENKELFAT, C. (2005). Cocaine craving, euphoria, and self-administration: A preliminary study of the effect of catecholamine precursor depletion. *Behavioral Neuroscience, 119(6),* 1619–1627.

LI, Y., KOLB, B., & ROBINSON, T. E. (2003). The location of persistent amphetamine-induced changes in the density of dendritic spines on medium spiny neurons in the nucleus accumbens and caudate-putamen. *Neuropsychopharmacology, 28,* 1082–1085.

LINSKIE, R. (1977). *The learning process: Theory and practice.* New York: D. Van Nostrand.

LIPP, O. V., & DERAKSHAN, N. (2005). Attentional Bias to Pictures of Fear-Relevant Animals in a Dot Probe Task. *Emotion, 5,* 365–369.

LIPP, O. V., & WATERS, A. M. (2007). When Danger Lurks in the Background: Attentional Capture by Animal Fear-Relevant Distractors Is Specific and Selectively Enhanced by Animal Fear. *Emotion, 7,* 192–200.

LOGUE, A. W. (1988). A comparison of taste aversion learning in humans and other vertebrates: Evolutionary pressures in common. In R. C. Bolles & M. D. Beecher (eds.), *Evolution and learning* (pp. 97–116). Hillsdale, NJ: Lawrence Erlbaum Associates.

LØMO, T. (1966). Frequency potentiation of excitatory synaptic activity in the dentate area of the hippocampal formation. *Acta Physiologica Scandinavica, 68,* 128.

LORENZ, K. (1952). *King Solomon's ring.* New York: Crowell.

LORENZ, K. (1965). *Evolution and modification of behavior.* Chicago: University of Chicago Press.

LORENZ, K. (1970). *Studies in animal and human behavior* (Vol. 1). Cambridge, MA: Harvard University Press.

LU, B. (2003). BDNF and activity-dependent synaptic modulation. *Learning and Memory, 10,* 86–98.

LUBOW, R. E., & MOORE, A. U. (1959). Latent inhibition: The effect of nonreinforced preexposure to the conditioned stimulus. *Journal of Comparative and Physiological Psychology, 52,* 415–419.

LUMSDEN, C. J., & WILSON, E. O. (1981). *Genes, mind, and culture.* Cambridge, MA: Harvard University Press.

LUNDIN, R. W. (1974). *Personality: A behavioral analysis* (2nd ed.). New York: Macmillan.

LYNCH, G., & BAUDRY, M. (1984). The biochemistry of memory: A new and specific hypothesis. *Science, 224,* 1057–1063.

LYNCH, G., & BAUDRY, M. (1991). Reevaluating the constraints on hypothesis regarding LTP expression. *Hippocampus, 1,* 9–14.

MACCORQUODALE, K., & MEEHL, P. E. (1953). Preliminary suggestions as to a formalization of expectancy theory. *Psychological Review, 60,* 55–63.

MACDONALL, J. S. (1999). A local model of concurrent performance. *Journal of the Experimental Analysis of Behavior, 71,* 57–74.

MACDONALL, J. S. (2003). Reinforcing staying and switching while using a changeover delay. *Journal of the Experimental Analysis of Behavior, 79,* 219–232.

MACKINTOSH, N. J. (1973). Stimulus selection: Learning to ignore stimuli that predict no change in reinforcement. In R. A. Hinde & J. S. Hinde (eds.), *Constraints on learning.* London: Academic Press.

MACKINTOSH, N. J. (1975). A theory of attention: Variations in the associability of stimuli with reinforcement. *Psychological Review, 82,* 276–298.

MAHURIN, R. K. (1998). Neural network modeling of basal ganglia function in Parkinson's disease and related disorders. In R. W. Parks & D. S. Levine (eds.), *Fundamentals of neural network modeling: Neuropsychology and cognitive neuroscience* (pp. 331–355). Cambridge, MA: MIT Press.

MAIER, S. F., SELIGMAN, M. E. P., & SOLOMON, R. L. (1969). Pavlovian fear conditioning and learning helplessness: Effects on escape and avoidance behavior of (a) the CS-US contingency, and (b) the independence of the US and voluntary responding. In B. A. Campbell & R. M. Church (eds.), *Punishment and aversive behavior.* New York: Appleton-Century-Crofts.

MALONE, J. C. (1991). *Theories of learning: A historical approach.* Belmont, CA: Wadsworth.

MANTHEY, S., SCHUBOTZ, R. I., & VON CRAMON, D. Y. (2003). Premotor cortex in observing erroneous action: An fMRI study. *Brain Research. Cognitive Brain Research, 15(3),* 296–307.

MAROUN, M., & RICHTER-LEVIN, G. (2003). Exposure to acute stress blocks the induction of long-term potentiation of the amygdale-prefrontal cortex pathway *in vivo. Journal of Neuroscience, 23,* 4406–4409.

MARTIN, G. M., WALKER, K. M., & SKINNER, D. M. (2003). A single unstable visual cue impairs spatial learning in a water maze. *Learning and Motivation, 34,* 87–103.

MARX, M. H., & CRONAN-HILLIX, W. A. (1987). *Systems and theories in psychology* (4th ed.). New York: McGraw-Hill.

MAY, P., TIITINEN, H., ILMONIEMI, R. J., NYMAN, G., TAYLOR, J. G., & NAEAETAENEN, R. (1999). Frequency changes in human auditory cortex. *Journal of Computational Neuroscience, 6,* 99–120.

MCCLELLAND, J. L., & RUMELHART, D. E. (1988). *Explorations in parallel distributed processing: A handbook of models, programs and exercises.* Cambridge, MA: MIT Press/Bradford Books.

MCEWEN, B. S. (2001). Plasticity of the hippocampus: Adaptation to chronic stress and allostatic load. *Annals of the New York Academy of Sciences, 933,* 265–277.

MEDIN, D. L., & SHAFFER, M. M. (1978). Context theory of classification learning. *Psychological Review, 85,* 207–238.

MEEHL, P. E. (1950). On the circularity of the law of effect. *Psychological Bulletin, 47,* 52–75.

MEEK, R. L. (1977). The traditional in non-traditional learning methods. *Journal of Personalized Instruction, 2,* 114–119.

MELZACK, R., & THOMPSON, W. R. (1956). Effects of early experience on social behavior. *Canadian Journal of Psychology, 10,* 82–90.

METALINKOV, S. (1934). *Role du systeme nerveux et des facteurs biologiques et psychiques dans l'immunitie.* [The role of the nervous system and of biological and psychic factors in immunity.] Paris: Masson.

METALINKOV, S., & CHORINE, V. (1926). Role des reflexes conditionnels dans l'immunitie. [The role of conditional reflexes in immunity.] *Annales de l' Institut Pasteur, 40,* 893–900.

METCALFE, J., FUNNELL, M., & GAZZANIGA, M. S. (1995). Right-hemisphere memory superiority: Studies of a split-brain patient. *Psychological Science, 6,* 157–164.

MILLER, G. A. (1965). Some preliminaries to psycholinguistics. *American Psychologist, 20,* 15–20.

MILLER, N. E. (1969). Learning of visceral and glandular responses. *Science, 163,* 434–445.

MILLER, N. E. (1983). Behavioral medicine: Symbiosis between laboratory and clinic. In M. R. Rosenzweig & L. W. Porter (eds.), *Annual Review of Psychology, 34,* 1–31.

MILLER, N. E. (1984). *Bridges between laboratory and clinic.* New York: Praeger.

MILLER, N. E., & CARMONA, A. (1967). Modification of a visceral response, salivation in thirsty dogs, by instrumental training with water reward. *Journal of Comparative and Physiological Psychology, 63,* 1–6.

MILLER, N. E., & DOLLARD, J. C. (1941). *Social learning and imitation.* New Haven, CT: Yale University Press.

MILNER, B. (1959). The memory defect in bilateral hippocampal lesions. *Psychiatric Research Reports, 11,* 43–58.

MILNER, B. (1965). Memory disturbance after bilateral hippocampal lesions. In P. Milner & S. Glickman (eds.), *Cognitive processes and the brain.* Princeton, NJ: Van Nostrand.

MISHKIN, M., MALAMUT, B., & BACHEVALIER, J. (1984). Memories and habits: Two neural systems. In G. Lynch, J. L. McGaugh, & N. M. Weinberger (eds.), *Neurobiology of learning and memory* (pp. 65–77). New York: Guilford Press.

MOLTZ, H. (1957). Latent extinction and the fractional anticipatory response mechanism. *Psychological Review, 64,* 229–241.

MONTGOMERY, K. J., ISENBERG, N., & HAXBY, J. V. (2007). Communicative hand gestures and object-directed hand movements activated the mirror neuron system. *Social Cognitive and Affective Neuroscience, 2(2),* 114–122.

MOORE, B. R., & STUTTARD, S. (1979). Dr. Guthris and *Felis domesticus* or: Tripping over the cat. *Science, 205,* 1031–1033.

MOORE, J. W., & STICKNEY, K. J. (1980). Formation of attentional-associative networks in real time: Role of the hippocampus and implications for conditioning. *Physiological Psychology, 8,* 207–217.

MORGAN, C. L. (1891). *An introduction to comparative psychology.* London: W. Scott.

MOUNT, G. R., PAYTON, T., ELLIS, J., & BARNES, P. (1976). A multimodal behavioral approach to the treatment of alcoholism. *Behavioral Engineering, 33,* 61–66.

MOWRER, O. H. (1956). Two-factor learning theory reconsidered, with special reference to secondary reinforcement and the concept of habit. *Psychological Review, 63,* 114–128.

MOWRER, O. H. (1960). *Learning theory and behavior.* New York: Wiley.

MUELLER, C. G., & SCHOENFELD, W. N. (1954). Edwin R. Guthrie. In Estes et al. (eds.), *Modern learning theory* (pp. 345–379). New York: Appleton-Century-Crofts.

MÜHLBERGER, A., WIEDEMANN, G., HERRMANN, M. J., & PAULI, P. (2006). Phylo- and Ontogenetic Fears and the Expectation of Danger: Differences Between Spider- and Flight-Phobic Subjects in Cognitive and Physiological Responses to Disorder-Specific Stimuli. *Journal of Abnormal Psychology, 115,* 580–589.

MULLER, G. E., & PILZECKER, A. (1900). *Experimentelle Beitrdge Zur Lehre Vom Gedachtniss.* Leipzig.

MUNN, N. L., FERNALD, D. L., Jr., & FERNALD, P. S. (1972). *Introduction to psychology.* Boston: Houghton Mifflin.

MURDOCK, B. B., Jr. (1961). The retention of individual items. *Journal of Experimental Psychology, 62,* 618–625.

MURRAY, D. J. (1995). *Gestalt psychology and the cognitive revolution.* New York: Harvester Wheatsheaf.

NAKANISHI, S. (1992). Molecular diversity of glutamate receptors and implications for brain function. *Science, 258,* 597–603.

NANN-VERNOTICA, E., DONNY, E. C., BIGELOW, G. E., & WALSH, S. L. (2001). Repeated administration of the D1/5 antagonist ecopipam fails to attenuate subjective effects of cocaine. *Psychopharmacology, 155,* 338–347.

NICOL, C. J., & POPE, S. J. (1993). Food deprivation during observation reduces social learning in hens. *Animal Behaviour, 45,* 193–196.

NIXON, K., & CREWS, F. T. (2004). Temporally specific burst in cell proliferation increases hippocampal neurogenesis in protracted abstinence from alcohol. *Journal of Neuroscience, 25(43),* 9714–9722.

NOWEND, K. L., ARIZZI, M. N., CARLSON, B. B., & SALAMONE, J. D. (2001). D1 or D2 antagonism in nucleus accumbens core or dorsomedial shell suppresses lever pressing for food but leads to compensatory increases in chow consumption. *Pharmacology Biochemistry and Behavior, 69,* 373–382.

OBRIST, P. A., SUTTERER, J. R., & HOWARD, J. L. (1972). Preparatory cardiac changes: A psychobiological approach. In A. H. Black & W. F. Prokasy (eds.), *Classical conditioning II.* Englewood Cliffs, NJ: Prentice Hall.

ÖHMAN, A., FLYKT, A., & ESTEVES, F. (2001). Emotion drives attention: Detecting the snake in the grass. *Journal of Experimental Psychology: General, 131,* 466–478.

ÖHMAN, A., & MINEKA, S. (2001). Fear, phobias, and preparedness: Toward an evolved module of fear and fear learning. *Psychological Review, 102,* 483–522.

ÖHMAN, A., & MINEKA, S. (2003). The malicious serpent: Snakes as a prototypical stimulus for an evolved module of fear. *Current Directions in Psychological Science, 12,* 5–9.

ÖHMAN, A., & SOARES, J. J. F. (1993). On the automatic nature of phobic fear: Conditioned electrodermal responses to masked fear-relevant stimuli. *Journal of Abnormal Psychology, 102,* 121–132.

ÖHMAN, A., & SOARES, J. J. F. (1994). "Unconscious anxiety": Phobic responses to masked stimuli. *Journal of Abnormal Psychology, 103,* 231–240.

ÖHMAN, A., & SOARES, J. J. F. (1998). Emotional conditioning to masked stimuli: Expectancies for aversive outcomes following nonrecognized fear-irrelevant stimuli. *Journal of Experimental Psychology: General, 127,* 69–82.

OLDS, J. (1955). Physiological mechanisms of reward. In M. R. Jones (ed.), *Nebraska symposium on motivation.* Lincoln: University of Nebraska Press.

OLDS, J., & MILNER, P. (1954). Positive reinforcement produced by electrical stimulation of septal area and other regions of rat brain. *Journal of Comparative and Physiological Psychology, 47,* 419–427.

OLTON, D. S. (1992). Tolman's cognitive analyses: Predecessors of current approaches in psychology. *Journal of Experimental Psychology, General, 121,* 427–428.

ORNSTEIN, R. E. (1997). *The right mind: Making sense of the hemispheres.* New York: Harcourt Brace.

PALMER, T. D., MARKAKIS, E. A., WILLHOITE, A. R., SAFAR, F., & GAGE, F. H. (1999). Fibroblast growth factor 2 activates a latent neurogenic program in neural stem cells from diverse regions of the adult CNS. *Journal of Neuroscience, 19,* 8487–9497.

PALMER, T. D., RAY, J., & GAGE, F. H. (1995). FGF-2 responsive neuronal progenitors reside in proliferative and quiescent regions of adult rodent brain. *Molecular and Cellular Neuroscience, 6,* 474–486.

PAVLOV, I. P. (1927). *Conditioned reflexes.* London: Oxford University Press.

PAVLOV, I. P. (1928). *Lectures on conditioned reflexes.* New York: Liveright.

PAVLOV, I. P. (1941). *Conditioned reflexes and psychiatry.* New York: International.

PAVLOV, I. P. (1955). *Selected works.* Moscow: Foreign Languages Publishing House.

PEARCE, J. M., & BOUTON, M. E. (2001). Theories of associative learning in animals. *Annual Review of Psychology, 52,* 111–139.

PEARCE, J. M., & REDHEAD, E. S. (1995). Supernormal conditioning. *Journal of Experimental Psychology: Animal Behavior Processes, 21,* 155–165.

PETERSON, L. R., & PETERSON, M. J. (1959). Short term retention of individual verbal items. *Journal of Experimental Psychology, 58,* 193–198.

PETRI, H. L., & MISHKIN, M. (1994). Behaviorism, cognitivism, and the neuropsychology of memory. *American Scientist, 82,* 30–37.

PETRINOVICH, L. (1997). Evolved behavioral mechanisms. In M. E. Bouton & M. S. Fanselow (eds.), *Learning, motivation, and cognition: The functional behaviorism of Robert C. Bolles* (pp. 13–30). Washington, DC: American Psychological Association.

PETRINOVICH, L., & BOLLES, R. C. (1954). Deprivation states and behavioral drive discrimination in the rat. *Journal of Comparative and Physiological Psychology, 47,* 450–453.

PHILLIPS, D. C., & ORTON, R. (1983). The new causal principle of cognitive learning theory: Perspectives on Bandura's "reciprocal determinism." *Psychological Review, 90,* 158–165.

PHILLIPS, J. L., Jr. (1975). *The origins of intellect: Piaget's theory* (2nd ed.). San Francisco: Freeman.

PHILLIPS, J. L., Jr. (1981). *Piaget's theory: A primer.* San Francisco: Freeman.

PIAGET, J. (1966). *Psychology of intelligence.* Totowa, NJ: Littlefield, Adams.

PIAGET, J. (1970a). *Genetic epistemology* (E. Duckworth, trans.). New York: Columbia University Press.

PIAGET, J. (1970b). Piaget's theory. In P. H. Mussen (ed.), *Carmichael's manual of child psychology* (Vol. 1). New York: Wiley.

PIAGET, J. (1973): *The child and reality: Problems of genetic psychology* (A. Rosin, trans.). New York: Penguin Press.

PIAGET, J., & INHELDER, B. (1969). *The psychology of the child* (H. Weaver, trans.). New York: Basic Books.

PINKER, S. (1994). *The language instinct: How the mind creates language.* New York: William Morrow and Company.

PINKER, S. (1997). *How the mind works.* New York: Norton.

PLOTKIN, H. (1998). *Evolution in mind: An introduction to evolutionary psychology.* Cambridge, MA: Harvard University Press.

POPPER, K. (1963). *Conjectures and refutations.* New York: Basic Books.

PREMACK, D. (1959). Toward empirical behavior laws: Vol. I. Positive reinforcement. *Psychological Review, 66,* 219–233.

PREMACK, D. (1962). Reversibility of the reinforcement relation. *Science, 136,* 255–257.

PRESSEY, S. L. (1926). A simple apparatus which gives tests and scores and teaches. *School and Society, 23,* 373–376.

PRESSEY, S. L. (1927). A machine for automatic teaching of drill material. *School and Society, 25,* 549–552.

QUINLAN, P. T. (1991). *Connectionism and psychology: A psychological perspective on new connectionist research.* Chicago: University of Chicago Press.

RACHLIN, H. (1976). *Behavior and learning.* San Francisco: Freeman.

RACHLIN, H. (1991). *Introduction to modern behaviorism* (3rd ed.). San Francisco: Freeman.

RACHLIN, H., & GREEN, L. (1972). Commitment, choice and self-control. *Journal of the Experimental Analysis of Behavior, 17,* 15–22.

RAMACHANDRAN, V. S. (2000). Mirror neurons and imitation learning as the driving force behind "the great leap forward" in human evolution. Accessed June 5, 2007 at http://www.edge.org/3rd_culture

RAMACHANDRAN, V. S., & BLAKESLEE, S. (1998). *Phantoms in the brain.* New York: HarperCollins.

RASHOTTE, M. E., & AMSEL, A. (1999). Clark L. Hull's behaviorism. In W. O'Donohue & R. Kitchener (eds.), *Handbook of behaviorism* (pp. 119–158). San Diego, CA: Academic Press.

RAZRAN, G. (1961). The observable unconscious and the inferable conscious in current Soviet psychophysiology. *Psychological Review, 68,* 81–147.

RAZRAN, G. (1965). Russian physiologists' psychology and American experimental psychology. *Psychological Bulletin, 63,* 42–64.

REISS, B. F. (1946). Genetic changes in semantic conditioning. *Journal of Experimental Psychology, 36,* 143–152.

RENALDI, R., POCOCK, D., ZEREIK, R., & WISE, R. A. (1999). Dopamine fluctuations in the nucleus accumbens during maintenance, extinction, and reinstatement of intravenous D-amphetamine self-administration. *Journal of Neuroscience, 19,* 4102–4109.

RESCORLA, R. A. (1966). Predictability and number of pairings in Pavlovian fear conditioning. *Psychonomic Science, 4,* 383–384.

RESCORLA, R. A. (1967). Pavlovian conditioning and its proper control procedures. *Psychological Review, 74,* 72–80.

RESCORLA, R. A. (1971). Variation in the effectiveness of reinforcement and nonreinforcement following prior inhibitory conditioning. *Learning and Motivation, 2,* 113–123.

RESCORLA, R. A. (1988). Pavlovian conditioning: It's not what you think. *American Psychologist, 43,* 151–160.

RESCORLA, R. A. (2002). Effect of following an excitatory-inhibitory compound with an intermediate reinforcer. *Journal of Experimental Psychology: Animal Behavior Processes, 28,* 163–174.

RESCORLA, R. A., & HETH, C. D. (1975). Reinstatement of fear to an extinguished conditioned stimulus. *Journal of Experimental Psychology: Animal Behavior Processes, 1,* 88–96.

RESCORLA, R. A., & WAGNER, A. R. (1972). A theory of Pavlovian conditioning: Variations in the effectiveness of reinforcement and non-reinforcement. In A. H. Black & W. F. Prokasy (eds.), *Classical conditioning II.* Englewood Cliffs, NJ: Prentice Hall.

RIESEN, A. H. (1947). The development of visual perception in man and chimpanzee. *Science, 106,* 107–108.

RIMM, D. C., & MASTERS, J. C. (1979). *Behavior therapy.* New York: Academic Press.

RINGEN, J. (1999). Radical behaviorism: B. F. Skinner's philosophy of science. In W. O'Donohue & R. Kitchener (eds.), *Handbook of behaviorism* (pp. 159–178). San Diego, CA: Academic Press.

RIZZOLATTI, G., FADIGA, L., GALLESE, V., & FOGASSI, L. (1996). Premotor cortex and the recognition of motor actions. *Cognitive Brain Research, 1,* 131–141.

RIZZOLATTI, G., FOGASSI, L., & GALLESE, V. (2001). Neurophysiological mechanisms underlying the understanding and imitation of action. *Nature Reviews Neuroscience, 9,* 661–670.

ROBERTS, A. H. (1994). "The powerful placebo" revisited: Implications for headache treatment and management. *Headache Quarterly, 5,* 209–213.

*ROBINSON, D. N. (1981). *An intellectual history of psychology* (rev. ed.). New York: Macmillan.

ROBINSON, D. N. (1986). *An intellectual history of psychology* (paperback text edition). Madison: University of Wisconsin Press.

ROBINSON, S., SANDSTROM, S. M., DENENBERG, V. H., & PALMITER, R. D. (2005). Distinguishing whether dopamine regulates liking, wanting, and/or learning about rewards. *Behavioral Neuroscience, 119(1),* 5–15.

ROBINSON, T. E., & BERRIDGE, K. C. (2000). The psychology and neurobiology of addiction: An incentive-sensitization view. *Addiction, 95(Suppl2),* S91–S117.

ROBINSON, T. E., & BERRIDGE, K. C. (2001). Incentive sensitization and addiction. *Addiction, 96,* 103–114.

ROBINSON, T. E., & BERRIDGE, K. C. (2003). Addiction. *Annual Review of Psychology, 54,* 25–53.

ROMANES, G. J. (1882/1897). *Animal intelligence.* London: Kegan Paul, Trench.

ROMANES, G. J. (1884). *Mental evolution in animals.* New York: Appleton-Century-Crofts.

ROMANES, G. J. (1885). *Mental evolution in man.* London: Kegan Paul.

ROSENZWEIG, M. R., & BENNETT, E. L. (1978). Experiential influences on brain anatomy and brain chemistry in rodents. In G. Gottlieb (ed.), *Studies on the development of behavior and the nervous system* (pp. 289–387). New York: Academic Press.

ROVNER, B. W. (2002). The Charles Bonnet syndrome: Visual hallucinations caused by vision impairment. *Geriatrics, 57,* 45–46.

ROZIN, P., & FALLON, A. E. (1981). The acquisition of likes and dislikes for foods. In J. Solms & R. L. Hall (eds.), *Criteria of food acceptance* (pp. 35–48). **Zurich,** Switzerland: Forster Verlag AG.

RUJA, H. (1956). Productive psychologists. *American Psychologist, 11,* 148–149.

RUMELHART, D. E., MCCLELLAND, J. L., & PDP RESEARCH GROUP. (1986). *Parallel distributed processing* (Vols. 1 and 2). Cambridge, MA: MIT Press/Bradford Books.

SALAMONE, J. D., & CORREA, M. (2002). Motivational views of reinforcement: Implications for understanding the behavioral functions of nucleus accumbens dopamine. *Behavioral Brain Research, 137,* 3–25.

SALAMONE, J. D., CORREA, M., MINGOTE, S., & WEBER, S. M. (2003). Nucleus accumbens dopamine and the regulation of effort in food-seeking behavior: Implications for studies of natural motivation, psychiatry, and drug abuse. *Journal of Pharmacology and Experimental Therapeutics, 305(1),* 1–8.

SALAMONE, J. D., COUSINS, M. S., & BUCHER, S. (1994). Anhedonia or anergia? Effects of haloperidoland nucleus accumbens dopamine depletion on instrumental response selection in a T-maze cost/benefit procedure. *Behavioural Brain Research, 65,* 221–229.

SALAMONE, J. D., KURTH, P., MCCULLOUGH, L. D., & SOKOLOWSKI, J. D. (1995). The effects of nucleus accumbens dopamine depletions on continuously reinforced operant responding: Contrasts with the effects of extinction. *Pharmacology Biochemistry and Behavior, 50,* 437–443.

SALTZ, E. (1971). *The cognitive bases of human learning.* Homewood, IL: Dorsey Press.

SAPOLSKY, R. M. (2000). Glucocorticoids and hippocampal atrophy in neuropsychiatric disorders. *Archives of General Psychiatry, 57,* 925.

SARTAIN, Q. A., NORTH, J. A., STRANGE, R. J., & CHAPMAN, M. H. (1973). *Psychology: Understanding human behavior* (4th ed.). New York: McGraw-Hill.

SCHADE, J. B., & BAXTER, C. F. (1960). Changes during growth in volume and surface area of cortical neurons in the rabbit. *Experimental Neurology, 2,* 158–178.

SCHEIBEL, A. B., CONRAD, T., PERDUE, S., TOMIYASU, U., & WECHSLER, A. (1990). A quantitative study of dentrite complexity in selected areas of the human cortex. *Brain and Cognition, 12,* 85–101.

SCHRAMM, W. (1964). *The research on programmed instruction: An annotated bibliography.* Washington, DC: U.S. Office of Education (OE-34034).

SCHUMAN, E. M., & MADISON, D. V (1991). A requirement for the intercellular messenger nitric oxide in long-term potentiation. *Science, 254,* 1503–1506.

SCHWARTZ, B., WASSERMAN, E. A., & ROBBINS, S. J. (2002). *Psychology of learning and behavior* (5th ed.). New York: Norton.

SCOVILLE, W. B., & MILNER, B. (1957). Loss of recent memory after bilateral hippocampal lesions. *Journal of Neurology, Neurosurgery, and Psychiatry, 20,* 11–21.

SEARS, R. R. (1944). Experimental analysis of psychoanalytic phenomena. In J. McV. Hunt (ed.), *Personality and the behavior disorders.* New York: Ronald Press.

SEARS, R. R., MACCOBY, E. E., & LEVIN, H. (1957). *Patterns of child rearing.* New York: Harper & Row.

SEARS, R. R., WHITING, J. W. M., NOWLIS, V., & SEARS, P. S. (1953). Some child-rearing antecedents of aggression and dependency in young children. *Genetic Psychology Monographs, 47,* 135–236.

SEJNOWSKI, T. J., & ROSENBERG, C. R. (1987). Parallel networks that learn to pronounce English text. *Complex Systems, 1,* 145–168.

SELIGMAN, M. E. P. (1969). Control group and conditioning: A comment on operationism. *Psychological Review, 76,* 484–491.

SELIGMAN, M. E. P. (1970). On the generality of the laws of learning. *Psychological Review, 77,* 406–418.

SELIGMAN, M. E. P. (1972). Phobias and preparedness. In M. E. P. Seligman & J. L. Hager (eds.), *Biological boundaries of learning.* New York: Appleton-Century-Crofts.

SELIGMAN, M. E. P. (1975). *Helplessness.* San Francisco: Freeman.

*SELIGMAN, M. E. P., & HAGER, J. L. (eds.). (1972). *Biological boundaries of learning.* New York: Appleton-Century-Crofts.

SELIGMAN, M. E. P., & MAIER, S. F. (1967). Failure to escape traumatic shock. *Journal of Experimental Psychology, 74,* 1–9.

SEWARD, J. P., & LEVY, N. J. (1949). Sign learning as a factor in extinction. *Journal of Experimental Psychology, 39,* 660–668.

SHAPIRO, D., TURKSY, B., GERSON, E., & STERN, M. (1969). Effects of feedback and reinforcement on the control of human systolic blood pressure. *Science, 163,* 588–589.

SHARPLESS, S., & JASPER, H. (1956). Habituation of the arousal reaction. *Brain, 79,* 655–680.

SHEFFIELD, F. D., & ROBY, T. B. (1950). Reward value of a non-nutritive sweet taste. *Journal of Comparative and Physiological Psychology, 43,* 471–481.

SHELLICK, S., & FITZSIMMONS, G. (1989). Biofeedback: An exercise in self-efficacy. *Medical Psychotherapy: An International Journal, 2,* 115–124.

SHEPARD, R. N. (1992). The advent and continuing influence of mathematical learning theory: Comment on Estes and Burke. *Journal of Experimental Psychology, General, 121,* 419–421.

SHERMAN, J. G. (1992). Reflections on PSI: Good news and bad. *Journal of Applied Behavior Analysis, 25,* 59–64.

SHERMAN, P., & REEVE, K. (1997). Forward and backward: Alternative approaches to studying human social evolution. In L. Betzig (ed.), *Human nature: A critical reader* (pp. 147–158). New York: Oxford University Press.

SHORS, T. J., MIESEGAES, G., BEYLIN, A., ZHAO, M., RYDEL, T., & GOULD, E. (2001). Neurogenesis in the adult is involved in the formation of trace memories. *Nature, 410,* 372–376.

SHUWAIRI, S. M., ALBERT, M. K., & JOHNSON, S. P. (2007). Discrimination of possible and impossible objects in infancy. *Psychological Science, 18(4),* 303–307.

SIEGEL, S. (1979). The role of conditioning in drug tolerance and addiction. In J. D. Keehn (ed.), *Psychopathology in animals: Research and clinical implications.* New York: Academic Press.

SKINNER, B. F. (1938). *The behavior of organisms: An experimental analysis.* Englewood Cliffs, NJ: Prentice Hall.

SKINNER, B. F. (1948). *Walden Two.* New York: Macmillan.

SKINNER, B. F. (1950). Are theories of learning necessary? *Psychological Review, 57,* 193–216.

SKINNER, B. F. (1951). How to teach animals. *Scientific American, 185,* 26–29.

SKINNER, B. F (1953). *Science and human behavior.* New York: Macmillan.

SKINNER, B. F. (1954). The science of learning and the art of teaching. *Harvard Educational Review, 24,* 86–97.

SKINNER, B. F. (1956). A case history in scientific method. *American Psychologist, 11,* 221–233.

SKINNER, B. F. (1957). *Verbal behavior.* Englewood Cliffs, NJ: Prentice Hall.

SKINNER, B. F. (1958). Teaching machines. *Science, 128,* 969–977.

SKINNER, B. F. (1960). Pigeons in a pelican. *American Psychologist, 15,* 28–37.

SKINNER, B. F. (1967). In E. G. Boring & G. Lindzey (eds.), *A history of psychology in autobiography.* New York: Naiburg.

SKINNER, B. F. (1971). *Beyond freedom and dignity.* New York: Knopf.

SKINNER, B. F. (1974). *About behaviorism.* New York: Knopf.

SKINNER, B. F. (1984). The shame of American education. *American Psychologist, 39,* 947–954.

SKINNER, B. F. (1986). What is wrong with daily life in the Western world? *American Psychologist, 41,* 568–574.

SKINNER, B. F. (1987). *Upon further reflection.* Englewood Cliffs, NJ: Prentice Hall.

SMEDSLUND, J. (1961). The acquisition of conservation of substance and weight in children: I. Introduction. *Scandinavian Journal of Psychology, 2,* 11–20.

SPENCE, K. W. (1936). The nature of discrimination in animals. *Psychological Review, 43,* 427–449.

SPENCE, K. W. (1937). The differential response in animals to stimuli varying within a single dimension. *Psychological Review, 44,* 430–444.

SPENCE, K. W. (1942). The basis of solution by chimpanzees of the intermediate size problem. *Journal of Experimental Psychology, 31,* 257–271.

SPENCE, K. W. (1952). Clark Leonard Hull: 1884–1952. *American Journal of Psychology, 65,* 639–646.

SPENCE, K. W. (1956). *Behavior theory and conditioning.* New Haven, CT: Yale University Press.

SPENCE, K. W. (1960). *Behavior theory and learning: Selected papers.* Englewood Cliffs, NJ: Prentice Hall.

SPENCE, K. W., & LIPPITT, R. (1940). "Latent" learning of a simple maze problem with relevant needs satiated. *Psychological Bulletin, 37,* 429.

SPERRY, R. W. (1961). Cerebral organization and behavior. *Science, 133,* 1749–1757.

SPERRY, R. W. (1964). The great cerebral commissure. *Scientific American, 210,* 42–52.

SPOONER, F., JORDAN, L., ALGOZZINE, B., & SPOONER, M. (1999). Student ratings of instructions in distance learning and on-campus classes. *Journal of Educational Research, 92,* 132–140.

SPRINGER, S. P., & DEUTSCH, G. (1985). *Left brain, right brain* (rev. ed.). San Francisco: Freeman.

SPURZHEIM, G. (1834). *Phrenology, or the doctrine of mental phenomena.* Boston: Marsh, Capen, & Lyon.

SQUIRE, L. R. (1992). Memory and the hippocampus: A synthesis from findings with rats, monkeys, and humans. *Psychological Review, 99,* 143–145.

STADDON, J. (1995, February). On responsibility and punishment. *Atlantic Monthly,* 88–94.

STADDON, J. E. R. (1988). Learning as inference. In R. C. Bolles & M. D. Beecher (eds.), *Evolution and learning* (pp. 59–77). Hillsdale, NJ: Lawrence Erlbaum Associates.

STADDON, J. E. R., & CERLUTTI, D. T. (2003). Operant conditioning. *Annual Reviews of Psychology, 54,* 115–144.

STANOVICH, K. E. (2001). *How to think straight about psychology* (6th ed.). Boston: Allyn & Bacon.

STANTON, P. K. (1996). LTD, LTP, and the sliding threshold for long-term synaptic plasticity. *Hippocampus, 6,* 35–42.

STAUBLI, U., & LYNCH, G. (1987). Stable hippocampal long-term potentiation elicited by "theta" pattern stimulation. *Brain Research, 444,* 153–158.

STEVENSON-HINDE, J. (1973). Constraints on reinforcement. In R. A. Hinde & J. Stevenson-Hinde (eds.), *Constraints on learning.* New York: Academic Press.

STEWART, J., & KOLB, B. (1994). Dendritic branching in cortical pyramidal cells in response to ovariectomy in adult female rats. *Brain Research, 654,* 149–154.

SUEDFIELD, P., & COREN, S. (1989). Perceptual isolation, sensory deprivation, and rest: Moving introductory psychology texts out of the 1950s. *Canadian Psychology, 30,* 17–29.

SULLOWAY, F. J. (1996). *Born to rebel: Birth order, family dynamics, and creative lives.* New York, Pantheon.

TAYLOR, J. A. (1951). The relationship of anxiety to the conditioned eyelid response. *Journal of Experimental Psychology, 41,* 81–92.

TERRACE, H. S. (1963). Errorless transfer of a discrimination across two continua. *Journal of the Experimental Analysis of Behavior, 6,* 223–232.

THOMAS-OLLIVIER, V., REYMANN, J. M., LEMOAL, S., SCHUCK, S., LIEURY, A., & ALLAIN, H. (1999). Procedural memory in recent-onset Parkinson's disease. *Dementia and Geriatric Cognitive Disorders, 10,* 172–180.

THORNDIKE, E. L. (1898). Animal intelligence: An experimental study of the associative processes in animals. *Psychological Review* [Monograph Suppl.] *2(81).*

THORNDIKE, E. L. (1901). The mental life of the monkeys. *Psychological Review Monograph, 3(15).*

THORNDIKE, E. L. (1905). *The elements of psychology* (2nd ed.). New York: Seiler.

THORNDIKE, E. L. (1906). *The principles of teaching: Based on psychology.* New York: Seiler.

THORNDIKE, E. L. (1911). *Animal intelligence.* New York: Macmillan.

THORNDIKE, E. L. (1912). *Education, a first book.* New York: Macmillan.

THORNDIKE, E. L. (1913a). *Educational psychology: Vol. 1. The psychology of learning.* New York: Teachers College Press.

THORNDIKE, E. L. (1913b). *Educational psychology: Vol. 2. The original nature of man.* New York: Teachers College Press.

THORNDIKE, E. L. (1922). *The psychology of arithmetic.* New York: Crowell-Collier and Macmillan.

THORNDIKE, E. L. (1924). Mental discipline in high school studies. *Journal of Educational Psychology, 15,* 1–22, 83–98.

THORNDIKE, E. L. (1932). *The fundamentals of learning.* New York: Teachers College Press.

THORNDIKE, E. L. (1940). *Human nature and the social order.* New York: Macmillan.

THORNDIKE, E. L. (1949). *Selected writings from a connectionist's psychology.* New York: Appleton-Century-Crofts.

THORNDIKE, E. L., & WOODWORTH, R. S. (1901). The influence of improvement in one mental function upon the efficiency of other functions. *Psychological Review, 8,* 247–261, 384–395, 553–564.

THORPE, W. H. (1963). *Learning and instinct in animals* (2nd ed.). Cambridge, MA: Harvard University Press.

TIGER, L. (1979). *Optimism: The biology of hope.* New York: Simon and Schuster.

TIMBERLAKE, W. (1980). A molar equilibrium theory of learned performance. In G. H. Bower (ed.), *The psychology of learning and motivation* (Vol. 14, pp. 1–58). San Diego, CA: Academic Press.

TIMBERLAKE, W. (1983). Appetitive structure and straight alley maze running. In R. Mellgren (ed.), *Animal cognition and behavior* (pp. 165–222). Amsterdam: North Holland Press.

TIMBERLAKE, W. (1997). An animal centered, causal-system approach to the understanding and control of behavior. *Applied Animal Behaviour Science, 53,* 107–129.

TIMBERLAKE, W. (1999). Biological behaviorism. In W. O'Donohue & R. Kitchener (eds.), *Handbook of behaviorism* (pp. 243–284). San Diego, CA: Academic Press.

TIMBERLAKE, W. (2001). Integrating niche-related and general process approaches in the study of learning. *Behavioural Processes, 54,* 79–94.

TIMBERLAKE, W. (2002). Niche-related learning in laboratory paradigms: The case of maze behavior in Norway rats. *Behavioural Brain Research, 134,* 355–374.

TIMBERLAKE, W., & ALLISON, J. (1974). Response deprivation: An empirical approach to instrumental performance. *Psychological Review, 81,* 146–164.

TIMBERLAKE, W., & FARMER-DOUGAN, V. A. (1991). Reinforcement in applied settings: Figuring out ahead of time what will work. *Psychological Bulletin, 110,* 379–391.

TIMBERLAKE, W., & LUCAS, G. A. (1989). Behavior systems and learning: From misbehavior to general principles. In S. B. Klein & R. R. Mowrer (eds.), *Contemporary learning theories: Instrumental conditioning theory and the impact of biological constraints on learning* (pp. 237–275). Hillsdale, NJ: Erlbaum.

TIMBERLAKE, W., & SILVA, K. M. (1995). Appetitive behavior in ethology, psychology, and behavior systems. In N. Thompson (ed.), *Perspectives in ethology* (pp. 211–253). New York: Plenum Press.

TIMBERLAKE, W., & WHITE, W. (1990). Winning isn't everything: Rats need only food deprivation not food reward to traverse a radial arm maze efficiently. *Learning and Motivation, 21,* 153–163.

TIPPETT, L. J., & FARAH, M. J. (1998). Parallel distributed processing models in Alzheimer's disease. In R. W. Parks & D. S. Levine (eds.), *Fundamentals of neural network modeling: Neuropsychology and cognitive neuroscience* (pp. 319–415). Cambridge, MA: MIT Press.

TOLMAN, E. C. (1932). *Purposive behavior in animals and men.* New York: Naiburg.

TOLMAN, E. C. (1938). The determiners of behavior at a choice point. *Psychological Review, 45,* 1–41.

TOLMAN, E. C. (1942). *Drives toward war.* New York: Appleton-Century-Crofts.

TOLMAN, E. C. (1945). A stimulus-expectancy need-cathexis psychology. *Science, 101,* 160–166.

TOLMAN, E. C. (1949). There is more than one kind of learning. *Psychological Review, 56,* 144–155.

TOLMAN, E. C. (1959). Principles of purposive behavior. In S. Koch (ed.), *Psychology: A study of a science* (Vol. 2). New York: McGraw-Hill.

TOLMAN, E. C., & HONZIK, C. H. (1930). Introduction and removal of reward, and maze performance in rats. *University of California Publications in Psychology, 4,* 257–275.

TOLMAN, E. C., RITCHIE, B. F., & KALISH, D. (1946a). Studies in spatial learning. 1. Orientation and the short-cut. *Journal of Experimental Psychology, 36,* 13–24.

TOLMAN, E. C., RITCHIE, B. F., & KALISH, D. (1946b). Studies in spatial learning. 11. Place learning versus response learning. *Journal of Experimental Psychology, 36,* 221–229.

TOOBY, J., & COSMIDES, L. (1990). The past explains the present: Emotional adaptations and the structure of ancestral environments. *Ethology and Sociobiology, 10,* 29–49.

TOOBY, J., & COSMIDES, L. (1992). Psychological foundations of culture. In J. H. Barkow, L. Cosmides, & J. Tooby (eds.), *The adapted mind* (pp. 19–136). New York: Oxford University Press.

UNDERWOOD, B. J., & KEPPEL. G. (1962). One-trial learning? *Journal of Verbal Learning and Verbal Behavior, 1,* 1–13.

VAKIL, E., & HERISHANU-NAAMAN, S. (1998). Declarative and procedural learning in Parkinson's disease patients having tremor or bradykinesia as the predominant syndrome. *Cortex, 34,* 611–620.

VANDERWOLF, C. H., KRAMIS, R., GILLESPIE, L. A., & BLAND, B. G. (1975). Hippocampal rhythmical slow activity and neocortical low voltage fast activity: Relations to behavior. In R. L. Isaacson & K. H. Pribram (eds.), *The hippocampus. Vol. 2. Neurophysiology and behavior.* New York: Plenum Press.

VERPLANCK, W. S. (1954). Burrhus F. Skinner. In Estes et al. (eds.), *Modern learning theory* (pp. 267–316). New York: Appleton-Century-Crofts.

VOEKS, V. W. (1950). Formalization and clarification of a theory of learning. *Journal of Psychology, 30,* 341–363.

VOIGT, T., OPITZ, T., & DOLABELA DE LIMA, A. (2005). Activation of early silent synapses by spontaneous synchronous network activity limits the range of neocortical connections. *Journal of Neuroscience, 25(18),* 4605–4615.

VON SENDEN, M. V. (1932). *Raum-und gestaltauffassung bei operierten blindgeborenen vor und nach der operation.* Leipzig: Barth.

VORONIN, L. L., & CHERUBINI, E. (2004). "Deaf, mute, and whispering" silent synapses: Their role in synaptic plasticity. *Journal of Physiology, 557(1),* 3–12.

VYAS, A., MITRA, R., RAO, S., & CHATTARJI, S. (2002). Chronic stress induces contrasting patterns of dendritic remodeling in hippocampal and amygaloid neurons. *Journal of Neuroscience, 22,* 6810–6818.

WAGNER, A. R. (1961). Effects of amount and percentage of reinforcement and number of acquisition trials on conditioning and extinction. *Journal of Experimental Psychology, 32,* 234–242.

WAGNER, A. R. (1963). Conditioned frustration as a learned drive. *Journal of Experimental Psychology, 64,* 142–148.

WAGNER, A. R. (1969). Stimulus selection and a "modified continuity theory." In G. H. Bower & J. T. Spence (eds.), *The psychology of learning and motivation* (Vol. 3). New York: Academic Press.

WAGNER, A. R. (1971). Elementary associations. In H. H. Kendler & J. T. Spence (eds.), *Essays in neobehaviorism: A memorial volume to Kenneth W. Spence.* Englewood Cliffs, NJ: Prentice Hall.

WAGNER, A. R. (1978). Expectancies and the priming of STM. In S. H. Hulse, H. Fowler, & W. R. Honig (eds.), *Cognitive processes in animal behavior.* Hillsdale, NJ: Erlbaum.

WAGNER, A. R., & RESCORLA, R. A. (1972). Inhibition in Pavlovian conditioning: Application of a theory. In R. A. Boakes & M. S. Halliday (eds.), *Inhibition and learning.* New York: Academic Press.

WALKER, E. L. (1969). Reinforcement—"the one ring." In J. T. Tapp (ed.), *Reinforcement and behavior.* New York: Academic Press.

WALTERS, G. C., & GRUSEC, J. E. (1977). *Punishment.* San Francisco: Freeman.

WATSON, J. B. (1908). Imitation in monkeys. *Psychological Bulletin, 5,* 169–178.

WATSON, J. B. (1913). Psychology as the behaviorist views it. *Psychological Review, 20,* 158–177.

WATSON, J. B. (1925). *Behaviorism.* New York: Norton.

WATSON, J. B. (1926). Experimental studies on the growth of the emotions. In C. Murchison (ed.), *Psychologies of 1925.* Worcester, MA: Clark University Press.

WATSON, J. B. (1936). John B. Watson. In C. Murchison (ed.), *History of psychology in autobiography* (Vol. 3). Worcester, MA: Clark University Press.

WATSON, J. B., & McDOUGALL, W. (1929). *The battle of behaviorism.* New York: Norton.

WATSON, J. B., & RAYNER, R. (1920). Conditioned emotional reactions. *Journal of Experimental Psychology, 3,* 1–14.

WATSON, R. I. (1978). *The great psychologists* (4th ed.). Philadelphia: Lippincott.

WEIMER, W. B. (1973). Psycholinguistics and Plato's paradoxes of the Meno. *American Psychologist, 28,* 15–33.

WERTHEIMER, M. (1912). Experimentelle studienfiber das sehen von bewegung. *Zeitschrift Für Psychologie, 61,* 161–265.

WERTHEIMER, M. (1959 [1945]). *Productive thinking,* enlarged ed. by Max Wertheimer, ed. Michael Wertheimer. New York: Harper & Row.

WERTHEIMER, M. (1980). Gestalt theory of learning. In G. M. Gazda & R. J. Corsini (eds.), *Theories of learning: A comparative approach.* Ithasca, IL: Peacock.

WILCOXON, H. C., DRAGOIN, W. B., & KRAL, P. A. (1971). Illness-induced aversions in rat and quail: Relative salience of visual and gustatory cues. *Science, 171,* 826–828.

WILLIAMS, B. A., & McDEVITT, M. A. (2002). Inhibition and superconditioning. *Psychological Science, 13,* 454–459.

WILLIAMS, D. R., & WILLIAMS, H. (1969). Auto-maintenance in the pigeon: Sustained pecking despite contingent non-reinforcement. *Journal of the Experimental Analysis of Behavior, 12,* 511–520.

WILSON, E. O. (1975). *Sociobiology: The new synthesis.* Cambridge MA: Harvard University Press.

WILSON, E. O. (1988a). *Consilience: The unity of knowledge.* New York: Knopf.

WILSON, E. O. (1988b). *On human nature.* Cambridge, MA: Harvard University Press.

WILSON, M., & KNOBLICH, G. (2005). The case for motor involvement in perceiving conspecifics. *Psychological Bulletin, 131(3),* 460–473.

WINDHOLZ, G. (1992). Pavlov's conceptualization of learning. *Amercan Journal of Psychology, 102,* 459–469.

WOLPE, J. (1958). *Psychotherapy by reciprocal inhibition.* Stanford, CA: Stanford University Press.

WOODWORTH, R. S. (1938). *Experimental psychology.* New York: Henry Holt.

ZEAMAN, D. (1949). Response latency as a function of the amount of reinforcement. *Journal of Experimental Psychology, 39,* 466–483.

ZENER, K. (1937). The significance of behavior accompanying conditioned salivary secretion for theories of the conditioned response. *American Journal of Psychology, 50,* 384–403.

ZENTALL, T. R. (2003). Imitation by animals: How do they do it? *Current Directions in Psychological Science, 12,* 91–95.

ZIRKLE, G. A. (1946). Success and failure in serial learning: I. The Thorndike effect. *Journal of Experimental Psychology, 36,* 230–236.

ZUBEK, J. P. (1969). *Sensory deprivation: Fifteen years of research.* New York: Appleton-Century-Crofts.

Name Index

Subject Index

A

Absolute theory, 267
Abstract modeling, 343–344
Accommodation, 284–285, 286, 295–296
Acquisition of behavior, 343
Action potential, 379
Acts, 209–210
Actual environment, 336–337
Adaptation, 406–408
Additive stimulus relationships, 243–244
Advantageous comparison, 340
Advertising, associative shifting and, 62
Age, 314
Agency, 350–352
Aggression
  media influence on, 348–349
  punishment and, 90
Altruistic behavior, 409, 428–429
  kin selection and, 425–426
Ambiguity, 277
Analogy
  definition of, 21
  response by, 60–61
Animal spirits, 33
Animal subjects, 18–19. *See also* Behaviorism
  in evolution research, 39
  observational learning in, 327–328
  before Thorndike, 51–52
  Tolman and, 302
Annoying state of affairs, 57–58
Anterograde amnesia, 373
Anthropomorphization, 51
Anticipatory frustration stimulus, 156
Antisocial behavior, 348–349
Anxiety, as drive in learning, 143
Anxiety hierarchies, 199
Apperception, 42
Appetite, 315
Aptitude testing, 126–127
Arousal function of a stimulus, 367
Arousal theory, 367–368

Array model, 242–248
Assimilation, 284–285, 286, 295–296
Association, principle of, 209, 223
Associationism, 31
  doctrine of, 269–271
  Ebbinghaus on, 39–41
  Hobbes in, 33–34
Associationistic paradigm, 46–47
Associative shifting, 62, 214
Associative strength, 239
Attention, 189–190, 206–207
Attentional processes, 331–332, 335
Attitudes, 59
Attribution of blame, 341
Autoclitic behavior, 104
Autoshaping, 113–115, 415–416
Avoidance conditioning, 8, 146, 414
Axons, 378–379

B

Back-propagation systems, 396–398
Backward conditioning, 171, 186
Backward masking, 421–422
Bandura's theory, 323–358
Basal ganglia, 374
Behavior
  beliefs and, 262–263
  chaining, 86–87, 139–140, 209
  copying, 326
  imitative, 326–327
  learning and change in, 1–7
  matched-dependent, 326
  molar, 257
  molecular, 257
  operant, 75
  respondent, 75
  same, 326
  self-regulated, 337–339
  species-specific, 5
  technology of, 106–107
  unlearned, 129–130
Behavioral economics, 99–103
Behavioral environment, 262–263
Behavioral potentiality, 1
Behavioral production processes, 333

Behaviorism, 44–46, 72–125, 438–439
  biological, 418–419
  chaining in, 86–87
  contingency contracting in, 104–105
  cumulative recording and, 79
  discriminative operants in, 83–84
  educational practices and, 115–116
  extinction in, 81–82
  generalized reinforcers in, 85–86
  Gestalt and, 256–257
  lever-pressing conditioning in, 80
  Little Albert experiment, 195–197
  on misbehavior, 111–115
  positive and negative reinforcers in, 88
  punishment in, 88–91
  purposive, 301
  radical, 75
  reinforcement schedules in, 93–103
  relativity of reinforcement in, 107–111
  respondent and operant behavior in, 75
  secondary reinforcement in, 84–85
  shaping in, 80–81
  Skinner boxes in, 78–79
  spontaneous recovery and, 82
  superstitious behavior and, 82–83
  technology of behavior in, 106–107
  on transposition, 267–268
  type S and type R conditioning in, 75–76
  verbal behavior and, 103–104
Behavior therapy, 196–197
Belongingness, 64–65
Binet Testing Laboratory, 282–283
Biofeedback, 158–160
Biological behaviorism, 418–419
Blind spots, 261–262
Bliss,Lømo, 380–382